THE IMPORTANCE
OF SCRUTINY

Other books by the editor

A Century of Hero-Worship, 1944
The Playwright as Thinker, 1946
Bernard Shaw, 1947

Translations of Bertolt Brecht
The Private Life of the Master Race, 1944
Parables for the Theatre (with Maja Bentley), 1948

Eric Bentley is the author of
The Life of the Drama **(1964)**
and other books.

THE IMPORTANCE OF SCRUTINY

Selections from
SCRUTINY: *A Quarterly Review,*
1932–1948

EDITED BY
ERIC BENTLEY

NEW YORK UNIVERSITY PRESS

1964

Copyright, 1948, by George W. Stewart, Publisher, Inc.

Library of Congress Catalog Card Number: 57-7726

MANUFACTURED IN THE UNITED STATES OF AMERICA

To
JOHN CROWE RANSOM
for his sixtieth birthday
in friendship

CONTENTS

	PAGE
Acknowledgements	xi
Introduction, by Eric Bentley	xiii

I
SCRUTINY AND MODERN CULTURE

Three Editorials:
  (I) *Scrutiny*: a Manifesto 1
  (II) Retrospect of a Decade 5
  (III) After Ten Years 8

Criticism and Literary History
  (I) A Review, by F. R. Leavis 12
  (II) A Comment, by F. W. Bateson 16
  (III) A Rejoinder, by F. R. Leavis 20

Literary Criticism and Philosophy
  (I) A Letter, by René Wellek 23
  (II) A Reply, by F. R. Leavis 30

The Discipline of Letters: A Sociological Note,
  by Q. D. Leavis 41

II
THREE GREAT CRITICS

Samuel Johnson, by F. R. Leavis 57
Coleridge, by F. R. Leavis 76
Matthew Arnold, by F. R. Leavis 88

III
THREE GREAT POETS

Shakespeare
  (I) *As You Like It,* by James Smith 99

(II) *Henry V*, by D. A. Traversi	120
(III) The Ambiguity of *Measure for Measure*, by L. C. Knights	141
(IV) The Greatness of *Measure for Measure*, by F. R. Leavis	150
(V) Shakespeare Criticism, by L. C. Knights	163
(VI) Statistical Criticism, by R. G. Cox	166

Coleridge
- (I) The Poetry of Coleridge, by Marius Bewley . . . 169
- (II) The Theme of *The Ancient Mariner*, by D. W. Harding 174

Dickens
- Dickens, Drama, and Tradition, by R. C. Churchill . 182

IV
FOUR VERSIONS OF DRAMA

Tragic Philosophy, by George Santayana 203
Tragedy and the "Medium," by F. R. Leavis 214
Notes on Comedy, by L. C. Knights 227
Music and the Dramatic, by W. H. Mellers 238

V
A MODERN MISCELLANY

W. H. Auden
- Auden's Inverted Development, by R. G. Lienhardt . 249

Cyril Connolly
- From Playground to Grave, by R. G. Lienhardt . . . 255

T. S. Eliot
- (I) *Collected Poems 1909-1935*, by D. W. Harding . 262
- (II) *East Coker*, by W. H. Mellers 267
- (III) *Little Gidding*, by D. W. Harding 269
- (IV) *Selected Essays*, by Edgell Rickword 273
- (V) *After Strange Gods*, by F. R. Leavis 276
- (VI) *Essays Ancient and Modern*, by F. R. Leavis . . 283

	PAGE
(VII) *The Idea of a Christian Society*, by D. W. Harding	287
(VIII) *Points of View*, by R. O. C. Winkler	291

E. M. Forster
   E. M. Forster, by F. R. Leavis 295

Rémy de Gourmont
   Rémy de Gourmont—Precursor, by G. D. Klingopulos 311

T. E. Hulme
   The T. E. Hulme Myth, by H. A. Mason 314

James Joyce
   Joyce and the Revolution of the Word, by F. R. Leavis 316

Rudyard Kipling
   A Case for Kipling? by Boris Ford 324

D. H. Lawrence
   The Wild, Untutored Phoenix, by F. R. Leavis . . . 338

Marcel Proust
   Introduction to Proust, by Martin Turnell . . . 344

I. A. Richards
   (I) I. A. Richards, by D. W. Harding 349
   (II) Dr. Richards, Bentham, and Coleridge, by F. R. Leavis 360

Virginia Woolf
   (I) Mrs. Woolf and Life, by W. H. Mellers 378
   (II) Caterpillars of the Commonwealth Unite!, by Q. D. Leavis 382

Appendix A: Leavis and *The Calendar* 393

Appendix B: The Contents of *Scrutiny*, Volumes I to XIX (1932–1953) 407

ACKNOWLEDGEMENTS

I have to thank all my authors for permission to reprint their work; also two London publishing houses—Chatto & Windus and Lawrence & Wishart—for leave to use material belonging to them; Morton D. Zabel, Samuel H. Monk, and Lionel Trilling, who guided my choice in areas where I am no expert; my wife, Maja Tschernjakow Bentley, for preparing Appendix B (among many other things less easy to pin down); and, of course, F. R. Leavis, who helped me in every possible way (though he is embarrassed at the large quantity of his own writing that I insisted on choosing).

A word of apology is due to those who, in controversies printed here, have allowed Mr. Leavis to have the last word. Mr. Wellek wrote me that he would not today endorse all that he wrote in the essay here reprinted; no doubt, Mr. Leavis's other contenders would like to say this and/or to make a further rejoinder. I wish to apologize also to those *Scrutiny* contributors who are here represented inadequately or not at all. If my aim had indeed been to "represent" everyone who has made valuable contributions to *Scrutiny* this book must be accounted a total failure. But what I aimed at was a certain range and a certain coherence in subject-matter—quite irrespective of authorship.

E. B.
1948

INTRODUCTION

Each generation of original writers, we are told, has to create the taste by which it is understood. Certainly, one can see that a new critical method has grown up alongside modern literature, a method that is now entering even the colleges and affecting the educational system. The New Criticism, John Crowe Ransom has called it. Among its most celebrated products—most celebrated among literary people in America at least—are *Seven Types of Ambiguity* by William Empson, and *The Double Agent* by R. P. Blackmur. But the method has been carried to numbers that these books will never reach by Cleanth Brooks and Robert Penn Warren in their freshman text-book, *Understanding Poetry*.

Now, it is good to know *Understanding Poetry*, and it is better to know Empson and Blackmur, but I am worried by American ignorance of a writer who may in the long run prove more significant, F. R. Leavis, editor of the quarterly review, *Scrutiny*.

I

The New Criticism stems from such books as T. S. Eliot's *The Sacred Wood* (1920) and J. Middleton Murry's *The Problem of Style* (1925). One could even trace it further back. Eliot and Murry are linked with the previous age, especially through the writer whom Eliot called "the critical consciousness of a generation," Rémy de Gourmont. From him comes the very title of Murry's book and many direct quotations in Eliot's. If we look back at *La Culture des Idées* and *Le Problème du Style*, we soon find—among much that is obvious or merely modish—the few things that were grist to the mill of Murry and Eliot. Perhaps, indeed, the few things are one thing, one word—*sensibility*. In view of what *Scrutiny* would later have to say about technique and pedagogy, it is interesting that Gourmont wrote on style largely to refute a contemporary pedagogue who had produced a treatise *L'art d'écrire enseigné en vingt leçons*. Gourmont said that style cannot be transmitted at all (let alone in twenty lessons) because it is the expression of the stylist's own sensibility. Here are some of his dicta, which, incidentally, support my hint that Gourmont was the link between the nineties and the twenties:

> L'art est incompatible avec une préoccupation morale ou religieuse.
>
> ... le style seul n'est rien. ... La pensée est l'homme même. Le style est la pensée même.
>
> Le style est une spécialisation de la sensibilité.
>
> Les mots les plus inertes peuvent être vivifiés par la sensibilité.
>
> Les mots n'ont de sens que par le sentiment qu'ils renferment.
>
> Flaubert incorporait toute sa sensibilité à ses oeuvres; et, par sensibilité, j'entends, ici comme partout, le pouvoir général de sentir tel qu'il est inégalement développé en chaque être humain. La sensibilité comprend la raison elle-même, qui n'est que de la sensibilité cristallisée.

Murry's *Problem of Style* contains many applications of Gourmont's ideas. Its limitation is that none too much is added. Eliot's *Sacred Wood* is another matter. Eliot had a much finer mind than Gourmont's and used it. Quotation from a fashionable French author always goes down well—beyond that, Gourmont was for Eliot merely a starting-point. The latter added far too many ideas to summarize here, and since his book has to be read by all those who tackle this one, I need not make the attempt. It is enough to remind the reader of some essential problems which Eliot here helps us to think clearly about. In what way is poetry the efflux of personality? In what way is the poet related to past and present? Very terse and lucid answers are suggested in the now famous essay, "Tradition and the Individual Talent." Then there is the matter of the "objective correlative," the matter of character in literature, and, of course, the many particular topics announced in the table of contents. To show how Eliot can take Gourmont's ideas and develop them, one need only set against the above dicta of the latter the following sentences of the former:

> The true generalization is not something superposed upon an accumulation of perceptions; the perceptions do not, in a really appreciative mind, accumulate as a mass, but form themselves as a structure; and criticism is the statement in language of this structure; it is a development of sensibility.
>
> To create a form is not merely to invent a shape, a rhyme or rhythm. It is also the realization of the whole appropriate content of this rhyme or rhythm.

... the effort of the philosopher proper, the man who is trying to deal with ideas in themselves, and the effort of the poet, who may be trying to *realize* ideas, cannot be carried on at the same time. But this is not to deny that poetry can be in some sense philosophic. The poet can deal with philosophic ideas, not as matter for argument, but as matter for inspection.

I. A. Richards, whose *Principles of Literary Criticism* came out in 1924, is the last of those whom one cannot avoid listing as among the founders of the New Criticism. Although today *Principles* seems to have merit only in spite of its setting in scientistic psychology and philosophy, merit that is located in two or three chapters of the total thirty-five, one must remember that the setting was probably influential in getting the book a hearing and thus in getting modern literature a hearing. Again, *Practical Criticism* (1929) is alternately inconclusive (we never are given *correct* analyses of the poems) and pretentious (we are told to meditate on the immensity of the universe). Yet this book, too, is significant—for its simplest qualities: for the initial idea of the experiment and the admission which it compels that *our* common reader is not Dr. Johnson's. If Richards's title—*Practical Criticism*—is an inaccurate description of his book, which contains little or no actual criticism of a mature sort, it is a useful pointer to the actual problem: how could the New Criticism be more than a theory held by a couple of eminent writers? How could it be a school of practice? A pervasive influence?

Some say—and others deny—that Richards's most telling answer to these queries was not to be found in his books but in his lecture-halls and college-rooms. Though there is no such thing as a "Cambridge school of criticism," most would agree that whatever approximation to such a school exists can be traced back to the twenties and to Richards. And what the university was to Richards, the literary periodical had been to Murry and Eliot. For two years after the First World War, *The Athenaeum* was a literary weekly. With Murry editing it and Eliot contributing to it, it must be regarded as one of the prime sources of the New Criticism.

Thus far I have been noting agreement among Gourmont, Murry, Eliot, and Richards, a sort of common front *against* vulgar error and *for* a New Criticism. All were concerned to assert that literature was not less important in this unliterary age than formerly, to point from the many things that literature is connected with to the thing that it is, to defend, as Eliot put it, the integrity of literature. The central idea of the New Criticism—"stick close to the text"—is modestly suggested in *The Sacred Wood*:

> This essay ["Tradition and the Individual Talent"] proposes to halt at the frontier of metaphysics or mysticism, and confine itself to such practical conclusions as can be applied by the responsible person interested in poetry.

This was Eliot in 1920. And for a time even Murry and Richards kept fairly close to literature. Later all three declined to "halt at the frontier" any longer. To the 1928 edition of *The Sacred Wood* Eliot appended a curious preface in which he pooh-poohs the book as but a record of an earlier time. He has "passed on," he tells us, "to a larger and more difficult subject" . . . "that of the relation of poetry to the spiritual and social life of its time and of other times." *The Sacred Wood* is simply an "introduction" to this subject. I do not think Eliot's dealings with the "larger and more difficult subject" have been very satisfactory. What is more relevant here—and perhaps in general—is that after the early twenties Eliot ceased to be a critic of the first rank. It was not only that he wrote on literature less often, but that—preoccupied, no doubt, with larger and more difficult things—he wrote on it less well. He became respectable.

One's regret that Eliot is lost to criticism is offset, of course, by the knowledge that he is not lost to poetry. Middleton Murry, lost to criticism, was lost to all literature; and outside literature his efforts are no more impressive than Eliot's. (Test this by comparing *The Athenaeum* with *The Adelphi*, and *The Adelphi* in the twenties with *The Adelphi* in the forties). I. A. Richards, of course, cannot so easily be written off the books. At Harvard he is still very much inside the educational world. But is he interested in anything so special as criticism? Has he not indulged his desire to save the world as rashly as Murry? It would be very fine to save the world, of course. Only these men do *not* save it. They only brandish rather improbable notions in its face. Attempting more, they achieve less, perhaps, than when they cultivated their garden—for there can be no doubt that it is *theirs* by right—the garden of criticism.

This is where F. R. Leavis comes in. If anyone of our time has believed in cultivating that garden, it is he. We realize how deep his devotion must have been when we reflect that he began and continued his critical work in the decade of all decades when men were distracted from such things: the thirties. There was at least

INTRODUCTION   xvii

one other Englishman who was equal to the task in the twenties—
Edgell Rickword, who, as leading spirit and one of the editors of
The Calendar of Modern Letters (1925-1927), carried on the business of criticism while Murry and Eliot turned to "larger" things.
In the thirties Rickword became a Communist. Contributing to
C. Day Lewis's book *The Mind in Chains*, he seems to have bowed
his way out of literature. *His* mind was in chains.
   One of F. R. Leavis's few direct contacts with British letters
prior to 1930 is his Introduction, not written till 1933, to *Towards
Standards of Criticism*, a collection of excerpts from *The Calendar.*
Appearing below as Appendix A, it is self-explanatory. It shows how
Scrutiny—the very name might have been lifted from a series of
articles in the earlier magazine *—carries on where *The Calendar*
left off, just as, one might say, *The Calendar* carries on where *The
Athenaeum* left off. To be sure, there were many other literary
magazines in this period: but did any of them exercise quite the
central critical function of these? On the left, so to speak, were the
naughty Bohemian magazines of Ezra Pound and Wyndham Lewis;
on the right, the solemn elder-statesmanly magazines of Murry and
Eliot. More necessary than either of these *genres,* surely, is a critical
organ that simply and sheerly criticizes old and new literature without naughtiness, without solemnity. That is evidently what Rickword thought. That is what Leavis was to think.
   Murry's *Athenaeum* and Rickword's *Calendar* each lived for a
couple of years. Richards built no continuing school of criticism at
Cambridge: he was so often not there. *Scrutiny,* on the other hand,
has appeared continuously since 1932 and is still strong. Without
any of the large-scale assistance that American critical journals get
(*Scrutiny* has never paid a contributor one penny), it has survived
the Depression and the Second World War. Moreover, though Mr.
Leavis is still very much a prophet without honour in his own
country (and in his own university), he has contrived to make
Downing College a centre of literary study in accordance with the
principles of *Scrutiny.*

II

   How much importance should we attach to this achievement?
Not too much, many of our contemporaries will suggest. Eliot and
Richards and Rickword are not unrepresentative of our time in

───────────
* The series was called "Scrutinies." So were two volumes of essays which Rickword compiled.

preferring to turn to a "larger" world than that of criticism. More recently C. S. Lewis has written of "the real frivolity, the solemn vacuity" of valuing literature as literature. W. H. Auden has called literature itself frivolous. Now, when literature is not respected as literature, it is respected, if at all, either as homiletics or as light recreation or as both. One cannot pretend to be surprised. Throughout history, this not very high opinion of the arts has probably been general. Aristotle was an exception among the Greeks, as S. H. Butcher has shown, in not valuing literature chiefly for its "message." He would have been an exception in almost every period down to and including that of Oliver Allston.* This, however, is not to say that he was wrong.

It seems possible that past culture took the arts so much for granted that their value was seldom clearly estimated. The theorists were content with pious commonplace. We today cannot take the arts for granted. We have destroyed the old aristocratic culture, which, for all its faults, had a place for the arts, and have created a culture of commodities, which, to be sure, has a place for everything —upon one condition: that everything become a commodity. Thus there is one sort of literature that flourishes today as never before: commodity literature, as promoted by the book clubs and publishers' salesmen.

If we view literature as a frivolity, it is natural that we should give it up and rush off to die in Spain. If we view it as homiletic, it is equally natural that we should stay at home and formulate the opinions of Oliver Allston. But if we actually find value in literature as literature, we have to make ourselves conscious of that attachment to the arts which up to now has been taken for granted. This is not a process which has yet to begin. It began, I think, in the Romantic movement. Was it not in legitimate self-defence that the Romantic poets began to define the status of the artist and declare it a high one? True, the dignity of the artist came, in the Victorian Age, to mean the dignity of a rather Allstonian type of sage; men always fall back into that *in*dignity. But such a movement as Aestheticism—Art for Art's Sake—came in its turn to chastise the sages. The Aesthetic movement is by now notoriously discredited, and not least in modernist circles. Yet it lies, as I have intimated, behind Gourmont, and therefore behind modernism. It is no longer necessary to praise or dispraise it. But one should see

---

* For the benefit of British readers I should explain that Oliver Allston is a character through whom Van Wyck Brooks attacked modern taste.

that it cannot be brushed off, and that it was a part of a much larger movement of the human spirit, the movement through which the need for a defence and redefinition of culture has become conscious. Matthew Arnold, who, I suppose, has seldom been called an aesthete, very explicitly maintained that poetry has a special claim to status in the modern era. I have in mind a passage which Arnold used to quote from himself, and which I. A. Richards quoted in *Science and Poetry*:

> The future of poetry is immense, because in poetry, where it is worthy of its high destinies, our race, as time goes on, will find an ever surer and surer stay. There is not a creed which is not shaken, not an accredited dogma which is not shown to be questionable, not a received tradition which does not threaten to dissolve. Our religion has materialized itself in the fact, in the supposed fact: it has attached its emotion to the fact, and the fact is failing it. But for poetry the idea is everything.

These sentences of Arnold's could reasonably be attacked on several grounds. But, whether Arnold here solves the religious question to our satisfaction or not, his words do put us in mind of the modern cultural question and of the crying need for art. Long before the nineties, Hebbel observed that art was "the highest form of life." Is not one of the meanings of Henry James's work that, if we become more civilized, morals will become an aesthetic matter?

Even those who do not agree that the arts are more important today than formerly will admit, I hope, that they are not *less* important; and even this is to grant that the arts will require more attention than formerly, the anti-artistic pressures of the modern world being so prodigious. In the aristocratic society of former times, the ruling class was much the same thing as the educated class: your great statesman, your Chatham, spoke the same language as your man of letters, your Johnson, your Burke. Thus, the average member of this class could be regarded as a qualified reader. Modern non-aristocratic society contains no class that has inherited the old culture. We have only an *intelligentsia* recruited from all classes. A member of the modern *intelligentsia* enters European culture as a working-class scholarship boy enters Oxford: he has to learn consciously and from the beginning what, under happier circumstances, he would unconsciously have already made part of his being.

Hence the explicitness of the New Criticism—perhaps one ought to say the New Pedagogy—hence its preoccupation with the rudiments, the grammar, of art. Some people are offended with this explicitness—"after all, we know how to read," they say. Others are over-impressed by it. They note that there is nothing in the whole history of criticism like the analyses in, for example, this book. One of them, Mr. R. W. Stallman, concludes that the New Criticism is "an achievement . . . the like of which has not been equalled by literary critics in our time or in any previous period of our literary history." Not equalled? Not attempted, either, and not *needed*. The New Criticism does not tell us many things that would have been beyond Samuel Johnson's range. It tells us things that he would have considered too obvious to need saying.

It is our misfortune that they are not too obvious today. For modern men and women do *not* know how to read. When we confront those who have been to the best schools and have had the best opportunity to live the good life—that is to say, when we confront highly selected undergraduates—what do we find? The answer is in Richards's *Practical Criticism*: we find total helplessness in the face of the simplest works of art, total incomprehension. It is natural, perhaps, that when a boy or girl is first asked to discuss a work of art he will be completely baffled. Can one say to him: "Well, watch how professionals write about literature and do likewise"? One cannot. For professionals are chiefly either scholars who write solely on the background of literature or belletrists who skate—often very dexterously—over its surface. The professor who delivers a daily literary lecture and the "critic" who writes a weekly literary article are usually people who have learnt to master the occasion by avoiding the subject. The student is left with the lines of *Phèdre* staring him blankly in the face. Neither professor nor "critic" says much, if anything, about them. The histories of literature include them in some larger category, brush them off with a single epithet.

What have the universities been doing? In the past they professed an interest in literature. But it was for a long time an interest in ancient literature only, and in that literature viewed in a very unliterary way. Latin and Greek were supposed to be for the gentleman what hard labour is to the convict. One might call this the penitentiary view of literature. Now, when Greek and Latin were the penitentiary subjects, English literature could be a delightful playground. And on all counts a playground is preferable to a prison. English had an advantage over Greek that many were sorry to see the end of when, a generation ago, English became a "subject" in the great British universities.

INTRODUCTION xxi

There are those whose memory of the playground dies hard. With an elegance acquired in Bloomsbury or elsewhere, they dedicate their professional efforts to dilettantism. Affronted by this, and determined to make English as "hard" a subject as Greek and Latin, other professors erect a new prison. If there can be nothing fully equivalent, in a language you already know, to the rigours of Greek and Latin grammar, Anglo-Saxon and Linguistics and the Historical Approach would make an impressive substitute. The pedant would be a match for the dilettante.

I need not labour familiar points. We all know that literature has become one of the least useful of all academic subjects, with the result that it now attracts the wrong kind of students, students with little interest in the arts but with a considerable facility in learning by rote. A less familiar point—and perhaps my main one in this introduction—is that the New Criticism, applied as a pedagogy, affords something of a remedy. And in that application so far, no one has played a larger part than F. R. Leavis.

Leavis is one of the few people who welcomed English as a serious university subject, and welcomed it for what it is, not for what you can turn it into or reduce it to. He agreed with the dilettantes that literature is an art. He agreed with the pedants that it is a legitimate area for hard work. But the hard work was to be applied precisely to understanding the art. While English literature remains a playground, one cannot possibly appreciate its extent, its greatness, or its complexity. Hard work must go into this appreciation. If the modern mind is as confused and disorderly as Richards's experiment indicated, the very effort to rescue it from confusion and disorder would be an arduous and educative process. Learning to read well would be a discipline, a discipline of what Gourmont had called the sensibility, that is, a discipline of the intellect and the feelings taken—as they must be taken in the arts—together.

I must refer those who wish to know exactly what Leavis has said and done about it to the rest of the present book and to two books, especially, of Leavis's *Revaluation* and *Education and the University*. Here I shall only issue some warnings against misapprehension. In *Revaluation* Leavis reappraised so many English poets that the book as a whole amounts to a new view of English poetic tradition. The reappraisal, reiterated in other books such as Cleanth Brooks's *Modern Poetry and the Tradition*, is now familiar to many people who have never even heard of Leavis: hence the new view is sometimes regarded as a new orthodoxy, and those who do know of Leavis sometimes think of him as one who hands out opinions to the young. They miss the point. It may be a fact that some young people have "stolen" their opinions from Leavis. How could he stop them? The important thing is to remember that such stealing is clean contrary to Leavis's principles. He is not another Irving Babbitt. If there is a bed-rock of doctrine, an absolute, at the bottom of his work, it is not a philosophical system, but a doctrine as to procedure, a methodological absolute. Even the method is far from peculiar or idiosyncratic. The assumption is that literature means something, that the meaning or content is bound up with the style or form, and may therefore be discovered by the trained sensibility. Literature means letters, humane letters, men's words. The best literature, as we have already been taught, is the best words in the best order. Literary study, Leavis concludes, means a study of the words and their order. To use Ezra Pound's phrase, literature is "language charged with meaning to the utmost possible degree." Reading literature, Leavis concludes, means being sensitive to the charge, the energy, which the poet gives to his words.

Far from offering a new philosophy of art, or even insisting on a particular old one, Leavis might be described as the anti-philosophical critic. "No theoretical discussion should be allowed to go on for long at any distance from critical practice," he writes in "How to Teach Reading." People say one should examine one's assumptions, but the literary critic who says this more than three times ends up as a philosopher, and seldom a good philosopher. Here philosophy plays the perennial part of "the larger and more difficult subject" that lures critics to give up criticism. If we are trying to demonstrate that criticism is itself a discipline we should not give it up for philosophy, even for the philosophy of criticism. In the *Scrutiny* group of writers are men of radically different philosophies.

Leavis is not, of course, asking critics to stop short, to hedge and hesitate. On the contrary, he would protest, I think, that all too much of what passes for New Criticism in America is inconclusive and inadequate. Since the famous Brooks and Warren text-book came out, there has been much expounding and explaining which is good as far as it goes. But Leavis always assumed that understanding is complete only when it is pushed as far as appraisal of the thing understood. This is another reason why, in an age of wishy-washy broad-mindedness, he is thought dogmatic. Actually

Leavis is no neo-classic, setting up "objective" criteria by which we are all bound to render the same verdicts; art would be a dull thing if we could measure it out in neo-classic coffee-spoons. On the other hand, judgement is the summation of criticism. And some degree or kind of objectivity is presumed by it. For if all judgements are equally valid, there is just my predilection and yours and the other man's, and we are not in the human realm at all; we are in a sub-human chaos. Whether "order" is interpreted by the philosophers to be something pre-existing or something man-made we have to insist on having it. Aesthetic judgement is difficult and risky, but scarcely more difficult and risky than judgement in other realms, where we grant its necessity.*

III

Whenever I find myself relaxing into the belief that all this is now accepted by sensible people, I recall the account of literature, criticism, education, and the university given a few years ago by an eminent writer whom I respect, C. S. Lewis. In *Rehabilitations* (note the anti-Leavisian title), Lewis proposes that the universities pursue "learning" as distinct from "education." Education ("what will do me most good?") is, we are told, the business of the schools. Learning ("what do I most want to know?") is a man's independent investigation of any "tract of reality." Although he regards guidance in the choice of subject-matter as an insult to the student's adulthood, Lewis is prepared to be just as firm as any educationist in laying down what the boundaries of the "tract" are to be in English studies:

> The tap-root, Anglo-Saxon, can never be abandoned. The man who does not know it remains all his life a child among real English students.
> There is an intrinsic absurdity in making current literature a subject of academic study, and the student who wants a tutor's assistance in reading the works of his own contemporaries might as well ask for a nurse's assistance in blowing his own nose.

Having done my stint of Anglo-Saxon, I am presumably entitled to dissent from the view that those who have not done theirs must remain children "among real English students." Both the passages I have quoted from Lewis suggest that he has a very unsatisfactory conception of two central matters: tradition and taste. A sense of

---

* See "Poetic vs. Rhetorical Exegesis: the case for Leavis against Richards and Empson," by H. M. McCluhan, *The Sewanee Review*, Spring, 1944.

tradition implies a sense of the oneness of past and present. The antiquarian who is interested only in the past is therefore making the same kind of mistake as the journalist who is interested only in the present. The kind of traditionalism which puts Anglo-Saxon before modern English seems to me antiquarian.

Not that this is exactly what Lewis does. He assumes that we shall read and understand modern literature anyway—in leisure moments. In other words, he likes to regard literature as a playground in areas where it is definitely not a prison. Is this feasible? Is reading new literature as easy as blowing one's nose? And (if Lewis would turn this question into a condemnation of modern obscurity) was new literature *ever* as easy as blowing one's nose? Is not the new by definition the unfamiliar and is it not therefore hard to assimilate? Lewis seems to take literature for something much simpler than it actually is. That is, he is able to over-simplify the matter of taste as much as he over-simplifies the matter of tradition. He is able to overlook facts.

For, as a matter of brute fact, our students are *not* educated when they enter the university. Both in England and America the universities exist today primarily for educational purposes. Educationally, the use of literature is that it can train discrimination or taste. In the training of taste it seems reasonable to start from the student's own world, from the present. This would be true in any period. In our period we have, I think, the special and extra reason that certain modern authors are particularly instructive in a literary way—that is, they afford the best possible discipline for the growing mind. I am thinking of writers like Henry James and T. S. Eliot.

We come back again, inevitably, to the question of the function of literature. That is where the deepest difference between a Lewis and a Leavis lies. To Lewis what is all-important is religion. Literature may helpfully subserve religion—that is, it may be edifying—or it may be among the amenities of the good life—that is, it may be amusing. It's prison or playground. Leavis, on the other hand, is more in the Arnoldian tradition. Shall we say, then, that he substitutes literature for religion? Such a formula is roughly true, I think, except for certain implications of the word *substitute*: one need not assume that religion is fundamental and that everything else a man is attached to is mere *ersatz*. The point is not necessarily that literature is *all*-important, but that it is important. Important for a whole society. The function of the writer—socially considered—is to stand guard over the language.

INTRODUCTION

In discussing the relation of literature to general ideas, Leavis again endorses some words of Ezra Pound:

> It [literature] has to do with the clarity of any and every thought and opinion. It has to do with maintaining the very cleanliness of the tools, the health of the very matter of thought itself.

Leavis himself says:

> To those who take a serious interest in literature it must often seem as if their interest were curiously irrelevant to the modern world; curiously, because a serious interest in literature starts from the present and assumes that literature matters, in the first place at any rate, as the consciousness of the age.

Believing this, and believing in "education" rather than in "learning," Leavis is bound to esteem what Arnold called "the remnant" and what our pseudo-democratic age sneers at as the "superior few":

> In any period it is upon a very small minority that the discerning appreciation of art and literature depends: it is (apart from cases of the simple and familiar) only a few who are capable of unprompted, first-hand judgement. They are still a small minority, though a larger one, who are capable of endorsing such first-hand judgements by genuine personal response.

Some people will enjoy asserting that the editors of *Scrutiny* see themselves as the "very small minority" and their pupils as the "small minority, though a larger one." Yet should one be scornful if someone tries to practise what he preaches? At least one should understand that *Scrutiny* is run frankly as a collaboration of colleagues and students, not as an "open" metropolitan magazine with offices in a skyscraper. The uniformity of attitude which some object to is the defect of a quality without which there could not be such a magazine at all: unity of purpose. If it is to have character a literary review has to stand for something. It has to fight. It is therefore likely to seem arrogant and ill-natured. Yet, for all the talk of a new orthodoxy, *Scrutiny* has not been stupidly partisan. While American critics, once they have accepted a modernist author, tend to be overawed by him, *Scrutiny* has been severely critical of the same men it has championed, men such as Eliot and Pound, Joyce and Henry James. While literary people in general waited till recently to discover that Lawrence was great, and that Aldous Huxley is not great, *Scrutiny* made the correct appraisals from the start. While literary people followed the fashion of the decade—

cynicism in the twenties, Marxism in the thirties, Existentialism and Crisis Theology in the forties—*Scrutiny* kept up a steady fire against the cliques, both academic and metropolitan. The tone of *Scrutiny* may not always be what could be desired. "It's too personal, too insulting," people say. The trouble is that sensibility is a personal matter. Tell a critic he is guilty of an error of fact, and he can still think himself a great man. Tell him he is guilty of an error of taste, and he feels his existence threatened. Perhaps *Scrutiny* could be more kindly in such matters. Perhaps this and perhaps that. I could easily write another essay on "Where I Disagree with *Scrutiny*." I should like even more to attempt yet another essay on the limitations of the New Criticism in general: John Crowe Ransom, who invented the term, has recently and rightly called for a broader definition of it. But these are not the essays that are needed here and now. For *Scrutiny* has not yet been granted a fair hearing. To help it get one I have prepared this book.

Readers will form their own opinion. Having worked over the whole file of *Scrutiny*, 1932-1948, I may be permitted to wonder if any other magazine contains so much useful analysis of literature—and by a useful analysis I mean simply one that helps you to grasp a work for yourself, as most of the "critical" works at present cluttering our libraries do not. I should add that this introduction of mine is entirely unofficial: the editors of *Scrutiny* are not committed to it. If only because, in England at any rate, the *Scrutiny* circle is often dismissed as a mutual-admiration society, it is possible that a statement from an outsider like myself—I have never met Mr. Leavis or written for *Scrutiny*—might carry some weight.

ERIC BENTLEY
1948

PART I

SCRUTINY AND MODERN CULTURE

Three Editorials

(1) *SCRUTINY*: A MANIFESTO

The first number of a review is not, of course, an ideal place in which to discuss the best Method of Conducting a Critical Journal. To do so provides openings for irony, and caution would suggest that we creep into print meekly. But such a course is impossible; the age is illiterate with periodicals, and no ordinary reasons will excuse an addition to the swarm. Policy, as well as honesty, demands that if we imagine ourselves to have a valid reason for existence, we should state it.

The general dissolution of standards is a commonplace. Many profess to believe (though fewer seem to care) that the end of Western civilization is in sight. But perhaps even the Spenglerian formula, in its deterministic nonchalance, represents an emotional as much as an intellectual reaction; and if optimism is naïve, fatalism is not necessarily an intelligent attitude. Intelligence has an active function.

Those who are aware of the situation will be concerned to cultivate awareness and will be actively concerned for standards. A review is necessary that combines criticism of literature with criticism of extra-literary activities. We take it as axiomatic that concern for standards of living implies concern for standards in the arts.

At this point we remind ourselves of the recent history of critical journalism. In England during the last two decades no serious critical journal has been able to survive in the form in which it was conceived; and how many have been able to survive in any form? *The Calendar of Letters*, which deserved the whole-hearted support of the educated, lasted less than three years. And more recently *The Nation*, itself the grave of *The Athenaeum*, has suffered a euphemistic extinction. There are survivors, but they have for the most part steadily lowered their level of appeal. There is no need to describe the more blatant signs—gossiping essays, inferior criticism, competitions, and cross-word puzzles. In America there is *The Hound and Horn, The Symposium,* and *The New Republic,* all of which remind us that America is not inhabited solely by Babbitts. *The New Republic* in particular combines literary criticism with sensitive attention to modern affairs. But these papers have no English counterparts, and the ordinary man receives far less help from the better-class journals and the critics than, in a civilized community, he has a right to expect.*

* * * *

The reader will have gathered by now that *Scrutiny* is not to be a purely literary review. But what exactly, he may wonder, is meant by that hint of a generous interest in "modern affairs" at large? There are politics, for instance. Well, a devotion to them at the party level is, no doubt, somewhere necessary. But something else is necessary—and prior: a play of the free intelligence upon the underlying issues. This is to desiderate a cultivated historical sense, a familiarity with the "anthropological" approach to contemporary civilization exemplified by *Middletown,* and a catholic apprehension of the humane values. When we say that the political ambition of *Scrutiny* is indicated here, we incur criticism from two sides: to the effect that our ambition is amusing and that we are too remote from practice to interest anyone really alive to the plight of the world. As for the former criticism, a glance round at current journalism suggests that, at any rate, to be too ambitious will be something of a novel fault. As for the latter, the impotence of the practical mind to do anything essential in practice is being so thoroughly demonstrated that the retort needs no pressing.

Scrutiny, then, will be seriously preoccupied with the movement of modern civilization. And if we add that it will direct itself especially upon educational matters the reader will realize that there may, after all, be a fairly close approach to practice.

* * * *

Where literary criticism is concerned we can be immediately practical and political. The first duty is to publish good criticism

---

* There is, of course, *The Criterion,* of which it is difficult to speak without respect. It is still the most serious as it is the most intelligent of our journals. But its high price, a certain tendency to substitute solemnity for seriousness, and, during the last two years, a narrowing of its interests prevent it from influencing more than a small proportion of the reading public. It is necessary, but not the *unum necessarium.*

judiciously directed. And inseparable from this is a conscious critical policy, if anything is to be effected in the present state of culture. For today there are anti-high-brow publics and "modernist" publics, but there is no public of Common Readers with whom the critic can rejoice to concur. He cannot leave his standards to look after themselves. When Mr. Eliot's *Ash Wednesday* appeared it received one intelligent review, in an American paper.* Mr. Empson's *Seven Types of Ambiguity* apparently caused nothing but bewilderment in the minds of nearly all its reviewers. On the other hand, *Jew Süss* received a noisy welcome in the press ("Everybody who respects himself has read it," said Mr. Arnold Bennett); and *Dusty Answer* was said to "reveal new possibilities for literature." There is no need to multiply examples. They can be found in almost any number of *The Times Literary Supplement* (where at one time it was possible to find criticism), in the columns of the Sunday papers and elsewhere.

And when criticism defaults, the loss is not merely the reader's. Of late years important works of art have appeared, serious books of criticism have been written, but their reception has been such as to discourage further production on the part of their creators, if not to make creation impossible; for in spite of the romantic conception of the poet as a bird (preferably a skylark) singing to please himself in glorious isolation, the artist does depend in large measure on the prevailing standard of taste. On occasions he may be able to ignore his age and its demands, but in the past the relation between artist and patron (the person or persons for whom he writes, builds, carves, etc.) has been of great importance in determining the use of talent. There is no reason to suppose that it will be otherwise in the future.

* * * *

It goes without saying that for the majority neither the present drift of civilization nor the plight of the arts is a matter for much concern. It is true there are many who are interested in one or the other without seeing any connexion between them; but it is only a small minority for whom the arts are something more than a luxury product, who believe, in fact, that they are "the storehouse of recorded values" and, in consequence, that there is a necessary relationship between the quality of the individual's response to art and his general fitness for a humane existence. The trouble is not that such persons form a minority, but that they are scattered and unor-

---

* By Allen Tate in *The Hound and Horn*.

ganized. Every year, for instance, intelligent young men and women go down from the universities and are swallowed by secondary and public schools. Their interests wilt in the atmosphere of the school common-room, and isolation makes their efforts to keep themselves informed of "the best that is known and thought in the world" unnecessarily depressing and difficult. Others besides schoolmasters are in the same position. *Scrutiny* has been founded on the assumption that a magazine in which such men and women can exchange and refine their ideas, and which provides a focus of intellectual interests, will perform a service attempted by no other paper.

* * * *

It would perhaps be wisest not to define the programme of *Scrutiny* too narrowly until intentions can be judged by performance. But if the case which we have outlined above is to be something more than a gesture of dissatisfaction, it is necessary that we should at least indicate the policy which we intend to follow.

Scrutiny will print critical articles on literature and the arts and on various significant aspects of contemporary life. In both these departments of criticism, analysis and interpretation will be with a view to judgement—from a standpoint which will have been made clear when one or two numbers have been published.

Besides essays in literary criticism, a few carefully selected books will be reviewed each quarter, of the sort that is so frequently passed over by the newspaper supplements and the monthly magazines or inadequately treated. Occasionally there will be reviews of books which have appeared in the past and which have suffered an unjust disregard; and it may seem profitable to analyse certain popular successes. In each case consistent standards of criticism will be applied.

A pervasive interest of the magazine will find expression in disinterested surveys of some department of modern life in an attempt to increase understanding of the way in which civilization is developing. In the collection of material it is hoped to secure the co-operation of readers who are in a favourable position for observation.

Related to this kind of analysis are the articles which we have planned on various aspects of education—the teaching of English in schools and universities, the training of teachers, and similar subjects. Traditional methods of education are being subjected at present to fairly rigorous criticism and a certain amount of over-hauling; criticism which sees educational problems as part of the larger problems of general culture is, however, still necessary. To say that the life of a country is determined by its educational ideals is a commonplace; but it is a commonplace that is passively accepted more often than it is acted upon.

Scrutiny will also publish original compositions. Since, however, more people are able to write good criticism than good verse or short stories, we commit ourselves to no large or constant proportion of creative work.

In conclusion, we wish to make it clear that active co-operation from readers is invited. All contributions will be carefully considered, in order to make current the best of that kind of criticism which is now so often confined to isolated groups and private discussion. We have long been told that *les clercs* have betrayed their function. It would be more nearly true to say that their voice cannot be heard above the confused noises made by the self-appointed sponsors of civilization. We do not know how long this will be so. Meanwhile the attempt is worth making to provide a focus of ideas and a centre of resistance for those who accept the case presented in this manifesto.

* * * *

We have a critical policy. This does not mean that all articles printed in *Scrutiny* will be identical in outlook. In particular, the points of view of articles with immediate practical bearings may differ considerably from each other, and they will not necessarily coincide with editorial opinion. For instance, the reader need not draw from an essay on public schools any conclusions regarding our own attitude to them. We shall publish articles which—whether we agree with them entirely or not—are of intrinsic importance, which help to clear up current confusions and suggest a new approach to standards.

(1932)

(II) RETROSPECT OF A DECADE

In opening our ninth year at such a time as this, the mere bringing out of the new issue, with the implied intention to carry on while that remains possible, seems manifesto enough. The importance of the function that *Scrutiny*, in its own necessarily modest way, exists to serve is today generally granted. Eight years ago, we recall, things were different. The purpose of *Scrutiny*, as we conceived it, was plainly enough set forth in the first issue, but that didn't inhibit the choruses and reiterated "Show your colours!" There was a simple choice to be made, and not to make it and proclaim it was to be guilty of pusillanimity. We remember as representative of the prevailing assumptions and indicative of the pressure of the environment at that time this comment on our "political attitude," made with malicious intent by an eminent young intellectual: "Well, of course, you're as little Communist as you dare be."

The assumption that not to be Communist required courage was at that time a natural one. The pressure was certainly tremendous —to wear red or some colour recognized as its opposite. But that had been a reason for starting *Scrutiny*, and could only be one for continuing to feel that the undertaking was worth persisting with. There was never, as a matter of fact, any hesitation or inexplicitness about our anti-Marxism, this negative being a corollary of our positive position. And our positive position was that, though without doubt the human spirit was not to be thought of as expressing itself in a void of "freedom," unconditioned by economic and material circumstances, nevertheless there was a great need to insist on the element of autonomy and to work for the preservation of the humane tradition—a tradition representing the profit of a continuity of experience through centuries of economic and material change. Further, it was an essential part of our position, as we conceived it, *not* to be as positive as some people—possible sympathizers —would desire: we intended *Scrutiny* to stand for the humane tradition as something to be fostered apart from any particular religious creed; and the fostering of a free play of critical intelligence we thought of as essential to the tradition. In this sense *Scrutiny* invites the description "liberal."

Such a position could hardly be stigmatized as Fascist. But we got a good deal of free advertisement in young-intellectual organs, which used to attack *Scrutiny* for "playing into the enemy's hands" by encouraging "irresponsibility" in the intelligent young and distracting from a clear perception of the clear-cut issues. As the decade wore on we got less advertisement of this kind: Marxist intellectuals became more and more occupied with explaining that Marxist criticism was not what in these attacks it had very militantly represented itself to be. And then, of course, quite recently the Marxist decade came to its sharp close: that chapter ended before the chronological period was quite out.

But Marxist the decade decidedly was. It was also, in literature, a very barren decade. Compare it with the 1920's. The 1920's were the decade of Joyce, Eliot, D. H. Lawrence, Virginia Woolf, E. M.

Forster, T. F. Powys, the effective publication of *Mauberley*, the discovery of Hopkins, and the advent of Yeats as a major poet. The 1930's started with a poetic renascence. Now at their close one is driven to judge that the making accessible of Isaac Rosenberg (who has not yet been "discovered," in spite of his great superiority in interest over Wilfred Owen) was a more important event in English poetry than any emergence of a new poet. In the novel there was *The Root and the Flower;* but what else is there to mention—at any rate, of cis-Atlantic origin?

The prevalent Marxizing and the barrenness might well seem to be in obviously significant relation, Marxist doctrines about literature and art being what they are. But it would, of course, be unsubtle to insist much on the suggestion of simple cause-and-effect. If the young intelligentsia yielded so readily to the satisfactions of an easy salvationism, explanations may no doubt be reasonably looked for in the menacing state of the world. Politico-economic problems filled the prospect, and unless you supposed you knew of a very simple solution, you could hardly suppose you knew of one at all. Certainly, the kind of political distraction that characterized the decade was very bad for creative work.

But there is one aspect of the unfavourable state of civilization that especially concerns *Scrutiny* and its specific function. In all ages, no doubt, there have been cliques and coteries, and young writers have founded mutual-admiration societies and done their best to make these coincident with the literary world—the world that determines current valuations. But has there ever before been a time when the young aspirant, graduating from his university group, could immediately and without any notable sense of a change find himself in a fraternity that effectively "ran" contemporary letters— "ran" them so effectively that he could make a name and a career without even coming in sight of adult standards? The existence of such a state of affairs will be found amply recorded and documented in the eight volumes of *Scrutiny*. The disastrous consequence may be pointed to in the representative career of W. H. Auden, distinguished by his promise at the beginning of the decade.

No one would expect reminders of the nature of standards to be received with gratitude. It seems worth noting, however, in further illustration of the decade, that a little research in back-files will reveal the young, predominantly Left-inclined, *élite* incongruously cocking their snooks at *Scrutiny* from the pages of *The Criterion*— the only attention *Scrutiny* ever got in that promisingly styled organ.

It may perhaps be permissible to record too that, because of such performances there, where we had once looked for judicial criticism by more philosophical standards than ours, we have on occasion thought it necessary to abstain from reviewing books that certainly ought otherwise to have been reviewed: we were anxious not to give the least colour of countenance to the prevailing gang-warfare notion of critical exchange. But to have to confess failure to that extent was a disappointment, for without a serious critical interplay there can hardly be said to be the beginning of a functioning contemporary criticism.

On the other hand, we feel that the history of the decade has justified the intentions with which we started. And, conscious as we are of many inadequacies, it would be dishonest to pretend that, as far as one organ can hope to maintain the function of criticism, *Scrutiny* appears to us, when we turn over the back volumes, to have fallen discreditably short in its attempt at maintaining it. Moreover, to have brought and kept together something of an intellectual community, however small, seems to us to have been worth the labour. We shall carry on while we can.

(1940)

(III) AFTER TEN YEARS

In this number, on wartime paper and a crowded page, *Scrutiny* completes its tenth year. To persist under present conditions implies (among other things) some assurance of function. The belief that the function served by *Scrutiny* is not less a matter of proper concern now than it was in time of peace has been given encouragement in a good many hortatory messages. We have been reminded that, while the handful of serious reviews coming from America— they were never very generally accessible on this side of the Atlantic, but their existence mitigated the sense of vacancy—has, since the American entry into the war, been suddenly reduced to the point where we must fear a complete extinction, here there has been nothing to set against the loss of *The Criterion;* and that, further, this country fosters the export of books and takes official steps to bring home to the world that there is an English literature and a living British culture. However, it is not the special difficulties of the moment that we are inclined to stress, but the difficulties of the past, and the fact that *Scrutiny* has continued for ten years; it seems to us not merely something done but, in a sense, something proved.

A brief recall of the situation of ten years back will explain this feeling. As a serious critical organ, maintaining a continuity of the critical function above the level of mere journalism, *The Criterion* stood alone. A flourishing criticism is a matter of co-operation—the co-operation that is constituted by difference, tension, and interplay; but *The Calendar of Modern Letters,* defunct in 1927, had had no successor, and the history of that brilliant and lively organ made it quite plain that no successor could be expected. When in discussions of the "cultural situation" one made this point it often met with the reply that there was nothing here for sorrow; a preoccupation with cultural matters that wasn't politically serious (or seriously political) deserved neither attention nor respect—"politically serious," of course, meant something of the Marxizing kind. This was the onset of the period of *Left Review, New Writing,* and *The Mind in Chains.* And to this argument and this philosophy one saw little satisfaction in theoretical replies.

To ask what can be done is to ask what opportunity lies in front of you in your own particular situation. Those concerned in founding *Scrutiny* were situated at a university. A university of its very nature (or "idea"), if it is one at all, asserts a contrary view of cultural tradition to the Marxian; a view of cultural tradition as representing the active function of human intelligence, choice, and will; that is, as a spiritual force that can direct and determine. The promoters of *Scrutiny* didn't say that they were bent, in their zeal on behalf of the "function of criticism," on vindicating at the same time "the idea of a university": they may well have felt that to put it in those terms would have been presumptuous and impolitic (they were none of them of any academic importance). But in planning to do in their own way what clearly couldn't be done in the old, they were consciously appealing to the idea that it was more than ever the *raison d'être* of a university to be, amid the material pressures and dehumanizing complications of the modern world, a focus of humane consciousness; a centre where, faced with the specializations and distractions in which human ends lose themselves, intelligence, bringing to bear a mature sense of values, should apply itself to the problems of civilization. They were in fact heroically bent on refuting the adjective "academic." And perhaps they will be pardoned if, on a proper occasion for formal retrospect, they seem to be making a lot of a very little; they will perhaps be for a moment indulged in the complacencies of the private perspective. They can, at any rate, say that *Scrutiny* has been run, by unpaid collaboration, from a base at a university and has been run now for ten years.

Of course, that it should be in any narrow sense a university organ was contrary to the essence of the plan, which aimed (short of paying "staff" and contributor) at discharging the function of a metropolitan critical review. (And we don't think that *Scrutiny* will be found to have been notably more provincial than the metropolitan "literary world"—but this is, after all, a very modest assertion.) But without the base at a university, and the accompanying opportunities for recruitment, and for enlisting collaboration and support in other universities and in the academic world generally, *Scrutiny* couldn't have been kept going (apart from occasional gifts, amounting to a very small fraction of the expenses, it has been unsubsidized). These conditions of success have had their expression in the pages of *Scrutiny* in the attention given from time to time to the question of education, especially to that of "liberal education" as it concerns the university. But the essential thing on all counts has been the attempt to carry on, in the way described, the general function of criticism.

In his address last year to the Malvern Conference, Mr. T. S. Eliot, referring (in flattering terms) to an article in *Scrutiny* by one of the editors, used the term "humanist" of those of us who have associated ourselves with what may be called the general editorial point of view (we consider it part of the function of *Scrutiny* to represent a diversity of views, as almost any quarter's issue will make pretty manifest). When Mr. Eliot says "humanist" he intends, of course, a critical judgement; he is reporting an inadequacy in the nature of our preoccupation with the problems we discuss. Without going here into the intended force of Mr. Eliot's charge of incompleteness, it is perhaps worth repeating that we don't suppose ourselves to be doing anything more in *Scrutiny* than say: here are some things that need attending to; here is a kind of attention, and here a kind of approach, that is necessary. For instance, it seems to us important that the difference between a play by Mr. Eliot and a play by Miss Dorothy Sayers should be generally recognized, and we see no reason for believing that, without a preoccupation somewhere with the kind of approach represented by *Scrutiny*, there is likely to be anywhere an adequate insistence on such differences. The theoretical difficulty that Mr. Eliot raises about the grounds of our preference for an ideal of civilization different from that dominant in Germany leaves us convinced that we have grounds enough to go upon.

Practical difficulties increase, and so, unhappily, do the occasions for apology: we are late again with this number and, after the re-avowals of large and high intentions above, are the more embarrassedly conscious of other shortcomings that seem inseparable from carrying on under present conditions. But the word still is: we shall carry on while we can.

(1942)

Criticism and Literary History

(1) A REVIEW, by F. R. Leavis

English Poetry and the English Language, by F. W. Bateson

Mr. Bateson introduces his essay with some just criticism of the academic study of literature. The essay itself constitutes a much more radical criticism. For the unprofitable issue of an intention and an initiative in themselves so admirable must be charged to academic deficiencies. A critic as interested and energetic as Mr. Bateson ought not to have been able to be so unprovided with the elementary tools for his job, so unprepared by the elementary training, and so unaware of his plight.

But "critic," one gathers, is a description that he would repudiate. The nature of the distinction that, in his opening pages, he tries to elaborate between the critic and the literary historian is not clear, but he certainly intends a separation, and he calls his book "An Essay in Literary History." Yet the kind of history that he undertakes could be successfully attempted only by a critic and would then be essentially literary criticism. For by "history" he means something more than the usual compilation for the use of examinees—names, titles, dates, "facts about," irrelevancies, superficial comments, and labour-saving descriptions; and he is determined that it shall be *literary* (his italics) history. But his notion of this remains vague:

> His objection to regarding literature as a function of the social organism is the literary critic's objection—not that it cannot be done, but that it can only be done by disregarding those elements in literature that distinguish good writing from bad. In the last resort, therefore, the literary historian stands or falls only in so far as he satisfies, or fails to satisfy, the literary critic. If the interpretation he proposes does not clarify the central and universal significance of the literature he is treating, it is worthless. His history may be excellent social history or economic history, but there is one thing it will not be: it will not be *literary* history.

Mr. Bateson assumes that he can, as a literary historian, take over the necessary criticism (betraying innocent assumption—where does he suppose this criticism is to be found?) and "satisfy the literary critic" without being one himself. And, looking round for something in terms of which he can safely "interpret" the history of poetry, he settles here:

> It is to words therefore, their history and science, that I invite the historian of poetry to turn. I suggest that poetry develops *pari passu* with the words it uses, that its history is a part of the general history of language, and that its changes of style and mood are merely the reflection of changing tendencies in the uses to which language is being put.

"Words" for him is a simple term; "denotation" and "connotation" suffice for his perception of complexities (Dr. Richards's "paradigm of the fluctuations of the word *word*" would have come to him as an inhibiting revelation). But even with a more adequate analytic equipment he could not, except as a literary critic making a distinctively literary-critical approach, have written a more essentially *literary* history—a history, that is, unobnoxious to the considerations on which he dismisses the "social" and "economic."

There can be no simple directions—no helpful ones—for writing the literary history that, when his thought is clarified, Mr. Bateson is desiderating (his "words" and "language" do not provide the guidance he supposes them to). The essential thing about such a history will be the focus, the centre of interest: the centre of interest will always be in literature, the focus always upon literary values. But "literary values" is an unsatisfactory phrase; it says no more here than that the kind of attention, the discrimination, the eye for significance, will be the literary critic's.

Such a history—a history of English poetry—will be undertaken because the works of certain poets are judged to be of lasting value— of value in the present. When it takes account of other works it will not be because such works were published, had once perhaps a public, and are habitually referred to in histories of literature. It will take account of changes in taste and fashion, but will not confuse its business with that of a history of taste and fashion. Judgements of poetic value will determine and control its attention none the less strictly because its attention will not be confined to valuable poetry. As Mr. Bateson says:

> The English poets are not suspended in a vacuum. They have relations and connexions both with each other and with the general life of their times, and it should be possible to illustrate and define those inter-connexions without falling into the verbose inanities of "influences" and "tendencies."

The "illustrating" and "defining," one must add, will be a part of a strictly critical process—a process of evaluating, and of bringing out the significance of what is judged to be valuable. The desiderated "history" will be as much a work of criticism as a critique of a single poet is.

Such a history, then, could be accomplished only by a writer interested in, and intelligent about, the present. It would, for one thing, be an attempt to establish a perspective, to determine what of English poetry of the past is, or ought to be, alive for us now. The motive to it would be inseparable from an interest in the problems of contemporary poets—in the problems of their relation to tradition and to the contemporary world, Mr. Bateson's grounds for "deliberately omitting to consider Mr. W. B. Yeats and Mr. T. S. Eliot"—"The one is an Irishman, the other an American, and the language they maltreat with such masterly virtuosity is not exactly English, but a sweeter and less stubborn instrument, a *dead* language"—are of a piece with his judgement that Mr. A. E. Housman benefited by "the language's gains in precision" in the twenty years before *A Shropshire Lad*: "*A Shropshire Lad* has exactly those qualities of directness, concision, and inevitability that Hopkins's style just misses."

The relation of poetry to the language of its time, and also the state of that language (if a phrase that covers such a multitude of questions says anything at all), are obviously essential considerations. Mr. Bateson tends to be satisfied with considering ideas about language. Thus he explains the loose tautological fluency of the Elizabethans by the contemporary idea of "linguistic flux"—an idea due to the constant importation of new words. "They had an uneasy feeling all the time that their vocabulary was slipping away from under them, and suspecting and distrusting it, they did not dare to confide the whole of their meaning to a single word or phrase." But who from a reading of the verse itself could bring away any other impression than that the poets delight in their prolix fluency, and cultivate it for its own sake, being not much troubled with any particular burden of meaning? Their practice is to be explained in terms of literary convention—in terms of a young tradition that had not yet struck roots in contemporary life: mere "poetry," the excitement of having it at all, was, for a while, good enough.

The most important development of the period, the development that brought the full vitality of the age into poetry and produced a poetry representing a marvellous new use of the language, Mr. Bateson takes no note of. "But the drama and the novel," he tells us, "are relatively impure forms of literature" (also, "I hold that drama, including poetic drama, is essentially a form of prose, because its *media* are not words but ideas. . . ."). Nevertheless, how the advantages of the "impurity" by which Marlowe, Shakespeare, Jonson, Tourneur, Middleton, and others profited might be regained for poets—this should be the underlying preoccupation of Mr. Bateson's ideal historian. Not that it need be obtruded, or even explicit, anywhere. But it would direct and inform the eye with which the historian observed the changing conditions determining, from age to age, the use of genius and talent (in the foreground of the field of attention coming those that fall under the head of literary tradition—the current heritage of conventions, technical proclivities, habits of expression and approach).

In considering the eighteenth century, for instance, he would not, as Mr. Bateson does, make Thomson, Young, Gray, and Collins mainly an opportunity for elaborating an account of "the baroque style" ("The baroque style is rapid and inexact: it is rapid because inexact"). Instead he would notice that these poets represent a poetic tradition bearing a much less satisfactory relation to contemporary life than that borne either by the Metaphysical tradition or by the tradition that includes Pope and Johnson; and he would inquire how it was that so unsatisfactory a tradition came to prevail, making poets "literary" and "poetical" in pejorative senses of those terms.

In the nineteenth century he would find himself considering similar problems: how came the Romantic tradition (on which, in its first phase, one's comment is that, though alive with the vitality of the age, it made so disappointing a use of the talents belonging to it) to result in a Victorian poetry so essentially turned away from the contemporary world and cut off from the sources of vitality? He would not find the differences between Tennyson and the Pre-Raphaelites as important as Mr. Bateson makes them. Pre-Raphaelite poetry, Mr. Bateson tells us, "had been made possible by the vagueness of Mid-Victorian English; its function disappeared when the language became precise again." What this language was that became precise again (and by what agency) he does not tell us; and he nowhere discusses the relation between Victorian poetry and the English spoken in the age. But: "Hopkins was too early. The language had not increased sufficiently in precision by then for the massive concrete poetry of Hopkins to be possible at all without very special precautions. The clumsy, and, as one feels, unnecessary, concentration of his style was in fact necessary in 1876." And: *"A Shropshire Lad* had exactly those qualities of directness, concision, and inevitability that Hopkins's style just misses."

These three quotations show the essential themes—or what should have been such for Mr. Bateson—completely missed.

(1935)

(II) A COMMENT, by F. W. Bateson

Dear Sirs,

Dr. F. R. Leavis's review of my *English Poetry and the English Language* raises an issue of more importance than the merit or demerit of my essay. I mean the relation between literary history and literary criticism. The subtitle of my book is "An Experiment in Literary History," and I have devoted more than half my Introduction to defining, or attempting to define, what I conceive to be the essential differences between the two activities. Dr. Leavis, however, will have none of this. If I understand him he will not allow that there can be any such thing as literary history. A literary history, he writes, "could be successfully attempted only by a critic and would then be essentially literary criticism."

I think Dr. Leavis is demonstrably wrong, but as he found my exposition of the opposite point of view "vague" and "not clear" (it was entirely theoretical) I should like, with your permission, to state the case for literary history in different and more concrete terms. It will be necessary to begin with some rather elementary considerations. Dr. Leavis will, I hope, agree that the majority of propositions about literature, other than mere statements of fact, can be subsumed in a final analysis under two types. The formula for Type I, a simple example of which would be Dryden's tribute to Waller ("Unless he had written, none of us could write"), might be "A derives from B." And similarly Type II, which is exemplified by Arnold's dictum that "The best of Addison's composition (the 'Coverly Papers' in *The Spectator*, for example) wears better than the best of Pope's," could be reduced to "A is better than B," or even just "A is good." Now, of these two propositions the first is what I should call literary history, whereas the second only is, strictly speaking, literary criticism. But the labels are less important than a realization that the two types of proposition represent two different orders of truth. For the formula "A derives from B" really implies a further "and I can prove it"; on the other hand, the critic's formula "A is better than B" can only be expanded into "I am convinced that A is better than B." Arnold could not *prove* that Addison wears better than Pope. He was merely stating an *opinion*, and in order to make his opinion more plausible all that he could do, and did do, was to produce some additional *opinions* on the nature of eighteenth-century prose and verse. But the dependence of Dryden's poetry on Waller's is not an opinion, but a *fact*. Its truth or falsehood can be tested by a simple examination of the relevant evidence; *e.g.*, that provided by parallel passages, just as a fact is tested in a court of law.

The analysis can be taken a step further. A critical judgement, such as that cited from Arnold, is the expression of an immediate intuition. In its entirety it is necessarily inexplicable and incommunicable. Arnold, if one comes to think of it, was comparing the total impression made on him by years of familiarity with Addison's prose not only with the analogous impression he had of Pope's verse but also with his more diffused feeling of what in general constitutes good writing. And the half-conscious balancing of all these impressions against each other *resulted* in the dictum. But the process by which that result was obtained is inevitably mysterious. To compel an assent to such a judgement it would be necessary for Arnold's reader to have already read Addison and Pope in precisely the same way and against precisely the same literary background as Arnold himself possessed. And this is clearly an impossibility. An element of faith on the reader's part and of impressiveness or persuasiveness on the writer's must always enter into the effective propagation of every form of literary criticism. For a literary historian, on the other hand, and for the readers of literary historians, life is much simpler. Here there are no difficulties of communication at all. A historical thesis, such as Dryden's remark already quoted, either proves or disproves itself. The historian has simply to present his reader with the evidence upon which he has himself based his conclusion, and if the evidence proves to be trustworthy and adequate his reader can have no alternative except to concur in it. All in fact that is required is some mutually acceptable rules of evidence.

In the light of these considerations I can now return to Dr. Leavis's assertion that literary history is "essentially literary criticism." Dr. Leavis's paradox can mean three different things. He may mean: (1) that a historical proposition ("Pope derives from Dryden") is indistinguishable from a critical proposition ("Pope is better than Dryden"); or (2) that a historical proposition is just not worth making; or (3) that historical propositions are of subsidiary importance and can be taken by the critics in their stride. But (1) is nonsense, and the strict application of (2) would make any continuous survey of literature an impossibility. It is (3) therefore that Dr. Leavis probably intends, and (3) has a certain plausibility. No doubt, in a sense, critical propositions *are* more valuable than historical propositions. But, though the historian may be subordinate to the critic, Dr. Leavis is forgetting that the historian is none the less indispensable to him. Without the historians of literature where would Dr. Leavis be? Without texts, without commentaries, without biographical or technical information—in a word, without half the data out of which his judgements emerge. If we can read the Elizabethan dramatists today without undue difficulty, who have we to thank? The critics or the historians? Lamb or Dyce, Swinburne or Bullen? And let it not be imagined that any but a very exceptional critic can do the historians' work himself. The qualifications of a good critic and a good historian are, as I hope I have made clear, very different. The intuitions of the critic emerge from a temperament worlds away from the sober evidence-weighing of the historian. Taste, literary skill, a certain self-confidence, and finally an imperious urge to impose order upon the chaos of contemporary opinion—these are perhaps the desiderata of criticism. Literary history, on the other hand, demands the more prosaic virtues only of curiosity, learning, patience, and accuracy. May I say, without offence, that I look in vain for these qualities in Dr. Leavis?

But, though I think nothing is gained by denying that literary history and literary criticism are different disciplines, employing different methods and requiring different aptitudes in their exponents, I should be the last to agree to a total divorce between the two activities. On the contrary, I believe that criticism and scholarship are both suffering today from their ignorance and suspicion of each other. I wrote my book very largely in the hope that, in a small way, it might help to bridge the gulf between them. I wanted to show the critics that a scholar could be aware of their problems, though my approach had necessarily to be different from theirs; I wanted to show the scholars that their standards of exactitude and adequacy of documentation need not be sacrificed in a work of somewhat more ambitious scope than they usually venture on. Perhaps I was guilty of a certain presumptuousness. Dr. Leavis's review has left me in no doubt that I have failed to impress one critic whose opinions I respect. Nevertheless, I am still not convinced that

I was not right. Our critics *ought* to be more scholarly and our scholars more critical. But that goal cannot be reached simply by pretending that criticism and scholarship are the same thing. What I desiderate is not a deletion of the frontiers between the two professions, but a more intimate co-operation between them. At present, with one or two lonely exceptions, the critics and scholars just don't know what the other is doing. How many of the subscribers to *Scrutiny* and *The Criterion* are also readers of the *Review of English Studies* and the *Modern Language Review*? *Scrutiny* is not the place for me to discuss the deficiencies of some of our leading English scholars in, but I am tempted, without prejudice to the beam in their eyes, to consider for a moment a mote in the eye of the most eminent and influential of living critics, Mr. Eliot.

The Sacred Wood is so good a book that it must seem impertinent to say that it ought to have been better. That is, however, the unpalatable truth. Mr. Eliot's ignorance of or indifference to the requirements of scholarship has given his essays a regrettable capriciousness. Some of his observations are reckless almost to the point of impudence. I must content myself with one example, selected almost at random, from "Some Notes on the Blank Verse of Christopher Marlowe":

> The rapid long sentence, running line into line . . . marks the certain escape of blank verse from the rhymed couplet, and from the elegiac or rather pastoral note of Surrey, to which Tennyson returned. If you contrast these two soliloquies with the verse of Marlowe's greatest contemporary, Kyd—by no means a despicable versifier—you see the importance of the innovation:
>
> > *The one took sanctuary, and, being sent for out,*
> > *Was murdered in Southwark as he passed*
> > *To Greenwich, where the Lord Protector lay.*
> > *Black Will was burned in Flushing on a stage;*
> > *Green was hanged at Osbridge in Kent . . .*
>
> which is not really inferior to:
>
> > *So these four abode*
> > *Within one house together; and as years*
> > *Went forward, Mary took another mate;*
> > *But Dora lived unmarried till her death.*
> > (TENNYSON, *Dora*)

What would a scholar's reactions be to this passage? In the first place, I suppose, he would want to know what was meant by Tennyson's "return" to Surrey. Tennyson's blank verse, though less varied than Marlowe's, is not end-stopped like Surrey's, and the long sentence is, as it happens, a prominent feature of it. In the second place our scholar would protest, I believe, against the unqualified attribution of *Arden of Feversham* (from which Mr. Eliot's quotation comes) to Kyd. The attribution is still entirely conjectural. It is possible, too, that he would hesitate to accept *tout court* the description of Kyd as "Marlowe's greatest contemporary." Shakespeare, after all, was born in the same year as Marlowe and they were rivals during more than half the latter's dramatic career. A more serious matter is the confusion of the deliberate naïveté of Tennyson's *Dora* with the artlessness of *Arden*. Tennyson's poem (which Mr. Eliot incidentally misquotes) is a clever, if hollow, pastiche of Wordsworth; its fault, as Arnold pointed out, is *simplesse,* an affected simplicity. To say that it "is not really inferior to" the crude metrical prose of the Elizabethan dramatist is about as helpful as saying that chalk is not really inferior to cheese.

My moral is, I trust, fairly obvious. Literary history and literary criticism both have a perfectly good right to exist, and each can learn something from the other. If Dr. Leavis will try to persuade his fellow critics to adopt a somewhat less arrogant attitude towards scholarship, I will see if I can induce some of our scholars to think less harshly of him—and perhaps even to read his books.

I am, your obedient servant,
F. W. Bateson

(1935)

(III) A REJOINDER, *by F. R. Leavis*

I did not intend to give Mr. Bateson any excuse for supposing that I despise scholarship and I am sorry if I have given him any. I intended to criticize his scholarship for being incomplete; to insist that it was inadequate for his undertaking because (*a*) it relied fundamentally upon such difficult concepts as "word" and "language" without, apparently, any realization of the difficulty or any acquaintance with the relevant analysis, and (*b*) it was insufficiently informed and guided by criticism. The proposition I in fact made was not of the generality that Mr. Bateson imputes: "the kind of history that he undertakes," I said, "could be successfully attempted only by a critic and would then be essentially criticism" (in another context I might have said, without inconsistency, that it could be successfully attempted only by a scholar). I have no doubt at all that there may be histories consisting, in so far as they have any use, of mere statements of facts about works of literature—works the assumed values of which the historian takes as fact too, without asking how it came to be fact or what here is the nature of the fact (though even the purest "historian" would, if one can imagine him sufficiently aware, find himself faced with awkward questions when fixing the edge, for his purposes, of literature: we all know where Martin Tupper comes, but conventional valuation isn't universally so helpful).

The parenthesis, "in so far as they have any use," slipped in because actually I know of no literary history that doesn't make a show of criticism. And any history that deals in influences is committed to criticism—as Mr. Bateson, in his own way, is committed. This general proposition will surprise Mr. Bateson—or, rather, he will feel, and perhaps rightly, that it justified his ascribing to me the more general proposition. It brings me, at any rate, to my essential point against him: the radical distinction he invokes, the distinction that he reduces to the difference between fact and opinion, seems to me extraordinarily uncritical (I hope he won't think this begging the question). What is this "fact" of "the dependence of Dryden's poetry on Waller's"? I should like to see by what "sober evidence-weighing" Mr. Bateson would set out to establish it. The only evidence he specifies is "that provided by parallel passages"—by which, indeed, Dryden can be proved to have read Waller just as he can be proved to have read Cowley and Milton. But the most sober weighing can go no further, except in terms of critical judgements of a most complex and delicate order: "dependence" in any sense that can interest anyone interested in poetry —anyone who knows at first hand, and not as a fact accepted on authority, why Dryden should be worth studying—is still to be determined, estimated, defined, or pooh-poohed.

Mr. Bateson can suppose his position reasonable only because he invokes an absurdly simple notion of criticism: the critic, he suggests, says, pointing to this or that work which lies there for him, the historian, and all of us as a common fact, "this is good" or "bad." Actually, Mr. Bateson as a literary historian can have access to the works he proposes to deal with—to his most essential facts— only if he is sufficiently a critic; only by an appropriate and discriminating response to them; a response, that is, involving the kind of activity that produces value-judgements. And these judgements are not, in so far as they are real, expressions of opinion on facts that can be possessed and handled neutrally (so to speak). The jobs, it follows, both of the scholar and the critic are (if they do them properly) more arduous than either commonly cares to recognize. I especially deplore Mr. Bateson's attitude because it encourages a lazy notion of criticism. The critic should be at least as arduously concerned for "fact" as the scholar; not merely because he should pay due attention to the relevant facts of scholarship, but because he should be controlled by the determination to justify his treating as a fact of the public world something that cannot be tripped over, passed from hand to hand, brought into a laboratory, or, in any literal sense, pointed to (*e.g., Macbeth, Wuthering Heights, Sailing to Byzantium*). This means not self-confidence, but cultivated self-mistrust; not assertiveness, but disciplined and strenuous humility and docility—means "curiosity," "patience," and "accuracy." So Mr. Bateson will see what a hard knock he gives me when he finds me devoid of these last three virtues ("learning" I knew I hadn't a great deal of, though I have tried hard to acquire what is relevant to my interests).

As for Dyce and Bullen, towards them I feel gratitude and respect; towards Lamb and Swinburne, when adduced as critics, very much the opposite.

As for Mr. Eliot, I have myself been in the habit of making certain critical comments on the passage that Mr. Bateson criticizes; but I suspect that Mr. Eliot might reply to Mr. Bateson's criticisms that, as they stand, they combine pedantry with inaccuracy.

And as for Mr. Bateson's book, I did not think it necessary to say in my review (what I say now) that I found it well worth disagreeing with and that I was grateful for the opportunity.

(1935)

Literary Criticism and Philosophy

(1) A LETTER, by René Wellek

Dear Dr. Leavis:

I have read your new book, *Revaluation,* with much admiration and profit. It seems the first consistent attempt to rewrite the history of English poetry from the twentieth-century point of view. Spenser, Milton, Shelley, Tennyson, the Pre-Raphaelites, the Georgians recede into the background, and Donne, Dryden, Pope, Wordsworth, and Keats in part, Hopkins, the later Yeats, T. S. Eliot, etc., move into the foreground. Your book teems with acute critical observations and brilliant interpretations of texts. I think there will be little quarrel with your chapters on the seventeenth century, on Pope, on the eighteenth century, and on Keats. If I may venture, however, some fundamental criticisms (and there would be no reason to write unless I had something to say), I could wish that you had stated your assumptions more explicitly and defended them systematically. I do not doubt the value of these assumptions and, as a matter of fact, I share them with you for the most part, but I would have misgivings in pronouncing them without elaborating a specific defence or a theory in their defence. Allow me to sketch your ideal of poetry, your "norm" with which you measure every poet: your poetry must be in serious relation to actuality, it must have a firm grasp of the actual, of the object, it must be in relation to life, it must not be cut off from direct vulgar living, it should not be personal in the sense of indulging in personal dreams and fantasies, there should be no emotion for its own sake in it, no afflatus, no mere generous emotionality, no luxury in pain or joy, but also no sensuous poverty, but a sharp, concrete realization, a sensuous particularity. The language of your poetry must not be cut off from speech, should not flatter the singing voice, should not be merely mellifluous, should not give, *e.g.,* a mere general sense of motion, etc. You will recognize, of course, in this description tags from your book chosen from all chapters, and the only question I would ask you is to defend this position more abstractly and to become conscious that large ethical, philosophical, and, of course, ultimately, also aesthetic *choices* are involved.

My further criticism would be directed to one of the consequences of your assumption. Your insistence on a firm grasp on the actual predisposes you in the direction of a realist philosophy and makes you unappreciative of a whole phase of human thought: idealism as it comes down from Plato. This makes you underrate the coherence and even the comprehensibility of the romantic view of the world. I would like to demonstrate this by an analysis of a few examples from your chapters on the Romanticists.

You compare, *e.g.*, the structure of Blake's *Introduction* to the *Songs of Experience* with Eliot's *Ash Wednesday*, and consider Blake's poem as so ambiguous as to have no "right sense" at all (p. 141). Actually, I think, the poem has only one possible meaning, which can be ascertained by a study of the whole of Blake's symbolical philosophy. Here is my paraphrase: the poet is addressing Mankind, Fallen Man, who in Blake is frequently enough symbolized by the Earth. "Man!" he says, "listen to the voice of the poet who has the gift of prophecy because he has listened to the voice of God. In spite of his fall Man might yet control the universe ('the starry pole')." Now the bard is quoted as saying: "Arise from your slumber. Morning is near. But in the meantime you can wait armed with Reason, limited by Time and Space." Or to comment on every difficulty in detail: not the Holy Word of the *Bard* is calling the lapsed soul, as you say (p. 141). The Bard claims only to have heard the voice of God who once (in the garden of Eden) called the lapsed soul who then was weeping in the evening dew. Delete "and" (in line 7), which was inserted only because of the rhythm, and the sense is quite clear. The word "dew," by the way, has a special significance in Blake, and if you compare the very similar scene in *Vala* ("Ninth Night," 1. 371, etc.) you find there phrases like "the dew of death," which are obviously relevant. "The dewey grass" in line 12 of our poem is also symbolic. "Dew," or any water, in Blake represents matter, the grass, for obvious reasons, flesh. The next "that" cannot possibly refer to God, but to the soul or to Man, who after his rebirth might control the "starry pole." There is no need to evoke "Lucifer." Earth, identical with Man and soul, should arise out of matter ("dewey grass" is the same as "slumberous mass"). The twinkling stars in Blake mean always the light of Reason, and the watery shore the limit of matter or of Time and Space. The identification of Earth and Man in this poem is explicitly recognized by Blake in the illustration to this very poem, which represents a masculine figure lying upon the "watery shore" and, with the "starry floor" as a background, painfully lifting his head. There may be discussion how hard this or that symbol of Blake should be pressed, but the structure seems to me in no way to resemble *Ash Wednesday,* and the syntax is quite clear. One of the difficulties is the punctuation in your version: in the first edition there is no semi-colon after "sees," no comma after "Soul," a colon after "dew," commas after "heard" and "Word," etc.

The chapter on Wordsworth, excellent as it is in fine critical discrimination, shows the same lack of interest in romantic philosophy. I cannot see why the argument of Canto II of *The Prelude* could not be paraphrased, and I cannot possibly consider Mr. Empson's analysis of a passage from *Tintern Abbey* as satisfactory (*Seven Types of Ambiguity*, 1930, p. 191 *ff.*). There is no difficulty with this passage except possibly in the words "something far more deeply interfused." The question "than what?" put by Mr. Empson can be answered only by "than you would think, than it is usually (*i.e.,* in theism) understood." A "presence," a "sense sublime," a "motion and a spirit," are all different terms for the something "impelling all thinking things, all objects of all thought." This last phrase does not, as Mr. Empson suggests, imply "determinism" or even "predestination," but means simply that this something, this spirit, sets in motion both human minds and all objects of these minds. The sense of the passage becomes quite clear if we see it in the light of the whole of Wordsworth's philosophy; *e.g.,* if we read of "the one interior life that lives in all things . . . in which all beings live with God, themselves are God, existing in the mighty whole" (from a *Note-book* of only slightly later date, Sélincourt's edition of *The Prelude,* p. 512). I grant that we today may not be impressed by these speculations, but they are the very life-blood of a great European tradition descended from Plato, and they are still considered valid and valuable by many prominent thinkers. I recall, *e.g.,* A. N. Whitehead's interesting comments on Wordsworth's philosophy of nature (*Science and the Modern World,* 1926, p. 103), where the eminent mathematician, logician, and speculative philosopher commends Wordsworth precisely because "he grasps the whole nature in the tonality of the particular instance." Whitehead quotes "Ye Presences of Nature in the sky" (from *The Prelude,* I, line 464) as expressing most clearly a feeling for nature, "exhibiting entwined prehensive unities, each suffused with modal presences of others." Bradley's comparison with Hegel does not seem to me absurd, and

I have myself shown (in my book on *Kant in England,* 1931, p. 159 *ff.*) that traces of Kantian thought can be found in Wordsworth (indirectly through Coleridge). The debt to Hartley to which you refer and which you consider rightly as external (p. 158) was really much slighter and more transient than it would appear from a book like Beatty's. So, contrary to your own conclusion (p. 164), I would maintain the coherence, unity, and subtlety of Wordsworth's thought. I would be chary about using the term ultimate validity, but Wordsworth's thoughts on nature, etc., seem to me equally satisfying (and actually of the very same general tendency) as the thought of Schelling or Hegel on these questions. This stress on the "defensibility" (is there such a word in the English language?) of Wordsworth's philosophy of nature implies that Wordsworth's thought is not reducible to the Arnoldian conception or to Mr. Empson's astonishing assertion that he has no "other inspiration than the mountains as a totem or a father-substitute" *(loc. cit.,* p. 26). Arnold notoriously ignored the poetical thought of Wordsworth, and his anthology of Wordsworth is worth looking at as it shows how exclusively he stressed the pastoral and idyllic side in Wordsworth. Mr. Empson has possibly traced part of Wordsworth's conception to its psychological source in childhood experiences, but it is an ordinary "fallacy of origins" to dispose of the actual contents and value of thought by reducing it to individual experience. Whatever the value of Wordsworth's conception of Nature, it seems to me essential to his ideas on human sanity and spiritual health which you state so admirably. "Nature" is part of his whole view of the world and cannot be artificially isolated.

The same criticism applies, I think, also to your paper on Shelley. I have, first, some doubts on individual points. Your analysis of the second stanza of the *Ode to the West Wind* presses, I think, some of the metaphors too hard. The comparison of loose clouds with earth's decaying leaves does not seem to me merely vague and general (p. 205). A defence could suggest that the parallel can be made plausible by imagining Shelley lying in his boat and seeing in the loose clouds the counterpart of the leaves swimming in the stream or even seeing clouds mirrored in the water together with the leaves. These are the "tangled boughs of Heaven and Ocean," which I don't think could have been suggested merely by leaves, but rather allude to the old mystical conception of the two trees of Heaven and Earth intertwining.

Your objections against Shelley's stress on inspiration seem to me exaggerated. One cannot deny the share of the unconscious in the creative process, and sudden "inspiration" must be of necessity more prominent in a writer of songs compared to a dramatist, a novelist, or a composer of symphonies, where the share of conscious work must be larger. Shelley, I think, overstressed the "inspiration" in obvious reaction to eighteenth-century ideas on composing poetry and in answer to Peacock's essay, which is written from a completely rationalist point of view. Shelley himself revised his work continually, and one can find at least two or three earlier stages of the *Ode* in his *Note-books* (ed. Buxton Forman, 1911, Vol. I, 164); *e.g.*, line five was originally "On the blue deep of the aerial stream," then "blue deep" was changed to "blue depth" and then to "blue surface." "Stream" was replaced by "billows" before the "surge" to which you object was adopted.

I cannot see the slightest confusion in the opening paragraph of *Mont Blanc*. It states an epistemological proposition quite clearly. "There is nothing outside the mind of man, the receptive function of the stream of consciousness is very much larger than the tiny active principle in mind which itself is determined by the huge flood of external impressions." So or similarly could one state the contents in abstract terms which in Shelley are expressed in two similes: first the external impressions are compared to a huge stream ever varied into which at a secret point the active principle flows, and then this active principle is compared to a feeble brook among high mountains which has seemingly a much louder voice because of the intermingling and surrounding sounds of waterfalls, winds, and woods. I cannot see that the "metaphorical and the actual," "the real and the imagined," are confused, as you say (p. 212), and the "inner" and "outer" are confused only in the sense that, according to Shelley (and all subjective idealists), there is simply no "outer" accessible to our mind. Shelley—in distinction from Fichte, etc.—is of the opinion that the active contribution of our mind is only slight but still existent, as can be further shown by verses in the very same poem:

> My own, my human mind, which passively
> Now renders and receives fast influencings,
> Holding an unremitting interchange
> With the clear universe of things around   [1. 37].

Here we have again, in spite of the stress on the passivity of the mind, a clear conception of the give-and-take, of an interchange, between the creative and the purely receptive principles of mind, a complete commentary on the passage explained above. The passage you quote (p. 213) in contrast from Wordsworth's *Prelude* (VI, 631*ff*.) has philosophically nothing to do with the introduction of Shelley's *Mont Blanc*. It merely asserts the romantic conception of a symbolic meaning in the physiognomy of Nature.

I would not like to defend *When the lamp is shattered*, which seems to me a poor poem in any case. But still I think you make the poem out to be worse than it is. You do not seem to have interpreted rightly the meaning of the question beginning "O Love" in stanza 3. The poet merely asks Love why she chooses the frailest thing, *i.e.*, the human heart, as her cradle, home, and bier. Love is born, resides, and dies in the heart. This does not seem to be anything unconventional, but still it saves the poem from your charge of containing "banalities about the sad lot of woman" (p. 221), as woman, in my interpretation, is never mentioned at all. "The weak one" which is "singled to endure what is once possessed" is not necessarily of feminine sex at all, but simply the heart for which complete forgetfulness of former happiness would be less painful than the burden of memory. Stanza 4 addresses Love again, and *"its passions"* refer to the passion of the heart.

These notes are made only to support my main point: Shelley's philosophy, I think, is astonishingly unified and perfectly coherent. After an early stage of eighteenth-century materialism he turned to idealism in a subjective version. It is outside the scope of these notes to determine what exactly were the different influences which moulded his thoughts. Berkeley or Berkeley through Drummond, Plato, the neo-Platonists, the Gnostics, Spinoza, Shaftesbury, or the animistic philosophy of nature developed by E. Darwin and H. Davy from Newton are the names which can be found among his wide reading, and they are obviously his spiritual ancestry. (*cf., e.g.*, the two books by Carl Grabo, *A Newton among Poets*, 1930, and *The Meaning of the Witch of Atlas*, 1936, which contain much material on these questions and interpret many obscure passages in Shelley.) Shelley's conception of the world as a phenomenal flux behind which the unreachable absolute ("the white radiance of eternity") is only dimly perceived pervades also his imagery and symbols as the veils, and streams, boats, caverns, the gnostic eagles and serpents. Another consequence of this idealism is one pervading characteristic of his style, which psychologists call "synaesthesia" *i.e.*, the seeing of sounds and hearing of colors, which is not a mere idiosyncrasy but is based on a widespread psychological type and appears in the poetry of many ages, especially in the Baroque and the Romantic ages. (There is a whole series of papers with hundreds of quotations also from English poetry in the *Deutsche Vierteljahrschrift*, Vols. IX and XVI.) This fusing of the spheres of the different senses in Shelley is exactly paralleled in his rapid transitions and fusions of the emotions, from pleasure to pain, from sorrow to joy. Shelley would like us similarly to ignore or rather to transcend the boundaries of individuality between persons just as Indian philosophy or Schopenhauer wants us to overcome the curse and burden of the *principium individuationis*. Here is, of course, the place of Shelley's mysticism which belongs organically to the whole view of the world expounded here. The intellectual honesty, consistency, and, at the particular time and place, originality of his thought cannot, I think, be reasonably doubted. I am not sure whether this intellectual system in Shelley's poetry says anything in favour of its value as poetry, but I think it should meet a good deal of the criticism against him, which seems to me to exaggerate the "confusion" of his style because it underrates the thought implied. I do not think that psychological considerations on the make-up of the personality of the poet can contribute anything to his defence. Mr. Herbert Read seems to have achieved the opposite of what he wanted when he stressed the pathological features in Shelley's character. Still I think you condemn too rashly as signs of "viciousness" and "corruption" Shelley's marked interest in details of decay and death (p. 216). The "sinister" elements are in Shelley, it is true, sometimes expressed in the language of sensational romanticism (graveyard poetry and Gothic romance), but the interest itself, which you may call morbid, is so very widespread throughout the history of humanity and even so marked in much great poetry (Donne, Baudelaire, etc.) that it seems to me nothing peculiarly damaging for Shelley can be made out of it.

All these remarks could have only one purpose: to show that the romantic view of the world, though it found in England only one prominent philosopher, Coleridge, underlies and pervades the poetry of Blake, Wordsworth, and Shelley, elucidates many apparent difficulties, and is, at least, a debatable view of the world. Your book, or rather the very limited part I have been discussing, raises anew the question of the poet's "belief" and how far sympathy with this belief and comprehension of it are necessary for an appreciation of the poetry. A question which has been debated a good deal, as you know, and which I would not like to solve too hastily on the basis of your book.

Yours sincerely,
René Wellek

(1937)

(II) A REPLY, by F. R. Leavis

I must thank Dr. Wellek not merely for his explicit compliments (which, coming from a dissentient critic, are especially gratifying), but for bringing fundamental criticism to my work, and above all for raising in so complete a way an issue that a reviewer or two had more or less vaguely touched on—an issue of which no one can have been more conscious than myself, who had seen the recognition of it as an essential constituent of what I naturally (whatever the quality of my performance) hoped for: an appreciation of my undertaking. Dr. Wellek points out, justly, that in my dealings with English poetry I have made a number of assumptions that I neither defend nor even state: "I could wish," he says, "that you had made your assumptions more explicitly and defended them systematically." After offering me a summary of these assumptions, he asks me to "defend this position abstractly and to become conscious that large ethical, philosophical, and, of course, ultimately, also aesthetic *choices* are involved."

I in my turn would ask Dr. Wellek to believe that if I omitted to undertake the defence he desiderates it was not from any lack of consciousness: I knew I was making assumptions (even if I didn't—and shouldn't now—state them to myself quite as he states them) and I was not less aware than I am now of what they involve. I am interested that he should be able to say that, for the most part, he shares them with me. But, he adds, he would "have misgivings in pronouncing them without elaborating a specific defence or a theory in their defence." That, I suggest, is because Dr. Wellek is a philosopher; and my reply to him in the first place is that I myself am not a philosopher, and that I doubt whether in any case I could elaborate a theory that he would find satisfactory. I am not, however, relying upon modesty for my defence. If I profess myself so freely to be no philosopher it is because I feel that I can afford my modesty; it is because I have pretensions—pretensions to being a literary critic. And I would add that even if I had felt qualified to satisfy Dr. Wellek on his own ground I should have declined to attempt it in that book.

Literary criticism and philosophy seem to me to be quite distinct and different kinds of disciplines—at least, I think they ought to be (for while in my innocence I hope that philosophic writing commonly represents a serious discipline, I am quite sure that literary-critical writing commonly doesn't). This is not to suggest that a literary critic might not, as such, be the better for a philosophic training, but if he were, the advantage, I believe, would manifest itself partly in a surer realization that literary criticism is not philosophy. I pulled up just short of saying "the two disciplines . . .," a phrase that might suggest too great a simplification: it is no doubt possible to point to valuable writing of various kinds representing varying kinds of alliances between the literary critic and the philosopher. But I am not the less sure that it is necessary to have a strict literary criticism somewhere and to vindicate literary criticism as a distinct and separate discipline.

The difficulty that one who approaches with the habit of one kind of discipline has in duly recognizing the claims of a very different kind—the difficulty of reconciling the two in a working alliance—seems to me to be illustrated in Dr. Wellek's way of referring to the business of literary criticism: "Allow me," he says, "to sketch your ideal of poetry, your 'norm' with which you measure every poet . . ." That he should slip into this way of putting things seems to me significant, for he would on being challenged agree, I imagine, that it suggests a false idea of the procedure of the critic. At any rate, he gives me an excuse for making, by way of reminder, some elementary observations about that procedure.

By the critic of poetry I understand the complete reader: the ideal critic is the ideal reader. The reading demanded by poetry is of a different kind from that demanded by philosophy. I should not find it easy to define the difference satisfactorily, but Dr. Wellek knows what it is and could give at least as good an account of it as I could. Philosophy, we say, is "abstract" (thus Dr. Wellek asks me to defend my position "more abstractly"), and poetry "concrete." Words in poetry invite us not to "think about" and judge, but to "feel into" or "become"—to realize a complex experience that is given in the words. They demand not merely a fuller-bodied response, but a completer responsiveness—a kind of responsiveness that is incompatible with the judicial, one-eye-on-the-standard approach suggested by Dr. Wellek's phrase: "your 'norm' with which you measure every poet." The critic—the reader of poetry—is indeed concerned with evaluation, but to figure him as measuring with a norm which he brings up to the object and applies from the outside is to misrepresent the process. The critic's aim is, first, to realize as sensitively and completely as possible this or that which claims his attention; and a certain valuing is implicit in the realizing. As he matures in experience of the new thing he asks, explicitly and implicitly: "Where does this come? How does it stand in relation to . . .? How relatively important does it seem?" And the organization into which it settles as a constituent in becoming "placed" is an organization of similarly "placed" things, things that have found their bearings with regard to one another, and not a theoretical system or a system determined by abstract considerations.

No doubt (as I have admitted) a philosophic training might possibly—ideally would—make a critic surer and more penetrating in the perception of significance and relation and in the judgement of value. But it is to be noted that the improvement we ask for is of the critic, the critic as critic, and to count on it would be to count on the attainment of an arduous ideal. It would be reasonable to fear—to fear blunting of edge, blurring of focus, and muddled misdirection of attention: consequences of queering one discipline with the habits of another. The business of the literary critic is to attain a peculiar completeness of response and to observe a peculiarly strict relevance in developing his response into commentary; he must be on his guard against abstracting improperly from what is in front of him and against any premature or irrelevant generalizing—of it or from it. His first concern is to enter into possession of the given poem (let us say) in its concrete fullness, and his constant concern is never to lose his completeness of possession, but rather to increase it. In making value-judgements (and judgements as to significance), implicitly or explicitly, he does so out of that completeness of possession and with that fullness of response. He doesn't ask, "How does this accord with these specifications of goodness in poetry?"; he aims to make fully conscious and articulate the immediate sense of value that "places" the poem.

Of course, the process of "making fully conscious and articulate" is a process of relating and organizing, and the "immediate sense of value" should, as the critic matures with experience, represent a growing stability of organization (the problem is to combine stability with growth). What, on testing and retesting and wider experience, turn out to be my more constant preferences, what the relative permanencies in my response, and what structure begins to assert itself in the field of poetry with which I am familiar? What map or chart of English poetry as a whole represents my utmost consistency and most inclusive coherence of response?

From this consistency and this coherence (in so far as I have achieved them) it should, of course, be possible to elicit principles and abstractly formulable norms. Dr. Wellek's first criticism of me is (to give it its least exceptionable force) that I haven't proceeded to elicit them; that, having written the book I undertook to write, I haven't gone on to write another book in which I develop the theoretical implications of the first (for it would be essentially a matter of two books, even if there were only one binding). To this I make again my modest reply that I doubt, in any case, my capacity to satisfy Dr. Wellek in this respect. And I add again that I do not think my modesty has any adverse bearing on my qualifications for writing the book I did undertake to write. The cogency I hoped to achieve was to be for other readers of poetry—readers of poetry as such: I hoped, by putting in front of them in a criticism that should keep as close to the concrete as possible my own developed "coherence of response," to get them to agree (with, no doubt, critical qualifications) that the map, the essential order, of English poetry seen as a whole did, when they interrogated their experience, look like that to them also. Ideally I ought perhaps (though, I repeat, I should not put my position in quite the terms Dr. Wellek ascribes to me) to be able to complete the work with a theoretical statement. But I am sure that the kind of work that I have attempted comes first, and would, for such a theoretical statement to be worth anything, have to be done first.

If Dr. Wellek should still insist that I ought, even if I declined to elaborate the philosophy implicit in my assumptions, at any rate to have been more explicit about them, I can only reply that I think I have gone as far in explicitness as I could profitably attempt to go, and that I do not see what would be gained by the kind of explicitness he demands (though I see what is lost by it). Has any reader of my book been less aware of the essential criteria that emerge than he would have been if I had laid down such general propositions as: "poetry must be in serious relation to actuality, it must have a firm grasp of the actual, of the object, it must be in relation to life, it must not be cut off from direct vulgar living, it should be normally human..."? If, as I did, I avoided such generalities, it was not out of timidity; it was because they seemed too clumsy to be of any use. I thought I had provided something better. My whole effort was to work in terms of concrete judgements and particular analyses: "This—doesn't it?—bears such a relation to that; this kind of thing—don't you find it so?—wears better than that," etc. If I had to generalize, my generalization regarding the relation between poetry and "direct vulgar living" or the "actual" would run rather in the following way than in that suggested by Dr. Wellek: "traditions, or prevailing conventions or habits, that tend to cut poetry in general off from direct vulgar living and the actual, or that make it difficult for the poet to bring into poetry his most serious interests as an adult living in his own time, have a devitalizing effect." But I cannot see that I should have added to the clarity, cogency, or usefulness of my book by enunciating such a proposition (or by arguing it theoretically). Again, I did not say that the language of poetry "should not flatter the singing voice, should not be merely mellifluous," etc. I illustrated concretely in comparison and analysis the qualities indicated by those phrases, pointed to certain attendant limitations, and tried to show in terms of actual poetic history that there were serious disadvantages to be recognized in a tradition that insisted on such qualities as essential to poetry. In fact, though I am very much aware of the shortcomings of my work, I feel that by my own methods I have attained a relative precision that makes this summarizing seem intolerably clumsy and inadequate. I do not, again, argue in general terms that there should be "no emotion for its own sake, no afflatus, no mere generous emotionality, no luxury in pain and joy"; but by choice, arrangement, and analysis of concrete examples I give those phrases (in so far, that is, as I have achieved my purpose) a precision of meaning they couldn't have got in any other way. There is, I hope, a chance that I may in this way have advanced theory, even if I haven't done the theorizing. I know that the cogency and precision I have aimed at are limited; but I believe that any approach involves limitations, and that it is by recognizing them and working within them that one may hope to get something done.

Dr. Wellek has a further main criticism to bring against me: it is that my lack of interest in philosophy makes me unfair to the poets of the Romantic period. I hope he will forgive me if I say that his demonstration has, for me, mainly the effect of demonstrating how difficult it is to be a philosopher and a literary critic at the same time. The positive aim of his remarks he sums up as being "to show that the romantic view of the world . . . underlies and pervades the poetry of Blake, Wordsworth, and Shelley, elucidates many apparent difficulties, and is, at least, a debatable view of the world."—

"The romantic view of the world," a view common to Blake, Wordsworth, Shelley, and others—yes, I have heard of it; but what interest can it have for the literary critic? For the critic, for the reader whose primary interest is in poetry, those three poets are so radically different, immediately and finally, from one another that the offer to assimilate them in a common philosophy can only suggest the irrelevance of the philosophic approach.

My attitude toward Blake Dr. Wellek, I think, misunderstands. He certainly misrepresents my verdict on the particular poem, the *Introduction* to *Songs of Experience*. The comparison with *Ash Wednesday* has a context in the chapter to which the note challenged by Dr. Wellek is appended, and, so far from arguing that Blake's poem is "so ambiguous as to have no 'right sense,' " I have in that note the explicit aim of showing how Blake, with his astonishingly original technique, achieves something like the extraordinary precision of *Ash Wednesday*. And in general, where Blake is concerned, my intention is the reverse of a slighting one. My view of the poem, in fact, seems to me more favorable than that implied by Dr. Wellek, who says: "Actually, I think the poem has only one possible meaning, which can be ascertained by a study of the whole of Blake's symbolical philosophy." I myself, a literary critic, am interested in Blake because it is possible to say with reference to some of his work that his symbolical philosophy is one thing, his poetry another. I know that even in his best poetry symbolism appears, and I was aware of symbolism in the poem I picked on; but I judged that I might fairly avoid a large discussion that seemed inessential to the point I was proposing to make.

I will say now, though, that when in Blake's poetry his symbols function poetically they have, I believe, a life that is independent of his "symbolical philosophy": for instance, "Earth," "starry pole," "dewey grass," and "wat'ry shore," in the *Introduction* to *Songs of Experience,* seem to me to have a direct evocative power. Knowledge of Blake's arbitrary assignment of value to a symbol may often help to explain why he should have written as he has done here, there, and elsewhere; I do not believe that it will ever turn what was before an unsuccessful poem into a good one. And I think *Hear the voice of the Bard!* decidedly a good one. Dr. Wellek's account of it seems to me to justify my assumption that I could fairly discuss the poem without talking about symbols; for I cannot see that his account tends to invalidate mine. I cannot, in fact, see why he should suppose it does. Or rather, I see it is because he assumes that what we are elucidating is a text of symbolical philosophy—written as such and to be read as such.

The confidence of his paraphrase made me open my eyes. It is a philosopher's confidence—the confidence of one who in the double strength of a philosophic training and a knowledge of Blake's system ignores the working of poetry. The main difference, one gathers, between the philosopher and the poet is that to the poet there may be allowed, in the interests of rhythm and formal matters like that, a certain looseness, a laxity of expression: "Delete 'and' (in line 7), which was inserted only because of the rhythm, and the sense is quite clear"—yes, immediately clear, if one derives from a study of "the whole of Blake's symbolical philosophy" the confidence to perform these little operations. But I myself believe that in this poem Blake is using words with very unusual precision—the precision of a poet working as a poet.

And it is this precision that Dr. Wellek ignores in his paraphrase and objects to my noticing:

> In spite of his fall Man might yet control the universe ("the starry pole"). . . . The next "that" cannot possibly refer to God, but to the soul or to Man, who after his rebirth might control the "starry pole." There is no need to evoke Lucifer.

"Man" capable of controlling the universe may surely be said to have taken on something of God, and may be, I suggest, in Blake's syntax—in his peculiar organization of meaning—not so sharply distinguishable from God as Dr. Wellek's notion of "clear sense" and "one possible meaning" demands. And if "fallen, fallen light" does not for Dr. Wellek bring into the complex of associations Lucifer—

> *from morn*
> *To noon he fell, from noon to dewy eve,*
> *A summer's day, and with the setting sun,*
> *Dropt from the zenith like a falling star*
> *On Lemnos, the Aegean isle*

—then I think we have an instance of the philosopher disabling the critic; an instance of the philosophical approach inducing in the reader of poetry a serious impercipience or insensitiveness. Blake is not referring to abstract ideas of Man and rebirth; he works in the concrete, evoking by a quite unproselike (that was my point) use of associations a sense of a state of desolation that is the more grievous by contrast with an imagined state of bliss, in which Man, in harmonious mastery of his full potentialities, might be godlike—an unfallen and unsinful Lucifer (Milton, we remember, was of the Devil's party without knowing it).

> The twinkling stars in Blake mean always the light of Reason, and the watery shore the limit of matter or of Time and Space. The identification of Earth and Man in this poem is explicitly recognized by Blake in the illustration to this very poem, which represents a masculine figure lying upon the "watery shore" and, with the "starry floor" as a background, painfully lifting his head.

—I would call Dr. Wellek's attention to the poem, *Earth's Answer*, immediately following that which is under discussion. It opens:

> Earth raised up her head
> From the darkness dread and drear.
> Her light fled,
> Stony dread!
> And her locks cover'd with grey despair.
>
> 'Prison'd on wat'ry shore,
> 'Starry Jealousy does keep my den:
> 'Cold and hoar,
> 'Weeping o'er,
> 'I hear the father of the ancient men.'

I quote these stanzas as a way of suggesting to him that his neat and confident translation of symbols will not do (I am not saying that "Reason" and "Jealousy" could not be reconciled), and that even an argument from one of Blake's illustrations may not be as coercive as Dr. Wellek supposes.

Again, where Wordsworth is concerned, Dr. Wellek seems to misunderstand my intention. "So, contrary to your own conclusion (p. 164)," he says, "I would maintain the coherence, unity, and subtlety of Wordsworth's thought."—Well, I had heard of and read about Wordsworth's thought, which, indeed, has received a great deal of notice, but my business was with Wordsworth's poetry; I never proposed, and do not propose now, to consider him as a philosophic thinker. When I look up p. 164 in my book I find this as the only passage Dr. Wellek can be referring to:

> His philosophizing (in the sense of the Hartleian studies and applications) had not the value he meant it to have; but it is an expression of his intense moral seriousness and a mode of that essential discipline of contemplation which gave consistency and stability to his experience.

In saying that Wordsworth's philosophizing hadn't the value he meant it to have I was pointing out that it hadn't the relation he supposed to his business as a poet, and my analysis still seems to me conclusive. Dr. Wellek merely says in general terms that it isn't conclusive for him: "I cannot see why the argument of Canto II of *The Prelude* could not be paraphrased." It can, I freely grant, be very easily paraphrased if one brings to it a general knowledge of the kind of thought involved and an assumption that poets put loosely what philosophers formulate with precision. For would Dr. Wellek in prose philosophy be satisfied with, or even take seriously, such looseness of statement and argument as Wordsworth's in his philosophic verse? If so, he has a very much less strict criterion for philosophy as philosophy than I have for poetry as poetry. Even if Wordsworth had a philosophy, it is as a poet that he matters, and if we remember that even where he offers "thought" the strength of what he gives is the poet's, we shall, as critics, find something better to do than supply precision and completeness to his abstract argument.

I do not see what service Dr. Wellek does either himself or philosophy by adducing Chapter V of *Science and the Modern World*. That an eminent mathematician, logician, and speculative philosopher should be so interested in poetry as Professor Whitehead there shows himself to be is pleasing; but I have always thought the quality of his dealings with poetry to be exactly what one would expect of an authority so qualified. I will add, perhaps wantonly and irrelevantly, that the utterances of Professor Whitehead's quoted by Dr. Wellek look to me like bad poetry; in their context no doubt they become something different, but I cannot see why even then they should affect a literary critic's view of Wordsworth and Shelley.

When Dr. Wellek comes to Shelley he hardly makes any serious show of sustaining his case against me and the weakness of his own approach is most clearly exposed. He is so interested in philosophy that he pays no real attention to my analyses of poetry. Take, for instance, his suggested interpretations of points in the *Ode to the West Wind*: it is not merely that they are, it seems to me, quite unacceptable; even if they were otherwise, they would make no substantial difference to my carefully elaborated analysis of the way in which Shelley's poetry works. And why should Dr. Wellek suppose that he is defending Shelley in arguing that "the tangled boughs of Heaven and Ocean" may allude to "the old mystical conception of the two trees of Heaven and Earth intertwining"? Not that I attack the *Ode to the West Wind;* I merely illustrate from it the characteristic working of Shelley's poetry.

Nor do I attack *Mont Blanc*. When Dr. Wellek says, "I cannot see the slightest confusion in the opening paragraph of *Mont Blanc*," he seems to me to be betraying an inappreciation of Shelley —an inappreciation explained by the approach intimated in his next sentence: "It states an epistemological proposition quite clearly." Now, to me the opening paragraph of *Mont Blanc* evokes with great vividness a state of excited bewilderment and wonder. The obvious Wordsworthian element in the poem suggests a comparison with Wordsworth, and, regarding as I do the two poets, not as stating epistemological propositions or asserting general conceptions, but as reacting characteristically to similar concrete occasions, the comparison I actually make seems to me justified. When Dr. Wellek tells me that the passage I quote from *The Prelude* "has philosophically nothing to do with the introduction of Shelley's *Mont Blanc*," he merely confirms my conviction that philosophy and literary criticism are very different things.

Having described certain Shelleyan habits, I go on to point out that these carry with them a tendency to certain vices; vices such that, in diagnosing them, the literary critic finds himself becoming explicitly a moralist. I conduct the argument very carefully and in terms of particular analysis, and I cannot see that Dr. Wellek makes any serious attempt to deal with it. I cannot see why he should think that his alternative interpretation of the third stanza of *When the lamp is shattered* makes that poem less bad in any of the ways in which I have judged it adversely. But I do see that, *not* reading as a literary critic, he fails to respond with his sensibility to the peculiarly Shelleyan virtue, the personal voice, of the last stanza, and so fails to realize the force of my radical judgement on the poem (I cannot recapitulate the whole argument here).

Actually, of course, Dr. Wellek's attention is elsewhere than on Shelley's poetry and my analysis. "These notes," he slips into saying, "are made only to support my main point: Shelley's philosophy, I think, is astonishingly unified and perfectly coherent." I do not consider it my business to discuss that proposition, and Dr. Wellek has given me no grounds for judging Shelley's poetry to be anything other than I have judged it to be. If, in reply to my charge that Shelley's poetry is repetitive, vaporous, monotonously self-regarding, and often emotionally cheap, and so, in no very long run, boring, Dr. Wellek tells me that Shelley was an idealist, I can only wonder whether some unfavourable presumption has not been set up about idealism. Again, it is no consolation for disliking the characteristic Shelleyan vapour to be told:

> This fusing of the spheres of the different senses in Shelley is exactly paralleled in his rapid transitions and fusions of the emotions, from pleasure to pain, from sorrow to joy. Shelley would like us similarly to ignore or rather to transcend the boundaries of individuality between persons just as Indian philosophy or Schopenhauer wants us to overcome the curse and burden of the *principium individuationis*.

Of course, according to that philosophy poetry may be a mistake or illusion, something to be left behind. But Dr. Wellek will hardly bring it against me that I have been unfair to Shelley's poetry out of lack of sympathy with such a view.

Unfairness to poets out of lack of interest in their philosophy he does, of course, in general charge me with. His note concludes:

> Your book . . . raises anew the question of the poet's "belief" and how far sympathy with this belief and comprehension of it are necessary for an appreciation of the poetry. A question which has been debated a good deal, as you know, and which I would not like to solve too hastily on the basis of your book.

I will only comment, without wishing to question the justice of this conclusion, that Dr. Wellek seems to me to assume too easily that the poet's essential "belief" is what can be most readily extracted as such from his works by a philosopher.

(1937)

The Discipline of Letters
A Sociological Note

by Q. D. Leavis

In *Scrutiny Volume XI, Number 4* we examined the university career of a peculiarly gifted man, the late A. C. Haddon, who combined the abilities of a specialist opening up a new field of knowledge with those of an exceptionally inspiring teacher. It was a career that could hardly be called successful by worldly standards. Chance has given us the opportunity to complete the findings by contrast: we may now inspect the record of a man whom in our time an ancient university has delighted to honour.

It must be said first that this collection * of the late George Gordon's letters, made by his widow, seems intended primarily to show that he was an affectionate relative and had many distinguished friends. It is what emerges incidentally that matters, for it is of course in his public and representative capacities, as professor of literature and of poetry, that we are concerned with him here. He has in fact no other importance, since there is, as the blurb tactfully puts it, a "scarcity of more formal monuments to his learning and literary craftsmanship."

Gordon was the able Scots student who collects firsts and prizes by cannily directed industry. Coming from Glasgow as already a brilliant classic, after skimming through History and Greats he saw possibilities, as others have done, in the more recent department of English and transferred his attentions thither—English studies being, apart from the linguist's claims on them, notoriously the prerogative of your classic (generally of your not-good-enough classic). So he attracted Raleigh's attention by editing a typically academic collection of essays, *English Literature and the Classics,* to which he himself contributed a piece on Theophrastus; this, he wrote, convinced Raleigh that he would do for the English School. With Raleigh's backing he secured an English fellowship at Magdalen and managed before his fellowship ran out to land with it the Chair of English at Leeds, from whence he returned to succeed Raleigh as Merton Professor of Literature in 1922. In 1928 he became

* *The Letters of G. S. Gordon, 1902-1942.*

President of Magdalen, and subsequently Vice-Chancellor, but his merely academic offices, except as symptoms of success, are beside the point. We must note rather his election to the Oxford Chair of Poetry in 1934, his appointment to the original Selection Committee of the Book Society along with Walpole and Priestley (as to which he wrote, "I couldn't wish for better company"), his election to the various literary societies that carry social prestige, his undertaking a series of popular fifteen-minute broadcast talks on great literature, his editing a selection of *Times'* third leaders, etc. In contrast to Haddon, who achieved so much with so little public assistance, Gordon, in spite of every worldly opportunity in the way of financial endowment, social sanction, and professional backing, has left nothing except a few published lectures and addresses. Nevertheless, they have their interest and their place in literary history. For though they are not literary criticism they do give us an insight into the conditions which control literary studies in the universities and are therefore of the greatest value at this moment for us. For if any educational reform as a whole is to be achieved in this country after the war—and everything suggests that attempts in that direction will be made—it must centre on the universities, and there on the humanities. It is impossible to discuss such subjects in the air, without relation to the academic world which conditions them. And that sociology of the academic world which was desiderated in *Scrutiny Volume XI, Number 4* would certainly need to take note of the history of George Gordon. In contrast to Haddon, he was a green-bay-tree specimen: what enabled him to flourish? What sources of satisfaction did he provide for his order? we must ask. We may conveniently start by examining his record with respect to literature, for sociology and literary criticism are mutually enlightening.

His chief productions are his two inaugural lectures, *The Discipline of Letters*, delivered before the University of Oxford in 1923, and *Poetry and the Moderns*, delivered in the same circumstances in 1934. Both are professions of belief, with a difference: between them the deluge had occurred, as far as literary criticism is concerned. As late as 1923 Gordon, who evidently lived in a literary backwater, was unaware of any challenge to what he stood for. The discipline of letters, he proclaims, is represented by the Oxford School of English. This is twofold. On the one hand, linguistic-philological studies as an end in themselves. On the other, scholarship—the ideal of perfect editing, that is, a frivolous one which is hostile to any real standards in literature, since any text long enough dead is equally meet to be edited, the credit consists in producing the perfect index, etc., to a piece of writing not necessarily worth publishing in the first place. Or in Gordon's own words—and the jargon is characteristic—"In this University Mercury and Philologia, after many deeds of settlement (for the lady has been difficult), are partners, I hope, for life." He followed this up by an attack on the Royal Commission's *Report on English,* apparently because that proposed that English should take the place traditionally occupied by classics, and should in short be taken seriously as an educational and cultural study. To take literature seriously, he declared, is "an affront to life." An inexplicable attitude for a professor of English literature to strike in his inaugural lecture? But before we look further into this extraordinary position we will attend his next public appearance on an almost identical occasion.

Poetry and the Moderns, eleven years later, reveals the formerly complacent academic uneasy; if he is dimly aware that he has not a leg to stand on, so to speak, he is still feeling around for a stance to maintain his self-esteem. We note he invokes for support his friends and predecessors, Bridges, de Sélincourt, Garrod, Raleigh; with the like-minded to back him he takes up a position of superiority to what he cannot understand and feels as a threat to his prestige. The lecture is nothing but a series of appeals to his audience to respond in the cheapest way; he is out to capitalize the stock responses of the herd, he jeers in order to elicit sniggers of approval, and so on. The lecture is of course only memorable as one contribution to the academic war against contemporary poetry and literary criticism which, raging from about 1925 for a dozen years or more, will in a century or so no doubt become a subject for sanctioned literary research. That campaign looks negligible now, but it was conducted with every expression of malice, misrepresentation, and personal spite that the academic pen and tongue could command—the scholarly conscience having nothing to do with a critical conscience, or with any other kind, it would appear. We notice in Gordon's lecture that the focus of his ill-will is Mr. T. S. Eliot, and this was generally so, because as poet and literary critic Mr. Eliot represented a challenge which the "lovers of a continuous literary decorum" could neither overlook nor hope to take up without disaster: some of them envied his success as a poet and all were jealous of his literary influence. Hence the choice of an attack on "the moderns" as a subject for an inaugural lecture. But even in 1934 it was too late; the tide of public opinion had already turned. Even then Professor Claude Colleer Abbott was editing the letters of Gerard Manley Hopkins (Oxford, 1935) with the implication that they were as important as Keats's—to value highly the poems of Hopkins was another way to incur academic odium, Bridges, in reluctantly and patronizingly editing them, having indicated the permissible degree of admiration. And when in 1937 Mr. A. Humphry House, also of Oxford, produced an expensive edition of Hopkins's *Note-books and Papers,* in themselves of no particular interest, with all the panoply of scholarship including biographies of everyone mentioned in the text and bibliographies of the MSS., etc., well, if the citadel had not actually fallen, at least solidarity had been sacrificed. Or perhaps only consistency, for that section of the academic party which had put on record its opinion that any critic who thought Hopkins a considerable poet was thereby "certifiable" was at least put out of countenance. But Gordon had an instinct against risking being caught out on a limb: he ends by manœuvring into the favourite post-die-hard academic position. He ends with a profession, not this time of the Discipline of Letters (Mercury wedded to Philologia), but of broad-mindedness. He manages to put the critics he is attacking, instead of himself, in the attitude of intolerance by the usual trick of misrepresentation and even invention. We shall return to this later.

Altogether it is a curious history for a professor of English literature and worth investigating. The *Letters* recently published illuminate it considerably. Gordon succeeded Raleigh at Oxford and was formed by him, so we must go a stage further back, to the case of Raleigh himself. For Raleigh was not only the first professor of English literature at Oxford; he became a cult. His idiosyncrasies became the mould of form and his prejudices and prepossessions were standardized. We can see that while Raleigh made the Oxford English School he never took literature seriously, apart from its succubus, scholarship. He is an example of the most dangerous kind of academic, the man who hasn't enough ability to set up on his own as a creative artist and bears literature a grudge in consequence. His letters run on humorously about whatever poet he is writing on (Shakespeare, Blake, and Wordsworth figure in turn as Bill)—the effect is to place himself on a level with them or whatever literary figure he writes about. His lectures seem to have been dramatic readings studded with epigrams. His professorial writings are all, implicitly or explicitly, about the inferiority of literature to life, an antithesis which he propagated continually, and he is seen perpetually anxious to show that he was not a don, not a professional man of letters, not a serious teacher of literature (though he was quite willing to accept a comfortable living by undertaking to be all three). These characteristics, combined with a denigration of all literary criticism (which did not prevent him from publishing a number of books and resenting adverse reviews of them) when contrasted with his unquestioning belief in the virtues of good mixing in the best company, combine to make an unpleasant impression. A life devoted to teaching literature in this spirit is bound to become uneasy. By 1906 he was declaring "I begin to hate criticism. Nothing can come of it," and he seems before then to have been conscious of the futility of his kind of English studies. "If I am accused on Judgement Day of teaching literature, I shall plead that I never believed in it and that I maintained a wife and children," he wrote in 1921. This is an attitude by no means confined to Raleigh or Oxford, and is seen, characteristically, to produce a cynicism about the academic function that is, to put it in the lowest terms, unnecessary (readers may prefer a stronger adjective). It is not necessary to acquiesce, as the Raleighs do, on the grounds that there is no alternative. "We go to Glasgow about the 10th to get my ridiculous degree," he wrote once. "I call it ridiculous because I have been in the kitchen where these things are cooked." This is not a healthy scepticism; it is an excuse for taking a hand in the cooking as well as for benefiting by it. The next step is to make the Wodehouses free of the ridiculous degree.

This is Gordon's academic heredity. He shows what happens to ability when it is exposed to the atmosphere of classical studies pursued without any standards other than those of scholarship and of social snobbishness. One is not surprised to learn from his letters that the important things in life are (1) good mixing—a good man is one who likes a good dinner and knows the right people; and (2) scholarship for its own sake. We see too that one corollary to the latter belief is that ability to edit a text is the only and sufficient test of academic fitness, hence the man who has edited any insignificant text is qualified to practice literary criticism and to direct literary studies. We see Gordon, through his letters, filling all the university posts he can, at home and aboard, with men who have proved their right to "a senior post" by editing something, and with every conviction of righteousness spreading despair and blight on university students of English throughout the British Commonwealth. We see him believing, as he was taught by Raleigh, that the summit of achievement in modern English is represented by the writings of Charles Lamb and Robert Louis Stevenson—to write on Elia is "the last test and pledge"; he is "steeped in the *Letters* . . . I have read them for fifteen years; and the only fault I find in them is that they make all other Letters seem poor and thin. Even Stevenson must not be read till some time has elapsed; or he seems a green boy" (1920). The other great figure in this gallery is Johnson. I say figure because it is not Johnson's prose writings and poetry whose value is recognized; it is the club figure which can be used for purposes of solidarity (though, of course, Johnson's club and Johnson's personality were not of that kind). Lamb, Stevenson, and Johnson evidently united to form an ideal centre, and in so far as Gordon had any particular taste it was for mannered prose with a "personal" content, while archaizing and pastiches and light verse seem to have been the accepted form for academic *jeux d'esprit*. It was not incompatible with such tastes that he should have sponsored Sir Hugh Walpole's novels and P. G. Wodehouse, joined the former in his anti-high-brow battles, and have done his best to keep the academic world clear of the infection of modern literature. That he should reject the real poetry of his time while affecting to find virtue in the academic verse of Bridges also follows. It is not surprising, either, that he should believe that otherwise poetry has, so to speak, run its race: "We still have our cellars, with all the old vintages from Chios to Chilswell." Bridges's "experiments"—academic tinkering with metrics and spelling, devoid of a personal rhythm—are the kind he can sanction, recognizing in them a respectable ancestry. In this museum Milton is inevitably, as Leslie Stephen says he was even in Johnson's time, "a tabooed figure" for criticism.

A bird's-eye view of the culture I have tried to describe is available in the form of an elegant little book of essays published in 1920, R. W. Chapman's *Portrait of a Scholar*. Gordon wrote to the author when it appeared, "I find in these essays not only something that has never been so well expressed, but the flower of a mode of life for you and me seven or eight years old." Here we find essays on trivial subjects turned with that playfulness which so becomes a scholar ("Silver Spoons," "Proper Names in Poetry") or serious ones treated in the style of Elia ("Thoughts on Spelling Reform" begins: "I protest I know little of phonetics"). One is tempted to pause and Veblenize the spectacle. For instance, consider the significance of book-collecting in this culture—it has no more relation to literature than stamp-collecting, but carries a far higher *cachet* in respect to the greater income and esoteric knowledge needed. It would never occur to anyone in this group to refuse to acquiesce in such a merely conventional value; to question it even would be in bad taste. Spoons and furniture are valuable only if they are old, as certain books only because they are rare; hence contemporary poetry could not by definition be any good unless made on strict classical models and in every way reminiscent of them. Modern letters can only have value if they pretend to be old—Elia and R. L. S. will pass, but never Dickens, who is deplored for lacking "style"; the best living writers of English prose, we are told, "having regard to their manner only" (!), are Bridges, Raleigh, Belloc, E. V. Lucas, and Masefield; "their prose is good because their models are good . . . seventeenth- and eighteenth-century models [which they] have found adequate to the most exacting demands of their twentieth-century form and invention." For such a group with such values and preconceptions a live contemporary use of language as that of a Hopkins or Eliot, the real art of a Conrad and Henry James, will fall on deaf ears, and the most genuinely witty, urbane, and brilliant critic, Santayana, will make no impression. Real literature is necessarily closed to them, and they are aware of it only to resent it.

To look with Veblen's eyes at this "mode of life," as Gordon rightly called it, is at least to make one point—that its social standards and its conventional literary and cultural values are only different aspects of the same mentality. To threaten its security in any way, by casting aspersions against the genuineness of a literary idol like Landor or Milton or by suggesting that the social structure needs revision, is to get the same reaction. Gordon's letters about the General Strike (that deplorable episode in the history of the universities when undergraduates in plus-fours and fellows of colleges marched off in organized gangs to break the workers' strike) are almost unbelievable. Particularly instructive is his gloating over the defeat of Labour and his savage jibes at the ecclesiastics who tried to exert a Christian influence over the middle class (when the bishops called upon educational authorities like Gordon for support he told them to go to hell). He concludes: "We've had the Great Strike, and in some ways it's going to be as valuable as the Great War. . . . We shall feel the benefit of the public object lesson to Labour for the rest of our lifetime at least." We notice that religion is conceived entirely as a social institution to which it is necessary to conform (of course, one has one's children christened, and goes to church sometimes because then one gets better servants). This fury at the bishops who tried to implement the theoretical implications of the Established Church in an economic crisis exactly corresponds to the emotional reaction to literary critics who refused to play the game of letters and actually tried to replace the counters by real values. These forms of behaviour are just as much "flowers" of that "mode of life" as *Portrait of a Scholar*. This "mode of life" has a vested interest in the profession of letters identical with its economic interests. A life devoted to the humanities means not following a vocation but taking up the genteelest profit-making pursuit, one which confers a high caste on its members; literary appreciation must obey the same laws as other expressions of social superiority. The Discipline of Letters is seen to be simply the rules of the academic English club. Only thus can we account for the curious spectacle of a professor of poetry and literature inaugurating his terms of office by insulting the greatest living poet (*Ash Wednesday* had appeared four years earlier) and decrying literary criticism, by denouncing state proposals to take seriously the study of literature as an educational process, and declaring that in his university at least literature should be studied only in its aspects of philology and scholarship, while post-graduate work should be restricted to learning to edit texts. The pusillanimity of the academic character outside the sciences is a matter of common experience; it is a product of the club spirit, no doubt; so that when a Gordon gives tongue so boldly we may be sure he knows the whole pack is ready to yelp with him.

Clearly Gordon had this value for the society to which he belonged, that while he served as a public figure going through the motions expected of a scholar and a gentleman he was also a mouthpiece for its instinctive attitudes of self-protection. What oft was thought but ne'er so well expressed was the academic reception of his *Poetry and the Modern World*. We noticed, in summarizing this later inaugural lecture, how his position had changed from the complacent insolence of *The Discipline of Letters*. Now he would like to be on both sides at once, and though he cannot conceal his hatred of all that Eliot stood for he makes a great show of open-mindedness, as in extending cautious (but ludicrously undiscriminating) patronage to the young Oxford poets. Let us appreciate every dead poet equally (so long as we are not asked to think less highly of, say, Milton and the Romantic movement than we have always understood it to be correct to think), he says, and let us not take seriously any poet now alive (except to raise our hats to our classically sanctioned Bridges and Housman). It is "the literary groups now vocal" who exhibit "narrowness and intolerance," he complains and ends on this rather plaintive note.

This was a cunning move, obviously more serviceable than the last-ditch foaming-at-the-mouth attitude. It kept pace with the quiet ratting that was occurring at this time on the Hopkins controversy, and inaugurated the shift of opinion about "the modern movement" that was noticeable very soon after. For such a social group, though it does not move or alter essentially, has to modify its facial expression from time to time in order to survive. Take the affair of Hopkins, which we have outlined—by the time Mr. House had published the fruits of his scholarly labours what bad taste it would have been to suggest that they were superfluous! The critics, that is, had succeeded in persuading the great world that they were right about Hopkins and the academic club wrong, and Hopkins had become a classic in face of the club's persistent blackballing. (This is the mysterious process known in the text-books as "having stood the test of time.") Hopkins had to be incorporated into the conventional pantheon. But if the club finds it politic to make concessions, it will only make them on its own terms. In the matter of Hopkins, Professor Abbott's introduction to the letters is a transparent example of its technique of accommodation without reconstitution. Hopkins could not be radically altered, because he was dead; he could only be misrepresented. A more recent instance is Lord David Cecil's *The English Poets,* where Hopkins is linked with Patmore, the palm being given to the latter, whereas "Hopkins is difficult not for his thoughts but for his mode of expression"; conversely Bridges is jacked up by pairing him off with Yeats. The opposite process is used to write down Eliot, who is dismissed in the same breath as Auden and Spender; the "new school led by T. S. Eliot" is pronounced to be a dead end, while "the main English tradition" in modern poetry, we are told, is kept going by Dorothy Wellesley and W. J. Turner (who, oddly enough, edit the series in which Lord David's book appears), the Sitwells and Ruth Pitter. It is obvious that these are not judgements of literary criticism but gestures of social solidarity—the only kind of criticism that isn't Bad Form.

But let us consider another example of this principle at work. One of the few entertaining spectacles in this last depressing decade has been that of the academics who had shown themselves most hostile to modern literary criticism recognizing that Eliot had achieved a lasting position in spite of them; but while desiring a place on the platform alongside him they couldn't afford to show too glaring an inconsistency. We may well ask how this came about. Mr. Eliot had in fact become respectable for extra-literary reasons (there is not greater proof of respectability than the clerical audiences drawn by *The Rock*), while his poetry and essays had won through to the general educated public on their own merits, assisted by the "narrow and intolerant critics." Thus the former literary Bolshevik (*ut* Dean Inge) became fit even to preside over the Classical Association. Mr. Eliot has accordingly become incorporated into the cannon of accepted Literature—which must be accepted and may not be criticized; and those critics who only recently were outlawed for daring to insist that *The Sacred Wood* and *The Waste Land* were important are now rebuked by the same pens for venturing to disagree with later critical pronouncements of his. The academics, that is, have not changed their skins at all, merely camouflaged them. They still object, as they always have objected, to the practice of real literary criticism, which necessarily menaces their self-esteem and professional reputation. The sociologist would note that for them it is unforgivable to be too far ahead of public opinion; even after public opinion has caught up with, and forced the club to endorse, the discoveries of the pioneering critic, his original offence remains and he will bear always the stigma of harbouring dangerous views. Gordon's protective device has become the modern academic's wear. He does not deny that there may be something in latter-day writers, only, he says, we must be tolerant. This in practice means that you may acclaim Eliot's *Collected Poems* if you will do the same for *The Testament of Beauty;* you may be interested in Kafka and Conrad if you will grant that Wodehouse and Sayers are equally incomparable; you may take Eliot's literary criticism seriously only if you will allow Lamb's to be just as good. Well, isn't that a handsome enough offer?

No, for the literary critic and the educationist will insist that the question they must put to academic authority remains what it always was: are we or are we not to be allowed to apply real standards, to work with real values instead of currency-counters? Apparently the answer still is that we are not. It was Henry James who declared that "the confusion of kinds is the inelegance of letters and the stultification of values."

Gordon's death did not then mark the end of the epoch in academic literary history that Raleigh inaugurated. Every university school of English appears to have its Gordons, and they predominate. Mr. C. S. Lewis's programme for an English school (in *Rehabilitations*) and his defence of it does not differ from Gordon's *Discipline of Letters* sixteen years earlier, either in tone or content, nor did he seem aware of the damaging criticism to which his assumptions and arguments are open. *Rehabilitations* was warmly received in academic quarters, where Mr. Lewis was credited with brilliant wit and a powerful intellect, and from thence came assertions that a blow had been struck for the cause. A really up-to-date intellectual, combining the scholarly virtues with critical genius, had taken service under them, we were given to understand. If there had been the slightest indication of originality in Mr. Lewis's outlook or of criticism of the *status quo* in his programme, what outraged bellows would have come from that herd instead! We may conclude that the academic club will go on recruiting its kind so long as it has a stranglehold on appointments in nearly every university, and will continue to put up *à la mode* Gordons to maintain its supremacy. It is useless, we may deduce and must point out, for state schemes of educational reform at the university level to be broached without considering the realities of the situation. The reforms must be directed to the right quarters.

We started by presenting a question: what does the academic world gain by endowing and countenancing a Gordon and snubbing and starving a Haddon? We can now see that it gains immediately in a psychological sense, because a Gordon enables a bankrupt and decrepit tradition to feel that it can not only stand on its legs but can actually hold up its head and cut a fine figure after all. Whereas a Haddon makes it uncomfortable, painfully aware of deficiencies and the possibility of having to return to the Button Mould. The existence on its doorstep of a Haddon becomes a reproach and therefore an intolerable nuisance. No wonder he had occasion to complain of the stepmotherly behaviour of his Alma Mater. But in the long run, we may predict, it will be the Gordons who are the disability. An impatient revolutionary movement in education, the new order that is more than likely to follow the peace, will be tempted to send the whole system down the drain, not only the academic club but the humanistic studies that they have discredited. It would be hard to justify a claim that a university school of English, as described by Raleigh, Gordon, Mr. C. S. Lewis, is of value to the community or the individual. There is no future for an order that is incarnated in a Gordon; and it deserves the fate it has invited. But is it not possible to make some attempt to salvage English studies? The first step, clearly, is to take them out of the hands of the old-style academic who, in the name of the discipline of letters, bans any attempted interest by the young in the finest poetry and novels and the most profitable criticism of their own time while welcoming the corrupters of standards, and who forces on the student an intolerably arbitrary view of poetry and the history of our literature. And this is the more indefensible when we look into the authority on which this academic's claims to competence are based.

The claims are ultimately made in the name of the classical tradition, that your genuine humanist is the familiar classic scholar and gentleman that the academic could once claim to be. When English schools were first formed, the classically trained were the only academics available with which to supplement the philologists. But if the classic ever was the salt of literary criticism (the evidence for it seems totally lacking), that salt has long since lost its savour. It has long been untrue to imply that the personnel of the academic English club is made up of such legendary people. The caste privileges of the classic scholar and gentleman are now claimed, and the prejudices propagated, by those who are rarely the first, often have no real title to the second—and as for the third, perhaps that need not be discussed. The theory is one employed now by all sorts of intellectual incapables to disguise their inferiority. Though this is a process of evolution not unknown to the social historian, I believe, it none the less leaves its supporters in a weak position. And even if the theoretical claims are occasionally substantiable, is there not something more to be said, and urgently in need of saying, about the fitness of the classic for directing English studies? Gordon started with some natural endowment; his career seems to suggest that his training qualified him for nothing except the editing of classical texts. He could bring nothing but prejudice and an assurance of superiority to his new department, that air of saying gracefully something profound and final which disguises saying nothing, the style of *Times* third leaders and *Times Literary Supplement* leading articles, which are notoriously the work of Greats products and their Cambridge equivalents. But how much more vicious when higher English studies are handled in the same spirit! Naturally enough, the believers in this kind of "discipline" do not like the criticism that shifts something, the teaching that stimulates and matures. The natural reaction of the academic English club, so constituted, has been that since they are incapable of doing anything themselves as directors and producers of literary studies, nobody else shall if they can help it (they are quite willing to help each other to help it, an activity which the organization of the academic world, as one large club, is peculiarly fitted to promote).

The stultifying effect on English studies of such a régime has long been apparent. The moral is that English studies must be cut free from the classical-scholarly tradition in every respect and at every level; must point out firmly that the ability to edit texts and make piddling comments on them is no more qualification by itself for an English university post than a certificate of librarianship, since it is an ability that can be readily acquired by quite stupid people with no interest in literature; and recruit new blood from, and enter into new connexions with, the live studies instead of dead ones. A new deal for English could be initiated at once on the basis of the experimental English college and courses that were long ago outlined in *Scrutiny*. With the aid of the allied studies—other modern literatures, particularly French, and the social sciences (history, anthropology, psychology, sociology, but cultural history and sociology in particular)—new and uniquely equipped specialists would be turned out whose centre in literary criticism and training in the methods and disciplines of other specialisms would enable them to work further and further into adjacent fields of knowledge with the most fruitful results. And it would equip them to do the work which the mere scholar trained only to edit texts cannot do but which literary criticism must get done. And there is work which other specialisms—psychology, sociology, history—notoriously need done and which only the trained literary critic can safely undertake, work which is waiting to be done because no one who is not a literary critic, in our special sense, can undertake it at all. A simple example lies to hand, in Raleigh's literary remains. Raleigh had most of his life contemplated writing a book on Chaucer. He never wrote it, and we know why. "The Chaucer has got only so far, that I have mapped out and defined a lot of things that I should like to know and don't. 'What the philologists should tell us and don't,' 'What students of French poetry should tell us and don't';—these are hardly chapter titles" (*Letters*, 1903). Gordon, a much less intelligent man than Raleigh, characteristically comments (Preface to Raleigh's posthumous *On Writing and Writers*, 1926): "They are the private chapter titles of more than one unwritten book on Chaucer, nor can it well be otherwise while the tradition of his text remains uncertain." Nor could it well be otherwise if the text were as certain as that of today's newspaper. What Raleigh wanted the philologist and the French mediaeval scholar to tell him was what only a literary critic could, who was incidentally a philologist and a specialist in early French poetry. Raleigh had come up against questions which no amount of scholarly information alone can determine; they can be "settled" only by the methods of literary criticism. There is no good book on Chaucer's poetry because no first-class literary critic happens to have had sufficiently intense an interest in Chaucer to go to the immense trouble of acquiring the incidental specialisms and absorbing the masses of "factual matter" that would equip him to decide *as a literary critic* the critical problems Chaucer raises. And until such a critic does there will not be the book on Chaucer we all need, let what Bentley of mediaeval studies there ever may be edit the text, or if the authentic text were suddenly revealed from heaven. There is a similar difficulty about Donne—everyone has had the experience of consulting the great edition—for which we are all deeply grateful to Professor Grierson—and finding that there is no light thrown in the notes, the scholarly and textual notes, on our difficulties. This in my experience is true of all edited texts from the Elizabethan dramatists right down to so apparently straightforward a specimen as Jane Austen's novels. The real difficulties of reading the text, the critical problems, seem to be outside the editor's province, or he is unaware of them because like most scholars he is not a literary critic, too often not even an intelligent reader. That Shakespeare texts cannot be finally determined by "scientific" editing is now generally admitted. I don't mean that we should send scholarship packing—of course we can't do without it—but that we should insist that scholarship in the narrow sense is recognized for the tool it can only be and a useful tool only when in the right hands. "I can hire mathematicians, but mathematicians can't hire me," said Edison.

What English studies need, then, is not more scholarship but fresh contacts, cross-fertilization—a W. H. Rivers of the complex of cultural subjects of which the study of literature forms part, and the intellectual disciplines of which it can profitably draw upon to enrich its method. Failing his appearance, we can at least reorganize English studies on such a basis. Besides being educational in a real sense, so that English studies would be freed from that sense of futility so widely complained of by university students, it would give post-graduate and "research" students a real field of useful work. And other studies would profit. But can anyone be so optimistic as to believe that any university reform less violent than a bloody revolution would make such a programme possible?

(1943)

PART II
THREE GREAT CRITICS

Samuel Johnson
by F. R. Leavis

Johnson's critical writings are living literature as Dryden's (for instance) are not: they compel, and they repay, a real and disinterested reading, that full attention of the judging mind which is so different an affair from the familiar kind of homage—from that routine endorsement of certified values and significances with which the good student, intent on examination-success, honors his set texts. Dryden too, it may be protested, deserves something better. No doubt; but to read Dryden critically can only serve to bring out, in the comparison with Johnson, the difference between classical documents and classical literature. Johnson's criticism, most of it, belongs with the living classics: it can be read afresh every year with unaffected pleasure and new stimulus. It is alive and life-giving.

One can say so much with confidence, and yet not be ready to say off-hand just what it is that gives Johnson's criticism its value. What do we read it for? Not for enlightenment about the authors with whom it deals (though it may impart some), and not for direct instruction in critical thinking. We might perhaps say that we read it for the vigor and weight that it shares with all Johnson's writings —the vigor that comes from a powerful mind and a profoundly serious nature, and the weight that seems to be a matter of bringing to bear at every point the ordered experience of a lifetime. This, however, is too general an answer to be satisfying: Johnson's critical writings exhibit very notably the characteristic wisdom, force, and human centrality of the great moralist, but they have also a value that is peculiarly of and for literary criticism—their specific interest is in and of that field. Johnson is always a great moralist, but in criticism he is a classic *qua* critic.

When we read him we know, beyond question, that we have here a powerful and distinguished mind operating at first hand upon literature. This, we can say with emphatic conviction (the emphasis registering the rarity), really *is* criticism. The critic knows what he means and says it with unescapable directness and force ("deliberately, not dogmatically"), and what he says is clearly the expression of intense and relevant interest. This in itself, we can see, is enough to give Johnson's critical writings a distinctive value in the field of criticism, however difficult it may be to define and assess the profit to be got by frequenting them. They offer us that rare thing, the criticism of a qualified critic, for Johnson is decidedly and impressively that, whatever the limits of his qualifications.

And here, at this last prompting, we move toward a sharper definition of his peculiar interest and significance: they are conditioned by the very fact of his being limited—limited, as he is, so decidedly and specifically. The limitations are commonly both misunderstood and overstressed. He had defects of sensibility, we gather, analogous to his well-known myopia. This myopia, in fact, has been adduced as partly explaining and excusing his deplorable lack of sympathy with the more poetical developments in eighteenth-century poetry: he couldn't be interested in Nature since he couldn't see her beauties. Now that fashions in taste have changed, this particular physical incapacity is less likely to be invoked, but the "defective ear" with which he is credited seems commonly to be thought of as an analogous incapacity afflicting this other organ: the ear has its defect as the eye its myopia. The analogy, of course, won't survive a moment's thought. Nevertheless, many who will recognize it at once to be absurd—disclaiming, perhaps, having ever entertained it—will not have thought of rejecting the implication (conveyed in the phrase) that Johnson's "defective ear" is a matter of mere privation.

What is most striking about Johnson's "ear," as about his other characteristics, is something positive. That "ear" is the product of a training—a training in a positive taste. "Taste" is a not altogether happy word, since it suggests something in the nature of a connoisseur's palate. The taste that matters is the operative sensibility, the discriminating "touch," through which, in exploration and critical response, a fine and inclusive organization engages. Johnson's "ear" is of that order. His training has been in a great positive tradition; a tradition so congenial to him, massively idiosyncratic as he is, that it takes on in him a highly personal quality. We see it as a literary tradition when we talk of "taste" and "ear," but its positiveness is a matter of its being so much more than literary: the very decided conventions of idiom and form engage comprehensive unanimities regarding morals, society, and civilization. At no other period of English history have literary interests been governed by a literary tradition so positive. Johnson, an indubitably real critic, first-hand and forceful, writes from within it, and here we have the peculiar interest of his case.

The nature of the "defect" of his "ear" comes out plainly enough in his comments on Milton's blank verse:

> The musick of the English heroick line strikes the ear so faintly that it is easily lost, unless all the syllables of every line co-operate together: this co-operation can be only obtained by the preservation of every verse unmingled with another, as a distinct system of sound; and this distinctness is obtained and preserved by the artifice of rhyme. The variety of pauses, so much boasted by lovers of blank verse, changes the measures of an English poet to the periods of a declaimer; and there are only a few skillful and happy readers of Milton, who enable their audience to perceive where the lines end or begin. *Blank verse,* said an ingenious critick, *seems to be verse only to the eye.*
>
> Poetry may subsist without rhyme, but English poetry will not often please. . . . Blank verse . . . has neither the easiness of prose, nor the melody of numbers, and therefore tires by long continuance . . . what reason could urge in its defence, has been confuted by the ear.

This seems final enough: blank verse, in theory and in practice, is deplorable. But—

> But, whatever be the advantage of rhyme, I cannot prevail on myself to wish that Milton had been a rhymer; for I cannot wish his work to be other than it is. . . .

Milton, that is, is powerful enough to prevail over the critic's training. The critic reports the resistance and the favourable judgement together, giving more space to the resistance, by way of bringing out the power of Milton's genius. Johnson's very positive training (for that is what the taste, or "ear," of so disciplined a critic represents) impels him to ask for something that Milton doesn't offer, and he feels the impulsion even while acclaiming what Milton gives. We see the same thing in his remarks on Milton's diction:

> This novelty has been, by those who can find nothing wrong in Milton, imputed to his laborious endeavours after words suitable to the grandeur of his ideas. *Our language,* said Addison, *sunk under him.* But the truth is, that, both in prose and verse, he had formed his style by a perverse and pedantick principle. He was desirous to use English words with a foreign idiom. This in all his prose is discovered and condemned; for there the judgment operates freely, neither softened

by the beauty, nor awed by the dignity of his thoughts; but such is the power of his poetry, that his call is obeyed without resistance, the reader feels himself in captivity to a higher and nobler mind, and criticism sinks in admiration.

In this case the tension between acceptance and questioning criticism is likely to seem to most readers wholly respectable and unquaint. Johnson's strong Augustan training hasn't tended to disqualify him here, or to make just appreciation more difficult for him than it is for us. And, reverting to the question of blank verse, it is perhaps worth insisting on the force of that "strong": Johnson represents the Augustan strength of eighteenth-century tradition. The author of *The Vanity of Human Wishes* has, as critic, no weakness—this will perhaps be generally recognized nowadays as a fair way of putting it—for the Miltonizing habit of his age: his taste is that of Goldsmith, who refers to "the disgusting solemnity of blank verse." But, faced with *Paradise Lost,* Johnson can tell the difference between Milton and eighteenth-century Miltonics, his distaste for which will hardly be urged against him as a disability: the passage, quoted above, in which he "cannot prevail upon himself to wish that Milton had been a rhymer" concludes:

> . . . yet, like other heroes, he is to be admired rather than imitated. He that thinks himself capable of astonishing, may write blank verse; but those that hope only to please, must condescend to rhyme.

It is when we come to his treatment of *Lycidas* that we have something we can bluntly call disability, and the nature of it deserves to be precisely noted. His judgement is unhesitating and downright:

> . . . the diction is harsh, the rhymes uncertain, and the numbers unpleasing. What beauty there is, we must therefore seek in the sentiments and images. It is not to be considered as the effusion of real passion; for passion runs not after remote allusions and obscure opinions. . . . Where there is leisure for fiction there is little grief.
>
> In this poem there is no nature, for there is no truth; there is no art, for there is nothing new. Its form is that of a pastoral, easy, vulgar, and therefore disgusting: whatever images it can supply, are long ago exhausted; and its inherent improbability forces dissatisfaction on the mind.

The "diction is harsh . . . the numbers unpleasing"; that looks like "stark insensibility." Whatever it is, it is not a mere lapse, provoked (say) by the content of the poem. Of the songs in *Comus,* a work of which Johnson approves, he says: "they are harsh in their diction, if not very musical in their numbers." Those surprising judgements, imputing "harshness" and lack of "music," are to be explained by reference to the cultivated predilection, the positive "ear," with which they are correlated. It is the "ear" critically formulated in Johnson's appraisal of the place in poetic history of Denham and Waller. The "smoothness" and "softness" of numbers ascribed to them are inseparably bound up with "elegance" and "propriety": "it cannot be denied that he [Waller] added something to our elegance of diction, and something to our propriety of thought." In the *Life* of Dryden Johnson tells us:

> The new versification, as it was called, may be considered as owing its establishment to Dryden; from whose time it is apparent that English poetry has had no tendency to relapse to its former savageness.

A little earlier in the same *Life* we have had the predicate "harsh" elucidated:

> There was therefore before the time of Dryden no poetical diction, no system of words at once refined from the grossness of domestick use, and free from the harshness of terms appropriated to particular arts. Words, too familiar, or too remote, defeat the purpose of a poet. From those sounds which we hear on small or on coarse occasions we do not easily receive strong impressions or delightful images; and words to which we are nearly strangers, whenever they occur, draw that attention on themselves which they should transmit to things.

The "ear," then, that judges *Lycidas* and the songs in *Comus* to be harsh in diction and unmusical is an organ that engages and brings to bear the whole complex of Augustan criteria. "Elegance" and "propriety" involve "politeness." Johnson's sense of "music" carries with it inseparably a demand for the social movement and tone so characteristic of Augustan verse, and the demand for these is an implicit introduction of the associated norms, rational and moral.

> Poetical expression includes sound as well as meaning: *Musick,* says Dryden, *is inarticulate poetry;* among the excellences of Pope, therefore, must be mentioned the melody of his metre. [*Life* of Pope].

But Johnson has no use for "music" apart from meaning:

> From poetry the reader justly expects, and from good poetry always obtains, the enlargement of his comprehension and elevation of his fancy.... [*Life* of Waller]

There is always to be a substance of statement in verse, and it is fair to say that the music Johnson demands is a music of meaning as much as of sound. Of this passage of Waller's—

> *O could I flow like thee, and make thy stream*
> *My great example, as it is my theme!*
> *Though deep, yet clear; though gentle, yet not dull;*
> *Strong without rage, without o'erflowing full*

—a passage of which he tells us that it has been a model of versification "for a century past," he says:

> So much meaning is comprised in so few words; the particulars of resemblance are so perspicaciously collected, and every mode of excellence separated from its adjacent fault by so nice a line of limitation; the different parts of the sentence are so accurately adjusted; and the flow of the last couplet is so smooth and sweet; that the passage, however celebrated, has not been praised above its merits. [*Life* of Denham]

On the other hand, in the *Life* of Pope, we find this significant note:

> I have been told that the couplet by which he declared his own ear to be most gratified, was this:
>
> > *Lo, where Maeotis sleeps, and hardly flows*
> > *The freezing Tanais through a waste of snows.*
>
> But the reason of this preference I cannot discover.

Johnson, that is, has no leaning towards the taste, so decidedly alive in the eighteenth century, for Spenserian-Tennysonian melodizing, the incantatory play of mellifluousness in which sense is subordinated.

When he comes to *Lycidas* he has no need to stop his ears against the music; the incantation, so acceptable to most of us, doesn't work for him—"the diction is harsh, the rhymes uncertain, and the numbers unpleasing." The trained hearkening for another music has immunized him. He attends undistracted to the sense—attends critically, and we can't imagine him doing otherwise; which may be a limitation in him, but is certainly of the essence of his strength. The burden of *Paradise Lost* is such as to overcome all prepossessions against the kind of versification; the "music" can overcome the trained "ear." Of *Comus* he cay say:

> . . . it exhibits . . . his power of description and his vigour of sentiment, employed in the praise and defence of virtue. A work more truly poetical is rarely found.

But what does *Lycidas* yield if, as the duly responding reader does not, but as Johnson must, we insist on reading it for its paraphrasable substance?

We know that they never drove a field and that they had no flocks to batten; and though it be allowed that the representation may be allegorical, the true meaning is so uncertain and remote, that it is never sought because it cannot be known when it is found.

This poem has yet a grosser fault. With these trifling fictions are mingled the most awful and sacred truths such as ought never to be polluted with such irreverent combinations.

It is difficult to see how, granted the approach, Johnson's essential criticism can be disposed of. The answer, of course, is that the approach is inappropriate and the poem a different kind of thing from any appreciable by Johnsonian criticism. One may perhaps add, in fairness to Johnson, whose approach does at any rate promote this recognition, that it is a lesser thing than post-Johnsonian taste has tended to make it.

When we come to his treatment of Shakespeare, Johnson's limitations appear both more seriously disabling and more interesting, for his training gets more radically in the way of appreciation than where Milton is concerned. The critic for whom the Augustan use of language is the undisputed norm cannot come to terms with the Shakespearian use. He understands and he doesn't understand. He describes the Shakespearian use with characteristic strength and vivacity:

> It is incident to him to be now and then entangled with an unwieldy sentiment, which he cannot well express, and will not reject; he struggles with it a while, and if it continues stubborn, comprises it in words such as occur, and leaves it to be disentangled and evolved by those who have more leisure to bestow upon it.
>
> Shakespeare regarded more the series of ideas, than the words.*
>
> <div align="right">[<i>Preface</i>]</div>

That such descriptions carry with them in Johnson's mind a severely adverse judgement we know well enough; the evidence abounds: "the offspring of his throes is tumour, meanness, tediousness and obscurity": "he has corrupted language by every mode of depravation"—it is easy to accumulate passages and tags of like import. Yet again and again the description itself, in its lively aptness, implies a measure of appreciation. This is most notably so in the well-known place in *The Rambler* where Johnson passes his strictures on lowness in *Macbeth*:

---

* *Cf.* ". . . that fulness of idea, which might sometimes load his words with more sentiment than they could conveniently convey, and that rapidity of imagination . . ." (*Proposals*).

Words which convey ideas of dignity in one age are banished from elegant writing or conversation in another, because they are in time debased by vulgar mouths, and can be no longer heard without the involuntary recollection of unpleasing images.

When Macbeth [the speaker is really Lady Macbeth] is confirming himself in the horrid purpose of stabbing his king, he breaks out amidst his emotions into a wish natural for a murderer:

> —*Come, thick night!*
> *And pall thee in the dunnest smoke of hell,*
> *That my keen knife see not the wound it makes,*
> *Nor Heaven peep through the blanket of the dark,*
> *To cry, Hold, hold!*

In this passage is exerted all the force of poetry; that force which calls new powers into being, which embodies sentiment, and animates matter; yet, perhaps, scarce any man now peruses it without some disturbance of his attention from the counteraction of the words to the ideas.

Johnson, of course, enforcing that "counteraction" with particularized commentary, goes on to stigmatize the lowness of "dun" ("an epithet now seldom heard but in the stable"), of "knife" ("an instrument used by butchers and cooks in the meanest employments"), and of "peeping through a blanket." Yet when he concludes that "in this passage is exerted all the force of poetry" he is not, for the sake of paradox, indulging in rhetorical licence. It is not his habit to use words lightly, and how much he means what he says comes out in what follows: "that force which calls new powers into being, which embodies sentiment, and animates matter." The felicity of these phrases is not accidental, and can we say that the critic who finds them when trying to express his sense of the peculiar exploratory creativeness and metaphorical concreteness of Shakespeare's poetry doesn't appreciate the Shakespearian use of language?

The potency of the training, the strong positiveness of the criteria, by virtue of which appreciation stultifies itself in an accompanying perversity of rejection, appears the more strikingly. Nothing could be more unlike the Shakespearian use of English than that in which Johnson's mind and sensibility have been formed. For him, in this the typical Augustan, expression in poetry as in prose is a matter of stating—of stating with point, elegance, and propriety. It is significant that, asked for a definition of the "wit" that is common to Pope (who, of course, has more than one kind and is more than an Augustan poet), Johnson, Goldsmith, and Crabbe, together with the Gray of the *Impromptu* and the *Elegy* and the Cowper of *The Castaway,* one naturally replies in some such formula as this: "a neatness and precision of *statement*, tending towards epigram." When Johnson says that "Shakespeare regarded more the series of ideas, than the words," he is thinking of the problems, grammatical and logical, with which Shakespeare in his mature styles confronts the analyst. What D. W. Harding says of Rosenberg's handling of language (see *Scrutiny*, Vol. III, No. 4) applies to Shakespeare's—it is, in fact, the essentially poetic use:

> He—like many poets in some degree, one supposes—brought language to bear on the incipient thought at an earlier stage of its development. Instead of the emerging idea being racked slightly so as to fit a more familiar approximation of itself, and words found for *that*, Rosenberg let it manipulate words almost from the beginning, often without the controls of logic and intelligibility.

Shakespeare's "thoughts," concretely realized moments in the development of the dramatic poem (itself a marvellously concrete and complex whole), are apt to be highly specific and, so, highly complex—which is to say, compressed and licentious in expression: hence the occasions for Johnson's vigours and rigours of censure. The Augustan cannot conceive the need for such a use of language. The ideas he wants to express are adequately provided for—and this is true of poetry as of prose—in the common currency of terms, put together according to the conventions of grammar and logic. He doesn't feel that the current concepts of ordinary discourse muffle or misrepresent anything he has to convey. His business is, while observing the ordinary rules in arranging them, to achieve further a formal pattern of meaning-structure and versification. He can express himself congenially in modes that are in such a sense and at such a level social that this pattern (like Augustan idiom itself) suggests formal conventions of social manners and public deportment. It is an age in which everyone of any cultivation knows so well what Reason, Truth, and Nature, the presiding trinity, are that no one feels any pressing need of definitions (and here we have an essential mark of a strong positive culture). It is not an age in which the poet feels called on to explore further below the public surface than conventional expression takes cognizance of, or to push in any way beyond the frontiers of the charted. He has no impulse to indulge in licentious linguistic creation, nor does it occur to him that such indulgence may ever with any propriety be countenanced.

And what, in such a convention, makes the poet's compositions poetry? The pattern, primarily—the extremely formal pattern which, involving metre, rhyme, and sense-organization, involves so much and asserts itself so dominantly. It virtually involves the decorum that might have been listed as a separate head; the decorum that Johnson vindicates in his commentary on the passage of *Macbeth*. Given movement, tone, and idiom so essentially suggestive of formal deportment and company manners, it is not surprising that the obligatory decorum should be so delicate and intolerant and the '"low" it cannot abide be stigmatized so arbitrarily (it must seem to us).

There is, where Johnsonian Augustanism is concerned, a third head to be added, that of generality—the peculiar kind of generality prescribed in the well-known passage of *Rasselas*:

> "The business of a poet," said Imlac, "is to examine, not the individual, but the species; to remark general properties and large appearances. He does not number the streaks of the tulip or describe the different shades in the verdure of the forest; he is to exhibit in his portraits of nature, such striking and prominent features, as recall the original to every mind; and must neglect the minuter discriminations, which one may have remarked, and another have neglected, for those characteristics which are alike obvious to vigilance and to carelessness."

Pope, of course, can be particular enough, but there is only one Pope, and, although *the* great Augustan, he transcends Augustanism too much to be the type Augustan, and it is fairly plain as the eighteenth century wears on that Augustanism tends inherently towards this generality, the relation of which to decorum comes out clearly in Johnson's censure of "dun," "knife," and "blanket." The relation appears again in this significantly phrased stricture on Cowley:

> The fault of Cowley, and perhaps of all the writers of the metaphysical race, is that of pursuing his thoughts to their last ramification, by which he loses the grandeur of generality; for of the greatest things the parts are little; what is little can be but pretty, and by claiming dignity becomes ridiculous.

More radically, a thoroughgoing rejection of the Shakespearian use of language, and, consequently, of all concrete specificity in the rendering of experience, would seem very much to imply the quest of a compensating poetic generality. Johnson remarks (again in the *Life* of Cowley):

> Great thoughts are always general, and consist in positions not limited by exceptions, and in descriptions not descending to minuteness. . . . Those writers who lay on the watch for novelty could have little hope of greatness; for great things cannot have escaped former observation.

They should have known that the poet can only aim at achieving, in the "grandeur of generality," *What oft was thought, but ne'er so well express'd.*

Remembering *The Vanity of Human Wishes,* one hesitates to say that this use of language is essentially unpoetic—though the essentially poetic is certainly the Shakespearian, its antithesis. What one can, however, say is that the use Johnson favours and practises —the only use he really understands—is essentially undramatic. And here we have his radical limitations as a critic of the drama and his radical incapacity as a dramatist (he being in both respects representative of his age). We may see the *literary* bias expressed in his characteristic formula, "A dramatick exhibition is a book recited with concomitants that increase or diminish the effect," as, in an age in which elevated drama (by Shakespeare or by Home) is an opportunity for Garrick, and declamatory histrionic virtuosity the best the theatre has to offer, wholly respectable. The assumption that a work of art in words is to be judged as literature has in any case much to be said for it, whatever complications unrecognized by Johnson may attend on the qualifying "dramatic." Yet, as I have remarked before in these pages, when one re-reads *Irene*—so patently conceived as a book to be recited, and leaving so wholly to the concomitants the hopeless task of making it a theatre-piece—one realizes that, nevertheless, "literary bias" misses what is most interesting in Johnson's case. That he has no sense of the theatre, and worse, that he cannot present or conceive his themes dramatically—these criticisms one doesn't need to urge. The point one finds oneself making is that his essential bent is undramatic in a sense that goes far deeper than the normal interest of the "dramatic critic." The weakness of *Irene* sends one back to consider the nature of the strength of his best verse.

The Vanity of Human Wishes is great poetry; but it is a mode that, above, just escaped being called essentially unpoetic: it is certainly as undramatic as good poetry can be. Johnson—and in this he is representative of his age—has neither the gift nor the aim of catching in words and presenting to speak for themselves significant particularities of sensation, perception, and feeling, the significance coming out in complex total effects, which also are left to speak for themselves; he starts with general ideas and general propositions and develops them by discussion, comment, and illustration. The failure in dramatic conception so patent in *Irene* is correlated with the essential qualities of *The Vanity of Human Wishes.* When he attempts drama, the conditions that enable Johnson in his characteristic poetry of statement, exposition, and reflection to give his moral declamation the weight of lived experience and to charge his eighteenth-century generalities with that extraordinary and characteristic kind of concreteness—

> *Unnumber'd suppliants crowd Preferment's gate,*
> *Athirst for wealth, and burning to be great;*
> *Delusive Fortune hears th' incessant call,*
> *They mount, they shine, evaporate, and fall*

—these conditions fail him. In blank verse the wit and the patterned social movement are absent, and with them the Johnsonian weight. His characters declaim eloquent commonplaces—he cannot make them do anything else; but the dramatic aim has robbed them of the familiar strength and substance; the great moralist, reduced to making a show of speaking through his *personae,* is less than himself.

The point I am making is that Johnson's limitations as a critic have positive correlatives. But they are not the less limitations, and seriously disabling ones. With his radically undramatic habit we may reasonably associate his bondage to moralistic fallacy—his censure of Shakespeare's indifference to poetic justice and Shakespeare's general carelessness about the duty to instruct:

> His first defect is that to which may be imputed most of the evil in books or in men. He sacrifices virtue to convenience, and is so much more careful to please than to instruct, that he seems to write without any moral purpose. From his writings indeed a system of social duty may be selected, for he that thinks reasonably must think morally; but his precepts and axioms drop casually from him; he makes no just distribution of good or evil, nor is always careful to shew in the virtuous a disapprobation of the wicked; he carries his persons indifferently through right and wrong, and at the close dismisses them without further care, and leaves their examples to operate by chance. This fault the barbarity of his age cannot extenuate; for it is always a writer's duty to make the world better, and justice is a virtue independent on time and place.

Not really appreciating the poetry, he cannot appreciate the dramatic organization; more generally, he cannot appreciate the ways in which not only Shakespeare's drama but all works of art *act* their moral judgements. For Johnson a thing is stated, or it isn't there.

It is as well, perhaps, to insist on the inability to appreciate Shakespearian poetry—for in spite of the stress laid above on the paradoxical kind of appreciation Johnson shows in describing, inability is what, in sum, we have to recognize. Corroboration, if it were needed, is to be seen in the taste for declamatory eloquence exemplified in his starring of the passage from *The Mourning Bride* (in the *Life* of Congreve): "If I were required to select from the whole mass of English poetry the most poetical paragraph, I know not what I could prefer. . . ." The paragraph is eighteenth-century eloquence of a kind that Johnson's own account suggests well enough:

> He who reads these lines enjoys for a moment the powers of a poet; he feels what he remembers to have felt before, but he feels it with great increase of sensibility; he recognizes a familiar image, but he meets it again amplified and expanded, embellished with beauty, and enlarged with majesty.

This incapacity of Johnson's involves, in the criticism of Shakespearian drama, limitations more disabling than his moralism. He ranks Shakespeare's genius supremely high, of course, but it is interesting to note where he lays the stress:

> Shakespeare is above all writers, at least above all modern writers, the poet of nature; the poet that holds up to his readers a faithful mirrour of manners and of life.

> This therefore is the praise of Shakespeare, that his drama is the mirrour of life; that he who has mazed his imagination in following the phantoms which other writers raise up before him, may here be cured of his delirious extasies, by reading human sentiments in human language, by scenes from which a hermit may estimate the transactions of the world, and a confessor predict the progress of the passions. [*Preface*]

What Johnson acclaims in Shakespeare, it might be said, is a great novelist who writes in dramatic form (and this, if we add an accompanying stress on the bard who provides opportunities for histrionic declamation, is the eighteenth-century attitude in general). To use the time-honoured phrase, he values Shakespeare—and extols him in admirably characteristic terms—for his "knowledge of the human heart"; and the *Preface to Shakespeare* should be a *locus classicus* for the insufficiency of an appreciation of Shakespeare's "knowledge of the human heart" that is not at the same time an appreciation of the poetry. That Johnson's mode of exhibiting such insufficiency is "period" doesn't make the illustrative and monitory value of the relation to Bradley's less, but the reverse; and now that Bradley's itself begins to look "period" to Professor Dover Wilson, there are more recent modes that can be brought into the critical series.

Johnson's case is clear enough: the radical insufficiency correlated with his abstraction of the "drama" from the "poetry"—with his failure to see the dramatic genius as a poetic and linguistic genius—appears when he exalts the comedies above the tragedies:

> He therefore indulged his natural disposition, and his disposition, as Rhymer has remarked, led him to comedy. In tragedy he often writes, with great appearance of toil and study, what is written at last with little felicity; but in his comick scenes, he seems to produce without labour what no labour can improve. In tragedy he is always struggling after some occasion to be comick; but in comedy he seems to repose, or to luxuriate, as in a mode of thinking congenial to his nature. In his tragick scenes there is always something wanting, but his comedy often surpasses expectation or desire. His comedy pleases by the thoughts and the language, and his tragedy for the greater part by incident and action. His tragedy seems to be skill, his comedy to be instinct.

It is quite unequivocal. A couple of pages further on in the *Preface* he reverts to the theme; there is no need to quote again. The appreciation of Shakespeare's dramatic genius—of his "knowledge of the human heart" and his depth and range in rendering life—that exalts the comedies above the tragedies is a calamitously defective appreciation.

The gross obviousness of the defect goes with the very strength of Johnson's criticism. What he says of Shakespeare might be adapted to himself as critic:

> Shakespeare, whether life or nature be his subject, shews plainly, that he has seen with his own eyes; he gives the image which he receives, not weakened or distorted by the intervention of any other mind;* the ignorant feel his representations to be just, and the learned see that they are compleat.

Johnson is not invariably just or complete; but the judgement—and he never fails to judge—is always stated with classical force and point, and based beyond question on strong first-hand impressions. He addresses himself deliberately and disinterestedly to what is in front of him; he consults his experience with unequivocal directness and always has the courage of it. Concerned as he is for principle, he refers with characteristic contempt to "the cant of those who judge by principle rather than perception" (*Life* of Pope). There is

---

* Contrast this, on Milton: "But his images and descriptions of the scenes or operations of Nature do not seem to be always copied from original form, nor to have the freshness, raciness, and energy of immediate observation. He saw Nature, as Dryden expresses it, *through the spectacles of books*; and on most occasions calls learning to his assistance."

always, he says, "an appeal open from criticism to nature" (*Preface*) and:

> It ought to be the first endeavour of a writer to distinguish nature from custom; or that which is established because it is right, from that which is right only because it is established.

It is significant for "nature" he tends to substitute the term "experience." For instance, in the number of *The Rambler* (156) from which the last extract comes, having adduced the orthodox objection to "tragicomedy," he asks:

> But will not experience show this objection to be rather subtile than just? Is it not certain that the tragick and comick affections have been moved alternately with equal force; and that no plays have oftener filled the eyes with tears, and the breast with palpitation, than those which are variegated with interludes of mirth?

The "mingled drama" has succeeded in practice, and that would seem to dispose of the rules. It is true that Johnson then draws back:

> I do not however think it safe to judge of works of genius merely by the event.

He is not prepared to say that success is necessarily self-justifying: there is always principle to be considered. And he goes on to suggest that "perhaps the effects even of Shakespeare's poetry might have been yet greater, had he not counteracted himself," but kept the rules. This is pretty obviously a formal conservative scruple rationalizing itself. Yet there is nothing timid about Johnson's appeal to experience, and the relation in his criticism between experience and authority (predisposed as he is to the idea of authority) has nothing in common with that reconciliation between Nature and the Rules which Pope, representative here of last-phase Neo-classicism, effects with such elegant ease in his *Essay*. In fact, Johnson's recourse to experience is so constant and uncompromising and so subversive of Neo-classic authority that it is misleading to bring him under the Neo-classic head.

The strength and the limitations together, in criticism, of Johnsonian "'experience" come out best of all, perhaps, in his treatment of the unities. Here the terms are downright and the dismissal is blunt (*Preface*):

> Such is the triumphant language with which a critick exults over the misery of an irregular poet, and exults commonly without resistance or reply. It is time therefore to tell him by the authority of Shakespeare,

> that he assumes, as an unquestionable principle, a position which, while his breath is forming it into words, his understanding pronounces to be false. It is false, that any representation is mistaken for reality; that any dramatick fable in its materiality was ever credible, or, for a single moment was ever credited.
>
> The truth is, that the spectators are always in their senses, and know, from the first act to the last, that the stage is only a stage, and that the players are only players. They came to hear a cerain number of lines recited with just gesture and elegant modulation. The lines relate to some action, and an action must be in some place; but the different actions that compleat a story may be in places very remote from each other; and where is the absurdity of allowing that space to represent first Athens, and then Sicily, which was always known to be neither Sicily nor Athens, but a modern theatre?

This kind of common sense, being common sense and a real resort to experience, is adequate to the dismissal of so unreal a structure as the doctrines of the unities. But, of course, for a satisfactory account of the experience of the theatre more is needed: "that the spectators are always in their senses" is an incomplete truth, and misleading in its incompleteness. And even if Johnson had found the theatre more congenial than he does we shouldn't have looked to him for anything of adequate subtlety—anything of the order of "that willing suspension of disbelief which constitutes poetic faith." The subtlety of analysis that Coleridge, with his psychological inwardness, is to bring into criticism is not at Johnson's command. But it can be said that Johnson, with his rational vigour and the directness of his appeal to experience, represents the best that criticism can do before Coleridge.

The deficient analysis has an obvious manifestation in his moralism. It leads also to his appearing sometimes to be exhibiting his moralistic disability where the appearance is deceptive, being imposed by the idiom he cannot escape.

> The end of writing is to instruct; the end of poetry is to instruct by pleasing. [*Preface*]

This way (not invented by Johnson) of resolving the dilemma represented by the traditional question, "Is it the business of art to please or instruct?," doesn't bring emancipation from the false analysis that the question involves. He knows, as his critical practice unfailingly exemplifies, that his business when faced with a set of verses is to judge whether they are good poetry or not, and that this is a different matter from judging whether they are salutary as instruction: he knows that something more is involved. But, admirably preoccupied as he is with technical examinations and judgements of sensibility, he can't, when asked what this something more is, rise above—or go deeper than—an answer in terms of "please." Pleasure added to instruction: that, though his perception transcends it, is the analysis to which the critical idiom he inevitably uses is tied. When he has occasion to insist on the serious function of poetry, the vocabulary of "instruction" is his inevitable resort.

In the *Life* of Gray, for instance, we read:

> To select a singular event, and swell it to a giant's bulk by fabulous appendages of spectres and predictions, has little difficulty, for he that forsakes the probable may always find the marvellous. And it has little use: we are affected only as we believe; we are improved only as we find something to be imitated or declined. I do not see that *The Bard* promotes any truth, moral or political.

This might be taken for a clear instance of the most indefensible didacticism. Yet the context—indeed, the tone of the passage itself—makes it plain enough that what we have here is Johnson's way of saying that for a mature, accomplished, and cultivated mind such as Gray's to be playing this kind of game and exhibiting itself in these postures is ridiculous. It will be noted that his criticism proceeds by way of common-sense analysis to a final dismissing judgement of sensibility:

> These Odes are marked by glittering accumulations of ungraceful ornaments; they strike, rather than please; the images are magnified by affectation; the language is laboured into harshness. The mind of the writer seems to work with unnatural violence. *Double, double, toil and trouble.* He has a kind of strutting dignity, and is tall by walking on tiptoe. His art and his struggle are too visible, and there is too little appearance of ease and nature.

The judgement is surely unanswerable. Johnson is a better critic of eighteenth-century poetry than Matthew Arnold. In dealing with that, at any rate, he has an advantage in his training. To be trained in so positive a tradition is to have formed strong anticipations as to the kind of discrimination one will have to make, and within the field to which the anticipations are relevant they favour quickness of perception and sureness of judgement. (An analogy: the "native" tracker owes his skill not to a natural endowment of marvellously good sight, but to analogous anticipations: knowing the kind of thing to look for, he is quick to perceive, and being habituated to the significance of the various signs, he is quick to appraise and interpret.) Johnson's disapproval of Gray's Pindaric sublimities goes with his disapproval of Miltonics. For him—and who today will disagree?—Miltonics represent the weakness of taste in his age. Now that we no longer search the eighteenth century for what is congenial to Victorian-romantic taste—for poetry from the "soul"—we can see that the Pindaric ambition consorts with the same weakness. Drawing inspiration from the Miltonic side of Dryden, it applies resonant externalities of declamation to conventional ideas of the exalted. What Johnson singles out for praise is Gray's Augustan classic—for the *Elegy* is Augustan in its strength: it has Augustan movement and the accompanying Augustan virtues of neat, compact, and dignified statement. The terms in which he extols it are significant:

> The *Churchyard* abounds with images which find a mirrour in every mind, and with sentiments to which every bosom returns an echo. The four stanzas beginning *Yet even these bones,* are to me original: I have never seen the notions in any other place; yet he that reads them here, persuades himself that he has always felt them. Had Gray written often thus, it had been vain to blame, and useless to praise him.

These stanzas, Johnson judges, have the virtues of *What oft was thought, but ne'er so well express'd*: that is, he extols the *Elegy* as classical statement—as giving moving and inevitable form to the human commonplaces.

His treatment of Gray, who has not even yet fully emerged from the Arnoldian transfiguration, has counted for much in the traditional notion of the arbitrary Great Cham as criticism, narrow, dogmatic, and intolerant. Actually, it illustrates his excellence as a critic of eighteenth-century verse.

In stressing Johnson's sureness and penetration within the limits of the field to which his training properly applies, it will not do to suggest that his distinction as a critic is confined within those limits. The truth is far otherwise. How notably he transcends them in discussing Shakespeare has already been suggested, and admirers of the *Preface* (not the only relevant document) know that there is much more to adduce. Perhaps the most striking demonstration of his uninhibited versatility of critical response is to be found in his *Life* of Cowley. That he should pick on Cowley as the best of the Metaphysicals—"Cowley adapted it [the "metaphysick style"], and excelled his predecessors, having as much sentiment, and more musick"—is, of course, an instance of Augustan limitation: Cowley is nearer than the others, and, in his transitional quality, which relates him more closely to Dryden and Rochester than to Donne, more accessible to Augustan sympathy. But, on the other hand, it has to be recognized that, as a Metaphysical, he deserves no more than Johnson concedes; so far as he is concerned, the estimate is just:

> Yet great labour, directed by great abilities, is never wholly lost; if they frequently threw away their wit upon false conceits, they likewise sometimes struck out unexpected truth: if their conceits were farfetched, they were often worth the carriage. To write on their plan, it was at least necessary to read and think. No man could be born a metaphysical poet, nor assume the dignity of a writer, by descriptions copied from descriptions, by imitations borrowed from imitations, by traditional imagery, and hereditary similes, by rhyme, and volubility of syllables.

It is not for "period" disabilities that the eighteenth-century critic who writes this seems most remarkable. And the free and powerful intelligence compels recognition in the whole immediately accompanying discussion of Metaphysical characteristics. So powerful an intelligence, associated with so intense an interest both in letters and in human nature, could no more be narrow than shallow. Here is a concluding example of Johnson's quality:

> To his domesticks [Swift] was naturally rough; and a man of rigorous temper, with that vigilance of minute attention which his works discover, must have been a master that few could bear.

In spite of what was said in the opening of this essay, such a passage might very well be pondered for the illumination it throws on the "works." The implications constitute a very salutary corrective to the still current sentimentalization of Swift.

(1944)

Coleridge

by F. R. Leavis

That Coleridge was a rarely gifted mind is a commonplace. It is perhaps equally a commonplace that what he actually accomplished with his gifts, the producible achievement, appears, when we come to stock-taking, disappointingly incommensurate. That "perhaps" registers a hesitation: judges qualified in the religious and intellectual history of the past century might, I think, reply that actually Coleridge was a great power, exercising influence in ways that must be credited to him for very notable achievement, and that we cannot judge him merely by reading what is extant of him in print. My concern, however, is with the field of literary criticism. That his performance there justifies some disappointment is, I believe, generally recognized. But I believe too that this recognition stresses, in intention, rather the superlativeness of the gifts than shortcoming in the performance. The full disparity, in fact, doesn't get clear recognition very readily; there are peculiar difficulties in the way— at least, these are the conclusions to which, after reconsidering the body of Coleridge's work in criticism, I find myself brought.

The spirit of that reconsideration had better be made plain at once. Let me start, then, by reminding the reader of the introduction to the standard scholarly edition of *Biographia Literaria*. The ninety pages or so are devoted almost wholly to discussing Coleridge's relation to Kant and other German philosophers. Now, it seems clear to me that no head of study that involves discussions of Coleridge's indebtedness to, or independence of, Kant, Schelling, the Schlegels, or Fichte has any claims on the attention of the literary student; it is from his point of view a solicitation to unprofitable expenditures. If in a work recommended to him as directly relevant to the problems of literary criticism any such solicitations seem likely to engage or confuse him he had better be warned against them. It follows then, if this is so, and if J. Shawcross's introduction is relevant to the work it precedes, that the docile student ought certainly to be warned against a large part of *Biographia Literaria*. It may be that, as Shawcross suggests, "Coleridge's philosophy of art" has not "received in England the consideration which it deserves." But Coleridge's philosophy of art is Coleridge's philosophy, and though no doubt he has an important place in the history of English thought, not even the student of philosophy, I imagine, is commonly sent to Coleridge for initiations into key-problems or for classical examples of distinguished thinking. And the literary student who goes to Coleridge in the expectation of bringing away an improved capacity and equipment for dealing critically with works of literature will, if he spends much time on the "philosophy of art," have been sadly misled.

It is by way of defining the spirit of my approach that I assert this proposition, the truth of which seems to me evident. Actually, of course, its evidence gets substantial recognition in established academic practice: the student usually starts his reading—or at least his serious reading—of *Biographia Literaria* at Chapter XIV. Nevertheless, since the appropriate distinction is not formulated and no sharp separation can be made in the text, the common effect of the perusal can hardly be clarity—or clear profit. It is certain, on the other hand, that Coleridge's prestige owes a great deal to the transcendental aura; his acceptance as a master of "theoretical criticism" is largely an awed vagueness about the philosophy—a matter of confused response to such things as

> The primary IMAGINATION then, I consider, to be the living power and prime agent of all human Perception, and as a repetition in the finite mind of the eternal act of creation in the infinite I AM.

The essential distinction ought to be plain enough to us, but that Coleridge himself should not have made it sharply and have held firmly to it cannot, given the nature of his genius, surprise us; on the contrary, even if he had been a much more orderly and disciplined worker than he was we still couldn't have expected in his work a clear separation between what properly claims the attention of the literary critic and what does not. "Metaphysics, poetry and facts of mind," he wrote, "are my darling studies." The collocation of the last two heads suggest the sense in which Shelley's phrase for him, "a subtle-souled psychologist," must often, when he impresses us favourably in the literary-critical field, seem to us an apt one, and, on the other hand, it is difficult not to think of the first head as a nuisance. Yet we can hardly suppose that we could have had the psychologist without the metaphysician; that the gift of subtle analysis could have been developed, at that date, by a mind that shouldn't also have exhibited something like the Coleridgean philosophic bent. But that makes it not less, but more necessary to be firm about the distinction that concerns us here.

I had better at this point indicate more fully the specific equipment that might seem to have qualified Coleridge for great achievements in literary criticism—to be, indeed, its modern instaurator. The "subtle-souled psychologist," it seems not superfluous to emphasize, was intensely interested in literature. He was, of course, a poet, and the suggestion seems to be taken very seriously that he indulged the habit of analytic introspection to the extent of damaging the creative gift he turned it upon. However that may be, it is reasonable to suppose that the critic, at any rate, profited. The psychological bent was associated with an interest in language that expresses itself in observations such as lend colour to I. A. Richards's enlistment of Coleridge for semasiology. But, as in reviewing *Coleridge on Imagination* [pages 360-377 below] I had occasion to remind Dr. Richards, who lays stress on those of Coleridge's interests which might seem to fall outside the compass of the literary critic, these interests went, in Coleridge, with a constant wide and intense cultivation of literature:

> O! when I think of the inexhaustible mine of virgin treasure in our Shakespeare, that I have been almost daily reading him since I was ten years old—that the thirty intervening years have been unintermittingly and not fruitlessly employed in the study of the Greek, Latin, English, Italian, Spanish and German *belle lettrists*, and the last fifteen years in addition, far more intensively in the analysis of the laws of life and reason as they exist in man—and that upon every step I have made forward in taste, in acquisition of facts from history or my own observation, and in knowledge of the different laws of being and their apparent exceptions from accidental collision of disturbing forces,—that at every new accession of information, after every successful exercise of meditation, and every fresh presentation of experience, I have unfailingly discovered a proportionate increase of wisdom and intuition in Shakespeare. . . .*

The "analysis" and the "laws" mentioned hardly belong to literary criticism, but it is easy to assemble an impressive array of characteristic utterances and formulas that promise the literary critic's own concern with principle:

> The ultimate end of criticism is much more to establish the principles of writing than to furnish *rules* how to pass judgment on what has

---

* I quote from the Everyman volume, *Essays and Lectures on Shakespeare*, but see T. H. Raysor, *Coleridge's Shakespearean Criticism*, Vol. I, p. 210.

been written by others; if indeed it were possible that the two should be separated. [*Biographia Lit.*, Ch XVIII]

You will see, by the terms of my prospectus, that I intend my lectures to be, not only "in illustration of the principles of poetry," but to include a statement of the application of those principles, "as grounds of criticism on the most popular works of later English poets, those of the living included." [*Coleridge's Shakespearean Criticism*, II, p. 63]

It is a painful truth that not only individuals, but even whole nations, are ofttimes so enslaved to the habits of their education and immediate circumstances, as not to judge disinterestedly even on those subjects, the very pleasure arising from which consists in its disinterestedness, namely, on subjects of taste and polite literature. Instead of deciding concerning their own modes and customs by any rule of reason, nothing appears rational, becoming, or beautiful to them, but what coincides with the peculiarities of their education. In this narrow circle, individuals may attain to exquisite discrimination, as the French critics have done in their own literature; but a true critic can no more be such without placing himself on some central point, from which he may command the whole, that is, some general rule, which, founded in reason, or the faculties common to all men, must therefore apply to each—than an astronomer can explain the movements of the solar system, without taking his stand in the sun. And let me remark, that this will not tend to produce despotism, but, on the contrary, true tolerance, in the critic. [See Raysor, *Coleridge's Shakespearean Criticism*, I, p. 221.]

These things seem the more significant for being thrown out by the way, suggesting a radical habit of mind, the literary critic's concern to *ériger en lois*—his proper concern with the formulation of principle. They add greatly to the impressiveness of the account that can be elaborated of Coleridge's qualifications for a great achievement in criticism. My own experience is that one can easily fill a lecture on Coleridge with such an account, and that the impressiveness of the qualifications has a large part in one's impression of a great achivement. The qualifications are obvious, but the achievement isn't readily sized up.

What, in fact, can be said of it after a resolute critical survey? Asked to point to a place that could be regarded as at the centre of Coleridge's achievement and indicative of its nature, most admirers would probably point to the famous passage on imagination at the end of Chapter XIV of *Biographia Literaria*:

The poet, described in *ideal* perfection, brings the whole soul of man into activity, with the subordination of its faculties to each other, according to their relative worth and dignity. He diffuses a tone and spirit of unity, that blends, and (as it were) *fuses,* each into each, by that synthetic and magical power, to which we have exclusively appropriated the name of imagination. This power, first put into action by the will and understanding, and retained under their irremissive, though gentle and unnoticed, control (*laxis effertur habenis*) reveals itself in the balance or reconciliation of opposite or discordant qualities: of sameness, with difference; the general, with the concrete; the idea, with the image; the individual, with the representative; the sense of novelty and freshness, with old and familiar objects; a more than usual state of emotion with more than usual order; judgment ever awake and steady self-possession, with enthusiasm and feeling profound or vehement; and while it blends and harmonizes the natural and the artificial, still subordinates art to nature; the manner to the matter; and our admiration of the poet to our sympathy with the poetry.

It is an impressive passage—perhaps too impressive; for it has more often, perhaps, caused an excited sense of enlightenment than it has led to improved critical practice or understanding. The value we set on it must depend on the development and illustration the account of imagination gets in such context as we can find for it elsewhere in Coleridge and especially in his own critical practice. The appropriate commentary according to general acceptance would, I suppose, bear on the substitution by Coleridge of an understanding of literature in terms of organism, an understanding operating through an inward critical analysis, for the external mechanical approach of the Neo-classic eighteenth century. That Coleridge has a place in literary history to be indicated in some such terms is no doubt true. And yet we ought hardly to acquiesce happily in any suggestion that the subsequent century exhibits a general improvement in criticism. What in fact this view—the academically accepted one, I believe—of Coleridge amounts to is that, of the decisive change in taste and literary tradition that resulted from the Romantic movement, Coleridge is to be regarded as the supreme critical representative.

And it has to be recognized that, in effect, his "imagination" does seem to have amounted to the Romantic "creative imagination." This much, at any rate, must be conceded: that, though justice insists that Coleridge's account of the creative process is not that given by Shelley in his *Defense of Poetry,* nevertheless Coleridge's influence did not, in the subsequent century, avail to make the Romantic tradition, of which he was an acclaimed founding father, aware of the difference, From whom, for instance, does that "soul" descend in which, according to Arnold (who—and it is one of his claims to honor—was much less satisfied than Coleridge with the notion of poetry as the product of the inspired individual), "genuine poetry" was "conceived and composed"? Arnold can hardly be said to have favoured Shelleyan notions, and yet, if we conclude that it descends from the soul "brought into activity" by the poet who is described in Chapter XIV of *Biographia Literaria,* we are hardly recommending Coleridge.

In any case, Coleridge's historical importance isn't at the centre of my concern. My concern is with the intrinsic interest of his extant critical work—with his achievement in that sense. A critic may have an important place in history and yet not be very interesting in his writings: Dryden seems to me a case in point. Coleridge, on the other hand, may be more interesting than the claims made for him as an influence suggest. What credit we give for the interesting possibilities of that passage on imagination depends, as has been said, on the way the account is developed and illustrated.

The Fancy-Imagination contrast hardly takes us any further. Coleridge does little with it beyond the brief exemplification that cannot be said to justify the stress he lays on the two faculties he distinguished. I. A. Richards's attempt, in *Coleridge on Imagination,* to develop the distinction is a tribute not to Coleridge but to Bentham. The best that can be said for Coleridge is that, though he was undoubtedly serious in positing the two faculties, actually the distinction as he illustrates it is a way of calling attention to the organic complexities of verbal life, metaphorical and other, in which Imagination manifests itself locally: Fancy is merely an ancillary concept. And Coleridge certainly gives evidence of a gift for critical analysis:

> *Look! how bright a star shooteth from the sky;*
> *So glides he in the night from Venus' eye!*

How many images and feelings are here brought together without effort and without discord, in the beauty of Adonis, the rapidity of his flight, the yearning, yet hopelessness, of the enamoured gazer, while a shadowy ideal character is thrown over the whole. [See *Coleridge's Shakespearean Criticism,* I, p. 213.]

A good many passages of this kind could be quoted, showing a capacity for a kind of sensitive analytic penetration such as will hardly be found in any earlier critic.

But "capacity"—again it is evidence of qualifications we are adducing. What corresponding achievement is there to point to? The work on Shakespeare constitutes the nearest thing to an impressive body of criticism, and everyone who has tried to read it through knows how disappointing it is. Coleridge didn't inaugurate what may be called the Bradley approach, but he lends his prestige to it. Of course, his psychologizing is pursued with nothing of Bradley's system—he never carries through anything with system. On the other hand, he has things to offer that are beyond Bradley's range. The subtle-souled psychologist appears to advantage, for example, in the analysis, if not of Hamlet's character, of the effects, at once poetic and dramatic, of the opening of the play. There are various notes of that kind and a good many acute observations about points in the verse. In short, when we take stock of what there is to be said in favour of the Shakespeare criticism, we again find ourselves considering, not achievement, but evidence of a critical endowment that *ought* to have achieved something remarkable. Even those who rate it more highly would, I imagine, never think of proposing the work on Shakespeare to the student as a classical body of criticism calculated to make much difference to his powers of appreciation or understanding.

What is, I suppose, a classical document is the group of chapters on Wordsworth in *Biographia Literaria*. But if they are that it is at least partly for reasons of historical interest, because Coleridge on Wordsworth is Coleridge on Wordsworth, and not because of achieved criticism of a high order contained in them. The treatment of the poetry, however interesting, hardly amounts to a profound or very illuminating critique. The discussion of poetic diction provides, of course, more evidence of Coleridge's peculiar gifts, especially in the argument about metre in Chapter XVIII. That Coleridge perceives certain essential truths about poetic rhythm and metre—truths that are not yet commonplaces, at any rate in academic literary study—is plain. But anything approaching the satisfactory treatment of them that he seems pre-eminently qualified to have written he certainly doesn't provide. His virtue is represented by this:

> Secondly, I argue from the EFFECTS of metre. As far as metre acts in and for itself, it tends to increase the vivacity and susceptibility both of the general feelings and of the attention. This effect it produces by the continued excitement of surprise, and by the quick reciprocations of curiosity still gratified and still re-excited, which are too slight indeed to be at any one moment objects of distinct consciousness, yet become considerable in their aggregate influence. As a medicated atmosphere, or as wine during animated conversation, they act powerfully, though themselves unnoticed. Where, therefore, cor-

respondent food and appropriate matter are not provided for the attention and feelings thus aroused, there must needs be a disappointment felt; like that of leaping in the dark from the last step of a staircase, when we had prepared our muscles for a leap of three or four.

This fairly earns the tribute that I. A. Richards pays Coleridge in *The Principles of Literary Criticism,* in the chapter on "Rhythm and Metre" (one of the useful parts of that book). But though the paragraph quoted tends to confer credit upon the context of technical-looking analysis, it doesn't really gain anything from that context, the rigorously and ambitiously analytic air of which doesn't justify itself, despite an element of interesting suggestion.

And this seems the moment to make the point that Coleridge's unsatisfactoriness isn't merely what stares at us in the synopsis of *Biographia Literaria*—the disorderliness, the lack of all organization or sustained development: locally too, even in the best places, he fails to bring his thoughts to a sharp edge and seems too content with easy expression. Expression came, in fact, too easily to him; for a man of his deep constitutional disinclinations to brace himself to sustained work at any given undertaking, his articulateness was fatal. He could go down to the lecture-hall at the last minute with a marked copy of Shakespeare and talk—talk as much as he talked anywhere and at any time. And what we read as Coleridge's writings comes from that inveterate talker, even when the text that we have is something he actually wrote and not reported discourse.

Perhaps the habit of the lecture-hall accounts for such things as the definition of a poem in Chapter XIV of *Biographia Literaria*:

> The final definition then, so deduced, may be thus worded. A poem is that species of composition, which is opposed to works of science, by proposing for its immediate object pleasure, not truth; and from all other species (having *this* object in common with it) it is discriminated by proposing to itself such delight from the *whole,* as is compatible with a distinct gratification from each component *part.*

That, I am afraid, is representative of a good deal in Coleridge, though it seems to me quite unprofitable. And at the end of the same chapter is this well-known pronouncement:

> Finally, GOOD SENSE is the BODY of poetic genius. FANCY is its DRAPERY, MOTION its LIFE, and IMAGINATION the SOUL that is everywhere, and in each; and forms all into one graceful and intelligent whole.

It comes, characteristically enough, just after the famous passage on imagination, which is of another order altogether.

The immediately succeeding chapter (XV) seems to me to show Coleridge at his best. It is headed, "The specific symptoms of poetic power elucidated in a critical analysis of Shakespeare's *Venus and Adonis* and *Lucrece*," and this heading is significant: it suggests with some felicity the nature of Coleridge's peculiar distinction, or what should have been his peculiar distinction, as a critic. He speaks in his first sentence, referring no doubt mainly to the passage on imagination, of "the application of these principles to purposes of practical criticism." Actually, principle as we are aware of it here appears to emerge from practice; we are made to realize that the "master of theoretical criticism" who matters is the completion of a practical critic. The theory of which he is master (in so far as he is) doesn't lead us to discuss his debt to Kant or any other philosopher; it comes too evidently from the English critic who has devoted his finest powers of sensibility and intelligence to the poetry of his own language.

This commentary is prompted by, specifically, the second head of the chapter:

> A second promise of genius is the choice of subjects very remote from the private interests and circumstances of the writer himself. At least I have found that, where the subject is taken immediately from the author's personal sensations and experiences, the excellence of a particular poem is but an equivocal mark, and often a fallacious pledge, of genuine poetic power.

The general considerations raised are immediately relevant to that central theme of T. S. Eliot's criticism, impersonality. But they are presented in terms of particular analysis, and the whole passage is a fine piece of practical criticism:

> In the *Venus and Adonis* this proof of poetic power exists even to excess. It is throughout as if a superior spirit more intuitive, more intimately conscious, even than the characters themselves, not only of every outward look and act, but of the flux and reflux of the mind in all its subtlest thoughts and feelings, were placing the whole before our view; himself meanwhile unparticipating in the passions, and actuated only by that pleasurable excitement which had resulted from the energetic fervour of his own spirit in so vividly exhibiting what it had so accurately and profoundly contemplated. I think I should have conjectured from these poems that even then the great instinct, which impelled the poet of the drama, was secretly working in him,

prompting him by a series and never broken chain of imagery always vivid and, because unbroken, often minute; by the highest effort of the picturesque in words, of which words are capable, higher perhaps than was ever realized by any other poet, even Dante not excepted; to provide a substitute for that visual language, that constant intervention and running comment by tone, look and gesture, which in his dramatic works he was entitled to expect from the players. His Venus and Adonis seem at once the characters themselves, and the whole representation of those characters by the most consummate actors. You seem to be told nothing but to see and hear everything. Hence it is, that from the perpetual activity of attention required on the part of the reader; from the rapid flow, the quick change, and the playful nature of the thoughts and images; and above all from the alienation, and, if I may hazard such an expression, the utter *aloofness* of the poet's own feelings from those of which he is at once the painter and the analyst; that though the very subject cannot but detract from the pleasure of a delicate mind, yet never was poem less dangerous on a moral account. Instead of doing as Ariosto, and as, still more offensively, Wieland has done, instead of degrading and deforming passion into appetite, the trials of love into the struggles of concupiscence Shakespeare has here represented the animal impulse itself, so as to preclude all sympathy with it, by dissipating the reader's notice among the thousand outward images, and now beautiful, now fanciful circumstances, which form its dresses and its scenery; or by diverting our attention from the main subject by those frequent witty or profound reflections, which the poet's ever active mind had deduced from, or connected with, the imagery and the incidents. The reader is forced into too much action to sympathize with the merely passive of our nature. As little can a mind thus roused and awakened be brooded on by mean and indistinct emotion, as the low, lazy mist can creep upon the surface of a lake, while a strong gale is driving it onward in waves and billows.

It will have been seen that, incidentally, in the sentence about "the perpetual activity of attention required on the part of the reader" and the further observations about the "action" into which the reader is forced, Coleridge has given an account of the element of "wit" that is in *Venus and Adonis*.

Though the other heads of the chapter contain nothing as striking, we tend to give full credit to what is best in them. In the first and third, for instance, Coleridge makes it plain (as he has already done in practical criticism) that the "imagery" that matters cannot be dealt with in terms of "images" conceived as standing to the verse as plums to cake; but that its analysis is the analysis of complex verbal organization:

It has therefore been observed that images, however beautiful, though faithfully copied from nature, and as accurately represented in words, do not of themselves characterize the poet. They become proofs of original genius only as far as they are modified by a predominant passion; or by associated thoughts or images awakened by that passion; or when they have the effect of reducing multitude to unity, or succession to an instant; or lastly, when a human and intellectual life is transferred to them from the poet's own spirit.

But there would be little point in further quotation of this kind. Such imperfectly formulated things hardly deserve to be remembered as classical statements, and nothing more is to be adduced by way of justifying achievement than the preceding long quotation. And there is nowhere in Coleridge anything more impressive to be found than that. We are left, then, with the conclusion that what we bring from the resurvey of his critical work is impressive evidence of what he might have done.

A great deal more space, of course, could be occupied with this evidence. Some of the most interesting is to be found in *Coleridge's Miscellaneous Criticism* (T. H. Raysor's collection), where, in the form of marginalia, odd notes, table-talk, and so on, there are many striking judgements and observations. There are, for instance, the pages (131 *ff.*) on Donne—pages that incline one to comment that if Coleridge had had real influence the vogue of Donne would have started a century earlier that it did. (Of *Satire* III, *e.g.*, he says: "If you would teach a scholar in the highest form how to *read*, take Donne, and of Donne this satire.") He is sound on Beaumont and Fletcher: "Beaumont and Fletcher write as if virtue or goodness were a sort of talisman or strange something that might be lost without the least fault on the part of the owner"—and he refers to "the too poematic-minus-dramatic nature" of Fletcher's versification. He is good on Swift: "In short, critics in general complain of the Yahoos; I complain of the Houyhnhnms." He is acutely severe on Scott. In fact, the volume as a whole repays exploration. Elsewhere there are the various notes on dramatic and poetic illusion, of which those in *Coleridge's Shakespearean Criticism*, Vol. I (pp. 199 *ff.*), should be looked up, though the best-known formulation "that willing suspension of disbelief for the moment, which constitutes poetic faith," occurs in *Biographia Literaria* (Ch. XIV).

But to revert to the depressing conclusion: Coleridge's prestige is very understandable, but his currency as an academic classic is something of a scandal. Where he is prescribed and recommended it should be with far more by way of reservation and caveat (I have come tardily to realize) than most students can report to have received along with him. He was very much more brilliantly gifted than Arnold, but nothing of his deserves the classical status of Arnold's best work.

(1940)

Matthew Arnold

by F. R. Leavis

"And I do not like your calling Matthew Arnold Mr. Kidglove Cocksure. I have more reason than you for disagreeing with him and thinking him very wrong, but nevertheless I am sure he is a rare genius and a great critic." *

The note of animus that Hopkins here rebukes in Bridges is a familiar one where Arnold is concerned: it characterizes a large part of recorded comment on him. Raleigh's essay in *Some Authors* is (if we can grant this very representative *littérateur* so much distinction) a convenient *locus classicus* for it and for the kind of critical injustice it goes with. But one may be quite free from such animus or from any temptation to it—may welcome rather than resent that in Arnold by which the Raleighs are most antagonized—and yet find critical justice towards him oddly difficult to arrive at. He seems to present to the appraising reader a peculiarly elusive quantity. At least, that is my experience as an admirer, and I am encouraged in generalizing by the fact that the experience of the most important literary critic of our time appears to have been much the same.

In *The Sacred Wood,* speaking of Arnold with great respect, Mr. Eliot calls him "rather a propagandist for criticism than a critic," and I must confess that for years the formula seems to me unquestionably just. Is Arnold's critical achievement after all a very impressive one? His weaknesses and his irritating tricks one remembers very well. Is it, in fact, possible to protest with any conviction when we are told (in the later essay, "Arnold and Pater" in *Selected Essays*)?—

> Arnold had little gift for consistency or for definition. Nor had he the power of connected reasoning at any length: his flights are either short flights or circular flights. Nothing in his prose works, therefore, will stand very close analysis, and we may very well feel that the positive content of many words is very small.

And yet, if the truth is so, how is it that we open our Arnold so often, relatively? For it is just the oddity of Arnold's case that,

* *The Letters of Gerard Manley Hopkins to Robert Bridges,* XCVIII.

while we are apt to feel undeniable force in such judgements as the above, we nevertheless think of him as one of the most lively and profitable of the accepted critics. Let us at any rate seize on the agreement that as a propagandist for criticism he is distinguished. On the view that has been quoted the first two essays in *Essays in Criticism: First Series* would be the texts to stress as exhibiting Arnold at his strongest, and they have, indeed, seemed to me such. And re-reading confirms the claim of "The Function of Criticism at the Present Time" and "The Literary Influence of Academies" to be remembered as classical presentments of their themes. The plea for critical intelligence and critical standards and the statement of the idea of centrality (the antithesis of "provinciality") are made in memorable formulations of classical rightness:

> . . . whoever sets himself to see things as they are will find himself one of a very small circle; but it is only by this small circle resolutely doing its own work that adequate ideas will ever get current at all.
>
> All the world has, or proposes to have, this conscience in moral matters. . . . And a like deference to a standard higher than one's own habitual standard in intellectual matters, a like respectful recognition of a superior ideal, is caused, in the intellectual sphere, by sensitiveness of intelligence.
>
> . . . not being checked in England by any centre of intelligent and urbane spirit . . .
>
> M. Planche's advantage is . . . that there is a force of cultivated opinion for him to appeal to.
>
> . . . a serious, settled, fierce, narrow, provincial misconception of the whole relative value of one's own things and the things of others.

Arnold's distinction as a propagandist for criticism cannot be questioned. At the same time, perhaps, it must be admitted that these essays do not involve any very taut or subtle development of an argument or any rigour of definition. They are pamphleteering—higher pamphleteering that has lost little of its force and relevance with the passage of time.

Yet it must surely be apparent that the propaganda could hardly have had its virtue if the pamphleteer had not had notable qualifications in criticism. The literary critic, in fact, makes a direct appearance, a very impressive one, in the judgement on the Romantics, which, in its time, remarks Mr. Eliot * (who elsewhere justly pronounces it incontrovertible), "must have appeared start-

---
* *The Use of Poetry and the Use of Criticism*, p. 104.

lingly independent." It seems plain that the peculiar distinction, the strength, represented by the extracts given above, is inseparable from the critical qualifications manifested in that judgement: the sensitiveness and sure tact are essentially those of a fine literary critic.

But does any actual performance of Arnold's in set literary criticism bear out the suggestion at all convincingly? Again it is characteristic of his case that one should be able to entertain the doubt. How many of his admirers retain very strongly favourable impressions of the other series of *Essays in Criticism?*—for it is to this, and to the opening essay in particular, "The Study of Poetry," that the challenge sends one back. For myself, I must confess to having been surprised, on a recent re-reading of that essay, at the injustice of my recollection of it. The references to Dryden and Pope tend (in my experience) to bulk unfairly, and, for that reason and others, there is a temptation to talk too easily of the essay as being chiefly memorable for having standardized Victorian taste and established authoritatively what, in the academic world, has hardly ceased to be the accepted perspective of poetic history. And it is, actually, as a review of the past from the given-period angle that the essay claims its classical status. But it is classical—for it truly is—because it performs its undertaking so consummately. Its representative quality is of the highest kind, that which can be achieved only by vigorously independent intelligence. If it is fair to say that Arnold, in his dismissal of Dryden and Pope by the criterion of "soul" and his curious exaltation of Gray, is the voice of the Romantic tradition in his time, we must note too that he is the same Arnold who passed the "startlingly independent" judgement on the Romantics. And with whatever reservations, protests, and irritations we read "The Study of Poetry," it is impossible in reading it (I find) not to recognize that we have to do with an extraordinarily distinguished mind in complete possession of its purpose and pursuing it with easy mastery—that, in fact, we are reading a great critic. Moreover, I find that in this inconsequence I am paralleled by Mr. Eliot. He writes in *The Use of Poetry and the Use of Criticism* (p. 118), in the mainly depreciatory chapter on Arnold:

> But you cannot read his essay on *The Study of Poetry* without being convinced by the felicity of his quotations: to be able to quote as Arnold could is the best evidence of taste. The essay is a classic in

English criticism: so much is said in so little space, with such economy and with such authority.

How is this curious inconsistency of impression—this discrepancy of report which, I am convinced, many readers of Arnold could parallel from their own experience of him—to be explained? Partly it is, I think, that, taking critical stock at a remove from the actual reading, one tends to apply inappropriate criteria of logical rigour and "definition." And it is partly (a not altogether separable consideration) that the essay "dates" in various ways; allowances have certainly to be made with reference to the age to which it was addressed, certain things "date" in the most damaging sense, and it is easy to let these things infect one's general impression of the "period" quality of the essay.

The element that "dates" in the worst sense is that represented by the famous opening in which Arnold suggests that religion is going to be replaced by poetry. Few now would care to endorse the unqualified intention of that passage, and Arnold as a theological or philosophical thinker had better be abandoned explicitly at once. Yet the value of the essay does not depend on our accepting without reservation the particular terms in which Arnold stresses the importance of poetry in those introductory sentences, and he is not disposed of as a literary critic by pointing out that he was not theologian or philosopher; nor is it proved that he was incapable of consistency and vigour of thought. Many who deplore Arnold's way with religion will agree that, as the other traditions relax and social forms disintegrate, it becomes correspondingly more important to preserve the literary tradition. When things are as already they were in Arnold's time, they make necessary, whatever else may be necessary too, the kind of work that Arnold undertook for "Culture"—work that couldn't have been done by a theologian as such. No doubt Arnold might have been able to do it even better if he had had the qualifications that actually he hadn't; he would at any rate have known his limits better, and wouldn't have produced those writings of his which have proved most ephemeral and which constitute the ground on which Mr. Eliot charges him with responsibility for Pater. But his actual qualifications were sufficiently remarkable and had their appropriate use. His best work is that of a literary critic, even when it is not literary criticism: it comes from an intelligence that, even if not trained to some kinds of rigour, had its own discipline; an intelligence that is informed by a mature and delicate sense of the humane values and can manifest itself directly as a fine sensibility. That function some who most disapprove of Arnold's religious position readily grant.* Failure to recognize—or to recognize unequivocally—an admirable performance of the function in "The Study of Poetry" may be partly explained by that opening of the essay: Arnold, after all, issues the distracting challenge, however unnecessarily.

The seriousness with which he conceived the function and the importance he ascribed to poetry are more legitimately expressed in the phrase, the best-known tag from the essay, "criticism of life." That it is not altogether satisfactory the animadversion it has been the object of must perhaps be taken to prove: at best we must admit that the intention it expresses hasn't, to a great many readers, made itself satisfactorily clear. Nevertheless, Arnold leaves us with little excuse for supposing—as some of his most eminent critics have appeared to suppose—that he is demanding doctrine or moral commentary on life or explicit criticism. Nor should it be necessary to point out that all censure passed on him for having, in calling poetry "criticism of life," produced a bad definition is beside the mark.† For it should be obvious to anyone who reads the phrase in its context that Arnold intends, not to define poetry, but, while insisting (a main concern of the essay) that there are different degrees of importance in poetry, to remind us of the nature of the criteria by which comparative judgements are made.

Why Arnold should have thought the insistence and the reminder worth while and should have hit on the given phrase as appropriate for his purpose is not difficult to understand if we think of that Pater with whom, as noted above, he has been associated.

> "Art for Art's sake" is the offspring of Arnold's culture; and we can hardly venture to say that it is even a perversion of Arnold's doctrine, considering how very vague and ambiguous that doctrine is.

At any rate, we can certainly not say that "Art for Art's sake" is the offspring of Arnold's "criticism of life." In fact, Arnold's phrase is sufficiently explained—and, I think, vindicated—as expressing an intention directly counter to the tendency that finds its consummation in "Art for Art's sake." Aestheticism was not a sudden development: the nature of the trend from Keats through Tennyson and Dante Gabriel Rossetti was, even in Arnold's mid-career, not unapparent to the critic who passed the judgement on the great

---

* See, *e.g.*, *Poetry and Crisis*, by Martin Turnell.
† See, *e.g.*, J. M. Robertson's curious performance in *Modern Humanists Reconsidered*, referred to by Mr. Eliot.

Romantics. The insistence that poetry must be judged as "criticism of life" is the same critic's reaction to the later Romantic tradition; it puts the stress where it seemed to him that it most needed to be put.

In so far as Arnold ever attempts to explain the phrase it is in such terms as those in which, in the essay on Wordsworth, he explains why it is that Wordsworth must be held to be a greater poet than the "perfect" Gautier. But with no more explanation than is given in "The Study of Poetry" the intention seems to me plain enough for Arnold's purposes. To define the criteria he was concerned with, those by which we make the more serious kind of comparative judgement, was not necessary, and I cannot see that anything would have been gained by his attempting to define them. His business was to evoke them effectively (can we really hope for anything better?), and that, I think, he must be allowed to have done. We may, when, for example, he tells us why Chaucer is not among the very greatest poets, find him questionable and provoking, but the questions are profitable and the provocations stimulate us to get clear in our own minds. We understand well enough the nature of his approach; the grounds of his criticism are sufficiently present. Pressed for an account of the intention behind the famous phrase, we have to say something like this: we make (Arnold insists) our major judgements about poetry by bringing to bear the completest and profoundest sense of relative value that, aided by the work judged, we can focus from our total experience of life (which includes literature), and our judgement has intimate bearings on the most serious choices we have to make thereafter in our living. We don't ordinarily ask of the critic that he shall tell us anything like this, or shall attempt to define the criteria by which he makes his major judgements of value. But Arnold appears to challenge the demand and so earns reprobation for not satisfying it. By considering the age to which he was addressing himself we are able to do him justice; but if in this way he may be said to "date," it is not in any discreditable sense.

There is still to be met the pretty general suspicion to which Mr. Eliot gives voice when he says [*] that Arnold "was apt to think of the greatness of poetry rather than of its genuineness." It is a suspicion that is the harder to lay because, with a slight shift of accent, it turns into an unexceptionable observation:

---
[*] *The Use of Poetry*, etc., p. 110.

The best of Arnold's criticism is an illustration of his ethical views, and contributes to his discrimination of the values and relations of the components of the good life.*

This very fairly accords due praise while suggesting limitations. We have, nevertheless, to insist that, but for Arnold's gifts as a literary critic, that criticism would not have had its excellence. And when the suspicion takes such form as the following,† some answer must clearly be attempted:

> Yet he was so conscious of what, for him, poetry was *for*, that he could not altogether see it for what it is. And I am not sure that he was highly sensitive to the musical qualities of verse. His own occasional bad lapses arouse the suspicion; and so far as I can recollect he never emphasizes this virtue of poetic style, this fundamental, in his criticism.

Whatever degree of justice there may be in these suggestions, one point can be made at once: some pages of "The Study of Poetry" are explicitly devoted to considering "genuineness"—the problem of how the critic makes those prior kinds of judgements, those initial recognitions of life and quality, which must precede, inform, and control all profitable discussion of poetry and any evaluation of it as "criticism of life." Towards the close of the essay we read:

> To make a happy fireside clime
> To weans and wife,
> That's the true pathos and sublime
> Of human life.

> There is criticism of life for you, the admirers of Burns will say to us; there is the application of ideas to life. There is undoubtedly.

And Arnold goes on to insist (in terms that would invite the charge of circularity if we were being offered a definition, as we are not) that the evaluation of poetry as "criticism of life" is inseparable from its evaluation as poetry; that the moral judgement that concerns us as critics must be at the same time a delicately relevant response of sensibility; that, in short, we cannot separate the consideration of "greatness" from the consideration of "genuineness." The test for "genuineness" Arnold indicates in this way:

> Those laws [of poetic truth and poetic beauty] fix as an essential condition, in the poet's treatment of such matters as are here in question, high seriousness;—the high seriousness which comes from absolute

---
* *Criterion*, Vol. III, p. 162.
† *The Use of Poetry*, etc., p. 118.

> sincerity. The accent of high seriousness, born of absolute sincerity, is what gives to such verse as
>
> > *E'n la sua volontate è nostra pace* . . .
>
> to such criticism of life as Dante's, its power. Is this accent felt in the passages which I have been quoting from Burns? Surely not; surely, if our sense is quick, we must perceive that we have not in those passages a voice from the very inmost soul of the genuine Burns; he is not speaking to us from these depths, he is more or less preaching.

This passage is old-fashioned in its idiom, and perhaps "high seriousness" should be dismissed as a mere nuisance. But "absolute sincerity," a quality belonging to the "inmost soul" and manifested in an "accent," an "accent that we feel if our sense is quick"—this phrasing, in the context, seems to me suggestive in a wholly creditable and profitable way. And actually it has a force behind it that doesn't appear in the quotation: it is strengthened decisively by what has come earlier in the essay.

The place in question is that in which Arnold brings out his critical tip, the "touchstone." Whatever that tip may be worth, its intention should be plain. It is a tip for mobilizing our sensibility; for focussing our relevant experience in a sensitive point; for reminding us vividly of what the best is like.

> Of course we are not to require this other poetry to resemble them; it may be very dissimilar.
>
> The specimens I have quoted differ widely from one another, but they have in common this: the possession of the very highest poetical quality.

It is only by bringing our experience to bear on it that we can judge the new thing, yet the expectations that we bring, more or less unconsciously, may get in the way; and some readers may feel that Arnold doesn't allow enough for the danger. But that he means to allow for it and envisages the problem with the delicate assurance of a fine critic is plain.

What, however, we have particularly to mark—the main point of turning back to this place in the essay—is what follows. Arnold, while protesting that "It is much better simply to have recourse to concrete examples," ventures, nevertheless, to give some critical account, "not indeed how and why" the characters of a high quality of poetry arise, "but where and in what they arise." The account is characteristic in its method and, I think, notably justifies it.

> They are in the matter and substance of the poetry and they are in its

manner and style. Both of these, the substance and matter on the one hand, the style and manner on the other, have a mark, an accent of high beauty, worth and power.

And the succeeding couple of pages might seem to be mainly a matter of irritating repetition that implicitly admits an inability to get any further. Nevertheless, there is development, and the varied reiteration of associated terms, which is certainly what we have, has a critical purpose.

> We may add yet further, what is in itself evident, that to the style and manner of the best poetry their special character, their accent, is given by their diction, and, even yet more, by their movement. And though we distinguish between the two characters, the two accents, of superiority, yet they are nevertheless vitally connected one with the other. The superior character of truth and seriousness, in the matter and substance of the best poetry, is inseparable from the superiority of diction and manner marking its style and movement.

It is plain that, in this insistent association of "accent," "diction," and "movement" in the equally insistent context, Arnold is offering his equivalent of Mr. Eliot's "musical qualities of verse" and of Dr. Richards's "rhythm." * His procedure is a way of intimating that he doesn't suppose himself to have said anything very precise. But he seems to me, all the same, to have done the appropriate directing of attention upon poetry—and that was the problem —not less effectively than the other two critics.

Inquiry, then, into the main criticisms that have been brought against "The Study of Poetry" yields reports decidedly in Arnold's favour. If he speaks in that essay with economy and authority, it is because his critical position is firmly based, because he knows what he is setting out to do, and because he is master of the appropriate method. The lack of the "gift for consistency or for definition" turns out to be compensated for, at his best, by certain positive virtues: tact and delicacy, a habit of keeping in sensitive touch with the concrete, and an accompanying gift for implicit definition— virtues that prove adequate to the sure and easy management of a sustained argument and are, as we see them in Arnold, essentially those of a literary critic.

However, it must be confessed that none of the other essays in that volume can be called a classic in English criticism. The "Milton" is a mere ceremonial address. (But it may be noted at this point that the reader who supposes Arnold to have been an

---

* *Science and Poetry*, p. 40.

orthodox idolater of Milton will be surprised if he turns up in *Mixed Essays* the essay called "A French Critic on Milton"). The "Gray" dates most of all the essays in the series—dates in the most damaging sense; though it may be said to have gained in that way a classical status as a document in the history of taste. Neither the "Keats" nor the "Shelley" makes any show of being a model critique of poetry; but, nevertheless, the rarely gifted literary critic is apparent in them. It is apparent in his relative placing of the two poets. "Shelley," he says, "is not a classic, whose various readings are to be noted with earnest attention." And the reasons he gives for his low valuation, though they are not backed with particular criticism, seem to me unanswerable. On Keats he is extraordinarily just, in appreciation both of the achievement and of the potentiality —extraordinarily just, if we think of the bias that "criticism of life" is supposed to imply. The critic's quality comes out in some notable phrases:

> But indeed nothing is more remarkable in Keats than his clear-sightedness, his lucidity; and lucidity is in itself akin to character and to high and severe work.

> Even in his pursuit of "the pleasures of song," however, there is that stamp of high work which is akin to character, which is character passing into intellectual production.

The "Wordsworth," with all its limitations, is at any rate a distinguished personal estimate, and though by a Wordsworthian, and by the critic who spoke of poetry as the "application of ideas to life," exhibits its salutary firmness about the "philosophy."

But what has to be stressed is his relative valuation of the great Romantics: Wordsworth he put first, then Byron (and for the right reasons), then Keats, and last Shelley. It is, in its independence and its soundness, a more remarkable critical achievement than we easily recognize today. (The passage on the Romantics in the "Heine" essay should not be overlooked.)

If any other particular work of his is to be mentioned, it must be the long essay "On Translating Homer." It was, as Saintsbury points out,[*] an extraordinarily original undertaking at the time, and it was carried out with such spirit and intelligence that it is still profitable reading.

The actual achievement in producible criticism may not seem a very impressive one. But we had better inquire where a more im-

---
[*] *Matthew Arnold*, p. 68.

pressive is to be found. As soon as we start to apply any serious standard of what good criticism should be, we are led towards the conclusion that there is very little. If Arnold is not one of the great critics, who are they? Which do we approach with a greater expectation of profit? Mr. Eliot himself—yes, and not only because his preoccupations are of our time; his best critical writing has a higher critical intensity than any of Arnold's. Coleridge's pre-eminence we all recognize. Johnson?—that Johnson is a living writer no one will dispute, and his greatness is certainly apparent in his criticism. Yet that he imposes himself there as a more considerable power than Arnold isn't plain to me, and strictly as a critic—a critic offering critical value—he seems to me to matter a good deal less to us. As for Dryden, important as he is historically, I have always thought the intrinsic interest of his criticism much overrated: he showed strength and distinction in independent judgement, but I cannot believe that his discussion of any topic has much to offer us. We read him (if we do) because of his place in literary history, whereas we read Arnold's critical writing because for anyone who is interested in literature it is compellingly alive. I can think of no other English critic who asks to be considered here, so I will say finally that, whatever his limitations, Arnold seems to me decidedly more of a critic than the Sainte-Beuve to whom he so deferred.

(1938)

PART III

THREE GREAT POETS

Shakespeare

(1) AS YOU LIKE IT, *by James Smith*

It is a commonplace that Jaques and Hamlet are akin. But it is also a commonplace that Jaques is an intruder into *As You Like It,* so that in spite of the kinship the plays are not usually held to have much connexion. I have begun to doubt whether not only *As You Like It* and *Hamlet,* but almost all the comedies and the tragedies as a whole are not closely connected, and in a way which may be quite important.

Recent criticism of Shakespeare has directed itself with profit upon the tragedies, the "problem plays," and certain of the histories. The early comedies, on the other hand, have either been disparaged or entirely overlooked. Yet the same criticism owes part of its success to a notion of what it calls Shakespeare's "integrity"; his manifold interests, it has maintained, being co-ordinated so as rarely to thwart, regularly to strengthen one another. Hence he was alert and active as few have been, while his writing commanded not part but the whole of his resources.

Such a notion seems sound and proves useful. Belief in an author's integrity, however, ought to forbid the dismissal of any part of his work, at least its hasty dismissal. The comedies, to which he gave a number of years of his life, are no insignificant part of Shakespeare's. If it is true that they shed no light on the tragedies nor the tragedies on them, it would seem he deserves credit for a unique dissipation rather than concentration of his powers.

It is of course comprehensible that the comedies should be shunned. To some readers they are less inviting than the tragedies, to all they are more wearisome when their study is begun. Not only are the texts in a state of comparative impurity; the form itself is impure. Being less serious than tragedy—this, I am sure, is disputed, but would suggest that the word has a number of meanings—being less serious than tragedy, comedy admits of interludes and side-shows; further, the material for the side-shows is not infrequently such that it might be material for the comedy itself. Decision is important, but not always easy whether or not it should be disregarded.

The desultory nature of the following notes may, I hope, be forgiven, partly because of complications such as these, partly because of contemporary distractions which leave no time for elaboration. I start with Jaques's melancholy, in respect of which alone he has been likened to Hamlet.

It is, I think, most accessible to study in his encounter with Rosalind at the beginning of Act IV. Having abundant leisure he needs a companion to while it away. "I prethee, pretty youth," he says, "let me be better acquainted with thee." But Rosalind, who has heard unfavourable reports, is by no means eager to comply: "They say you are a melancholy fellow." As for that, replies Jaques, his melancholy is at least sincere, for it is as pleasing to him as jollity to other men: "I doe love it better then laughing." But sincerity is irrelevant unless to deepen his offence. As there is an excess of laughter so there is of sadness which should not be pleasing to anybody:

> Those that are in extremity of either, are abhominable fellowes, and betray themselves to every moderne censure, worse than drunkards.

The rebuke is no more than a rebuke of common sense. Your melancholy, objects Rosalind, is not justifiable merely because it is your melancholy, for it may be one of the things which, though they exist, ought not to do so. But the rebuke is none the less pertinent, common sense implying a minimum of alertness and Jaques being afflicted with languor. Either as cause or as consequence of his state he is blind and fails to see, or is stupid and fails to ponder obvious truths.

The force of the rebuke is to be noticed. From Shakespeare, mediaeval rather than modern in this as other matters, drunkards receive no more than temporary tolerance: Falstaff is in the end cast off, Sir Toby beat about the coxcomb. And the respect which they receive is not even temporary. Wine and wassail make

> . . . Memorie, the Warder of the Braine
> . . . a Fume, and the Receit of Reason
> A Lymbeck only;

the sleep they produce is "swinish," by them nature is "drenched."

A drunkard as such forfeits not only his manhood but his humanity. Nor does Rosalind's "modern" mean what the word does now, "modish" or what has been invented of late. Rather it is that which has always been the mode, and which stands plain to reason so that there never was need to invent it. In this play, for example, the justice is described as

Full of wise sawes and moderne instances

—of instances which belong to proverbial wisdom, apt and sound so that they have become trite. What Rosalind is saying is that Jaques by his melancholy is turned into a beast, and that an old woman would be less ignorant, less pitiable, than he.

Taken aback for the moment, he can think of nothing to reaffirm his liking: "Why, 'tis good to be sad and say nothing." Crudely, however, so that he lays himself open to the crude retort: "Why, then, 'tis good to be a poste." And it would seem to be this which finally rouses him to a defence.

His melancholy, he begins, is not like others Rosalind has heard of:

> I have neither the Schollers melancholy, which is emulation; nor the Musitians, which is fantasticall; nor the Courtiers, which is proud; nor the Souldiers, which is ambitious . . .

and so on. Jaques's melancholy has its source not in private hopes, anxieties, and disappointments, but in what is of wider importance, as it is in the world outside. "It is a melancholy," he continues, "of mine owne"—one, that is, which he is the first to discover—"compounded of many simples, extracted from many objects." Or, in other words, it is "the sundrie contemplation of my travells, in which [m]y often rumination wraps me in a most humorous sadnesse."

Jaques's meaning may not be quite clear, and I do not think it is or can be, but his intention would seem to be so. By boasting of originality, breadth, and freshness of information he hopes to impress, perhaps to intimidate, the youthful Rosalind. But she mistakes, and I suspect purposely, his drift: as she is intelligent enough to distrust originality, she is subtle enough to challenge it in this way. Seizing on the word "travels" she exclaims:

> A traveller: by my faith you have great reason to be sad; I feare you have sold your owne lands, to see other mens; then to have seene much, and to have nothing, is to have rich eyes and poore hands.

She ventures after all, that is, to assimilate his melancholy to other people's, suggesting that it may be due to poverty, which is a private anxiety. But Jaques rejects with scorn the notion that his travels have on a balance brought him anything but profit: "I have gain'd," he insists, "my experience." Once more he is implying that something, because it exists, has a title to do so; that his experience, as it has been gained, was necessarily worth the gaining. Once more therefore, and if possible more vigorously this time, she appeals to common sense for his condemnation. Whatever profit he imagines he has brought back from his travels, there is something which the merest stay-at-home could tell him is a loss:

JAQUES: I have gain'd my experience.
ROSALIND: And your experience makes you sad: I had rather have a foole to make me merrie, then experience to make me sad, and to travaile for it too.

Whether or not Rosalind is aware of it, this second rebuke is of peculiar force as addressed to Jaques. Of all characters it is he alone who, in previous scenes, has expressed complete satisfaction in the company of Touchstone, the fool. He has gone even further, and claimed that nowhere but in folly ought satisfaction to be found:

>   . . . *Oh noble foole,*
>   *A worthy foole: Motley's the onely weare* . . .
>   . . . *O that I were a foole,*
>   *I am ambitious for a motley coat.*

Yet now he has to be reminded that there is an office which fools can perform. About his conduct it seems there is a grave inconsistency, for at one time he countenances factitious gaiety, at another equally factitious gloom.

If it stood alone, such an inconsistency might be puzzling; but it has a companion, which also serves to explain it. In claiming in his interchange with Rosalind that all experience is worth while, Jaques is claiming in effect that no experience is worth anything at all. In asserting that, in the present, there are no reasons why he should do one thing rather than another—why, for example, he should be merry rather than mope—he is shutting his eyes to reasons why, in the future, one thing rather than another should be done. In other words he is posing as a sceptic, and scepticism is an inconsistent doctrine. Though a belief itself, it denies the possibility of belief; it denies to man the possibility of action, though by his nature he cannot refrain from acting. And it is because Jaques, in his more alert moments, is aware of this second inconsistency that he commits the first. He seeks shelter in the motley to persuade himself that, though he acts and cannot help doing so, he nevertheless does nothing. For if his actions are mere folly they are of no account and as good as nothing at all.

It is, however, only at rare moments, as, for example, when stirred by a first meeting with Touchstone, that Jaques is alert. For the greater part of his time he is characterized by the languor already referred to: which keeps him from making sustained efforts, even that which (as he is not wholly unintelligent) being a fool requires. Instead of concerning himself to justify his scepticism, he quietly submits to it; and his submission is his melancholy, his "sadness." A man in whose eyes the world contains nothing of value cannot be spurred to action either by the sight of objects he wishes to obtain or by the thought of ideals he hopes to realize. The only action open to him—and as he is human, he cannot remain wholly inert—no more than half deserves the name, for in it he is as much passive as active. He needs, so to speak, to be betrayed into action—to be propelled into it from behind, by agencies of which he is not completely aware. Such agencies are the mechanism of habit, or a conspiracy of circumstance. In comedy, where characters are not relentlessly harassed by circumstance, they are able continually to yield to habit.

The travels to which Jaques refers the origin of his scepticism are equally likely to have been its consequence, for travel and exploration degenerate into habit. When the senses are dazzled by a ceaseless and rapid change of objects, the intellect has no time to discriminate between them, the will no occasion for choice, so that in the end a man becomes capable of neither. The habit is then a necessity to life, which at the same time and to the same extent has slackened, becomes languid. It concerns itself only with the surface of objects, while their substance is neglected. Jaques's decision in Act V proceeds from a habit of this kind:

> *The Duke hath put on a Religious life . . .*
> *To him will I.*

His pretext is that

> *. . . out of these convertites*
> *There is much matter to be heard, and learn'd.*

But his reason, rather than to learn, is to avoid learning. He quits the court for the monastery much as amateur students, threatened with the labour of mastering a subject, abandon it for the preliminaries of another—usually as different as possible. If during the course of the play, Jaques does not engage on travel, it should be remembered that he frequently changes, not his surroundings, but his interlocutor. He indulges the habit of gossip, which is that of a traveller immobilized. That he has abundant leisure for gossip is only natural: time hangs heavy on a sceptic's hands, for whom the world contains nothing that can take it off.

It hangs heavy on Hamlet's, and this is the most obvious point of resemblance between him and Jaques. "I have of late," Hamlet complains, "lost all my mirth, forgone all custome of exercise"; and he goes on to give general reasons. They imply scepticism of a kind: the earth and sky, he says, seem but a "foule and pestilent congregation of vapours," such as do not encourage enterprise: man himself has come to appear but the "Quintessence of dust," with whom he would not willingly have commerce. In the same way, to refer to another tragedy, time hangs heavy on Macbeth's hands, at least as he draws near his end. Neither sight nor sound can rouse his interest, nor could it be roused by any conceivable sight or sound. He finds himself incapable of believing in the reality even of his wife's death: the report of it, he suggests, should be kept from him until tomorrow. But at the same time he knows that tomorrow will find him as insensible, as incredulous, as today.

Scepticism of a kind: but it is immediately obvious that Hamlet speaks with a disgust or an impatience, Macbeth with a weariness, which to Jaques are unknown. Even in this matter in which alone they are similar, their dissimilarity is yet greater. Anticipating a little, it might be said that Macbeth and Hamlet lead a fuller, a more complete life than Jaques; they are, that is, more conscious of themselves, and rather than languid are continuously, perhaps, feverishly alert.

One consequence is that they cannot easily be betrayed into action. Whereas Jaques looks back without regret, even with complacency, on his travels, it is only with reluctance that Macbeth lapses into the habit of fighting for fighting's sake:

> *Why should I play the Roman Foole, and dye*
> *On mine owne sword? whiles I see lives, the gashes*
> *Do better upon them.*

Sentiment and rhythm are flat to extinction, Macbeth is speaking sullenly. What he is about to do may be better than nothing; it is all he can do; nevertheless, it is no more than might be done by a common bully, by an animal. For them it might be a full life; for himeslf, Macbeth admits, its can be no more than the slackened half-life of habit. Similarly the "custome of exercise" and all custom have lost their hold on Hamlet; for him to act he needs to be surprised by extraordinary circumstance.

Nevertheless, as has been said, neither he nor Macbeth is idle. The energy which their state of mind forbids they should employ on the world, they employ on the state of mind itself; so that not only the inconsistency, the evil (what Rosalind meant by the "beastliness") of scepticism is continually before them. They see it is not the solution to a problem, but rather a problem which presses to be solved; not the tempering of feeling and the invigoration of thought, but the denial of both. They not only reject Jaques's flight into folly, which was to preserve scepticism; they agonize over the sort of reflection with which, in both languid and alert moments, Jaques is lulled. "And all our yesterdayes," exclaims Macbeth in despair at what forces itself upon him as the nothingness of man,

> *And all our yesterdayes have lighted Fooles*
> *The way to dusty death;*

" 'tis but an hour agoe," observes Jaques with satisfaction,

> *'Tis but an hour agoe, since it was nine,*
> *And after one houre more, 'twill be eleven,*
> *And so from houre to houre, we ripe, and ripe,*
> *And then from houre to houre, we rot, and rot . . .*

or rather Touchstone observes this, from whom Jaques is quoting. Touchstone is by profession and conviction a fool, the seriousness of whose statements will come up for consideration later; Jaques is as little serious as, in a quotation, it is possible to be. He is echoing more sound than sense; the latter he has not plumbed (the movement, the rhythm, show it), and the statement he has made no more than half his own—fitting accompaniment and expression of a half-life of habit. Elsewhere he compares human life to a theatrical performance as though, in harmony with his scepticism, to stress its unreality; but very soon, in harmony with his languor, the theatre begins to appear a substantial, for all he cares, a permanent structure. Performances in it last a long time, so that it is possible to make a full display of talent:

> ... *one man in his time playes many parts,*
> *His Acts being seven ages.*

And then Jaques recites the ages, diverting himself with objects separated on this occasion not in space but in time. When the same comparison occurs to Macbeth he is so overwhelmed with the notion of unreality that he does not allow even the actor to act: the latter "struts and frets . . . upon the Stage," struts and frets not for a full performance but only for "his houre . . . and then is heard no more." In Macbeth's verse the comparison flares up and extinguishes itself in indignation at what it implies of man's lot:

> *. . . It is a Tale*
> *Told by an Ideot, full of sound and fury*
> *Signifying nothing.*

That of Jaques continues to demean itself elegantly even when describing in detail man's end:

> *Sans teeth, sans eyes, sans taste, sans everything.*

Once again the rhythm and the movement show that Jaques is meaning little of what he says; that, a true traveller once more, he is occupied with the surface only, not the substance of objects before him.

If I may look aside or ahead for a moment, I would venture to suggest that the essential difference between comedy and tragedy may perhaps be this sort of difference: not one of kind, I mean, but of degree. As far as I can see, it is possible and even probable that tragedy and comedy—Shakespearean comedy, at any rate—treat of the same problems, comedy doing so (to repeat the word) less seriously. And by "less seriously," I may now explain, I mean that the problems are not forced to an issue: a lucky happening, a lucky trait of character (or what for the purposes of the play appears lucky), allowing them to be evaded. As, for example, conditions in Arden and conditions of his own temper preserve Jaques from fully realizing the nature and consequences of his scepticism: to Rosalind, to the reader, it is obvious that his interests are restricted, his vigour lessened, but he is never put to the test. Hamlet, on the other hand, in a similar spiritual state, is called upon to avenge a father, foil an uncle, and govern a kingdom. And when at last chance forces him into action it is not only that he may slaughter, but also that he may be slaughtered: in other words, not that in spite of his disability he may achieve his end, but that because of it he may fail. In *Othello* hardly an accident happens which does not lend plausibility to Iago's deceit, so that the problem posed by human malice on the one hand, human ignorance on the other, cannot but be faced; in *Much Ado* there is a final accident—and a very obvious one, for its name is Dogberry—which unmasks Don John. In *Lear* accident of the wildest form unites with malice and with the elements to convince a human being of his imbecility; in *The Winter's Tale* accident equally wild serves to hide that imbecility, if not from Leontes (who is, however, encouraged to forget it), at least from Florizel. In comedy the materials for tragedy are procured, in some cases heaped up; but they are not, so to speak, attended to, certainly not closely examined. And so what might have caused grief causes only a smile, or at worst a grimace.

I apologize for speculations of this kind, which can only remain gratuitous until it is known more exactly what comedy, more especially what *As You Like It,* is about. At least one other resemblance, possibly an important one, between it and the tragedies, calls, I think, for attention. As Hamlet's melancholy is caused by the sin of others and Macbeth's by sins of his own, so Jaques—if the Duke is to be trusted—has not only travelled, but been

> . . . *a Libertine,*
> *As sensuall as the brutish sting itself.*

And the cure for all three, according to each of the three plays, is very much the same. Fortinbras reproaches Hamlet, and Hamlet reproaches himself, with lacking a "hue of resolution," which, as it is "native," is a defect he should not possess; Macbeth contrasts the division of counsels within him, suspending activity, with the strong monarchy or "single state" enjoyed in the healthy man by the reason. Similarly, Rosalind confronts Jaques with the desirability of what she calls merriment or mirth: from her remark already quoted it is obvious she does not mean laughter, not at any rate laughter without measure, and therefore not laughter in the first place. For the confusion of Jaques it is necessary she should speak emphatically; in a conversation which irks her she is to be excused if she is brief. Were the occasion other, or were she given to reflection, she might perhaps describe this "mirth" more closely —as something similar to her own "alertness," which has already drawn attention: the prerequisite of common sense, and what in more recent times, according to the sympathies and perspicacity of the speaker, has been known either as "vitality" or "faith." The meaning of "mirth" in fifteenth- and sixteenth-century devotional books should be borne in mind, and its meaning on the lips of, say, Saint Thomas More. Hamlet, it will be remembered, noted as first among his distressing symptoms that he had "lost all his mirth."

This scene at the beginning of Act IV sheds light, I do not think it would be too much to claim, on all that Jaques says or does. If so, it is important to a not inconsiderable part of the play, and in that at least Jaques cannot be an intruder. For his quips and monologues, however loose in their immediate context, have a dependence on this dialogue, to which he is indispensable. He is so not only by what he says, but also by what he causes to be said to him. I am going to suggest that, in spite of the familiar verdict, he is no more of an intruder anywhere. For the rest of the play consists largely of situations which, if he is taken as primary melancholic, might be described as modelled on that in which he finds himself with Rosalind. Either she or a temporary ally or deputy of hers— frequently Corin the Old Shepherd—faces and condemns a succession of characters who, like Jaques, are incapable of or disposed to action. Silvius, Touchstone, Orlando, the Duke, each has a melancholy of his own; and so too has Rosalind, in so far as she is in love with Orlando. But not even that escapes her judgement, since she can judge it disguised as someone other than herself. Add that the minor characters occasionally condemn or at least reprove one another, and it is possible to gain some notion of the pattern which Shakespeare seems to have intended for *As You Like It*. A single motif is repeated, giving unity to the whole; but at the same time it varies continually, so that the whole is complex.

Such, I think, was Shakespeare's intended pattern: unfortunately it has been either obscured by revision, or incomplete revision has failed to impress it clearly on the play. The theory of the New Cambridge editors must no doubt be accepted, that there are at least two strata of text, an early and a late. This is a difficulty of the kind referred to, that a student must expect from textual impurities in a comedy. But certain portions of the pattern are sufficiently clear to give, to a careful reader, some idea of the whole.

Take, for example, the relations obtaining between the Old Shepherd, on the one hand, and Jaques and Touchstone, on the other. Touchstone has been much sentimentalized, partly because of his wits, partly because of a supposed loyalty to Celia. But his wit has been treated as though it were a mere interlude, a diversion for the reader as well as for the Duke; whereas little else would seem more closely knit into the play. And as will be suggested, this is the reverse of sentimental. As for Touchstone's loyalty, it would seem to be mentioned only in Celia's line,

> He'll go along o'er the wide world with mee.

It may have had importance in an earlier version, but in that which has survived Shakespeare is no more concerned with how the characters arrive in Arden—whether under Touchstone's convoy or not —than how they are extricated from it. Touchstone's loyalty is about as interesting to him, and should be as interesting to the reader, as Oliver's green and gold snake.

What is interesting is a disingenuous reply which Touchstone gives to the question: "And how like you this shepherds life?" He pretends to make distinctions where it is impossible there should be any:

> Truely . . . in respect of it selfe, it is a good life; but in respect that it is a shepherds life, it is naught. In respect that it is solitary, I like it verie well: but in respect that it is private, it is a very vile life . . .

A shepherd's life, no more than other things, can be distinguished from itself, nor can what is solitary be other than private. What Touchstone is saying is that he neither likes nor dislikes the shepherd's life, while at the same time he does both; or, in other words, that towards the shepherd's life he has no feelings whatever. And, in truth, towards all things, if not quite all, Touchstone is as apathetic as Jaques. He too has his melancholy, as has been said: and naturally resembling Jaques more than Hamlet or Macbeth, he too accepts distraction from a habit. It is not the ceaseless search for novelty or gossip, but what he calls "philosophy" or the barren intercourse of a mind with itself. He multiplies distinction like the above, or pursues similarities based solely on sound or letter, neglecting the meaning of a word. The result is scepticism in a very practical sense, such as unchecked would destroy language and all possibility of thought. Even the old Shepherd is not slow to realize this, for his sole reply to the blunt question, "Has't any Philosophie in thee . . .?" is to recite a number of obvious truths:

> I know the more one sickens, the worse at ease he is: and that hee that wants money, meanes, and content, is without three good friends. That the propertie of raine is to wet, and fire to burne . . .

and so on. However obvious, they are at least truths, at least significant; and he concludes:

hee that hath learned no wit by Nature, nor Art, may complaine of dull breeding, or comes of a very dull kindred.

In other words: he who cannot behave in a more responsible way than Touchstone is an idiot. But "idiot is what I mean by a philosopher"—

Such a one is a naturall philosopher

rejoins Touchstone, indifferent enough to his diversion not to claim that it is more than it is.

He proceeds to indulge in it at length. The Shepherd, he says, is damned because he has not been to court, court manners being good and what is not good being wicked. Too patiently the Shepherd replies with a distinction which, as it is he and not Touchstone who makes it, is of primary importance:

> those that are good manners at the Court, are as ridiculous in the Countrey, as the behaviour of the Countrie is most mockeable at the Court.

But this is brushed aside, and Touchstone emphasizes his perversity by changing the order in which court and country are ranked. Henceforward, he decrees, they shall be on a level, or rather the court shall be the more wicked. In despair the Shepherd retires from a conversation in which words, as they have so variable a meaning, have as good as no meaning at all:

> You have too Courtly a wit, for mee, Ile rest.

Had he said "too philosophical a wit" his point might have been more immediately clear; but for him, no doubt as for Touchstone, court and "philosophy" are closely allied.

To justify himself he adds the following description:

> Sir, I am a true Labourer, I earne that I eate: get that I weare; owe no man hate, envie no mans happinesse; glad of other mens good[,] content with my harme: and the greatest of my pride, is to see my Ewes graze, and my Lambes sucke.

Of himself, that is, he claims to go about his own affairs, and to go about them with the mirth or minimum of serenity demanded by Rosalind. He has no need of "incision"—whatever that may mean— or of any other remedy to conduct himself like an adult being; whereas Touchstone, who suggests the remedy, has at the moment no affairs, appears to be able to conceive of no affairs to go about at all.

For Shepherd and audience the conversation is over. To them it seems that Touchstone is defeated beyond recovery; not, however, to Touchstone himself. He insists on adding a last word, and in doing so hints at one of the things to which he is not yet wholly indifferent, in respect of which therefore he parts company with Jaques. Mention of ewes and sucking lambs spurs him on to the following:

> That is another simple sinne in you, to bring the Ewes and the Rammes together, and to offer to get our living by the copulation of Cattle, to be bawd to a Belwether, and to betray a shee-Lambe of a twelvemonth to a crooked-pated olde Cuckoldly Ramme, out of all reasonable match. If thou bee'st not damn'd for this, the divell himselfe will have no shepherds, I cannot see how else thou shouldst escape.

About this there are two things to be noticed: first, that it is nasty, and, secondly, that it is the nastier because it falls outside the conversation. Touchstone is no longer endeavouring to prove anything about country and court, whether sound or fantastic: he assimilates the sexual life of men to that of beasts solely because it seems of itself worth while to do so. Yet this should not cause surprise: if in this passage he appears to exalt the latter, elsewhere in deeds as well as words he is diligent to degrade the former.

Upon their first arrival in Arden, when he and Rosalind overhear Silvius's complain, Rosalind sighs:

> *Jove, Jove, this Shepherds passion*
> *Is much upon my fashion.*

"And mine," exclaims Touchstone, adding, however, immediately, "but it growes somewhat stale with mee." That is, he is impatient of the elaborations and accretions received by the sexual desire, when a persistent subject in an otherwise healthy mind. His next appearance is as the wooer of Audrey, a country wench who thanks the gods that she is "foul," and whom no elaborations have been necessary to win. Her desire to be a "woman of the world," in other words a married woman, is ingenuous and no more a secret from Touchstone than from anyone else.

It is by no means to her discredit, nor would it be to Touchstone's, if, gratifying her desire, he thereby eased his own and was thankful. But the opposite is true. He is neither eased, nor does he spare an occasion, public or private, of pouring ridicule on the ingenuousness of which he has taken advantage. It is as though, aware that he can no longer hope for desire to be restrained, he sought to humiliate it with the least attractive object, then proceeded to revenge himself upon the object for his own lack of restraint. Audrey protests that she is "honest" or chaste; but that, he answers, has had no share in drawing his attentions:

> AUDREY: Would you not have me honest?
> TOUCH: No truly, unlesse thou wert hard favour'd . . .
> AUDREY: Well, I am not faire, and therefore I pray the Gods make me honest.
> TOUCH: Truly, to cast away honesty upon a foule slut, were to put good meate in an uncleane dish . . . But be it, as it may bee, I will marrie thee . . .

To a large extent this conversation, like most of Touchstone's, is mere playing with words; but in so far as it has any meaning, it is that the word "honesty" deserves only to be played with. And when at last he brings himself to mention honesty with an air of seriousness, it is not that she but that he himself may be praised:

> . . . a poore virgin sir, an il-favor'd thing sir, but mine owne, a poore humour of mine sir, to take that that no man else will: rich honestie dwels like a miser sir, in a poore house, as your Pearle in your foule oyster.

He is presenting her to the Duke as his intended: and, since her exterior has nothing to explain his choice, hints that an explanation is to be found within. That is, he is claiming for himself the credit due to perspicacity.

Unfortunately he puts forward at the same time a claim to modesty, thus showing with how little seriousness he is continuing to speak. Did he value honesty at all, he would not represent the choice of it as a sacrifice; nor would he describe Audrey, its exemplar, as a "poor thing." His modesty, it should further be noticed, itself suggests confusion or deceit, for not only does it permit of advertisement, it is advertised not at Touchstone's expense but at someone else's. He does not in one respect decry himself so that he may be exalted in another; rather in order to exalt himself he decries his future wife. The first would in any case be tiresome, as is all inverted vanity; but the second, as a hypocritical form of selfishness, is contemptible.

Given that Touchstone is a man of sense, a performance like this can be due only to his attempting two things at once, and two things not very compatible one with another. As usual he is seeking to ridicule Audrey; but at the same time, I think, to recommend himself to the Duke. While sharing all Jaques's objections to purposeful activity, he is without Jaques's income: he must provide himself with a living or must starve. And scepticism and melancholy being essentially unnatural, no one starves for their sake. At Touchstone's entry on the stage it was hinted that the Duke might be willing to appoint a jester:

> Good my Lord, bid him welcome: This is the Motley-minded Gentleman, that I have so often met in the Forrest: he hath bin a Courtier he sweares. . . . Good my Lord, like this fellow.

And the Duke is well known to be, in Jaques's word, "disputatious." It is solely to please him that Touchstone, among his other preoccupations, does what he can to handle the notions "honesty" and "modesty"; were he speaking to a crony or to himself they would not enter his head, no more than the euphuistic apologue about oysters with which he ends.

A similar reason is to be advanced for his string of court witticisms which follow, about the causes of a quarrel and the degree of a lie. So long as to be tiresome, the modern reader is tempted to dismiss it as an interlude; it is not, however, wholly without dramatic excuse. At the stage reached by his candidature, Touchstone thinks it proper to give an exhibition of professional skill. And that, too, he makes subserve his sexual passion: having drawn all eyes to himself, for a moment he directs them to Audrey:

> Upon a lye, seven times removed: (beare your bodie more seeming Audrey) . . .

and so she is ridiculed once more.

It seems likely he obtains his appointment: at any rate he makes the impression he desires. "He is very swift and sententious," says the Duke.

> He uses his folly like a stalking-horse, and under the presentation of that he shoots his wit.

Which of course is just what the real Touchstone never does, in spite of what the critics say. The judgement of the Old Shepherd is sounder, that Touchstone's folly has no purpose at all, or, if any that of discrediting and ruining purpose. And so is Jaques sounder, when he recognizes in Touchstone's folly the cover for his scepticism.

It is interesting, and significant of the subtle pattern which Shakespeare intends to weave—a pattern not only of intrigue but of ideas—that the Duke, who is thus easily gulled when Touchstone assumes a virtue, protests immediately when required to accept as a virtue Touchstone's vice. Jaques describes to him, and asks for himself, the liberty of railing which Touchstone enjoys:

> ... *weed your better judgements*
> *Of all opinion that grows ranke in them,*
> *That I am wise. I must have liberty*
> *Withall, as large a Charter as the winde,*
> *To blow on whom I please, for so fooles have.* ...
> *Invest me in my motley: Give me leave*
> *To speake my mind.*

Such impunity, the Duke sees, can have no results of the kind Jaques promises:

> ... *I will through and through*
> *Cleanse the foule bodie of the' infected world* ...

but only evil for himself and others:

> *Fie on thee. I can tell what thou wouldst do.* ...
> *Most mischeevous foule sin.*

And he proceeds to diagnose it correctly. Only a man ruined by evil, he suggests, confines himself to the correction of evil; for this implies not that evil finds him peculiarly sensitive, but that he is insensitive both to evil and to good. To good, because he neglects and therefore runs the risk of destroying it; to evil, because he seeks no relief from what should stifle and nauseate. Brutalized to this degree, Jaques can see no reason why others should not be brutalized too:

> ... *all the' imbossed sores, and headed evils,*
> *That thou with license of free foot hast caught,*
> *Would'st thou disgorge into the generall world.*

The portrait is drawn in high colour, but Hamlet would recognize it. Jaques presumably does not, being, as has been said, less alert and therefore less perspicacious; but here unfortunately there is a cut in the text of *As You Like It*.

Further instances of this Shakespearean subtlety are two scenes in which Jaques and Touchstone, usually allies, are brought, if not into conflict, into contrast. As Touchstone is as acutely sensitive to the brutish sting as ever Jaques may have been in the past, in the present he can on occasion be resolute as Jaques is not. In response to the sting he can make conquest of Audrey, browbeat William for her possession:

> . . . abandon the society of this Female, or Clowne thou perishest . . . I will kill thee a hundred and fifty wayes, therefore tremble and depart.

William obediently trembles. But it is Jaques of all characters whom Shakespeare chooses to administer a rebuke to Touchstone for this; as though to make it clear that if he condemns inertia he does not, with a crudeness familiar in more recent times, advocate precipitancy; if he deplores apathy, he does not commend brute appetite. When Touchstone contemplates a hedge-marriage so that he might have "a good excuse hereafter" to leave his wife, it is Jaques who prevents him:

> And will you (being a man of your breeding) be married under a bush like a beggar? Get you to church. . . .

And at the final leave-taking it is Jaques who foretells to Touchstone a future of wrangling, a "loving voyage . . . but for two moneths victuall'd."

At the opposite pole to the characters hitherto considered, tolerating no elaboration in love, stand Silvius and Phebe, who seek to conform their lives to the pastoral convention, one of the fullest elaborations known. The scenes in which they appear are perhaps too short to have the effect intended, now that the convention, if not forgotten, is no longer familiar. But to an Elizabethan the sentiments and the verse—the former largely echoes, external as well as internal, to the play: the latter easy yet mannered—would suffice to evoke a wealthy tradition. A modern judges of this perhaps most readily by the apostrophe to Marlowe:

> *Dead Shepherd, now I [f]ind thy saw of might,*
> *Who ever lov'd that lov'd not at first sight?*

No incongruity is intended or feared from his introduction with fleece and crook: the tradition being rich enough to absorb him, vigorous enough to assert even beside him its actuality.

And also the apostrophe may serve to dispel some of the mist which has hung about pastoral in England since the seventeenth century, and notably since the attack of Johnson. Though actual, pastoral need not be realistic; and to apply to it realistic canons as he did is to misconceive it entirely. It is not an attempt to portray a shepherd's life: but in its purity—though frequently, of course, it is impure—to portray a life in which physical misery is reduced to a minimum or has disappeared. Traditionally such a life is called a shepherd's: in which, therefore, man is held to enjoy every happiness, if only his desires will let him. But as become clear with the progress of the pastoral, his desires will not. Removed from the danger of physical pain those of the intellect and the imagination become the acuter; in particular the passion of love, with neither social pressure nor economic necessity inclining it in any direction, becomes incalculable in its vagaries. It remains an ever open source of calamity. A tragic note of undertone is thus inseparable from pastoral, and if subdued is only the more insistent. It is in permanent contrast with the composure or gaiety of the rest of the score.

By their share in a tradition of this kind, the Silvius and Phebe scenes have a claim to be effective out of all proportion to their length; and the effect they are intended to produce is in the first place a serious, not a comic one. That there is a close connexion between Shakespearean tragedy and comedy, I have already stated, is one of my assumptions in this paper.

As the Old Shepherd is contrasted with Touchstone, so he is with Silvius. When the latter pours out his complaints, Corin's attitude is far from one of incomprehension:

> *Oh* Corin, *that thou knew'st how I do love her.*
> *—I partly guesse; for I have lov'd ere now.*

Far also from impatience, for the complaints are not of the briefest; far, however, from approval. To put the matter at its crudest, Silvius is not prudent in his conduct:

> *That is the way to make her scorne you still.*

And however charitably Corin listens to the recital of another's extravagances, he has no regret that now he is rid of his own:

> *How many actions most ridiculous*
> *Hast thou been drawne to by thy fantasie?*
> *—Into a thousand that I have forgotten.*

His attitude seems to be that Silvius's extravagances will pass with time as his own have passed; meanwhile they may at least be tolerated, for they are decent.

Touchstone's reaction to the meeting with Silvius has already been noticed. Rosalind's is somewhat more complicated:

> *Alas poor Shepherd searching of* [*thy wound*],
> *I have by hard adventure found my own.*

She approves of the premises on which the pastoral convention is based, both that the wound of love is genuine and that it is sharp and serious. But the assumption that therefore it is deserving of sole attention, or that by receiving such attention it can in any way be cured, she criticizes as does Corin, and less patiently. It conflicts with the common sense, for which she is everywhere advocate, and which requires either as condition or as symptom of health a wide awareness of opportunity, a generous assumption of responsibility. By confining his attention to love, Silvius is restricting both, frustrating his energies like the other melancholics. That Rosalind should be less patient than Corin is natural, as she is younger: she cannot trust the action of time upon Silvius, when as yet she is not certain what it will be upon herself.

For she too is tempted by love, and in danger of the pastoral convention. Though she rebukes Silvius and Phebe from the outset, she does so in language more nearly approaching theirs than ever she approached Jaques's. But the luck of comedy, which (it has been suggested) stifles problems, is on her side, causing Phebe to fall in love with her. She needs only to reveal herself as a woman, and the folly of pastoralism—as a convention which allows freedom to fancy or desire—comes crashing to the ground. Taught by such an example and by it teaching others, she pronounces the judgement that if Silvius and Phebe persist in love yet would remain rational creatures, they must get married.

It is the same judgement she pronounced on all lovers in the play. Of the four who are left, two only call for separate consideration: herself and Orlando.

Orlando has achieved an extravagance but, unlike Silvius, not a decent one; his verse, even in Touchstone's ears, is the "right Butter-womans ranke to Market." As Touchstone is concerned only to destroy he finds criticism easy, but specimens of the verse prove he is not wholly unreliable. And therefore Rosalind chooses to deal with Orlando in prose:

> These are all lies, men have died from time to time, and wormes have eaten them, but not for love.
> —I would not have my right *Rosalind* of this mind, for I protest her frowne might kill me.
> —By this hand, it will not kill a flie.

Her purpose once again is to disabuse her interlocutor about the supposed supreme importance of love. And to do so effectively she makes use at times of a coarseness almost rivalling Touchstone's:

> What would you say to me now, and I were your verie, verie Rosalind?

> —I would kisse before I spoke.
> —Nay, you were better speak first, and when you were gravel'd, for lacke of matter, you might take occasion to kisse: verie good Orators when they are out, they will spit, and for lovers, lacking (God warne us) matter, the cleanliest shift is to kisse.

Not that she agrees with Touchstone, except materially. She may say very much the same as he says, but her purpose is different. It is not to deny that desire, no more than other things, has value; but to assess its proper value, by no means so high as Orlando thinks.

She can undertake to do so with some sureness, and command some confidence from the reader, because she herself has first-hand acquaintance with desire. All criticisms passed on others are also criticisms on herself, and she is aware of this (or if not, as on one occasion, Celia is at hand to remind her). The consequences for the play are manifold. First the criticisms, which as applying to other persons might seem scattered, are bound together as applying to her; over the pattern of the repeating motif, such as has been already described, she superposes as it were another pattern, or encloses it in a frame. Then the final criticism, or judgement which resumes them all, is seen to issue from the body of the play itself, not to be imposed on it by author or authority from without. Finally a breadth and a sanity in the judgement are guaranteed. If Rosalind freely acknowledges in herself the absurdities she rebukes in others—"Ile tell thee *Aliena*," she says, "I cannot be out of sight of Orlando: Ile goe find a shadow and sigh till he come"—in return she transfers to others her own seriousness and suffering:

> O coz, coz, coz; my pretty little coz, that thou didst know how many fathom deepe I am in love: but it cannot bee sounded: my affection hath an unknowne bottome, like the Bay of Portugall.

Or in a phrase which has a foretaste or reminiscence of Donne:

> One inche of delay more, is a South-sea of discoverie. I pre-thee tell me, who it is quickly, and speake apace.

The final judgement would seem to run somewhat as follows. As Rosalind says to Orlando at their first meeting: "Love is purely a madnesse, and I tel you, deserves wel a darke house, and a whip, as madmen do"; it is, however, a madness which, owing to the number of victims, there are only two ways of controlling. One is to "forsweare the ful stream of the world, and to live in a nooke merely Monasticke"—and this way does not generally recommend itself. The second, then, must be adopted, which is marriage. Above all, whines and cries such as combine to a chorus in Act V must be prevented:

> ... *tell this youth what 'tis to love.*
> —*It is to be all made of sighes and teares,*
> *And so am I for* Phebe.
> —*And I for* Ganimed.
> —*And I for* Rosalind.
> —*And I for no woman.*
> —*It is to be all made of faith and service,*
> *And so am I for* Phebe ...

da capo three times. Rosalind, though as lover she joined in, as critic and judge rejects it as "the howling of Irish wolves against the Moone." To it the alacrity of Oliver and Celia are to be preferred: "They are in the verie wrath of love, and they will together. Clubbes cannot part them."

If once again this seems reminiscent of Touchstone, and of Touchstone at his worst, the distinction already drawn should be remembered. The same words can mean different things on Touchstone's lips and on Rosalind's. She is not inciting her fellow characters to marriages which shall hold only until the "blood breaks," but to "high wedlock," which is "great Juno's crown," and a "blessed bond"—the masquing song, though possibly not by Shakespeare, aptly summarizes certain of the play's sentiments. Further, that Rosalind and Touchstone agree on a single topic, even a topic so important as the qualities of desire, does not mean that one of them is not superior to the other. Rosalind is very obviously the superior: not, however, in respect of the topic on which she and Touchstone agree. She is distinguished and privileged beyond him, not because she knows desire—rather that confounds both him and her—but because she is, whereas he is not, at the same time many things besides. She is not only a capable manager of her own life, but a powerful influence for good on the lives of others. And finally a word may be put in for Touchstone himself. If Shakespeare, as has been said, does not condemn apathy in order to commend lust, neither does he disapprove of lust in order to advocate Puritanism. Touchstone is on the way to tragedy because he has allowed desire to get out of control; had he controlled it, he would have built up a life more satisfactory than do those who, while living in the world, neglect desire altogether or overmuch. And therefore he remains a positive critic even in his failure and to some extent because of it; it is proper not only that he himself should rebuke Orlando, but also that Rosalind, taking, it would seem, words from his lips, should rebuke large groups of people.

If *As You Like It* is planned at all in the way I have suggested, the least title it deserves is, I think, "unsentimental." But for common practice I would go further and call it "unromantic"; and suggest that, to get the measure of its unromanticism, no more is necessary than to read it alongside its source, Lodge's *Rosalynde*. And the title "unromantic" would possibly be confirmed by an investigation of the Duke's melancholy, which in this paper it has not been possible to investigate.

There is little time to return to the topic from which the paper started, the relation namely between the tragedies and the comedies. But perhaps it is obvious that, conceived as unromantic, the early comedies are a fitting preparation for the "problem plays," while from these to the tragedies is but a step.

(1940)

(II) HENRY V, by D. A. Traversi

There are, among Shakespeare's plays, those which seem to have eluded criticism by their very simplicity. Among them is certainly *Henry V*. It is not, by Shakespearean standards, a difficult play. There is no closely woven web of imagery to disentangle, no elusive personal "symbolism" to be explained. The plot is plainly historical and the underlying purpose, a study in the conditions and limitations of successful kingship, clearly defined. Yet few plays have been so unfortunately received. Some critics—and among them the best—have passed the play by, treated it with a suggestion of boredom; whilst for others, less discerning, it has become a mine of commonplaces and a quarry for patriotic texts. Either view ignores, among other things, the fact that *Henry V* does not stand alone. Shakespeare's interest in political conduct and its human implications was, at this period, intense and continuous. The general theme of *Henry V*, already approached in *Richard II* and developed in the two parts of *Henry IV*, is the establishment in England of an order based on consecrated authority and crowned successfully by action against France. The conditions of this order, which is triumphantly achieved by the new king, are moral as well as political. The crime of regicide, which, by breeding internal scruples and nourishing external revolt, has stood between Bolingbroke and the attainment of peace, no longer hangs—unless as a disturbing memory—over *Henry V,* and the crusading purpose which has run as an unfulfilled nostalgia through the father's life is replaced by the reality, at once brilliant and ruthless, of the son's victorious campaign.

This, as critics have not always realized, is less a conclusion than a point of departure for the understanding of *Henry V*. It was the conditions of kingship, rather than its results, that really interested Shakespeare, whose emphasis falls, not upon the King's success, but upon the sacrifice of common humanity which it involves. It is significant that he takes up almost immediately the theme of Henry's "miraculous" transformation from dissolute prince to accomplished monarch and gives it a setting of political intrigue which barely conceals the underlying irony. The opening scene is, in this respect, full of meaning. A bill is to be passed, as prelude to the new reign, which will deprive the Church of "the better half" of her temporal possessions; and the bishops of Canterbury and Ely, with pondered diplomatic cunning, are debating the possibility of evading a measure which would "drink deep," which would, indeed, "drink the cup and all." The remedy lies, to Canterbury's mind, in the virtues of the King, who is "full of grace and fair regard," and moreover, most conveniently, "a true lover of the holy church." In words which deliberately underline the incredible, the unmotivated nature of the change so suddenly wrought in Henry, Canterbury proceeds to describe these virtues:

> *Never was such a sudden scholar made;*
> *Never came reformation in a flood*
> *With such a heady currance, scouring faults;*
> *Nor never Hydra-headed wilfulness*
> *So soon did lose his seat, and all at once,*
> *As in this king.*

Never, indeed; and there is something unreal, more than a hint of deliberate exaggeration in the studied artificial phrases with which the Archbishop proceeds to particularize the royal gifts:

> *Turn him to any course of policy,*
> *The Gordian knot of it he will unloose,*
> *Familiar as his garter; that, when he speaks,*
> *The air, a chartered libertine, is still,*
> *And the mute wonder lurketh in men's ears,*
> *To steal his sweet and honey'd sentences.*

The apparent servility of the prelate ends by casting an indefinable doubt upon the very reformation he is describing. That Henry should be able so suddenly to undo "the Gordian knot" of policy may pass, but that he should do it negligently, "familiar as his garter," passes belief: and the suggestion of cloying persuasiveness behind the reference to "his sweet and honey'd sentences" makes us question, not only the sincerity of the speaker, but that of Henry himself. The thing, to be true, must be a miracle; and "miracles," as Canterbury himself points out in a most damaging conclusion, "are ceased."

Shakespeare's treatment of Henry's transformation needs to be considered in the light thrown upon it by the preceding plays. Finding it, of course, in his sources, he seems to have fastened upon it from the first as peculiarly relevant to his purpose. Prince Hal's first soliloquy at once foreshadows it and explains its animating spirit:

> *So, when this loose behaviour I throw off*
> *And pay the debt I never promised,*
> *By how much better than my word I am,*
> *By so much shall I falsify men's hopes;*
> *And like bright metal on a sullen ground,*
> *My reformation, glittering o'er my fault,*
> *Shall show more goodly and attract more eyes*
> *Than that which hath no foil to set it off.*
> *I'll so offend, to make offence a skill,*
> *Redeeming time when men least think I will.*
> [*Henry IV—Part I.* Act I, Sc. II]

The note of calculation, therefore, is present from the first, and as the Prince's character develops through the two plays dealing with his father's reign, it is most noticeably deepened and intensified by contrast with Falstaff. Shakespeare not only accepted the artistic difficulty involved in the Prince's rejection of his former friend; he wove it into the structure of his play. The cleavage between the two men is only a projection of one, fundamental to his purpose, between unbridled impulse, which degenerates into swollen disease, and the cold spirit of successful self-control, which inevitably becomes inhuman. The Falstaff of Part II is given an altogether new burden of lechery, age, and disease. When King Henry denounces him as "So surfeit-swell'd, so old, and so profane," he makes a true criticism which would not have seemed excessive to an Elizabethan audience; and he backs it with the austerity of a great religious tradition when he adds:

> *Make less thy body hence, and more thy grace.*

Yet, though we must take the King's words at their own value, the same applies to Falstaff's criticisms of the royal family. Lancaster, whose deceit wins a victory over the rebels at Gaultree Forest, in his eyes "a young, *sober-blooded boy*," one of those who "when they marry, get wenches." The flexibility and richness of Falstaff's prose in a succession of phrases like "apprehensive, quick, forgetive, full of nimble, fiery, and delectable shapes" only emphasizes by contrast the coldness, almost the perversion, which characterizes the successful kings and generals of these plays. Prince Hal in *Henry IV—Part II* strikes a note of calculating vulgarity, which he regards as a necessary condition of his success. His remark to Poins—"My appetite was not princely got"—is highly typical. It implies a contrast between the natural sensual processes ("appetite," of course, in connexion with the consuming desires of the "blood," is a word which constantly interested Shakespeare) and the indifference to humanity which is required of the princely state. This contrast, as it affects the mature King, is the theme of *Henry V*.

It is a theme, once more, closely related to Shakespeare's maturing interests and destined to unfold itself progressively in his great series of tragedies. The problem of political unity, or "degree," and that of personal order are brought in the course of these historical plays into the closest relationship. Just as the state, already in *Henry IV—Part II*, is regarded in its divisions as a diseased body ravaged by a consuming fever of its various members, so is the individual torn between the violence of his passions and the direction of reason; and just as the political remedy lies in unquestioned allegiance to an authority divinely constituted, so does personal coherence depend upon the submission to reason of our uncontrolled desires. The link between the two states, political and personal, is provided in these plays by concentration upon the figure of the King. The problem of the state becomes, in a very real sense, that of the individual at its head. The King, who rightly demands unquestioning allegiance from his subjects, is first called upon to show, through the perfection of his self-control, a complete and selfless devotion to his office. The personal implications of that devotion are considered in *Henry V*.

It demands, in the first place, an absolute measure of self-domination. Called upon to exercise justice and shape policies for the common good, the King can allow no trace of selfishness or frailty to affect his decisions. He must continually examine his motives, subdue them in the light of reason; and this means that he is engaged in a continual struggle against his share of human weakness. This struggle, as I have already suggested, is presented in terms of one between passion and the controlling reason. The mastery of passion and its relation to action are themes which *Henry V* shares with most of the plays written by Shakespeare at this time. Such control, admittedly essential in a king, is infinitely dangerous in its possible consequences. It turns easily, almost inevitably, to cruelty and selfishness. Sonnet XCIV is decisive on this point:

> *They that have power to hurt and will do none,*
> *That do not do the thing they most do show,*
> *Who, moving others, are themselves as stone,*
> *Unmoved, cold, and to temptation slow;*
> *They rightly do inherit heaven's graces.* . . .

The gap, so momentous and yet so slight, between Hamlet's rather abstract longing for the man "that is not passion's slave," and Angelo, who emphasizes his self-control and ends by an abject surrender to the claims of "blood," is here openly stated. The virtuous man is he who, without exercising it, has "power to hurt," the man who is cold, slow, impassive as stone before the claims of his own humanity. He seems, indeed, in full possession of his impulses, but his control is only separated by a continual and conscious effort from cruelty and the satisfaction of desires which long denial has set increasingly on edge. The similarity of the King's position is obvious. He too has power to hurt and may easily abuse it: he too, whilst moving others, must keep the firmest check upon his impulses and watch sleeplessly over his judgement. And he too—we might add—may easily fall from his position of vigilance into an unrestrained and savage indulgence. If this is the just man, in short, Henry V is fairly representative of him.

The circumstances of Henry's first appearance before his court make this clear. The subject under discussion is the action shortly to be taken by the freshly united kingdom against the realm of France. The idea of war had obviously been already accepted. Henry does not, in reality, look for disinterested advice. He prompts the subservient Archbishop, at each step, not without a touch or irony, to the expected answer:

> *My learned lord, we pray you to proceed*
> *And justly and religiously unfold*
> *Why the law Salique that they have in France*
> *Or should or should not bar us in our claim.* . . .

And then, when the matter has been expounded to his satisfaction:

> *May I with right and conscience make this claim?*

The King's mind, in short, is already made up, and his decision only awaits public confirmation. The perfunctory flatness of Canterbury's exposition, which no one could possibly hear without indifference, contrasts most forcibly with the rhetoric with which he and his fellow-courtiers underline what is obviously a foregone conclusion:

> *Gracious lord,*
> *Stand for your own; unwind your bloody flag;*
> *Look back into your mighty ancestors.*

Already, however, another theme of deeper significance has made itself felt in Henry's utterances: the theme of the horrors of war and, by implication, of the responsibility which weighs upon the king who would embark upon it:

> *Therefore take heed how you impawn our person,*
> *How you awake our sleeping sword of war:*
> *We charge you, in the name of God, take heed;*
> *For never two such kingdoms did contend*
> *Without much fall of blood; whose guiltless drops*
> *Are everyone a woe, a sore complaint*
> *'Gainst him whose wrongs give edge unto the swords*
> *That make such waste in brief mortality.*

Most of Shakespeare's conception of the King is already implicit in this speech. Throughout the play, Henry is not deaf to the voice of conscience. It pursues him, in fact, with almost superstitious insistence to the very eve of Agincourt, when the memory of his father's crime against his sovereign is still present in his mind:

> *Not to-day, O Lord,*
> *O, not to-day, think not upon the fault*
> *My father made in compassing the crown.* [IV, i]

Bolingbroke's misdeed is by now only a memory, but here, at the outset of Henry's proposed enterprise in France, the same kind of misgiving is already present. The awareness that his victories must be bought at a terrrible price in bloodshed and human suffering remains with him throughout the play; but—and here is the flaw essential to the character—so does his readiness to shift the responsibility upon others, to use their complacence to obtain the justification he continually, insistently requires. Take heed, he warns the prelate, "how *you* impawn our person," "how *you* awake the sleeping sword of war"; for

> we will hear, note, and believe in heart
> That what you speak is in your conscience wash'd
> As pure as sin in baptism.

Henry's political success is definitely associated, in the mind of Shakespeare, with this ability to override his conscience. Once Canterbury has spoken, once the dutiful moral echo has been duly obtained, the very ruthlessness which seems to have disturbed him at the opening of the scene enters into his own rhetorical utterance:

> Now we are well resolved; and, by God's help,
> And yours, the noble sinews of our power,
> France being ours, we'll bend it to our awe,
> Or break it all to pieces.   [I, ii]

The reference to conscience, the inevitable preface to each of Henry's utterances, remains in the propitiatory aside "by God's help": but, once it has been uttered, the sense of power implied in the cumulative force of "sinews" joined to the verbs "bend" and "break" takes possession of the speech. This overriding—for, in the last analysis, it is nothing else—of conscience by the will to power is a process which constantly repeats itself in Henry's utterances.

But there is, in Shakespeare's interpretation of the character, a further subtlety of analysis. As the play proceeds, we become increasingly aware that there is in Henry an uneasy balance, already reminiscent of Angelo, between unbridled passion and cold self-control. The latter element, exercised even to the exclusion of normal human feeling, has been present in him from the first. Prince Hal shows it, as we have already noted, in his first soliloquy, when he announces his utilitarian attitude to the company he is keeping, and it is strongly felt, of course, in the rejection of Falstaff. Such control is, indeed, an essential part of his political capacity; but it has behind it, in addition to the strain of inhumanity, an unmistakable sense of constraint which makes itself felt in his greeting to the French ambassador:

> We are no tyrant, but a Christian king;
> Unto whose grace our passion is as subject
> As are our wretches fettered in our prisons.

The harshness of the comparison is, to say the least of it, remarkable. Such self-control is necessarily precarious; the passions, held in subjection, "fettered," treated with a disdain similar to that which, as Prince Hal, he has already displayed to normal human feelings when his success as monarch depended upon the renunciation of his past, may be expected to break out in forms not altogether creditable. Almost at once, in fact, they do so. The French ambassadors, in fulfilling their mission by presenting him with the Dauphin's tennis-balls, touch upon Henry's most noticeable weakness: they expose him to ridicule and, worst of all, they refer—by the observation that "You cannot revel into dukedoms here"—to the abjured but not forgotten past. Henry's reaction, in spite of the opening affirmation of his self-control, takes the form of one of those outbursts which are habitual with him whenever his will is crossed. As when France was to be "bent" or "broken," his rhetoric, measured and even cold on the surface, is full of accumulated, irrepressible passion:

> *When we have match'd our rackets to these balls,*
> *We will in France, by God's grace, play a set*
> *Shall strike his father's crown into the hazard.*

The reference to "God's grace," rarely omitted from Henry's utterances, clearly befit a "Christian king"; but the note of resentment which rises through the speech and finally takes complete control of it is undeniably personal. It rankles in the utterance until the real motive, scarcely concealed from the first, becomes at last explicit:

> *We understand him well,*
> *How he comes o'er us with our wilder days*
> *Not measuring what use we made of them.*

The personal offence, once mentioned, banishes every consideration of conscience. The horrors of war, the slaughter and misery attendant upon it, are mentioned once again, but only—as so often in Henry—that he may disclaim responsibility for them. The tone of the utterance rises to one of ruthless and triumphant egoism:

> *But I will rise there with so full a glory*
> *That I will dazzle all the eyes of France,*
> *Yea, strike the Dauphin blind to look on us.*
> *And tell the pleasant prince this mock of his*
> *Hath turned his balls to gun-stones; and his soul*
> *Shall stand sore charged for the wasteful vengeance*
> *That shall fly with them: for many a thousand widows*
> *Shall this his mock mock out of their dear husbands;*
> *Mock mothers from their sons, mock castles down;*
> *And some are yet ungotten and unborn*
> *That shall have cause to curse the Dauphin's scorn.*

"*I* will rise there": "*I* will dazzle all the eyes of France." The Dauphin's gibe has set free Henry's fettered passions, and they ex-

press themselves frankly in a cumulative vision of destruction. The
tone of the utterance—the impact of the verb "strike," the harsh
referance to the balls which have been turned to gun-*stones*, the
sense of irresistible, ruinous force behind "mock castles down"—reflects the new feeling and reminds us of the later, more masterly
picture of Coriolanus in action.* The sense of power, inhuman and
destructive, is at last unleashed in the King. The responsibility for
coming events, already assumed by the Archbishop, has now been
further fastened upon the Dauphin, and Henry is in a position to
wind up the picture of his coming descent upon France with a
phrase that incorporates into his new vehemence the convenient
certainty of righteousness—

> *But all this lies within the will of God,*
> *To whom I do appeal.*

No doubt the conviction is, as far as it goes, sincere; for the will of
God and the will of Henry, now fused in the egoistic passion released by the Dauphin's jest, have become identical.

It is not until the opening of the third act that the characteristic
qualities of Henry's utterances and preparations are openly translated into action. The poetry of war in this play deserves careful
attention, for much of it is unmistakably associated with the element of constraints already noted in Henry himself. The rhetoric
with which the King incites his man to battle before the walls of
Harfleur has about it a strong flavour of artificiality and strain.
There is about his picture of the warrior something grotesque and
exaggerated, which almost suggests the caricature of a man:

> *. . . imitate the action of the tiger;*
> *Stiffen the sinews, summon up the blood,*
> *Disguise fair nature with hard-favour'd rage;*
> *Then lend the eye a terrible aspect;*
> *Let it pry through the portage of the head*
> *Like the brass cannon; let the brow o'erwhelm it*
> *As fearfully as doth a galled rock*
> *O'erhang and jutty his confounded base,*
> *Swill'd with the wild and wasteful ocean.*
> *Now set the teeth and stretch the nostril wide,*
> *Hold hard the breath and bend up every spirit*
> *To his full height.* [III, 1]

There is about this incitation something forced, incongruous, even
slightly absurd. The action of the warrior is an imitation, and an

---
* *E.g.*, *Coriolanus*, Act II, Scene II.

imitation of a wild beast at that, carried out by a deliberate exclusion of "fair nature." The blood is to be "summoned up," the sinews "stiffened" to the necessary degree of artificial bestiality, whilst the involved rhetorical comparisons which follow the references to the "brass cannon" and the "galled rock" strengthens the impression of unreality. In stressing the note of inhumanity, Shakespeare does not deny the poetry of war which he expresses most fully in certain passages from the various prologues of this play; * but, as later in *Coriolanus*, he balances the conception of the warrior in his triumphant activity as "a greyhound straining at the leash" against that, not less forcible, of a ruthless and inhuman engine of destruction. The mastery of phrase and rhythm is far less developed, the prevailing tone far more immature, than in the Roman tragedy; but the immaturity which is reflected in the convolutions of the verse is not such that the critical purpose cannot make itself felt. The ruthlessness, as well as the splendour of the warrior, are given in *Coriolanus* an expression incomparably finer; but both are already present and fully conscious in the earlier play.

Henry's treatment of the governor and citizens of Harfleur, immediately after this apostrophe, relates this conception of the warrior more clearly to strains already apparent in the King's own character. Shakespeare, not for the first time, places the two scenes together to enforce a contrast. The words in which Henry presents his ultimatum are full of that sense of conflict between control and passion which is so prominent in his first utterances. The grotesque inhumanity of his words is balanced, however, by a suggestion of tragic destiny. Beneath his callousness is a sense that the horrors of war, once unloosed, once freed from the sternest self-control, are irresistible. His soldiers, he warns the governor, are still held uneasily in check. "The cool and temperate wind of grace," whose control over passion has already been indicated by Henry as the distinctive mark of a Christian king, still exercises its temporary authority; but "licentuous wickedness"—the adjective is noteworthy —and "the filthy and contagious clouds" of "*heady* murder" threaten to break out at any moment. In his catalogue of the horrors of unbridled war, stress is laid continually upon rape and the crimes of "blood." The "fresh-fair virgins" of Harfleur will become the victims of the soldiery, whose destructive atrocities are significantly referred to in terms of "liberty"—

---
* *E.g.*, Prologues to Act III and Act IV.

> *What rein can hold licentuous wickedness*
> *When down the hill he holds his fierce career?*

The process of evil, once unleashed, proceeds along courses fatally determined; but Henry, as usual, having described them in words which lay every emphasis upon their horror, disclaims all responsibility for them just as he had once disclaimed all responsibility for the outbreak of the war. The whole matter, thus taken out of his hands, becomes indifferent to him:

> *What is't to me,* when you yourselves are cause,
> *If your pure maidens fall into the hand*
> *Of hot and forcing violation?*

Yet this very assertion of indifference implies, at bottom, a sense of the tragedy of the royal position. Only this denial of responsibility, Shakespeare would seem to say, only the exclusion of humanity and the acceptance of a complete dualism between controlling "grace" and the promptness of irresponsible passion, make possible that success in war which is, for the purposes of this play, the crown of kingship.

For it would be wrong to suppose that Shakespeare, in portraying Henry, intends to stress the note of hypocrisy. His purpose is rather to bring out certain contradictions, human and moral, which seem to be inherent in the notion of a successful king. As the play proceeds, Henry seems to be increasingly, at least in the moral sense, the victim of his position. The cunning calculations of the Archbishop, with which the play opens, have already given us a hint of the world in which he moves and which he has, as King, to mould to his own purposes; and the treasonable activities of Cambridge, Grey, and Scroop are further indications of the duplicity with which monarchs are fated by their position to deal. The complexity of the situation explains the curiously equivocal tone of the reference to loyalty in the scene (II, ii). It seems strange that Exeter should say that the King has "dull'd and cloy'd" his followers with his gracious favours; and the political instability which Henry has inherited from his father is implied in the dubious tone, combining acidity and sweetness, of Grey's statement that—

> *these that were your father's enemies*
> *Have steep'd their galls in honey.*

There are numerous parallels for this imagery of the palate, this sensibility to contrasted tastes, in *Troilus and Cressida,* parallels which—in plays of the same period—are certainly significant. Somewhere at the heart of this court, as in the heroic world of Troy, there is a fundamental fault which must constantly be allowed for by a successful king. It appears to Henry, in his dealings with the conspirators, as something deep-rooted enough to be associated with the original Fall of man:

> *Seem they religious?*
> *Why, so did'st thou: or are they spare in diet,*
> *Free from gross passion or of mirth or anger,*
> *Constant in spirit, not swerving with the blood,*
> *Garnish'd and decked in modest complement,*
> *Not working with the eye without the ear,*
> *And put in purged judgment trusting neither?*
> *Such and so finely bolted didst thou seem:*
> *And thus thy fall hath left a kind of blot,*
> *To mark the full-fraught man and best indued*
> *With some suspicion. I will weep for thee;*
> *For this revolt of thine, methinks, is like*
> *Another fall of man.* [II, ii]

It is remarkable that Henry, in meditating upon this betrayal, should return once more to that theme of control, of freedom from passion, which is so pre-eminent in his own nature. Much in the expression—notably the references to "diet" and purging and the presence of adjectives like "garnish'd" and "bolted" drawn from material processes to express a moral content—recalls the problem plays. There is the same tendency to labour in the versification and the same struggle to convey by a difficult concentration of imagery a spiritual condition that obstinately refuses to clarify itself in the expression. By concentrating on the functioning of the body, and on the sense of mutual divergence between eye, ear, and judgement in the infinitely difficult balance of the personality, Shakespeare sets spiritual control in contrast with a sense of anarchy which proceeds, most typically, from his contemplation of physical processes. "Gross passion"—the adjective is significant—is associated with the irrational "swerving of the blood," and the judgement which controls it needs to be "purged" by fasting ("spare in diet") before it can attain a scarcely human freedom from "mirth or anger." By emphasizing the difficult and even unnatural nature of such control, Shakespeare casts doubt, at least by implication, upon that of Henry himself; but it is also seen to be necessary, inseparable from his office. The administration of justice, upon which depends order within the kingdom and success in its foreign wars, demands in the monarch an impersonality which is almost tragic and borders on the inhuman. The state must be purged of "treason lurking in its way" before it can be led, with that single-mindedness of purpose which we have already found to involve in Henry a definite sacrifice of common humanity, to the victorious enterprise in France.

It will be clear by now that *Henry V* represents, however tentatively, a step in the realization of themes only fully developed in the tragedies. Inheriting from his material a conception of Henry as the victorious king, perfectly aware of his responsibilities and religiously devoted to the idea of duty, Shakespeare seems to emphasize the difficulties of the conception, the obstacles, both personal and political, which lie between it and fulfilment. These difficulties, however, never amount to a questioning of the royal judgement. Even in his decisive debate with Williams and Bates on the eve of Agincourt (IV, 1), where the implications of his power are most searchingly discussed, the King's right to command is never in doubt. The claims of authority, which are as fundamental to the Shakespearean conception of the body politic as are those of judgement and control of the moral idea, must still be made and accepted. Henry's soldiers, in spite of their pessimistic view of the military situation, accept them without reserve. For Bates the duty of a subject lies simply in loyal execution of the royal will, and the responsibility for wrong action, if wrong there be, rests beyond the simple soldier with the King; "we know enough if we know we are the king's subjects." Williams is more sceptical in his estimate of the King's judgement, but his scepticism, far from eating into the mind and sapping the will to action, is simply the reflection of a sturdy and independent character. It is, in other words, closer in spirit to Falstaff's unprejudiced observations upon "honour" than to the corroding scepticism of the "problem" plays. Replying to Henry's assertion that the cause is just with a doubtful "that's more than we know," he never really questions the postulate that the subject is bound to obedience. Indeed, he openly asserts that this is so. To disobey, as he puts it, "were against all proportion of subjection"; and the emphasis is still upon the "proportion" to be observed in the relationship between king and subject, between the directing head and the executive body, and upon the proper submission necessary to successful military effort. Henry, of course, accepts this view of his position. Indeed, the temper of the play, still strictly political and patriotic, does not permit him to do otherwise: but the manner of his acceptance, modified as it is by a consistently sombre estimate of human possibilities, is decidedly tragic in spirit.

For the arguments of his followers, though they do not lead Henry to question his own authority, force him to reflect deeply upon the weaknesses which even kings cannot overcome. It is the tone of these reflections that he approaches more nearly than ever before to the spirit of later plays: "The king is but a man as I am; the violet smells to him as it doth to me; . . . all his senses have but human conditions: his ceremonies laid by, in his wickedness he appears but a man; and though his affections are higher mounted than ours, yet when they stoop they stoop with the like wing." There is about the argument a universality which transcends the royal situation. Men, differentiated by vain "ceremony," are united in their common wickedness, and the most notable feature of human behaviour is its domination by sensual weakness, its helplessness before the universal stooping of the affections.* In this aspect, at least, the King's shares the failings of his men; and just because he is so like them, just because his senses too have but human conditions, are constantly liable to break through the guard of rigid self-control, there is something precarious and disproportionate in his absolute claim upon the allegiance of his followers. The royal isolation is further underlined by Williams when he points out the spiritual consequences of a conflict for which the King, as unquestioned head of his army, is alone responsible: "For how can they" (soldiers) "charitably dispose of anything when blood is their argument? Now, if these men do not die well, it will be a black matter for the king that led them to it!" These words repeat once more, but with a greater urgency, a preoccupation with the horrors of war which Henry has already expressed, even if he succeeded in shaking off responsibility for them, to the French ambassadors and to the governor of Harfleur. They repeat them, moreover in terms of that friction between flesh and spirit which is so prominent in

---

* The reference to the violet and its smell in connexion with corrupt sensuality can be paralleled by the words of Angelo:

> . . . *it is I*
> *That, lying by the violet in the sun,*
> *Do as the carrion does, not as the flower,*
> *Corrupt with virtuous season.*
> [*Measure for Measure*, II, II]

the King himself. The words of Williams imply, in fact, beyond the religious sense of responsibility which derives from the traditional conception of Henry's character, a contrast—already familiar to us—between the Christian law of "grace" or "charity" and the "blood"-spurred impulse to destruction that threatens it in the acts of war with the consequences of unleashed brutality. The connexion between this conflict of flesh and spirit and the tendency of human societies, states, and families alike, to dissolve by the questioning of "degree" into individual anarchy, is not established in this play as it is in the tragedies which follow. But Hamlet himself might have reflected like Henry on the precarious basis of human pretensions, and Angelo defined in similar terms the catastrophic realization of it brought about by his fatal encounter with Isabella. Had Henry once followed his line of speculation far enough to doubt the validity of his motives for action, or—on the other hand—had he given free play to the sinister impulses he dimly recognizes in himself, the resemblance would have been complete; as it is, there is only a premonition, a first indication of possibilities brought more fully to light in later plays.

For the moment, Henry counters the disturbing implications of Williams's argument by pointing out that soldiers "purpose not their death, when they purpose their services." His sombre view of human nature, however, impresses itself upon the King, attaches itself to his own meditations, and is profoundly echoed in his own words. Connecting war with sin, and in particular with overriding passion, he repeats the tone of earlier statements: "Besides, there is no king, be his cause never so spotless, if it come to the arbitrament of swords, can try it out with all unspotted soldiers: some peradventure have on them the guilt of premeditated and contrived murder; some, of beguiling virgins with the broken seals of perjury." The result is, in part, a fresh emphasis upon meticulous self-examination as a means of conserving spiritual health—"therefore should every soldier in the wars do as every sick man in his bed, wash every mote out of his conscience"—and, in the soliloquy which brings the scene to an end, one of those outbursts of nostalgic craving for release which have appeared already in the Second Part of *Henry IV* and will be repeated with a new, more directly *physical* apprehension of existence in Hamlet's soliloquies and the Duke's incitations to Claudio in *Measure for Measure*.

> *What infinite heart's ease*
> *Must kings neglect, that private men enjoy.*

The craving for "heart's ease" in this long speech is still, generally speaking, what it is in *Henry IV*: a desire to be freed from the burden of an office in which human purposes seem fatally divorced from human achievement. The development of the verse is still painstaking, leisurely in the expansion of its long periods, and a little rhetorical; but there are moments, generally traceable to characteristic touches of imagery, which anticipate the association in *Hamlet* of this familiar nostalgia with a desire to be free from the intolerable incumbrances, the "fardels," the " things rank and gross in nature," by which the flesh persistently, fatally seems to obstruct the unimpeded workings of the spirit. Greatness is a "fiery fever" which consumes its royal victim like a bodily disease, and the contrasted peace of the humble subject is described with a curious ambiguity of tone:

> *Not all these, laid in bed majestical,*
> *Can sleep so soundly as the wretched slave,*
> *Who with a body fill'd and vacant mind*
> *Gets him to rest, cramm'd with distressful bread.*

In the association of peace with bodily fullness and vacancy of mind, in the impression, harshly and directly physical, behind "fill'd" and "cramm'd," there is a distinct suggestion of certain descriptions of satiated, idle contentment in plays as far apart as *Troilus and Cressida* and *Coriolanus*.* Here already such imagery represents a kind of residue standing, intact and irreducible, in direct contrast to the King's unceasing emphasis on the need for spiritual discipline. It is no more than a suggestion, unabsorbed as yet into the main imaginative design of the play; but, tentative as it is, it does stand in a certain relationship to the clash of flesh and spirit, "passion" and "grace," which exacts continual vigilance from Henry, and which is slowly moving through these developments of imagery towards more open realization.

A similar potential cleavage, and one which is given clearer dramatic expression, can be traced in the treatment of the two sides drawn up in battle at Agincourt. Shakespeare differentiates between the French and English forces in a way which dimly anticipates the balance held in *Troilus and Cressida* between Greeks and Trojans: though it is true that here the unfavourable estimate of the English, which is scarcely compatible with the spirit of the story, is expressed only in the words of their enemies. The English are

---
* I have indicated the importance of imagery of the same type in both these plays in *Scrutiny* Vol. VI, No. 4, and Vol. VII, No. 3.

still morally worthy of their victory, but the French account of them at least anticipates the possibility of criticism. The French, combining a touch of the insubstantial chivalry of Hector and Troilus with a more than Trojan emptiness, are, like the Trojans, defeated; the English, represented by them as gross and dull-witted, are as undeniably successful as the Greeks. In his treatment of the French nobility, Shakespeare seems to be turning a popular satirical conception to fresh purposes. The Dauphin's description of his horse (III, vii), which is typical of many French utterances, combines a certain elemental lightness with a deliberate euphuistic hollowness of phrase: "It is a beast for Perseus; he is pure air and fire, and the dull elements of earth and water never appear in him." The contrast between the opposed elements is typical, but so is the reference just below to the conventional love poetry of the courts. For the Dauphin goes on to say that he once wrote in praise of his horse a sonnet beginning "Wonder of nature," to which Orleans retorts, "I have heard a sonnet begin so to one's mistress"; and the Dauphin, oblivious to the reversal of values involved, comments—"Then did they imitate that which I composed to my courser, for my horse is my mistress." The world implied by such remarks is clearly, in embryo, that of the early scenes of *Troilus*: a world far less seriously treated and with much less evidence of a dominating and clearly conceived purpose, but already light, sceptical, and revealing a fundamental moral carelessness, a society which views with cynicism the graceful phrase-making of its own members. Equally significant are the slighting references of the French to the heavy wits and bodies of the English, references which already bear some similarity to Shakespeare's treatment of "the dull, brainless Ajax" and Achilles, his rival in ponderous inaction. At one point the criticism is enforced by a comparison between the qualities and effects of wine and water:

> Can sodden water,
> A drench for sur-rein'd jades, their barley-broth,
> Decoct their cold blood to such valiant heat? [III, v]

The difference is described here—and this is the most interesting thing about a passage which might otherwise pass for nothing more than a piece of popular satire on national humours—in terms of "blood." Hot blood, sensual, frivolous, and ineffective in its verbal pretensions to nobility, meets the cold fixity of purpose which it affects to despise, and is hopelessly defeated. Without overstressing the importance of these passages, we may hold that there are elements in this picture which Shakespeare will soon use with greater intellectual consistency and for more serious purposes. Meanwhile, the Constable contemptuously refers to the King of England and "his fat-brain'd followers" as empty in the head—for "if their heads had any intellectual armour they could never wear such heavy headpieces"—and dependent for their courage on the fact that they have left "their wits with their wives"; but, like the Greeks in *Troilus* and more deservedly, they prevail. Shakespeare's handling of the battle carries on this conception. The French, trusting in a thin and rhetorical belief in their own aristocratic superiority, rush hastily and incompetently to their deaths; the English, deriving their spirit from their King, win the day by perseverance and self-control. Self-control, however, which is—as in Henry himself—not without a suggestion of harshness and inhumanity. Henry's righteousness does not prevent him from inflicting merciless reprisals on his prisoners, and there is something sardonic about Gower's comment that "the king, most worthily, hath caused every soldier to cut his prisoner's throat. O 't is a gallant king" (IV, vii). By such excellence, Shakespeare would seem to say, must wars be won.

There is, indeed, a good deal of throat-cutting in this play. The King's ruthlessness, which is a logical consequence of his efficiency, needs to be seen against the human background which Shakespeare provides for it, most noticeably in the comic scenes which turn on the behaviour of the common soldiery. There is little room in *Henry V* for the distinctive note of comedy. Shakespeare's delineation of character is as clear-cut as ever, and his dialogue abundantly if discreetly flavoured with the sense of humanity; but there is about these humorous scenes a certain desiccated flatness that contrasts sharply with the exuberance of earlier plays. We may detect in these scenes, if we will, an increasing interest in Ben Jonson's handling of "humour" to fit a new kind of moral purpose. Bardolph, Pistol, and the others, no longer enlivened by contact with Falstaff, quarrel like curs, and their jokes turn largely upon the bawdy-houses which will inevitably swallow them up when they return to England, and upon the cutting of throats. "Men may sleep, and they may have their throats about them at that time; and some say knives have edges" (II, ii). Nym's remark, itself dark and enigmatic, is prefaced by a sombre, fatalistic "things must be as they may," which modifies the comic sententiousness of the speaker and implies a certain resigned acceptance of the ordering of things. The humorous conception of the character is toned down to fit in with a spirit no longer essentially humorous; and this applies not only to Nym, but to his companions-in-arms. Fluellen and Gower, Williams and Bates, are distinguished, not by comic vitality or by the penetration of their comments on men and events, but by their qualities of common sense, by a tough sense of loyalty and dedication to the work in hand; and it is by their devotion to the strictly practical virtues and by the definition of their various national idiosyncrasies that they live. This is no longer the world of *Henry IV—Part I*. Falstaff himself, out of place in such company, is remembered only in his death, serving as a kind of measure by contrast with which Shakespeare emphasized his changing vision of humanity. His death—it is worth noting—is ascribed directly to the King, who "has killed his heart"; and Nym, repeating that phrase of resignation which conveys so much more than he realizes of the spirit of this new world, relates Henry's treatment of him to an obscure, inherent fatality. "The King is a good King; but it must be as it may; he passes some humours and careers" (II, 1). In a play where the touchstone of conduct is political success, and in which humanity has to accommodate itself continually to the claims of expediency, there is no place for Falstaff. Shakespeare had already recognized this and prepared for the necessary change in the "rejection" which had brought the previous play to a close; and now, in *Henry V*, his death affects us tragically as the last glimpse of another and less sombre world. His companions who remain, and whose life in previous plays was largely a reflection of his vitality, must now accommodate themselves to the times. They do so—and this is significant in defining Shakespeare's attitude to Henry's war —by abandoning domestic crime to follow their King to France. War, and its prospects of plunder, are for them no more and no less than a means of livelihood and an alternative to preying upon one another. As Bardolph puts it—"We must to France together; why the devil should we keep knives to cut one another's throats?" (II, 1).

In the comic scenes which present Henry's campaign against a background of drab reality, Shakespeare sets this sober view of human nature against the King's rhetorical incitations to patriotic feeling. The arrangement of the scenes is, as usual, not accidental. The behaviour of Nym, Bardolph, and Pistol before Harfleur (III, 11) reads with double force after Henry's stress on breeding and the patriotic virtues. The general tone of the soldierly meditations is familiar enough and recalls Falstaff's observations at Shrewsbury.

"The knocks are too hot"—as Nym puts it—"and for mine own part, I have not a case of lives"; whilst the Boy's comment—"I would give all my fame for a pot of ale and safety"—makes him the inheritor, at least for a moment, of the philosophy of his master. But the Shakespearean attitude to war in this play implies, beyond this familiar appeal to common sense, a further element scarcely suggested in *Henry IV—Part I,* although it is in process of development in the sequel to that play. The values towards which Shakespeare is now feeling his way are tragic and essentially moral. Even in Pistol's flamboyant bravado and evident cowardice, there is a new note of reflection, a serious reference to the wastage of invaluable human lives—"Knocks come and go; God's vessels"—the phrase, for all its comic solemnity, is not unaffected by the sense of religious seriousness—"drop and die." Striking too, though in another direction, is the repeated emphasis upon stealing in the scenes which portray the invading army. Henry's Englishmen, "the noblest English" who are to be a copy to "men of grosser blood," are the same who "will steal anything and call it purchase." They steal, not in the spirit of the earlier Falstaff defying "the rusty curb of old father antic the law," but to keep body and soul together or in simple obedience to their innate cupidity; and in the intervals of stealing, there are abundant opportunities for the throat-cutting which is so great a part of the military vocation. As Macmorris reminds his fellows, "there is throats to be cut and works to be done," so that Henry's treatment of his prisoners in the hour of battle, far from being an isolated incident, simply gives a polite sanction to the common reality of war.

The presence of these elements in his army imposes certain necessities upon the King in the fulfilment of his responsibilities. Cupidity in man is balanced by uncompromising rigour in the maintenance of elementary moral law. Besides being ready to inflict suffering upon his enemies, Henry has to enforce good conduct among his own men. When Bardolph, adding sacrilege to theft, steals a pax from a French church, Henry has no hesitation in ordering him to be hanged (III, VI); for discipline, as the faithful and competent Fluellen observes, "is to be used," and the offender should die, even "if he were my brother." In imposing discipline upon his men, Henry has to make the sacrifices called for by his office. Once more justice requires authority to be ready to cut across human feeling; and once more the dominating impression is one of political expediency. Even the enforcement of honesty in this play has its basis in sober calculation. Henry, in confirming the sentence passed upon the thief, leaves the last word to diplomacy: "for when lenity and cruelty play for a kingdom, the gentler gamester is the soonest winner." Moral principle, coming into contact with political reality, translates itself inevitably into a question of expediency; and it is expediency, the condition of successful leadership, which is—whatever his deepest desires—the touchstone of Henry's conduct.

Perhaps we can now understand why *Henry V*, as I suggested at the opening of this essay, has been most generally popular when imperfectly understood. Its concessions to human feeling are too few, its presiding spirit too discouraging to compel enthusiasm. It ends, on every level, in a decided pessimism which somehow fails to attain the note of tragedy. Pistol, speaking the last word for the cut-throats of the play, leaves us with a gloomy and uncompromisingly realistic vision of his future which the sober common sense of Fluellen and the other soldiers does not sufficiently lighten:

> *Doth Fortune play the huswife with me now?*
> *News have I, that my Doll is dead i' the spital*
> *Of malady of France;*
> *And there my rendezvous is quite cut off.*
> *Old do I wax; and from my weary limbs*
> *Honour is cudgelled. Well, bawd I'll turn,*
> *And something lean to cutpurse of quick hand.*
> *To England will I steal, and there I'll steal:*
> *And patches will I get unto these cudgell'd scars,*
> *And swear I got them in the Gallia wars.* [V, i]

Nor is the political conclusion, which shows peace following on the English triumph, much more encouraging. Henry's wooing of Katharine, distant and consistently prosaic in tone, befits what is after all never more than a political arrangement undertaken in a spirit of sober calculation. It may have satisfied the demands of patriotic orthodoxy at Elizabeth's court; but Shakespeare had the gift of fulfilling obligations of this kind without being deterred from his deeper purposes, and this conclusion can hardly have been meant to do more. The inspiration of *Henry V* is, if anything, critical, analytic, exploratory. As we read it, a certain coldness takes possession of us as it took possession, step by step, of the limbs of the dying Falstaff; and we too, in finishing this balanced, sober study of political success, find ourselves in our own way "babbling of green fields."

(1941)

(III) THE AMBIGUITY OF *MEASURE FOR MEASURE*
by L. C. Knights

I

It is probably true to say that *Measure for Measure* is that play of Shakespeare's which has caused most readers the greatest sense of strain and mental discomfort. "More labour than elegance" was Dr. Johnson's way of expressing his sense of something forced in "the grave scenes" (he found "the light or comic part . . . very natural and pleasing"), whilst to Coleridge the whole play was "painful," and even, a few years later, "hateful, though Shakespearean throughout." The most obvious reason for this discomfort is to be found in the conflicting attitudes towards the main characters that seem to be forced upon us, and it is easy to list questions of personal conduct for which it is impossible to find a simple answer. (What, to take one example, are we to think of Isabella? Is she the embodiment of a chaste serenity, or is she, like Angelo, an illustration of the frosty lack of sympathy of a self-regarding puritanism?) Hazlitt's explanation of the painful impression created by the play, that "our sympathies are repulsed and defeated in all directions," is, however, only part of the truth. It is not merely that the play is a comedy, so that the "general system of cross-purposes between the feelings of the different characters and the sympathy of the reader" can be in part attributed to the needs of the plot—complication, suspense, and a conventionally happy ending; the strain and conflict goes much deeper than that, being in fact embedded in the themes of which the characters are made the mouthpiece.

Like many other Elizabethan plays, *Measure for Measure* has an obvious relation to the old moralities. It is too lively and dramatic—too Elizabethan—to be considered merely as a homiletic debate, but it turns, in its own way, on certain moral problems, the nature of which is indicated by the recurrent use of the words "scope," "liberty," and "restraint." What, Shakespeare seems to ask, is the relation between natural impulse and individual liberty, on the one hand, and self-restraint and public law on the other?

The mainspring of the action is, of course, the sexual instinct; Claudio is condemned "for getting Madam Julietta with child," Angelo discovers the force of suppressed impulse, and most of the lesser characters seem to have no other occupation and few other topics of conversation but sex. Angelo, on the one hand, and Mrs.

Overdone and her clients, on the other, represent the extremes of suppression and licence, and towards them Shakespeare's attitude is clear. The figure of Angelo, although a sketch rather than a developed character study, is the admitted success of the play. In few but firm lines we are made aware that his boasted self-control is not only a matter of conscious will ("What I will not, that I cannot do"), but of a will taut and strained. The Duke speaks of him as "a man of stricture and firm abstinence," and the unfamiliarity of the word "stricture" ensures that its derivation from *stringere*, to bind together or to strain, shall contribute to the meaning of the line. In his "gravity" ("Wherein, let no man hear me, I take pride") there is an unpleasantly self-conscious element— summed up in Claudio's exclamation, "The prenzy Angelo!" which relates him to the objects of Shakespeare's irony in the sonnet about "lilies that fester":

> *Unmoved, cold, and to temptation slow:*
> *They rightly do inherit heaven's graces,*
> *And husband nature's riches from expense.*
> *They are the lords and owners of their faces,*
> *Others, but stewards of their excellence.*

It is the unnaturalness and rigidity of his ideal that is insisted on. That it is unnatural is stressed not only by Lucio—"this ungenitured agent will unpeople the province with continency; sparrows must not build in his house-eaves because they are lecherous"—but by the Duke:

> *Lord Angelo is precise;*
> *Stands at a guard with envy; scarce confesses*
> *That his blood flows, or that his appetite*
> *Is more to bread than stone.*

Once the precarious balance is upset it is the despised "blood"— an uncontrolled and unrelated sensual impulse—that runs away with him:

> *I have begun,*
> *And now I give my sensual race the rein:*
> *Fit thy consent to my sharp appetite . . .*

His lust, like his forced chastity, is felt as something **excessive**, urgent, and disproportionate in its demands:

> *Why does my blood thus muster to my heart,*
> *Making both it unable for itself,*
> *And dispossessing all my other parts*
> *Of necessary fitness?*

And the relation between the two extremes is further emphasized by the gratuitous cruelty of his demands on Isabella:

> ... *redeem thy brother*
> *By yielding up thy body to my will,*
> *Or else he must not only die the death,*
> *But thy unkindness shall his death draw out*
> *To lingering sufferance;*

for the savagery of this had been foreshadowed, before his own temptation, not only in his peremptory harshness to Juliet (II, ii), but in the sadism of his parting words to Escalus, when the latter was about to try the offenders from the suburbs: "I'll take my leave ... Hoping you'll find good cause to whip them all."

Lucio and his associates, on the other hand, follow their impulses without scruple or restraint. They have a natural vitality, expressing itself at times in a certain raciness of comment ("Heaven grant us its peace, but not the King of Hungary's"); and it is the "fantastic" Lucio who urges the easily discouraged Isabella to further efforts to save her brother's life. "Those pleasant persons" —as Hazlitt calls them—Lucio, Pompey, and Froth, are often referred to as an example of Shakespeare's sympathy for scoundrels; but although we are not required to get up any moral steam about their vices, the artistic handling is cool and clear. The note of frothy triviality, struck in the first conversation between Lucio and "two other like gentlemen" (I, ii), is never absent from their talk for long. They sufficiently represent the "scope" or "liberty" that, it is postulated, has made "Vienna" what it is.

Neither Angelo nor the traffickers in sex are the source of the sense of uneasiness that we are trying to track down. It is Claudio —who is scarcely a "character" at all, and who stands between the two extremes—who seems to spring from feelings at war with themselves, and it is in considering the nature of his offence that one feels most perplexity. Soon after his first appearance, led by a gaoler, he is accosted by Lucio:

LUCIO: *Why how now, Claudio! Whence comes this restraint?*
CLAUDIO: *From too much liberty, my Lucio, liberty:*
　　　　　As surfeit is the father of much fast,
　　　　　So every scope by the immoderate use
　　　　　Turns to restraint. Our natures do pursue,
　　　　　Like rats that ravin down their proper bane,
　　　　　A thirsty evil, and when we drink we die.
LUCIO: *If I could speak so wisely under an arrest, I would send*

>   for certain of my creditors. And yet, to say the truth,
>   I had as lief have the foppery of freedom as the mor-
>   tality of imprisonment. What's thy offence, Claudio?
> CLAUDIO: What but to speak of would offend again.
> LUCIO: What, is it murder?
> CLAUDIO: No.
> LUCIO: Lechery?
> CLAUDIO: Call it so.

That Shakespeare was aware of an element of sententiousness in Claudio's words is shown by Lucio's brisk rejoinders. The emphasis has, too, an obvious dramatic function, for by suggesting that the offence was indeed grave it makes the penalty seem less fantastic; and in the theatre that is probably all one notices in the swift transition to more explicit exposition. But on coming back to the lines with fuller knowledge of what is involved it is impossible to avoid the impression of something odd and inappropriate. Apart from the fact that Claudio was "contracted" to Juliet, he does not seem to have "surfeited," and he was certainly not a libertine: his "entertainment" with Juliet was, we learn, "most mutual"—they were in love with each other—a fact that is emphasized again later (II, III, 24-28), when the Duke makes it a matter of special reproach to Juliet: "Then was your sin of heavier kind than his." And consider the simile by which Claudio is made to express feelings prompted, presumably, by his relations with the woman who—except for "the denunciation ... of outward order"—is "fast my wife":

> Our natures do pursue,
> Like rats that ravin down their proper bane,
> A thirsty evil, and when we drink we die.

The illustrative comparison has, we notice, three stages: (I) rats "ravin down" poison, (II) which makes them thirsty, (III) so they drink and—the poison taking effect—die. But the human parallel has, it seems, only two stages: prompted by desire, men quench their "thirsty evil" in the sexual act and—by terms of the new proclamation—pay the penalty of death. The act of ravening down the bane or poison is thus left on our hands, and the only way we can dispose of it is by assuming that "our natures" have no need to "pursue" their "thirsty evils," for it is implanted in them by the mere fact of being human. This of course is pedantry and—you may say— irrelevant pedantry, for Shakespeare's similes do not usually demand a detailed, point-by-point examination, and the confusion between desire (thirst) and that from which desire springs does not lessen the general effect. The fact remains, however, that there is some slight dislocation or confusion of feeling, comparable, it seems to me, to the wider confusion of Sonnet 129, "The expense of spirit in a waste of shame . . ." (for not even the excellent analysis by Robert Graves and Laura Riding in their *Survey of Modernist Poetry*, pp. 63-81, can make me feel that the sonnet forms a coherent whole). And even if you accept the simile as completely satisfactory, nothing can prevent "our natures" from receiving some share of the animus conveyed by "ravin," a word in any case more appropriate to lust than to love, and so used by Shakespeare in *Cymbeline*:

> *The cloyed will—*
> *That satiate yet unsatisfied desire, that tub*
> *Both fill'd and running—ravening first the lamb,*
> *Longs after for the garbage.*

The sentiments expressed here concerning what, compared with Angelo's abstinence and Lucio's sexuality, looks like a natural relationship, are not the only ones voiced in the course of the play. Shakespeare in fact dramatizes various attitudes, and one would say that our estimate of their relative validity depended on our sense of the character embodying them were it not that some of the characters are themselves either ambiguous or without much dramatic substance. Angelo's unqualified contempt for Juliet—

> *See you the fornicatress be remov'd:*
> *Let her have needful, but not lavish, means*

—is sufficiently "placed," as are Pompey's remarks about "the merriest usury"; and Lucio, embodying a vulgar flippancy that blurs all distinctions, is obviously not disinterested when, pleading for "a little more lenity to lechery," he complains of Angelo, "What a ruthless thing is this in him, for the rebellion of a codpiece to take away the life of a man!" But we can feel no such certainty about the Duke or Isabella, who are sure enough of themselves: each of them is disposed to severity towards "the sin" (II, iv, 28-36; III, i, 148) of Claudio and Juliet, and the Duke seems to regard it as an instance of the "corruption" that boils and bubbles in the state: "It is too general a vice, and severity must cure it" (III, ii, 103). To Escalus, who, so far as he is anything, is simply a wise counsellor, the "fault" (II, i, 40) is venial; and the humane Provost describes Claudio as

> *a young man*
> *More fit to do another such offence,*
> *Than die for this.*   [II, iii, 13-15]

Yet even in the Provost's sympathy there are overtones from a different range of feelings; and the excuse he finds for Claudio, "He hath but as offended in a dream" (II, II, 4), seems to echo once more the sonnet on lust:

> Made in pursuit and in possession so,
> Had, having, and in quest, to have extreme.
> A bliss in proof and prov'd and very woe,
> Before a joy propos'd, behind a dream.

The play of course is only "about" Claudio to the extent that he is the central figure of the plot; he is not consistently *created*, and he only lives in the intensity of his plea for life. But I think it is the slight uncertainty of attitude in Shakespeare's handling of him that explains some part, at least, of the play's disturbing effect. Shakespeare, we know, had a deep sense of the human worth of tradition and traditional morality, but his plays do not rely on any accepted scheme of values. Their morality (if we call it that) springs from the unshrinking exploration of—the phrase is Marston's— "what men were, and are," and the standard is, as we say loosely, nature itself. In the period immediately preceding the greatest plays—the period of *Measure for Measure, Troilus and Cressida, Hamlet,* and perhaps some of the Sonnets—analysis is not completely pure, and an emotional bias seems to blur some of the natural, positive values which in *Macbeth* or *Lear* are as vividly realized as the vision of evil.

II

The theme of liberty and restraint has, in *Measure for Measure,* another and more public aspect. The first full line of the play is, "Of government the properties to unfold," and the working out of the new severity of the law against licence leads to an examination of more general questions—the relations of law and "justice," of individual freedom and social control, of governors and governed. Here again one finds not only divided sympathies but the pressure of feelings that fail to reach explicit recognition, as in the Duke's lines about the folly of keeping laws on the statute book but not enforcing them:

> We have strict statutes and most biting laws,
> The needful bits and curbs to headstrong steeds,
> Which for this fourteen years we have let slip;
> Even like an o'er grown lion in a cave,
> That goes not out to prey. Now, as fond fathers,

> *Having bound up the threat'ning twigs of birch,*
> *Only to stick it in their children's sight*
> *For terror not to use, in time the rod*
> *Becomes more mock'd than fear'd; so our decrees,*
> *Dead to infliction, to themselves are dead,*
> *And liberty plucks justice by the nose;*
> *The baby beats the nurse, and quite athwart*
> *Goes all decorum.*

What one first notices here is the crisp and lively description of the disorder resulting from official negligence; but behind this there are more complex feelings. If the offenders are "weeds," they are also full of natural energy, like the horse that needs the curb; whilst the concluding lines suggest mischief or childish tantrums rather than deliberate wickedness. And if the unenforced law is ludicrous —"a scarecrow," as Angelo says (II, I, 1)—the law and the law-makers are not exactly amiable. If the Duke's metaphors are given due weight ("biting," "prey," "rod," etc.), one begins to sympathize with Lucio's feelings about "the hideous law" (I, IV, 63), especially when, a few lines later, the Duke is explicit that to enforce the laws is, now, "to strike and gall" the people. It is, however, a postulate of the play that laws are necessary; and although Shakespeare's deep —and characteristically Elizabethan—sense of social *order* is not expressed here with the same force as it is elsewhere, it is not, I feel, simply Angelo who thinks of the law as "all-building." It is when this epithet is restored to its context that the underlying dilemma of the play becomes apparent: the full phrase is,

> *the manacles*
> *Of the all-building law*   [II, IV, 93-94]

Once more, Shakespeare presents various possible attitudes and points of view. The perplexity of the ordinary man confronted with the application of the laws to a particular fellow human is expressed by Escalus when, towards the end of Act II, Scene I, he reverts to Angelo's explicit instruction that Claudio shall "be executed by nine to-morrow morning":

> ESCALUS: *It grieves me for the death of Claudio;*
>   *But there's no remedy.*
> JUSTICE: *Lord Angelo is severe.*
> ESCALUS: *It is but needful:*
>   *Mercy is not itself, that oft looks so;*
>   *Pardon is still the nurse of second woe.*
>   *But yet, poor Claudio! There is no remedy.*

Whilst laws are necessary, they must be enforced; yet one's readiness to accept the logic of this is qualified by various considerations already, in the same scene, brought to our attention. Elbow, chosen constable by his neighbours for seven years and a half, is not simply a stock figure of fun: those who are concerned for the validity of the law can hardly ignore the fact that its instruments may be as foolish as he. "Which is the wiser here?" says Escalus, confronted with Elbow, Froth, and Pompey. "Justice or Iniquity?" Again, how many escape the law!

> Some run from brakes of vice and answer none,
> And some condemned for a fault alone.

"Robes and furr'd gowns hide all," as the mad king says in *Lear*. More important still, those who make or administer the laws may be as corrupt, at least in thought, as those they sentence. This is what Escalus urges on Angelo at the beginning of the scene, and the exchange between them leads to the heart of the problem.

> ESCALUS: Let but your honour know,
> Whom I believe to be most strait in virtue,
> That, in the working of your own affections,
> Had time coher'd with place or place with wishing,
> Or that the resolute acting of your blood
> Could have attain'd the effect of your own purpose,
> Whether you had not, sometime in your life,
> Err'd in this point which now you censure him,
> And pull'd the law upon you.
>
> ANGELO: 'Tis one thing to be tempted, Escalus,
> Another thing to fall. I not deny,
> The jury, passing on the prisoner's life,
> May in the sworn twelve have a thief or two
> Guiltier than him they try; what's open made to justice,
> That justice seizes: what know the laws
> That thieves do pass on thieves?

Angelo, self-righteous and unsubtle, claims that the law is impersonal: equating law with justice, he complacently overlooks the fact that justice has a moral basis; and that morality is concerned with men's thoughts and desires, not merely with their acts. When, in the following scene (II, II), Isabella takes up this theme—

> How would you be,
> If He, which is the top of judgment, should
> But judge you as you are?

—she is met with the same answer: "It is the law, not I, condemns your brother." Given Angelo's premise, that law *is* justice, his further contention, that any deviation from strict law involves injustice to "those . . . which a dismiss'd offence would after gall," is unassailable. Isabella, when her plea for mercy fails, takes the only course open to her and attacks the human motive that sets the logical machine in motion,

> Hooking both right and wrong to the appetite,
> To follow as it draws. [II, IV, 176-177]

Claudio has already made some bitter comments on "the demi-god Authority," and Isabella, in words that remind us once more of *Lear*, now forces the personal, as opposed to the purely formal, issue:

> So you must be the first that gives this sentence,
> And he, that suffers . . .
> Could great men thunder
> As Jove himself does, Jove would ne'er be quiet,
> For every pelting, petty officer
> Would use his heaven for thunder; nothing but thunder!

That, really, is as far as we get. That Angelo has to reverse his former opinion and to tell himself,

> Thieves for their robbery have authority
> When judges steal themselves,

is not a full answer to the questions we have been forced to ask; and it is significant that the last two acts, showing obvious signs of haste, are little more than a drawing out and resolution of the plot. Angelo's temptation and fall finely enforce the need for self-knowledge and sympathy which seems to be the central "moral" of the play,* and which certainly has a very direct bearing on the problems of law and statecraft involved in any attempt to produce order in an imperfect society. But the problems remain. Important in any age, they had a particular urgency at a time when established social forms were being undermined by new forces, and Shakespeare —who in several plays had already pondered "the providence that's in a watchful state"—was to return to them again with a developed insight that makes most political thought look oddly unsubstantial. The development was, of course, to be in the direction indicated by *Measure for Measure*—the continued reduction of abstract "questions" to terms of particular human motives and particular human

---

* Mr. Wilson Knight's essay in *The Wheel of Fire* is headed, aptly, "Measure for Measure and the Gospels."

consequences, and the more and more explicit recognition of complexities and contradictions that appear as soon as one leaves the realm of the formal and the abstract. But in this way the paradox of human law—related on one side to justice and on the other to expediency—is felt as confusion rather than as a sharply focussed dilemma. The reader exclaims with Claudio,

> *Whether the tyranny be in his place,*
> *Or in his eminence that fills it up,*
> *I stagger in*   [I, II, 164-166]

I hope that no one, reaching the end of this examination, will feel that it would have been more appropriate if *Measure for Measure* had been written by Mr. Shaw. The play itself—and this is a sign of its limitations—tends to force discussion in the direction of argument; but I certainly do not wish to imply that its admitted unsatisfactoriness is due to Shakespeare's failure to provide neat answers for Social Problems. Even when, later, he probes far more deeply the preoccupations that have been touched on here, he offers no solutions. *Lear, Coriolanus, Antony and Cleopatra*—each is a great work of clarification, in which there is the fullest recognition of conflicting "truths"; in these plays, therefore, there is that element of paradox which seems inseparable from any work of supreme honesty. In *Measure for Measure* the process of clarification is incomplete, and one finds not paradox but genuine ambiguity.

(1942)

(IV) THE GREATNESS OF *MEASURE FOR MEASURE*
by F. R. Leavis

Re-reading, both of the above and of *Measure for Measure*, has only heightened my first surprise that such an argument about what seems to me one of the very greatest of the plays, and most consummate and convincing of Shakespeare's achievements, should have come from the author of "How Many Children Had Lady Macbeth?" * For I cannot see that the "discomfort" he sets out to explain is other in kind than that which, in the bad prepotent tradition, has placed *Measure for Measure* both among the "unpleasant" ("cynical") plays and among the unconscionable compromises of the artist with the botcher, the tragic poet with the slick provider of bespoke comedy. In fact, Knights explicitly appeals to the "ad-

---
* Reprinted in *Explorations* (1947).

mitted unsatisfactoriness" of *Measure for Measure*. The "admitted unsatisfactoriness," I find myself with some embarrassment driven to point out (he quotes Hazlitt and Coleridge, and might have followed up with Swinburne, the Arden editor, Sir Edmund Chambers, Mr. Desmond McCarthy, the editors of the New Cambridge Shakespeare, and innumerable others), has to be explained in terms of that incapacity for dealing with poetic drama, that innocence about the nature of convention and the conventional possibilities of Shakespearean dramatic method and form, which we associate classically with the name of Bradley.

It is true that Knights doesn't make the usual attack on the character and proceedings of the Duke, and tell us how unadmirable he is, how indefensible, as man and ruler. Nor, in reading this critic, do we find cause for invoking the kind of inhibition that has certainly counted for a lot in establishing the "accepted" attitude towards *Measure for Measure*—inhibition about sex: he doesn't himself actually call the play "unpleasant" or "cynical." But that "sense of uneasiness" which "we are trying to track down"—what, when we have followed through his investigations, does it amount to? It focusses, he says, upon Claudio, or, rather, upon Claudio's offence:

> It is Claudio—who is scarcely a "character" at all, and who stands between the two extremes—who seems to spring from feelings at war with themselves, and it is in considering the nature of his offence that one feels most perplexity.

I am moved to ask by the way what can be Knights's critical intention in judging Claudio to be "scarcely a 'character' at all." I think it worth asking because (among other things) of his judgement elsewhere that Angelo is a "sketch rather than a developed character study." True, he says this parenthetically, while remarking that Angelo is the "admitted success of the play"; but it is an odd parenthesis to have come from the author of "How Many Children Had Lady Macbeth?" It seems to me to have no point, though an unintentional significance.

But to come back to Claudio, whom Knights judges to be "not consistently *created*": it is plain that the main critical intention would be rendered by shifting the italics to "consistently"—he is not "created" (*i.e.,* "scarcely a 'character' ") and, what's more significant, not consistent. This inconsistency, this "uncertainty of handling," we are invited to find localized in the half-dozen lines of

Claudio's first address to Lucio—here Knights makes his most serious offer at grounding his argument in the text:

> From too much liberty, my Lucio, liberty:
> As surfeit is the father of much fast,
> So every scope by the immoderate use
> Turns to restraint. Our natures do pursue,
> Like rats that ravin down their proper bane,
> A thirsty evil, and when we drink we die.

What problem is presented by these lines? The only problem I can see is why anyone should make heavy weather of them. Knights finds it disconcerting that Claudio should express vehement self-condemnation and self-disgust. But Claudio has committed a serious offence, not only in the eyes of the law, but in his own eyes. No doubt he doesn't feel that the offence deserves death; nor does anyone in the play, except Angelo (it is characteristic of Isabella that she should be not quite certain about it). On the other hand, is it difficult to grant his acquiescence in the moral conventions that, barring Lucio and the professionals, everyone about him accepts? A Claudio who took an advanced twentieth-century line in these matters might have made a more interesting "character"; but such an emancipated Claudio was no part of Shakespeare's conception of his theme. Nor, I think Knights will grant, are there any grounds for supposing that Shakespeare himself tended to feel that the prescription of pre-marital chastity might well be dispensed with.

No perplexity, then, should be caused by Claudio's taking conventional morality seriously; that he should do so is not in any way at odds with his being in love or with the mutuality of the offence. And that he should be bitterly self-reproachful and self-condemnatory, and impute a heavier guilt to himself than anyone else (except Isabella and Angelo) imputes to him, is surely natural: he is not a libertine, true (though a pal of Lucio's); but, as he now sees the case, he has recklessly courted temptation, has succumbed to the uncontrollable appetite so engendered, and as a result brought death upon himself, and upon Juliet disgrace and misery. Every element of the figurative comparison will be found to be accounted for here, I think, and I can't see anything "odd" or "inappropriate" about the bitterness and disgust.

Further, Knights's own point should be done justice to: "The emphasis has, too, an obvious dramatic function, for, by suggesting that the offence was indeed grave, it makes the penalty seem less fantastic; and in the theatre that is probably all one notices in the swift transition to more explicit exposition." The complementary point I want to make is that nowhere else in the play is there anything to support Knights's diagnostic commentary. The "uncertainty of attitude" in Shakespeare's handling of Claudio, and uncertainty manifested in a "dislocation or confusion of feeling," depends on those six lines for its demonstration: it can't be plausibly illustrated from any other producible passage of the text. And I don't think anyone could have passed from those lines to the argument that adduces Sonnet 129 and the passage from *Cymbeline,* and ends in references to *Hamlet* and *Troilus and Cressida,* who was not importing into *Measure for Measure* something that wasn't put there by Shakespeare. The importation seems to me essentially that which is provided by what I have called the bad prepotent tradition. Taking advantage of the distraction caused by the problems that propose themselves if one doesn't accept what *Measure for Measure* does offer, that tradition naturally tends to smuggle its irrelevancies into the vacancies one has created. It must be plain that the references to *Hamlet* and *Troilus and Cressida* implicitly endorse the accepted classing of *Measure for Measure* with the "unpleasant," "cynical," and "pessimistic" plays.

The strength of the *parti pris* becomes very strikingly apparent when we are told, of the Provost's sympathetic remark,

Alas!
He hath but as offended in a dream.

that "it seems to echo once more the sonnet on lust." I am convinced it couldn't have seemed to do so to anyone who had not projected on to the text what he finds it giving back. When the word "dream," without any supporting context, can set up such repercussions, we have surely a clear case of possession by the idea or predetermined bent. The intention of the Provost's remark is plain enough: he is merely saying that the offence (morals are morals, and we don't expect a Provost to say, or think, there has been *no* offence) can't be thought of as belonging to the world of real wrong-doing, where there is willed offending action that effects evil and is rightly held to accountability. The Provost, that is, voices a decent, common-sense humanity.

Isabella takes a sterner moral line. But why this should give rise to perplexity or doubt about the attitude we ourselves are to take towards Claudio I can't see. Then I don't agree that she is not sufficiently "placed." Without necessarily judging that she is to be regarded with simple repulsion as an "illustration of the frosty lack of sympathy of a self-regarding puritanism," we surely know that her attitude is not Shakespeare's, and is not meant to be ours. With the Duke it is different. His attitude, nothing could be plainer, *is* meant to be ours—his total attitude, which is the total attitude of the play. He, then, is something more complex than Isabella; but need it conduce to a "sense of strain and mental discomfort" when, speaking as a Friar, he shows himself "disposed to severity towards 'the sin' of Claudio and Juliet"; or when, speaking both as a Friar and to Lucio, he says, "It is too general a vice, and severity must cure it"? To impersonate a reverend friar, with the aim, essential to the plot, of being taken for a reverend friar, and talk otherwise about the given "natural relation"—we might reasonably have found uncertainty of handling in that. As it is, the disguised Duke acts the part, so that the general confidence he wins, including Isabella's, is quite credible.

The criticism that the Duke's speech, "Reason thus with life . . . ," "ignores the reality of emotion" was anticipated (as Knights, by mentioning in the same foot-note Claudia's "retort to the equally 'reasonable' Isabella," reminds us) by Shakespeare himself. The duly noted superiority of Claudio's speech on death to the Duke's (on which, at the same time, I think Knights is too hard) is significant, and it is, not insignificantly, in the same scene. A further implicit criticism is conveyed through Barnadine, who is not, for all the appreciative commentary of the best authorities, a mere pleasing piece of self-indulgence on Shakespeare's part: of all the attitudes concretely lived in the play, the indifference to death displayed by him comes nearest to that preached by the Friar. Those illusions and unrealities which he dismisses, and which for most of us make living undeniably positive and real, have no hold on Barnadine; for him life is indeed an after-dinner's sleep, and he, in the wisdom of drink and insensibility, has no fear at all of death. And towards him we are left in no doubt about the attitude we are to take: "Unfit to live or die," says the Duke, voicing the general contempt.

In fact, the whole context, the whole play, is an implicit criticism of that speech; the speech of which the Arden editor, identifying the Friar-Duke quite simply and directly with Shakespeare, says representatively, on the page now beneath my eye: "There is a **terrible and morbid pessimism in this powerful speech on 'unhealthy-mindedness' that can have only escaped from a spirit in sore** trouble." Actually, no play in the whole canon is remoter from "morbid pessimism" than *Measure for Measure,* or less properly to be associated in mood with *Hamlet* or *Troilus and Cressida.* For the attitude towards death (and life, of course) that the Friar recommends is rejected not merely by Claudio, but by its total context in the play, the varied positive aspects of which it brings out—its significance being that it does so. In particular this significance appears when we consider the speech in relation to the assortment of attitudes towards death that the play dramatizes. Barnadine is an unambiguous figure. Claudio shrinks from death because, once he sees a chance of escape, life, in spite of all the Friar may have said, asserts itself, with all the force of healthy natural impulse, as undeniably real and poignantly desirable; and also because of eschatological terrors, the significance of which is positive, since they are correlatives of established positive attitudes (the suggestion of Dante has often been noted). Isabella can exhibit a contempt of death because of the exaltation of her faith. Angelo begs for death when he stands condemned, not merely in the eyes of others, but in his own eyes, by the criteria upon which his self-approval has been based; when, it may fairly be said, his image of himself shattered, he has already lost his life.

The death penalty of the Romantic comedy convention that Shakespeare starts from he puts to profoundly serious use. It is a necessary instrument in the experimental demonstration upon Angelo:

> hence shall we see,
> If power change purpose, what our seemers be.
>
> [I, III, 53]

The demonstration is of human nature, for Angelo is

> man, proud man,
> Drest in a little brief authority,
> Most ignorant of what he's most assured,
> His glassy essence . . .   [II, II, 117]

Of that nature of the issue we are reminded explicitly again and again:

> If he had been as you, and you as he,
> You would have slipped like him . . .   [II, II, 64]

> How would you be
> If He, which is the top of judgment, should
> But judge you as you are? O! think on that.   [II, II, 75]

> *Go to your bosom;*
> *Knock there, and ask your heart what it doth know*
> *That's like my brother's fault: if it confess*
> *A natural guiltiness such as is his,*
> *Let it not sound a thought upon your tongue*
> *Against my brother's life.* [II, ii, 136]

The generalized form in which the result of the experiment may be stated is, "Judge not, that ye be not judged"—how close in this play Shakespeare is to the New Testament Wilson Knight (whose essay in *The Wheel of Fire* gives the only adequate account of *Measure for Measure* I know) and R. W. Chambers (see *Man's Unconquerable Mind*) have recognized. But there is no need for us to create a perplexity for ourselves out of the further recognition that, even in the play of which this is the moral, Shakespeare conveys his belief that law, order, and formal justice are necessary. To talk in this connexion of the "underlying dilemma" of the play is to suggest (in keeping with the general purpose of Knights's paper) that Shakespeare shows himself the victim of unresolved contradictions, of mental conflict, or of uncertainty. But, surely, to believe that some organs and procedures of social discipline are essential to the maintenance of society needn't be incompatible with recognizing profound and salutary wisdom in "Judge not, that ye be not judged," or with believing that it is our duty to keep ourselves alive to the human and personal actualities that underlie the "impersonality" of justice. Complexity of attitude isn't necessarily conflict or contradiction; and, it may be added (perhaps the reminder will be found not unpardonable), some degree of complexity of attitude is involved in all social living. It is Shakespeare's great triumph in *Measure for Measure* to have achieved so inclusive and delicate a complexity, and to have shown us complexity distinguished from contradiction, conflict, and uncertainty with so sure and subtle a touch. The quality of the whole, in fact, answers to the promise of the poetic texture, to which Knights, in his preoccupation with a false trail, seems to me to have done so little justice.

To believe in the need for law and order is not to approve of any and every law; and about Shakespeare's attitude to the particular law in question there can be no doubt. We accept the law as a necessary datum, but that is not to say that we are required to accept it in any abeyance of our critical faculties. On the contrary, it is an obvious challenge to judgement, and its necessity is a matter of the total challenge it subserves to our deepest sense of responsibility and our most comprehensive and delicate powers of discrimination. We have come now, of course, to the treatment of sex in *Measure for Measure,* and I find myself obliged to insist once more that complexity of attitude needn't be ambiguity, or subtlety uncertainty.

The attitude towards Claudio we have dealt with. Isabella presents a subtler case, but not, I think, one that ought to leave us in any doubt. "What," asks Knights, "are we to think of Isabella? Is she the embodiment of a chaste serenity, or is she, like Angelo, an illustration of the frosty lack of sympathy of a self-regarding puritanism?" But why assume that it must be "either/or"—that she has to be merely the one or else merely the other? It is true that, as Knights remarks, *Measure for Measure* bears a relation to the morality; but the Shakespearean use of convention permits far subtler attitudes and valuations than the morality does. On the one hand, Isabella is clearly not a simple occasion for our feelings of critical superiority. The respect paid her on her entry by the lewd and irreverent Lucio is significant, and she convincingly establishes a presence qualified to command such respect. Her showing in the consummate interviews with Angelo must command a measure of sympathy in us. It is she who speaks the supreme enunciation of the key-theme:

> *man, proud man,*
> *Drest in a little brief authority . . .*

On the other hand, R. W. Chambers is certainly wrong in contending that we are to regard her with pure uncritical sympathy as representing an attitude endorsed by Shakespeare himself.

To begin with, we note that the momentary state of grace to which her influence lifts Lucio itself issues in what amounts to a criticism—a limiting and placing criticism:

> Lucio: *I hold you as a thing ensky'd and sainted:*
> *By your renouncement an immortal spirit,*
> *And to be talked with in sincerity,*
> *As with a saint.*
> Isab.: *You do blaspheme the good in mocking me.*
> Lucio: *Do not believe it. Fewness and truth, 'tis thus:*
> *Your brother and his lover have embrac'd:*
> *As those that feed grow full, as blossoming time*
> *That from the seedness the bare fallow brings*
> *To teeming foison, even so her plenteous womb*
> *Expresseth his full tilth and husbandry.*
>
> [I, iv, 34]

This is implicit criticism in the sense that the attitude it conveys, while endorsed dramatically by the exalted seriousness that is a tribute to Isabella, and poetically by the unmistakable power of the expression (it comes, we feel, from the centre), is something to which she, with her armoured virtue, can't attain. We note further that this advantage over her that Lucio has (for we feel it to be that, little as he has our sympathy in general) comes out again in its being he who has to incite Isabella to warmth and persistence in her intercession for Claudio. The effect of this is confirmed when, without demanding that Isabella should have yielded to Angelo's condition, we register her soliloquizing exit at the end of Act IV, Scene ii; it is not credibly an accidental touch:

> Then, Isabel, live chaste, and, brother, die:
> More than our brother is our chastity.

The cumulative effect is such that it would need a stronger argument than R. W. Chambers's* to convince us that there oughtn't to be an element of the critical in the way we take Isabella's parting discharge upon Claudio:

Isab.: *Take my defiance:*
Die, perish! Might but my bending down
Reprieve thee from thy fate, it should proceed.
I'll pray a thousand prayers for thy death,
No word to save thee.
Claud.: *Nay, hear me, Isabel.*
Isab.:   *O! fie, fie, fie.*
Thy sin's not accidental, but a trade.
Mercy to thee would prove itself a bawd:
'Tis best that thou diest quickly.
                          [Going.
Claud.:   *O hear me, Isabella!*

It is all in keeping that she should betray, in the exalted assertion of her chastity, a kind of sensuality of martyrdom:

> were I under the terms of death,
> The impression of keen whips I'd wear as rubies,
> And strip myself to death, as to a bed
> That longing have been sick for, ere I'd yield
> My body up to shame.   [II, iv, 100]

Finally, it is surely significant that the play should end upon a hint that she is to marry the Duke—a hint that, implying a high valuation along with a criticism, aptly clinches the general presentment of her.

---
* In *Man's Unconquerable Mind*.

But at this point I come sharply up against the casual and confident assumption that we must all agree in a judgement I find staggering: "it is significant that the last two acts, showing obvious signs of haste, are little more than a drawing out and resolution of the plot." The force of this judgement, as the last sentence of Knights's first paragraph confirms, is that the "drawing out and resolution of the plot," being mere arbitrary theatre-craft done from the outside, in order to fit the disconcerting development of the poet's essential interests with a comedy ending that couldn't have been elicited out of their inner logic, are not, for interpretive criticism, significant at all. My own view is clean contrary: it is that the resolution of the plot of *Measure for Measure* is a consummately right and satisfying fulfilment of the essential design; marvellously adroit, with an adroitness that expresses, and derives from, the poet's sure human insight and his fineness of ethical and poetic sensibility.

But what one makes of the ending of the play depends on what one makes of the Duke; and I am embarrassed about proceeding, since the Duke has been very adequately dealt with by Wilson Knight, whose essay Knights refers to. The Duke, it is important to note, was invented by Shakespeare; in *Promos and Cassandra*, Shakespeare's source, there is no equivalent. He, his delegation of authority, and his disguise (themselves familiar romantic conventions) are the means by which Shakespeare transforms a romantic comedy into a completely and profoundly serious "criticism of life." The more-than-Prospero of the play, it is the Duke who initiates and controls the experimental demonstration—the controlled experiment—that forms the action.

There are hints at the outset that he knows what the result will be; and it turns out that he had deputed his authority in full knowledge of Angelo's behaviour towards Mariana. Just what he is, in what subtle ways we are made to take him as more than a mere character, is illuminatingly discussed in *The Wheel of Fire*. Subtly and flexibly as he functions, the nature of the convention is, I can't help feeling, always sufficiently plain for the purposes of the moment. If he were felt as a mere character, an actor among the others, there would be some point in the kind of criticism that has been brought against him (not explicitly, I hasten to add, by Knights—though, in consistency, he seems to me committed to it). How uncondonably cruel, for example, to keep Isabella on the rack with the lie about her brother's death!

I am bound to say that the right way of taking this, and everything else that has pained and perplexed the specialists, seems to me to impose itself easily and naturally The feeling about the Duke expressed later by Angelo—

> O my dread lord!
> I should be guiltier than my guiltiness,
> To think I can be undiscernible,
> When I perceive your grace, like power divine
> Hath look'd upon my passes,

the sense of him as a kind of Providence directing the action from above, has been strongly established. The nature of the action as a controlled experiment, with the Duke in charge of the controls, has asserted itself sufficiently. We know where we have to focus our critical attention and our moral sensibility: not, that is, upon the Duke, but upon the representatives of human nature that provide the subjects of the demonstration. This, we know, is to be carried to the promised upshot—

> hence shall we see,
> If power change purpose, what our seemers be,

which will be, not only the exposure of Angelo, but his exposure in circumstances that develop and unfold publicly the maximum significance.

The reliance on our responding appropriately is the more patently justified and the less questionable (I confess, it seems to me irresistible) in that we can see the promise being so consummately kept. The "resolution of the plot," ballet-like in its patterned formality and masterly in stage-craft, sets out with lucid pregnancy the full significance of the demonstration: "'man, proud man,'" is stripped publicly of all protective ignorance of "his glassy essence"; the ironies of "measure for measure" are clinched; in a supreme test upon Isabella, "Judge not, that ye be not judged" gets an ironical enforcement; and the relative values are conclusively established—the various attitudes settle into their final placing with regard to one another and to the positives that have been concretely defined.

I don't propose to do a detailed analysis of this winding-up—that seems to me unnecessary; if you see the general nature of what is being done, the main points are obvious. I will only refer, in illustration of the economy of this masterpiece in which every touch has significance, to one point that I don't remember to have seen noted. There is (as everyone knows) another invention of Shakespeare's besides the Duke—Mariana, and her treatment by Angelo. It wasn't, as R. W. Chambers thinks, merely in order to save Isabella's chastity that Shakespeare brought in Mariana; as the winding-up scenes sufficiently insist, she plays an important part in the pattern of correspondences and responses by which, largely, the moral valuations are established. In these scenes, Angelo's treatment of her takes its place of critical correspondence in relation to Claudio's offence with Juliet; and Claudio's offence, which is capital, appears as hardly an offence at all, by any serious morality, in comparison with Angelo's piece of respectable prudence.

Finally, by way of illustrating how the moral aspect of the play is affected by an understanding of the form and convention, I must glance at that matter of Angelo's escape from death—and worse than escape (". . . the pardon and marriage of Angelo not merely baffles the strong indignant claim of justice," etc.)—which has stuck in the throats of so many critics since Coleridge. One has, then, to to point out as inoffensively as possible that the point of the play depends upon Angelo's not being a certified criminal-type, capable of a wickedness that marks him off from you and me:

> *Go to your bosom;*
> *Knock there, and ask your heart what it doth know*
> *That's like my brother's fault: if it confess*
> *A natural guiltiness such as is his,*
> *Let it not sound a thought upon your tongue*
> *Against my brother's life.*
> *If he had been as you, and you as he,*
> *You would have slipp'd like him . . .*

There is a wider application than that the speaker intends—even critics aren't exempt. If we don't see ourselves in Angelo, we have taken the play and moral very imperfectly. Authority, in spite of his protest, was forced upon him, and there are grounds for regarding him as the major victim of the experiment. He was placed in a position calculated to actualize his worst potentialities; and Shakespeare's moral certainty isn't that those potentialities are exceptional. If any further argument should seem necessary for holding it possible, without offending our finer susceptibilities, to let Angelo marry a good woman and be happy, it may be said in complete seriousness that he has, since his guilty self-committals, passed through virtual death: perhaps that may be allowed to make a difference. It is not merely that immediate death has appeared certain, but that his image of himself, his personality as he has lived it for himself as well as for the world, having been destroyed, he has embraced death:

> *I am sorry that such sorrow I procure:*
> *And so deep sticks it in my penitent heart*
> *That I crave death more willingly than mercy:*
> *'Tis my deserving, and I do entreat it.*

So wide of the mark, then, is the judgement that, in this play, we have tragic development mechanically and incongruously resolved in a comedy ending. It may be said further that, if *Measure for Measure* is to be bracketed with any other play in particular, it should be, not *Troilus and Cressida,* but *Macbeth.* And, in fact, the point about Angelo may be made by saying he is in some important ways better qualified for the part of tragic hero than Macbeth is— just as there are reasons why, of the two plays, *Measure for Measure* should come more intimately home to the modern. There is something remote, romantic, and "costume" about the situation and crimes of the barbaric chieftain; and to show that Macbeth doesn't lack the necessary element of the sympathetic the critics have to exercise some ingenuity. It is surely easier for us to put ourselves in Angelo's place, and imagine ourselves exposed to his temptations. He is a victim (or is made one by the Duke's experiment) of the discrepancy between an ideal and the actual. Mariana's representation of—

> *They say best men are moulded out of faults,*
> *And, for the most, become much more the better*
> *For being a little bad.* [V, I, 442]

—is not to be taken as mere evidence of amiable feminine weakness. Isabella immediately afterwards—and it is not for nothing—reluctantly grants:

> *I partly think*
> *A due sincerity govern'd his deeds,*
> *Till he did look on me.*

The bright idea of a recent Cambridge production, the idea of injecting point, interest, and modernity into him by making him a twitching study in neurosis, was worse than unnecessary. But then if you can't accept what Shakespeare does provide you have, in some way, to import your interest and significance.

(1942)

(v) SHAKESPEARE CRITICISM

Art and Artifice in Shakespeare, A Study in Dramatic Illusion and Contrast by Elmer Edgar Stoll

Reviewed by L. C. Knights

There is a constant tendency in criticism towards the eccentric, and when time has familiarized the eccentricity ("Pope was no poet but a man of wit") unusual effort is required to demonstrate the inadequacy of "accepted truth." The importance of Professor Stoll is that he is one of those who have most clearly defined the eccentricity of a hundred and fifty years of Shakespeare criticism: "The play has been thought to be a psychological document, not primarily a play . . . and the characters have been taken for separable copies of reality." Whereas, indeed, "The plot is not so much a part of the characters as they are parts of the plot"; convention is more important than verisimilitude. This is salutary, and the account of Elizabethan dramatic conventions, both here and in *Shakespeare Studies,* forms an admirable corrective to the vagaries of the nineteenth-century criticism.

But in the present book Professor Stoll claims to offer something more than a corrective; he is "intent upon the positive": and it is of some importance that those who sympathize with his attacks on Romantic criticism (and have profited from them) should make plain the serious imperfections of his positive method, should explain why this very efficient grave-digger is an untrustworthy sponsor.

The four main chapters in *Art and Artifice* deal with the four great tragedies, and the chapter on *Hamlet* is by far the best. This is significant: *Hamlet* (can one still be misunderstood on this point?) is, as a work of art, imperfect; requires therefore more external explanation than the other three. Besides, partly for this reason, *Hamlet* has occasioned so many critical aberrations, even in the greatest of critics, that the work of destruction is both easier and more necessary than in the case of *Othello, Lear,* or *Macbeth.* Professor Stoll undermines the precarious Romantic structures with gusto, but he offers nothing in their place. Of his positive judgements this, of *Othello,* is a fair sample: "Since the tragedy does not, like the classical French, spring directly out of the hero's and heroine's own bosoms, it is, in its development, as in its origin, not a psychological study; but it is a more vivid imaginative spectacle, is—

'like the Pontic Sea'—a more irresistible dramatic current. It is a story ... it is a series of incidents, which show different aspects of the passion, and various stages of it, along its course; it is an *emotional* development—an eclipse, then an earthquake, then an avalanche." Beyond this seismological account there is no hint of what the emotional development—the poetry—is. At the end, "As his free soul ... thus shines forth again ... there is such an effect, heightened by music, as the theatre had not known or was again to know." The vagueness is pervasive; the same inability to seize any but the more obvious features of plot and situation constantly betrays itself. The only effect of Duncan's entry into the castle—that superbly delicate evocation of supernaturally sanctioned natural good—is, it seems, to make the Professor "sympathetic, anxious and excited. ... It is somewhat the same effect ... (to speak of lesser matters) as when Sherlock [Holmes?] smokes or reads."

For all the erudition, the underlying conception of drama is that of the illiterate playgoer ("And what other point of view are we entitled to take?"). "The core of tragedy," the present book begins, "is situation," and it is "the highly effective situation," the "effects of terror and surprise" that are stressed throughout. "Two things above all he sought—a striking situation and a vivid impression of personality." Professor Stoll's reaction to art is the thrill that comes from seeing "the struggle of the noble nature in the toils, the magnificent effect." "We tremble for Hamlet. ... We are anxious. ..." A discussion conducted in these terms leaves no room for poetry, for all that makes a Shakespeare play a subtly particular emotional experience.

Poetry is indeed mentioned fairly frequently, but the Professor's labyrinthine style is not the only indication that he is not particularly sensitive to it as a medium of emotional precision. There were some odd collocations in *Shakespeare Studies*—"Like Browning's, the touch of his hand is like an electric shock; and as with Browning and Dickens both, even the inanimate things it touches start and quiver. ... Though greater, Shakespeare is, like Browning, Balzac, Scott, and Dickens, too preoccupied with life to study perfection in art"—and the reference to "masters like Shakespeare and Beaumont" in the present volume shows complete unawareness of the gulf between them. It was, I believe, Mr. Logan Pearsall Smith who called Professor Stoll "a hard-boiled critic," but the conception of poetry displayed by this tough realist is the familiar one of "magic." "We believe, not as convinced, but as enchanted and enthralled." Poetic effect is indicated by the vaguest gestures, "He walks not soberly afoot, but flies. And Shakespeare is the greatest of the dramatists because the illusion he offers is the widest and highest, the emotion he arouses the most irresistible and overwhelming." But then, Professor Stoll had already recorded his conviction that Shakespeare "is far less restricted in his appeal, *less exacting in his demands upon the attention and understanding,* more popular, in short, than Ibsen."

The defect indicated here is radical; it explains all the other shortcomings. A critic whose sensibility is not minutely controlled by the word is not likely to be aware of the cardinal virtue of precision. *Shakespeare Studies,* one remembers, exhibited an equivocal use of such key-words as "self-consciousness" and "technique"; and in *Art and Artifice* it is plain that we are not meant to inquire too deeply into "the higher reality, the super truth." Humbler matters, such as "the identity or continuity of stroke or touch, or of fabric and texture," might, perhaps, have had a modicum of explanation.

And an undiscriminating response to poetry—to the word— means, inevitably, a conception of drama as "situation," and a discussion of it in terms only of general effect. *Hamlet* is "a story, not of Hamlet's procrastination ... but of a prolonged and artful struggle between him and the King." So, for that matter, was the *Ur-Hamlet.* The observation that "the central mechanism of the dramatic method [in *Macbeth* and *Othello*] lies in the contrast between the hero and his conduct" is not very helpful. What makes the play important as a particular experience, "so, and not otherwise," is the poetry. Stoll's words could be applied equally to plays with a similar subject matter written in the blank verse of Dryden. It is without surprise that we find (p. 147) an uncritical coupling of *Antony and Cleopatra* and *All for Love,* and (p. 31) evidence of a complete inability to appreciate the significance of *The Wheel of Fire.* According to the criteria that Professor Stoll supplies, a Shakespeare play—a matter of "situation" or of dramatic contrast—could obtain its *full* effect when acted on the stage. If we dissent from this view it is not from any Lamb-like squeamishness but for the reasons which Dryden prefixed to *The Spanish Friar:* "For the propriety of thoughts and words, which are hidden beauties of a play, are but confusedly judged in the vehemence of action: all things are there beheld as in a hasty motion, where the objects only glide before the eye and disappear. The most discerning critic can judge no more of these silent graces in the action than he who rides post through an unknown country can distinguish the situation of places, and the nature of the soil. . . . In short, those very words and thoughts, which cannot be changed, but for the worse, must of necessity escape our transient view upon the theatre; and yet without all these a play may take."

In a sense, Professor Stoll deserves a different review from this. A good deal of work remains to be done on Elizabethan dramatic conventions; especially we need an account of the relation of conventional elements and the "attempt at realism" in particular plays, and we need to know how far conventions were consciously accepted as such. (Mr. Eliot's note on "Four Elizabethan Dramatists" has some interesting—though sometimes misleading—suggestions.) But Professor Stoll has done the spade-work, and future research might well start from his observation that Shakespeare "observes not so much the probabilities of the action, or the psychology of the character, as the psychology of the audience." His books are valuable not only for their account of specific conventions—that of assumed madness, or of the slanderers believed, and so on—but for occasional remarks on the general value of a convention to the artist (for example, "the advantage of not provoking criticism, not arousing resistance"). But, and this explains the direction taken by this review, "convention" criticism of this kind **can never be "positive." Its function is the negative one of preventing the entire misleading approach.**

There are, then, many reasons why we should be grateful to Professor Stoll. It remains to add that we are not grateful to the Cambridge Press for introducing his work to this country in one of the most dazzling types that we have had the misfortune to read.

(1934)

(vi) STATISTICAL CRITICISM

Shakespeare's Imagery and What It Tells Us by Caroline F. E. Spurgeon

Reviewed by R. G. Cox

The idea that there are other approaches to Shakespeare than that of Bradley seems by now to have become completely respectable. At the same time, it is as if there had been a conspiracy to show up these other approaches as inherently tedious and pedantic.

Even Professor Wilson Knight's pertinent and stimulating analyses dwindled into the kind of irrelevant traffic in symbolism represented by *The Shakespearean Tempest*. Professor Spurgeon has gone one better: she has "listed and classified and counted every image in every play thrice over." She has even compiled illustrative charts and diagrams—there are seven in this book—which look like the statistical reports of the Empire Marketing Board.

The first obvious objection—what exactly is to be called an image, and of what?—is considered in an appendix, where it is explained that certain images have to be classified under two headings. But what could happen to, say, the passage in *Antony and Cleopatra*, Act IV, Scene xv:

> *O, see my women,*
> *The crown o' the earth doth melt. My lord!*
> *O, withered is the garland of the war*
> *The soldier's pole is fall'n: young boys and girls*
> *Are level now with men; the odds is gone,*
> *And there is nothing left remarkable*
> *Beneath the visiting moon.*

—where there is a complex imaginative fusion of images? "Any count of this kind," says Professor Spurgeon, "must to some extent be an approximate one, dependent on the *literary judgement* and methods of the person who has compiled it." I have italicized the phrase "literary judgement," because it is constantly suggested throughout the book that we have here something scientific, which can be weighed and measured, something tangible and objective, susceptible of a statistical approach which will rule out such nebulous quantities as the reactions of personal sensibility. In short, the method very easily becomes, like Robertson's verse tests, another will-o'-the-wisp offering an illusory, scientific short-cut instead of the more difficult path of personal evaluation.

That is the radical criticism of the whole undertaking. The only really valuable consideration of Shakespeare's imagery would involve a strictly critical approach: every image must be scrupulously related to its context, must be considered in the light of the sense, feeling, tone, intention, and rhythm of the passage in which it stands. But, as a matter of fact, the first half of the book is scarcely concerned with literature at all. There is one chapter comparing Shakespeare's imagery with that of five arbitrarily selected contemporaries (why include Dekker and Massinger?) and another with that of Marlowe and Bacon. The latter proves that the evidence of the images is against any identification of Shakespeare with Bacon: it all seems very unnecessary. The remaining chapters in this section are an attempt to reconstruct Shakespeare's character, starting from the assumption that a poet tends to give himself away in his images; there are chapters on his senses, his tastes and interests, and his thought. There may be something in all this, and the chapter on "Association of Ideas" may possibly assist in determining work of doubtful authorship, but in general it can only have the most rudimentary biographical interest. What permanent profit is there in knowing that a certain eddy referred to in *Venus and Adonis* is really under such and such a bridge in Warwickshire or that Shakespeare saw the martlets' nests of *Macbeth* on the walls of Berkeley Castle? There seems to be no doubt that Professor Spurgeon has forborne to dig.

Part II is more relevant to literary criticism, though even here reservations must be made. The section deals with "The Function of the Imagery as Background and Undertone in Shakespeare's Art," and it incorporates the earlier pamphlet, "Leading Motives in the Imagery of Shakespeare's Tragedies." This, in fact, remains the best thing in the book, for here there is some convincing attempt to show how in the mature plays the imagery was *used* to contribute to the total imaginative effect. The chapters on the comedies and the romances contain some useful observations, but that on the histories is less convincing. One cannot help feeling that Professor Spurgeon ought to have shown that such leading motives as she is able to discover in, for instance, the *Henry VI* plays or *Richard II* are quite insignificant in comparison with those of the mature tragedies. The whole of this section serves to show that there is no substitute for literary criticism. It is a depressing fact that so much of modern Shakespearean study seems to be little more than an industrious search for such a substitute.

(1935)

Coleridge

(1) THE POETRY OF COLERIDGE, by *Marius Bewley*

Of the bulky volume of poetry which Coleridge has left behind there are only several poems which are of sufficient merit to attract our attention still; but there is little poetry which one approaches critically with more hesitation than these. There is an understandable temptation to accept them at their popular value without making an effort to pass judgement on that evaluation. It is a matter neither for wonder nor censure that this should be so. The intimate familiarity that may be taken to exist between the ordinary reader of poetry and *The Ancient Mariner* or *Kubla Khan* is an added difficulty towards a critical consideration that would not, in any case, be easy. In *The Ancient Mariner* this difficulty exists in a suggestion of moral purpose—a suggestion so elusive that it is of no value, yet sufficiently present to implore our assent to pretensions that a more detailed examination must reject. There is, in short, an ambiguity of motive, of creative purpose, in the poem. It is doubtful if Coleridge himself was aware, when he composed *The Ancient Mariner,* of movements sprung from any loftier creative impulse than those to which he later referred in the *Biographia Literaria.* Speaking of those poems dealing with the supernatural which he undertook for the *Lyrical Ballads,* he there wrote, ". . . the excellence aimed at was to consist in the interesting of the affections by the dramatic truth of such emotions as would naturally accompany such situations, supposing them to be real." Such a motive, in the last analysis, was not substantially different from Mrs. Radcliffe's or Monk Lewis's.

One need not cavil at applying the term moralist to Coleridge. He was concerned with philosophy and religion and politics in a way that the merely frivolous can never be concerned with them, and particularly in establishing a vital relationship between them and the world. It would be remarkable if behind the explicit motive of *The Ancient Mariner* it were not possible to catch glimpses of an ulterior and possibly more real impulse at work. Coleridge's poetry may be rated on too high a level, but to assume that he approached it as a pedestrian task not essentially different from ledger work would be to do him an injustice. For good or ill Coleridge could not help drawing in some measure from his full sensibility. The *raconteur* of supernatural tales is, in *The Ancient Mariner,* not quite free from the moralist. The moral element is forgotten, if indeed it was ever recognized as present; it is changed, choked out by theatrical fripperies. All else is put aside in the fuller attention that is given to the merely dramatic motive. But although the moral motive is scotched, ineffectual fragments are still to be seen in odd corners of the poem as indications of that ambiguity which in the beginning was not absent from Coleridge's mind and which still tends to make one slightly puzzled in reading *The Ancient Mariner.*

I have suggested that this ambiguity is, then, a dispute between the dramatic and the moral motives in composition, and that from the beginning Coleridge exerted his full force on behalf of the first; that he succeeded in what he wished, but was only not sufficiently neat in disposing of the remains of the latter. The ineffective moral motive of *The Ancient Mariner* is a Christian one. It stresses the necessity of supernatural love as the order in creation. It is degraded and like an appendage when at last it comes to a head in the last stanza but two of the poem:

> He prayeth best, who loveth best
> All things both great and small;
> For the dear God who loveth us,
> He made and loveth all.

But disguised and unsatisfactory as its expression is, it is still the central idea of the whole poem, the core around which the action is developed, and without which the sequence of events would be meaningless. In tracing the play of this stunted moral motive, so much thrust into the background, against the length of the poem, a certain roughness of handling is necessitated. But if the interpretation seems arbitrary it is not meant to mark the boundaries of the motive with any precision, but only to point to its existence in the poem.

The transgression of the Ancient Mariner in killing the Albatross is a violation of that supernatural charity which should rule throughout creation. The sanctions which are imposed for the death of the Albatross do not seem remarkable when one reflects that the extraordinariness of the bird does not exist in its own right. It is necessary to bear in mind the stanza:

> *At length did cross an Albatross,*
> *Thorough the fog it came;*
> *As if it had been a Christian soul,*
> *We hailed it in God's name.*

In these lines the Albatross becomes, in effect, a person. It is given a kind of inviolability. It has been deliberately placed by the Ancient Mariner on the same plane of creation which he himself occupies, and the full play of the will to which this deliberation gives scope brings to the Ancient Mariner's act of violence a special guilt.

The punishment which the Ancient Mariner undergoes begins to abate when he is able to generate stirrings of love in the soul once again for created things. One can place this moral motive of the poem locally very well in the last two stanzas of Part IV. Speaking of the water snakes the Ancient Mariner says:

> *O happy living things! No tongue*
> *Their beauty might declare:*
> *A spring of love gushed from my heart*
> *And I blessed them unaware:*
> *Sure my kind Saint took pity on me*
> *And I blessed them unaware.*
>
> *The self-same moment I could pray;*
> *And from my neck so free*
> *The Albatross fell off, and sank*
> *Like lead into the sea.*

The moral motive is almost explicit at this point. It is at the beginning of Part V that this moral becomes operative in the positive sense. Up to this point the Ancient Mariner has been the active agent, but his will has not worked in harmony with the divine goodness, which now, through the operation of a supernatural mechanism, begins the work of regeneration in his soul. There follows quickly that passage in which the seraph band enters the bodies of the crew. It is one of the most dramatic passages in the poem. Bearing with its reminiscences of the Incarnation and the Resurrection, it is but a further insistence on the controlling principle of love which springs from God.

This interpretation, though it is obvious enough, is not the one most immediate and apparent. Indeed, it lies far back in the poem. We are likely to overlook it entirely, despite the kind of obviousness which it can claim, and it would make little difference but for the moral overtone which it strikes, and which reaches our ears like a faint echo suggesting a more considerable substance than search is likely to verify. The reader more probably assumes, for example, that the Albatross is a bird of sinister significance whose death liberates inexplicable threads of mystery to wave in the atmosphere. The sequence of action is, as a result, microscoped to a moral inconsequentiality from this point onwards. It was what Coleridge wanted. He even assists the reader to the interpretation by his marginal note referring to the bird of good omen. As the poem stands it is indeed the interpretation that should be made; but the moral motive which was sketched in above, ignored and distorted, hovers in the background and implies a moral integrity which does not exist.

The dramatic purpose of the poem is realized by means of the supernatural mechanism. But as this mechanism is a means to the dramatic fulfilment of the poem, it works also towards the failure of the moral motive. Still, the function which the machinery performs it performs well, and it is one which necessitated a mechanism of this order. The peculiar quality of the supernatural machinery consists in its being localized; one might almost say, *essentially* localized. If the supernatural is to be treated at all it is inevitable that it should be given extension, and to do this is to tie it down to a particular place. Yet it is not impossible that these necessary materializations should appeal to the reader only as inevitable symbols of states of being that cannot otherwise be expressed. Dante achieved this. But Coleridge places his supernatural beings against the geography of an unknown world in such a manner that their respective mysteries enforce each other. This means that while the mystery of the world is increased, that of the supernatural not only decreases but changes in character. There is little that more readily appeals to the imagination than the mysteries of unexplored realms. Today, when the mystery has been largely swept off the earth, those who still feel the appetite have to be satisfied with the somewhat prepared mystery of Sir James Jeans and the scientific popularizers of the last unexplored frontiers. But it isn't quite the same. The achievement of Coleridge is that he succeeds in re-creating an atmosphere of mystery that a long line of explorers from Vasco da Gama to Byrd have been at some effort to take from us.

This air of mystery is created by direct statement and by playing the supernatural against a terrestrial background. It is stated directly, for example, in lines such as,

> *We were the first that ever burst*
> *Into that silent sea.*

Coleridge's process of building up this air of mystery, inasmuch as it concerns itself with descriptions of "ice as green as emerald," the relative position of the sun, the rather weird effect of personifying and capitalizing "the STORM-BLAST," the suitably dramatic choice of the South Pole and then the Line as the course of the ship's voyage, and particularly the skeleton ship with its crew, Death and Life-in-Death, is sometimes theatrical, but it is innocent always. It is indeed this innocence that keeps the whole machinery at times from creaking. By innocence here I mean that accomplished lack of sophistication which is sometimes so characteristic of Coleridge. By felicitous touches Coleridge tapped forgotten emotional connotations. He is able to suggest fabulous mediaeval sea-monsters with some subtlety:

> *Yea, slimy things did crawl with legs*
> *Upon the slimy sea.*

But this direct statement of the geographical mystery is intensified by the familiar movements of the demons of the middle air through their element, by the skeleton ship, which, with its plunging and tacking and veering, gives the impression of being a constant inhabitant of the Pacific, by the Polar Spirit—in short, by that sense of supernatural population which seems to be a part of the background against which it moves. The atmosphere of *The Ancient Mariner* is heavily charged. The earth is a mysterious place, but its mystery is not, strictly speaking, the mystery of rocks and stones and trees. It is in good part the mystery of the spiritual beings who reside in them and whose identities are, for the poem's purposes, not clearly distinct.

To have succeeded in re-creating this air of mystery, or, more correctly, in creating this new air of mystery, is not after all a major achievement. It is comparatively trivial. Yet if we search for a more substantial value in *The Ancient Mariner* the search will not be fruitful. The moral value of the poem is sacrificed to the attainment of a somewhat frivolous distinction. The texture of the poetry itself is never adequate to its purpose, but it is not, for the most part, interesting. It is inflexible because it is manufactured to compass a certain preconceived effect, and one that, from Coleridge's own words, which were quoted above, is scarcely closed to suspicion. It is not likely that words of such impersonal calculation should have led on to poetic attempts whose roots were buried deep in the essential impulses of the man. The chief objection must be, I think, that *The Ancient Mariner* brings into play a machinery that is by its nature moral, but caricatures and deflects that machinery from its true purpose, that a smaller satisfaction may be realized. It is trivial, but it is not honestly so. Its pretentiousness is of a type that for a small effect debases a universe, and this is a charge of some gravity. It has lost its moral bearing and stands at the summit of a declivity at whose foot is *The Blessed Damozel*. . . .   (1940)

(II) THE THEME OF *THE ANCIENT MARINER* by D. W. Harding

The compelling quality of *The Ancient Mariner,* more than of many poems, is difficult to identify with any confidence. Marius Bewley seems right in dismissing as trivial those very aspects on which conventional adulation is based. And if one dissents from his final judgement some other account of the poem's appeal has to be offered. Mr. Bewley believes that uncertain fragments of a moral outlook, hints of a motive which Coleridge sacrificed to simpler ends, tempt us to attribute deep significance to what is mainly a trifling drama of the supernatural. Coleridge's effective motive, he thinks, "in the last analysis, was not substantially different from Mrs. Radcliffe's or Monk Lewis's."

He quotes Coleridge's own description of this motive: ". . . the excellence aimed at was to consist in the interesting of the affections by the dramatic truth of such emotions as would naturally accompany such situations, supposing them to be real." This formula covers several possibilities. One no doubt is such pastime reading as the melodramas of the supernatural. But equally the formula describes the vastly more significant "excellence" of dreams and fairy-tales. The question is always *what* imaginary situation is presented; whether the result is piffling or significant depends on that. In speaking of the situation I include the potentialities of the characters within it. For what matters in *The Ancient Mariner* is not just that a man was becalmed and haunted, but what sort of man he was. Naturally, he was Coleridge; for, as Mr. Bewley says, however detachedly he may have planned the poem, he "could not help drawing in some measure from his full sensibility."

The first thing, then, is to say what situations Coleridge presents in the poem, what his theme is. One could follow Maud Bodkin (in *Archetypal Patterns in Poetry*) and show the more or less unconscious symbolism of some of its features. But her analyses, relevant as I think they are, stress too much the detachable significance of parts of the poem and give too little attention to its unique whole. One still needs to say quite simply what it seems to be about.

The human experience around which Coleridge centres the poem is surely the depression and the sense of isolation and unworthiness which the Mariner describes in Part IV. The suffering he describes is of a kind which is perhaps not found except in slightly pathological conditions, but which, pathological or not, has been felt by a great many people. He feels isolated to a degree that baffles expression and reduces him to the impotent, repetitive emphasis which becomes doggerel in schoolroom reading:

> *Alone, alone, all, all alone,*
> *Alone on a wide, wide sea!*

At the same time he is not just physically isolated but is socially abandoned, even by those with the greatest obligations:

> *And never a saint took pity on*
> *My soul in agony.*

With this desertion the beauty of the ordinary world has been taken away:

> *The many men so beautiful!*
> *And they all dead did lie . . .*

All that is left, and especially, centrally, oneself, is disgustingly worthless:

> *And a thousand thousand slimy things*
> *Lived on; and so did I.*

With the sense of worthlessness there is also guilt. When he tried to pray,

> *A wicked whisper came, and made*
> *My heart as dry as dust.*

And enveloping the whole experience is the sense of sapped energy, oppressive weariness:

> *For the sky and the sea, and the sea and the sky*
> *Lay like a load on my weary eye,*
> *And the dead were at my feet.*

This, the central experience, comes almost at the middle of the poem. It is the nadir of depression to which the earlier stanzas sink; the rest of the poem describes what is in part recovery and in part aftermath. You need not have been a mariner in a supernatural Pacific in order to have felt this mood. Coleridge knew it well, and *Dejection* and *The Pains of Sleep* deal with closely related experiences.

A usual feature of these states of pathological misery is their apparent causelessness. The depression cannot be rationally explained; the conviction of guilt and worthlessness is out of proportion to any ordinary offence actually committed. In the story of *The Ancient Mariner* Coleridge finds a crime which, in its symbolic implications, is sufficient to merit even his suffering. The Mariner's sin, as Mr. Bewley and others have seen, was that in killing the Albatross he rejected a social offering. Why he did so is left quite unexplained. It was enough for Coleridge that this was a dreadful thing which one might do, and one did it. The Mariner wantonly obliterated something which loved him and which represented in a supernatural way the possibility of affection in the world:

> *The Spirit who bideth by himself*
> *In the land of mist and snow,*
> *He loved the bird that loved the man*
> *Who shot him with his bow.*

This for Coleridge was the most terrible possibility among the sins.

The depth of meaning it held for him is indicated in the curious self-exculpation with which he ends *The Pains of Sleep*. That poem is a fragment of case-history recounting three nights of bad dreams:

> *Fantastic passions! maddening brawl!*
> *And shame and terror over all!*
> *Deeds to be hid which were not hid,*
> *Which all confused I could not know*
> *Whether I suffered, or I did:*
> *For all seem'd guilt, remorse or woe . . .*

Characteristically, he assumed that these sufferings must be a punishment for something or other. Yet by the standards of waking life and reason he feels himself to be innocent. He never explicitly mentions what the supposed offence might be. But in the last two lines, when he protests his innocence, the terms in which he does so reveal implicitly what crime alone could merit such punishment:

> *Such punishments, I said, were due*
> *To natures deepliest stained with sin . . .*
> *But wherefore, wherefore fall on me?*

> *To be beloved is all I need,*
> *And whom I love, I love indeed.*

Why is he innocent of the fatal sin? Because he aims at nothing beyond affection and union with others, gives no allegiance to more individual interests in the outer world which might flaw his complete devotion. It is only in the light of the last two lines that the introductory section of the poem yields its meaning. Explaining that he is not accustomed to saying formal prayers before going to sleep, Coleridge continues:

> *But silently, by slow degrees,*
> *My spirit I to Love compose.*
> *In humble trust mine eyelids close,*
> *With reverential resignation . . .*

And then one realizes that he is protesting against being visited with the horrible dreams *in spite of* cultivating submissive affection and so guarding against the one sin that could merit such punishments.

The Ancient Mariner committed the sin. Yet Coleridge knew that by the ordinary standards of the workaday world his act was not, after all, very terrible. Hence the sarcastic stanzas which show the indifference of the other mariners to the real meaning of the deed. At first,

> *Ah wretch! said they, the bird to slay,*
> *That made the breeze to blow!*

And then,

> *'Twas right, said they, such birds to slay,*
> *That bring the fog and mist.*

And Coleridge's concern for the Mariner's unfortunate companions can hardly be called even perfunctory. It is not by the ordinary standards of social life, for the breach of ordinary social obligations, that Coleridge or the Mariner could be condemned; as in *The Pains of Sleep*, he protests his innocence by those standards. It is an irrational standard, having force only for him, by which he is found guilty. *The Ancient Mariner* allowed him to indicate something of this by means of the supernatural machinery. The small impulsive act which presses a supernatural trigger forms an effective parallel to the hidden impulse which has such devastating meaning for one's irrational, and partly unconscious, private standards. It is a fiction which permits the expression of real experience.

The total pattern of experience in *The Ancient Mariner* includes partial recovery from the worst depression. The offence for which the dejection and isolation were punishment was the wanton rejection of a very simple social union. One way to recovery is suggested in *The Pains of Sleep*. It is a return to a submissive sense of childlike weakness and distress:

> *O'ercome with sufferings strange and wild,*
> *I wept as I had been a child;*
> *And having thus by tears subdued*
> *My anguish to a milder mood* . . .

In *The Ancient Mariner* his sufferings have first to reduce him to a dreadful listlessness and apathy. He contrasts his condition then with the calm activity of the Moon going about her ordinary business in the universe, accompanied by the stars, which, unlike him, still have their right to be welcomed:

> In his loneliness and fixedness he yearneth towards the journeying moon, and the stars that still sojourn, yet still move onward; and everywhere the blue sky belongs to them, and is their appointed rest, and their native country and their own natural homes, which they enter unannounced, as lords that are certainly expected and yet there is silent joy at their arrival.

He has to reach complete listlessness—itself a sort of submission—before there is any chance of recovery. His state at the turning-point is in significant contrast to the desperate activity, the courageous snatching at hope in the direction from which he personally has decided salvation must come, which is suggested earlier by his watch for a sail and his final effort of hope:

> *I bit my arm, I sucked the blood,*
> *And cried, A sail! a sail!*

All this directed effort and expense of spirit is futile in the state of mind which Coleridge describes. Only when his individual striving has sunk to a low ebb does the recovery begin.

This naturally gives the impression, characteristic of such states of depression, that the recovery is fortuitous. It comes unpredictably and seemingly from some trivial accident. This part of the experience Coleridge has paralleled in the supernatural machinery of the tale by means of the dicing between Death and Life-in-Death. To the sufferer there seems no good reason why he shouldn't simply die, since he feels that he has thrown up the sponge. Instead, chance has it that he lives on.

The fact of its being Life-in-Death who wins the Mariner shows how incomplete his recovery is going to be. (This fact also makes it doubtful how far the poem can usefully be viewed as an expression of "The Rebirth Archetype" of Maud Bodkin's analysis.) Nevertheless, some degree of recovery from the nadir of dejection does unpredictably occur. It begins with the momentary rekindling of simple pleasure in the things around him, at the very moment when he has touched bottom in apathy:

> O happy living things! no tongue
> Their beauty might declare . . .

It is the beginning of recovery because what is kindled is a recognition not only of their beauty but also of the worth of their existence and, by implication, of his own. For he had previously associated himself with them—the thousand thousand slimy things —in denying their right to live when the men were dead:

> He despiseth the creatures of the calm. And envieth that they should live and so many lie dead.

The earlier exclamation, in the depths of self-condemnation, "The many men, so beautiful!" is not one of simple pleasures in the things around him. He is still absorbed in his self-contempt and uses his recognition of other men's beauty only as a further lash against himself. Or, to put it differently, when he was in the depths the only beauty he would consent to see was beauty dead and spoilt; the beauty still present in the world he denied.

His returning joy in living things comes, of course, from his changed attitude to himself and his willingness to look differently on the world. Coleridge made the point in *Dejection*:

> *O Lady! we receive but what we give*
> *And in our life alone does nature live . . .*
> *Ah! from the soul itself must issue forth*
> *A light, a glory, a fair luminous cloud*
>   *Enveloping the Earth—*
> *And from the soul itself must there be sent*
> *A sweet and potent voice, of his own birth,*
> *Of all sweet sounds the life and element!*

From this one turns to *The Ancient Mariner* at a later stage in the recovery:

> *Around, around, flew each sweet sound,*
> *Then darted to the Sun;*
> *Slowly the sounds came back again,*
> *Now mixed, now one by one.*

Still later the band of seraphs who

> *stood as signals to the land,*
> *Each one a lovely light*

can be associated with

> *A light, a glory, a fair luminous cloud.*

Coleridge accepts sound and light and colour as the simplest adequate expression of the beauty of the world which ebbed and flowed with his own spirits.

In consistent development of the general theme, the Mariner's recovery leads on to reunion with the very simple and humble kinds of social life. He joins the villagers in the formal expression of atonement with each other, and with the source of love, which he sees in their religious worship. But it would be a mistake to think of this as anything like full recovery. For one thing, he never again belongs to a settled community, but has to pass from land to land. For another thing, there is the periodic "abreaction" and confession that he has to resort to:

> *Since then, at an uncertain hour,*
> *That agony returns:*
> *And till my ghastly tale is told,*
> *This heart within me burns.*

More important than this sign of imperfect recovery is the contrast between the submissive sociability with which he must now content himself and the buoyancy of the voyager as he first set out:

> *The ship was cheered, the harbour cleared,*
> *Merrily did we drop*
> *Below the kirk, below the hill,*
> *Below the lighthouse top.*

Such a voyage (of the sort that fascinated Coleridge in Anson's narratives) entails a self-reliant thrusting-forth into the outer world and repudiates dependence on the comfort of ordinary social ties. But Coleridge's anxieties seem to have shown him this attitude taken beyond all bounds and leading to a self-sufficiency which would wantonly destroy the ties of affection. The Albatross is killed, and then the penalty must be paid in remorse, dejection, and the sense of being a worthless social outcast. Only a partial recovery is possible; once the horrifying potentiality has been glimpsed in human nature, Coleridge dare not imagine a return to self-reliant voyaging. Creeping back defeated into the social convoy, the Mariner is obviously not represented as having advanced through his suffering to a fuller life; and he no more achieves a full rebirth than Coleridge ever could. There is nothing but the crushed admission that he would, after all, have done better to have stayed at home in humble companionship. Even the vigour and excitement of the marriage feast are too daring for him; he needs submissive, trustful prayer to a great Father. And the unfortunate "moral"—"He prayeth best, who loveth best All things both great and small"—has at least this much aptness, that it stands at the opposite extreme to that wilful rebuttal of affection of which Coleridge sought so earnestly to assure himself that he was guiltless:

> *To be beloved is all I need,*
> *And whom I love, I love indeed.*

Viewing the poem from this angle, I see little sign of the confused motive which Mr. Bewley suspected. Coleridge's detached, conscious intentions in writing the poem were no doubt mixed (they certainly included that of defraying the cost of the walking tour on which it was planned). But the achievement, whatever the intention, has unity and coherence. True, the poem is not an allegory. There is no need to think that Coleridge could have paraphrased his theme either before or after writing. In this he may be contrasted with Cowper, also drawing upon Anson, in *The Castaway*. All we need suppose is that the fiction Coleridge produced made a special appeal to him and could be handled with special effectiveness because its theme and incidents allowed highly significant, though partly unconscious concerns to find expression. This is not to say that he was merely manipulating symbols. The concrete details of the fiction were not *less* but *more* vividly realized because they were charged with something else besides their manifest content.

(1941)

Dickens

DICKENS, DRAMA, AND TRADITION, by R. C. Churchill

I

As many different points of view have been taken of the genius of the author of *Martin Chuzzlewit* as Mr. Pecksniff required from his pupils in making elevations of Salisbury Cathedral. The only procedure, at this date, for anyone wishing to add to the lengthy list of Dickensian criticism is to select those questions upon which something, perhaps, remains to be said and deal with each separately. But the very confusion which would attend any attempt to view Dickens's labours as a whole has an attraction, and a certain value, provided it be put forward merely as an introduction to detailed study of individual points.

For the confusion reigns not only among his critics, but among his writings. It is not only that, almost as with Shakespeare, the critics have attributed to their author their own opinions, and from his "extremely varied published works" have presented to us a typical Victorian, a typical anti-Victorian, a Marxist, a Royalist, and so on. The conclusion to be drawn here is clear enough: that Dickens should be considered as a novelist, first to last, and judged by the standards of his art.

But this verdict introduces the problem rather than settles it. The confused idea of Dickens one would carry away after reading the opinions of (to name a few) Lewes, Taine, Gissing, Chesterton, Mr. Santayana, Mr. O'Faoláin, Mr. Jackson, Mr. Orwell, this confusion is nothing beside the heterogeneous mass of good, bad, and indifferent writing which the average Dickens novel itself presents.

Take, for instance, the novel we mentioned to begin with. If *Martin Chuzzlewit* be not universally thought Dickens's finest work (Chesterton preferred *Bleak House*, and Mr. Kingsmill, if I remember rightly, plumped for *Pickwick*), yet it has never been denied a place in the front rank. Gissing said that in it "every quality of Dickens is seen at its best," and that, apparently, was Dickens's own opinion when he began to write—he had "never had so much confidence in his powers." Yet we could hardly find a better example than *Chuzzlewit* for our contention. There can be few pieces of literature where the good and the bad jostle each other so closely. That the good predominates overwhelmingly is, of course, true, and an "expurgated" edition of the novel (inspired by motives rather different from Thomas Bowdler's) would not make it many pages shorter. But we have to admit that Dickens, by all evidence, thought it everywhere good; he "laughed and cried as he wrote." Though we still laugh, we find it difficult to share the tears.

The good is very good indeed. Whether Pecksniff be a "human being" or only the embodiment of a vice, we are confronted with the perfection of this presentation of hypocrisy. It is brilliant at a distance, from one's casual recollection, but the idea of the writer's comic genius becomes a certainty when we look at the detail, the actual language, with which this figure is given to us. One of the strangest paradoxes in the artistry of Dickens is that this most verbose of novelists, who gloried in his long-windedness and never used one word where ten would do, was also a master of the pithy, illuminating phrase. "With a phrase," says Eliot, "he can make a character as real as flesh and blood—'What a Life Young Bailey's was!'" He can also give us a couple of lines that say as much about the ruling vice of Mr. Pecksniff as the rest of the hypocrite's adventures put together. I am not thinking of the often-admired exhortation to his daughter Charity ("When I take my chamber candlestick to-night, remind me to be more than usually particular in praying for Mr. Anthony Chuzzlewit, who has done me an injustice"), but of his conversation with Mrs. Lupin at the Blue Dragon, when he pulls off his gloves to warm his hands before the fire—warming them, says Dickens, *"as benevolently as if they were somebody else's, not his,"* and his back "as if it were a widow's back, or an orphan's back, or an enemy's back, or a back that any less excellent man would have suffered to be cold."

Throughout, it is the detail which is so masterly. The ideas we hold in recollection of Mrs. Gamp, Young Bailey, Mr. Jefferson Brick, Mrs. Todgers, are clearly enough defined, but we have to turn to the actual text, the language in which these characters are presented to us and with which they speak, to get the proper value of their creation. It is always the *language* of Dickens that is so important; his genius was essentially dramatic. We may remember that Mrs. Gamp was a fat old woman who liked the bottle to be left on the mantelpiece so that she might put her lips to it when she was "so dispoged," but we are less likely to retain in our memory, as part of the effect she has had upon us, the epitaph (say) on her late husband—"the wooden leg gone likeways home to its account, which in its constancy of walking into wine-vaults, and never coming out again till fetched by force, was quite as weak as flesh, if not weaker." We may remember Mrs. Todgers well enough as a person, while forgetting that, when she embraced the Miss Pecksniffs, there was "affection beaming in one eye and calculation shining out of the other."

The deliberate and necessary distortion of language in which these characters move and speak fits their deliberately exaggerated forms; they are all several sizes larger than life, but the distortion is to scale. The popular idea of Dickens's characters, that they are, in a sense, different from George Eliot's, so *real,* so closely drawn from life, is (as Sean O'Faoláin and others have pointed out) the opposite of the truth. Micawber may have been based on Dickens's father, but the difference between them is the difference between Sairey Gamp and any garrulous old woman in one's own experience, between Young Bailey ("an abstract of all the stable-knowledge of time") and the precocious youngster Dickens relates meeting in America, between the Flora of *Little Dorrit* and the woman Dickens had once wished to marry. Between, if you like, Falstaff and Sir John Oldcastle.

As for the bad writing in *Chuzzlewit,* the vulgar pathetic touches are there, of course, as in almost everything he wrote, and may here perhaps be summed up in the phrase "Blessings on thy simple heart, Tom Pinch!" The laboured archness of the courtship between Ruth Pinch and John Westlock ("Oh, foolish, panting, timid little heart, why did she feign to be unconscious of his coming?")—yet a level I think possibly he might not have descended to so often had not a certain number of sheets to have been delivered regularly to the printer. But the apology is a lame one, and we have to admit the absolute lack of any critical discrimination in a writer who could produce such things. A better apology, as I hope to show, can be found in the vulgarity of the age that accepted them. For the moment the point to be made is simply the extraordinary difference in intelligence between the mind which produced the best parts of Gamp and Pecksniff and the American interlude, and the mind which produced the worst parts of Thomas Pinch, the mind being the same man's, writing the same book.

The difference cannot be explained simply by saying that the comic parts of *Chuzzlewit* are good and the "serious" or "sentimental" parts bad, because that is an over-simplifying of the case.

Pecksniff is a comic character, certainly, but Hypocrisy is not a comic thing; it would be stupidly sophisticated of us to deny that Dickens's avowed object in writing the novel was achieved. "The notion of taking Pecksniff for a type of character," Forster tells us, "was really the origin of the book, the design being to show, more or less by every person introduced, the number and variety of humours and vices that have their root in selfishness." With the accumulation of Pecksniff, the Miss Pecksniffs, Anthony and Jonas Chuzzlewit, old and young Martin, the object may be said to have been attained, and the unearthly goodness of Tom Pinch and Mark Tapley may presumably be explained by the need for a contrast, these two personifying unselfishness as clearly as the rest its opposite. The *unreality* of all the characters does not matter. What is significant is that whereas the distorted form given to comic characters like Pecksniff and Mrs. Gamp and Young Bailey becomes an artistic virtue, becomes great comedy, the distorted form given to the serious characters appears to act the other way, so that wicked people like Jonas are merely melodramatic and good people like the Pinches just vessels for sentimentality.

Why this should be so is not an easy question to answer, if indeed it is possible to answer it satisfactorily at all. Why should the comic distortion succeed and the serious distortion fail? A possible explanation lies in the connexion of Dickens with the stage. I think that possibly the serious characters should not be there at all, that the vices of Jonas should have been laughed at equally with Pecksniff's, that the whole thing should have been a Comedy of Humours like the play of Ben Jonson's Dickens admired so much. But for the moment we are concerned with this confusion of styles in *Chuzzlewit,* this discrepancy in taste. The novel is, of course, simply an exceptionally good example of what is to be found in nearly all Dickens's work. There is a high comic seriousness in the early pages of *Oliver Twist* and a low "serious" sentimentality later on. *Bleak House,* praised by Chesterton and undoubtedly one of Dickens's best, gives us the excellent comedy of Chadband and Guppy and the Snagsbys, the skilful melodrama of Chesney Wold, the satire on Chancery, the impressive delineation of London; but there is also the sillier side of the Dedlock story and the pathetic figure of the consumptive crossing-sweeper, who might have been presented with success had not so many tears fallen on the writer's manuscript ("Jo is it thou?"). The satire on the *nouveau riche* in *Our Mutual Friend* is offset by the incredible figures of Lizzie Hexham and

Eugene Wrayburn. The comic characters of *Dombey,* again, are only scarce plums in the stodgy suet of the sentimental theme.

One might cite nearly all the novels to the same purpose. Those least marred by sentimentality and melodrama are, I suppose, *Pickwick, Barnaby Rudge, Hard Times, Little Dorrit, Great Expectations;* but that does not necessarily mean they are the best. The humour of *Pickwick* is of an entirely different kind from that of *Chuzzlewit* and (in spite of the famous Trial Scene) the kind is lower; it is less subtle, in many places almost good enough for *Punch,* and one monologue by Mrs. Gamp is worth a whole chapter of Wellerisms. The virtue of *Pickwick* is that it maintains a level, is consistent, its farce only slightly spoilt by sentimentality; Mr. Pickwick is a "lovable" character, but Dickens does not shed blessings on his simple heart, as on Tom Pinch's; the book seems in comparatively good taste against the avalanche of sentiment that immediately followed it: *Oliver Twist, Nicholas Nickleby, The Old Curiosity Shop.*

If those novels of Dickens where his taste for sentiment and melodrama is least indulged were also those where his comic genius is at its height, we should have no difficulty in saying which are his finest works. But Mrs. Gamp adorns *Chuzzlewit,* Micawber rubs shoulders with Steerforth and Little Em'ly, Oliver leaves the workhouse not for the world but for the nineteenth-century stage-version of it. Therefore Dickens has no masterpiece (as George Eliot her *Middlemarch*), no sustained piece of writing where his virtues are unaccompanied by his faults. He is the one great novelist whom, even at his best, it is necessary occasionally to skip. But, though he probably wrote nothing that as a whole can compare with *Joseph Andrews* or *Tom Jones,* yet there are passages in *Oliver Twist,* in Martin Chuzzlewit, in *Little Dorrit,* which make even the fine comic genius of Fielding appear slight.

II

Dickens's interest in the theatre, and the influence of the theatre upon himself and his writings, have formed an important part of every biography, from John Forster's to Mr. Kingsmill's. The childhood recitations, the acting and stage-managing in amateur productions after he had become famous as novelist, the public readings of his works which were really a kind of acting (he added "stage-directions" to the copies he read from)—these are the most obvious points. But also connected with the question are his love of applause, his self-dramatization (shown in the persistency with which he kept up the legend of the Inimitable Boz, in the un-English flamboyancy of his dress, even in the famous flourish under his signature), and the effect of the theatre upon his actual writing. It is this last point we wish to discuss here.

He lived, of course, at a time when the drama in England had sunk to its lowest level. Edmund Kean, "the last of the great actors," died in 1833, and the very fact that this date seems important is significant, for it is not usually by its actors that one judges a period's drama. But, after Sheridan, who died in 1816, there is no distinguished name in playwriting till the close of the century, when Dickens had given his final reading of the Murder of Nancy and left unexplained the mystery of Edwin Drood. It was a period of stagnation in the drama, which had been declining gradually since the middle of the previous century, perhaps ever since Fielding, "driven out of the trade of Aristophanes" (as Shaw puts it) "took to that of Cervantes." Drury Lane, after Kean, gave itself over to grand spectacles, with real water on the stage, etc. The remnants of tragedy descended into melodrama, and the dregs of comedy dwindled into farce. There was no important dramatist on the Continent (I take it that Goethe's influence did not affect the stage) to give an impetus to the English theatre as Molière had done in the seventeenth century and Ibsen was to do later on—even had the notorious insularity of the Victorian character, deplored by Matthew Arnold, been susceptible to such an influence. So that melodrama, becoming more and more crude and appealing to less and less intelligent audiences, shared the stage with farce and with burlesque. The popularity of burlesque is not surprising in a period that saw the birth of *Punch,* and it would appear to have lasted many years, for we find that even Samuel Butler, a novelist supposedly out of tune with his time, makes the regenerate Ernest Pontifex "laugh heartily" at a skit on *Macbeth* and cry, "What rot Shakespeare is, after this!"

If we accept the proposition that the dramatic genius which might have gone into playwriting, had the theatre been in a more healthy state, spent itself instead, like Fielding's, on the novel, then we need to know why, on the face of it, Dickens would appear likely to have been so *bad* a dramatist. Not, of course, by the evidence of his amateur dramatic efforts, in which he was excelled by his friend Wilkie Collins, nor by the stage versions of his novels presented later on by Beerbohm Tree and others, but by the evidence of the novels themselves. How unlikely it seems, on the face of it, that the creator of Little Nell, Florence Dombey, Lizzie Hexham, Sydney Carton, to name a few of his less credible figures, would have been able to produce any drama that was not of the most melodramatic sort. And this is not to ignore Mr. Eliot's reminder that "you cannot define Drama and Melodrama so that they shall be reciprocally exclusive; great drama has something melodramatic in it, and the best melodrama partakes of the greatness of drama." For it would not, apparently, have been the "best melodrama."

But might it not have been the "best comedy"? Might not the creator of Mrs. Gamp, Pecksniff, Flora Finching, Jefferson Brick, Sapsea, Chadband, Busfuz, Micawber, have produced comedy nearer in kind to *The Alchemist* than to the usual Victorian farce? This seems as likely as the contention that he could not, by any evidence, have produced a serious play that would not have been grossly sentimental and melodramatic. So that we come back to the conundrum propounded by *Chuzzlewit*—why are the comic parts so good and the serious parts so bad? It is not enough, obviously, to say that he had a genius for comic writing, and that, with a flourishing theatre, this genius would probably have taken a dramatic instead of a prose fictional form. The question goes deeper: why should a writer so concerned with Virtue, Morality, Justice, etc., so seldom succeed in being serious; or, to put it more fairly, succeed usually on such a low level?

I believe we were not so far from a possible explanation when we mentioned just now the name of Fielding. Robert Walpole drove Fielding from the theatre by the institution of the censorship. The novels he subsequently wrote owed, as the title-page of *Joseph Andrews* too generously acknowledged, a large debt to Cervantes. But they must also have been influenced by his own dramatic experience; indeed, the influence of the stage upon his novels has even been urged as a point of criticism against them. So that we have a link, if a very slight one, to connect the novels of Fielding with the course of English stage comedy, from his own plays back (via Congreve, Wycherley, Dryden, and Massinger) to those of Ben Jonson. It is not, obviously, a point to be stressed; it is sufficient to note that a connexion of some sort must have existed. That the connexion extends to Dickens, we know, of course, from his early reading of Fielding mentioned in *Copperfield* and in Forster's *Life,* quite apart from the stylistic evidence of the novels.

So that the writer of comedy, actually in fiction but conceivably in drama, is connected, however slightly, with the masters of the art. There is no such connexion discoverable on the "serious side." What connects the Elizabethan-Jacobean tragedy with the Victorian melodrama is merely the long and tedious degeneration between the two, represented (at various stations down the line) by Shirley, Otway, Lee, Addison, Lillo, Knowles, etc. The dissociation, surely, is almost complete, even though the "best melodrama" may bear some slight resemblance to *Macbeth*. For his comedy, Dickens had the influence of Sterne, Smollett, Fielding, and Defoe, and through Fielding (however slender the connexion) the influence of the English stage right back to Ben Jonson and Shakespeare. For his "tragedy" he had the *William Tell* of Sheridan Knowles, the death of Le Fever in *Tristram Shandy*, and an appreciation of Shakespeare spoilt by the degenerate opinion of the times (*Punch*, burlesque, "the celebrated dramatic poet buried at Stratford," etc.)—spoilt also by his own "knowingness" about the stage.

He was a writer very much influenced by his surroundings, by the taste and sentiment of his time; this would be expected of one whose most obvious distinction was, as Santayana puts it, " a vast sympathetic participation in the daily life of mankind," who had the largest and most enthusiastic public of any writer before or (saving best-sellers) since. He could be critical of his time and its manner when the question was one of social reform; he wrote *Oliver Twist* and *Hard Times*. He could oppose the money-grabbing and the pretentiousness that were the darker side of "our commercial greatness"; he wrote *Little Dorrit* and *Our Mutual Friend*. He was not patient of the law's delay; he wrote *Bleak House*. But the things that did not arouse either his righteous indignation or his sense of the ridiculous slipped through his guard unobserved. The sentimentality and vulgarity of the age he accepted with open arms; he was an important part, himself, of that sentimentality and vulgarity; his love of the theatre became a liability as well as an asset when it took over *en masse* the conventions of its debased melodrama.

It remains to be seen wherein lie the assets and the liabilities. As *Chuzzlewit* reminded us, it is the language of Dickens which is always so significant, and so it is the actual speech of the characters, rather than any question of dramatic "improbabilities" or "coincidence" in the plot, that matters most when we wish to consider the influence, good or bad, of the stage.

Perhaps it is as well to get the bad over at once. When Ralph

Nickleby dies, crying to the church bell: "Lie on, with your iron tongue! Ring merrily for births that make expectants writhe, and marriages that are made in hell, and toll ruefully for the dead whose shoes are worn already! Call men to prayers who are goodly because not found out, and ring chimes for the coming-in of every year that brings this cursed world nearer to an end. No bell or book for me! Throw me on a dunghill, and let me rot there, to infect the air!"—when the villain of *Nickleby* dies like this, we are certainly (to borrow the phraseology of *Elizabethan Essays*) "in the presence of a vicious rhetoric" and a character "seeing himself in a dramatic light," and we are bound to be reminded of the dying speeches of some Elizabethan villains ("Tongue, curse thy fill, and die!"); but any notion that this, like Marlowe's *Jew*, is "savage comedy" is dispelled by a recollection of the rest of the book. If the whole novel were on the comic scale, then undoubtedly this would fit in; but what of the scene where Nicholas defends Smike from the cane of Squeers, a scene which is certainly meant to be taken seriously?—"Touch him at your peril! I will not stand by and see it done. My blood is up, and I have the strength of ten such men as you. Look to yourself, for by heaven I will not spare you if you drive me on!" Or his triumphant cry at the end: "You are caught, villains, in your own toils!"; or Ralph Nickleby's stagy hiss: "My curse, my bitter, deadly curse, upon you, boy!" This, surely, is about the crudest melodrama we get anywhere in Dickens. The unmasking of Pecksniff ("Hear me, rascal!") is comparatively credible, and by the time we get to *Copperfield* it is significant that the exposure of the villain is performed by a *comic* character, Micawber: "You Heep of infamy!"

We are forced, then, to the reluctant conclusion that, in the death of Ralph Nickleby, Dickens scarcely knew what he was doing. To bring the melodrama so near to the "Elizabethan comic," to the *Jew of Malta* and *Volpone,* required talent of an exceptional kind, but we get the justice of Eliot's general comment on Dickens, "*decadent* genius," when we admit that the success of this instance was not only out of keeping with the tone of the whole novel, but a throw-back to a kind of writing very much out of keeping with the tone of the time; "savage comedy" and saccharine sentiment made strange bedfellows, and the juxtaposition of the two is but another example of that confusion in Dickens's work we mentioned to begin with.

The normal melodrama of Dickens, that which is neither so

seriously comic as the death of Ralph Nickleby nor so comically serious as Nicholas defending Smike, can only be described as rather dull. At its best (*e.g.*, the death of Steerforth, the arrest of Jonas, the escape of Sikes) it is thrilling or affecting enough if we shut off the part of our mind that might criticize its quality; that is, it is skilful, but on a low level, whereas the comedy, at its best, is good by any standard. As for the speech of the serious characters, it is enough to remind ourselves of Lizzie Hexham, the heroine of *Our Mutual Friend*, who, as A. W. Ward put it, "has to discard the colour of her surroundings and talk the conventional dialect as well as express the conventional sentiments of the heroic world." This applies to nearly all the heroes and heroines of the novels, though the degree of unreality varies a good deal. (We can, I presume, take it for granted that, with his serious characters, Dickens was aiming at reality, and not using their heroic posturings for comic purposes.) Nothing was ever done again by Dickens as crude as Nickleby, but one cannot say that the serious characters became more credible as he went on, for Lizzie Hexham, one of the worst examples of the misplaced heroic, occurred in the last novel he completed. It is not quite with Dickens, as Mr. Frank Chapman pointed out with regard to Hardy,* that one could not say by their style which novels were written first; it is more a question of Dickens's having outgrown some of his cruder notions but not all of them, and equally of having placed in the crudest context some of his finest work.

Examples of the latter bring us at once to those aspects of his comic writing where the influence of the theatre, and of the theatre coupled with the eighteenth-century novelists, was an influence for good. For excellencies embedded in a melodramatic whole, we need look no further than *Oliver Twist*, the second novel he wrote. The workhouse section stands quite apart, in merit, from the rest, but even at the end of the novel there is at least one bright spot, when Mr. Bumble reappears to answer the charge of stealing the trinkets. "The law supposes," says Mr. Brownlow, "that your wife acts under your direction." "If the law supposes that," replies Bumble, "the law is a ass, a idiot. If that's the eye of the law, the law is a bachelor; and worst I wish the law is that his eye may be opened by experience—by experience."

We can agree with Mr. George Santayana that this kind of humour is not far from that of Aristophanes or Shakespeare. What

---
* See "Hardy the Novelist," *Scrutiny*, Vol. III, No. 1.

concerns us here is that such bright spots in Dickens nearly always occur when a comic character is *holding forth,* occupying the stage, so to speak, addressing the reader/audience as much as, if not more than, the other characters in the book. It is this extra-literary life of his characters which has earned Dickens his greatest applause and his heartiest abuse. On the one hand, we have the popular idea of his characters, that they are as real as life, as our own friends, a misconception based on this very fact, that the characters do protrude somehow beyond the novel; on the other hand, the criticisms of G. H. Lewes, Taine, and the rest complain of the *undevelopment* of the characters psychologically, Micawber "always presenting himself in the same situation, moved with the same springs," etc., and Mrs. Gamp "talking incessantly of Mrs. Harris." But both the uncritical delight and the hypercritical contempt seem indiscriminate when we relate this tendency to its probable source, the stage. G. H. Lewes, many of whose criticisms were very sound, sneered at Dickens for having once remarked that "every word said by his characters was distinctly *heard* by him." If we bear in mind the novelist's obsession with the theatre, the remark seems not so much the "hallucination" suggested by Lewes as a quite accurate description of Dickens's method of composition. Whether such a method of writing novels is the best, or is even a permissible one by finer standards, is really beside the point for the moment. What matters is that this fundamentally dramatic way of writing was responsible for nearly all that is best in his comic creation. It was the gift of the dramatist rather than the novelist which enabled Dickens to express the ramblings of a Mrs. Gamp and a Flora Finching, or the rhetoric of a Jefferson Brick and a General Choke, with enough exaggeration to astound. When Mrs. Gamp comes *"sidling and bridling* into the room," when she remarks that "rich folks may ride on camels but they won't find it easy to get through a needle's eye," when she remembers "the wooden leg gone likeways home to its account" and says after the quarrel with Betsy Prig that "the words she spoke of Mrs. Harris lambs could not forgive, no, nor worms forget"; when Flora Finching, describing her married life to Little Dorrit, says "ere we had yet fully detected the housemaid in selling the feathers out of the spare bed *Gout flying upward* soared with Mr. F. to another sphere"; when the Young Columbian defies the British Lion ("Bring forth that Lion! Alone, I dare him! I taunt that Lion! I tell that Lion, that Freedom's hand once twisted in his mane, he rolls a corse before me . . .")—when we come across such things as these, it is not surprising, if we are reminded as much of Mrs. Quickly and Pistol and the characters of *The Alchemist* as of Fielding or Sterne or Smollett. Here the talent for the theatre has succeeded in adorning the medium of the novel; here the tradition of English comic writing is taken up by another master; and there is now no question of "decadent genius," because the line of comedy is unbroken. What is remarkable, of course, is that Dickens should have been able to carry on this tradition while being also so much in tune with his own age; that he should, in one and the same novel (such as *Chuzzlewit*), give us this supreme type of comedy, with its almost Shakespearean "suggestiveness," side by side with the debased and sentimental forms popular in his day; and that he should not only share these more vulgar kinds of wit, but even be regarded as the chief exponent of them.

III

How far the vulgarity, the bad taste, to be found in Dickens's writing can be regarded as his own, and how far it is the literary manner of the age, is a question worth considering. The more we admire his genuine achievements (the comic we have glanced at and the serious concern us later on), the more, of course, we resent the artistic blots upon his work. There is nothing to be gained by denying their existence, though it is too often assumed that the bad writing is all equally contemptible, whereas the gradations between good and bad are many and sometimes the border-line between failure and success drawn so fine that it is difficult to come to any conclusion. To do Dickens common justice, it is necessary, after convicting him of vulgar tastes, to look at the vulgarity of the age he wrote in. We say "wrote in" rather than "lived in" because it is literary vulgarity we are chiefly concerned with, the bad literary taste of the time.

A comparison of Eliot's between a poem by Lord Herbert of Cherbury and one by Tennyson suggests itself as an opening. The difference between them, says Eliot, "is not a simple difference of degree between poets. It is something which had happened to the mind of England between the time of Donne or Lord Herbert of Cherbury and the time of Tennyson and Browning." We can apply this, by paraphrase, to Dickens. Contrasting him, not at his best but as his normal level, with (say) Fielding, we might say that the difference was not one of degree between novelists but of "something which had happened to the mind of England" between the time of Johnson, Fielding, and Gibbon and the time of Carlyle, Dickens, Thackeray, and Macaulay.

A history of the Sentimental in English literature would be a useful study; lacking it, we must be content here with a few random indications. If we think of the Man of Feeling of the late eighteenth century, of the worst parts of *Tristram Shandy* and the *Sentimental Journey*, of the decline in the theatre already noted, of the major part of Scott, of the worst but most popular side of Byron; if we couple all this with a hearty, manly, complacent kind of humour, the pedigree of which it would be difficult to trace; with the whimsicality of Charles Lamb; and with that degeneration of eighteenth-century English which would speak of "drawing the finny tribe from their native element" * and which popular nineteenth-century journalism first parodied and then took over seriously; if we bear this background in mind and add to it the spirit of cheap burlesque upon the stage and in periodicals like *Punch,* the gradual pressure upon literature of the ideals of a new commercial class, the strong Puritan reaction against the rakishness of the Regency, the start of the public-school ideal of a Gentleman (no longer the Philosopher of Addison, but the Sportsman of an Eton that ragged "mad Shelley"); above all, the swiftly increasing reading public; bearing this background in mind, it is surely not surprising that Dickens, coming to literature "self-made," almost the infant prodigy, the inimitable Boz, abnormally susceptible to his environment and abnormally desirous of applause, it is surely not surprising that he should become (at his worst, at any rate) the "half-educated writer for a half-educated public" and reveal "more genius than taste." The surprise should be reserved for the many occasions on which he did *not* conform to the taste of the time. "I like and admire it extremely," wrote Lord Jeffrey to Dickens of *The Battle of Life;* and of *The Chimes,* "The good and the brave are with you, and the truth also." And this is the voice—the Victorian voice—of one of the great pundits of the Great Review!

The finer elements in nineteenth-century literature (to conclude these generalizations) gave way, then, to the grosser. Tennyson and Browning reigned supreme in poetry, farce and melodrama and burlesque held the stage. As far as the general public was concerned, the novel meant Dickens, but we know that a more discriminate section took their Dickens with a pinch of salt; we have already quoted G. H. Lewes, and it cannot be denied that there was a group

---
* *The Modern Miniature,* an anonymous novel, 1790.

of writers hostile to his reputation. But I don't think it is possible to draw a definite line between novelists like Dickens and Wilkie Collins, on the one hand, and Thackeray, Trollope, and George Eliot, on the other. For one thing, we know that Dickens praised George Eliot and that Thackeray in his lectures praised Dickens. For another, when Thackeray started the *Cornhill,* its contributors included Trollope, G. H. Lewes, George Eliot, *and* Wilkie Collins, and might conceivably have included Dickens could we imagine Dickens writing for any other editor but himself.

But what of the gulf that separates Dickens from Jane Austen, for that is a definite division? Here, surely, we should be content with stating that the gulf exists. For, however fine a standard of artistic integrity we grant Jane Austen (and Mrs. Leavis's articles in *Scrutiny* give the standard a validity we had previously only vaguely acknowledged), and however obvious it is that such a standard Dickens certainly lacked, we should no more wish to condemn the latter by it than by the standard of Flaubert we should wish to condemn George Sand. Dickens was essentially a *public* writer, it was part of his theatrical instinct that he had to feel the sympathy of every man with him, and we should never forget the effect on a man of this temperament his immediate and unparalleled success must have had. He was a different kind of writer intrinsically from Jane Austen or Emily Brontë or the George Eliot of *Middlemarch,* and his incredible popularity simply widened the gulf. Perhaps one would not wish to claim as high a place in English literature for Dickens as for these three novelists, because any apology for his submission to the vulgarity of the age can only extenuate the offence, cannot condone it wholly. But one would have to add that some of Dickens's achievements (particularly in comedy) were not only beyond these writers' grasp but owed little to the taste of the time.

The point is one worth making. We began by saying that those faults in his writing which gratify his detractors' malice and shake his admirers' constancy should not be considered in isolation but against the literary background of the time. His position as a *public* writer makes this comparison essential; and, just as we need to look beneath the mechanical obscenity of Restoration drama for the occasional flash of wit, so out of the mass of this "period" and popular Dickens we must, for a proper appreciation, quarry the enduring parts. "Period" need not, in this connexion, necessarily imply a sneer; the very worst of Dickens is often merely an *exaggera-*

tion of a prevailing mode of thought, a prevailing manner of expression. One of his most obvious characteristics was this love of exaggeration, of hyperbole, and, coupling it with his leaning towards a decadent stage, it is not surprising that the bad taste and the vulgarity which make themselves felt in nine-tenths of the literature of the time should in *his* writings positively shout for recognition. The sickly sentiment of *Dombey* and *The Old Curiosity Shop* is merely an exaggeration of an increasingly popular mode, the logical (if vulgar) development of the Man of Feeling; the tender whimsicality that produced such figures as the Marchioness, the Doll's Dressmaker, Maggie in *Little Dorrit,* Tiny Tim, counts parts of *Shandy* as well as Lamb among its ancestors; and the more sentimental side of Dickens's social criticism, such as the death of Jo in *Bleak House* ("Dead, your Majesty. Dead, my lords and gentlemen . . . And dying thus around us every day."), goes along with the pathetic-indignant ballads of Thomas Hood ("One more unfortunate, weary of breath . . ."—"A shroud as well as a shirt . . ."). As for the hearty, back-slapping, "manly" tone that occasionally disfigures his pages, we need only remark that he shares the disfigurement with Scott, Landor, Hawthorne, Thackeray, Reade, and Browning. While the very worst piece of decadent Regency journalese that might be chosen from Dickens's sometimes appalling style would seem comparatively well written beside many pages of Carlyle's *French Revolution.*

To make up one's mind in regard to the best and the worst of Dickens is not very difficult; it is where he hovers on the brink of success that one hesitates to cast judgement. Jo in *Bleak House* might have "come off" had not Dickens gone so headlong after the pathetic effect; but that is a case which misses success by several pocket-handkerchiefs; what are we to say of the heroine of *Little Dorrit,* where the pathos is held so skilfully in check? Or of characters like Esther Summerson, who are only a shade too good to be true?

And the many occasions when the sentimental shakes hands with reality; when the pathetic merges into the satiric? It is easy to sneer at this confusion in Dickens, more difficult to analyse the effect it has on one. I can never come to a decision about the funeral of Anthony Chuzzlewit. There are so many small points, satiric or pathetic or both at once, that add to the impression of the whole: the satisfaction of the undertaker Mould at the avaricious but conscience-stricken Jonas's having ordered a procession regardless of expense; his professional delight giving way to his professional mourning for the deceased ("Quickly becoming depressed again, he sighed; looked into the crown of his hat, as if for comfort; put it on without finding any; and slowly departed"); the delight of Mrs. Gamp and the Mutes at the refreshments provided; the bandying of courtesies between Pecksniff and the Doctor; the one sincere mourner, Chuffey, being reproved by the rest for his indecent distress at the grave-side; the gradual composure of Jonas once the body has been buried; the whole of this accumulation of hypocrisy leading to the final paragraphs of the chapter, where "Mrs. Gamp went home to the bird-fancier's and was knocked up again that night for a birth of twins . . ." etc., and where, in the graveyard, "the night was dark and wet; the rain fell silently among the stagnant weeds and nettles. One new mound was there which had not been there last night. Time, burrowing like a mole below the ground, had marked his track by throwing up another heap of earth. And that was all."

If this chapter of *Chuzzlewit* be a failure, through striving too obviously after its effects, then it is a failure very near to success. The same border-line of achievement I seem to find in such things as the satire on Chancery in *Bleak House,* the return of the convict Magwitch in *Great Expectations,* the farewell to the Marshalsea in *Little Dorrit.* His love of exaggeration, his habit of over-emphasis, his desire to enforce a point already driven home, told heavily against Dickens's natural talent as a master of expression. But sometimes (and, strangely enough, where his passion for social justice was most strongly roused) he could write with remarkable restraint.

IV

"Figuratively speaking, I travel for the house of Human Interest brothers, and have rather a large connection in the fancy goods way." This celebrated epigram from the introduction to *The Uncommercial Traveller* indicates, if in a rather "whimsical" and self-satisfied manner, the nature of one side of Dickens's "interest in social reform." The inverted commas of the latter phrase suggest, perhaps, the distinction we wish to make between this "reporting" of social abuses and that very serious (even where sometimes apparently "comic") criticism of society which bears not merely the contemporary, particular reference, but the universal.

For the "interest in social reform" proper is matter for the historian rather than the literary critic, and can be appreciated by standards that have nothing to do with literature. It is as well to make this distinction, even if equally necessary to grant that it cannot be absolute. The *Uncommercial Traveller* and *American Notes* give us the reporting pure and simple, the candid survey of public institutions here and in the States, the writer's praise or censure resting securely on the facts recorded. Even where, as in the case of Negro slavery, Dickens's indignation lets loose a torrent of scornful words, the tirade is followed by a cool transcription of some of the slave-advertisements of the time: "Ran away, a negro woman and two children. A few days before she went off, I burned her with a hot iron on the left side of her face. I tried to make the letter M."—"Ran away, a negro named Arthur. Has a considerable scar across his breast and each arm, made by a knife; loves to talk much of the goodness of God."—"Ran away, a negro named WASHINGTON . . ." etc.

On the other hand, *Oliver Twist, Martin Chuzzlewit, Bleak House, Little Dorrit,* give us a Dickens whose criticism of society is part and parcel of his skill and virtue as a novelist. Between the two kinds, of perhaps almost equal interest to the historian and to the literary critic, lies that impressive production, *Hard Times.*

The distinction, we said, cannot be absolute. Someone said of Shakespeare that his finest poetry occurs in his most dramatic moments, and we shall find with Dickens that he is at his very best as a "social critic" when he is displaying his greatest talent as a novelist. *Oliver Twist* takes the same precedence over *The Uncommercial Traveller* and *American Notes* as Fielding's *Joseph Andrews* must over his *Proposal for the Poor.*

Oliver Twist is not one of the novels of Dickens that have worn particularly well. Like Keats's *Nightingale,* it has "suffered in the simplifying memory." It has about it the stigma of such low connexions as Beerbohm Tree's stage version, where it was served up as a typical Victorian melodrama, on the same level as *East Lynne.* But to classify it as such is to forget the way in which the story opens.

In his introduction to the *Everyman* edition, G. K. Chesterton described the early chapters of *Oliver* as "curious and important," and he was thinking chiefly of their contrast, in the matter of social criticism, with the "idealistic outbursts of the Great Reformers." But the descriptions of the reformed workhouse have a literary importance as well. "The Board established the rule," says Dickens, "that all poor people should have the alternative of being starved by a gradual process in the house or by a quick one out of it . . ." They also "undertook to divorce poor married people, in consequence of the great cost of a suit in Doctors' Common, and instead of compelling a man to support his family, as they had theretofore done, took his family away from him and made him a bachelor. There is no saying how many applicants for relief, under these last two heads, might have started up in all classes of society, but the board were long-headed men, and had provided for this difficulty. The relief was inseparable from the workhouse and the gruel, and that frightened people."

If we wish to appreciate this from the point of view of social criticism alone, we can turn up the historical parallel in Mr. and Mrs. Hammond's book *The Age of the Chartists,* where the system is discussed in remarkably similar terms: "They kept the mixed workhouse, but they classified the inmates, forbidding any communication between the different classes. In this way, husbands and wives, parents and children, were kept rigorously apart . . ."

But, from the point of view of Dickens as a novelist, what is the importance of the *Oliver* passage? Nothing, to begin with, could be less sentimental. The irony is refreshingly cool. The first sentence, indeed—"they established the rule that all poor people should have the alternative of being starved by a gradual process in the house or by a quick one out of it"—might almost have been written by Swift, certainly by Fielding. But the apparent detachment goes along with something very different. It was the particular genius of Dickens that he could always put his finger on the social evil which hurt the suffered the most. He was always "seeing people," thinking in terms of flesh and blood rather than in ideas or institutions, and such a bent of mind, it will be agreed, is essentially the artist's. He saw the Workhouse Board not as an institution, but as so many individuals anxious to assert their authority at someone's else's expense, as so many people given by the accident of fortune power over the lives and conduct of others, firmly convinced that their own good fortune meant virtue and the distress of the others vice. He was aware of the fact that the petty regulation (as in the passage quoted) was not only the one that hurt the pauper most keenly but the one the Board got the most pleasure out of inflicting. The exaggeration here is simply the necessary exaggeration of art, the necessary "fine excess."

The attitude of the Board, the relation between the workhouse authorities and the pauper, were to the novelist only examples of a universal theme, a theme not restricted to the nineteenth century or to workhouses alone. So that any appreciation of Dickens which restricts itself merely to the aptitude of his writing to the immediate social background is giving us a very small part of the real Dickens, no more than we should get of Shakespeare if we took Falstaff to be simply a commentary on the reign of Henry IV or of Swift if we took the satire of the horses to apply only to the politicians of Queen Anne.

What the Dickensian theme is a second quotation enforces. Mr. Sowerberry, the undertaker, is admiring the brass buttons on Mr. Bumble's coat. "Dear me, what a very elegant button this is, Mr. Bumble, I never noticed it before." "Yes, I think it is rather pretty," replies the beadle. "The die is the same as the parochial seal—the Good Samaritan healing the sick and bruised man. The board presented it to me on New Year's morning, Mr. Sowerberry; I put it on, I remember, for the first time, to attend the inquest on that reduced tradesman, who died in a doorway at midnight."

The very offhandedness of that reference points the moral implication. It is the very opposite of sentimentality, achieving in an economical effectiveness what a whole page of pathos might have failed to do. It is the carelessness here (and later on, when Bumble refers to "two Irish labourers and a coalheaver," as to so much cattle) that gives the irony its force. It is not only the character of Bumble that is shown by these remarks, but the habit of mind of the institution he represents—the refusal to take into account the individual.

Dickens is here using the resources of the novel towards a practical end which was largely realized some years later. But he is not less of a novelist because he is concerned so directly with social issues; on the contrary, he gains in stature as a writer, as an artist, by the manner in which he presents his criticism. If this were not so, such parts of his work would be as dead now as other nineteenth-century "novels with a purpose." The gift, the gift of the artist, for perceiving the fundamental beneath the particular, saves him. Most of the evils he represented in *Oliver* have long since been cleared away, but there remains the universal significance of the relation between Bumble's sort, personifying Authority, and the "two Irish labourers and a coalheaver," personifying Dependence. This is one of the fundamental themes of literature—"the insolence of office"—and it has never been better developed than in the novels of Fielding and Dickens. That offhanded reference of Bumble's to the "reduced tradesman, who died in a doorway at midnight" can only be compared with the celebrated parenthesis in *Joseph Andrews* on the kind-hearted postilion who lends the naked hero his coat—"A lad," said Fielding, "that hath since been transported for robbing a henroost."

It is this insistence on the personal, this hatred of the institution for its ignoring the human element ("classifying the inmates"), that is typical of all Dickens's writing on social justice. Like Cobbett, he was concerned not only for the welfare of the poor but for their dignity; unlike Cobbett, he did not see the remedy in economics. Probably he saw no remedies at all, save the fundamental Christian or moral one. In *Hard Times,* his most impressive statement of the problems of poverty, he insists merely upon a better understanding between the conflicting parties; not only between the maltreated labourer and the would-be reformer. "In an England gone mad about a minor theory," says Chesterton, "he reasserted the original idea—that no one in the state must be too weak to influence the state." It is a mistake to look in Dickens's writings for "solutions"; in *Hard Times* the view he takes is too long, and in *The Uncommercial Traveller* probably too short, to suit either the economist or the politician. It is the *presenting* of the case which we should naturally expect from a novelist embarked upon this theme, and *Hard Times* does that for us, unforgettably. The description of Coketown at the beginning of the book owes nothing to sentimentality:

> Let us strike the key-note, Coketown, before pursuing our tune. It was a town of red brick that would have been red if the smoke and ashes had allowed it . . . It was a town of machinery and tall chimneys, out of which interminable serpents of smoke trailed themselves for ever, and never got uncoiled. . . . It contained several large streets all very like one another, and many small streets still more like one another . . . You saw nothing in Coketown but was severely workful; the jail might have been the infirmary, the infirmary might have been the jail, the town-hall might have been either . . .

V

We have, then, an important part of Dickens's work which would contradict most of the generalizations one could make about him: cool irony instead of sentimentality or pathos, deliberate understatement instead of hyperbole. The recognition of these unexpected qualities should reinforce the idea of his diversity. No attempt to reconcile all the elements to be found in his writings would be likely to meet with success, and what we have attempted here, in connexion with the influence of the theatre and with the vulgarity of his age, can only be said to have drawn a few of the main strands together. We have not touched on his Comedy of the Grotesque (the Quilps, the Krooks, the Smallweeds); on his power of description, so impressive at its best (the Gordon Riots in *Barnaby*, the Fall of the Bastille in *A Tale of Two Cities*, the London of *Bleak House* and *Little Dorrit*), but at its worst a mere repetition of stale images and cheap effects; nor on that large question, his influence on English literature.

On the latter point, it must be admitted that the influence was partly for bad. Mr. O.Faoláin, in Mr. Verschoyle's symposium *The English Novelists*, gives an example of "Dickensian" journalese, and it is to be feared that on his most vulgar side the Inimitable Boz was only too imitable. Though more important novelists, such as George Eliot, Hardy, and Conrad, were to some extent affected by him, the main influence of Dickens must be admitted to have been on popular literature. Conan Doyle's *Firm of Girdlestone* is a particularly good example.

(1942)

PART IV

FOUR VERSIONS OF DRAMA

Tragic Philosophy
by George Santayana

In comparing a passage from *Macbeth* with one from the *Paradiso*, Mr. T. S. Eliot tells us that poetically the two are equally good, but that the philosophy in Shakespeare is inferior. By what standard, I am tempted to ask, may the poetic value of different types of poetry in different languages be declared equal? By the equal satisfaction, perhaps, that fills the critic's mind? But the total allegiance of a mature person, his total joy in anything, can hardly be independent of his developed conscience and his sense for ultimate realities. He cannot be utterly enchanted by what he feels to be trivial or false. And if he is not utterly enchanted, how should he recognize the presence of the supremely beautiful? Two passages could hardly be pronounced equal in poetic force if the ultimate suggestions of the one were felt to be inferior to those of the other.

Admitting, then, that poetry expressing an inferior philosophy would to that extent be inferior poetry, we may ask this further question: in what respect other than truth may philosophies be called inferior or superior? Perhaps in being more or less poetical or religious, more or less inspired? Sometimes a philosophy may spring up imaginatively, and in that sense may be inspired rather than strictly reasoned or observed, as the myths of Plato are inspired; but nobody would call such inspired philosophy *superior* unless he felt it to spring from the total needs and total wisdom of the heart; and in that case he would certainly believe, or at least hope, that this superior philosophy was true. How, then, should the poetic expression of this inspired philosophy not be conspicuously superior as poetry, and more utterly enchanting, than the expression of any other philosophy?

Let me postpone generalities and turn to the passages in question.

Lady Macbeth is dead. Macbeth foresees his own end. All the

prophecies flattering his ambition have been fulfilled, and after the mounting horror of his triumph he stands at the brink of ruin. Surveying the whole in a supreme moment, he consents to his destiny:

> *Tomorrow, and tomorrow, and tomorrow*
> *Creeps in this petty pace from day to day*
> *To the last syllable of recorded time;*
> *And all our yesterdays have lighted fools*
> *The way to dusty death. Out, out, brief candle!*
> *Life's but a walking shadow; a poor player*
> *That struts and frets his hour upon the stage,*
> *And then is heard no more. It is a tale*
> *Told by an idiot, full of sound and fury,*
> *Signifying nothing.*

Mr. Eliot says that this philosophy is derived from Seneca; and it is certain that in Seneca's tragedies, if not in his treatises, there is a pomp of diction, a violence of pose, and a suicidal despair not unlike the tone of this passage. But would Seneca ever have said that life signifies nothing? It signified for him the universal reign of law, of reason, of the will of God. Fate was inhuman, it was cruel, it excited and crushed every finite wish; yet there was something in man that shared that disdain for humanity, and triumphed in that ruthless march of order and necessity. Something superior, not inferior, Seneca would have said; something that not only raised the mind into sympathy with the truth of nature and the decrees of heaven, but that taught the blackest tragedy to sing in verse. The passions in foreseeing their defeat became prophets, in remembering it became poets; and they created the noblest beauties by defying and transcending death.

In Seneca this tragic philosophy, though magnificent, seems stilted and forced; it struts rhetorically like an army of hoplites treading down the green earth. He was the last of ancient tragedians, the most aged and withered in his titanic strength; but all his predecessors, from Homer down, had proclamied the same tragic truths, softened but not concealed by their richer medium. Some of them, like Virgil, had rendered those truths even more poignant precisely by being more sensitive to the loveliness of perishable things. After all, the same inhuman power that crushes us breeds us and feeds us; life and death are but two aspects of the same natural mutation, the same round of seed-time and harvest. And if all human passions must be fugitives, they need not all be unamiable: some are merry in their prime, and even smile at their own fading.

An accident of ritual led the ancients to divide tragedy sharply from comedy; I think it has been a happy return to nature in modern dramatists and novelists to intermingle the two. Comic episodes abound in the most tragic experience, if only we have the wit to see them; and even the tragic parts are in reality relieved by all sorts of compensations that stimulate our sense of life and prompt us to high reflection. What greater pleasure than a tear that pays homage to something beautiful and deepens the sense of our own profundity?

Not every part of this classic philosophy re-echoes in the pessimism of Macbeth. Shakespeare was not expressing, like Seneca, a settled doctrine of his own or of his times. Like an honest miscellaneous dramatist, he was putting into the mouths of his different characters the sentiments that, for the moment, were suggested to him by their predicaments. Macbeth, who is superstitious and undecided, storms excessively when he storms; there is something feverish and wild in his starts of passion, as there is something delicate in his perceptions. Shakespeare could give rein in such a character to his own subtle fancy in diction and byplay, as well as in the main to the exaggerated rhetoric proper to a stage where everybody was expected to declaim, to argue, and to justify sophistically this or that extravagant impulse. So at this point in *Macbeth,* where Seneca would have unrolled the high maxims of orthodox Stoicism, Shakespeare gives us the humours of his distracted hero; a hero nonplussed, confounded, stultified in his own eyes, a dying gladiator, a blinded lion at bay. And yet intellectually—and this is the tragedy of it—Macbeth is divinely human, rational enough to pause and survey his own agony, and see how brutish, how insignificant it is. He sees no escape, no alternative; he cannot rise morally above himself; his philosophy is that there is no philosophy, because, in fact, he is incapable of any.

Shakespeare was a professional actor, a professional dramatist; his greatness lay there, and in the gift of the gab: in that exuberance and joy in language which everybody had in that age, but he supremely. The Renaissance needed no mastering living religion, no mastering living philosophy. Life was gayer without them. Philosophy and religion were at best like travels and wars, matters for the adventurer to plunge into, or for the dramatist to describe; never in England or for Shakespeare central matters even in that capacity, but mere conventions or tricks of fancy or moods in individuals. Even in a Hamlet, a Prospero, or a Jaques, in a Henry VI or an

Isabella, the poet feels no inner loyalty to the convictions he rehearses; they are like the cap and bells of his fools; and possibly if he had been pressed by some tiresome friend to propound a personal philosophy, he might have found in his irritation nothing else to fall back upon than the animal despair of Macbeth. Fortunately, we may presume that burgherly comfort and official orthodoxy saved him from being unreasonably pressed.

That which a mastering living philosophy or religion can be, we may see at once by turning to the passage from Dante. In the lowest circle of Paradise, that of the inconstant moon, dwells the spirit of Piccarda, a lady who, having once been a nun but having been carried off and married by force, when later she became a widow preferred to continue her life in the world rather than return to her convent. Dante asks her if those who dwell in this part of Heaven ever desire to go higher, so as to see more and to love more. And she replies, No: for the essence of religious love is union with the order of creation. Perfect happiness would be impossible, if we were not perfectly happy in what God has given us; and in his will is our peace.

> *Frate la nostra volontà quieta*
> *virtù di carità, che fa volerne*
> *sol quel ch'avemo, e d'altro non ci asseta.*
> *Se disiassimo esser più superne,*
> *foran discordi li nostri disiri*
> *dal voler di colui che qui ne cerne:*
> *Che vedrai non capere in questi giri,*
> *s'essere in carità è qui necesse,*
> *e se la sua natura ben rimiri.*
> *Anzi è formale ad esto beato esse*
> *tenersi dentro alla divina voglia,*
> *per ch'una fansi nostre voglie stesse.*
> *Si che, come noi sem di soglia in soglia*
> *per questo regno, a tutto il regno piace,*
> *com'al lo re ch'a suo voler ne invoglia:*
> *E'n la sua volontade è nostra pace;*
> *ella è quel mare al qual tutto si move*
> *ciò ch'ella crea, e che natura face.*
> *Chiaro mi fu allor com'ogni dove*
> *in cielo è Paradiso, e si la grazia*
> *del sommo ben d'un modo non vi piove.*

I questioned at the beginning whether the poetic value of unlike things could be pronounced equal: and if now I compare this whole passage with the passage from *Macbeth* I find that to my sense they are incommensurable. Both are notable passages, if that is all that was meant; but they belong to different poetic worlds, appealing to and developing different sides of the mind. And there is more than disparity between these two worlds; there is contrariety and hostility between them, in as much as each professes to include and to subordinate the other, and in so doing to annul its tragic dignity and moral finality. For the mood of Macbeth, religion and philosophy are insane vapours; for the mood of Dante, Macbeth is possessed by the devil. There is no possible common ground, no common criterion of truth, and no common criterion even of taste or beauty. We might at best say that both poets succeed in conveying what they wish to convey, and that in that sense their skill is equal: but I hardly think this is true in fact, because in Shakespeare the medium is rich and thick and more important than the idea; whereas in Dante the medium is as unvarying and simple as possible, and meant to be transparent. Even in this choice passage, there are stretches of pure scholastic reasoning, not poetical at all to our sensuous and romantic apprehension; yet the studious and rapt poet feels himself carried on those wings of logic into a paradise of truth, where choir answers choir, and everything is beautiful. A clear and transparent medium is admirable, when we love what we have to say; but when what we have to say is nothing previously definite, expressiveness depends on stirring the waters deeply, suggesting a thousand half-thoughts, and letting the very unutterableness of our passion become manifest in our disjointed words. The medium then becomes dominant: but can this be called success in expression? It is rather success in making an impression, if the reader is impressed; and this effect seems essentially incomparable with that of pure lucidity and tireless exact versification in one chosen form. To our insecure, distracted, impatient minds, the latter hardly seems poetry.

Voltaire said that Dante's reputation was safe, because nobody read him. Nowadays that is hardly true; all superior persons read him a little, or read a great deal about him. He sets tempting problems for professional critics and antiquarians, and he appeals to archaistic taste, that flies for refuge into the fourth dimension, to everything that seems pure and primitive. But as living poetry, as a mould and stimulus for honest feeling, is Dante for us at all comparable to Shakespeare? Shakespeare, in passages such as this from *Macbeth*, is orchestrated. He trills away into fancy: what was daylight a moment ago suddenly becomes a candle: we are not thinking or reasoning, we are dreaming. He needs but to say "all our yesterdays," and presently the tedium of childhood, the tedium of labour and illness, the vacancy of friendships lost, rise like vague ghosts before us, and fill us with a sense of the unreality of all that once seemed most real. When he mentions "a poor player" we think at once of the poet himself, because our minds are biographical and our sympathies novelesque; we feel the misery and the lurid contrasts of a comedian's life; and the existence that just now seemed merely vain now seems also tempestuous and bitter. And the rhythms help; the verse struts and bangs, holds our attention suspended, obliges our thoughts to become rhetorical, and brings our declamation round handsomely to a grand finale. We should hardly have found courage in ourselves for so much passion and theatricality; but we bless Shakespeare for enabling us still to indulge in such emotions, and to relieve ourselves of a weight that we hardly knew we were carrying.

Nothing of the sort in the Italian: the simplest language, the humble vernacular, made pungent and to us often obscure only by an excess of concision and familiarity, or by allusions to events then on everybody's tongue. Dante allows his personal fortunes and hatreds to crop out in many places, perhaps quickening the interest of the modern gossip-loving reader. Yet these are incidental indiscretions, which the poet's own conscience might have regarded as blemishes. His work as a whole, and in intention, is that of a consecrated mind. A single thread of thought guides him, the eye is focussed on pure truth, on human wills illustrating the divine laws against which they profess to rebel; hell in the heart of earth, and earth enveloped in celestial harmonies. No occasion, as in modern edifying works, to avoid mentioning things unpleasant or to explain them away. Every detail is noted, not bashfully or apologetically, but with zest; when anything is wicked, its wickedness is exhibited and proved for our instruction. We learn the scientific complexity of the moral world, all plain facts, demonstrable truths, principles undoubted and certified. Mastered and chastened by this divine dispensation, what need should we feel of verbal opulence or lurid rhetoric? Not one rare epithet, not one poetic plum; instead, a childlike intellectual delight in everything being exact, limpid, and duly named, and dovetailed perfectly into everything else. Each word, each rhyme, files dutifully by in procession, white verses, three abreast, like choristers, holding each his taper and each singing in turn his appointed note. But what sweetness in this endless fugue, what simple exactitude, what devout assurance; and how unanimously these humble voices, often harsh and untutored if taken singly, rise together into a soaring canticle! The poetry, you might say, of industrious children, careful to make no mistake, but having nothing of their own to say, or not daring to say it. And indeed Dante's mind is busy, learned, and intense; exact even in allegory, as in a sort of heraldry; yet this very minuteness and pedantry are the work of love. Never was heart more tender or subtle or passionate; only that its intensity is all turned towards metaphysical joys, and transferred to an inward spiritual heaven.

I doubt whether either the beauty or the weakness of such poetry can be understood without understanding the nature of religion, as neither religious people nor irreligious people are likely to do; not the irreligious, because of insensibility, and not the religious, because of delusion. Still, a disinterested student, say of the origins of Christianity, ought to understand. Religion is not essentially a supplement to common knowledge or natural affection on the same level as the latter: it is not essentially a part of rational life, adjusted however gropingly to cosmic or social influences, and expressing them and their effects. Religion is rather a second life, native to the soul, developed there independently of all evidence, like a waking dream: not like dreams coming in sleep and composed largely of distorted waking impressions, but an autonomous other life, such as we have also in music, in games, and in imaginative love. In religion the soul projects out of her own impulses, especially when these are thwarted, the conditions under which she will regard herself as living. If she needs salvation, she will posit a saviour; if the thought of death offends her, she will posit resurrection or even immortality; if she is troubled at the injustice of fortune, she will posit previous crimes or original sins of her own, to explain her misery. If in general she wishes to impose her will where she is impotent, she will utter that will in prayers or imprecations, and posit an invisible power inclined to listen and able to help.

Now, such an inner fountain of life and thought is evidently akin to poetic inspiration. As in poetry, so in religion, imagination evokes a more or less systematic invisible world in which the passions latent in the soul may work themselves out dramatically. Yet there are differences. The profane poet is by instinct a naturalist. He loves landscape, he loves love, he loves the humour and pathos of earthly existence. But the religious prophet loves none of these things. It is precisely because he does not love them that he cultivates in himself, and summons the world to cultivate, a second more satisfying life, more deeply rooted, as he imagines, in the nature of things. Earthly images therefore interest him only as symbols and metaphors, or as themes for denunciation. He is hardly a poet in the ordinary sense, except in so far as (like Milton, for instance) he may owe a double allegiance, and be a profane poet altogether when he is a poet at all. Religion is often professed and intellectually accepted without ever having flowered in the soul, or being suspected to have any kinship with poetry. It may have withered into a forced and angry metaphysics or semi-political party doctrine, poetically deplorable.

The opposite is the case in Dante, whose poetry is essentially religious, as his religion is essentially poetical. We are in the presence of an overpowering inspiration, become traditional, become also learned and quasi-scientific, but still kindled by moral passion and fertile in poetic ideas. The Hebrew prophets had begun by denouncing that which was and proclaiming that which should be; but that which should be could evidently never become actual without a miracle and a total revolution in the world; so that prophecy turned to eschatology and to expectation of a Messiah. At this point pagan streams of inspiration began to mingle with the Hebraic stream. Perhaps the Messiah had already come. Perhaps he was to be no conquering monarch, but a god in disguise. Perhaps he had been crucified, as the spirit is always crucified. Perhaps his kingdom was not of this world. Were there not reports that Jesus, who had been crucified, had been seen, risen from the dead? Would he not surely come again with glory in the clouds of heaven? Transfigured by this new spiritual faith, many current legends and maxims were ascribed to Jesus, and beautifully set down in the Gospels. The fathers worked out the theology. The saints repeated the miracles and explored all the phases of ascetic and mystical experience. Nothing remained but for Dante, with exquisite fidelity and minuteness, to paint a total picture of the Christian universe. The whole substance of the universe was poetry; only the details could threaten to become prosaic; but this danger was removed, in the more important places, by Dante's extraordinary sensitiveness. He has had a revelation of his own in childhood, interrupted later by the false glare of the world, but finally restored in the form of religious wisdom and consecration. The fresh dew of poetry and love trembled upon everything. Indeed, for our modern feeling the picture is too imaginative, too visionary, soaked too much in emotion. In spite of the stern historical details, when we rub our eyes and shake off the spell, the whole thing seems childishly unreal. We can understand why Mr. Eliot feels this to be a "superior" philosophy; but how can he fail to see that it is false?

Inspiration has a more intimate value than truth and one more unmistakably felt by a sensitive critic, since inspiration marks a sort of springtide in the life of some particular creature, whereas truth impassively maps the steady merciless stretches of creation at large. Inspiration has a kind of truth of its own, truth to the soul; and this sincerity in intuition, however private and special it might be, would never conflict with the truth of things, if inspiration were content to be innocently free and undogmatic, as in music or lyric poetry. The inmost vegetative impulses of life might then come to perfect flower, feeling and celebrating their own reality without pretending to describe or command reality beyond, or giving any hostages to fortune. But, unfortunately, animals cannot long imitate the lilies of the field. Where life is adventurous, combative, and prophetic, inspiration must be so, too. Ideas, however spontaneous, will then claim to be knowledge of ulterior facts, and will be in constant danger of being contradicted by the truth. Experience, from being lyrical, will become tragic; for what is tragedy but the conflict between inspiration and truth? From within or, as we may fancy, from above, some passionate hope takes shape in the mind. We fall in love or hear a voice from heaven; new energies seem to leap up within us; a new life begins crowding the old life out, or making it seem dreary or wicked. Even when inspiration is not moral, but merely poetical, it kindles a secret fire and an inner light that put vulgar sunshine to shame. Yet not for long, nor for ever; unless we passionately shut ourselves up in the *camera obscura* of our first inspiration, and fear the darkness of other lights. The more profound and voluminous that first inspiration was, the more complete at last will be our astonishment and despair. We shall cry with *Le Cid*:

> Percé jusques au fond du coeur
> D'une atteinte imprévue aussi bien que mortelle . . .
> Je demeure immobile, et mon âme abattue
> Cède au coup qui me tue.

Tragedy must end in death: for any immortality which the poet or his hero may otherwise believe in is irrelevant to the passion that has absorbed him. That passion, at least, dies, and all he cares for dies with it. The possibility of ulterior lives or alien interests destined in future to agitate the world makes no difference to this drama in this soul; and the mention of those irrelevant sequels to this ruin, and to this tragic acceptance of ruin, would tinkle with a ghastly mockery at this supreme moment, when a man is entering eternity, his measure taken, his heart revealed, and his pride entire.

These considerations may help us to understand why Shakespeare, although Christianity was at hand, and Seneca, although a Platonic philosophy was at hand, based like Christianity on moral inspiration, nevertheless stuck fast in a disillusioned philosophy which Mr. Eliot thinks inferior. They stuck fast in the facts of life. They had to do so, whatever may have been their private religious convictions, because they were dramatists addressing the secular mind and concerned with the earthly career of passionate individuals, of inspired individuals, whose inspirations contradicted the truth and were shattered by it. This defeat, together with a proud and grandiloquent acceptance of it, is final for the tragic poet. His philosophy can build only on such knowledge of the world as the world can give. Even in the seventeenth century, when Christian orthodoxy was most severe, most intellectual, and most dominant, also most courtly and presentable to the worldly mind, Christianity was nevertheless strictly banished from the stage, except in a few expressly religious plays written for young ladies. Both Christian and pagan personages talked and felt throughout like thoroughly unregenerate mortals. To have allowed religion to shift the scenes, override the natural passions of men, and reverse the moral of the story would have seemed an intolerable anticlimax.

Nor does even Dante, who calls his vision a comedy, really escape this tragic reality. Existence is indeed a comedy, in that it is a series of episodes, each blind and inconclusive, though often merry enough, but all having their justification beyond themselves, in a cosmic muse which they help to make without knowing it. Nonetheless, the individual souls in Dante's hell and heaven speak the language of tragedy, either in desperate pride or in devout self-surrender. In either case, in eternity, they have no further hopes fears, or ambitions. Their lives *there* are simply the full knowledge of what their lives had been *here*. If the *Divine Comedy* had not had in it this sublime note of recollection, if it had attempted to describe new adventures and fanciful Utopias succeeding one another *ad infinitum,* it would not have been divine at all, but only a romantic medley like the second part of *Faust*. In Dante the hurly-burly is rounded out into a moral tale, into a joyful tragedy, with that sense of finality, of eternity, which Christian eschatology had always preserved.

I can think of only one tragedy in which religion might well play a leading part, and that is the tragedy of religion itself. The point would be to show that a second life of pure inspiration, freely bred in the soul out of moral impulses, must sooner or later confront the cold truth. The illusions then surrendered would not lose their poetic value, since their source would remain alive in the soul; and the element of deception involved might disappear insensibly, as it did in paganism, yielding with a good grace to an impartial philosophy. Such a philosophy need not be in the least hostile to inspiration. There is inspiration whereby there is mind. The sensuous images and the categories of thought on which common knowledge relies are themselves poetic and wholly original in form, being products of a kind of inspiration in the animal organism. But they are controlled in their significance and application by experiment in the field of action. Higher fictions are more loosely controlled by the experience of the heart. They are less readily revived or communicated. They flare up into passionate prophecies, take themselves for revealed truths, and come more often to a tragic end.

(1936)

Tragedy and the "Medium"

by F. R. Leavis

"Tragic Philosophy" exhibits Mr. Santayana's characteristic brilliance and wit—that rare wit (not rare in Mr. Santayana, of course) which is the focussed sharpness of illuminating intelligence. But it has striking weaknesses (or so I see them), and it is the considerations raised by one of them in particular that I am concerned with here. They are considerations that take me back to a point I made in discussing Johnson's criticism.*

Many admirers of Mr. Santayana besides myself must have been surprised at the way in which he plays off Macbeth's speech beginning "Tomorrow, and tomorrow, and tomorrow" against the passage attributed by Dante to Piccarda de Donati in which occurs the line:

> *E'n la sua volontade è nostra pace.*

True, earlier in the essay he has said that Shakespeare "like an honest miscellaneous dramatist . . . was putting into the mouths of his different characters the sentiments that, for the moment, were suggested to him by their predicaments." But he unmistakably slips into arguing as if Macbeth's comment on the plight to which the action has brought him may be taken as Shakespeare's just as Piccarda may be taken as speaking for Dante. Mr. Santayana's point, I recognize, is that Shakespeare hasn't a settled and coherent philosophy to set against Dante's—though "possibly if he had been pressed by some troublesome friend to propound a personal philosophy, he might have found in his irritation nothing else to fall back upon than the animal despair of Macbeth. Fortunately, we may presume that burgherly comfort and official orthodoxy saved him from being unreasonably pressed." But we are at the same time invited, unambiguously, to take Macbeth's speech as representing such substitute for a philosophy as Shakespeare, in this play, has to offer:

> I questioned at the beginning whether the poetic value of unlike things could be pronounced equal: and if now I compare this whole passage with the passage from *Macbeth* I find that to my sense they are incommensurable. Both are notable passages, if that is all that was

---

* See essay on Johnson, pages 57 to 75 above.

meant; but they belong to different poetic worlds, appealing to and developing different sides of the mind. And there is more than disparity between these two worlds; there is contrariety and hostility between them, in as much as each professes to include and to subordinate the other, and in so doing to annul its tragic dignity and moral finality. For the mood of Macbeth, religion and philosophy are insane vapours; for the mood of Dante, Macbeth is possessed by the devil. There is no possible common ground, no common criterion even of taste or beauty.

For the mood of Shakespeare, too, we are moved to retort, Macbeth is possessed by the devil: the tragic dignity and moral finality of Shakespeare's world are focussed in Macbeth's cry of "animal despair" only in so far as this refers us, inevitably (one would have thought), to the quite other effect of the total action—the total action in relation to which the speech has its significance. By his plunge into crime, taken in fatal ignorance of his nature—

> *If it were done, when 'tis done, then 'twere well*
> *It were done quickly*

—he has confounded "this little state of man" and the impersonal order from which it is inseparable. It is not on his extinction after a tale of sound and fury, signifying nothing, that the play ends, and his valedictory nihilism is the vindication of the moral and spiritual order he has outraged, and which is re-established in the close.

How, one asks, can Mr. Santayana have failed to see things so obvious? The answer follows immediately on the sentence of his last quoted:

> We might at best say that both poets succeed in conveying what they wish to convey, and that in that sense their skill is equal: but I hardly think this is true in fact, because in Shakespeare the medium is rich and thick and more important than the idea; whereas in Dante the medium is as unvarying and simple as possible, and meant to be transparent. Even in this choice passage, there are stretches of pure scholastic reasoning, not poetical at all to our sensuous and romantic apprehension; yet the studious and rapt poet feels himself carried on those wings of logic into a paradise of truth, where choir answers choir, and everything is beautiful. A clear and transparent medium is admirable, when we love what we have to say; but when what we have to say is nothing previously definite, expressiveness depends on stirring the waters deeply, suggesting a thousand half-thoughts and letting the very unutterableness of our passion become manifest in our disjointed words. The medium then becomes dominant: but can this be called success in expression? It is rather success in making an impression, if the reader is impressed . . .

The critic who falls so complete a victim to the word "medium" as Mr. Santayana here shows himself doesn't, it is plain, understand the poetic—and the essentially dramatic—use of language that Shakespeare's verse supremely exemplifies. He cannot, then, understand the nature of the organization that goes with that use of language: he cannot appreciate the ways in which the themes and significances of the play are dramatically presented. Take, for instance, this betraying sentence:

> So at this point in *Macbeth*, where Seneca would have unrolled the high maxims of orthodox Stoicism, Shakespeare gives us the humours of his distracted hero; a hero nonplussed, confounded, stultified in his own eyes, a dying gladiator, a blinded lion at bay.

We don't, when we are responding properly, say that "Shakespeare gives us Macbeth's speech": it comes to us, not from the author, but from the play, emerging dramatically from a dramatic context. It offers no parallel to Seneca's "'high maxims." And the "philosophy," moral significance, or total upshot of the play isn't stated but enacted. But for Mr. Santayana significance is a matter of "ideas," and "ideas" have to be stated, and so, looking for an epitomizing statement, he excises that speech from the organism to which it belongs, fixes it directly on Shakespeare, and gives us his surprising commentary.

We have only shifted the question a stage further back, of course. How can so subtle an intelligence as Mr. Santayana's have let itself be so victimized? The answer, I think, is that he is a philosopher. This is not to suggest that a philosopher can, for his own purposes, safely dispense with the ability to comprehend Shakespearean poetry. On the contrary, Mr. Santayana's inappreciation seems to me to go with a naïveté about the nature of conceptual thought that is common among philosophers, to their disadvantage as such. In venturing so far I may be merely exposing myself; but this, I am sure, must be said: to demand that poetry should be a "medium" for "previously definite" ideas is arbitrary, and betrays a radical incomprehension. What Mr. Santayana calls "Shakespeare's medium" creates what it conveys; "previously definite" ideas put into a "clear and transparent" medium wouldn't have been definite enough for Shakespeare's purpose. It is in place to quote again here a passage of D. W. Harding on Isaac Rosenberg that I quoted in considering Johnson:

> Usually when we speak of finding words to express a thought we seem to mean that we have the thought rather close to formulation and

use it to measure the adequacy of any possible phrasing that occurs to us, treating words as servants of the idea. "Clothing a thought in language," whatever it means psychologically, seems a fair metaphorical description of most speaking and writing. Of Rosenberg's work it would be misleading. He—like many poets in some degree, one supposes—brought language to bear on the incipient thought at an earlier stage of its development. Instead of the emerging idea being racked slightly so as to fit a more familiar approximation of itself, and words found for *that*, Rosenberg let it manipulate words almost from the beginning, often without insisting on the controls of logic and intelligibility.

The control over Shakespeare's words in *Macbeth* (for what Harding describes is the essentially poetic use of language, a use in which Shakespeare is pre-eminent) is a complex dramatic theme vividly and profoundly realized—not thought of, but possessed imaginatively in its concreteness, so that, as it grows in specificity, it in turn possesses the poet's mind and commands expression. To explain how so marvellous a definiteness of conception and presentment can have been missed by Mr. Santayana one has to invoke a training in inappropriate linguistic habits—inappropriate, that is, to the reading of Shakespeare: unable to relinquish irrelevant demands, the critic cannot take what is offered; misinformed and blinded by preconceptions, he cannot see what is there.

The case, readers will have noted, has much in common with Johnson's. Mr. Santayana, too, has a way of paradoxically appreciating while exhibiting his inability to appreciate like that I have pointed to in Johnson's dealings with Shakespeare:

> But as living poetry, as a mould and stimulus for honest feeling, is Dante for us at all comparable to Shakespeare? Shakespeare, in passages such as this from *Macbeth,* is orchestrated. He trills away into fancy: what was daylight a moment ago suddenly becomes a candle: we are not thinking or reasoning, we are dreaming. He needs but to say "all our yesterdays," and presently the tedium of childhood, the tedium of labour and illness, the vacancy of friendships lost, rise like vague ghosts before us, and fill us with a sense of the unreality of all that once seemed most real. When he mentions "a poor player" we think at once of the poet himself, because our minds are biographical and our sympathies novelesque; we feel the misery and the lurid contrasts of a comedian's life; and the existence that just now seemed merely vain now seems also tempestuous and bitter.

Can we say that the author of this cannot understand the Shakespearean use of language, and cannot therefore appreciate the nature and force of the Shakespearean "medium"? What we have here implies, surely, a pretty good analysis of the speech. But Mr. Santayana goes on:

> And the rhythms help; the verse struts and bangs, holds our attention suspended, obliges our thoughts to become rhetorical, and brings our declamation round handsomely to a grand finale. We should hardly have found courage in ourselves for so much passion and theatricality; but we bless Shakespeare for enabling us still to indulge in such emotions, and to relieve ourselves of a weight that we hardly knew we were carrying.

These sentences are perhaps not so unequivocal as Johnson's pejorative remarks, but it is nevertheless impossible not to take them as cancelling the appreciation. We relate them to these earlier sentences, and to their significant failure to distinguish between irresponsible exuberance and the mature Shakespearean mastery of language:

> Shakespeare was a professional actor, a professional dramatist; his greatness lay there, and in the gift of gab: in that exuberance and joy in language which everybody had in that age, but he supremely. The Renaissance needed no mastering living religion, no mastering living philosophy. Life was gayer without them.

The implications are plain enough. It would clearly be misleading to say that the critic who can express himself thus can properly appreciate Shakespeare's poetry. He clearly cannot appreciate the organization that has its local life in the verse. He has no inkling of the way in which the mastering living theme commands and controls the words.

It will have been noted that in the former of the two passages just quoted Mr. Santayana gives us an account of tragic catharsis. It is peculiarly interesting because in it he associated the cathartic effect with a poetic use (as he understands it) of language. We are bound to question his understanding, and in attempting to provide our own account of a poetic use we find ourselves exploring for a profounder and more satisfactory account of tragedy—of the tragic—that he implies here, or offers elsewhere in his essay. This, at any rate, is what, in my experience, gives the essay its peculiar value.

The view of the tragic implied in Mr. Santayana's account of catharsis seems a very limited one. Does Shakespearean tragedy, does the tragic in *Macbeth*, amount to no more than that? If so, where can we look for anything profounder? For surely the tragic experience is, or can be, a more important and serious matter than Mr. Santayana here suggests?

To postulate a "tragic experience" or "tragic effect" and then seek to define it is to lay oneself open to the suspicion of proposing a solemn and time-honoured academic game. Yet the critical contemplation of the profoundest things in literature does lead to the idea of such an experience, and we can see to it that the attempt at definition shall not be the kind of futility we associate with the Grand Style or the Sublime and the Beautiful. It need hardly be said, for instance, that what we are concerned with will not be found in all tragedies, or in most. And next, it is well to put aside the term "catharsis": its promptings don't seem to be at all helpful, and the exercise of refining upon, or interpreting away, Aristotle's medical metaphor may be left to the unfortunate student who knows that he may be required to "apply" the *Poetics* to Shakespeare, Webster, Racine, Ibsen, or Eugene O'Neill in the examination-room. If "calm" may properly be predicated of the tragic experience, it is certainly not "calm of mind, all passion spent" in the natural suggestion of that phrase. According to what seems valid in the current notion of the tragic, there is rather something in the nature of an exalting effect. We have contemplated a painful action, involving death and the destruction of the good, admirable, and sympathetic, and yet instead of being depressed we enjoy a sense of enhanced vitality.

I take this general account as granted—as recognized for sound as far as it goes. The conditions of something ostensibly answering to it are described by Mr. Santayana in his account of the Senecan tragic attitude or philosophy:

> Mr. Eliot says that this philosophy is derived from Seneca; and it is certain that in Seneca's tragedies, if not in his treatises, there is a pomp of diction, a violence of pose, and a suicidal despair not unlike the tone of this passage. But would Seneca ever have said that life signifies nothing? It signified for him the universal reign of law, of reason, of the will of God. Fate was inhuman, it was cruel, it excited and crushed every finite wish; yet there was something in man that shared that disdain for humanity, and triumphed in that ruthless march of order and necessity. Something superior, not inferior, Seneca would have said; something that not only raised the mind into sympathy with the truth of nature and the decrees of heaven, but that taught the blackest tragedy to sing in verse. The passions in foreseeing their defeat became prophets, in remembering it became poets; and they created the noblest beauties by defying and transcending death.

Mr. Santayana seems to imply (he says nothing crude, of course, and he shows considerable suppleness in presenting his case) that Seneca has an advantage over Shakespeare in this tragic philosophy, however the total comparison between the two poets may work out. Without granting this, we may at any rate feel that the formula for the tragic it represents, in Mr. Santayana's account of it, deserves pondering. It deserves pondering because, though clearly unsatisfactory, it has (we feel) something of the right form.

It is most clearly unsatisfactory because, in the terms in which it stands, it is equivocal. In spite of the "something superior, not inferior," it reminds us too much of "the bitter beauty of the universe and the frail human pride that confronts it for a moment undismayed." It is, in fact, not clearly enough distinguishable from "A Free Man's Worship":

> Brief and powerless is Man's life; on him and all his race the slow, sure doom falls pitiless and dark. Blind to good and evil, reckless of destruction, omnipotent matter rolls on its relentless way; for Man, condemned to-day to lose his dearest, tomorrow himself pass through the gate of darkness, it remains only to cherish, ere yet the blow falls, the lofty thoughts that ennoble his little day; disdaining the coward terrors of the slave of Fate, to worship at the shrine that his own hands have built; undismayed by the empire of chance, to preserve a mind free from the wanton tyranny that rules his outward life; proudly defiant of the irresistible forces that tolerate, for a moment, his knowledge and his condemnation, to sustain alone, a weary but unyielding Atlas, the world that his own ideals have fashioned despite the trampling march of unconscious power.*

The tragic experience, however it is to be defined, is certainly not anything that encourages, or permits, an indulgence in the dramatization of one's nobly suffering self. Mr. Santayana's Seneca, of course, doesn't propose anything as crude. Nevertheless, as we ponder the *"disdain* for humanity" and the *"defying* . . . death," it strikes us that the Senecan attitude as described is perilously ready to subside into something of a kindred order to the prose of "A Free Man's Worship": the differences aren't radical enough. We recall Mr. Eliot's observations (in "Shakespeare and the Stoicism of Seneca") on the Senecan influence in Elizabethan drama, and its relation to the trick of rhetorical self-boosting.

And whether Mr. Eliot is right or not in associating Othello's self-dramatizing habit with the Senecan influence, he gives us the cue for saying that the attitude represented by Othello's last speech is radically untragic. This is so obvious as to seem, perhaps, not worth saying: Othello, for those who don't join in the traditional sentimentalization of the play, is a very obvious case. The essential

---
* Bertrand Russell, *Mysticism and Logic*, p. 56.

TRAGEDY AND THE "MEDIUM"

point that has to be made is that his valedictory *coup de théâtre* represents a rhetorical inflation, a headily emotional glorification, of an incapacity for tragic experience that marks the ordinary moments of us all.

There is a passage in one of D. H. Lawrence's letters that came into my mind when this point was under discussion:

> I am so sick of people: they preserve an evil, bad, separating spirit under the warm cloak of good words. That is intolerable in them. The Conservative talks about the old and glorious national ideal, the Liberal talks about this great struggle for right in which the nation is engaged, the peaceful women talk about disarmament and international peace. Bertie Russell talks about democratic control and the educating of the artisan, and all this, all this goodness, is just a warm and cosy cloak for a bad spirit. They all want the same thing: a continuing in this state of disintegration wherein each separate little ego is an independent little principality by itself. What does Russell really want? He wants to keep his own established ego, his finite and ready-defined self intact, free from contact and connection. He wants to be ultimately a free agent. That is what they all want, ultimately—that is what is at the back of all international peace-for-ever and democratic control talks: they want an outward system of nullity, which they call peace and goodwill, so that in their own souls they can be independent little gods, referred nowhere and to nothing, little mortal Absolutes, secure from question. [*Letters*, p. 247]

The particular justice or injustice of these animadversions needn't be discussed: one wouldn't go to Lawrence for judicial fairness towards persons or parties, and there are necessary political and kindred activities at levels at which the characteristic Laurentian contribution may well appear the reverse of helpful or encouraging. But it is just his part, as he sees it, to insist—with a passionate insistence exasperating to energizers for movements and policies—that there are profounder levels; levels of experience that, though they tend constantly to be ignored, are always, in respect of any concern for life and health, supremely revelant. The most effective insistence would be tragic art. Lawrence, in fact, might fairly (for my present purpose) be said to be pronouncing of the attitudes he stigmatizes that they are incompatible with tragic experience.

At any rate, it is an essential part of the definition of the tragic that it breaks down, or undermines and supersedes, such attitudes. It establishes below them a kind of profound impersonality in which experience matters, not because it is mine—because it is to me it belongs or happens, or because it subserves, or issues in, purpose or will, but because it is what it is, the "mine" mattering only in so far as the individual sentience is the indispensable focus of experience. The attainment in literature of this level, and of organization at this level, would seem to involve the poetic use of language, or of processes that amount to that. By the "poetic" use of language I mean that which I described as "dramatic" in discussing Johnson's criticism and the limits to his appreciation of Shakespeare. For Johnson, I said, expression was necessarily statement; critically, he couldn't come to terms with the use of language, not as a medium in which to put "previously definite ideas," but for exploratory creation. Poetry as creating what it presents, and as presenting something that stands there to speak for itself, or, rather, that isn't a matter of saying, but of being and enacting, he couldn't properly understand. In this he is representative of the eighteenth century, and (the point was made in discussion) it is significant that that century, which went in so much for formal tragedy, should have shown itself so utterly incapable of attaining the tragic. The use of language for the expression of "previously definite" ideas needn't, of course, carry with it social and rational conventions as obviously limiting as the Augustan, but in proposing for the poet as his true business the lucid arrangement of ready-minted concepts Mr. Santayana proposes (it seems to me) limitations as essentially disabling for tragedy as the Augustan. It may not be altogether true to say that in such a use of language—in the business of expressing "previously definite" ideas—one is necessarily confined to one's "established ego," one's "ready-defined self." But it does seem as if the "tragic" transcendence of ordinary experience that can be attained by a mind tied to such a use must inevitably tend towards the rhetorical order represented by Mr. Santayana's account of Seneca's tragic philosophy (or—shall I say?—by the Senecan attitude as no doubt fairly conveyed by Mr. Santayana).

Such an attitude is really an exaltation of the "established ego," and, as we have seen, cannot be securely distinguished from the kind of attitude one strikes. The attainment of the level of experience at which emancipation from the "ready-defined self" is compelled involves an essentially different order of expression; one in which heightening is deepening, exaltation has nothing alcoholic about it, and rhetoric (as in *Othello*—for those who take what Shakespeare offers) is "placed."

It is interesting to see Yeats, in his own way and by his own characteristic approach, making the point in question. He rebels, in his aesthetically given youth, against the flatness of the dialogue in post-Ibsenian drama (see *Essays*). Modern naturalistic speech, he feels, precludes beauty and significance. We can never, of course, feel quite safe, reading these protests in Yeatsian prose, against a suggestion of *Rosa Alchemica* and *The Trembling of the Veil*. Nevertheless, he makes the necessary points and makes them firmly. You cannot, he notes, be passionate in educated modern speech: Ibsen in the attempt to overcome this difficulty invented a conventional rhetoric. Poetry, with attendant non-naturalistic conventions (see the essay on "Certain Noble Plays of Japan"), is necessary in order to provide the distance and the frame without which there can be no intensity of the right kind. And then we come to this ("The Tragic Theatre"): "I saw plainly what should have been plain from the first line I had written, that tragedy must always be a drowning, a breaking of the dykes that separate man from man. . . ." Yeats's intention in this, which is immediately related to his preoccupation with convention and the "medium," has unmistakably the directest relation to what I have been trying to say above.

We might further invoke as obviously relevant Nietzsche's insistence on the Dionysiac. But perhaps, after all, the Nietzschean witness had better be dispensed with; at the best it introduces a disturbing vibration. The Nietzschean context is uncongenial to the present purpose, and a glance at it prompts the remark that the tragic calm (if "calm" is the word), while not the product of any laxative catharsis, is not in the least the calm of the tensed and self-approving will.

The sense of heightened life that goes with the tragic experience is conditioned by a transcending of the ego—an escape from all attitudes of self-assertion. "Escape," perhaps, is not altogether a good word, since it might suggest something negative and irresponsible (just as "Dionysiac" carries unacceptable suggestions of the Dark Gods). Actually the experience is constructive or creative, and involves a recognizing of positive value as in some way defined and vindicated by death. It is as if we are challenged at the profoundest level with the question, "In what does the significance of life reside?," and found ourselves contemplating, for answer, a view of life, and of the things giving it value, that makes the valued appear unquestionably more important than the valuer, so that significance lies, clearly and inescapably, in the willing adhesion of the individual self to something other than itself. Here, for instance, is D. A.

Traversi writing on *Antony and Cleopatra* (with his relative valuation of which, I had better add by the way, I don't agree):

> For death, which had seemed in the Sonnets, and early tragedies to be incontrovertible evidence of the subjection of love and human values to Time, now becomes by virtue of Shakespeare's poetic achievement an instrument of release, the necessary condition of an experience which, though dependent upon Time and circumstance, is by virtue of its *value* and intensity incommensurate with them—that is "immortal." The emotions of Antony and Cleopatra are built upon "dungy earth," upon "Nilus' slime," and so upon Time which these elements by their nature imply; but, just as earth and slime are quickened into fire and air, whilst retaining their sensible qualities as constituent parts of the final experience, so Time itself becomes a necessary element in the creation of "immortality." [*Approach to Shakespeare*, p. 126]

I quote this for its relevant suggestiveness. It seems to me to compare very interestingly with the following passage from D. W. Harding (whose distinctive strength in criticism—I add, in case I should have appeared to be betraying metaphysical ambitions—goes with a psychologist's approach):

> Death in itself was not his concern, but only death at the moment when life was simplified and intensified; this he felt had a significance which he represents by immortality. For him it was no more than the immortality of the possibilities of life. This immortality and the value he glimpses in the living effort of war in no way mitigate his suffering at the human pain and waste. The value of what was destroyed seemed to him to have been brought into sight only by the destruction, and he had to respond to both facts without allowing either to neutralize the other. It is this which is most impressive in Rosenberg—the complexity of experience which he was strong enough to permit himself and which his technique was fine enough to reveal.*

I will not attempt to develop the kind of discussion of tragedy that the juxtaposition of these passages might seem to promise—or threaten. It suits my purpose rather to note the stress laid by Harding on "complexity" and "technique" (compare Traversi's "poetic achievement"—a phrase that sums up much preceding analysis of Shakespeare's verse), and to note further that he passes on to "impersonality":

> To say that Rosenberg tried to understand all that the war stood for means probably that he tried to expose the whole of himself to it. In one letter he describes as an intention what he obviously achieved: "I will not leave a corner of my consciousness covered up, but saturate

---

* *Scrutiny*, Vol. III, No. 4 ("The Poetry of Isaac Rosenberg").

myself with the strange and extraordinary new conditions of this life.
. . ." This willingness—and ability—to let himself be new-born into
the new situation, not subduing his experience to his established personality, is a large part, if not the whole secret, of the robustness which
characterizes his best work. . . . Here as in all the war poems his suffering and discomfort are unusually *direct;* there is no secondary distress arising from the sense that these things *ought not* to be. He was
given up to realizing fully what *was*. . . .
It was Rosenberg's exposure of his whole personality that gave his
work its quality of impersonality.

What Harding says about Rosenberg in these passages has clearly the closest relevance to tragedy. And it is especially significant for my theme that they belong to the essay containing that discussion of the poetic use of language which I have found so useful in defining the limitations, in respect of the tragic, of Johnson and (I suggest) Mr. Santayana.

This significance, my main concern in this note, will get a suitable parting stress, if we consider I. A. Richard's treatment of "impersonality," which has, on the surface, resemblances to Harding's. Dr. Richards deals with "impersonality" and tragedy together in the same chapter (XXXII) of *The Principles of Literary Criticism*. These pages (245-253) contain some of the most valuably suggestive things in the book, and if, for my convenience, I dwell on the weaknesses, I have at any rate the justification that they are entailed by Richards's essential neo-Benthamite ambition, which is irreconcilable with his best insight. (And I am urging that these pages should be read, or re-read).

The ambition asserts itself characteristically when Richards, having told us that, in the full tragic experience, the "mind does not shy away from anything, it does not protect itself with any illusion, it stands uncomforted, unintimidated, alone and self-reliant," goes on to pronounce toughly (p. 246):

> The joy which is so strangely at the heart of the experience is not an indication that "all's right with the world" or that "somewhere, somehow, there is Justice"; it is an indication that all is right here and now in the nervous system.

For him, of course, tragedy is the supreme instance of the inclusive organization of impulses: it is "perhaps the most general all-accepting, all-ordering experience known" (p. 247). Experience, for the purposes of the new science, must be reducible to unit impulses, so that evaluation may be quantitative. We are not, then, surprised when we read (p. 248):

This balanced poise, stable through its power of inclusion, not through the force of its exclusions, is not peculiar to Tragedy. It is a general characteristic of all the most valuable experiences of the arts. It can be given by a carpet or a pot or by a gesture as unmistakably as by the Parthenon, it may come about through an epigram as clearly as through a Sonata.

I must confess myself to have found, with surprise, that I had carried away a wrong impression from this passage—an impression that Richards actually pronounces the tragic experience to be obtainable from a carpet or a pot. But it is easy to see how I came to form it, the argument moving as it does, with so easy and uninhibited a transition. And it is not at all easy to see how Richards can satisfactorily explain the differences that divide any experience fitly to be called "tragic" from the most inclusively poised experience a carpet or a pot can be supposed to give. The scientifico-psychological ambition entails his taking his diagrams of poised and organized "impulses" or "appetencies" too seriously: he couldn't go on supposing he took his science seriously if he even began to recognize the remoteness of their relevance to concrete experiences.

This may seem, so late in the day, too obvious a kind of criticism to be worth reiterating; but I want to give it a special point in relation to my main argument. No theory of tragedy can amount to more than a blackboard diagram, a mere schematic substitute for understanding, unless it is associated with an adequate appreciation of the subtleties of poetic (or creative) language—the subtleties that are supremely illustrated in the poetry of Shakespeare. Such an appreciation if operative, would have inhibited Dr. Richards's reliance on his "impulses" and his "nervous system." This point is not the less worth making because he has always, in his neo-Benthamite way, been interested in language and the meaning of meaning. He has, since the phase represented by *The Principles of Literary Criticism,* specialized in semasiology. But no interest in language that is Benthamite in spirit, or controlled by a neo-Benthamite ambition, can afford to recognize the profoundest aspects of linguistic "communication"—those we find ourselves contemplating when we contemplate in the concrete the nature of tragic impersonality. Such an interest can no more be adequate to them than the utilitarian calculus—with its water-tight unit self, confined, for all self-transcendence, to external transactions with other selves—could engage in the kind of interest in moral issues taken by George Eliot.

(1944)

Notes on Comedy

by L. C. Knights

I

Labour-saving devices are common in criticism. Like the goods advertised in women's journals they do the work, or appear to do it, leaving the mind free for the more narcotic forms of enjoyment. Generalizations and formulae are devices of this kind. It is as easy and unprofitable to discuss the "essence" of the tragic and the comic modes as it is to conduct investigations in aesthetics which end with the discovery of Significant Form.

Comedy has provided a happy hunting-ground for the generalizers. It is almost impossible to read a particular comedy without the interference of critical presuppositions derived from one or other of those who have sought to define comedy in the abstract. In the first place, we all know that comedy makes us laugh. "Tragedy and comedy bear the same relation to one another as earnestness and mirth. Both these states of mind bear the stamp of our common nature but earnestness belongs more to the moral, and mirth to the sensual side. . . . The essence of the comic is mirth." Put in this form, the error is sufficiently obvious, but it lurks behind most of our generalizations about the nature of the comic and the function of comedy. Meredith's hypergelasts are enemies of the comic spirit, but his ideal audience all laugh, in their polite drawing-room way. "The test of true Comedy," he says, "is that it shall awaken thoughtful laughter."

Once an invariable connexion between comedy and laughter is assumed we are not likely to make any observations that will be useful as criticism. We have only to find the formula that will explain laughter and we know the "secret" of Jonson and Rabelais, Chaucer and Fielding, Jane Austen and Joyce. "Men have been wise in very different modes; but they have always laughed the same way." So if we are looking for a simple explanation we can refer to "a sudden glory," "incongruity," "the mechanical encrusted on the living," "tendency wit," or any of the other half-dozen solutions of the problem of laughter, none of which, however, will help us to become better, because more responsive, readers of Molière. There is evidence, on the other hand, that reading capacity is diminished by reliance upon any one of them. But it is time to clear away this particular obstruction. A neglected passage of *Timber* reads: "Nor is the moving of laughter always the end of Comedy. . . . This is truly leaping from the Stage to the Tumbrell again, reducing all wit to the original Dungcart." Comedy is essentially a serious activity.

After this particularly vulgar error the most common is that comedy is a Social Corrective, comic laughter a medicine administered to society to cure its aberrations from the norm of Good Sense. Meredith's celebrated essay, in which this theory is embedded, has been a misfortune for criticism. It has won eminence as a classic without even the merit of containing a sharply defined falsehood. The style is that of an inaugural lecture in a school of *belles-lettres*. The idle pose is betrayed by the key-words—"high fellowship," "the smile finely tempered," "unrivalled politeness," "a citizen of the selecter world"— and the theory emerges obscurely from the affected prose. "The comic poet is in the narrow field, or enclosed square, of the society he depicts"— a commonplace as true of any representational art as it is of comedy—"and he addresses the still narrower enclosure of men's intellects"—the implication is false; there is emotion in Jonson and Molière—"with reference to the operation of the social world upon their characters." With the aid of what has gone before we can make out the meaning. Comedy is "the firstborn of common-sense." "It springs to vindicate reason, common-sense, rightness and justice," and this Sir Galahad of the arts springs to attack whenever men "wax out of proportion, overblown, affected, pretentious, bombastical, hypocritical, pedantic; whenever it sees them self-deceived or hood-winked, given to run riot in idolatries . . . planning shortsightedly, plotting dementedly." There is nothing that can be said of such a theory except that it is of no use whatever in elucidating particular comedies and in forming precise judgments. But it has the ill effect of providing the illusion that we know all this is necessary about a comedy when we know very little. "The Comic Idea enclosed in a comedy makes it more generally perceptible and portable, which is an advantage." Exactly; there is no need to distinguish between the comedy of *Tom Jones* and *The Secret Agent* when we have this Comic Idea to carry around with us.

In Meredith's essay we hear much of "the mind hovering above congregated men and women" and we learn that the author was in love with Millamant, but if we look for particular judgements we find: "the comic of Jonson is a scholar's excogitation of the comic. . . . Shakespeare is a well-spring of characters which are saturated with the comic spirit . . . they are of this world, but they are of the world enlarged to our embrace by imagination, and by great poetic imagination. They are, as it were, . . . creatures of the woods and wilds . . . Jaques, Falstaff and his regiment, the varied troop of Clowns, Malvolio, Sir Hugh Evans and Fluellen—marvellous Welshmen!—Benedick and Beatrice, Dogberry and the rest, are subjects of a special study in the poetically comic." None of which helps us at all in understanding *Volpone* or *Henry IV*. We are not surprised when we find: "O for a breath of Aristophanes, Rabelais, Voltaire, Cervantes, Fielding, Molière!" as though these diverse writers had the same literary problems or solved them in the same way.

Profitless generalizations are more frequent in criticism of comedy than in criticism of other forms of literature. Since we continue to speak of the Comic Spirit after we have ceased to speak of the spirit of tragedy or the essence of the epic, that bogus entity may be held responsible. "It has the sage's brows, and the sunny malice of a faun lurks at the corners of the half-closed lips drawn in an idle wariness of half tension."

Meredith's essay serves as a warning that essays on comedy are necessarily barren exercises. The point is brought home if we consider how profitless it would be to compare one of Blake's *Songs of Experience* with a poem of Hopkins as Manifestations of the Lyric Impulse. As in all criticism the only generalizations which may be useful are those, usually short, based on sensitive experience of literature, containing, as it were, the distilled essence of experience, capable of unfolding their meaning in particular application, and those which suggest how the mind works in certain classes of experience. Of the latter kind one of the most fruitful occurs on page 209 of I. A. Richards's *Principles of Literary Criticism*: "Besides the experiences which result from the building up of connected attitudes, there are those produced by the breaking down of some attitude which is a clog and a bar to other activities." The breaking down of undesirable attitudes is normally part of the total response to a comedy. But to say this is to admit that all the work remains to be done in each particular case. We have to determine exactly how this breaking down is effected, exactly what attitude is broken down, and what takes its place.

Apply Dr. Richards's remark, with the necessary qualifications in each case, to *Volpone* and *Le Misanthrope*, and it is apparent how divergent the effects and methods of comedy may be. Jonson is concerned to create the mood which is the object of contemplation. He works by selection, distortion, and concentration, so that the attitude created by the interaction of Volpone, Corvino, Corbaccio, and the rest finally, as it were, blows itself up by internal pressure. The method is cumulative.

> *Good morning to the day; and next, my gold!*
> *Open the shrine, that I may see my saint.*
> *Hail the world's soul, and mine!*

The exaggeration reaches a climax in the attempted seduction of Celia:

> *See here, a rope of pearl; and each more orient*
> *Than the brave Aegyptian queen caroused:*
> *Dissolve and drink them. See, a carbuncle,*
> *May put out both the eyes of our St. Mark;*
> *A diamond would have bought Lollia Paulina,*
> *When she came in like star-light, hid with jewels.*

The world thus created, already undermined by the obscene songs and antics of the Dwarf, the Eunuch, and the Hermaphrodite, is demolished by the plots and counterplots of the final scenes. But the catastrophe is not mechanical: it represents on the plane of action the dissolution that is inherent in the swelling speeches of Volpone and Mosca:

> *I fear I shall begin to grow in love*
> *With my dear self, and my most prosperous parts,*
> *They do so spring and burgeon; I can feel*
> *A whimsy in my blood: I know not how,*
> *Success hath made me wanton.*

In *Volpone* the cathartic effect is relevant solely to the conditions of the play. Molière, on the other hand, is more directly satiric, drawing more directly upon the actual world for the attitudes which he refines and demolishes. The play is a pattern of varied satiric effects. How it works may be best discovered by comparing it with a direct satire such as the *Epistle to Arbuthnot*. The pitch and tempo of Pope's poem vary, but the tone is fairly consistent. In *Le Misanthrope*, on the other hand, the tone varies not only from character to character, but also within the limits of a single speech, of a few lines; and the speed with which the point of view shifts and the tone changes sets free the activity which breaks down the impeding attitudes. This is to confine our attention merely to one aspect of the play, but no criticism can be relevant which does not consider the peculiar mental agility required to follow the changes of this kind. Unlike *Volpone* the effects are repetitive (in kind, they are obviously not all the same) and a close examination of the tone and intention of each line in the first scene is the best way of discovering how the play as a whole should be read. Even to discover the points at which the author might be identified with the speaker is instructive.

It is obvious that the Social Corrective theory not only precludes discussion of a comedy in terms of the effects we have described, but prevents those who accept it from even realizing that such discussion is possible. Its inadequacy should be no less plain even if we admit, for the moment, that the function of comedy is "critical." Malvolio, Sir Tunbelly Clumsy, Squire Western, may be considered simply as failures judged by some social norm, but in many comedies the "criticism" is directed not only at the man who fails to live up to standard but also at the standard by which his failure is judged. In Shirley's *Love in a Maze* Sir Gervase Simple, reproached that he is dumb in the presence of his mistress, replies, "I cannot help it: I was a gentleman, thou knowest, but t'other day. I have yet but a few compliments: within a while I shall get more impudence, and then have at her." Here the object of criticism is not only the simpleton who has no court manners, but also the courtiers, acquaintance with whom he hopes will fill him with unmannerly boldness. The method of two-edged satire is of particular importance in a consideration of literature in relation to the social environment. Chapman's *The Widow's Tears* may serve as an example. Part of the play is concerned with a wife who, after expressing her horror of second marriages, yields to the first stranger who makes love to her on the, supposed, death of her husband, the stranger being her husband in disguise. The critics have seen here a satire on the frailty of woman, speaking of the "almost brutal cynicism" of the play. But the satire is directed not only at such frailty but at the contemporary attitude towards widowhood. "He that hath her," said Overbury of a remarried widow, "is but lord of a filthy purchase," and a minor moralist writes with approval of widows who have lived alone as they ought: "Their rooms bore the habit of mourning; funeral lamps were ever burning; no musical strain to delight the ear, no object of state to surprise the eye. True sorrow had there his mansion; nor could they affect any other discourse than what to their husbands' actions held most relation." The effect of the play is to cast doubts on the reasonableness of such an attitude. The speech in praise of the horn at the end of *All Fools* may be considered in relation to seventeenth-century marriage customs and cuckoldry. But the method is relevant when we are discussing plays, etc., as social documents rather than as literature independent of temporary conditions for their effect.

"Social Satire" is too vague and general to be of any use for the purpose of criticism. It needs to be defined in each instance in terms of the mental processes involved. The greatness of any comedy can only be determined by the inclusiveness, the coherence and stability of the resultant attitude; to define its method is the work of detailed and particular analysis, and abstract theories of comedy can at best only amuse. An examination of *Henry IV* will help to make this plain.

II

Henry IV does not fit easily into any of the critical schemata, though "incongruity" has served the critics in good stead. But, at any rate, since the time of Morgann, Falstaff has received a degree of sympathetic attention (how we love the fat rascal!) that distorts Shakespeare's intention in writing the two plays. We regard them as a sandwich—so much dry bread to be bitten through before we come to the meaty Falstaff, although we try to believe that "the heroic and serious part is not inferior to the comic and farcical." Actually each play is a unity, sub-plot and main plot co-operating to express the vision which is projected into the form of the play. And this vision, like that of all the great writers of comedy, is preeminently serious. It is symptomatic that Hazlitt, defending Shakespeare's tragedies against the comedies, said, "He was greatest in what was greatest; and his *forte* was not trifling."

The first speech of the King deserves careful attention. The brittle verse suggests the precarious poise of the usurper:

> *So shaken as we are, so wan with care,*
> *Find we a time for frighted peace to pant,*
> *And breathe short-winded accents of new broils*
> *To be commenced in stronds afar remote.*

The violence of the negative which follows suggests its opposite:

> *No more the thirsty entrance of this soil*
> *Shall daub her lips with her own children's blood:*
> *No more shall trenching war channel her fields,*

> Nor bruise her flowerets with the armed hoofs
> Of hostile paces.

"Thirsty" contains the implication that the earth is eager for more blood; and when the prophecy of peace ends with the lisping line, "Shall now, in mutual well-beseeming ranks," we do not need a previous knowledge of the plot or of history to realize that Henry is actually describing what is to come. The account of the proposed crusade is satiric:

> But this our purpose is a twelvemonth old, . . .
> Therefore we meet not now.

Throughout we are never allowed to forget that Henry is a usurper. We are given four separate accounts of how he gained the throne—by Hotspur (I, iii, 160-186), by Henry himself (III, ii, 39-84), by Hotspur again (IV, iii, 52-92), and by Worcester (V, i, 32-71). He gained it by "murd'rous subornation," by hypocrisy, his "seeming brow of justice," by "violation of all faith and troth." Words expressing underhand dealing occur even in the King's account to his son:

> And then I stole all courtesy from Heaven,
> And dress'd myself in such humility
> That I did pluck allegiance from men's hearts.

There is irony in the couplet that concludes the play:

> And since this business so fair is done,
> Let us not leave till all our own be won.

The rebels, of course, are no better. The hilarious scene in which the plot is hatched (I, iii, 187-302) does not engage much sympathy for the plotters, who later squabble over the expected booty like any long-staff sixpenny strikers. Their cause does not bear prying into by "the eye of reason" (IV, i, 69-72), and Worcester, for his own purposes, conceals "the liberal kind offer of the King" (V, ii, 1-25). But this is relatively unimportant; there is no need to take sides and "like Hotspur somewhat better than the Prince because he is unfortunate." The satire is general, directed against statecraft and warfare. Hotspur is the chief representative of chivalry, and we have only to read his speeches to understand Shakespeare's attitude towards "honour"; there is no need to turn to Falstaff's famous soliloquy. The description of the Mortimer-Glendower fight has just that degree of exaggeration which is necessary for not-too-obvious burlesque, though, oddly enough, it has been used to show that Hotspur "has the imagination of a poet." But if the image of the Severn—

> Who then, affrighted with their bloody looks,
> Ran fearfully among the trembling reeds,
> And hid his crisp head in the hollow bank—

is not sufficient indication, the rhyme announces the burlesque intention:
> He did confound the best part of an hour
> In changing hardiment with great Glendower.

There is the same exaggeration in later speeches of Worcester and Hotspur; Hotspur's "huffing part"—"by Heaven methinks it were an easy leap"—did not need Beaumont's satire. In the battle scene the heroics of "Now, Esperance! Percy! and set on," the chivalric embrace and flourish of trumpets are immediately followed by the exposure of a military dodge for the preservation of the King's life. "The King hath many marching in his coats."—"Another King! They grow like Hydra's heads."

The reverberations of the sub-plot also help to determine our attitude towards the main action. The conspiracy of the Percys is sandwiched between the preparation for the Gadshill plot and counterplot and its execution. Poins has "lost much honour" that he did not see the "action" of the Prince with the drawers. When we see the court we remember Falstaff's joint-stool throne and his account of Henry's hanging lip. Hotspur's pride in himself and his associates ("Is there not my father, my uncle and myself?") is parodied by Gadshill: "I am joined with no foot land-rakers, no long-staff sixpenny strikers . . . but with nobility and tranquility, burgomasters and great oneyers." The nobles, like the roarers, prey on the commonwealth, "for they ride up and down on her and make her their boots."

The Falstaff attitude is therefore in solution, as it were, throughout the play, even when he is not on the stage; but it takes explicit form in the person and speeches of Sir John. We see a heroic legend in process of growth in the account of his fight with the men in buckram. The satire in the description of his ragged regiment is pointed by a special emphasis on military terms—"soldiers," "captain," "lieutenant," "ancients, corporals . . . gentlemen of companies." His realism easily reduces honour to "a mere scutcheon." Prince Henry's duel with Hotspur is accompanied by the mockery of the Douglas-Falstaff fight, which ends with the dead and the counterfeit dead lying side by side. If we can rid ourselves of our realistic illusions and their accompanying moral qualms we realize how appropriate it is that Falstaff should rise to stab Hotspur's body and carry him off as his luggage on his back.

The satire on warfare, the Falstaff attitude, implies an axis of reference, which is of course found in the gross and vigorous life of the body. We find throughout the play a peculiar insistence on imagery deriving from the body, on descriptions of death in its more gruesome forms, on stabbing, cutting, bruising, and the like. We expect to find references to blood and death in a play dealing with civil war, but such references in *Henry IV* are far more pervasive than in a war play such as *Henry V*. In the first scene we hear of the earth "daubing her lips with her own children's blood." War is "trenching"; it "channels" the fields and "bruises" the flowers. "The edge of war" is "like an ill-sheathed knife" which "cuts his master." Civil war is an "intestinal shock," and battles are "butchery." We learn that the defeated Scots lay "balk'd in their own blood," and that "beastly shameless transformation" was done by the Welsh upon the corpses of Mortimer's soldiers. Later Hotspur mentions the smell of "a slovenly unhandsome corpse," and we hear of Mortimer's "mouthed wounds." So throughout the play. The dead Blunt lies "grinning," Hotspur's face is "mangled," and Falstaff lies by him "in blood." Falstaff's "honour" soliloquy insists on surgery, on broken legs and arms.

To all this Falstaff, a walking symbol, is of course opposed. "To shed my dear blood drop by drop i' the dust" for the sake of honour appears an imbecile ambition. Falstaff will "fight no longer than he sees reason." His philosophy is summed up when he has escaped Douglas by counterfeiting death: "S'blood! 'twas time to counterfeit, or that hot termagant Scot had paid me scot and lot too. Counterfeit? I lie, I am no counterfeit: to die is to be a counterfeit; for he is but the counterfeit of a man who hath not the life of a man; but to counterfeit dying, when a man thereby liveth, is to be no counterfeit, but the true and perfect image of life indeed." The same thought is implicit in the honour soliloquy.

Once the play is read as a whole, the satire on war and policy is apparent. It is useful to compare the first part of *Henry IV* with *King John* in estimating the development of Shakespeare's dramatic power. *King John* turns on a single pivotal point—the Bastard's speech on commodity, but the whole of the later play is impregnated with satire which crystallizes in Falstaff. Now, satire implies a standard, and in *Henry IV* the validity of the standard itself is questioned; hence the peculiar coherence and universality of the play. "Honour" and "state-craft" are set in opposition to the natural life of the body, but the chief body of the play is, explicitly, "a bolting-hutch of beastliness."—"A pox on this gout! or a gout on this pox, I should say." Other speeches reinforce the age-and-disease theme which, it has not been observed, is a significant part of the Falstaff theme. Hotspur pictures the earth as an "old bedlam"

> *pinch'd and vex'd*
> *By the imprisoning of unruly wind*
> *Within her womb.*

Again, he says:

> *The time of life is short;*
> *To spend that shortness basely were too long,*
> *If life did ride upon a dial's point,*
> *Still ending at the arrival of an hour.*

The last two lines imply that no "if" is necessary; life does "ride upon a dial's point," and Hotspur's final speech takes up the theme of transitoriness:

> *But thought's the slave of life, and life time's fool:*
> *And time, that takes survey of all the world,*
> *Must have a stop.*

There is no need to emphasize the disease aspect of Falstaff (Bardolph's bad liver is not merely funny). He "owes God a death." He and his regiment are "mortal men." It is important to realize, however, that when Falstaff feigns death he is meant to appear actually as dead in the eyes of the audience; at least the idea of death is meant to be emphasized in connexion with the Falstaff-idea at this point. No answer is required to the Prince's rhetorical question,

> *What! old acquaintance! could not all this flesh*
> *Keep in a little life? Poor Jack, farewell!*

The stability of our attitude after a successful reading of the first part of *Henry IV* is due to the fact that the breaking-down process referred to above is not simple but complex; one set of impulses is released for the expression of the Falstaff-outlook; but a set of opposite complementary impulses is also brought into play, producing an effect analogous to that caused by the presence of comedy in *King Lear* * (compare the use of irony in *Madame*

---
* See the admirable essay on "Lear and the Comedy of the Grotesque" in *The Wheel of Fire*, by G. Wilson Knight.

Bovary). *Lear* is secure against ironical assault because of the irony it contains; *Henry IV* will bear the most serious ethical scrutiny because in it the "serious" is a fundamental part of the "comic" effect of the play. (The second part of *Henry IV* is no less interesting. No one has yet pointed out that drunkenness, lechery, and senile depravity (in II, iv, for example) are *not* treated by Shakespeare with "good-natured tolerance." Shakespeare's attitude toward his characters in *2 Henry IV* at times approaches the attitude of Mr. Eliot towards Doris, Wauchope, etc., in *Sweeney Agonistes*. Northumberland's monody on death (I, i) needs to be studied in order to understand the tone of the play.)

This summary treatment of a play which demands further elucidation on the lines suggested is, I think, sufficient to illustrate the main points of the notes on comedy which precede it. No theory of comedy can explain the play; no theory of comedy will help us to read it more adequately. Only a morbid pedantry would be blind to the function of laughter in comedy, but concentration upon laughter leads to a double error: the dilettante critic falls before the hallucination of the Comic Spirit, the more scientifically minded persuade themselves that the jokes collected by Bergson and Freud have something to do with the practice of literary criticism.

(1933)

Music and the Dramatic
by W. H. Mellers

I

In speaking of the relation between music and drama one runs the risk of confusing a number of different things; it is therefore necessary to be as clear as possible about one's terms at the outset. By "drama" one generally means a representation of life and action intended for performance on a stage by living actors: in speaking of music-drama, or opera, one may mean that such a representation is illustrated by the *addition* of music so that the music merely intensifies the action; or one may mean that the visual representation in such a performance is merely a specific example of some conception of human experience which the music is presenting in general terms, and is therefore an aid to listening which masquerades as a distraction.

Euphuistically one also speaks of music as "dramatic" when no visual representation is involved but simply when the music seems to express emotions of an immediacy such that they suggest or imply a number of imaginary protagonists in a series of events (say the battle of the Tragic Hero with Fate or Destiny) which have the unity of interest of a play. This is a loose interpretation of the word "dramatic" as applied to music, but in some ways it is the most important and the most frequently employed. To consider in some detail this relation between music and the dramatic is certainly the most fundamental, and probably the only pertinent approach to an aesthetic of opera, for it is useless to discuss operatic music and non-operatic music as though they were activities distinct and separable.

II

If the notorious opposition between Classical and Romantic means anything at all it means, I would say, something like this. By "classical" music we mean music which "objectifies" a body of personal experiences which will usually be sanctioned by tradition. Technically this experience will most often be incarnated in forms which are predominantly melodic and built on the bases of the intervals which the human voice, owing to the nature of the harmonic series, instinctively sings (in normal circumstances it is impossible to sound a single tone without, for instance, also sounding the octave and twelfth above fairly prominently); and in forms which are polyphonic because, if it be granted that the essence of music is melody, then the formal products of polyphonic structure are *ipso facto* the inherently musical ones. Often, too, this sort of music will be contrapuntal because counterpoint is the means of organizing polyphony, and such technical organization is obviously inseparable from the organization of experience which we call objectivity—inseparable, that is, if the music is alive. It is apposite here to refer, among many others, to Haydn, Mozart, Beethoven, Schubert, Verdi, Glinka, all composers who, towards the end of their lives, turned to a renewed study of counterpoint as a preparation for their most mature and representative work.

By "romantic" music, on the other hand, we mean music that is personal in the subjective, introspective sense, music which, glorifying personal feeling, tends to be anti-traditional and therefore inclines, technically, away from the inherently musical melodic-polyphonic forms towards forms which (like the symphonic poem and the *Leitmotiv* music-drama) depend more on literary and pictorial associations. Such forms make their effect by a reliance on the "dramatic" vividness of harmony considered not as the logical result of a confluence of melodic voices but rather as a sequence of chordal blocks marking so many rhetorical points in a musical argument. (This rhetorical conception of harmony later becomes associated with the exploitation of orchestral "colour.") Classical music will usually be founded on a stable tonality because tonalities are built up by tradition and by the melody-motives the human voice sings naturally—and we must remember that in a sense equal tempered diatonicism is less stable than the more flexible system of the so-called ecclesiastical modes in that it is more artificial: romanticism in music tends to be associated with the *disruption* of tonalities, as in the chromaticism of Gesualdo, Liszt, Wagner, and Schönberg.

Of course, no hard-and-fast line can be drawn between the two types, and it is absurd to suggest that "classical" music—in the sense in which I have used the term—can never be "dramatic." Vittoria will achieve dramatic effects of the utmost poignancy by the placing of a simple triad or by an unexpected distribution of vocal sonorities. Monteverde writes homophonic harmonic passages directly designed for the dramatic thrill, and the modulations of Haydn or Scarlatti will be as dramatic as they are ungrammatical. Bach or Schütz will be as anguished in their chromaticism as Mozart is piercingly sweet. But just as, with all these composers, the "dramatic" effect is merely a part of a more complex total response, so the technical device is used merely as part of a traditional technique which is in each case—I think it may safely be said—fundamentally vocal, and there is no reliance on the harmonic thrill, or upon sensation, in and for itself. The "revolutionary" Monteverde never finally abjured the principles of his forebears, and the significance of the often-celebrated rhapsodic "romanticism" of Bach's *Chromatic Fantasia* lies in its being introductory to the magnificent *Fugue*. Only when a composer's sensibility tends to depart from a human centrality and sanity does he relinquish the formal principles, usually polyphonic, of musical tradition. Machaut, Palestrina, Bach, Haydn, Mozart, Fauré, and on the whole Berlioz I would list as typical "classical" composers; Gesualdo, Liszt, Wagner, Chopin, Berg, and (more equivocally) the Beethoven of the *Appassionata,* as typical romanticists. Brahms occupies a half-way house, and his importance lies most in the fact that he kept the true musical tradition alive at a time when it was hardly fashionable.

I list these names merely indicatively and without wishing to suggest that there is any point in pigeonholing artists; what I do want to suggest is that this balance or oscillation between the inherently musical, on the one hand, and the extra-musical conception of emotional autobiography (incarnated most obviously in "dramatic" harmony), on the other, has been a force of great potency in the evolution of musical history and one which has a direct bearing on the development of opera. I think we shall understand more clearly how the two attitudes act together and against one another if we examine for a moment an element of them both which we have not yet specifically considered, namely rhythm.

III

For all music, with the possible exception of such a static *tour de force* as Erik Satie's *Socrate,* implies in some degree physical movement. It may be that "classical" music tends to cultivate the plastic assymetrical rhythms inherent in the human singing voice, whereas "romantic" music tends to exploit the dramatic effect of violently contrasted physical movements of the kind exemplified in the dance; and it may be that it is a bad thing for music to become so intimately associated with the dance that it loses its linear independence and restricts its melody to the extra-musical demands of metre. But at the same time the rhythmic vitality of Vittoria as of Bach depends on a continual tension between (vocal) rhythm and (dance) metre, just as a piece of mature Shakespearean blank verse depends on a tension between metre and the rhythm of speech. The two elements are mutually interdependent, and during the history of music the dance has fought more or less impartially now on the side of the human voice and of inherent musicality, now on the side of dramatic truth and harmonic experiment. The physical movement of the dance is the common denominator which is shared by music and the drama equally; it is the source from which the fountain of opera springs.

IV

The dance has always been a step ahead of music. It was a highly organized ritualistic art before European music was born as expressive melody; by the time music had developed as a great religious art, the dance was turning away from ritual towards the pursuance of display upon the stage. It carried music, via popular religious art and the puppet-show, with it; the Renaissance, "the time at which the modern world was born," saw also the emergence of the exhibitionism of classical ballet. The "organic" relation between music and the dance gave place to the exquisite filigree of a sophisticated entertainment.

That the ambivalence which we have observed between music and the dramatic was implicit in the dance itself in its contrasted elements of pantomime and perfection of abstract design is testified by the numerous contemporary disputes, culminating in that between Noverre and Angiolini, as to the degree of conventionalism desirable. But it was not until words were introduced into spectacular entertainment in an attempt to imitate the drama of the Greeks that the problem of dramatic truth forcibly asserted itself. Musicality and the "dramatic," abstract design and pantomime, the stylized singer's opera and the ideal of dramatic realism, aria and recitative, solo dance and mime, all these are examples of the same fundamental dichotomy. Where the convention is stylized and sophisticated the human voice and perfection of design hold sway; when realism is encouraged the voice is reduced to a condition of intensified declamation and the drama is embodied in the harmony and sonority of the orchestra. (Italians such as Puccini preserved the voice's claim to—at least—equality only by vulgarizing its musical qualities beyond recognition.) If opera is too completely musical, as in the *opera seria* of Alessandro Scarlatti, Cesti, Handel, Marcello, or Puccini, with its stylized *da capo* aria, it may be boring because the representational, extra-musical part of it seems unnecessary, a fortuitous visual titillation: if the opera is too realistic it may be boring because the musical part of it will then seem absurd. The *verismo* of the latter-day Wagnerians cannot escape this charge, nor can some of the music-drama of Wagner himself, although he fortunately seldom followed through the implications of his theories but rather tried to seek dramatic justification for the lyrical moments of his work. Probably the only successful "realistic" opera is that of Mussorgsky and Dargomijsky (but not Borodin, who is comparatively Italianate), where the exoticism of the subject itself provides a convention and where the emotion involved are "primitive" and violent enough to give heightened speech-movement a musical validity. The danger implicit in a realistic interpretation of the verbal text is that the opera may over-emphasize the topical and local rather in the same way as "romantic" music over-stresses the element of personality. The ideal opera, like "classical" music, will not ignore the immediate dramatic situation, but will transcend it by reincarnating it in purely musical terms of more than topical and local application.

To say that singer's opera is artificial and realistic opera natural is, then, patently over-simple. An opera of Puccini is not necessarily less "real" than an opera of Gluck because it is less "like life"; what matters is that a convention should be employed sensitively and without confusion of values. Monteverde approached the sensitive compromise in his *Orfeo* and *Incoronazione di Poppaea* when he combined the aristocratic masque, the symphonic *ritornelli*, and the complex polyphonic madrigal of (say) the brilliant Orazio Vecchi with the passionate homophonic declamation and the bold modulations of his dramatic recitative—recitative so lyrical as to approach more nearly to song than to intensified speech.

Gluck, too, attained it in some measure since for all his insistence on naturalism he inherited the stylization of the courtly ballet of Cambert, while his vocal technique purified and perhaps etiolated but did not destroy the florid vocal organism of his predecessors. When Gluck remarked that "a misplaced *appoggiatura*, a shake, a roulade, can destroy the effect of an entire scene," he admitted by implication that, artistically placed, these ornaments were desirable.

Iphigénie en Tauride may be a masterpiece of psychological subtlety, but its quality of exquisite moral elevation is directly proportional to the beautiful purity of its music. Even Rameau, who was regarded as a die-hard revolutionary by reason of his barbarous and cacophonous harmonic experiments, derives much of the shapeliness of his *arioso* from the courtly melody of Lully, though he has a finer potency, while his "realistic" harmonies often tend to fall into *cliché*, one chordal construction to represent "fear," another to represent "horror," so that they led not so much in the direction of realism as to a narrower form of convention. Berlioz's wonderful *Les Troyens* adapts the technique of Gluck to a wider canvas; it is interesting to note how he introduced into his inherently musical anti-Wagnerian treatment of the opera stylized *pantomimes expressives* in the manner of Spontini and Méhul.

V

Rameau repented of his notoriously brusque aphorism, *"La mélodie naît de l'harmonie,"* when, towards the end of his career, he remarked that if he were twenty years younger he would abandon some of his harmony and adopt Pergolesi and the Italian vocal school as his model. Lecerf de la Viéville, at the time of Lully's heyday, and Jean-Jacques Rousseau in the latter half of the eighteenth century, complained of the too-blatant obtrusiveness of the orchestra (". . . But the accompaniment would rend the rocks! Pretty compensation! Is it the orchestra who is the hero? No, it is the singer . . ."); while even Mozart, whose orchestration so subtly underlines the vocal contour, explicitly stated that the voice took precedence over all. Only in Mozart's operas—and in the late Shakespearean operas of Verdi—has the ideal fusion, the musical-dramatic compromise, been successfully accomplished. Mozart was, it is true, fortunate in that the degree of stylization implicit in *opera buffa* was fairly clearly defined through its derivation from *Singspiel* and the *commedia dell'arte*, so that Mozart's flexible genius was able to exploit this conventionalism both in the interests of musicality and of psychological acumen: but the way in which he uses the elaborate musical polyphony of the concerted aria to convey the attitudes of a number of characters to a situation, and their attitudes to each other's attitudes to the situation simultaneously, is a miracle of musical-*cum*-psychological compression and a proof that the inherently musical potentialities of the human voice can convey, in the hands of a genius, all the gallant flourish and tragic pathos of a group of dramatic protagonists, and much more besides. Here the great artist turns to advantage all the resources, even the apparent limitations of his medium.

Desdemona's terrible cry at the end of the "Willow" song is another example of the fusion of dramatic and musical effect; here is the perfect collaboration of the text, the singer, and the orchestra. "I have tried to give Boïto's verses the most true and significant accents in my power," Verdi remarked, and the passions, the hatreds, the sensual and supersensual loves of human beings have never been delineated with greater intensity and power. Yet through all this human drama the soaring fountain of melody has a golden richness and nobility that belongs unmistakably, despite its different idiom, to the same world as the long supple lines of Alessandro Scarlatti or of Marcello's *Didone,* the work which Verdi admired above all the achievements of Baroque opera. Not since Marenzio and Giovanni Gabrieli had Italian music attained to such fiery brilliance, such sensuous glitter, and such etherial solemnity; this music indeed "needs youthfulness of the senses, impetuousness of the blood, fullness of life."

If *Otello* seems to be at once singer's opera and realistic opera, the position occupied by *Falstaff* is perhaps still more significant. Sir John is a Shakespearean Falstaff, conceived "in the round." But the atmosphere of the opera is essentially unrealistic, magical, fantastic, with a witty translucence and a quivering radiance like the play of sunlight upon water. Even in the exquisite music given to the young lovers Verdi's critical agility is operative—the aristocracy of the music comes from his ability to stand back from his emotions, covertly to parody himself. The kaleidoscopic melodic construction, the shimmering vivacity of the orchestration, are a sublimation of Cimarosa and Pergolesi; the fairy music is a quintessence of the fanciful, quite distinct from the fairy music of Weber or Mendelssohn; and the final fugue is a master-stroke, summing up the spirit of gossamer-like fancy in a framework of aloof and aristocratic intellectuality. Here the most inherently musical and classical of all forms becomes the logical consummation of a stylized drama that is an epitome of Mediterranean culture. At once human and supernatural, this work is the ideal realization of the ethos of the early classical opera of Monteverde.

No opera is more fruitful with intimations of the future than *Falstaff*. A study of the score marked a turning-point in the career of Busoni, and although it may seem a far cry from the fanciful vision of *Falstaff* to the mystical vision of Busoni's *Faust,* the texture of the music, with its spontaneous contrapuntal flow, is surprisingly similar in both works, and both, being preoccupied with magic rather than the realistic, are related to the tradition of the puppet-show and of the *commedia dell'arte.* No one, however, seems to have followed up Busoni's tentative experiments, and to the average twentieth-century composer who manifests no power of sustained melodic line and little understanding of the basic principles of the human voice, some modification of the Wagnerian symphonic still offers the path of least resistance. So fine and sensitive a musician as Alban Berg seems to have felt, in composing that macabre Wagnerian aftermath, *Wozzeck,* that the symphonic opera left much to be desired from the point of view of the musically significant form, and to have endeavoured to ameliorate its deficiencies by imposing an excessively elaborate musical formalism arbitrarily on top of music which remains in essence expressionistic. Very rarely symphonic opera may itself attain to an adequate stylization; *Tristan* possibly does, and certainly *Pelléas et Mélisanda.* But the Debussy opera is a unique case, and although the restrained declamation of the voice and the sensitive colouring of the orchestra emphasize the nuances of the verbal text with a delicacy and precision which has never been paralleled, the atmosphere of the play as a whole is so remote, fantastical, and musical in conception that it cannot be regarded as a realistic drama "illustrated" by music; rather is it poetry dissolving into music, somewhat like Shakespeare's *The Tempest,* except that here it is the musician who creats the metamorphosis rather than the poet.

Dukas, in his superb *Ariane et Barbe-Bleue,* worked out an interesting compromise of the Wagnerian *Leitmotiv-cum-*symphonic method with the utmost austerity of orchestration and with vocal lines which, although declamatory, have tremendous range and virility. Fauré's *Pénélope* develops this compromise further, for here hints of the *leitmotiv* are subservient to a restrained, subtle lyricism which is an aristocratic sublimation of the French *mélodie,* to a delicate manipulation of orchestral sonorities, and to a stylized "classical" mastery of counterpoint, exemplified particularly in canonic finales. The fantastic operas of Janáček are on the whole an eccentric (though very powerful) phenomenon, since, starting from speech-rhythm somewhat in the manner of Mussorgsky, they developed in an increasingly agonized and disrupted fashion towards an esoteric symbolism which may, like the later work of

Bartók, be expressive of the plight of the contemporary human consciousness in spiritual isolation, but which certainly does little towards solving the problem of the "biographical" and musical balance in opera.

VI

Figaro, Don Juan, Falstaff, Pelléas, prove that opera may be an adequate as well as an intermittently beautiful form. But, being a sophisticated entertainment, its conventions do not evolve of themselves; they require thought, careful consideration. In an age in which opera is (comparatively speaking) a commercial proposition, there is usually little time for thought; today there is plenty of time to think but few people to listen to the operas that have been thought about. But I do not believe that the problem is *fundamentally economic,* or that opera is in a relatively more desperate plight than the other "serious" arts; there is a more than fortuitous link between apparent economic difficulties and artistic ones—the inability of most composers today to think in terms of the human voice, their propensity to substitute rhetoric for sustained melodic line. No doubt this is why many intelligent contemporary composers who found the symphonic opera uncongenial—who realized that Wagner's interweaving of "pregnant thematic fragments" in some of his later work bears about as much relationship to genuine polyphony as margarine to butter—turned not to the stylization of the singer's opera but to the stylization of ballet. The disillusion of the puppet-tragedy of Stravinsky's *Petrouchka* leads in its extreme form to the "cubist" preoccupation with *things* which is exemplified in Satie's *Parade, Mercure,* and *Relâche.* In a sense the abstract design, the symmetrical melodic and rhythmic patterns of Satie's ballets mark the culmination of a tendency which had been developing ever since the swan-song of the Italian virtuoso vocal tradition—which is the elegiac melody of Bellini—merged into the great slow waltz tunes of Tchaikovsky's classical ballet.

The dance, as we have seen, may encourage a flourishing vocal tradition where there is one; but I do not think, despite the fact that Vaughan Williams's *Job,* musically one of the finest works of the twentieth century, was conceived as a "masque for dancing," that it can provide an adequate substitute for such a tradition. It is significant that Albert Roussel, in his *Padmâvatî, La Naissance de la Lyre,* and *Aenéas,* should have reintroduced the voice into a convention that is basically the stylization of the *dance.* With his free and plastic melodic sense, combined with his agile response to physical movement, no composer could have been better fitted to effect this re-creation of an art-form, the *opéra-ballet,* which had been moribund since the time of Rameau. From the point of view of the *future* of the relation between music and the stage, *Padmâvatî* and *Aenéas* seem to me probably the most important productions of the twentieth century.

(1940)

PART V

A MODERN MISCELLANY

W. H. Auden

AUDEN'S INVERTED DEVELOPMENT
For the Time Being, by W. H. Auden

Reviewed by R. G. Lienhardt

It is becoming apparent that any claim to poetic importance which Auden may have in the future will rest upon effects produced almost casually in his early work. His experiments have been immensely more promising than his achievement, and the fact that his poetry has not profited by them rather indicates that his efforts have not been directed towards improving his poetry, but towards something at the best extraneous to it, and at the worst extremely damaging. It has become increasingly obvious with each new publication that this poet's greatest difficulty lies in determining quite what he wishes to express and in formulating an appropriate attitude towards it, and that, at any time, his equipment for dealing with his matter, in a technical sense, is vastly in excess of what is required. The correct answer to this problem, for Auden, would have been to admit to himself that he could range safely only in a limited field, and to confine himself to saying the comparatively little that he could say personally, and to reduce and refine his effects to the minimum necessary for complete individual expression. Instead of this, he has attempted to assimilate more and more general ideas, to write verse based upon human experience quite outside his individual scope, and hence to write at second hand. His technical facility has been lavished upon the expression of sentimental regrets, boyish fantasies, and unbalanced, immature enthusiasms. Few poets can have started writing with such superficial promise of accomplishment, have developed so completely their early weaknesses, and shelved so definitely their early strength. One is thus forced to the conclusion that Auden has occasionally written a few lines worth preserving as a by-product of his conscious application to his task—a view which is supported by a glance through his work. For only such a series of casual successes will explain the absence of any single, successful poem, and yet the appearance throughout of occasional successful passages. Further, it will be noted that those qualities which make for success remain undeveloped throughout—that the better parts of his later work are not an advance on the better parts of his earlier work, whereas his faults develop in a predictable way and connect quite simply with weaknesses already revealed. He has thus undergone an inverted process of development, natural enough in a poet impervious to criticism from outside the group which formed his ideal public, and which existed on a basis of mutual admiration which a more independent poet would have found an embarrassment.

Reading *Paid on Both Sides,* one becomes aware of moral issues suggested but not fully defined or worked out in the poetry—there is a residue which one feels one has not quite grasped, a meaning beyond the literal meaning of the words on the page, suggested, but persistently elusive. Images come to have enormous symbolical significance, an action appears to be in progress between protagonists of immense importance.

> *O how shall man live*
> *Whose thought is born, child of one farcical night,*
> *To find him old? The body warm but not*
> *By choice, he dreams of folk in dancing bunches,*
> *Of tart wine spilt on home-made benches,*
> *Where learns, one drawn apart, a secret will*
> *Restore the dead; but comes thence to a wall.*
> *Outside on frozen soil lie armies killed*
> *Who seem familiar, but they are cold.*

Here there appear to be possibilities; a situation is partly realized in an urgent and supple idiom, and there appears to be a reserve of meaning which might eventually make itself apparent. But as one reads on one discovers that the qualified success of this and later poems depends upon ambiguity—that when a point is reached at which a definite formulation of an attitude or an issue is made, one is confronted with a shallow commonplace, something vaguely defined in terms of "love," "beauty," or "good." Just as throughout his work the indefinite evil forces, to which he seems extremely sensitive, resolve themselves into nothing more than a succession of images of disease, sterility, or cruelty, so his positive values are the merest indications of conventional virtues. In fact, there is no imaginative life whatsoever in Auden's treatment of moral conflict, and it is a verbal fluency, incorporating a number of effectively juxtaposed images, appearing to make a general impression by putting together a number of smaller impressions united at the most by compatible moods, which gives a specious vitality to much of his earlier work. He is consequently at his weakest when he is most explicit, when the suggestiveness of his language has to give way to a bald statement. Then the alarming paucity of idea beneath the surface of his impressionistic facility reveals itself, and in his yearning for

> *New styles of architecture, a change of heart*

one realizes that Auden is attempting to diagnose the spiritual malady of an age with the experiential equipment of the man in the street. Again, it becomes more and more obvious throughout Auden's work that his morbidity and disillusion, which have always the insecurity of pose, are in fact nothing more than a fashionable accretion, perhaps unconscious and unavoidable, and that fundamentally he is committed to an easy materialistic optimism, that somewhere and somehow agents for good are at work, though what the "good" is and how these indefinite virtuous ends are to be achieved is more than he can tell us. We know that "It is time for the destruction of error," but after the inevitable, and sometimes effective, sequence of related images which follow that announcement in the poem from which it is extracted, all we discover is that the "death of the old gang" is a necessary preliminary, and that after

> *The old gang to be forgotten in the spring*
> *The hard bitch and the riding master,*
> *Stiff underground . . .*

we may see

> *deep in a clear lake*
> *The lolling bridegroom, beautiful, there.*

What success this has depends upon its lack of explicitness, and it is therefore not surprising that *For the Time Being*, which is in places the most explicit work he has produced yet, if in places the most ambiguous, should also be much the least satisfactory.

For the Time Being consists of two compositions of indeterminate *genre*, with a persistent suggestion of having been adapted for broadcasting. The first, called *The Sea and the Mirror*, is an attempted extension of *The Tempest* into regions more uncertainly defined, both geographically and philosophically, than Prospero's island. The second is the title-piece of the whole and is described as "A Christmas Oratorio." Both are dramatized and have prose inserts of considerable length, in which the essentials of the situation being treated are discussed very tediously with the audience. Here, much of the poet's intention, already apparent from the verse, is unnecessarily emphasized, and much that remained obscure in the verse is presented with no added clarity in laboured and ungainly prose. In both works he indulges his increasing taste for general philosophical propositions, concerns himself with much deeper issues than he is at all competent to do justice to, and becomes involved in a complex of ideas which he has neither the intellectual sweep nor the emotional integrity to assimilate as a poet. The first poem is much the less explicit of the two, and is accordingly the more successful; but here the allegorical figures have such a wide possible field of reference, and the indications of any definite level at which the poem is to be understood as a whole is so vague, that the whole point of allegory is lost, the meaning too dependent on individual construction. (A reviewer in one of the literary weeklies, for example, connected Prospero with Democracy.) Instead of working out his general ideas in particular and concrete terms throughout the poem, so that the interplay of concepts and qualities becomes something accessible to the mind and feelings at once, the poet provides his familiar association of images and metaphors, but with no suggestion of any coherent imaginative scheme for the whole. In consequence, there is a superficial suggestion throughout that some impressive action is being worked out, but on closer examination the significance of it evaporates, and one is left with the theme of the resolution of the duality of Ariel and Caliban, with other characters from *The Tempest* who may mean this, that, or the other, according to the general construction which the reader puts on the main theme. There are occasional passages of pleasant imagery which excite no complaint, unless it be that even here Auden's rhythms are becoming flaccid and his language more reflective than active. Above all there is a persistent inflated manner which one can trace back without difficulty to earlier work in which the poet permitted himself to preach too unguardedly. Compare, for example:

> *Greed showing shamelessly her naked money,*
> *And all Love's wandering eloquence debased*

> *To a collector's slang, Smartness in furs,*
> *And Beauty scratching miserably for food* . . .

with his more recent

> *O blessed be bleak exposure on whose sword*
> *Caught unawares, we prick ourselves alive!*
> *Shake Failure's bruising fist* . . .

There can be few clearer signs of lack of poetic vitality than these automatically produced catalogues of abstract qualities, all doing something conventionally appropriate or with conventionally suitable attributes, but no more vivid or disturbing than if they had remained in the dictionary. At the best, they are dull; at the worst, they are absurd, as when the Star of the Nativity in the second poem invites one to

> *Hear tortured Horror roaring for a Bride* . . .

The habit of using capital letters for emphasis, where true emphasis would be achieved by a well-managed sentence construction and rhythm, is one which has grown on Auden. It results not infrequently in an appearance of extraordinary pretentiousness, emphasized by the complete flatness of the straightforward unambiguous statement, as in the following:

> *Sin fractures the Vision, not the Fact; for*
> *The Exceptional is always usual*
> *And the Usual exceptional.*
> *To choose what is difficult all one's days*
> *As if it were easy, that is faith* . . .

"A Christmas Oratorio," from which the last quotation comes, is an example of how bad Auden can be when it comes to treatment of clearly defined moral issues—in this case the theme of the Nativity, with comments by a Narrator who is, presumably, the detached observer of the action, pointing the moral but by no means adorning the tale. There is no space here to quote examples of his lapses of taste, his lack of proportion which makes him self-important when he wishes to be serious, frivolous or even nasty when he wants to be witty. His values, uncertain and unsystematized, represent nothing appreciably solid or coherent. This subject, if it is to be treated tolerably, demands either genuine simplicity or genuine sophistication in the artist. The poet who writes at one end of the scale:

> *Come to our well-run desert*
> *Where anguish arrives by cable*
> *And the deadly sins may be bought in tins*
> *With instructions on the label . . .*

and at the other:

> *He is the Way.*
> *Follow him through the land of Unlikeness;*
> *You will see rare beasts, and have unique adventures*

has neither qualification. For it is in just that irresponsible spirit of undefined but "unique" adventure that he approaches his material—the Nativity, *The Tempest,* the Oedipus legend in *The Ascent of F. 6.*

That Auden started his career with apparently unusual gifts cannot be denied; and even this volume displays, in places, snatches of his old accomplishment. But it has no chance when set against his determination to write on a grand scale with the mental equipment only of a minor poet. If his seriousness of purpose were part of his nature instead of yet another, if unconscious, attitude, his tendency to the cheap, commonplace, and exhibitionistic might not persist. But it is clear from this volume that his separation from the circle in which that tendency was formed came too late to enable him to discard his public character and see what values of his own he could substitute for those of the group which made his reputation.

(1945)

Cyril Connolly

FROM PLAYGROUND TO GRAVE

The Unquiet Grave, by Palinurus
The Condemned Playground, Essays 1927-1944,
by Cyril Connolly

Reviewed by R. G. Lienhardt

Both Mr. Connolly and Palinurus are interested in the same way in literature, and in those considerations of a general sort which must arise when quality is discussed. Theirs too, one is justified in supposing, is the only type of success which those who cover similar ground are at present able to achieve. They have contrived to diffuse their type of culture and their critical habits amongst a far wider public than any other contemporary literary group with pretensions to seriousness. In doing so, they have come to represent the only class of modern critical writers whose practice has some of the prestige value of a limited commercial success. Among those readers who now wish to discriminate, the sorts of judgements made by Palinurus and Mr. Connolly would probably receive general assent. At the level at which we are discussing literature and its ancillary problems, Palinurus and Mr. Connolly, along with those men of letters who may be relied upon to receive their work with enthusiasm, stand for the contemporary common reader at his most articulate. They have helped to create a certain demand for that which they consider to be of value, and at once represent and control the taste of a very large proportion of the serious reading public. As types of the common reader, their judgements confirm his and may decide his. Should he prove refractory, they have more chance than most of suggesting to him what opinion is best, from the points of view of both taste and advantage. With this in mind, one is inclined to take these two volumes seriously, and in the case of *The Unquiet Grave,* at least, one hopes more seriously than it was intended. Yet, Palinurus presents this work without a hint of oblique criticism of the type of mind which it displays. A writer with his pretensions can rarely have dished up his shortcomings with so little garnish.

The enthusiasm with which *The Unquiet Grave* was originally received is preserved on the dust-cover in lengthy quotations from early reviews. One comment, including the phrase "a superb gift for words and epigrams," was made on the wireless; the others come from well-known pens in the most widely read literary columns. The book is praised because its author is said to be "enchantingly clever," his prose style is said to be "taut and supple, disciplined and sensuous," and he is considered, in this "beautifully written book," to have made "a genuine addition" to the "world's stock of profitable introspection." The quotations above are from four different hands. His prose style, wit, and introspection are in fact those features of this work of Palinurus which should be discussed. *The Unquiet Grave* is a loosely composed mixture of self-examination, confession, reminiscence, quotation, and aphorism, a "word-cycle" vaguely connected in structure with the story of Palinurus, the pilot of Aeneas. Its prose style is in the aesthetic "fine writing" tradition. It has strong affinities with George Moore and Pater, and, in those passages containing general comments of a philosophical nature, owes something to E. M. Forster and to some of the essays of Virginia Woolf. Another debt is to that current literary journalism which exploits the critic's personality and tends to sacrifice coherence in the presentation of ideas to a "well-turned" phrase. Now, if you like that sort of thing, then that is what you like, and there might be no point in displaying its defects again here. Considering, however, the extreme adulation this work has received, it is perhaps desirable to express one dissentient view. The pretensions of the author may now be discussed with reference to his performance. His first sentence runs as follows:

> The more books we read, the sooner we perceive that the true function of a writer is to produce a master-piece, and that no other task is of any consequence.

This is followed by a list of works to which Palinurus would give the name "master-piece"—works written by twelve writers, amongst whom are Horace, Virgil, Montaigne, Villon, Pope, and Baudelaire. After considering these, Palinurus returns to his primary interest, himself, and reflects:

> Even though none of the conditions for producing a master-piece be present . . . [the compiler of the list] . . . can at least attempt to work at the same level of intention as the Sacred Twelve. Spiritualise the Earthbound, Palinurus, and don't aim too high.

How far he is able to work at the level of intention which he prescribes for himself may best be judged by three samples of his work, the first showing the quality of his prose when he consciously attempts to write well, the second exemplifying his "enchanting" cleverness, and the third in his philosophical manner.

> There, in his Tumulus, lies the last Celtic prince, wrapped in his race's age-long death-wish; his great vault stones carved with indecipherable warnings; runes of serpents and oak-leaves, of wave eddies and wind-patterns, finger prints of giant hands—O powerless to save! And that night at Vannes, the cave-wedding—Summoque ululárunt vertice Nymphae. She with sad grave gem-like beauty, and happiness soon to be thrown away.

> Hôtel de l'Université for American College girls, Hôtel de Londres with its chestnut tree in the courtyard, Hôtel Jacob for wasting much time; Hôtel de Savoie, Hôtel Delambre, Hôtel de la Louisiane; central heated Stations of the Cross . . .

> . . . it is no answer to say that we are meant to rid ourselves of self: religions like Christianity and Buddhism are desperate strategems of failure, the failure of men to be men. They may be operative as escapes from a problem, as flights from guilt, but they cannot turn out to be a revelation of our destiny. What should we think of dogs' monasteries, hermit cats, vegetarian tigers?

The first, suggesting everything and stating nothing, is a mere gesture in the direction of Pater, even to the cadence and the wholesale adoption of his "poetic" and insipid vocabulary. I hope that the taste of the second advertises its quality sufficiently in the quotation. The third pretends to be an argument, but in fact the terms mean nothing, since the author has no definition of what he means by the nature of man ("the failure of men to be men" is the phrase which blandly begs the question). There is no point in quoting more. The reader whose reaction is still uncertain may as well buy a copy of *The Unquiet Grave* and try out the cumulative effect of pages of similar comment.

Lastly, consider the nature of Palinurus's "profitable introspection." Here is a typical passage:

> August 30th. Morning tears return; spirits at their lowest ebb. Approaching forty, sense of total failure; not a writer but a ham actor whose performance is clotted with egotism . . .

One does not doubt that this is how he imagines he feels—he forgets very frequently the level of intention at which he wishes to appear to work. This is the way in which his sense of guilt, frustration, anxiety, the bad and bitter feeling which he calls *Angst* shows itself; the effects of this self-dissatisfaction, when self is the prime interest, are "misery, disgust, tears, guilt." There are, however, "temporary cures":

> Temporary cures. (1) Lunch with a new friend, literary talk, gossip, *i.e.* appeals to vanity; (2) Art (Renoir landscapes), the true escape into *Timelessness;* (3) The office personality, (Alibi Ike); (4) Old friends, relationships dating from before the Fall.

Emotion manifested and dispelled at this level scarcely merits further comment here. Self-examination without discipline or definite purpose beyond discovering self, is likely to discover very little, but with a great deal of fuss. Palinurus examines himself and his perceptions with reference to nothing beyond a makeshift and uncertain system of values, built upon the very moods and sensations which it proposes to describe and evaluate. Palinurus has an aphorism covering the matter:

> Complacent mental laziness is the English disease.

One can only assume charitably that he does not realize the extent to which so deliberate a self-revelation makes him appear disingenuous and dishonest. Nor is his reception by those whose comments appear to recommend him likely to draw his attention to the ease with which such an impression can be created.

Mr. Cyril Connolly's collection of essays and articles is a selection of those products of seventeen years of writing and thinking which seem to him most worth preserving. It contains a number of essays written chiefly as literary journalism, reviews and so on, some parodies, a fragment of a diary, and other casually written scraps which have recommended themselves to him. Mr. Connolly believes that "the distinction between true criticism and creation is non-existent," that his merits as a critic are "somewhat practical and earthy," and he wishes that he had not "written brightly, because I was asked to do, about so many bad books." (It would be interesting to know who asked him to do this.) The title of this book is suggested by, first, "the literary scene of the 1930's," and second, "that leafy *Spielraum* of Chelsea where I worked and wandered." Like Palinurus, he owes something to E. M. Forster, whose conception (in *What I Believe*) of an "aristocracy of the sensitive, the considerate and the plucky" leads to the deliberate and politic cultivation of a version of these qualities, and thence to a type of presumptuousness conflicting with Mr. Forster's ideal code of personal behaviour. In the critical field too, Mr. Forster, as transmuted by Mr. Connolly, might not easily recognize himself. Mr. Connolly's own conception of his qualities as a critic makes a passage like the following, from his introduction, even more surprising. He refers to himself as "a low-swung basset, who hunts by scent and keeps his nose to the ground," yet writes:

> . . . for Art is man's noblest attempt to preserve the Imagination from Time, to make unbreakable toys of the mind, mud-pies which endure . . .

The connection with Forster is apparent, though I cannot remember, even in *The Longest Journey*, any Forsterian character having flown his kite so high. (Mr. Connolly thinks, at one point, that *The Longest Journey* is Mr. Forster's second-best novel.)

Mr. Connolly's system of values may be said to be founded on the premises and attitudes stated and implied in Mr. Forster's pamphlet. He has that rather dramatized conception of a sensitive minority isolated in a wicked and chaotic world, trying by a scepticism concerning ideologies, a belief in personal relationships, and the sensitiveness recognizable as such in "the leafy *Spielraum* of Chelsea," to preserve the values of civilized life. The result is an emphasis on personality which personality alone cannot bear. An over-simplified view of the sorts of issues which the practice of criticism involves is one result. Take, for example, the following:

> The authors I most enjoy writing about are, first, those great, lonely, formal artists who spit in the eye of their century, and after them the wild and exquisitely gifted young writers who come to an untimely end through passion, and lastly those wise epicureans who combine taste with the gossiping good sense of the world, and whose graceful books are but the shadow of their intimate communion with their friends or with nature.

Some of this may be applicable in some cases to the features of individual writers and may constitute a legitimate, if dull, sort of criticism. But note what Mr. Connolly has done. He has observed, in his reading, that he enjoys responding most to certain qualities in large numbers of writers, responses which, in fact, become his stock-in-trade of critical reaction, as his fondness for words like "exquisite" and "graceful" shows. On his fondness for these sensations in reading he builds a system, in which the qualities which excite them become standards of judgement. What he fails to realize is that the qualities in question are not isolable and lose their authenticity when they become an object in themselves, and not, as they are in the authors from whom he would derive them, the comparatively superficial features of much profounder and more complex preoccupations. One need only consider Baudelaire as "one of those great, lonely formal artists who spit in the eye of their century" to realize that criticism on this basis leaves out almost everything worth saying, the desired sensation produced by reading him being so overwhelming that the critic wishes only to read into his work the qualities he most admires. Sensitiveness, though the word is becoming difficult to use, is, of course, indispensable to a critic, but it cannot be self-consciously pursued alone without becoming a travesty of itself. Mr. Connolly never brings his own range of personal reaction into comparative relationship with any coherent system of values. He tends to extract from what he reads simply a confirmation of a personal fantasy, the sensation which he parodies in a sentence in one of his articles:

> "But this is *me*," I remember saying, holding up a slim volume. "Why haven't I been told about this before, Dadie? Who is this T. S. Eliot?"

This is a parody. Yet, does it differ essentially from his reaction to reading Joyce?

> ... for me any criticism of *Ulysses* will be affected by a wet morning in Florence, when in the empty library of a villa with the smell of wood-smoke, the faint eves-drip, I held the uncouth volume dazedly open in the big arm-chair—Narcissus with his pool before him.

If what I have already said about the dangers inherent in this form of criticism by mood and sensation be true, it would be right to expect that Mr. Connolly can scarcely succeed as the "low-swung basset" of criticism, that when he stops capitalizing his pleasant sensations and turns to make a statement, a certain poverty of thought will be apparent. He parodies at one point a type of common and commonplace criticism:

> ... she seems to be a writer of very delicate intention, and has brought to a difficult subject a restraint, a distinction ...

Compare this with his own serious comment on Evelyn Waugh:

> He has a fresh, crisp style, a gift for creating character, a mastery of dialogue, a melancholy and dramatic sense of life ...

Different *clichés*, but each says as much as the other. It would have been much wiser for Mr. Connolly to leave his parodies out, since, quite apart from their essential triviality, they are not easily distinguishable from his normal manner, except by the absence of highly coloured chunks of prose. Yet even in his parodies he rarely pillories the jejune literary chit-chat which appears again and again in his criticism. An example:

> Henry James, semi-complete. I get an inconceivable pleasure from a Henry James book when I am able to finish it, but too often I can only flounder on a few yards and then have to retreat. . . . For others in this plight I recommend his long short stories. . . . Another remedy is to read anecdotes of Henry James.

I would suggest that the real remedy, for Mr. Connolly, is to leave Henry James alone, since there are so many other novelists from whom he derives satisfaction—for example:

> . . . All Miss Elizabeth Bowen's ironical and delicate studies, and all Rosamond Lehman, another natural writer, and *Frost in May*, by Antonia White, *Orphan Island,* the best novel of Miss Macaulay . . .

It may be objected that this volume has been written over seventeen years and that much that was at first original and may now appear commonplace; it may also be said that some of this is good in intention and the work of a younger and less developed writer than the present Mr. Connolly. The fact remains that, though some of *The Condemned Playground* was written in 1927, it was collected and given its author's blessing in 1944 and consequently is not unjustly treated as representative. I have left out most of his worst lapses in quoting and generally have dealt with only a few of his many vulnerable points. Even this would scarcely have been worth doing had one not had in mind the conditions under which the common reader is reading today and the conditions under which the young writer is writing. Those conditions would be improved if it were possible to make more of the reading public appreciate the full significance of the title of the first part of *The Unquiet Grave* and to compare it with what follows. The title is, *"Ecce Gubernator."*

(1945)

T. S. Eliot

(1) *Collected Poems 1909-1935*, by T. S. Eliot

Reviewed by D. W. Harding

This new volume is an opportunity, not for a review—for "The Poetry of T. S. Eliot" begins to have the intimidating sound of a tripos question—but for asking whether anything in the development of the poetry accounts for the change in attitude that has made Mr. Eliot's work less *chic* now than it was ten years ago. Perhaps the ten years are a sufficient explanation—obvious changes in fashionable feeling have helped to make the sort-of-Communist poets popular. But, on the other hand, it may be that these poets gratify some taste that Mr. Eliot also gratified in his earlier work but not in his later. If so, it is surely a taste for evocations of the sense of protest that our circumstances set up in us; for it seems likely that at the present time it is expressions of protest in some form or other that most readily gain a poet popular sympathy. And up to *The Waste Land* and *The Hollow Men* this protest—whether distressed, disgusted, or ironical—was still the dominant note of Mr. Eliot's work, through all the subtlety and sensitiveness of the forms it took. Yet already in these two poems the suggestion was creeping in that the sufferers were also failures. We are the hollow men, but there are, besides,

> *Those who have crossed*
> *With direct eyes, to death's other Kingdom.*

And in all the later work the stress tends to fall on the regret or suffering that arises from our own choice or our inherent limitations, or on the resignation that they make necessary. Without at the moment trying to define the change more closely, one can point out certain characteristics of the later work which are likely to displease those who create the fashions of taste in poetry today, and which also contrast with Mr. Eliot's earlier work. First, it is true that in some of the poems (most obviously in the choruses from *The Rock*) there are denunciations and preaching, both of which people like just now. But there is a vital difference between the denunciation here and that, say, in *The Dog Beneath the Skin*: Mr. Eliot doesn't invite you to step across a dividing line and join him in guaranteed rightness—he suggests at the most that you and he should both try, in familiar and difficult ways, not to live so badly. Failing to make it sound easy, and not putting much stress on the fellowship of the just, he offers no satisfaction to the craving for a life that is ethically and emotionally *simpler*.

And this characteristic goes with a deeper change of attitude that separates the later work from the earlier. Besides displaying little faith in a revolt against anything outside himself, Mr. Eliot in his recent work never invites you to believe that everything undesirable in you is due to outside influences that can be blamed for tampering with your original rightness. Not even in the perhaps over-simple *Animula* is there any suggestion that the "simple soul" has suffered an avoidable wrong for which someone else can be given the blame. Mr. Eliot declines to sanction an implicit belief, almost universally held, which lies behind an immense amount of rationalization, self-pity, and childish protest—the belief that the very fact of being alive ought to ensure your being a satisfactory object in your own sight. He is nearer the more rational view that the process of living is at its best one of progressive dissatisfaction.

Throughout the earlier poems there are traces of what, if it were cruder and without irony and impersonality, would be felt at once as self-pity or futile protest: for example,

> *Put your shoes at the door, sleep, prepare for life.*
> *The last twist of the knife.*

or,

> *Wipe your hand across your mouth, and laugh;*
> *The worlds revolve like ancient women*
> *Gathering fuel in vacant lots.*

or again,

> *The nightingales are singing near*
> *The Convent of the Sacred Heart,*
>
> *And sang within the bloody wood*
> *When Agamemnon cried aloud,*
> *And let their liquid siftings fall*
> *To stain the stiff dishonoured shroud.*

Obviously this is only one aspect of the early poetry, and to lay much stress on it without qualification would be grotesquely unfair to *Gerontion* especially and to other poems of that phase. But it is a prominent enough aspect of the work to have made critics, one might have thought, more liable to underrate the earlier poems

than, with fashionable taste, the later ones. For there can be no
doubt of the greater maturity of feeling in the later work:

> And I pray that I may forget
> These matters that with myself I too much discuss
> Too much explain
> Because I do not hope to turn again
> Let these words answer
> For what is done, not to be done again
> May the judgment not be too heavy upon us

This may be called religious submission, but essentially it is the
submission of maturity.

What is peculiar to Mr. Eliot in the tone of his work, and not
inherent in maturity or in religion, is that he does *submit* to what
he knows rather than welcoming it. To say that his is a depressed
poetry isn't true, because of the extraordinary toughness and resili-
ence that always underlie it. They show, for instance, in the quality
of the scorn he expresses for those who have tried to overlook what
he sees:

> . . . the strained time-ridden faces
> Distracted from distraction by distraction
> Filled with fancies and empty of meaning
> Tumid apathy with no concentration
> Men and bits of paper . . .

But to insist on the depression yields a half-truth. For though acceptance and understanding have taken the place of protest, the
underlying experience remains one of suffering, and the renunciation is much more vividly communicated than the advance for the
sake of which it was made. It is summed up in the ending of *Ash
Wednesday*:

> Blessèd sister, holy mother, spirit of the fountain, spirit
>   of the garden,
> Suffer us not to mock ourselves with falsehood
> Teach us to care and not to care
> Teach us to sit still
> Even among these rocks,
> Our peace in His will
> And even among these rocks
> Sister, mother
> And spirit of the river, spirit of the sea,
> Suffer me not to be separated
> And let my cry come unto Thee.

This is the cry of the weaned child, I suppose the analyst might
say; and without acquiescing in the genetic view that they would

imply, one can agree that weaning stands as a type-experience of much that Mr. Eliot is interested in as a poet. It seems to be the clearer and more direct realization of this kind of experience that makes the later poems at the same time more personal and more mature. And in the presence of these poems many who liked saying they liked the earlier work feel both embarrassed and snubbed.

However, all of this might be said about a volume of collected sermons instead of poems. It ignores Mr. Eliot's amazing genius in the use of words and rhythms and his extraordinary fertility in styles of writing, each "manner" apparently perfected from the first and often used only once (only once, that is, by Mr. Eliot, though most are like comets with a string of poetasters laboriously tailing after them). One aspect of his mastery of language may perhaps be commented on here because it reaches its most remarkable expression in the latest of the poems, *Burnt Norton*. Here most obviously the poetry is a linguistic achievement, in this case an achievement in the creation of concepts.

Ordinarily our abstract ideas are over-comprehensive and include too wide a range of feeling to be of much use by themselves. If our words "regret" and "eternity" were exact bits of mosaic with which to build patterns much of *Burnt Norton* would not have had to be written. But

> . . . *Words strain,*
> *Crack and sometimes break, under the burden,*
> *Under the tension, slip, slide, perish,*
> *Decay with imprecision, will not stay in place,*
> *Will not stay still.*

One could say, perhaps, that the poem takes the place of the ideas of "regret" and "eternity." Where in ordinary speech we should have to use those words, and hope by conversational trial-and-error to obviate the grosser misunderstandings, this poem is a newly created concept, equally abstract but vastly more exact and rich in meaning. It makes no statement. It is not more "about" anything than an abstract term like "love" is about anything: it is a linguistic creation. And the creation of a new concept, with all the assimilation and communication of experience that that involves, is perhaps the greatest of linguistic achievements.

In this poem the new meaning is approached by two methods. The first is the presentation of concrete images and definite events, each of which is checked and passes over into another before it has developed far enough to stand meaningfully by itself. This is, of course, an extension of a familiar language process. If you try to observe introspectively how the meaning of an abstract term—say "trade"—exists in your mind, you find that after a moment of blankness, in which there seems to be only imageless "meaning," concrete images of objects and events begin to occur to you; but none by itself carries the full meaning of the word "trade," and each is faded out and replaced by another. The abstract concept, in fact, seems like a space surrounded and defined by a more or less rich collection of latent ideas. It is this kind of definition that Mr. Eliot sets about here—in the magnificent first section, for instance—with every subtlety of verbal and rhythmical suggestion.

And the complementary method is to make pseudo-statements in highly abstract language, for the purpose, essentially, of putting forward and immediately rejecting ready-made concepts that might have seemed to approximate to the concept he is creating. For instance:

> *Neither from nor towards; at the still point, there the dance is,*
> *But neither arrest nor movement. And do not call it fixity.*
> *Where past and future are gathered. Neither movement from*
>   *nor towards,*
> *Neither ascent nor decline.*

Or:

> *Not the stillness of the violin, while the note lasts,*
> *Not that only, but the co-existence,*
> *Or say that the end precedes the beginning,*
> *And the end and the beginning were always there*
> *Before the beginning and after the end.*
> *And all is always now.*

In neither of these methods is there any attempt to state the meaning by taking existing abstract ideas and piecing them together in the ordinary way. Where something approaching this more usual method is attempted, in the passage beginning "The inner freedom from the practical desire," it seems a little less successful; admirable for the plays, where the audience is prominent, it fails to combine quite perfectly with the other methods of this poem. But it is Mr. Eliot himself who, by the closeness of his approach to technical perfection, provides a background against which such faint flaws can be seen.

(1936)

(II) *East Coker*, by T. S. Eliot

Reviewed by W. H. Mellers

... To read over the first page of *East Coker* is to realize that we have before us the work of a real poet, and that the distinction of the movement is something personal to Mr. Eliot, something which only he could have accomplished:

> ... *there is a time for building*
> *And a time for living and for generation*
> *And a time for the wind to break the loosened pane*
> *And to shake the wainscot where the fieldmouse trots*
> *And to shake the tattered arras woven with a silent motto.*

It is a genuine and distinguished movement; and yet it is perhaps the most spineless, the most nerveless, the most painfully weary movement in which a distinguished poetry has ever been created. There was life and power, even if largely of a negative order, in Mr. Eliot's apprehension of the degradation of the Waste Land, and there was a resilient clarity in *Ash Wednesday*'s perception of the garden within the desert. But here Eliot writes, proleptically, as an old man, a poetry that is in essence passive. There is a flicker of restrained agony in such a vision as this:

> ... *as, when an underground train, in the tube, stops too long between stations*
> *And the conversation rises and slowly fades into silence*
> *And you see behind every face the mental emptiness deepen*
> *Leaving only the growing terror of nothing to think about* ...

and there is a bitterness of disillusion in the passages on age:

> *What was to be the value of the long looked forward to,*
> *Long hoped for calm, the autumnal serenity*
> *And wisdom of age? Had they deceived us*
> *Or deceived themselves, the quiet-voiced elders,*
> *Bequeathing us merely a receipt for deceit?*

where the characteristically epigrammatic close injects a sudden tremor into the verse's incantatory movement. Yet the only conviction—if one can use so positive a term—that emerges is that things temporal, the uneasy nerves that trouble Mr. Eberhart,* are ultimately of no account, that "the only wisdom we can hope to acquire / Is the wisdom of humility: humility is endless." With

---

* Mr. Mellers has been reviewing Richard Eberhart's *Song and Idea* and William Empson's *The Gathering Storm*.—E. B.

reference to *Ash Wednesday* one might speak of resignation; here there is nothing to be resigned to:

> I said to my soul, be still, and wait without hope
> For hope would be hope for the wrong thing; wait without love
> For love would be love of the wrong thing; there is yet faith
> But the faith and the love and the hope are all in the waiting.

Because it is honest *East Coker* is not a depressing poem; but it is the most gloomy verse that Mr. Eliot has given us.

Whether or not it is an important contribution to twentieth-century poetry, I am sure that it was necessary for Mr. Eliot to write it. One can easily enough point to its shortcomings. The tendency to abstraction that was typical of *Burnt Norton* is perhaps more prevalent, and its significance less clearly defined:

> (There is, it seems to us,
> At best only a limited value
> In the knowledge derived from experience . . .)

and there is a cumulative insistence on certain mannerisms which suggests that Mr. Eliot is not only here and there imitating himself ("What you do not know is the only thing you do know," etc.) but also those who in the first place borrowed their modes from him ("Where you lean against a bank while a van passes, / And the deep lane insists on the direction / Into the village . . ." And compare the stanzas of section 4). Yet one cannot unequivocally deplore this since Mr. Eliot shows that he is clearly conscious of what he is doing:

> You say I am repeating
> Something I have said before. I shall say it again.

Perhaps *East Coker* is best regarded not as a poem—not as a system of "concepts" as was *Burnt Norton,* to which in some respects it seems to form a sequel—but rather as a number of passages of poetry alternating with talk about, discussion of, the experience the poetry is incarnating. In it Mr. Eliot is trying himself out in this mode or that, looking back at the modes he has adopted in the past and asking what it all comes to. Glibly enough, one might retort that the answer seems to be Not Much, until, remembering the magnificent sequence of *Gerontion, The Waste Land, Ash Wednesday,* and the *Ariel* poems, and the history of civilization during the generation in which Mr. Eliot has been writing, one realizes that it isn't we who have the right to smile. Mr. Eliot says that he stands "in the middle way" and that "old men ought to be explorers" ("through the cold dark and the empty desolation"): he may have found, in trying to learn to use words, that "every attempt is a wholly new start and a different kind of failure / Because one has only learned to get the better of words / For the thing one no longer has to say," but he reveals, in this peculiarly autobiographical document, that same moral integrity and that same seriousness of mind which have made his work one of the chief bulwarks in our time against "the general mess of imprecision of feeling."

> Like cats in airpumps, to subsist we strive
> On joys too thin to keep the soul alive.

This quotation from Young's satires stands as epigraph to Mr. Empson's volume, and it states very neatly not only Mr. Empson's own position but that, perhaps, of all contemporary poets. The dissatisfied tone of Mr. Empson's notes would seem to indicate that he finds it difficult to preserve his "joy" in that precariously serious wit which created *To an old lady;* Mr. Eberhart's tendency to regress to childhood suggests that he finds it difficult to maintain his delicate balance between the joys of the senses and the interests of the adult; while the limp, weary movement of *East Coker* suggests that Mr. Eliot, who has long ago seen through Wit and long ago learned as an adult to discipline the senses, is beginning to wonder where lies the joy that should come of experience. The integration of the poetic experience—the creation of the poem as a whole—is a problem that is inseparable from this search for the soul's joy, and we know how many of our poets have chosen to ignore the problem; how Mr. Empson and Mr. Eberhart have in more subtle (and very different) ways learned to evade it; and how Mr. Eliot in *East Coker* seems content merely to admit that the problem does exist, that it's one he has been preoccupied with in the past and may have to tackle again in the future. One hopes he will, for it is difficult to see where else those who are concerned about poetry today are likely to find direction and sustenance.

(1940)

(III) *Little Gidding,* by T. S. Eliot
Reviewed by D. W. Harding

The opening of the poem speaks of renewed life of unimaginable splendour, seen in promise amidst the cold decline of age. It offers no revival of life-procession; it is a springtime, "But not in time's covenant." If this "midwinter spring" has such blooms as the snow on hedges,

> Where is the summer, the unimaginable
> Zero summer?

With the sun blazing on the ice, the idea of pentecostal fire, of central importance in the poem, comes in for the first time, an intense, blinding promise of life and (as later passages show) almost unbearable.

The church of Little Gidding introduces another theme of the poem. Anchored in time and space, but for some people serving as the world's end where they can fulfil a purpose outside time and space, it gives contact with spiritual concerns through earthly and human things.

A third theme, important to the whole poem, is also stated in the first section: that the present is able to take up, and even give added meaning to, the values of the past. Here, too, the pentecostal idea comes in:

> And what the dead had no speech for, when living,
> They can tell you, being dead: the communication
> Of the dead is tongued with fire beyond the language
>   of the living.

Section II can be regarded as the *logical* starting-point of the whole poem. It deals with the desolation of death and the futility of life for those who have had no conviction of spiritual values in their life's work. First come three sharply organized rhyming stanzas to evoke, by image and idea but without literal statement, our sense of the hopeless death of air, earth, fire, and water, seen not only as the elements of man's existence but as the means of his destruction and dismissal. The tone having been set by these stanzas, there opens a narrative passage describing the dreary bitterness in which a life of literary culture can end if it has brought no sense of spiritual values. The life presented is one, such as Mr. Eliot's own, of effort after clear speech and exact thought, and the passage amounts to a shuddering "There but for the grace of God go I." It reveals more clearly than ever the articles in *The Criterion* did, years ago, what it was in "humanism" that Mr. Eliot recoiled from so violently. What the humanist's ghost sees in his life are futility, isolation, and guilt on account of his self-assertive prowess— "Which once you took for exercise of virtue"—and the measure of aggression against others which that must bring.

The verse in this narrative passage, with its regular measure and insistent alliteration, so effective for combining the macabre with the urbane and dreary, is a way to indicate and a way to control the pressure of urgent misery and self-disgust. The motive power of this passage, as of so much of Mr. Eliot's earlier poetry, is repulsion. But in the poem as a whole the other motive force is dominant: there is a movement of feeling and conviction outwards, reaching towards what attracts. The other parts of the poem can be viewed as working out an alternative to the prospect of life presented in this narrative.

Section III sees the foundation for such an alternative in the contact with spiritual values, especially as they appear in the tradition of the past. Detachment (distinguished from indifference) allows us to use both our own past and the historical past in such a way as to draw on their present spiritual significance for us without entangling us in regressive yearning for a pattern which no longer is:

> History may be servitude,
> History may be freedom. See, now they vanish,
> The faces and places, with the self which, as it could, loved them,
> To become renewed, transfigured, in another pattern.

Once we accept the significance of the spiritual motives and intentions of the past, even the faction connected with the church and community of Little Gidding leaves us an inheritance; we can be at one with the whole past, including the sinning and defeated past, for its people were spiritually alive.

> All touched by a common genius,
> United in the strife which divided them.

But the humanist's fate cannot be escaped in so gentle and placid a way; a more formidable ordeal is waiting. In contrast to the leisurely meditation of section III, the fourth section is a forceful passage, close-knit with rhyme, and incisive. Its theme is the terrifying fierceness of the pentecostal experience, the dove bringing fire. This is not the fire of expiation, such as the humanist had to suffer. It is the consuming experience of love, the surrender to a spiritual principle beyond us, and the only alternative to consuming ourselves with the miserable fires of sin and error. This pentecostal ordeal must be met before the blinding promise seen in "midwinter spring" can be accepted.

The final section develops the idea that every experience is integrated with all the others, so that the fullness of exploration means a return, with better understanding, to the point where you started. The theme has already been foreshadowed in Section III, where detachment is seen to give liberation from the future as well as the past, so that neither past nor future has any fascination of a kind that could breed in us a reluctance to accept the present fully.

The tyranny of sequence and duration in life is thus reduced. Time-processes are viewed as aspects of a pattern which can be grasped in its entirety at any one of its moments:

> *The moment of the rose and the moment of the yew-tree*
> *Are of equal duration.*

One effect of this view of time and experience is to rob the moment of death of any over-significance we may have given it. For the humanist of Section II life trails off just because it can't manage to endure. For the man convinced of spiritual values life is a coherent pattern in which the ending has its due place and, because it is part of a pattern, itself leads into the beginning. An over-strong terror of death is often one expression of the fear of living, for death is one of the life-processes that seem too terrifying to be borne. In examining one means of becoming reconciled to death, Mr. Eliot can show us life, too, made bearable, unfrightening, positively inviting:

> *With the drawing of this Love and the voice of this Calling*
>
> > *We shall not cease from exploration*
> > *And the end of all our exploring*
> > *Will be to arrive where we started*
> > *And know the place for the first time.*

Here is the clearest expression of a motive force other than repulsion. Its dominance makes this poem—to put it very simply—far happier than most of Mr. Eliot's.

Being reconciled to death and the conditions of life restores the golden age of unfearful natural living and lets you safely, without regression, recapture the wonder and easy rightness of certain moments, especially in early childhood:

> *At the source of the longest river*
> *The voice of the hidden waterfall*
> *And the children in the apple-tree*
> *Not known, because not looked for*
> *But heard, half-heard, in the stillness*

> *Between two waves of the sea.*
> *Quick now, here, now, always—*
> *A condition of complete simplicity*
> *(Costing not less than everything)*

The whole of this last section suggests a serene and revitalized return from meditation to one's part in active living. It includes a reaffirmation of that concern with speech which has made up so much of Mr. Eliot's work and which could have been the bitter futility that it is for the ghostly humanist. The reaffirming passage (introduced as a simile to suggest the integrated patterning of all living experience) is an example of amazing condensation, of most comprehensive thinking given the air of leisured speech—not conversation, but the considered speech of a man talking to a small group who are going to listen for a time without replying. It is one example of the intellectual quality of this poem. In most of Mr. Eliot's poems the intellectual materials which abound are used emotionally. In much of this poem they are used intellectually, in literal statement which is to be understood literally (for instance, the opening of Section III). How such statements become poetry is a question outside the range of this review. To my mind they do, triumphantly, and for me it ranks among the major good fortunes of our time that so superb a poet is writing.

(1943)

(IV) *Selected Essays,* by T. S. Eliot
Reviewed by Edgell Rickword

This substantial and comely volume contains the greater part of Mr. Eliot's influential criticism. There is about half of *The Sacred Wood,* the three essays from the crucial *Homage to Dryden* pamphlet, and the Dante study entire. The additions on the literary side include essays on Middleton, Heywood, Tourneur, and Ford; two excellent studies of Senecan influence on Elizabethan drama, a rather discouraged dialogue on Dramatic Poetry, and an essay on Baudelaire.

The novelty in the essays on the dramatists and on Baudelaire is the appearance of Mr. Eliot as an appreciator of moral essences. In this encroachment on the domain of such verbose critics as Mr. Murry and Mr. Fausset, he is not, of course, trying to put across an individual conception of morality; tradition governs this as much as it does taste. Mr. Eliot's tradition of morality is the most respectable of all, and when he says that "the essence of the tragedy of *Macbeth* is the habituation to crime," one could do nothing but assent if it were not that the italics show that he is not referring to the man but to the play. Again, he tells us, "in poetry, in dramatic technique, *The Changeling* is inferior to the best plays of Webster. But in the moral essence of tragedy, it is safe to say that in this play Middleton is surpassed by one Elizabethan alone, and that is Shakespeare." But even if that is a safe thing to say, the way of saying it is not free from danger. For after subtracting the poetry and the dramatic technique what is there left by which the moral essence may be apprehended? Again, in the essay on Baudelaire he writes: "In his verse, he is now less a model to be imitated or a source to be drained than a reminder of the duty, the consecrated task, of sincerity." But is our sensation of the poet's sincerity anything more than one of the reactions attendant on the poem's successful communication? Is anything really clarified by talking of a technical as if it were a moral achievement? It seems a pity that an essay that at the outset affirms the importance of Baudelaire's prose works should not have given some consideration to *L'Art Romantique* and *Curiosités esthétiques,* which illuminate Baudelaire's poetic much more than the diaries do. The "revelations" in the *Journaux Intimes,* written later than the majority of the poems, are perhaps rather specious intellectualizations, the violent efforts of a man to whom convictions of that sort were a novelty, to create a "strong personality" for himself; their fortrightness is deceptive, I think. But Mr. Eliot "hazards" an illuminating conjecture when he suggests "that the care for perfection of form, among some of the romantic poets of the nineteenth century, was an effort to support, or to conceal from view, an inner disorder." And he goes on to say: "Now the true claim of Baudelaire as an artist is not that he found a superficial form, but that he was searching for a form of life." I quote this, firstly because it is a good saying in itself, and also because the form of expression is comparatively new in Mr. Eliot's work. As it stands it is paradoxical. Not quite so paradoxical as Mr. G. K. Chesterton methodically is, but surprisingly near it. It marks a cleavage between Mr. Eliot's earlier and later criticism. It oversteps the conscious limitations of his earlier method. It must be every ambitious critic's aim to resolve the dichotomy between life and art; and every superficial critic does it constantly with negligent ease. Whether Mr. Eliot has the philosophical stamina, as he certainly has the poetic sensitiveness, for such a task remains to be seen.

The latter part of this volume is mainly occupied by essays on attitudes rather than works, and here Mr. Eliot is heavily engaged with the Martin Marprelates of today and yesterday, some of them within the Church, like Viscount Brentford, and some outside it. The outsiders are, in general, those who believe that art, culture, reason, science, the inner-light or what-not, may constitute efficient substitutes for organized religion. Arnold, Pater, Aldous Huxley, Bertrand Russell, Middleton Murry, and some American humanists who loom more sinisterly in Mr. Eliot's consciousness than seems necessary over here provide a variety of scapegoats. His diagnosis of the disease that must ensure the ultimate instability of all such eclectic systems built up from "the best that has been thought and done in the world" is devastatingly acute. The antidote is provided in "Thoughts after Lambeth."

This volume leaves us then, except for tentative branchings-out, as far as literature is concerned much where we were after the publication of *Dante*. One should not, perhaps, grumble at that; but the impression given by this heterogeneous mass is not so profound as that given by the slim volumes that found their way into the world more quietly. The essays on general subjects dilute that impression, for Mr. Eliot is not as astounding a thinker as he is a literary critic. His thinking is adequate to his own emotional needs, as a good poet's always is, but it has not much extra-personal validity. One may contrast the peroration of "Thoughts after Lambeth":

> The World is trying the experiment of attempting to form a civilized but non-Christian mentality. The experiment will fail; but we must be very patient in awaiting its collapse; meanwhile redeeming the time: so that the Faith may be preserved alive through the dark ages before us; to renew and rebuild civilization, and save the World from suicide,

with Berdyaev's lucid and virile exposition of a similar conviction in his *Un Nouveau Moyen Age*.

I must try to say briefly why Mr. Eliot's earlier work seems to me more valuable than his later, or it may seem that I underrate it just because its conclusions are unsympathetic to me. The intelligence displayed in the later essays might be matched by several of his contemporaries; the literary sensibility of the earlier essays is not matched by any of them. "Literary sensibility" is a horrible phrase and it does not sound a very impressive faculty, but when one considers how very few people there are actually capable of responding to poetry or word-order generally without prompting from its prestige, or message, or because the objects named evoke a pleasant response, perhaps the possession of this gift may be appreciated at its proper value. It is only the beginning, of course, but its absence vitiates the other critical faculties. Sometimes, when it is present, there is an absence of the co-ordinating faculty and thus the response is deprived of any significance beyond that of a pleasurable sensation. It was the presence of these faculties in unison which differentiated Mr. Eliot's earlier criticism from the "appreciative" convention in vogue at the time. The method at which he aimed, and which he practised with such delicate skill, is perhaps best described by a quotation he used from Rémy de Gourmont—"*ériger en lois ses impressions personnelles.*" If Mr. Eliot has for the time being gone outside literature, the loss is very much to literature; no doubt there is a compensation somewhere. But literature, in spite of wireless and cinema, is still the life-blood of the time; we are not sots or sadists by accident, and one should not be too fatalistic about the approaching dark ages. If literary criticism is not one of the means Mr. Eliot envisages of redeeming the time, nothing can obscure the value of his example. As our writings are, so are our feelings, and the finer the discrimination as to the value of those writings, the better chance there is of not being ashamed of being a human being.

(1933)

(v) *After Strange Gods: A Primer of Modern Heresy,* by T. S. Eliot

Reviewed by F. R. Leavis

After Strange Gods, like the last set of printed lectures, is clearly not a book the author would choose to have written, and one is tempted to pass it by with a glance at the circumstances of production. Yet the weaknesses, the embarrassing obviousness of which is partly to be explained by those circumstances, cannot, after all, be dismissed as having no significance. Mr. Eliot is too distinguished, his preoccupations have too representative an importance, and the subtitle of the book, recalling as it does an old and notorious promise, invites us to consider their presentment here as embodying a certain maturity of reflection.

His themes are orthodoxy and tradition, and, as one would expect, he says some memorable things. Tradition, for example, he describes admirably as "the means by which the vitality of the past enriches the life of the present." And when he describes "the struggle of our time" as being "to concentrate, not to dissipate; to renew our association with traditional wisdom; to re-establish a vital connexion between the individual and the race . . . ," one again assents with pleasure. But when he goes on, "the struggle, in a word, against Liberalism," it seems an odd summary.

Mr. Eliot's stress in this book, of course, falls explicitly upon the religious needs of the age. And, with conscious inadequacy, holding on to what one is sure of, one agrees that "to re-establish a vital connexion between the individual and the race" means, in a civilization that more and more, at higher and lower levels, fosters the chauffeur-mentality, reviving what it may be crude to call the religious sense—the sense that spoke in Lawrence when he said, "Thank God I am not free, any more than a rooted tree is free." It is the sense, perhaps it may be said, a perception of the need to cultivate which made Dr. I. A. Richards, in the book in which he speculates about a future in which we shall "have learned enough about our minds to do with them what we will" and "the question 'What sort of mind shall I choose to be?' would turn into an experimental matter" (*Practical Criticism*, p. 347), invent his "ritual for heightening sincerity" (*ibid.*, p. 290)—that invention the crudities of which Mr. Eliot is, if not excessively, perhaps unnecessarily severe upon in *The Use of Poetry and the Use of Criticism*.

What would be the drift of Mr. Eliot's comments on the present kind of fumbling inadequacy one knows well enough. The relevance of this, for instance, is plain: "When morals cease to be a matter of tradition and orthodoxy—that is, of the habits of the community formulated, corrected, and elevated by the continuous thought and direction of the Church—and when one man is to elaborate his own, then *personality* becomes a thing of alarming importance." Mr. Eliot has no need to talk hesitantly about the "need for a religious sense"; he adheres to a religion and can point to his Church and recite its dogmas.

Nevertheless, those of us who find no such approach to tradition and orthodoxy possible can only cultivate the sense of health they have. "The number of people in possession of any criteria for distinguishing between good and evil," writes Mr. Eliot, "is very small." As we watch his in use, we can only test them by reference to our own surest perceptions, our own most stable grounds of discrimination. When, for instance, he says that he is "applying moral principles" to literature, we cannot accept those principles as *alternatives* to the criteria we know. "What we can try to do," he says, "is to develop a more critical spirit, or rather to apply to authors critical standards that are almost in desuetude." The first phrase is strictly accurate: we could recover such standards only by the development—*as* the development—of a more critical spirit out of the capacity for discrimination that we have already. To put it another way: moral or religious criticism cannot be a substitute for literary criticism; it is only by being a literary critic that Mr. Eliot can apply his recovered standards to literature. It is only by demonstrating convincingly that his application of moral principles leads to a more adequate criticism that he can effect the kind of persuasion that is his aim. In these lectures, if he demonstrates anything, it is the opposite: one can only report that the criticism seems painfully bad—disablingly inadequate, often irrelevant, and sometimes disingenuous.

And it has, more generally, to be said that since the religious preoccupation has become insistent in them Mr. Eliot's critical writings have been notable for showing less discipline of thought and emotion, less purity of interest, less power of sustained devotion, and less courage than before. All this must be so obvious to those who read him (except to the conventional and academic who, having reviled him, now acclaim him) that there is no need to illustrate—the only difficulties in doing so would be to select and to stop. Mr. Eliot himself can hardly be happy when he contemplates his recent references to, say, Arnold and Professor Housman, and his references in the present book to Hopkins and Meredith.

These comments one makes, in all humility, as essential to the issue: they are to enforce the point of saying that it is not as a substitute or an alternative that what Mr. Eliot nowadays offers us could recommend itself, but only as a completion, and this it is far from seeming. One may at any rate venture that health—even religious health—demands a more active concern for other things than formal religion than Mr. Eliot now shows or encourages. Indeed, it seems reasonable to restate in terms of Mr. Eliot's situation his expressions of fear regarding Lawrence, fear that Lawrence's work "will appeal not to what remains of health in them ["the sick and debile and confused"], but to their sickness."

There is hardly any need to be more explicit: it must be plain why for those preoccupied with orthodoxy, order, and traditional forms Lawrence should be especially a test. I do not—need it be said?—mean a "test" in the sense that one knows beforehand what the "right" reaction is (it will certainly not be acceptance). What one demands is a truly critical attitude—a serious attempt to discriminate and evaluate after an honest and complete exposure to Lawrence. Mr. Eliot has in the past made me indignant by endorsing, of all things, Mr. Middleton Murry's *Son of Woman* while at the same time admitting to a very imperfect acquaintance with Lawrence's work. *After Strange Gods* exhibits something much more like a critical attitude; there has obviously been a serious attempt to understand in spite of antipathy.

> It is characteristic of the more interesting heretics, in the context in which I use the term, that they have an exceptionally acute perception, or profound insight, of some part of the truth; an insight more important often than the inferences of those who are aware of more, but less acutely aware of anything. So far as we are able to redress the balance, effect the compensation, ourselves, we may find such authors of the greatest value.

This is not explicitly said of Lawrence; but it suggests fairly Mr. Eliot's implied estimate of him: he is spoken of with respect, as (what he obviously is) "a very much greater genius" than Hardy, and there is "a very great deal to be learned" from him. We are decidedly far away from the imagined "frightful consequences" of Lawrence the don at Cambridge, "rotten and rotting others." It would, indeed, have been ungracious to recall this unhappy past if Mr. Eliot's attitude now had been consistently or in general effect critical, to be agreed or disagreed with. But it is not; its main significance still lies in its being so largely and revealingly uncritical —and so equivocally so.

> The first [aspect of Lawrence] is the ridiculous: his lack of sense of humour, a certain snobbery, a lack not so much of information as of the critical faculties which education should give, an incapacity for what we ordinarily call thinking. Of this side of Lawrence, the brilliant exposure by Mr. Wyndham Lewis in *Paleface* is by far the most conclusive criticism that has been made.

The charge of snobbery (repeated elsewhere in the book and accompanied by a most unfortunate tone) may be passed by; what damage it does is so obviously not to the object. But why, one asks, this invocation of Mr. Wyndham Lewis? With all his undeniable talent, is he qualified to "expose" any side of Lawrence? No one who can read will acclaim Lawrence as a philosopher, but "incapacity for what we ordinarily call thinking"—does not this apply far more to Mr. Wyndham Lewis than to Lawrence? Mr. Lewis stands, in a paradoxically high-pitched and excited way, for common sense; he offers us, at the common-sense level, perceptions of an uncommon intensity, and he is capable of making "brilliant" connexions. But "what we ordinarily call thinking" is just what he is incapable of—consider, for instance, the list of names brought together under the "Time-philosophy" in *Time and Western Man*. His pamphleteering volumes are not books; their air of sustained and ordered argument is a kind of bluff, as the reader who, having contrived to read one through, can bring himself to attempt a summary of it discovers. If, on the other hand, Lawrence does not offer intellectual order or definition or an intellectual approach, to speak of him as incapable of thinking is to mislead. In the same way the phrases "lack of intellectual and social training" and "soul destitute of humility" seem to me misleading in suggestion; and I think that, if Mr. Eliot goes on reading Lawrence—and especially the *Letters*—in a serious attempt to understand, he may come to wonder whether such phrases are quite consistent with humility in the critic.

When we look up Mr. Wyndham Lewis's "brilliant exposure" of Lawrence in *Paleface,* we discover that it is an "exposure" of Lawrence and Mr. Sherwood Anderson together. Now, the primitivistic illusion that Mr. Wyndham Lewis rightly attacks was indeed something that Lawrence was liable to (and could diagnose). Just how far, in any critical estimate, the stress may be fairly laid there is a matter for critical difference. But that Lawrence's importance is not anything that can be illuminated by assimilating him, or any side of him, to Mr. Sherwood Anderson is plain on Mr. Eliot's own showing: "Lawrence lived all his life, I should imagine, on the spiritual level; no man was less a sensualist. Against the living death of material civilization he spoke again and again, and even if these dead could speak, what he said is unanswerable." If Lawrence was this, how comes Mr. Eliot to be using Mr. Wyndham Lewis against him?—Mr. Wyndham Lewis, who, though he may stand for Intelligence, is as completely without any religious sense, as unqualified to discriminate between the profound insight and the superficial romantic illusion, as anyone who could have been hit on. His remarkable satiric gift is frustrated by an unrestrained egotism, and Mr. Eliot might have placed him along with Mr. Pound among those whose hells are for other people: no one could with less injustice be said to be destitute of humility.

Mr. Eliot no doubt thought he was merely using Mr. Wyndham

Lewis to mark off a weaker side of Lawrence from "the extraordinary keen sensibility and capacity for profound intuition" which made Lawrence so irreconcilable and potent an enemy of the idea that "by tolerance, benevolence, inoffensiveness and a redistribution or increase of purchasing power, combined with a devotion, on the part of an *élite*, to Art, the world will be as good as anyone could require. . . ." Mr. Eliot, unhappily, was mistaken. From the two sentences of supreme praise quoted in the last paragraph he goes on: "As a criticism of the modern world, *Fantasia of the Unconscious* is a book to keep at hand and re-read. In contrast to Nottingham, London or industrial America, his capering redskins of *Mornings in Mexico* seem to represent Life." *Mornings in Mexico* is Mr. Wyndham Lewis's text, and it is one of the very inferior books. If it represented Lawrence and the *Fantasia* deserved to be bracketed with it, or if the "capering redskins" (betraying phrase) represented Lawrence's "capacity for profound intuition," then Lawrence would not deserve the praise Mr. Eliot gives him—so equivocally.

This equivocalness, this curious sleight by which Mr. Eliot surreptitiously takes away while giving, is what I mean by the revealingly uncritical in his attitude towards Lawrence. It is as if there were something he cannot bring himself to contemplate fairly. And the index obtruded in that over-insistence on Lawrence's "sexual morbidity" refuses to be ignored. It is an odd insistence in one whose own attitudes with reference to sex have been, in prose and poetry, almost uniformly negative—attitudes of distaste, disgust, and rejection. (Mr. Wyndham Lewis's treatment of sex, it is worth noting, is hard-boiled, cynical, and external.) The preoccupation with sex in Lawrence's work is, no doubt, excessive by any standard of health, and no doubt psychologists, if they like, can elicit abnormalities. But who can question his own account of the preoccupation?—"I always labour at the same thing, to make the sex relation valid and precious, not shameful." And who can question that something as different as this from Mr. Eliot's bent in the matter is necessary if the struggle "to re-establish a vital connexion between the individual and the race" is to mean anything?

Lawrence's concern for health far transcends what is suggested by any talk of sex. His may be "not the last word, only the first"; but the first is necessary. His justification is given in these remarks from *After Strange Gods* (p. 18):

> We become conscious of these items, or conscious of their importance, usually only after they have begun to fall into desuetude, as we are

aware of the leaves of a tree when the autumn wind begins to blow them off—when they have separately ceased to be vital. Energy may be wasted at that point in a frantic endeavour to collect the leaves as they fall and gum them onto the branches: but the sound tree will put forth new leaves, and the dry tree should be put to the axe. . . . Our second danger is . . . to aim to return to some previous condition which we imagine as having been capable of preservation in perpetuity, instead of aiming to stimulate the life which produced that condition in its time.

The tree will not put forth new leaves unless the sap flows. The metaphor, of course, is susceptible of more than one translation, but the very choice of it is nevertheless an involuntary concession to Lawrence. To "stimulate the life" in Lawrence's way is not all that is needed, but is, nevertheless, as the phrase itself conveys, indispensable.

It is the way our sympathy flows and recoils that really determines our lives. And here lies the importance of the novel, properly handled. It can inform and lead into new places the flow of our sympathetic consciousness, and it can lead our sympathy away in recoil from things gone dead. Therefore the novel, properly handled, can reveal the most secret places of life—for it is in the *passional* secret places of life, above all, that the tide of sensitive awareness needs to ebb and flow, cleansing and refreshing.

Mr. Eliot complains of a lack of moral struggle in Lawrence's novels; here we have Lawrence's reply, and his justification of the earlier description of him as an "extremely serious and improving" writer. No one will suggest that in Lawrence we have all we need of moral concern, but, as *After Strange Gods* reminds us, a preoccupation with discipline—the effort towards orthodoxy—also has its disabilities and dangers. These are manifest in the obvious and significant failures in touch and tone. It may be prejudice that makes one find something distasteful in the habitual manner of Mr. Eliot's references during the past half-dozen years to Baudelaire and Original Sin. But such disasters as that "curtain" to the second lecture in the present volume leave no room for doubt.

No one who sees in what way Lawrence is "serious and improving" will attribute the sum of wisdom, or anything like it, to him. And for attributing to him "spiritual sickness" Mr. Eliot can make out a strong case. But it is characteristic of the world as it is that health cannot anywhere be found whole; and the sense in which Lawrence stands for health is an important one. He stands at any rate for something without which the preoccupation (necessary as it is) with order, forms, and deliberate construction cannot produce health.

(1934)

(VI) *Essays Ancient and Modern,* by T. S. Eliot
Reviewed by F. R. Leavis

To many who are aware of a great indebtedness to Mr. Eliot every new prose book of his that comes out nowadays is something for a painfully apprehensive approach. They have too much reason for fearing that they will find themselves condemning him by criteria, their way to which, looking back, they recognize as representing in a considerable degree his influence. *Essays Ancient and Modern* is not altogether new; the dust-jacket may be cited:

> This book takes the place of *For Lancelot Andrewes,* which is out of print. The Essay on Thomas Middleton is omitted because it has already been published in *Elizabethan Essays* and other essays omitted because the author does not think them good enough. Five new essays, not previously collected, have been added.

The essay on Middleton seems to me certainly no better than the essay on Crashaw that has been suppressed. The new essay on Tennyson seems to me the worst essay in literary criticism that Mr. Eliot has yet published. It opens:

> Tennyson is a great poet, for reasons that are perfectly clear. He has three qualities which are seldom found together except in the greatest poets: abundance, variety, and complete competence.

And what follows does not make these sentences look any more like the utterance of an interested and disinterested mind that knows what it thinks and is concerned to say it as clearly and precisely as possible. The flabbiness to which the air of brisk directness merely calls attention is pervasive. Later on we read:

> . . . even the second-rate long poems of that time, like *The Light of Asia,* are better worth reading than most modern long novels.

We immediately think of a reverse proposition that would be equally undiscussible and equally profitable.

We have already been told in the first paragraph that Tennyson "had the finest ear of any English poet since Milton." In spite of all that comes between we are still surprised (because of that eminently quotable first clause, which will have a currency that Mr.

Humbert Wolfe, whose "interesting essay" Mr. Eliot respectfully dissents from, could not have given it) when we read:

> Tennyson is the great master of metric as well as of melancholia; I do not think that any poet in English has ever had a finer ear for vowel sound, as well as a subtler feeling for some moods of anguish.

But it is not an occasional vulgarity of phrasing that is the worst offence; far worse is the subtlety of statement that disguises critical indolence and gives endorsement to time-honoured critical (or anti-critical) fallacies:

> The surface of Tennyson stirred about with his time; and he had nothing to which to hold fast except his unique and unerring feeling for the sounds of words. But in this he had something that no one else had. Tennyson's surface, his technical accomplishment, is intimate with his depths. . . .

If that last sentence means anything, either Tennyson's depths are not those of a great poet or Mr. Eliot ought not to have been content to talk so much, so redundantly, and so loosely about Tennyson's technical accomplishment as a matter of a fine ear for vowel sound and an unerring feeling for the sounds of words. Actually, Tennyson's feeling for the sounds of words was extremely limited and limiting: the ear he had cultivated for vowel sound was a filter that kept out all "music" of any subtlety or complexity and cut him off from most of the expressive resources of the English language. To bring English as near the Italian as possible could not have been the preoccupation of a great English poet, however interesting the minor poetry that might come of it. The term "metric" that Mr. Eliot has sponsored seems calculated to rehabilitate the discredited fallacies of the prosodic approach.

These fallacies are peculiarly hard to shift, the incapacities associated with the phrase "fine ear" are inveterate, in the normal product of a classical education. Why this should be so Coleridge virtually explains in the first chapter of *Biographia Literaria;* and Wordsworth, in the following lines, suggests the condition of a classical training's being something one may properly be concerned to preserve:

> *In fine,*
> *I was a better judge of thoughts than words,*
> *Misled in estimating words, not only*
> *By common inexperience of youth,*
> *But by the trade in classic niceties,*
> *The dangerous craft of culling term and phrase*

> *From languages that want the living voice*
> *To carry meaning to the natural heart;*
> *To tell us what is passion, what is truth,*
> *What reason, what simplicity and sense.*

The training in Latin and Greek must not be made a substitute for training in English. It would seem to be axiomatic that if one does not bring an educated sensibility from one's literary studies, what one brings away should not be called a humane education. And it would seem to be equally axiomatic that it is only in one's own language that one's sensibility can, in the first place, be educated. And the result of the assumption that if Latin and Greek are looked after the rest will look after itself is the cultivated classic who thinks that Mr. Belloc writes good prose and that it is a mark of a liberal good taste to account Miss Dorothy L. Sayers literature. The recognition that English must be looked after involves the recognition that it must be looked after at the university level—or, at any rate, that it is not merely and patently stupid to suppose so.

In Mr. Eliot's essay on "Modern Education and the Classics," however, we read:

> The universities have to teach what they can to the material they can get: nowadays they even teach *English* in England.

Merely that. Or rather, a little further on Mr. Eliot adds this (having dismissed *economics* and *"philosophy* when divorced from *theology"*):

> And there is a third subject, equally bad as training, which does not fall into either of these classes, but is bad for reasons of its own: the study of *English Literature,* or, to be more comprehensive, the literature of one's own language.

Of these reasons, Mr. Eliot says nothing whatever.

To those who have been working at the problems of a modern humane education, and discussing the place of English in it, he must sound ill-mannered and ill-tempered. For of such work and such discussion he cannot be altogether ignorant. And he must know that conclusions opposite to his own have been come to by persons ostensibly better qualified to conclude and pronounce. At any rate, one may suggest that he ought now, in common decency, to read the official report on *The Teaching of English in England,* or, more simply, Mr. George Sampson's *English for the English,* and tell us why he disagrees.

When we re-read his essay to discover what he himself advocates we still find him, for all the *ex cathedra* manner, curiously vague, general, and negative. He dissociates himself in large terms from all kinds of company, but for his account of what he positively wants gives us nothing but this:

> It is high time that the defence of the classics should be dissociated from objects which, however excellent under certain conditions and in a certain environment, are of only relative importance—a traditional public-school system, a traditional university system, a decaying social order—and permanently associated where they belong, with something permanent: the historical Christian Faith.

It would be very interesting indeed to be told just how, in Mr. Eliot's view, the classics are permanently associated with the historical Christian Faith, and what are the conclusions for education —just what and how, for instance, the monastic teaching orders he desiderates would teach. But we cannot really believe that Mr. Eliot will ever tell us more. If he does not, however, we cannot take his interest in education very seriously.

There is, in fact, something very depressing about the way in which, nowadays, he brings out these orthodox generalities, weightily, as substitutes for particularity of statement, rigour of thought, and various other virtues we have a right to expect of him. We no longer expect them, unfortunately. So that when, writing on "Religion and Literature," he starts with the proposition that

> Literary criticism should be completed by criticism from a definite ethical and theological standpoint,

we do not expect to be able to read with the sympathy that ought to be possible what follows. We expect to find that, in spite of anything that may be said or implied to the contrary, we are being offered something as a *substitute*. "We" stands for readers who agree, or rather urge, that serious literary criticism leads outside itself and are intent on following it, but do not know of any fixed base "outside" from which to move in the opposite direction. In the nature of the case we cannot, as Mr. Eliot himself has pointed out, hope to engage conclusively in argument with those who have such a base. But, however little they may be impressed, we have to insist that what looks to us like weak thinking, failure in critical disinterestedness or courage, bad judgement, and so on, we must judge as such, and that a "definite ethical and theological standpoint" is the reverse of recommended to us when its adoption has been accompanied by a decline in the virtues we can recognize.

The essay on "Religion and Literature" is too general to have much force for any readers but those who agree with Mr. Eliot already (to such indeed it is addressed). The rest of us must take it in relation to other things in the book—such things as the essays on Tennyson and education. And we in any case find it odd that Mr. Eliot should have had to learn from Mr. Montgomery Belgion (see the foot-note on p. 100) that the fiction we read may affect our behaviour to our fellows, and odd that he should be able to refer to "such delightful fiction as Mr. Chesterton's *Man Who Was Thursday* or his *Father Brown*" and say: "No one admires and enjoys these things more than I do." Of Mr. Chesterton Mr. Eliot himself once remarked that his cheerfulness reminds us not so much of Saint Francis as of a bus-driver slapping himself on a wintry day to keep warm. That will seem to most educated and sensitive people a very kind way of indicating the level of Mr. Chesterton's art and propaganda.

(1936)

(vii) *The Idea of a Christian Society*, by T. S. Eliot

Reviewed by D. W. Harding

Addressed to Christians, this book is largely about—and obviously meant to influence—those neutral others who support "a culture which is mainly negative, but which, so far as it is positive, is still Christian." Mr. Eliot believes that we must now choose between working for a new Christian culture and accepting a pagan one, whether Fascist or Communist; unless we aim at a positively Christian society we are committed "to a progressive and insidious adaptation to totalitarian worldliness for which the pace is already set." Democracy is not an alternative to totalitarian government; it is fundamentally, though perhaps less forthrightly, just as materialistic and pagan. In intention it merely neglects its Christians and has no coherent system of allegiances to a pagan ideal, but it is none the less developing an increasingly complete network of institutions which invite un-Christian conduct from the Christians who find their everyday life set amongst them.

In pointing out the unsatisfactory features of our society Mr. Eliot can count on wide respect and agreement. In his attack on flabbiness of mind, on the lowering of standards in literature and "culture" in the narrower sense, on the substitution of a mob led by propaganda in place of a community, and in the sort of concern he shows for education, Mr. Eliot implicitly agrees with much that has been expressed in *Scrutiny* for the last seven years; in his disgust at the financial control of politics and his dismay at the plight of agriculture he is on ground familiarized by social-credit reformers and their allies. In common with many other thinkers, Mr. Eliot believes that any remedy for these disorders must involve the establishment of a true community, one in which non-materialist values will find an important place and not just survive in chinks and crannies. Again, like many other thinkers he describes these values as "religious." The society he wants, therefore, is a "religious-social community," and at this point he is implicitly in sympathy with ideas that have been put forward in (for me) unfortunate terms by MacMurray. The new responsiveness to the social interests of man (sensitively expressed in technical psychology by Ian Suttie) is at the present time as obligatory for intellectuals as a concern with psycho-analytic discoveries was in the 1920's; and it is equally unbalanced; but its temporary currency further extends the range of appeal now possessed by valuable ideas of the kind Mr. Eliot puts forward.

His emphasis is markedly on the communal: "I have tried," he writes, "to restrict my ambition of a Christian society to a social minimum: to picture, not a society of saints, but of ordinary men, of men whose Christianity is communal before being individual." And his ideal is a community in which social custom is maintained by religious sanction: "a Christian community is one in which there is a unified religious-social code of behaviour."

It is at this point that the non-Christian's doubts begin to focus. Such societies have been known; and stagnation, oppression, and intolerant regimentation have characterized them. Mr. Eliot, it is true, acknowledges from time to time the need for toleration of the non-Christian and, presumably, toleration within limits of those who question the accepted religious-social code of behaviour and its supporting beliefs. But such toleration has not usually marked the effectively Christian societies of the past. Crude and unfashionable as it is—and bad taste though it may seem to the associates of Christian intellectuals—I decline to forget Galileo and his humbler fellow-victims throughout the Christian centuries, or even the attitude of the contemporary Roman Catholic Church to contraceptives. Religious sanction for social custom and customary belief has always produced such things, and there is no good reason to expect a change. "To the unreasoning mind," says Mr. Eliot with sedate surprise, "the Church can often be made to appear to be the enemy of progress and enlightenment." It may indeed; and count me among the unreasoning.

I cannot doubt that such a society as Mr. Eliot wants would be heavily overbalanced towards conservation and stability, at the cost of plasticity and exploration. I believe that greater plasticity and bolder exploration of human possibilities are more urgently needed. Talk, with which we half frighten and half flatter ourselves, about the hectic speed of the changes which humanity is undergoing in our century is excited blah. Human nature is, as it always was, remarkably stodgy and in crying need of greater plasticity.

People cannot be plastic, however, unless they are relatively free from anxiety and from guilty fear of the possibilities of their own nature; and freedom from anxiety and guilt is not a thing whose possibility Mr. Eliot convincingly believes in. It is true that he says, "We need to recover the sense of religious fear, so that it may be overcome by religious hope," but the fear very evidently takes first place and goes along with "the evil which is present in human nature at all times and in all circumstances."

All alternatives to this spirit seem to be brought under the heading of what Mr. Eliot calls Liberalism, and hates. His attack is made rather chaotic by sketchy suggestions of the relation between this spirit and political and religious liberalism, and by the unargued conviction that this general spirit is responsible for all the particular social disorders which disturb him.

But the tags are of little account, and what matters is recognizing the distinction between the "liberal" spirit and the "Christian" spirit as Mr. Eliot understands them. As so often happens, it can best be expressed in the paradigm which childhood offers. The "liberal" spirit is the child who explores his world without prejudice and sees no reason to stop exploring; he finds neither the world fundamentally hostile nor himself fundamentally inadequate. The "Christian" spirit is the child with an intuitive conviction of the world's hostility and his own unworthiness, who (at his best, which Mr. Eliot stands for) concentrates on fortifying himself to overcome —to overcome the world and himself simultaneously. Mr. Eliot's tense and guarded insecurity, beleaguered by the world, is well expressed in his condemnation of "Liberalism" as "'something which tends to release energy rather than accumulate it, to relax, rather than to fortify."

The only alternative he sees to Christianity or paganism is a constant departure from, in the sense of a mere rejection of, all positive convictions. This may have been the character of some movements which have been called Liberal. But it is not the only alternative to the religious spirit. What Mr. Eliot ignores or implicitly denies is the possibility of being content with moving on, in a direction given you by the past, to something which has now for the first time become possible and is even more satisfying than your past activities were. This, which is exploration, seems so unsafe to the Christian that he denies its very possibility. His peace of mind depends on the conviction that he knows what he is ultimately aiming at; all his activity must be directed towards a goal which he has already postulated. By this means he escapes the insecurity of being in the strict sense an explorer and becomes instead a pilgrim.

In some temperaments, including apparently Mr. Eliot's, this conviction of an ultimate goal serves paradoxically to reinforce a peculiar gloom. The goal they postulate must be described as unattainable on this earth, since, of course, it is in the nature of human activity that each new development reveals a new and unattained possibility. Simultaneously with becoming better than we were we realize that we could be better than we are. To the explorer this seems an unsurprising and undisturbing fact. But by concentration on their postulated goal, those of Mr. Eliot's spirit can see our every advance almost exclusively in the guise of a relative failure. Observe where the emphasis falls in the following passage: "But we have to remember that the Kingdom of Christ on earth will never be realized, and also that it is always being realized; we must remember that whatever reform or revolution we carry out, the result will always be a sordid travesty of what human society should be—though the world is never left wholly without glory." The satisfaction of advancing at all is recognized dimly; the satisfaction of seeing that further advance is possible is converted into a disappointment. What is vividly felt is "the evil which is present in human nature at all times and in all circumstances." It is this which turns the explorer into an anxious pilgrim.

(1939)

(VIII) *Points of View* (edited by John Hayward)
Reviewed by R. O. C. Winkler

This selection from Mr. Eliot's prose writings is made under four heads—"literary criticism," "dramatic criticism," "individual authors," and "religion and society." Mr. John Hayward's efforts at book-making have in the past been attended with considerably more success than is customary in such cases; his achievement in this case is less unequivocal. A circular accompanying the review copy suggests that the selection might be suitable for use in schools; the shortcomings that I have in mind can best be focussed by saying that that is exactly what it isn't. One can sympathize with Mr. Hayward's difficulties; he was being asked to fill a non-existent gap. To select passages of "prose" representative of an author's style and thought is all very well when the author is a C. E. Montague or a Lytton Strachey, whose whole work might have been written with an eye to being selected from; but the essence of Mr. Eliot's best critical practice, one might have thought, was its application to the specific situation, its unwillingness to leave a generalization in the air without tying it down to some particular piece of verse or some particular poet. But when you are reconnoitring an author's work for salient points, it is inevitably the generalization that takes the eye and the *ad hoc* criticism that is pruned off. And so we find a series of little gobbets of a page or two or three apiece, headed (titles by Mr. Hayward) "Poetic Imagery," "Metrical Innovation," "Dissociation of Sensibility," and the school-boy or -girl who reads this book will find, not the careful scrutiny of language that brought to light a whole age and revealed new possibilities to our own age, but a series of slogans ("tough reasonableness beneath the slight lyric grace") divorced from the situation which they elucidated so brilliantly, like a series of formulae with no experimental data—very few science masters would subscribe to that kind of teaching.

A note at the beginning mentions, though, "the author's approval"; and one might ask whether there is nothing in Mr. Eliot's development to justify Mr. Hayward's surgery. No attempt is made to present Mr. Eliot's ideas as developing; a quotation about tradition from *After Strange Gods* immediately precedes "Tradition and the Individual Talent." But this last appears, happily, almost in full; and the other selections are sufficiently diverse to obtain some bird's-eye view of the shift of Mr. Eliot's ideas.

The essay "Tradition and the Individual Talent" is among those demonstrating Mr. Eliot's method at its best. " 'Interpretation,' " he says in "The Function of Criticism," "is only legitimate when it is not interpretation at all, but merely putting the reader in possession of facts which he would otherwise have missed." This is the genuine disinterestedness of science, as opposed to the pseudo-science of the literary-criticism-branch-of-psychology type; and it is this quality that pervades the early essays—"Andrew Marvell," "The Metaphysical Poets," and the one I am considering. It controls the ordering of the prose, and is the chief source of its vigour. The sense in reading that every word in every sentence is significant, and that any omission would leave a hole in the structure, derives from Mr. Eliot's desire to circumscribe exactly the situation he is dealing with; to use words as a scientist might use symbols, putting the reader in possession of facts which he, Eliot, is in possession of, by reproducing them with as complete accuracy as the language available is capable of. The central ideas, of "impersonality," and of the "historic sense," are of the same kind as scientific hypotheses; not critic-as-artist creations, but principles of investigation, armed with which the reader can penetrate without confusion fields of verse hitherto regarded as treacherous and obscure. Mr. Eliot reclaimed seventeenth-century verse from obscurity in the same sense in which an engineer reclaims a swamp, or in which Galileo reclaimed the stellar universe from the astrologers.

The author of "Tradition and the Individual Talent" was an empiricist. The apparent large-scale logical cohesion of the essay dissolves away on close inspection. Although the argument has the appearance of being the work of a distinguished theoretician examining the specific case, it turns out to be the great experimentalist turning over his results to the student. Yet the sense that more than *ad hoc* guidance is possible, that there are general principles somewhere anterior, haunts the essay and haunts its author. He feels he cannot let the matter rest there, and goes in search of underlying assumptions. The direction in which they lie is clear enough; the province of ethics is one from whose bourne very few literary critics return safely. And with the passage of years we see Mr. Eliot withdrawing from the hand-to-hand fight with fact, the absorbing attention to the word on the page, and struggling to make his peace with morality.

The shift of attention is marked by a change of subject. The seventeenth century disappears from the field in favour of the nineteenth and twentieth, where, less hampered by exact knowledge, the moralist finds a freer hand. Mr. Eliot himself draws attention to the change when it is well under way. "The lectures," he says in the "Preface" to *After Strange Gods,* "are not designed to set forth, even in the most summary form, my opinions of the work of contemporary writers: they are concerned with certain ideas in illustration of which I have drawn upon the work of the few modern writers whose work I know. I am not primarily concerned either with their absolute importance or their importance relative to each other. . . . I ascended the platform of these lectures in the role of moralist." And the avowed object of *After Strange Gods* was to produce a Revised Version of "Tradition and the Individual Talent." He says, significantly, "The problem, naturally, does not seem to me so simple as it seemed then, nor could I treat it now as a purely literary one." And we see something of the extent of the departure from the former practice when we read, "the chief clue to the understanding of most contemporary Anglo-Saxon literature is to be found in the decay of Protestantism." The recipe now for comprehension—it is implicit in the whole concept of "orthodoxy"—is to ask no questions, but throw your witches in and see if they drown, and run no risk of endangering your principles: a reversal of the earlier practice. It is no longer possible to say of Mr. Eliot what Mr. Eliot said of Blake: "because he was not distracted, or frightened, or occupied in anything but exact statements, he understood." Mr. Eliot is distracted by the ethical generalizations he wished to consolidate, and his object is no longer to understand, but to convert. His language now loses its analytic nicety, and masses itself to persuade, cajole, bludgeon, as he attacks the unseen Satanic opponent. "But as the majority is capable neither of strong emotion nor of strong resistance, it always inclines to admire passion for its own sake, unless instructed to the contrary; and if somewhat deficient in vitality, people imagine passion to be the surest evidence of vitality" (*After Strange Gods*). Failure to agree to the proclaimed principle can only produce an impasse: "I confess that I do not know what to make of a generation that ignores these considerations." When he returns to the seventeenth century now, the subject he chooses is Pascal's *Pensées,* and his criteria of relevance have changed remarkably. "It is no concern of this essay," he says, "whether the Five Propositions condemned at Rome were really maintained by Jansenius in his book *Augustinus,* or whether we should deplore or approve the consequent decay ... of Port-Royal." With this we can readily concur; but it is unlikely that we should have in mind the reason which immediately follows: "It is impossible to discuss the matter without becoming involved as a controversialist either for or against Rome." Even if one accepts this as true, it is hardly the kind of circumstances which one would expect to concern a disinterested critic.

From this time on Mr. Eliot's Penelope is in sight. In "Religion and Literature" he makes clear that the time for equivocation has passed. "In ages like our own ... it is ... necessary for Christian readers to scrutinize their reading, especially of works of the imagination, with explicit ethical and theological standards." And the nature of the majority of problems is settled in advance: education, for example ("Modern Education and the Classics"): "Education is a subject which cannot be discussed in a void: our questions raise other questions, social, economic, financial, political. And the bearings are on more ultimate problems even than these: to know what we want in education we must know what we want in general, we must derive our theory of education from our philosophy of life. The problem turns out to be a religious problem." One somehow suspected that it would. As Mr. Eliot stands with top hat on the table and sleeves rolled at the elbow, it would be surprising if the rabbit failed to emerge. It is not surprising, then, to find that *The Idea of a Christian Society* is almost exclusively preoccupied with generalization, and when the particular judgement occurs its context is prescribed: "It would perhaps be more natural, as well as in better conformity with the Will of God, if there were more celibates and if those who were married had larger families." The wheel has come full circle. Mr. Eliot has re-emerged from the thickets of ethical controversy, and can apply himself to the specific case with complete assurance. To realize the most abstract of ideas through the agency of the immediate occasion has been and is one of the most powerful motive forces in Mr. Eliot's verse; but to bring *Marina* or *East Coker* to mind here isn't to convince oneself that Mr. Eliot's critical practice has been improved by being brought into conformity with his poetic practice.

The worst, then, that one can fairly say of Mr. Hayward's selections is that he has accepted a *fait accompli*. If generalization is to become Mr. Eliot's critical *métier,* then this is merely a fitting garland in his honour; but to those who ten years ago thought him the most distinguished critic that English literature had seen for over a century, it will seem a poor funeral wreath. (1941)

E. M. Forster

E. M. FORSTER, *by F. R. Leavis*

The problem with which E. M. Forster immediately confronts criticism is that of the oddly limited and uncertain quality of his distinction—his real and very fine distinction. It is a problem that Miss Macaulay * doesn't raise. In fact, she doesn't offer a critique; her book is rather a guide, simply and chattily descriptive, to the not very large corpus of Mr. Forster's work. Nor does she provide the biographical information that, however impertinently in one sense of the adverb, we should like to have and that we might have been led by the publisher's imprint to hope for, however faintly. We should like to have it because it would, there is good reason for supposing, be very pertinent to the problem facing the critic. Still we do, after all, without extra-critical pryings or importings, know quite a lot about the particular *milieu* and the phase of English culture with which Mr. Forster's work is associated; enough, perhaps, to discuss with some profit the extent to which, highly individual as it is, it is also, in its virtues and its limitations, representative.

The inequality in the early novels—the contrast between maturity and immaturity, the fine and the crude—is extreme; so extreme that a simple formula proposes itself. In his comedy, one might carelessly say, he shows himself the born novelist; but he aims also at making a poetic communication about life, and here he is, by contrast, almost unbelievably crude and weak. Yet, through his strength in these novels, it is true, comes out in an art that suggests comparisons with Jane Austen, while it is in the element, the intention, relating them most obviously to *The Celestial Omnibus*, that he incurs disaster, the formula is too simple. For one thing, to lump the four pre-war novels together is clumsy; a distinction has to be made. There is no disastrous weakness in the first of them, *Where Angels Fear to Tread*, or in *A Room with a View* (which, in order of publication, comes third). And the distinction here isn't one of "comedy" as against "poetry" or "comedy-*cum*-poetry." For though the art of the "'born novelist" has, in these two novels, a character-

---
* *The Writings of E. M. Forster,* by Rose Macaulay.

istically spinsterly touch, that novelist is at the same time very perceptibly the author of *The Celestial Omnibus,* the tales in which suggest, in their poetic ambition—they may fairly be said to specialize in "poetry"—no one less than they do Jane Austen. Italy, in those novels, represents the bent of interest that Pan and the other symbols represent in the tales, and it is a bent that plays an essential part in the novelist's peculiar distinction. Pre-eminently a novelist of civilized personal relations, he has at the same time a radical dissatisfaction with civilization—with the finest civilization of personal intercourse that he knows; a radical dissatisfaction that prompts references to D. H. Lawrence rather than to Jane Austen.

In his treatment of personal relations the bent manifests itself in the manner and accent of his preoccupation with sincerity—a term that takes on, indeed, a different value from that which it would have if Jane Austen were our subject. His preoccupation with emotional vitality, with the problem of living truly and freshly from a centre, leads him, at any rate in intention, outside of the limits of consciousness that his comedy, in so far as we can separate it off, might seem to involve—the limits, roughly, that it is Jane Austen's distinction to have kept. The intention is most obvious in his way of bringing in, in association, love and sudden death; as, for instance, in Chapter IV of *A Room with a View* (see pp. 54-58). It is still more strikingly manifested in *Where Angels Fear to Tread.* There Italy figures much more substantially and disturbingly as the critical challenge to the "civilization" of Mr. Forster's cultivated English people, and what may be called for the moment the Lawrencian bent is more pronounced. There is the scene (Ch. VII) in which passionate paternal love, a kind of elemental hunger for continuance, is enacted in the devotion of the caddish and mercenary Italian husband to the baby: and the baby it is that, in this book, suffers the violent death. There follows the episode in which the Italian tortures Philip Herriton by wrenching his broken arm. Yet none of Mr. Forster's books is more notable for his characteristic comedy, with its cool, sedate, and rather spinsterly poise. And there is, nevertheless, no discrepancy or clash of modes or tones: *Where Angels Fear to Tread* is decidedly a success. It seems to me the most successful of the pre-war novels.

A Room with a View is far from being a failure, but, though the themes here might seem to be much less dangerous, there are certain weaknesses to be noted. There is, as Miss Macaulay points out, a curious spinsterish inadequacy in the immediate presentation of love (in *Where Angels Fear to Tread,* significantly, serious love between the sexes doesn't come in, at any rate immediately). And old Mr. Emerson, though not a disaster, does lead one to question the substantiality of the wisdom that he seems intended to represent. Nevertheless, *A Room with a View* is a charming and very original book—extremely original and personal, yet decidedly, and more unreservedly than *Where Angels Fear to Tread,* provoking comparisons with Jane Austen.

The reference above to D. H. Lawrence was, of course, an overemphasis, but as a way of calling attention to Mr. Forster's peculiar distinction among Edwardian novelists it can perhaps be justified. If we have to agree that he shows the influence of Meredith (see, for instance, the story called "Other Kingdom" in *The Celestial Omnibus,*) that is not to make the originality and the distinction less remarkable. The critic who deals so damagingly with Meredith in *Aspects of the Novel* is potentially there in the genuineness of the element in Mr. Forster's early novels that sets them apart by themselves in the period of Arnold Bennett, Wells, Galsworthy, and (one might add) Conrad. For Mr. Forster's "poetic" intention is genuine and radical, even if in expression it may manifest itself as a surprising immaturity; and actually, in *Where Angels Fear to Tread* and *A Room with a View* it for the most part commands a touch that is hardly to be distinguished from that of the comedy.

Or perhaps it would have been better to say "is commanded by"; for when, coming to the other two pre-war novels, *The Longest Journey* and *Howards End,* we ask how it is that they should be so much less successful, we notice at once how the contrast brings out the sure easy poise, in *Where Angels Fear to Tread* and *A Room with a View,* of the artist's—the "born novelist's"—control. The art of the comedy is a distancing art—

"Foreigners are a filthy nation," said Harriet.

—and it is a tribute to the novelist's skill that we should have no disturbing sense of a change in mode and convention when we pass to effects quite other than those of comedy. That is, the whole action is framed and distanced. Lilia, Gino's silly tragic victim in *Where Angels Fear to Tread,* Philip Herriton, commissioned to retrieve the baby, Miss Abbott, and the rest are all simplified figures, seen from outside; it is only in a very qualified way that they engage us (though they engage us enough for a measure of poignancy). The complexity of the situation we see as such: though we are interested and sympathetic, we are hardly worried. The critical scenes and episodes towards the end are, of course, not undisturbing; yet we are immersed in them—the detachment, though modified, still holds. In this effect the Italian setting, exotic and quaint—its people seen as another kind from us—has its part; it lends itself beautifully to the reconciliation of the "comedy" with the "poetry" and of tragic intensity with detachment.

The other two novels are much less the artist's: in them the imposing or seeking of any such conditions of a detached and happily poised art has been precluded by the author's essential interest. *The Longest Journey,* perhaps one may without impertinence observe, has plainly a good deal of the autobiographical about it, and it offers, in the presentment of its themes, a fullness and intimacy of realization. True, we find there too the characteristic comedy (notably in all that concerns Mr. Herbert Pembroke), but we can no longer say the success of this carries with it a general success. In fact, there are discrepancies, disharmonies, and disturbing shifts that go a long way towards justifying the formula thrown out and withdrawn in the second paragraph of this note. The poised success of the comedy in its own mode serves to emphasize the immaturity, the unsureness, and sometimes the crudity of the other elements, with which it wouldn't have been easily congruent even if they had in themselves justified the intention they represent.

Passionate love and, close upon it, sudden death come early in this book:

> He had forgotten his sandwiches, and went back to get them. Gerald and Agnes were locked in each other's arms. He only looked for a moment, but the sight burnt into his brain. The man's grip was the stronger. He had drawn the woman on to his knee, was pressing her, with all his strength, against him. Already her hands slipped off him, and she whispered, "Don't—you—hurt—." Her face had no expression. It stared at the intruder and never saw him. Then her lover kissed it, and immediately it shone with mysterious beauty, like some star. [p. 51]

Gerald is a brutal and caddish minor-public-school Apollo and Agnes a suburban snob, but this glimpse is for Rickie, the hero, a revelation:

> He thought, "Do such things actually happen?" and he seemed to be looking down coloured valleys. Brighter they glowed, till gods of pure flame were born in them, and then he was looking at pinnacles of virgin snow. While Mr. Pembroke talked, the riot of fair images increased. They invaded his being and lit lamps at unsuspected shrines. Their orchestra commenced in that suburban house, where he had to

> stand aside for the maid to carry in the luncheon. Music flowed past him like a river. He stood at the springs of creation and heard the **primaeval monotony. Then an obscure instrument gave out a little phrase.** The river continued unheeding. The phrase was repeated, and a listener might know it was a fragment of the Tune of tunes . . . In full unison was love born, flame of the flame, flushing the dark river beneath him and the virgin snows above. His wings were infinite, his youth eternal . . .

Then, a dozen pages later (p. 62):

> Gerald died that afternoon. He was broken up in the football match. Rickie and Mr. Pembroke were on the ground when the accident took place.

It is a key-experience for Rickie. Its significance is made explicit—perhaps rather too explicit. This memory of pure uncalculating passion as a kind of ultimate, invested by death with an awful finality and something like a religious sanction, becomes for Rickie a criterion or touch for the real, a kind of test for radical sincerity, in his questing among the automatisms, acquiescences, blurs, and blunted indifference of everyday living:

> He has no knowledge of the world . . . He believes in women because he has loved his mother. And his friends are as young and ignorant as himself. They are full of the wine of life. But they have not ·tasted the cup—let us call it the teacup—of experience, which has made men of Mr. Pembroke's type what they are. Oh, that teacup! [p. 74]

The theme of *The Longest Journey* is Rickie's struggle to live by the truth of the wine while being immersed in knowledge of the world.

Rickie writes stories like Mr. Forster's in *The Celestial Omnibus*. There is a note of ironic indulgence in the references to them: Rickie is very young. The direct and serious expression that the novelist offers us of the bent represented by such stories is in terms of a character, Stephen Wonham,

> a man dowered with coarse kindliness and rustic strength, a kind of cynical ploughboy. [p. 217]

He is the illegitimate child (comes the shattering revelation) of Rickie's mother and a young farmer, of whom we are told

> people sometimes took him for a gentleman until they saw his hands.

It is a Lady Chatterley-and-the-keeper situation that is outlined, though Robert is too much idealized to be called a Lawrencian character. Stephen, product of a perfect passionate love (cut short by death), grows up among the villagers and shepherds a kind of heroic boor, devoid of the civilized graces and refinements, representative of physical and spiritual health:

> ... looked at the face, which was frank, proud and beautiful, if truth is beauty. Of mercy or tact such a face knew little. It might be coarse, but . . . [p. 243]

He loves horse-play and can be a drunken blackguard, but he is incapable of anything other than direct sincerity: he would, as Ansell says, "rather die than take money from people he did not love." He moves roughshod through the latter part of the action, violating suburban flower-beds, outraging gentilities, and breaking through the pretences, self-deceptions, and timid meannesses of respectability.

> He only held the creed of "here am I and there are you," and therefore class-distinctions were trivial things to him. [p. 292]

When Rickie, having suspected him of intent to blackmail, offers apology and atonement, this is how Stephen replies:

> "Last Sunday week," interrupted Stephen, his voice suddenly rising, "I came to call on you. Not as this or that's son. Not to fall on your neck. Nor to live here. Nor—damn your dirty little mind! I meant to say I didn't come for money. Sorry, sorry. I simply came as I was, and I haven't altered since . . ." "*I* haven't altered since last Sunday week. I'm—" He stuttered again. He could not quite explain what he was . . . His voice broke. "I mind it—I'm—*I* don't alter—blackguard one week—live here the next—I keep to one or the other—you've hurt something most badly in me I didn't know was there." [pp. 281-2]

In short, it isn't easy to feel that the novelist in this essential part of his undertaking has attained a much more advanced maturity than the Rickie of the stories. Of course, what he had undertaken is something incomparably more difficult, and the weakness of the "poetic" element is made to look its worst by contrast with the distinction of what is strongest in the novel. Still, the contrast is there, and it is disastrous. What Mr. Forster offers as the centre of his purpose and intends with the greatest intensity of seriousness plainly cannot face the test of reality it challenges. Uninhibited by the passage about "knowledge of the world" and the "cup of experience" quoted above, the reader has to remark that Mr. Forster shows himself, for a writer whose touch can be so sure, disconcertingly inexperienced. An offence, even a gross one, against the probabilities, according to "knowledge of the world," of how people act and talk isn't necessarily very serious. But such a scene as that (Ch. XXVII) in which Ansell, the Cambridge philosopher, defying headmaster, headmaster's wife, and prefects, addresses the assembled boys at Sawston School—

> "This man"—he turned to the avenue of faces—"this man who teaches you has a brother" [etc.]

—reflects significantly on the ruling preoccupation that, in the born novelist, could have led to anything so crudely unreal. And of all that in *The Longest Journey* centers in Stephen one has to say that, if not always as absurd, it is, with reference to the appropriate standard, equivalently unreal. The intention remains an intention; nothing adequate in substance or quality is grasped. And the author appears accordingly as the victim, where his own experience is concerned, of disabling immaturities in valuation: his attributions of importance don't justify themselves.

A ready way of satisfying oneself (if there were any doubt) that "immaturity" is the right word is to take note of the attitude towards Cambridge (after which one of the three parts of the novel is named). Rickie, a very innocent and serious young man, found happiness at Cambridge and left it behind him there, and that this phase of his life should continue to be represented, for him, by an innocent idealization is natural enough. But Rickie in this respect is indistinguishable from the author. And if one doesn't comment that the philosophic Ansell, representative of disinterestedness and intelligence and Cambridge, is seen through the hero-worshipping Rickie's eyes, that is because he is so plainly offered us directly and simply by the novelist himself in perfect good faith.

Howards End (1910), the latest of the pre-war novels and the most ambitious, is, while offering again a fullness and immediacy of experience, more mature in the sense that it is free of the autobiographical (a matter, not of where the material comes from, but of its relation to the author as it stands in the novel) and is at any rate fairly obviously the work of an older man. Yet it exhibits crudity of a kind to shock and distress the reader as Mr. Forster hasn't shocked or distressed him before.

The main theme of the novel concerns the contrasted Schlegels and Wilcoxes. The Schlegels represent the humane liberal culture, the fine civilization of cultivated personal intercourse, that Mr. Forster himself represents; they are the people for whom and in whom English literature (shall we say?—though the Schlegels are especially musical) exists. The Wilcoxes have built the Empire; they represent the "short-haired executive type"—obtuse, egotistic, unscrupulous, cowards spiritually, self-deceiving, successful. They are shown—shown up, one might say—as having hardly a redeeming characteristic, except that they are successful. Yet Margaret, the elder of the Schlegel sisters and the more mature intelligence, marries Mr. Wilcox, the head of the clan; does it coolly, with open eyes, and we are meant to sympathize and approve. The novelist's attitude is quite unambiguous: as a result of the marriage, which is Margaret's active choice, Helen, who in obeying flightily her generous impulses has come to disaster, is saved and the book closes serenely on the promise of a happy future. Nothing in the exhibition of Margaret's or Henry Wilcox's character makes the marriage credible or acceptable; even if we were to seize for motivation on the hint of a panicky flight from spinsterhood in the already old-maidish Margaret, it might go a little way to explain her marrying such a man, but it wouldn't in the least account for the view of the affair the novelist expects us to take. We are driven to protest, not so much against the unreality in itself, as against the perversity of intention it expresses: the effect is of a kind of *trahison des clercs*.

The perversity, of course, has its explanation and is not so bad as it looks. In Margaret the author expresses his sense of the inadequacy of the culture she stands for—its lack of relation to the forces shaping the world and its practical impotence. Its weaknesses, dependent as it is on an economic security it cannot provide, are embodied in the quixotic Helen, who, acting uncompromisingly on her standards, brings nothing but disaster on herself and the objects of her concern. The novelist's intention in making Margaret marry Mr. Wilcox is not, after all, obscure. One can only comment that, in letting his intention satisfy itself so, he unintentionally makes his cause look even more desperate than it need: intelligence and sensitiveness such as *Howards End* at its finest represents need not be so frustrated by innocence and inexperience as the unrealities of the book suggest. For "unreality" is the word: the business of Margaret and Henry Wilcox is essentially as unrealized as the business of Helen and the insurance clerk, Leonard Bast—who, with his Jackie, is clearly a mere external grasping at something that lies outside the author's first-hand experience (though his speech, like that of Miss Avery's genteel niece, is consummately caught: the born novelist's gift so apparent in *A Passage to India* is remarkable from the outset).

And the Wilcoxes themselves, though they are in their way very much more convincingly done, are not adequate to the representative part the author assigns them—for he must be taken as endorsing Margaret's assertion to Helen that they "made us possible": with merely Mr. Forster's Wilcoxes to represent action and practice as against the culture and the inner life of the Schlegels there could hardly have been civilization. Of course, that an intellectual in the twentieth century should pick on the Wilcox type for the part is natural enough; writing half a century earlier, Mr. Forster would have picked on something different. But the fact remains that the Wilcoxes are not what he takes them to be, and he has not seen his problem rightly: his view of it is far too external and unsubtle.

At the same time it is subtler than has yet been suggested. There is the symbolism that centres in Howards End, the house from which the book gets its title. Along with the concern about the practical insignificance of the Schlegels' culture goes a turning of the mind towards the question of ultimate sanctions. Where lie—or should lie—the real source of strength, the springs of vitality, of this humane and liberal culture, which, the more it aspires to come to terms with "civilization" in order to escape its sense of impotence, needs the more obviously to find its life, strength, and authority elsewhere?

The general drift of the symbolism appears well enough here:

> The sense of flux which had haunted her all the year disappeared for a time. She forgot the luggage and the motorcars, and the hurrying men who know so much and connect so little. She recaptured the sense of space which is the basis of all earthly beauty, and, starting from Howards End, she attempted to realize England. She failed—visions do not come when we try, though they may come through trying. But an unexpected love of the island awoke in her, connecting on this side with joys of the flesh, on that with the inconceivable. . . . It had certainly come through the house and old Miss Avery. Through them: the notion of "through" persisted; her mind trembled towards a conclusion which only the unwise have attempted to put into words. [p. 202]

Yes, but the author's success in the novel is staked on his effectively presenting this "conclusion" by means of symbols, images, and actions created in words. And our criticism must be that, without a more substantial grasp of it than he shows himself to have, he was, as it turns out, hardly wise in so committing himself. The intention represented by Howards End and its associates, the wych-elm, the pig's teeth, Old Miss Avery and the first Mrs. Wilcox, remains a vague gesturing in a general—too general—direction, and the close of the book can hardly escape being found, in its innocent way, sentimental.

The inherent weakness becomes peculiarly apparent in such prose as this:

> There was a long silence during which the tide returned into Poole Harbour. "One would lose something," murmured Helen, apparently to herself. The water crept over the mud-flats towards the gorse and the blackened heather. Branksea Island lost its immense foreshores, and became a sombre episode of trees. Frome was forced inward towards Dorchester, Stour against Wimborne, Avon towards Salisbury, and over the immense displacement the sun presided, leading it to triumph ere he sank to rest. England was alive, throbbing through all her estuaries, crying for joy through the mouths of all her gulls, and the north wind, with contrary motion, blew stronger against her rising seas. What of soil, her sinuous coast? Does she belong to those who have moulded her and made her feared by other lands, or to those who have added nothing to her power, but have somehow seen her, seen the whole island at once, lying as a jewel in a silver sea, sailing as a ship of souls, with all the brave world's fleet accompanying her towards eternity? [p. 172]

Mr. Forster's "poetic" communication isn't all at this level of poeticality (which, had there been real grasp behind his intention, Mr. Forster would have seen to be Wilcox rather than Schlegel), but it nevertheless lapses into such exaltations quite easily. And the "somehow" in that last sentence may fairly be seized on: there the intention that can thus innocently take vagueness of vision in these matters for a virtue proclaims its inadequacy and immaturity.

In closing on this severe note my commentary on the pre-war novels I had perhaps better add explicitly (in case the implication may seem to have got lost) that they are all, as I see them, clearly the work of a significantly original talent, and they would have deserved to be still read and remembered, even if they had not been the early work of the author of *A Passage to India*.

In *A Passage to India* (1924), which comes fourteen years later (a remarkable abstention in an author who had enjoyed so decided a *succès d'estime*), there are none of these staggering discrepancies. The prevailing mood testifies to the power of time and history. For the earlier lyrical indulgences we have (it may fairly be taken as representative) the evocation of Mrs. Moore's reactions to the caves ("Pathos, poetry, courage—they exist, but are identical, and so is filth," etc.—see pp. 149-151). The tone characterizing the treatment of personal relations is fairly represented by this:

> A friendliness, as of dwarfs shaking hands, was in the air. Both man
> and woman were at the height of their powers—sensible, honest, even
> subtle. They spoke the same language, and held the same opinions,
> and the variety of age and sex did not divide them. Yet they were dis-
> satisfied. When they agreed, "I want to go on living a bit," or, "I don't
> believe in God," the words were followed by a curious backwash as if
> the universe had displaced itself to fill up a tiny void, or as though
> they had seen their own gestures from an immense light—dwarfs talk-
> ing, shaking hands and assuring each other that they stood on the same
> footing of insight. [p. 265]

Of course, tone and mood are specifically related to the given theme and setting of the novel. But the Indian sky and the Anglo-Indian circumstances must be taken as giving a particular focus and frame to the author's familiar preoccupations (exhibiting as these naturally do a more advanced maturity).

Fielding, the central figure in the book, who is clearly very close to the author, represents in a maturer way what the Schlegels represented: what may still be called liberal culture—humanity, disinterestedness, tolerance, and free intelligence, unassociated with dogma or religion or any very determinate set of traditional forms. He might indeed (if we leave out all that *Howards End* stood for) be said to represent what was intended by Margaret's marrying Henry Wilcox, for he is level-headed and practical and qualified in the ways of the world. His agnosticism is explicit. Asked

> Is it correct that most people are atheists in England now?

he replies:

> The educated thoughtful people? I should say so, though they don't
> like the name. The truth is that the West doesn't bother much over
> belief and disbelief in these days. Fifty years ago, or even when you
> and I were young, much more fuss was made. [p. 109]

Nevertheless, though Fielding doesn't share it, the kind of preoccupation he so easily passes by has its place in *A Passage to India* as in Mr. Forster's other novels, and again (though there is no longer the early crudity) its appearances are accompanied by something unsatisfactory in the novelist's art, a curious lack of grasp. The first Mrs. Wilcox, that very symbolic person, and Miss Avery may be said to have their equivalents in Mrs. Moore and Ralph, the son of her second marriage. Mrs. Moore, as a matter of fact, is in the first part of the book an ordinary character, but she becomes after her death a vague pervasive suggestion of mystery. It is true that it is she who has the experience in the cave—the experience that concentrates the depressed ethos of the book—and the echo "undermines her hold on life," but the effect should be to associate her with the reverse of the kind of mysteriousness that after her death is made to invest her name. For she and the odd boy Ralph ("born of too old a mother") are used as means of recognizing possibilities that lie outside Fielding's philosophy—though he is open-minded. There is, too, Ralph's sister Stella, whom Fielding marries:

> She has ideas I don't share—indeed, when I'm away from her I think them ridiculous. When I'm with her, I suppose because I'm fond of her, I feel different, I feel half dead and half blind. My wife's after something. You and I and Miss Quested are, roughly speaking, not after anything. We jog on as decently as we can . . . [p. 320]

Our objection is that it's all too easy. It amounts to little more than saying, "There may be something in it," but it has the effect of taking itself for a good deal more. The very poise of Mr. Forster's art has something equivocal about it—it seems to be conditioned by its not knowing what kind of poise it is. The account of the Krishna ceremony, for instance, which is a characteristic piece by the sensitive, sympathetic, and whimsically ironic Mr. Forster, slides nevertheless into place in a general effect—there are more things in heaven and earth, Horatio—that claims a due impersonality. How radical is this uncertainty that takes on the guise of a sureness and personal distinction of touch may be seen in Mr. Forster's prose when a real and characteristic distinction is unmistakably there. Here is an instance:

> The other smiled, and looked at his watch. They both regretted the death, but they were middle-aged men who had invested their emotions elsewhere, and outbursts of grief could not be expected from them over a slight acquaintance. It's only one's own dead who matter. If for a moment the sense of communion in sorrow came to them, it passed. How indeed is it possible for one human being to be sorry for all the sadness that meets him on the face of the earth, for the pain that is endured not only by men, but by animals and plants, and perhaps by the stones? The soul is tired in a moment, and in fear of losing the little she does understand, she retreats to the permanent lines which habit or chance have dictated, and suffers there.

The touch seems sure in the first three sentences—in fact, but for one phrase, in the whole passage. Consider, for instance, how different an effect the second sentence would have out of its context: one would suppose it to be satiric in tone. Here, however, it is a means to the precise definition of a very different tone, one fatigued and depressed but sympathetic. The lapse, it seems to me, comes in that close of the penultimate sentence: ". . . plants, and perhaps by the stones." Once one's critical notice has fastened on it (for, significantly too, these things tend to slip by), can one do anything but reflect how extraordinary it is that so fine a writer should be able, in such a place, to be so little certain just how serious he is? For surely that run-out of the sentence cannot be justified in terms of the dramatic mood that Mr. Forster is offering to render? I suppose the show of a case might be made out for it as an appropriate irony, or appropriate dramatically in some way, but it wouldn't be a convincing case to anyone who had observed Mr. Forster's habit. Such a reader sees merely the easy, natural lapse of the very personal writer whose hand is "in." It may seem a not very important instance, but it is representative, and to say that is to pass a radical criticism.

Moreover, a general doubt arises regarding that personal distinction of style—that distinction which might seem to give Mr. Forster an advantage over, say, Mr. L. H. Myers (to take another novelist who offers some obvious points of comparison). The doubt expresses itself in an emphasis on the "personal."

> Ronny approved of religion as long as it endorsed the National Anthem, but he objected when it attempted to influence his life.

> Sir Gilbert, though not an enlightened man, held enlightened opinions.

> Ronny's religion was of the sterilized Public School brand, which never goes bad, even in the tropics.

> Incurably inaccurate, he already thought that this was what had occurred. He was inaccurate because he was sensitive. He did not like to remember Miss Quested's remark about polygamy, because it was unworthy of a guest, so he put it away from his mind, and with it the knowledge that he had bolted into a cave to get away from her. He was inaccurate because he desired to honour her, and—facts being entangled—he had to arrange them in her vicinity, as one tidies the ground after extracting a weed.

> What had spoken to her in that scoured-out cavity of the granite? What dwelt in the first of the caves? Something very old and very small. Before time, it was before space also. Something snub-nosed, incapable of generosity—the undying worm itself.

A larger assemblage of quotations (there would be no difficulty but that of space in going on indefinitely) would make the point fairly conclusively: Mr. Forster's style is personal in the sense that it keeps us very much aware of the personality of the writer, so that even where actions, events, and the experiences of characters are supposed to be speaking for themselves the turn of phrase and tone of voice bring the presenter and commentator into the foreground. Mr. Forster's felicities and his charm, then, involve limitations. Even where he is not betrayed into lapses of the kind illustrated above, his habit doesn't favour the impersonality, the presentment of themes and experiences as things standing there in themselves, that would be necessary for convincing success at the level of his highest intention.

The comparative reference to Mr. L. H. Myers thrown out above suggests a return to the question of Mr. Forster's representative significance. When one has recognized the interest and value his work has as representing liberal culture in the early years of the twentieth century, there is perhaps a temptation to see the weaknesses too simply as representative. That that culture has of its very nature grave weaknesses Mr. Forster's work itself constitutes an explicit recognition. But it seems worth while insisting at this point on the measure in which Mr. Forster's weaknesses are personal ones, qualifying the gifts that have earned him (I believe) a lasting place in English literature. He seems then, for one so perceptive and sensitive, extraordinarily lacking in (if the phrase will pass) force of intelligence; it is, perhaps, a general lack of vitality. The deficiencies of his novels must be correlated with the weakness so apparent in his critical and journalistic writings—*Aspects of the Novel*, *Abinger Harvest* *—the weakness that makes them representative in so disconcerting a way. They are disconcerting because they exhibit a lively critical mind accepting, it seems, uncritically the very inferior social-intellectual *milieu* in which it has developed. Mr. Forster, we know, has been associated with Bloomsbury—the Bloomsbury which (to confine ourselves to one name) produced Lytton Strachey and took him for a great writer. And these writings of Mr. Forster's are, in their amiable way, Bloomsbury. They are Bloomsbury in the valuations they accept (in spite of the showing of real critical perception), in the assumptions they innocently express, and in pervasive accent.

It might, of course, be said that it is just the weakness of liberal culture—"bourgeois," the Marxist would say—that is manifested by

---
* See *Scrutiny*, Vol. V, No. 1, p. 100.

Bloomsbury (which certainly had claims to some kind of representative status). But there seems no need to deal directly with such a proposition here, or to discuss at any length what significance shall be given to the terms "liberal" and "culture." The necessary point is made by insisting that the weaknesses of Mr. Forster's work and of Bloomsbury are placed as such by standards implicit in what is best in that work. That those standards are not complete in themselves or securely based or sufficiently guaranteed by contemporary civilization there is no need to dispute: the recognition has been an essential part of the creative impulse in Mr. Forster. But that, in the exploration of the radical problems, more power than he commands may be shown by a creative writer who may be equally said to represent liberal culture appears well enough in *The Root and the Flower*—at least, I throw out this judgement as pretty obviously acceptable. In any case, I cannot see how what they both stand for can be dispensed with. They represent, these spokesmen of the finer consciousness of our time, the humane tradition as it emerges from a period of "bourgeois" security, of traditional forms and the loss of sanctions embarrassingly "in the air"; no longer serenely confident or self-sufficient, but conscious of being not less than before the custodian of something essential. It is, in these representatives, far from the complacency of "freedom of thought," but they stand, nevertheless, for the free play of critical intelligence as a *sine qua non* of any hope for a human future. And it seems to me plain that this tradition really is, for all its weakness, the indispensable transmitter of something that humanity cannot afford to lose.

These rather commonplace observations seemed worth making because of the current fashion of using "liberal" largely and loosely as a term of derogation: too much is too lightly dismissed with it. To enforce this remark it seems to me enough to point to *A Passage to India*—and it is an occasion for ensuring that I shall not, in effect, have done Mr. Forster a major critical injustice. For I have been assuming, tacitly, a general agreement that *A Passage to India*, all criticism made, is a classic: not only a most significant document of our age, but a truly memorable work of literature. And that there is point in calling it a classic of the liberal spirit will, I suppose, be granted fairly readily, for the appropriateness of the adjective is obvious. In its touch upon racial and cultural problems, its treatment of personal relations, and in prevailing ethos the book is an expression, undeniably, of the liberal tradition; it has, as such, its fineness, its strength, and its impressiveness; and it makes the achievement, the humane, decent, and rational—the "civilized"—habit, of that tradition appear the invaluable thing it is.

On this note I should like to make my parting salute. Mr. Forster's is a name that, in these days, we should peculiarly honour.

(1938)

Rémy de Gourmont

Rémy De Gourmont—Precursor

Rémy De Gourmont—Essai De Biographie Intellectuelle, by Garnet Rees

Reviewed by G. D. Klingopulos

The book on Gourmont one would like most to see would be written by someone old enough to have been influenced by him. As a research subject (from a British university) his importance is obscured by the amount of writing which has to be noticed. Dr. Rees, who is thorough, has to admit *"qu'on ne peut facilement saisir le principe directeur de son oeuvre."* By the two hundred and seventieth page the *principes* have not clearly emerged from Dr. Rees's quotations, and the mere listing of Gourmont's critical theories without much decisive comment only spreads the blanket of vagueness under which Dr. Rees has laid MM. T. S. Eliot *("le critique anglais qui a le mieux continué l'oeuvre de Gourmont"),* Ezra Pound, Aldous Huxley, Richard Aldington, and *"le grand critique anglais M. Arthur Symons."* Gourmont is tucked in. Mr. Middleton Murry's important *The Problem of Style*, which derives as much from Gourmont as from Wordsworth's "Preface," is not even noticed, although it would have suggested criticism of several of Gourmont's theories: for instance, of what Mr. Murry calls "the pictorial heresy" (*"La faculté maîtresse du style, c'est donc la mémoire visuelle"*), and of "symbol." Dr. Rees is not at all certain of the value or significance of the "symbolist movement" either in French or English. His account is so appreciative and impersonal that he can be said to have confined himself to linking up quotations; with such comments as *"Dans un art synthétique (le symbolisme) à un tel point, chaque mot doit jouer un rôle bien précis et le langage doit traduire par sa musique autant que par son sens, l'idée exacte du poète."*

The best of Gourmont's ideas have been so completely assimilated by later critics that one reads him for the first time either with surprise or disappointment. *La Culture des Idées, Le Chemin de*

Velours, and *Le Problème du Style* were written between 1900 and 1902, about twenty years before *The Sacred Wood* and *The Problem of Style.* Particularly memorable are the discussions of decadence, of *cliché,* of imitation, of metaphor, of realism, of plagiarism, pastiche, and sentimentality, which are still lively and more useful than much that has been written, with more show of science, since. Gourmont too had his science. The *cellules nerveuses* were his most constant "'illusions of fact" to which Mr. Eliot refers. The science is not pretentious so much as dogmatic, the dogmatic guess-work of an amateur, frequently impudent. Odds and ends of information from physiology and biology Gourmont put to the same use as Lawrence, with more impudence and less relevance. The simple and comic parallels of Fabre's *Insect Life* excited in him the cynicism of a dilettante. *"Du nouveau, encore du nouveau, toujours du nouveau: voilà le premier principe de l'art."* Dr. Rees leaves unexamined the abstractions in which Gourmont saw the only alternative to Belief—such as Novelty, Beauty, Strength, Intelligence, and devotes space to Gourmont as a philosopher. It is only by a loose application of terms that the title can be extended to him. Gourmont was much more intelligent than Anatole France, but like him *"il n'avait pas de système."* The dissociation of ideas is hardly this, but rather an essayist's formula. His culture of ideas and his scepticism are less important than his reliance on sensibility, on "sensations," which kept him out of aesthetics and gave him his wide range.

Much more could have been made of the *Promenades Littéraires* which illustrate Gourmont's procedure. To call it a method would be misleading, as Gourmont seems to have disdained any show of practical criticism and comparison of authors. He represents good taste rather than practice. His opinions are always suggestive, but cannot be imitated. His indifference to practice meant that his criticism was general and frequently lacked exactness. He did not care to "understand minutely." Contrast, for instance, his interest in Flaubert with Lawrence's. Flaubert is an excuse for considerations on the ideal artist and *"le but de l'activité propre d'un homme."* Gourmont's concern with Beauty, Symbols, and the impermanence of feelings should all have been considered together against his *"ériger en lois"* axiom in the *Lettres à L'Amazone.*

When Gourmont's subject is poetry or art in general, his ideas and the way he expresses them are more delicate and more final than anything in Matthew Arnold. For example:

... *Cependant, le vulgaire ressentira plus d'émotion devant la phrase banale que devant la phrase originale; et ce sera la contre-épreuve; au lecteur qui tire son émotion de la substance même de sa lecture s'oppose le lecteur qui ne sent sa lecture qu'autant qu'il peut en faire une application à sa propre vie, à ses chagrins, à ses espérances.*

But he is inconstant and repetitive, and is distracted by points of philology or other miscellaneous knowledge. Dr. Rees writes, "*Le pouvoir de généraliser semble manquer aux essayistes anglais: ils n'ont pas de facilité pour jouer avec les idées comme des prestidigitateurs.*" Pre-eminently Gourmont displays this facility, a facility in being so excited by an idea or theory, becoming so completely a champion, a rebel, or whatever else, that reality is lost and ideas become fantasy. As in his novels and poetry, Gourmont's tendency in criticism is to substitute fantasy for experience and thought. The distinction between fact and fiction, which Eliot desires, is slurred over. The critic becomes an exhibitor of fantasy and a public character. It is here that Gourmont suffers in comparison, again, with Arnold. The Frenchman appears, in his brilliance, less experienced, less fastidious, less wise.

(1940)

T. E. Hulme

THE T. E. HULME MYTH

T. E. Hulme, by Michael Roberts

Reviewed by H. A. Mason

T. E. Hulme was even in his lifetime the object of a cult which the publication of *Speculations* (which contains most of his writings) did apparently nothing to dispel. Perhaps the fragmentary nature of these writings, his untimely death in the war, his support of then fashionable ideas, are enough to excuse the special way he was thought of and written about. One must distinguish here between the praises of those personal friends whose opinions in various degrees command respect and the snobs who surrounded his reputation with an atmosphere so close that it was difficult to approach his work without bias.

As a thinker he was essentially an amateur. This quality secured him a hearing similar to that obtained by Dr. Richards's *Principles of Literary Criticism.* In *Speculations* we find the same dogmatic "incisive" style, the refreshingly unacademic contempt for authority, the zest in exposing what Hulme thought charlatanry (two quotations come to mind: "I consider it a duty, a very pleasant duty and one very much neglected in this country, to expose charlatans when one sees them" and "There is a tremendous amount of hocus-pocus about most discussions of poetry"), and together with all this an air of many-sidedness, of embracing several disciplines and of escaping from the academic specializations. Not that he was ever smug. In his trenchant distinctions and his welding together of distinctions made in different fields into apparently brilliant positions of startling clarity (the hard, dry "classical vision") he undoubtedly indulged a natural bent. Yet in so doing he actually blurred his meaning, and whatever of value can be found in his writings can only be reached by patiently untangling his syntheses and toning down his over-statements.

This work has been admiraby undertaken by Mr. Roberts. In a careful, but often verbose, exposition of the ideas to be found in *Speculations* he says, "most of his assertions are true in their proper field; the problem is to restate them in a way that will make their limitations clear." Yet he makes two important admissions: that the unity of Hulme's work is temperamental and "there is scarcely a single statement in Hulme that is not borrowed." One may then pardonably wonder why he undertook the writing of this book. For the philosophies of Bergson, Husserl, and Scheler, etc., if still insufficiently known in this country, are better dealt with technically and by experts; Hulme's aesthetic excursions are on Mr. Roberts's own showing unsatisfactory. One may legitimately doubt whether the great work on aesthetics Hulme planned would have been anything but good middleman work for Bergson and Lipps.

In short, I doubt whether Mr. Roberts can substantiate his claim that Hulme's great merit is that the ideas he borrowed were important. It seems much more likely from the extensive ad-libbing (to borrow a word from the Americans) Mr. Roberts allows himself that Hulme's positions were useful to him in working out problems that are preoccupying him. A convenient summary occurs on pp. 252-253. "Democracy and democratic progress are bound to fail if they do not rest on the religious or tragic outlook; but within the framework of a Christian polity, whose economy reflected the moral principles it professed, a form of democracy would be not only possible but also necessary, for democracy is the form of government that recognizes most openly the responsibility of the individual and the fact that all government rests on the consent of the governed. Progress towards such an end is not impossible. . . ." In reaching this conclusion Mr. Roberts is just and frank in pointing out Hulme's limitations. But he himself does not appear to realize how damaging he is to the Hulme myth. It is clear from this book, if it was not so before, that Hulme was of importance almost exclusively as a stimulating influence, and was possibly more valuable in conversations than in his writings. Many of his dicta can be found in different settings in, for example, the work of T. S. Eliot. But these ideas are only valuable when worked out and properly defined. It is by the success of those who are known to have come under his influence that Hulme will be esteemed.

(1938)

James Joyce

JOYCE AND "THE REVOLUTION OF THE WORD"

transition 22
transition I-VIII, XI-XIII, XV, XVIII
Anna Livia Plurabelle, by James Joyce
Haveth Childers Everywhere, by James Joyce
Two Tales of Shem and Shaum, by James Joyce
Our Exagmination Round His Factification for Incamination of Work in Progress, by Samuel Beckett and others
The Language of Night, by Eugene Jolas

Reviewed by F. R. Leavis

To judge the *Work in Progress,* in any bulk, not worth the labour of reading is not necessarily to identify oneself, with the late Poet Laureate. One may find some of the propositions with which the hierophants of the Mystic Logos seek to stagger the world commonplace—one may think Gerard Manley Hopkins the greatest poet of the Victorian age—and yet regret the use to which James Joyce has put his genius since he finished *Ulysses.* There is no question of appealing to even the *Oxford English Dictionary* or even the most modern English grammar as authorities. "In developing his medium to the fullest, Mr. Joyce is after all doing only what Shakespeare has done in his later plays, such as *The Winter's Tale* and *Cymbeline,* where the play-wright obviously embarked on new word sensations before reaching that haven of peacefulness" etc.— in demurring to such a proposition, and replying that Mr. Joyce is, after all, not doing only what Shakespeare has done, one's objection is not that he takes particular licences unprecedented in the plays.

Mr. Joyce's liberties with English are essentially unlike Shakespeare's. Shakespeare's were not the product of a desire to "develop his medium to the fullest," but of a pressure of something to be conveyed. One insists, it can hardly be insisted too much, that the study of a Shakespeare play may start with the words; but it was not there that Shakespeare—the great Shakespeare—started: the words matter because they lead down to what they came from. He was in the early wanton period, it is true, an amateur of verbal fancies and ingenuities, but in the mature plays, and especially in the late plays stressed above, it is the burden to be delivered, the precise and urgent command from within, that determines expression—tyrannically. That is Shakespeare's greatness: the complete subjection—subjugation—of the medium to the uncompromising, complex, and delicate need that uses it. Those miraculous intricacies of expression could have come only to one whose medium was for him strictly a medium; an object of interest only as something that, under the creative compulsion, identified itself with what insisted on being expressed: the linguistic audacities are derivative.

Joyce's development has been the other way. There is prose in *Ulysses*, the description, for instance, of Stephen Dedalus walking over the beach, of a Shakespearian concreteness; the rich complexity it offers to analysis derives from the intensely imagined experience realized in the words. But in the *Work in Progress*, it is plain, the interest in words and their possibilities comes first. The expositors speak of "Mr. Joyce's linguistic experiments"; and: "That he is following the most modern philological researches can be deduced from the passage . . ." (*transition 22*, p. 103). We are explicitly told that "words evoke in him more intense emotions than the phenomena of the outer world" (*Exagmination* etc., p. 153). Mustering his resources, linguistic and philological, (and, one hears, with the aid of the Interpreting Bureau), he stratifies his puns deeper and deeper, multiplies his associations and suggestions, and goes over and over his text, enriching and complicating.

"Few authors ever wrote a sentence with a more complete consciousness of every effect they wished to obtain" (*Exagmination* etc., p. 67)—but the wished effect (it would be self-evident, even without the successive versions extant of given passages) develops continually at the suggestion of the words; more and more possibilities of stratification and complication propose themselves. Working in this way, "inserting his new ideas continually in whatever part of the supple text they are appropriate" (*Exagmination* etc., p. 164), Mr. Joyce achieves complexities that offer themselves as comparable to Shakespeare's. But, achieved in this way, they betray at once their essential unlikeness. "The obscurity of that passage, its prolixity and redundancy, all are deliberately and artistically logical" (*Exagmination* etc., p. 55). Nothing could be "righter" than Shakespeare's effects, but they are irreconcilable with this kind of deliberate, calculating contrivance and with this external approach. They register the compulsive intensity and completeness with which

Shakespeare realizes his imagined world, the swift immediacy that engages at a point an inexhaustibly subtle organization. The contrast would still have held even if Shakespeare had had (as we are convinced he had not) to achieve his organization by prolonged and laborious experiment, and his immediacy with corresponding critical toil. The essential is that the words are servants of an inner impulse or principle of order; they are imperiously commanded and controlled from an inner centre.

In the *Work in Progress,* even in the best parts, we can never be unaware that the organization is external and mechanical. Each line is a series of jerks, as the focus jumps from point to point; for the kind of attention demanded by each one of the closely packed "effects" is incompatible with an inclusive, co-ordinating apprehension. The kind of accent and intonation with which a pun annnounces itself refuse to be suppressed; they are persistent and devastating. Many of the effects are undoubtedly interesting; *Anna Livia Plurabelle* is in some ways a very striking—and, rendered by Joyce himself, one can believe, a pleasing—performance. But in anything resembling an integrated effect a very large part indeed of the intended complexity must be lost: "It is possibly necessary to 'trance' oneself into a state of word-intoxication, flitting concept-inebriation," says one of the expositors (*Exagmination* etc., p. 114). The "meaning," or an impressive amount of it, can always be worked out at leisure, just as it was worked in (the opportunities that the *Work in Progress* offers for knowing elucidation insure it a certain popularity; it is surprising, Paris having long enough ago given the cue, that our undergraduate intellect stays content with the *Cantos*). But, at the best, the satisfaction provided even by *Anna Livia Plurabelle* is incommensurate with the implicit pretensions and with the machinery. It is significant that, for the English-speaking reader, so much of the satisfaction remains in the French translation published (with an amusing account of the method of translating) in the *Nouvelle Revue Française* (1931, Vol. XXXVI, p. 633).

To justify a medium much less obtrusive in pretensions than that of the *Work in Progress* Joyce would have had to have a commanding theme, animated by some impulsion from the inner life capable of maintaining a high pressure. Actually the development of the medium appears to be correlated with the absence of such a theme— to be its consequence. For in the earlier work, in *Ulysses* and before, the substance is clearly the author's personal history and the pressure immediately personal urgency; the historical particularity is explicit enough, and it is hardly impertinent to say that *Ulysses* is clearly a catharsis. But if one asks what controls the interest in technique, the preoccupation with the means of expression, in the *Work in Progress,* the answer is a reference to Vico; that is, to a philosophical theory.

"Vico proposed the making of 'an ideal and timeless history in which all the actual histories of all nations should be embodied,' " (*Exagmination* etc., p. 51). He also contemplated the formation of a "mental vocabulary" "whose object should be to explain all languages that exist by an ideal synthesis of their varied expressions. And now, after two centuries, such a synthesis of history and language, a task which seemed almost beyond human achievement, is being realized by James Joyce in his latest work" (*Exagmination* etc., p. 54). A certain vicious bent manifested itself very disturbingly in *Ulysses,* in the inorganic elaborations and pedantries and the evident admiring belief of the author in Stephen's intellectual distinction, and the idea of putting Vico's theory of history into the concrete would seem rather to derive from this bent than to be calculated to control it.

In any case, the idea would seem to be self-stultifying. The result in the *Work in Progress* of trying to put "'allspace in a notshall"—the "ideal" (but concrete) "and timeless history" in a verbal medium defying all linguistic conventions—is not orchestrated richness but, for the most part, monotonous non-significance. Forms, after all, in life and art, are particular and limiting, and *The Waste Land* probably goes about as far as can be gone in the way of reconciling concrete particularity with inclusive generality. Joyce's limitless ambition leads to formlessness, local and in survey. The "ideal history" would seem to be chaos, that which precedes form—or swallows it. In it, "movement is non-directional—or multi-directional, and a step forward is, by definition, a step back" (*Exagmination* etc., p. 22). H. C. E. (Humphrey Chimpden Earwicker) is glossed by "Here Comes Everybody"; but a multi-directional flux, though it may be said to have something like universality, has not the universality of a mythical figure. Joyce's medium, likewise, is not in the end rich. It may be the "esperanto of the subconscious"; if so, the subconscious is sadly boring.

As a matter of fact, Joyce's subconscious is worse than boring; it is offensively spurious. It is not that one objects to conscious management, which is inevitable. But conscious management in the

Work in Progress is not the agent of a deeply serious purpose; it serves in general an inveterate solemn ingenuity, and it is often the very willing pimp to a poor wit. "Cosmic humour" there may be, as the expositors allege, in the *Work in Progress;* there is certainly a great deal of provocation for D. H. Lawrence's reaction: "My God, what a clumsy *olla putrida* James Joyce is! Nothing but old fags and cabbage-stumps of quotations from the Bible and the rest, stewed in the juice of deliberate, journalistic dirty-mindedness—what old and hard-worked staleness, masquerading as the all-new!" There is more in the *Work in Progress* than that, but the spuriousness, the mechanical manipulation, is pervasive.

Lawrence, of course, objected to the whole thing; and his objection finds endorsement in the company Joyce keeps. It was fair to use the bits from his expositors quoted above, since it is not because he can get published nowhere else that he continues to appear in *transition;* he, at any rate tacitly, encourages them. We are free to assume that the "International Workshop for Orphic Creation" (as *transition* now describes itself) is under his patronage, and that he does not dissociate himself from his expositors when they issue manifestoes in favour of "The Vertigral Age":

> The Vertigral Age believes that we stand in direct line with the primeval strata of life.
>
> The Vertigral Age wants to give voice to the ineffable silence of the heart.
>
> The Vertigral Age wants to create a primitive grammar, the stammering that approaches the language of God.

Joyce (who gives "such a picture of the entire universe as might be registered in the mind of some capricious god") is said to have "desophisticated language" ("Vico applied to the problem of style"). It is, on the contrary, plain that the whole phenomenon is one of sophistication, cosmopolitan if not very subtle, and, so far from promising a revival of cultural health, is (it does not need Lawrence's nostril to detect) a characteristic symptom of dissolution. The "internationalization of language" acclaimed by Joyce's apostles is a complementary phenomenon to Basic English; indeed, we note with a surprised and pleased sense of fitness that Mr. C. K. Ogden has shown an active interest in the *Work in Progress*.

Their conception of the problem—"I claim for *transition*," says Mr. Eugene Jolas, "priority in formulating the problem on an international scope . . . and in giving it a dialectical substructure"—is ludicrously inadequate. "I believe," says Mr. Jolas, standing up for the artist, "in his right to audaciously split the infinitive." As if any amount of splitting infinitives, mimicking the Master, pondering Gertrude Stein and E. E. Cummings, and connoisseuring American slang could revivify the English language.

A brief reflection on the conditions of Shakespeare's greatness is in place here. He represents, of course, the power of the Renaissance. But the power of the Renaissance could never so have manifested itself in English if English had not already been there—a language vigorous enough to respond to the new influx, ferment, and literary efflorescence, and, in so doing, not lose, but strengthen its essential character. The dependence of the theatre on both court and populace ensured that Shakespeare should use his "linguistic genius"— he incarnated the genius of the language—to the utmost. And what this position of advantage represents in particular form is the general advantage he enjoyed in belonging to a genuinely national culture, to a community in which it was possible for the theatre to appeal to the cultivated and the populace at the same time.

A national culture rooted in the soil—the commonplace metaphor is too apt to be rejected: the popular basis of culture was agricultural. Mr. Logan Pearsall Smith shows how much of the strength and subtlety of English idiom derives from an agricultural way of life. The essential nature of the debt is well suggested by his notes on phrasal verbs. "For when we examine these phrasal verbs, we find that by far the greater number of them also render their meanings into terms of bodily sensation. They are formed from simple verbs which express the acts, notions, and attitudes of the body and its members; and these, combining with prepositions like 'up,' 'down,' 'over,' 'off,' etc. (which also express ideas of motion), have acquired, in addition to their literal meanings, an enormous number of idiomatic significations, by means of which the relations of things to each other, and a great variety of the actions, feelings and thoughts involved in human intercourse, are translated, not into visual images, but into what psychologists call 'kinaesthetic' images, that is to say, sensations of the muscular efforts which accompany the attitudes and motions of the body" (*Words and Idioms,* p. 250).

This strength of English belongs to the very spirit of the language—the spirit that was formed when the English people who formed it were predominantly rural. Why it should be associated with a rural order, why it should develop its various resources to the fullest there, Mr. Adrian Bell, illustrating the vigour and fineness of rustic speech in *Scrutiny Volume II, Number 1,* suggested: he showed "how closely the countryman's life and language grow together; they are like flesh and bone." They grow together just as mind and body, mental and physical life, have grown together in those phrasal verbs. And how much richer the *life* was in the old, predominantly rural order than in the modern suburban world one must go to the now oft-cited George Bourne (under both his names) for an adequate intimation. When one adds that speech in the old order was a popularly cultivated art, that people talked (so making Shakespeare possible) instead of reading or listening to the wireless, it becomes plain that the promise of regeneration by American slang, popular city-idiom, or the inventions of *transition*-cosmopolitans is a flimsy consolation for our loss.

It is an *order* that is gone—Mr. Bell records its last remnants—and there are no signs of its replacement by another: the possibility of one that should offer a like richness of life, of emotional, mental, and bodily life in association, is hardly even imaginable. Instead we have cultural disintegration, mechanical organization, and constant rapid change. There is no time for anything to grow, even if it would. If the English people had always been what they are now there would have been no Shakespeare's English and no comparable instrument: its life and vigour are no mere matter of vivid idioms to be matched by specimens of American slang (English, it may be ventured, has been more alive in America in the last century than in England mainly because of pioneering conditions, which are as unlike those of the modern city as possible).

At any rate, we still have Shakespeare's English: there is indeed reason in setting great store by the "word"—if not in the revolutionary hopes of Mr. Jolas and his friends. With resources of expression that would not have existed if Shakespeare's England had not been very different from his own, Gerard Manley Hopkins wrote major poetry in the Victorian age. We have poets in own own day, and James Joyce wrote *Ulysses.* **For how long a cultural tradition can be perpetuated in this way one wonders with painful tension. Language, kept alive and rejuvenated by literature, is certainly an** essential means of continuity and transition—to what? We are back at the question, which has been raised in *Scrutiny* before and will be again, if *Scrutiny* performs its function, whether there can be a culture based on leisure, and if so, what kind.

We can demand no more than the certitude that there are certain things to be done and cared for now. The line of reflection indicated above leads one to the unanswerable questions raised innocently by scientists who (in romantic or journalistic moments) speculate as to the complete transformation, physical and psychological, that Science will effect in Man.

(1933)

Rudyard Kipling

A CASE FOR KIPLING? by Boris Ford

. . . talked pure Brasenose to him for three minutes. Otherwise he spoke and wrote trade-English—a toothsome amalgam of Americanisms and epigram.—"The Village That Voted the Earth Was Flat."

Mr. Eliot's criticism, at the period when it was evidently a product of the same mind and interests as also created the poetry, was not only bodied in some of the most aristocratic prose of the century, but displayed an intelligence that gave his judgements a rare authority and confidence. Not, one must admit, that Mr. Eliot was ever a wholly reliable critic, and often one was compelled to modify or even disagree with particular valuations. But throughout the early work the direction of argument was evident, tending to the refashioning of obliterated standards, and above all to a conception of art and literature as the product of a lively interplay of individual integrity and social vigour.

In the course of the introductory essay to his choice of poems by Kipling, Mr. Eliot writes: "Having previously exhibited an imaginative grasp of space, and England in it, he now proceeds to a similar achievement in time"; and he quotes in support of this shift of activity the following tales: "An Habitation Enforced," "My Son's Wife," and "The Wish House." Now, what is striking about this particular judgement is not that it is so indefinite as to be hardly worth making, for it shares this blemish with the rest of the essay, but that Mr. Eliot should now practise a critical discipline that permits him to reproduce verbatim and without acknowledgement (that is, unconsciously) the indefinite judgements of others. For in his book on Kipling, Mr. Shanks writes: "England now gave him not merely consolation but a new extension of life. Whereas on his departure from India he had sought this extension in space, he now found it in time"; and he in turn quotes the following stories: "An Habitation Enforced," "Friendly Brook," "The Wish House," and "My Son's Wife." But one should not deduce from this that Mr. Eliot's essay is nothing but plagiarism of lesser critics, for much of it is a stylistic plagiarism of Mr. Eliot himself. There is the familiar air of subtle differentiation, coupled with the pervasive refusal to observe any precise demarcations. The tone has about it that judicious detachment which was once so suggestive of meaning but is now employed simply to disarm criticism and to enforce a personal view. Indeed, Mr. Eliot seems to feel himself in a new role, that of legal panjandrum, when he admits that readers unacquainted with Kipling "might perhaps imagine that I had been briefed in the cause of some hopelessly second-rate writer, and that I was trying, as an exhibition of my ingenuity as an advocate, to secure some small remission of the penalty of oblivion." And though Kipling, anxious to stand well with posterity, expressed some anxiety as to who, "when our story comes to be told, will have the telling of it," one feels that he would have hesitated before inviting the author of *Triumphal March* to undertake the task. In fact, Mr. Eliot has all too evidently briefed himself. And at least one of the clues to the enigma has already been suggested; whereas Mr. Eliot's best criticism related to his poetic interests, his critical concern for Kipling is accompanied by the admission that "part of the fascination of this subject is the exploration of a mind so different from my own." In fact, if the two minds are still (or so one hopes) poetically exclusive, as individuals one can detect a certain affiliation, or in the case of Mr. Eliot a would-be affiliation, between the men; unfortunately, it is the human rather than the artistic factor that seems to have predominated.

The main case against the claim that Kipling revealed an imaginative grasp on space and then on time is that the imagination he revealed in the process has far more in common with that of the industrial pioneer, the man who exploits the backward area, than with that of the artist, who by contrast opens up inner regions of individual feeling. By this I do not mean here to imply the usual criticism of Kipling, that he was the voice of British imperialism, but rather and more relevantly that his mind was a very crude instrument, seldom if ever in touch with finer spiritual issues, and that in consequence his grasp on anything at all delicate has about it the virtuosity of the Chinese juggler. He found, very early on in his career, that he possessed a facility for conveying the atmosphere of a people and the type-emotions of an individual, and he spent a lifetime exploiting and developing this talent. But essentially the process is that of the news-camera, of the highly efficient journalist eye, and the journalist ear and nose and palate as well. It is on this level, and not, for instance, as implying a concern analogous to Hopkins's struggle with language, that one has to understand Kipling's remark that "it is necessary that every word should tell, carry, weigh, taste and, if need be, smell." And exactly what this means in practice can be seen in *Kim,* which Mr. Eliot in fact quotes in this context and which he feels to be Kipling's "greatest book." This novel is so disarmingly superficial that even its less pleasant elements, those relating to the colour conflict, fail to give any sharp offence. And if indeed it seems to be one of his most satisfactory works, that is because the author's main interest is still (the book appeared in 1901) that of the boggle-eyed and fascinated initiate, and not yet that of the legislator. As he himself wrote: *"Kim,* of course, was nakedly picaresque and plotless—a thing imposed from without." However, most often his flights of imagination, whether in space or time, seem to me merely ineffectual. Mr. Eliot quotes at length, and with admiration, from "The Finest Story in the World"; and certainly it is a test-case, since here Kipling faces himself not only with the ordinary job of writing an efficient tale, but with the added task of hinting at the "finest story in the world," and of convincing his reader that it is as fine as the tale demands. Actually this "finest story" seems to consist of nothing but a set of historical-cameos of a fairly vivid and entirely trivial nature, and these distinct episodes are related to each other not with a view to illustrating historical continuity, but simply as a means to dramatizing a crude belief in metempsychosis. The quality of imagination displayed is that of the scenario-writer, and the tale as a whole is on the level of *The Strand Magazine.* For all Mr. Eliot's remark that Kipling "is almost 'possessed' of a kind of second-sight," his vision, whether of the normal or the psychic variety, remains consistently that of the journalist, and his reconstructions of the past have as little *artistic* interest as his descriptions of the present. Except for children, there seems little to be said on behalf of this imagination; but of course, though children probably do enjoy *Puck of Pook's Hill* and the *Jungle Books,* Kipling rather hoped that adults would like them too, and hence the claims, often made on their behalf by his admirers, that they reveal a mature and subtle sense of historical tradition. Mr. Eliot, before supporting such an idea, might profitably read through some of his own essays dealing with tradition and continuity.

That Kipling is essentially a journalist, almost the founder of modern journalism, seems generally admitted; and for most people his name is also associated with a reverence for the machine of British imperialism. In any ordinary sense of the terms, these charges cannot profitably be denied; though Mr. Eliot devotes a full page of equivocations to the matter, even to answering the accusation that Kipling was a fascist (which surely no one with a sense for chronological exactitude can have made) with the retort that fascism "from the truly Tory point of view is merely the extreme degradation of democracy"; and concluding, in reply to the suggestion that Kipling believed in racial superiority, by quoting his genuine sympathy for the Indians in *Kim,* despite the fact that the whole point of that book, or at least its climax, is Kim's assertion of superiority, at the moment of crisis, simply by virtue of his white parentage, and his subsequent willingness to use his Hindu affiliations in the service of the white foreigners. After one has said all that can be said for Kipling, as Mr. George Orwell has said it (see *Dickens, Dali and Others*), after one has admitted his historical value, or his verbal dexterity, or has commended him as a "great verse-writer" or as a "good bad poet," or has stressed his undoubted sense of national responsibility—after saying all this and a great deal else, one inevitably returns to what seem to me the two fundamental issues: that Kipling developed in the 1890's, and that he suffered the common disability of an artistic decadence, which is an atrophy of finer feeling. Ultimately all one's criticisms resolve themselves to this historical consideration, on the one hand, and to the moral issue, on the other. And because the case has been made repeatedly on the level of the particular, I wish here simply to consider the implications of these more general issues.

Perhaps the main feature of the last decade of the nineteenth century in this country was its internal irruption. One thinks too exclusively of the 1890's as the era of Dandyism and the Decadence, of Wilde and Beardsley, forgetting that it was also a period both of imperial expansion and of the new socialism, of Rhodes and of the Webbs. It was, in fact, a period of social disintegration. The gaudy triumphs of imperialism, culminating in Mafeking Night, fostered, in the energy released, a spirit of irresponsibility in the realm of ideas. The key-word of the decade was *new,* and this concern expressed itself in two main ways: in literature, and in art generally, the new was expressed in a cult of virtuosity, a search for the exotic and the rare, and in a taste for antithesis and epigram; while in the social and political sphere, it showed itself in a flowering of socialist and Fabian ideas, on the one hand, and, on the other, in a realization by imperialism of its unsuspected power and dominion. At a somewhat analogous period, Marlowe gives expression to a similar combination of circumstances, and if his liking for sonorous and exotic language and his idealization of the merchant-adventurer were not inimical to the production of fine art, that was due to a set of cultural circumstances, above all perhaps to a social homogeneity, that was no longer operative when Kipling came to the fore. The impoverishment of life left his work as shallow as Marlowe's had been vigorous, and the atomization of the social scene found him hovering between the superficially divergent worlds of art and politics, much as Wilde also toyed with socialism and Wells with literature. Kipling's early life in India gave him, almost inevitably, the imperial outlook and the colour prejudice. But he was also born of artistic parents, and became a close friend of Burne-Jones. And thus he came to satisfy his longings for a life of active service to the Empire, a life he was never able to experience except by proxy, through the medium of his writing. And to us the consequences of such a combination are not sympathetic. The Empire that Kipling glorified, with the devotion that he sought to evoke on its behalf, has since then split up and it is now in a state of flux. Mandalay has become the centre of an Allied reverse of the most critical importance, and a whole civilization has been endangered by a short battle fought out on the very road that symbolized so much romance for Kipling. And it is not irrelevant to mention these mundane considerations, in a way that would be quite out of place in the case of Marlowe's glorification of a nascent capitalism; because Kipling's writing proceeds on the level of the ephemeral, and as a journalist none of his work achieves that artistic detachment from the actual which alone could make his ideas live as Marlowe's live. And one can, in passing, only deplore that Mr. Eliot should have supposed that Kipling is in some way worthy of attention (not only, one presumes, literary attention), and that we should be invited to admire this embodiment of a world that it has become so imperative to alter. Indeed, one could advance a convincing case for prescribing, at least for the duration, the writings of a man who speaks of the troops as revealing "the intense selfishness of the lower classes," of officers whose virtue consists in God's having "arranged that a clean-run youth of the British middle classes shall, in the matter of backbone, brains, and bowels, surpass all other youths," and who says of the battle in which they are engaged that "the bucketing went forward merrily"; but Mr. Eliot seems not to be acquainted with this aspect of Kipling, or perhaps he does not appreciate that this is, to say the least, not the most satisfactory attitude that can be adopted in the present situation.

Kipling's affiliations with the literary decadence are evident in his interest in language. The inventories of gems or scents or colours that one finds in Wilde are matched by his inventories and descriptions of mechanical components. As Théophile Gautier said, "the decadent style is the last effort of language to express everything to the last extremity," and this accurately describes Kipling, too. His verse and his prose are very carefully put together, and Mr. Eliot observes that he "could manage even so difficult a form as the sestina." Moreover, it is perfectly true that Kipling had a knack of turning a phrase quite as effectively as Shaw or Whistler; he shared with them the contemporary love of verbal dexterity, and he had the advantage over them of possessing a vulgarer mind, a mind closer to the communal platitude. With the result that it is Kipling, rather than the accredited conversationalists of the decadence, who has added to our language so many of those "toothsome amalgams of Americanisms and epigrams" that in some quarters are thought so rare an acquisition.

But perhaps the most significant fact about the *fin-de-siècle* writers was their spiritual isolation. Nearly all of them, in greater or less degree, were sexually abnormal, and the eroticism of much of their writing, and their endless quest after elaborate sensation, masked an inner disorder and desolation whose real nature they fought to conceal. The whole conduct of their lives, with its affectation of dandyism and elaborate inconsequence, was a device, perhaps subconsciously practised to a great extent, to make tolerable a lack of personal contact with others. Whether it be in the writings of Wilde or Beerbohm, Francis Thompson or Davidson, or even Bernard Shaw, the same uneasiness is evident, and they all reveal a similar lack of confidence in the validity of individual relationships. Indeed, the Ivory Tower was less an island of art standing out of a sea of social activity than the very person of the isolated individual himself. And in this connexion it is important to remember how many of the dandies of the decadence ended their lives in the sanctuary of the Roman Catholic Church; the organization and the ritual enabled them to reconcile a longing for participation with a dependence on emotional indulgence. And it is impossible to read any quantity of Kipling's verse and prose without realizing immediately how similar was his case. "What distinguished Kipling from so many present-day writers," says Dr. Bonamy Dobrée (in *The*

Lamp and the Lute), "is precisely that he does not attempt to break down man's loneliness, seeing only futility in the balm of the 'personal relation.'" The moral of the tale "As Easy as A B C" is that democracy implies solidarity and co-operation; the only reply to this aberration is to "Order the guns and kill!" and then to retire in on oneself again. Unfortunately, this blissful after-condition is threatened by a sudden resurrection of democracy, "and when once it's a question of invasion of privacy, good-bye to right and reason in Illinois!" The same symptom is treated more pretentiously in one of the psychological tales, "In the Same Boat," where the drug-addicts only escape into normality by pooling their moral resources and struggling together against the recurrent crises. But Kipling emphasizes not so much their mutual dependence on each other's help as that such co-operation is strictly conditional on their mental disorder. When they manage to reach normality, their sense of joint effort and attraction, which alone had enabled them to achieve it, vanish, and "for the new-found life of him Conroy could not feel one flutter of instinct or emotion that turned to herward." And in a somewhat similar story, "The Brushwood Boy," the hero, whose "school was not encouraged to dwell on its emotions," only becomes inveigled into a love-affair as a result of repeated telepathic communications with the lady in question; and when, eventually, they meet and have to go through with it (or rather Kipling has to go through with it), the dialogue is arch and almost embarrassing in its artificiality. In fact, it was not that Kipling was isolated willingly or without regret, for one finds throughout his work the gravitation of one individual to another, even if this is described as the outcome of something abnormal; rather does one feel that an inner disability compelled him to this detachment from human sympathies, and that by way of compensation he forcibly identified himself with the larger structure of the British Empire and later of the English tradition. The sentiments that might normally have fastened on individuals were frustrated, and so they drove Kipling almost frantically, and quite obstinately, into participation in the great abstraction. As others have pointed out, Kipling took his imperialism not only seriously but even religiously, and it gave him the security and also the emotional outlet that we have noticed in the conversion to Rome of the dandies. Nothing is so typically decadent about Kipling as this spiritual isolation, and Mr. Dobrée has justly remarked (though to illustrate quite another point) that the Empire is Kipling's Catholic Church.

And this brings one to the second of the two issues fundamental to an understanding of Kipling, and it bears directly on all that has been said so far. For Kipling's journalism, his interest in the craft of writing, his isolation, and his religious attachment to the Empire are all fundamentally related to what I defined earlier as an atrophy of feeling. In his essay Mr. Eliot points out that "the changes in his poetry, while they cannot be explained by any usual scheme of poetic development, can to some extent be explained by changes in his outward circumstances," and elsewhere he confesses that "the critical tools which we are accustomed to use in analysing and criticising poetry do not seem to work." And this leads Mr. Eliot to offer a number of explanations of which even he seems sceptical: such as the theory that Kipling, as distinct from other poets, intends his poems "to *act*," or the theory, nowhere demonstrated, that he is "an integral prose-and-verse writer." But, were it not damaging to his general case, Mr. Eliot must surely have realized that development in art, and its critical analysis, is a matter of *emotional* growth, both extensively and intensively. And this is precisely what one fails to find either in Kipling's work as a whole or in his individual poems and stories. Like *Kim,* they are "things imposed from without," most often unfolding a given situation or panorama. And this lack of internal development gives even his most dramatic tales a certain dustiness in the mouth; the gritty detachment of the style and the flashes of emotionalism are not controlled by any sense of artistic logic, but proceed from a mind of set ideas and narrow sympathies. In fact, as one studies his life, one sees Kipling moving from prejudice to prejudice, from one tactlessness to another, and one cannot see even in his private affairs any accession of maturity or judgement. This debility he shares, as has been suggested, with the other writers of the decadence; and, as in their case, this throttling (and I feel it was not altogether a personal responsibility) of normal spontaneity of feeling was accompanied by an increasing concern with the mere machine of his art. To Mr. Edmund Wilson (see *The Wound and the Bow*) this appears puzzling: "It is the paradox of Kipling's career that he should have extended the conquests of his craftsmanship in proportion to the shrinking of the range of his dramatic imagination. As his responses to human beings became duller, his sensitivity to his medium increased." But there is no paradox in this, so long as one is not deceived by Kipling's "conquests of his craftsmanship." Personally I find his skill no more remarkable than

Somerset Maugham's or H. G. Wells's; indeed, it rapidly developed into a formula that is all too easily and frequently copied. In very little of his work does one feel that he is doing much more than send his polished machine along the railroad that suits his whim of the moment; certainly it is a well-oiled and powerful locomotive, and it draws its freight of inanimate ideas and inanimate individuals unerringly to a pre-arranged destination; but of its nature it keeps to its rails and observes the dictation of a time-table.

One of the inevitable outcomes of Kipling's lack of warm-blooded feeling (as distinct from his susceptibility to full-blooded emotion) is that his interest centres in things and ideas, and the internal working of his individuals is treated as a process distinct from character and personality. Seldom does one find any suggestion of innate life; the Irish Mulvaney, the Scots McTurk, the Anglo-Indian Mrs. Hauksbee, the American Zigler, or Pallant the English M.P., as well as the McAndrews and the troopers of the verse, are all of them actors on a carefully prepared stage-set; it is the drama they perform, rather than their own potentialities, that gives the story interest. And this explains the fact that Kipling appears to have had not much more interest in the thoughts and feelings of human beings than of animals and machines, or even in a pillow called Aunt Ellen. If one readily admits the virtuosity of the performance (for this seems simpler than to be niggling over such a triviality), yet one is still baffled to explain the interest in such stories as "The Maltese Cat" and ".007"; they only exemplify the kind of vulgarity that results from a concentration on the thing in itself. The whole undertaking was factitious; Kipling knew nothing at first hand about machines or animals, and his interest in them is essentially that of the advertising journalist who eventually "falls" for his own wares. And this enthusiasm for the machine, this interest in relationships in the abstract, is something quite different from the contemporary school of pylon-poets. It is one of the refuges of the shrinking sensibility and carries little or no social significance. And the other side to this escape into the inanimate is Kipling's resort to hysteria; the two attitudes represent complementary evasions of the problem of normal sympathetic existence.

The element of hysteria is pervasive. In one of two stories Kipling gets near to treating a story honestly, looking at its full-face; in "Without Benefit of Clergy," for instance, the relationship between the British official and the Indian girl is almost satisfying. But at the crucial moment Kipling looks away; fever and cholera carry off the girl and her child, and violence breaks into what now seems to have been no more than an indulgent day-dream. Either some violent happening is brought in to shatter the glimpsed normality, or else Kipling dispenses with even the glimpses of normality, and presents instead various forms of aberration. On the most harmless level this takes the form of the practical joke. *Stalky and Co.* can be accepted, if only with difficulty, because one fondly supposes that most things are possible with the adolescent; but Kipling soon abandons even this degree of plausibility, and one finds exactly the same conduct glorified in the Regimental Mess. In "The Tie," five officers beat up the civilian caterer, and this conduct is justified because all of them have been to the same school and thus his catering offence has disgraced not only the Mess but also the Alma Mater; and the tale ends with one of the officers "thinking over the moral significance of Old School ties and the British Social fabric." Or there is "The Honours of War," in which an officer, who has been assaulted by his brother officers for being serious about military theory, decides not to take ordinary action against the offenders; instead "he cast away all shadow of his legal rights for the sake of a common or bear-garden rag—such a rag as if it came to the ears of the authorities would cost him his commission. They were saved, and their saviour was their equal and their brother. So they chaffed and reviled him as such, till he again squashed the breath out of them, and we others laughed louder than they." Kipling seemed to value above all irresponsibility as between individuals (of the same sex, of course), perhaps as a relief from the tension of observing unquestioning loyalty to the Idea. And in "The Village That Voted the Earth Was Flat" his boyish thrill in the practical joke runs riot; the whole apparatus of the press, of advertising, and of the music-hall is manipulated to wreak vengeance on the offending Blimp, and in the end even the House of Commons has succumbed, "hysterical and abandoned." But the thing to observe about this apparently harmless taste for the practical joke, about these extravaganzas on group irresponsibility and self-release, is that beneath it all there smoulders a potentiality for individual hysteria. A very large number of the tales deal with the mind on the edge of madness. Some of them are ordinary enough, and in "The Woman in His Life" the patient recovers as a result of developing a mawkish affection for a dog. (In contrast to Lawrence, Kipling had the kind of psychological insight that one picks up second-hand in the smoke-room.) But most often these tales are not in the least harmless, and

Kipling's taste for hysteria seems to uncover a deep longing for some similar violence of feeling in himself, some means of escaping into the ideal life of ruthless activity. Mr. Eliot is very wide of the point when he supposes that only "those who do not believe in the existence of the Beast probably consider 'The Mark of the Beast' a beastly story." This tale seems to me beastly (surely the pun was unnecessary), not because one disbelieves in the Beast, but because Kipling's attitude towards it is so equivocal. One cannot avoid feeling that he is mainly concerned with the opportunities for violent description that the Beast theme offers, and also with the element of revenge that, so school-boyish an amusement in the tales already discussed, gradually emerges as a major principle in his philosophy. The leper, in this story, has branded Fleete with the mark of the beast, and gradually it transforms him altogether into a beast; in order to restore him back to humanity, the leper is captured and forced by torture to eradicate the mark. But the emphasis at the climax is all on the torture, and after carefully describing the instruments used, Kipling resorts melodramatically to a row of periods: "Strickland shaded his eyes with his hands for a moment and then we got to work. This part is not to be printed...." And one retains a feeling that ruthlessness is the only solution and that revenge with violence is sweet; and I find it strange that this appeals to an Anglo-Catholic.

Of course, for Kipling revenge *is* sweet, and most of his tales turn on feelings of revenge. In "Mary Postgate" Kipling writes with less detachment than in any of his tales that I have read. And as illustrating many of the points I have been making, not least Kipling's unsuitability for us at the present time, this story is worth consideration. Mary Postgate has been for a long time governess to Fowler, who joins up in the Flying Corps and is immediately killed on a trial flight; she comments: "It's a great pity he didn't die in action after he had killed somebody." She decides to burn all his belongings, and there follows one of Kipling's interminable and tasteless inventories, occupying a full page, describing the possessions that she collects for his pyre; the sense of loss is gradually intensified through this emphasis on the inanimate object, giving a hard, unsympathetic feeling to the proceedings. Mary Postgate then goes out for a walk and is present when a bomb dropped by a German plane kills a small girl. She returns to light her bonfire, and there, sitting at the foot of a tree with a broken back, is the pilot of the German machine which has just crashed. The story, as can be seen at once, is internally quite bogus; the whole thing is manipulated from the outside and for preconceived purposes. The remaining pages simply describe the ecstasy of Mary Postgate as she waits to hear the death-rattle of the German airman. In spite of the earlier comment, she now repeats to herself that "Wynn was a gentleman who for no consideration would have torn little Edna into those vividly coloured strips and strings"; and so she waits, refusing the man any help, until with an "increasing rapture" she perceives the end is near, and then "she closed her eyes and drank it in," smiling. The importance of this is, I think, twofold. Kipling quite candidly, like Mary Postgate, "ceased to think, and gave himself up to feel" when he undertook this story; and it seems as if he had always been ready to indulge his feelings of revenge and hysteria when he could. But, unfortunately for him, the opportunity could only seldom arise for a man who, like himself, had done little but dip his pen into experiences of this kind. And this, the second interesting factor, explains why the story operates through the agency of a woman. On the whole, Kipling despised women; but in one or two tales he is glad to use them to vent feelings that he would be ashamed to attribute to a man, and above all to describe as being possible to himself. And one feels, in this story, that he is quite conscious of vicarious enjoyment in dealing with a woman whom he can safely allow to be contradictory and irrational. Always devoid of finer feeling and emotional discipline, Kipling here virtually extols these blemishes and, through the medium of Mary Postgate's calculated indulgence, turns the crude sensation over lovingly in his mouth. In this tale he does openly what for the most part he holds down by means of the harsh he-man pose. And in this respect he is not only one of the founders of modern journalism, but also of the modern school of literary toughness. Kipling's contemporary counterpart, is Hemingway, who writes up-to-date Kiplingese, and who betrays, beneath the staccato, machine-like prose, a similar coarseness of feeling that tends towards sentimentality on the one hand and towards brutishness on the other. What Kipling reveals, in every line he wrote, is a sensibility entirely devoid of moral discipline and artistic honesty; the only discipline he observes is that of his ideal Subaltern, the product of a "school that was not encouraged to dwell on its emotions, but rather to keep in hard condition, and to avoid false quantities." It is in products of this kind of training that one finds, almost invariably, an outward tough obstinacy protecting a soft centre of self-distrust and potential hysteria.

To go further into the matter, or to support these generalizations with detailed analysis, would be to perform a task out of all importance to its intrinsic importance. Kipling, in fact, seems to me neither so disgusting, for the most part, as he has been painted, nor worth the interest that Mr. Eliot seeks to encourage. And this particularly applies to his verse. Mr. Eliot admits to knowing no writer "for whom poetry seems to have been more purely an instrument"; and the uses to which this instrument was put are no longer likely to appeal to people whose hopes and efforts are directed towards ensuring an outcome to the present struggle very different from the world that appealed to Kipling and indeed made him possible. We do not, on the whole, visualize the future "in the shape of a semi-circle of buildings and temples projecting into a sea of dreams," which for Kipling represented "the whole sweep and meaning of things and effort and origins throughout the Empire"; and the document and experience on which we hope to work are at any rate not the volumes of *Punch*, "from whose files I drew my modern working history."

Certainly Mr. Eliot should never have lowered himself to advocating a revival of interest in such a writer. Of course, one can see the attraction that Kipling might have for him: for Kipling was the popular success that Mr. Eliot will never be, he was anti-Liberal with a crude gusto that Mr. Eliot can never attempt to equal, and above all he rested within the Catholic Church of his Empire with a solid assurance and with a sense of fulfilment that will always be artistically denied to Mr. Eliot in his dealings with the Anglican brotherhood. If Mr. Eliot has been undoubtedly the most important name in literature during the period between the two wars, this has entailed a sacrifice that he seems decreasingly willing to make; that side of him which confesses to a taste for music-hall and Camembert, for cats and for Douglas Credit—in short, his strain of the dilettante, even, one might say, of the decadent—leads him to look wistfully at the confident and unabashed vulgarity of Kipling. Perhaps, above all, it is this unattainable mastery and this security within the enveloping aura of the larger structure that appeals to one so fraught with doubt and insecurity:

> *So here I am, in the middle way, having had twenty years—*
> *Twenty years largely wasted, the years of l'entre deux guerres—*
> *Trying to learn to use new words, and every attempt*

> *Is a wholly new start, and a different kind of failure . . .*
> *. . . There is only the fight to recover what has been lost*
> *And found and lost again and again: and now, under conditions*
> *That seem unpropitious.*

Kipling lacked this kind of honesty and hence he lacked any sense of this kind of problem; through a partly deliberate thickening of the hide he convinced himself that "The game is more than the player of the game, And the ship is more than the crew." In his poetry, at least, Mr. Eliot has never sought refuge by renouncing the integrity of his personal response and the guidance of his matured sensibility; and up to the present he has not succumbed to the appeal of the Thing and of the System, the lure of the Ship and the Game.

(1942)

D. H. Lawrence

THE WILD, UNTUTORED PHOENIX

Phoenix: the Posthumous Papers of D. H. Lawrence
Reviewed by F.R. Leavis

Lawrence is placed—is, in fact, distinctly *passé;* we are no longer (if we ever were) very much impressed by him. He had, of course, there's no denying it, a kind of genius, but to take him seriously as an intellectual and spiritual force, a force that could effect our attitude towards life and the problems of our time—it's amusing to think that there were once earnest souls who did so. Today, while recognizing the queerly limited gifts he dissipated, we hardly bother to smile at his humourless fanaticisms.

At least, that's the impression one gets from the literary world today (I mean the *milieu* in which fashions are set and worn and the higher reviewing provided for). Lawrence is decidedly out of favour—in fact, he was never in, for it was without permission that he won his fame, and he was patently not the kind of writer who would ever earn permission. *Phoenix* came out a year ago, but it is still worth calling attention to as an admirable reminder of the qualities that make our ruling literary intellectuals feel that his fame had better be encouraged to fade as quickly as possible.

Here, for instance, in this collection of dispersed papers, he appears as an incomparable reviewer (presenting, that is, a standard that our higher literary editors couldn't be expected to take seriously). We remember that neglected critical masterpiece, *Studies in Classic American Literature,* and may very well go on to ask what kind of gift it was that made D. H. Lawrence the finest literary critic of our time—a great literary critic if ever there was one. We know it can't have been intelligence; for Mr. Quennell's view that (in contrast to the superlatively intelligent Mr. Aldous Huxley) he was, though a genius, muddle-headed is generally accepted (and did not Mr. Eliot find in Lawrence "an incapacity for what we ordinarily call thinking"?).*

Yet here, in these reprinted reviews, we have Lawrence dealing

---
* *After Strange Gods,* p. 58.

under ordinary reviewing conditions (he needed the money) with books of all kinds—H. G. Wells, Eric Gill, Rozanov, Dos Passos, Hemingway, Baron Corvo, fiction, poetry, criticism, psychology—and giving almost always the impression of going straight to the centre with the masterly economy, the sureness of touch, of one who sees exactly what it is in front of him and knows exactly what he thinks of it. Here he is on H. G. Clissold Wells:

> His effective self is disgruntled, his ailment is a peevish, ashy indifference to *everything*, except himself, himself as centre of the universe. There is not one gleam of sympathy with anything in all the book, and not one breath of passionate rebellion. Mr. Clissold is too successful and wealthy to rebel, and too hopelessly peeved to sympathize. What has got him into such a state is a problem; unless it is his insistence on the Universal Mind, which he, of course, exemplifies. The emotions are to him irritating aberrations. Yet even he admits that even thought must be preceded by some obscure physical happenings, some kind of confused sensation or emotion which is the necessary coarse body of thought and from which thought, living thought, arises or sublimates.
>
> This being so, we wonder that he so insists on the Universal or racial *mind* of man, as the only hope of salvation. If the mind is fed from the obscure sensations, emotions, physical happenings inside us, if the mind is really no more than an exhalation of these, is it not obvious that without a full and subtle emotional life the mind itself must wither: or that it must turn itself into an automatic sort of grind-mill, grinding upon itself.

His critical poise is manifested in (*pace* Mr. Eliot) a lively ironic humour—a humour that for all its clear-sighted and mocking vivacity is quite without animus. For, idiosyncratic as Lawrence's style is, it would be difficult to find one more radically free from egotism.

> Professor Sherman once more coaxing American criticism the way it should go.
>
> Like Benjamin Franklin, one of his heroes, he attempts the invention of a creed that shall "satisfy the professors of all religions, and offend none."
>
> He smites the marauding Mr. Mencken with a velvet glove, and pierces the obstinate Mr. More with a reproachful look. Both gentlemen, of course, will purr and feel flattered. . . .
>
> So much for the Scylla of Mr. Mencken. It is the first essay in the book. The Charybdis of Mr. P. E. More is the last essay: to this monster the professor warbles another tune. Mr. More, author of the *Shelburne Essays,* is learned, and steeped in tradition, the very antithesis of the nihilistic stink-gassing Mr. Mencken. But alas, Mr. More is remote: somewhat haughty and supercilious at his study table. And even, alasser! with all his learning and remoteness, he hunts out the

risky Restoration wits to hob-nob with on high Parnassus; Wycherley, for example; he likes his wits smutty. He even goes and fetches out Aphra Behn from her disreputable oblivion, to entertain her in public.

The humour seems to me that of a man whose insight into human nature and human experience makes egotism impossible, and I find myself, in fact, in thus attributing to him an extraordinary self-awareness and intelligence about himself, seeming to contradict Mr. Eliot, who denies him "the faculty of self-criticism" (*op. cit.*, p. 59). Lawrence does indeed characteristically exhibit certitude and isn't commonly to be found in a mood of hesitation or self-condemnation (though his art is largely a technique of exploration—exploration calling for critical capacity as well as courage); but in purity of interest and sureness of self-knowledge he seems to me to surpass Mr. Eliot, even though he pays no respects to criteria that Mr. Eliot indicates as essential:

> A man like Lawrence, therefore, with his acute sensibility, violent prejudices and passions, and lack of intellectual and social training . . . [*After Strange Gods,* p. 59]

I have already intimated that the acuteness of Lawrence's sensibility seems to me (whatever Bloomsbury may have decided) inseparable from the play of supremely fine and penetrating intelligence. And if one is to agree that Lawrence lacked intellectual and social training, one would like to be shown someone who didn't or doesn't. It's true that he didn't go to Oxford or Harvard, and that his family was of a social class the sons of which, at that time, had little chance of getting to one of the ancient universities. But few readers of the memoir of Lawrence by E. T. will, I imagine, however expensive their own education, claim with any confidence that they had a better one than Lawrence had.

At school, and later at University College, Nottingham, whatever their faults (and he says some stringent things about the college), he got sufficient stimulus and sufficient guidance to the sources and instruments of knowledge to be able, in intercourse, social and intellectual, with his friends, to carry on a real education. They discussed their way eagerly over an extraordinary range of reading, English and French, past and contemporary (Lawrence hit on *The English Review,* then in its great days), and it is difficult to imagine adolescents who should have read more actively and to greater profit. For, belonging as they did to the self-respecting poor in a still vigorous part of the country, not only was their intellectual education intimately bound up with a social training (what respectable meaning Mr. Eliot, denying a "social training" to Lawrence, can be giving the phrase I can't guess); they enjoyed the advantage of a still persistent cultural tradition that had as its main drive the religious tradition of which Mr. Eliot speaks so contemptuously. And the setting of family life (quite finely civilized and yet pressed on by day-to-day economic and practical exigencies) in which these young people met and talked was in sight of—in immediate touch with—on one side, the colliery (Lawrence's father was a miner) and, on the other, the farm (Miriam's father was a small farmer). It seems to me probable that D. H. Lawrence at twenty-one was no less trained intellectually than Mr. Eliot at the same age; had, that is, read no less widely (even if lacking Greek), was no less in command of his capacities and resources and of the means of developing further, and had as adequate a sense of tradition and the nature of wisdom. And it seems to me probable that, even if less sophisticated than Mr. Eliot, he was not less mature in experience of life.

> Some can absorb knowledge, the more tardy must sweat for it. Shakespeare acquired more essential history from Plutarch than most men could from the whole British Museum.

Lawrence was not Shakespeare, but he had genius, and his genius manifests itself in an acquisitiveness that is a miraculous quickness of insight, apprehension, and understanding. The "information" that Mr. Eliot doesn't deny him ("a lack not so much of information as . . .") is more than mere information; he had an amazing range and wealth of living knowledge. He knew well at least four languages besides his own, and it is characteristic of him that in reviewing Cunninghame Graham's *Pedro de Valdivia* he not only shows a wide general knowledge of the Spanish conquests, but, referring to the original Spanish particular instances of Cunninghame Graham's rendering, censures him for "the peculiar laziness or insensitiveness to language which is so great a vice in a translator." What those qualified to judge think of Lawrence's dealings with painting I don't know, but he certainly shows an extremely wide and close acquaintance with it, deriving from an obviously intense interest. This appears notably, not only in the "Introduction to These Paintings," but also in the "Study of Thomas Hardy."

This long "Study of Thomas Hardy," perhaps, represents the kind of thing that Mr. Eliot has especially in mind when he charges

Lawrence with "an incapacity for what we ordinarily call thinking."
It is an early work and hasn't much to do with Hardy. Lawrence
frankly admits that he is using Hardy as an occasion and a means
and that his real purpose is to explore, refine, and develop certain
ideas and intuitions of his own. I found the study difficult to read
through; it is diffuse and repetitive, and Lawrence has dealt with
the same matters better elsewhere. Yet, in the persistent integrity
of this exploration the genius is manifest, and without this kind of
work we couldn't have had the later ease, poise, and economy and
the virtues in general that compel Mr. Eliot to say:

> As a criticism of the modern world, *Fantasia of the Unconscious* is a
> book to keep at hand and re-read.

If Lawrence's criticism is sound, that seems to me to be because
of the measure in which his criteria are sound, and because they
and their application represent, if not what we "ordinarily call
thinking," an extraordinarily penetrating, persistent, and vital kind
of thinking. He says (p. 611):

> What good is our intelligence to us, if we will not use it in the greatest issues? Nothing will excuse us from the responsibility of living: even death is no excuse. We have to live. So we may as well live fully. We are doomed to live. And therefore it is not the smallest use running into *pis allers* and trying to shirk the responsibility of living. We can't get out of it.
>
> And therefore the only thing is to undertake the responsibility with good grace.

It is Lawrence's greatness that he was in a position to say this; he
was, in fact, intelligent as only the completely serious and disinterested can be. Those who plume themselves on being intelligent
but find this notion of intelligence uncongenial will prefer Mr.
Wyndham Lewis—even a Wyndham Lewis who comes out for Hitler.

I was reminded of Mr. Wyndham Lewis by this in *Phoenix* (p. 271):

> Wyndham Lewis gives a display of the utterly repulsive effect people have on him, but he retreats into the intellect to make his display. It is a question of manner and manners. The effect is the same. It is the same exclamation: They stink! My God, they stink!

The Lawrence who thus places Wyndham Lewis seems to me the
representative of health and sanity. Mr. Eliot's reactions to Lawrence are, of course, at a different level from those referred to at
the end of the last paragraph, the common petty reactions of the

literary world, and the case that Mr. Eliot argues does, at its most respectable, demand serious attention. But it is odd that he should, in pronouncing Lawrence "spiritually sick," be able at the same time to invoke Wyndham Lewis's "brilliant exposure" and "conclusive criticism" of any side of Lawrence. And it is odd also that in the book in which he finds in Lawrence a lack of intellectual and social training he should be able to take Mr. Ezra Pound and Dr. I. A. Richards as representatives of the "highly educated and fastidious."

* * *

I hadn't intended to end on this note. But my attention has just been drawn to Mr. Eliot's essay in *Revelation*. He treats Lawrence there still more respectfully than in *After Strange Gods*, but can say:

> For Babbitt was by nature an educated man, as well as a highly well-informed one: Lawrence, even had he acquired a great deal more knowledge and information than he ever came to possess, would always have remained uneducated. By being "educated" I mean having such an apprehension of the contours of the map of what has been written in the past, as to see instinctively where everything belongs, and approximately where anything new is likely to belong; it means, furthermore, being able to allow for all the books one has not read and the things one does not understand—it means some understanding of one's own ignorance.

—Irving Babbitt, all one's divinations about whom have been confirmed by the reminiscences and memoirs of him that have appeared since his death! Babbitt, who was complacently deaf and blind to literature and art and completely without understanding of his incapacity; who, being thus in sensibility undeveloped or dead, can hardly, without misplacing a stress, be called intelligent! Even as Mr. Eliot quotes him and comments on him he appears as the born academic (is that what "by nature an educated man" means?), obtuse—Mr. Eliot seems almost to bring out the word—obtuse in his dogged and argumentative erudition.

How can Mr. Eliot thus repeatedly and deliberately give away his case by invoking such standards? It is an amazing thing that so distinguished a mind can so persistently discredit in this way a serious point of view.

(1937)

Marcel Proust

Introduction to Proust, by Derrick Leon
Reviewed by Martin Turnell

This book is ten years too late. In 1930 there might still have been a place for an introduction to Proust even at this level, but since the publication of Mr. Edmund Wilson's valuable essay in *Axel's Castle* there is none. A good deal of work has been done on Proust since his death, and though little of it is first-class, it cannot all be relegated to an unscholarly bibliography at the end of a book. There are also a number of facts that have to be taken into account by anybody writing about Proust. It is a fact, for example, that most of us no longer take the same pleasure in his novel that we once did; and the critic has to decide whether this is due to the same sort of snobbishness which has caused the temporary eclipse of Lawrence or whether it points to a very serious limitation in Proust's art. In 1920 Jacques Rivière, who was the finest French critic of his generation, wrote an essay on *"Marcel Proust et la Tradition Classique"* in which he argued that Proust's insight and his use of the French language made him the direct descendant of the great masters of the seventeenth century. Mr. Wilson, on the other hand, declares roundly that Proust was "the first important novelist to apply the principles of Symbolism to fiction." It seems to me that the truth lies somewhere between these two opinions, which are not as irreconcilable as they first appear. The French attach great importance to what they call a writer's *révélation psychologique,* and there are many pages of psychological analysis in Proust's work which remind us strongly of the seventeenth-century moralists; but his prose also reveals both the good and bad influence of Symbolism. The work of the writers of this movement undoubtedly contains a good many conceits, a good many images which are mere *jeux de mots;* but it did extend the resources of language, and the extraordinary account of Swann's evening at Madame de Saint-Euverte's—particularly the description of the guests with their monocles—where this influence is most marked, is something new in European fiction.

The most determined attack on Proust has come, as one might expect, from the Left. According to their views, he is the laureate of a dying society, the apologist of an aristocracy which has retained its privileges while abandoning the functions that once made it a useful part of the community. This view deserves consideration, but it needs to be stated in specifically literary terms and examined in close relation to the text of Proust's novel.

There are pages in Proust which look at first as though they might have come straight from Saint-Simon, the master with whom he has been most often compared:

> *Ayant passé d'une débauche presque infantile à la continence absolue datant du jour où il avait pensé au quai d'Orsay et voulu faire une grande carrière* [he writes of the disreputable diplomat, M. de Vaugoubert], *il avait l'air d'une bête en cage, jetant dans tous les sens des regards qui exprimaient la peur, l'appétence et la stupidité.*

Thirty pages later the same criticism is repeated in slightly different terms:

> *La carrière diplomatique avait eu sur sa vie l'effet d'une entrée dans les ordres. Combinée avec l'assiduité à l'Ecole des Sciences Politiques, elle l'avait voué depuis ses vingt ans à la chasteté du chrétien.*

What might pass in the first passage for a stroke of Saint-Simonian irony now appears as a note of frustration, as though the writer were attempting to solve a personal problem by caricaturing it in the person of another. This suspicion is strengthened by the crude description (at the same party) of the narrator's enthusiastic acceptance of a friend's invitation to visit—at some future unspecified date—a particularly smart brothel.

It is this note of frustration that provides a clue to the later volumes of *A la Recherche du temps perdu*. It is characteristic of Mr. Leon's innocence as a critic that he can describe Albertine as

> Attractive, charming, and intelligent, we see her subtly transformed from the boisterous hoyden of the Balbec promenade to the smart, alluring, cultivated and companionable young woman into which she blossoms as Marcel's mistress.

He finds her, it is true, "elusive" and "enigmatic," but it does not occur to him that this may be due to some flaw in Proust's art, and he has apparently never heard of the theory that she was a young man. This is an important point. Unless it is realized that Proust was profoundly homosexual the whole of *Sodome et Gomorrhe* is meaningless. There is, in the later volumes of the novel, a universal drift towards the cities of the plain, and its full horror can only be appreciated when the implications of the story of Albertine's imprisonment are grasped. Consider the following extracts from the beginning of *La Prisonnière*:

> ... Albertine, que d'ailleurs je ne trouvais plus guère jolie et avec laquelle je m'ennuyais, que j'avais la sensation nette de ne pas aimer ...
>
> Son charme un peu incommode était ainsi d'être à la maison moins comme une jeune fille, que comme une bête domestique qui entre dans une pièce, qui en sort, qui se trouve partout où on ne s'y attend pas ...
>
> Je n'aimais plus Albertine.
>
> Albertine s'était étonnamment dévelopée, ce qui m'était entièrement égal ...

When we ask why he was so determined to keep prisoner a woman whom he neither loved nor found attractive, this is the answer:

> J'avais pu séparer Albertine de ses complices et, par là, exorciser mes hallucinations ...

The whole story of this enforced detention of the woman is a curious and sinister myth of a crumbling society trying desperately and violently to convince itself of its own normality, to stop its drift towards perversion and collapse. The writer invents a woman whose vices are also his own; he congratulates himself on his forcible prevention of practices that he envies and, at the same time, by changing the object into a woman tries to conceal the roots of the evil from himself. Nor should we miss the significance of the consultations with the Duchesse de Guermantes over Albertine's clothes. It is not the adornment of the bride or the mistress, but a sort of fetishism—a solemn incensing of a twofold being who is the symbol of normality and perversity.

The figure of M. de Charlus has been praised as a great comic creation. There is, indeed, a savage farce about this account of the dissolution of the middle-aged homosexual; but when we look into it, we find that Proust's irony is by no means disinterested. He envies Morel, who under cover of an engagement to a pleasant and very normal young woman carries on his appalling intrigue with Charlus—does, in fact, what Proust would like to do.

This diagnosis leads to the conclusion that Proust is not the great social critic that he is sometimes said to be. He is too deeply involved to possess the necessary critical detachment, too submerged in a world of subjective fantasy to have any clear perception of positive values. When we compare Saint-Simon's summing up at the close of the *Mémoires*:

> . . . *comme au temps où j'ai écrit, surtout vers la fin, tout tournait à la décadence, à la confusion, au chaos, qui depuis n'a fait que croître, et que ces Mémoires ne respirent qu'ordre, règle, vérité, principes certains, et montrent à découvert tout ce qui y est contraire, qui régnant de plus en plus avec le plus ignorant, mais le plus entier empire, la convulsion doit donc être générale contre ce miroir de vérité.*

with:

> Mais, réveillant les sentiments d'attent jadis éprouvés à propos d'autres jeunes filles, surtout de Gilberte, quand elle tardait à venir, la privation possible d'un simple plaisir physique me causait une cruelle souffrance morale.

—we notice a striking difference in the use of words. In Saint-Simon the words *décadence, confusion, règle, vérité, principes certains,* have a precise meaning and the phrase *miroir de vérité* represents a positive standard by which the evils of the time are measured. There is nothing of the sort in Proust. The linking of *plaisir physique* with *souffrance morale* reveals a strange confusion of values, a moral blindness which accounts for many of the shortcomings of his art, for it is clear that the word *morale* is used simply to indicate a peculiarly intense sense of physical privation. Saint-Simon's appeal to the *miroir de vérité* is answered in another place by Proust's assertion that

> . . . *la vérité change tellement pour nous, que les autres ont peine à s'y reconnaître.*

For Proust "truth" meant psychological truth, which of its very nature is changing and inconstant. This provides a clue to his greatness. His work—particularly the early volumes dealing with his childhood's experience before he had become aware of his own sexual inversion—does reveal human nature to itself in a new way: it does mark an extension of sensibility which alters the potentialities of the novel; but he has no means of measuring or criticizing the value of his findings. Mr. Wilson compares the tone of his supposed denunciation of homosexuality to that of the Old Testament prophets and puts it down to Proust's Jewish blood. I find it difficult, for reasons that I have already given, to believe in the existence of Proust the moralist. There is a certain repugnance to homosexuality, but this springs from a primitive fear, a taboo against something unnatural. In other words, its source is instinctive and largely emotional. When we compare this attitude with the strict ethical orthodoxy of the close of Baudelaire's *Femmes damnées*, where the moral attitude is completely fused in the poetic image, we realize why Baudelaire's poetry has a maturity, a finality, for which we shall look in vain in Proust.

(1941)

I. A. Richards

(1) I. A. RICHARDS, *by D. W. Harding*

Conversational comments on Richards's work, favourable or unfavourable, seldom express opinions about his actual views; they seem more often than not to be reactions to the general tone of his writing. Nor can this aspect of his work be neglected in an attempt to formulate a more precise opinion: some peculiarity of tone, or some prevailing attitude, undoubtedly distinguishes him from most scientific and critical writers. It would be laborious to analyse this attitude in detail. As a handy label for it, the term "amateur" (with some of its implications) will perhaps do. It is suggested for one thing by the slight awe that he inspires in the virginally lay. But it has more important justification than this in two essential features of his work, namely in his insistence upon the significance for "normal practical life" of his special interests and in the buoyancy with which he rides over difficulties of detail by means of general principles.

Take, for instance, his basic hypotheses for criticism and consider the difficulty and labour that would be involved in proving them. Only the spirit of the amateur could enable Richards to express them with as little inhibition as he does.

> The first point to be made is that poetic experiences are valuable (when they are) in the same way as any other experiences. They are to be judged by the same standards. [*Science and Poetry*, p. 28]

> The greatest difference between the artist or poet and the ordinary person is found, as has often been pointed out, in the range, delicacy and freedom of the connections he is able to make between different elements of his experience. [*Principles of Literary Criticism*, p. 181]

> The ways then in which the artist will differ from the average will as a rule presuppose an immense degree of similarity. They will be further developments of organizations already well advanced in the majority. His variations will be confined to the newest, the most plastic, the least fixed part of the mind, the parts for which reorganization is most easy. [*Principles of Literary Criticism*, p. 196]

> It is in terms of attitudes, the resolution, inter-inanimation, and balancing of impulses . . . that all the most valuable effects of poetry must be described. [*Principles of Literary Criticism*, p. 113]

Nor has his confidence waned with time. He is still ready to assert (see *The Criterion* of October, 1932) that the explanation of the difference between good and less good experiences "is inevitably in terms of that order or disorder among 'impulses' (or however else you care to describe the elementary processes on which consciousness depends). . . ." Contrast the more "professional" attitude towards similar problems:

> Personally I do not think the problem of ethical valuation [of different cultures] is hopeless, but it need not necessarily be undertaken in a purely sociological inquiry. [M. Ginsberg, in *Studies in Sociology*]

> Moreover, in humanity as it exists at present it is not easy to decide that one physical type is better adapted than another, and, when it comes to deciding which emotional and intelligent types are better or worse, the situation becomes far too complicated to handle with any probability of success. [T. H. Morgan, in a paper in *The Foundations of Experimental Psychology*]

These quotations, I think, fairly represent the attitude of qualified specialists when they refer to ethical questions: not hopeless but . . . The contrast with Richards need not be stressed.

Three hypotheses, distinct although closely related, are expressed by Richards in the passages quoted. They are, roughly, (*a*) that art and the rest of human activity are continuous, not contrasting; (*b*) that art is the most valuable form of activity; and (*c*) that the value of any activity depends on the degree to which it allows of a balancing or ordering among one's impulses. It is the third which is fundamental and upon which the other two depend, and our attitude to his work in general must depend to a great extent upon the view we take of this account of value. The practical purpose of his account must not be overlooked: he is attempting to discover "a defensible position for those who believe that the arts are of value," and it is clear from the context that he intends primarily a position that can be defended against all those who regard art as something other than one of the practical affairs of life. He attempts in effect to meet the friendly and intelligent Philistine on his own ground. Hence his account of value is best regarded as a systematization based on certain assumptions which are not questioned by the people whom he has in mind. He assumes first that living activity is its own satisfaction and that any questioning of its "value" is bogus questioning. Next he implies a conception of quantity in living activity and assumes that a further unquestionable satisfaction arises as one becomes *more* alive; he takes as the unit of living activity the satisfied impulse, so that the value of an activity or attitude can be measured, hypothetically, in terms of the number of impulses it satisfies. Further, he adopts the view that in all living organisms there is an unquestionable effort after greater and greater differentiation and integration of experience.

The necessary limitations of such an account of value have to be recognized before its usefulness for particular purposes can be judged. It is clear that it cannot, even hypothetically, give us grounds for judgement when a difference of opinion rests on a fundamental constitutional difference between two people. Richards, for instance, condemns swindling and bullying because they lead to a thwarting of important social impulses: the implicit assumption is that the swindler and bully in question possess the "normal" social impulses. If they do not, then they cannot be condemned on these lines. You might as well try to convince a tiger of its misfortune in not being a buffalo. The numerical treatment of impulses will not help here: it would be flat dogma to assert that the man without social needs must achieve a lower total output of satisfied "impulses" than the man with them. And according to Richards it is the total number that matters, for the "importance" of an impulse is only another term for the number of other impulses that depend upon it. It is difficult to suppose that the tiger, given equal strength and good health, satisfied fewer "'impulses" (fewer of "the elementary processes on which consciousness depends") than the buffalo. This is only to point out that Richards's systematizing of value judgements cannot, even in theory, lead to agreement in evaluations unless the parties concerned have the same fundamental constitution. In point of fact Richards keeps his numerical conception in the background and implies that greater ordering or integration will of itself lead to the satisfying of more impulses.

> At the other extreme are those fortunate people who have achieved an ordered life, whose systems have developed clearing-houses by which the varying claims of different impulses are adjusted. Their free untrammelled activity gains for them a maximum of varied satisfactions and involves a minimum of suppression and sacrifice. [*Principles of Literary Criticism*, p. 53]

Similarly, in the much finer discussion of development in *Practical Criticism*, where he relates the sayings of Confucius on sincerity to modern biological views, it is the ordering alone that is insisted on. The implication here and throughout his work is that everyone begins with the same fundamental impulses, but that they and the secondary impulses dependent on them get muddled and disorganized, thwarting each other unnecessarily. He is profoundly convinced that the function of the arts is to bring back order. In the discussion of sincerity, moreover, he brings forward, perhaps not explicitly enough, the idea that art is not merely remedial (restoring an original order), but that it aids in positive development; aids, that is, the assumed effort of the living organism to become more finely differentiated in its parts and simultaneously more integrated. "Being more at one within itself the mind thereby becomes more appropriately responsive to the outer world." Fundamental difficulties confront anyone who attempts to grasp the full meaning of this integration and this appropriateness. But the essential feature of Richards's attitude to art is clear: he pins his faith to the possibility of its being shown to be a means of further progress along the lines of what we regard as biological advance. This is the essence of his defensible position for the arts. Its significance rests perhaps less on the usefulness of its contention than on the fact that it was formulated by a writer who is genuinely sensitive to poetry, not by one with convictions of its uplift value, not by a philosopher who felt that he "ought" somehow to provide art with a pedestal in his exhibition of the universe.

The practical usefulness of Richards's account of value in convincing the plain man of the value of poetry or in helping us to reach agreement over disputed points is doubtful. After outlining the theory Richards writes (*Principles of Literary Criticism*, p. 51), "We can now take our next step forward and inquire into the relative merits of different systematizations." This step remains to be taken, unless it consisted in the brief discussion which follows, on the importance of the social virtues. In practice, of course, Richards is able to give us no more help in making these judgements than, for instance, T. H. Morgan offers, in the passage quoted. One might innocently suppose that we should judge a work of art by assessing the number of impulses it satisfied. It is needless to point out that Richards has nowhere done this, nor even pointed out what main impulses any one work of art has satisfied in him. It is, of course, quite clear that "the impulse" will not serve in practice as a unit of measurement. Who can say what this smallest impulse is in terms of which the importance of the others must be expressed? There is obviously a vast gap between Richards's theory of value and any actual judgement one may make. To say that "It is in terms of attitudes the resolution, inter-inanimation, and balancing of impulses . . . that all the most valuable effects of poetry must be described" is perhaps as true, and just as helpful, as to say that it is in terms of the combination and disintegration of molecules that all the effects of modern warfare must be described. Even the difference between a pleasing and an irritating variation of rhythm is "a matter of the combination and resolution of impulses too subtle for our present means of investigation" [*Principles of Literary Criticism*, p. 138]. And in making up our minds about a poem, "We have to gather millions of fleeting semi-independent impulses into a momentary structure of fabulous complexity, whose core or germ only is given us in the words" (*Practical Criticism*, p. 317). And if his account of the basis of valuable experience has little practical significance for literary judgements, as a means of judging other arts it is more remote still. The greater part of his chapters on painting, sculpture, and music must be regarded as something very close to psychological eye-wash; he hardly makes the gesture of applying his main theory to these subjects. We have to conclude that this attempt to provide a conception (of a balance of impulses) which will establish continuity between the everyday standards of a civilization advanced enough to condemn the bully and swindler and the standards of its art critics fails through the remoteness and elusiveness of the common denominator chosen—the impulse.

This conclusion does not affect the significance of Richards's profound conviction of the value of poetry and his belief that this value is of the same kind as that implicitly recognized by the civilized Philistine. The significance lies in the fact that such a writer should have felt the need to meet the outside world of common sense and science on its own ground and justify his position by current standards. It is one sign of the uneasiness that those with special qualifications in the arts are experiencing. They cannot now confidently remain specialists, secure in the knowledge of fulfilling a recognized function. They have to become amateurs, looking at the matter from the point of view of the majority and attempting to prove that their function does exist before they can attack their own more specialized problems. This consideration may account for the kind of use to which Richards puts psychology. In the first place, it is a means of shaking the complacency of practical people, who are more uneasy at the hints of psycho-analysts than they are at the gibes or fury of artists.

> Human conditions and the possibilities have altered more in a hundred years than they had in the previous ten thousand, and the next

fifty may overwhelm us, unless we can devise a more adaptable morality. The view that what we need in this tempestuous turmoil of change is a Rock to shelter under or to cling to, rather than an efficient aeroplane in which to ride it, is comprehensible but mistaken. [*Principles of Literary Criticism*, p. 57]

Secondly, psychology as Richards uses it seems to help him in repudiating the pseudo-mystical monopolists of aesthetic theory whose ideas do more harm than good to his demand for the recognition of poetry as a practical assistance in living. It seems to confer authority on such a statement as ". . . the experience of 'seeing stars' after a bang on the nose is just as 'unique' as any act of musical appreciation and shares any exalted quality which such uniqueness may be supposed to confer" (*Principles of Literary Criticism*, p. 171). On the other hand, the work of psychologists on aesthetics has not been of the kind he has any use for; it has usually implied other standards than his in its approach to works of art, and it has done nothing to show the practical value of such art as it has dealt with. Hence his care to dissociate himself from the professional psychologists.

> Such more complex objects as have been examined have yielded very uncertain results, for reasons which anyone who has ever *both* looked at a picture or read a poem *and* been inside a psychological laboratory or conversed with a representative psychologist will understand. [*Principles of Literary Criticism*, p. 8]

And rather than be committed to existing psychological methods he draws still further on the already heavily mortgaged future of neurology. Musical effects, for instance:

> . . . belong to a branch of psychology for which we have as yet no methods of investigation. It seems likely that we shall have to wait a long while, and that very great advances must first be made in neurology before these problems can profitably be attacked. [*Principles of Literary Criticism*, p. 170]

But there is a marked change of tone in *Practical Criticism*. After reiterating his dissatisfaction with much of the psychological work on aesthetics, he goes on:

> The general reader, whose ideas as to the methods and endeavours of psychologists derive more from the popularizers of Freud or from the Behaviourists than from students of Stout or Ward, needs perhaps some assurance that it is possible to combine an interest and faith in psychological inquiries with a due appreciation of the complexity of poetry. Yet a psychologist who belongs to this main body is perhaps

the last person in the world to underrate this complexity. [*Practical Criticism*, p. 322]

Again, speaking of the harm done by the cruder psychologies:

> But the remedy of putting the clock back is impracticable. Inquiry cannot be stopped now. The only possible course is to hasten, so far as we can, the development of a psychology which will ignore none of the facts and yet demolish none of the values that human experience has shown to be necessary. An account of poetry will be a pivotal point in such a psychology.

His attitude here seems to be one of willingness to leave professional psychology to make its contribution to the problem in its own way, whereas the tendency before was to short-circuit psychological methods by dogmatizing about the essentials of the conclusions they must reach. The change may perhaps be related to the fact that in *Practical Criticism* Richards has a much more demonstrable function than he had in the earlier work. For one thing he can offer his work as a contribution to academic psychology:

> . . . to find something to investigate that is accessible and detachable is one of the chief difficulties of psychology. I believe the chief merit of the experiment here made is that it gives us this. [*Practical Criticism*, p. 10]

Further he offers his work as a contribution to education, and is able to show that even by existing educational standards such work as he has done here has an important and undeniable function.

> This, then, may be made a positive recommendation, that an inquiry into language . . . be recognized as a vital branch of research, and treated no longer as the peculiar province of the whimsical amateur. [*Practical Criticism*, p. 337]

It is undoubtedly in dealing with problems of communication that Richards comes most closely to grips with his material and least shows the characteristics of the amateur. But to say this ought not to suggest that his work falls into two isolated compartments, one concerned with evaluation and the other with communication, and that they can be appraised separately. It is in fact through a consideration of his theory of value and its limitations that the importance of his work on communication can best be seen.

The conclusion that his account of value gives a basis for agreement only when "normality" (or identical abnormality) is assumed might seem to leave us no defence against an endless variety of critical opinions, each justified by an appeal to a fundamental constitutional peculiarity in the critic. Since innate differences do, of course, exist, we must perhaps admit that in the end we shall have to recognize distinguishable "types" of critical opinion founded on psycho-physiological differences in the critics, and irreconcilable. But this is too remote a consideration to give "type" psychologists any excuse for extending their literary labelling. It is still possible to show that differences of opinion in literary matters frequently arise from errors of approach which even those who make them can be brought to recognize. With people who assert that they know what they like the one hope is to demonstrate to them that in point of fact they *don't,* that according to standards they themselves recognize elsewhere their judgement here is mistaken. As these inconsistencies are faced and abandoned, the possibility of agreement with other people grows greater. We cannot tell how far this principle may be pushed, but undoubtedly we have a very long way to go before innate psycho-physiological differences are the sole cause of disagreement between us. The most important part of Richards's work consists in extending the possibility of agreement. From one point of view it is work on problems of communication; from another it offers us exercise in attaining self-consistency in literary judgements and remotely approaching the "self-completion" that Richards sees as the ultimate form of valuable experience.

In this part of his work there are so many distinct contributions —close, fully illustrated discussions of actual instances—that little general comment is in place. Many of them offer a starting-point for further investigation; sometimes there seems a possibility of fresh preliminary discussion, where, as for instance in his treatment of intellectual truth in poetry and of rhythm, Richards does not seem free from ambiguities and shifts of ground; all draw attention to serious possibilities of misreading and misjudging, and all go towards stressing the same main theme, that the adequate reading of poetry is a discipline and not a relaxation.

The relation between the two aspects of his work is well set out by Richards himself:

> The whole apparatus of critical rules and principles is a means to the attainment of finer, more precise, more discriminating communication. There is, it is true, a valuation side to criticism. When we have solved completely, the communication problem, when we have got, perfectly, the experience, *the mental condition* relevant to the poem, we have still to judge it, still to decide upon its worth. But the later question

nearly always settles itself; or rather, our own inmost nature and the nature of the world in which we live decide it for us. Our prime endeavour must be to get the relevant mental condition and then see what happens. If we cannot then decide whether it is good or bad, it is doubtful whether any principles, however refined and subtle, can help us much. Without the capacity to get the experience they cannot help us at all. This is still clearer if we consider the use of critical maxims in teaching. Value cannot be demonstrated except through the communication of what is valuable.

The difficulty of demonstrating the rightness of an opinion even on these lines ought not to be underrated; over the Longfellow poem, for instance, it seems only to have been a drawn battle between Richards and the protocols. But a reliance on improved methods of reading as the most hopeful way of reaching agreement in literary judgements undoubtedly grows out of Richards's practice more naturally than does his explicit theory of value. The suspicion is left, however, that in making practical judgements he is assuming more principles of evaluation than one would expect from the passage just quoted. One weakness of Yeats's transcendental poetry, for instance, is "a deliberate reversal of the natural relations of thought and feeling . . ." (*Science and Poetry*, p. 74). His charge against Lawrence is rather similar. But *natural relations* . . . Lawrence might have detected a principle of criticism here. The fact is that principles of evaluation remain a necessity for the practising critic even when interpretation and understanding have been carried to their hypothetical limit. How large is the highest common factor in human natures, and how far can it be formulated into agreed ethical principles, are questions that will not be answered in the near future. Yet guesses have to be made: "To set up as a critic is to set up as a judge of values." This is a fact that receives less prominence in Richards's later work than it did in his earlier, and it is not surprising to find Father D'Arcy reminding him (in *The Criterion,* January, 1933) that we have to set out "'both to understand the meaning of others and the truth of what they say."

The importance of Richards's work on communication is unfortunately obscured for many people by their annoyance at a too frequent outcropping of the amateur spirit. This shows itself particularly as a romantic inflation of the significance of the topics, in the form of dark hints at the extent of our ignorance and the cataclysm that awaits us as The Theory of Interpretation is pushed further. Exploitation of the Tremendous Idea makes a peculiarly strong appeal to one side of the amateur: for one thing, every professional immediately has the ground cut from under his feet. No matter what a man's standing, and no matter how impressive the substance of his views, you can still regard him from an unassailable vantage-ground if only you happen to observe that he isn't capable of understanding what's said to him. This, according to Richards (in *The Criterion,* October, 1932), is the weak place in the armour of Max Eastman, T. S. Eliot, and Irving Babbitt. They are all

> . . . untrained in the technique of interpretation . . . this is not their fault since the proper training has not yet been provided . . . you must *understand* before you argue. . . . When the right training has been provided, our three champions here will be seen to be each journeying through and battling with his own set of mirages.

So much for Irving Babbitt, T. S. Eliot, and Max Eastman. The earlier work too occasionally betrays this anxiety to cut the ground from under the feet of those who might otherwise seem qualified to express an opinion:

> . . . neither the professional psychologist whose interest in poetry is frequently not intense, nor the man of letters, who as a rule has no adequate ideas of the mind as a whole, has been equipped for the investigation [into the nature of poetry]. Both a passionate knowledge of poetry and a capacity for dispassionate psychological analysis are required if it is to be satisfactorily prosecuted.
> It will be best to begin by . . . [*Science and Poetry,* p. 9]

It is probably, too, as an aspect of the amateur that we must interpret the curiously romantic tone that sometimes appears in Richards's writing. *Science and Poetry,* for example, leaves a strong impression of a thrilled responsiveness to the difficulties and hazards of "the contemporary situation," and also of some failure to get at grips with any definite problems that concern people. The latter is a serious failing here, for it prevents him from clinching his argument that poetry is of supreme value as a means of reorientation. The nearest he comes to specifying more closely "the contemporary situation" of which one may be "agonizingly aware" is in his discussion of the neutrality of nature and the impossibility of beliefs. But the former is surely not a concern of fundamental importance to most informed people nowadays, though in some moods they may feel chilled by it. And the impossibility of beliefs—except in some quite limited sense—seems itself to be impossible. Certainly T. S. Eliot has repudiated Richards's suggestion that *The Waste Land* is without beliefs; but apart from this repudiation it is impossible to see how any living activity can go on without beliefs in some sense, and we must suppose that Richards is speaking only of a special sort of belief. Indeed, he seems only to mean that most people have ceased to believe in the possibility of supernatural sanctions or aids. If this is all, the excitement apparent in his tone seems naïve.

> It is very probable that the Hindenburg line to which the defence of our traditions retired as a result of the onslaughts of the last century will be blown up in the near future. If this should happen a mental chaos such as man has never experienced may be expected. [*Science and Poetry*, p. 82]
> Consider the probable effects upon love poetry in the near future of the kind of inquiry into basic human constitution exemplified by psycho-analysis.

These are very bourgeois bogies. Their worst feature is the way they play into the hands of the would-be emancipated, those whom L. H. Myers has described in *Prince Jali*:

> . . . they depended basically upon a solid, shockable world of decorum and common sense. They had to believe that a great ox-like eye was fixed upon them in horror.

These defects of tone in Richards's writing cannot be passed over. In the first place they tend to attract the least desirable kind of audience, though the astringency and discipline of Richards's best work should be a sufficient safeguard against this. A more serious consideration is that they offer a needless obstacle to an appreciation by better readers of Richards's real significance. To sum up this significance one may indicate the two points of view from which Richards sees poetry: he sees it both as the practised reader who has acquired his standards of culture imperceptibly and as the plain man of common sense and faith in science who needs *convincing*, without a gradual process of education, that poetry might be of some importance to him. A large part of Richards's work can be regarded as an attempt to find common ground for these two points of view; to find a set of standards recognized by the second man which will lead logically to the position of the first. He sets to work in two ways; first by an explicit theory of value, second by showing up the kinds of mistakes that are likely to lead to an underestimation of poetry. The second method really consists in making explicit, and at the same time telescoping, the steps which those who adequately value poetry must at some time have taken, normally without having analysed them. This second method is obviously of enormous value to people already prepared to take poetry seriously;

it may well divert university students, for instance, from their otherwise almost inevitable progress towards the point from which they regard "the time when they read poetry" with slightly more wistful feelings than they have for "the time when they played Red Indians." But whether Richards's methods would be effective in convincing the intelligent and friendly Philistine is another matter. It may be that his work fulfills its purpose by giving those who already value poetry a new assurance that their concern for it is a development, and not a distortion, of "ordinary practical living." If this is one of its functions it bears witness to the growing need of those with minority views to justify themselves at the bar of the main community. The main community may not be convinced; perhaps the fundamental need is that the minority should be.

(1933)

(II) DR. RICHARDS, BENTHAM, AND COLERIDGE

Coleridge on Imagination, by I. A. Richards

Reviewed by F. R. Leavis

I admire and revere Coleridge and I am in favour of thinking about poetry—in favour, more generally, of applying intelligence to literature. I should like to have said that in these respects at least I was at one with Dr. Richards. But even if I had started reading without premonitions I should very early in this book have conceived a doubt whether Dr. Richards's Coleridge would turn out to be mine, or whether the relation between thinking and poetry promoted by Dr. Richards would be one I could be happy about. To be fair, I had better say at once that we differ, I think, less essentially about the nature of Coleridge's greatness than about the ways of applying intelligence to poetry: Dr. Richards's admiration for Coleridge and his use of him seem to me to be quite unrelated—or to have, merely, a relation such that, contemplating it, we (to borrow a characteristic phrase of Dr. Richards's) inevitably adopt a diagnostic attitude.

The doubts I should, even as a reader innocent of earlier acquaintance with Dr. Richards's work, have conceived would have taken disturbing forms and proportions by the time I had read the reference to Mr. Eliot that begins at the bottom of p. 3. If anyone may be said to have been for our time what Coleridge was for his, then it is Mr. Eliot. Mr. Eliot, like Coleridge, combined a creative gift with rare critical intelligence at one of those moments in poetic history when (if we can think of it as being sometimes otherwise), except in conjunction with rare critical intelligence, there could hardly be a prosperous creative gift—certainly not one capable of important achievement. To have improved the situation for other poets is an achievement of decided importance, and, by his poetry and his criticism together, it is Mr. Eliot's: if, as Dr. Richards thinks, we are living in, or on the point of living in, a Poetic Renaissance, that is to Mr. Eliot's credit in ways for which students of the Romantic movement will provide the parallels.

Though observant already of a tendency in Dr. Richards to be less generous towards Mr. Eliot than Mr. Eliot is habitually towards him, I was nevertheless surprised when, on p. 3, I read this:

> But I must delay first for a few pages to complain of the very common and rather lazy assumption that intellectual labour will not help the critic. I will quote from Mr. Eliot an example of what has become a general custom among literary men in discussing Coleridge. "Nor am I sure," he says, "that Coleridge learnt so much from German philosophers, or earlier from Hartley, as he thought he did; what is best in his criticism seems to come from his own delicacy and subtlety of insight as he reflected upon his own experience of writing and poetry" (*The Use of Poetry*, p. 80). Yes. But is it an accident that this very peculiar kind of insight is found in Coleridge? His philosophic preoccupations cannot be separated from it. The speculations and the insight incessantly prompt one another.

This already, I am afraid, will be judged to be subtle in an uncomplimentary sense of the term: the sentence quoted from Mr. Eliot does not justify—and does not any the more because of the ensuing reasonable commentary—the imputing to him of the "lazy assumption that intellectual labour will not help the critic." But when the commentary, having discoursed through a couple of paragraphs on the relation between Coleridge's philosophic preoccupations and his criticism, concludes: "Is there not something a little ridiculous in saying, 'What a fine critic! What a pity he thought so hard about Poetry!'?"—well, one can only hope that Dr. Richards hadn't noticed what kind of cue this would inevitably appear to the reader (who may take it or not). In any case, one reminds oneself that, though there are no doubt different ways of thinking profitably about poetry, Mr. Eliot's best criticism stands as an exemplar and a criterion of rigour, relevance, and purity of interest—a criterion that very little writing about poetry can afford to challenge.

Actually, the effect of Dr. Richards's book (in my opinion) is to justify Mr. Eliot's judgement. Indeed, even in conscious intention, Dr. Richards might seem again and again to corroborate—or, at any rate, to be insisting on a not obviously inconsonant distinction. On p. 11, for instance, he says:

> But the critical theories can be obtained from the psychology without complication with the philosophical matter. They can be given all the powers Coleridge found for them, without the use either literally, or symbolically, of the other doctrines. The psychology and the metaphysics (and theology) are independent. For Coleridge's own thought they were not; they probably could not be . . .

Dr. Richards's rejoinder lies, of course, in that last sentence—along with his case for giving a great part of his book to the metaphysics. He shows himself, as a matter of fact—and here is the return comment of the reviewer—to be much more interested in the "philosophical matter" than in the "critical theories."

If in his attitude towards the "philosophical matter" he seems (as in other respects in this book) to be having it so elusively "both ways," that is because his interest in it is essentially equivocal. The philosopher is no more likely to thank him for his defence of philosophy than Sir Arthur Quiller-Couch (see p. 8 ff.) to be converted by it. His interest in Coleridge's philosophical explorations is, it may fairly be said, in the interests of Bentham's Theory of Fictions, the aim of the book being to show how out of that theory may be developed a science "to take" (as Mr. C. K. Ogden puts it in his introduction to Bentham's treatise) "the place of philosophy." Dr. Richards, of course, makes the claim formally for Coleridge and the study of poetry: Coleridge (as interpreted by an avowed Benthamite) "succeeded in bringing his suggestions to a point from which, with a little care and pertinacity, they can be taken on to become a new science" (p. 43).

More than a little pertinacity is demanded by Dr. Richards's more abstruse and ambitious chapters (notably VII and VIII)— chapters that justify or otherwise the ambition of the book. An adequate criticism of them would have to come from a critic with a philosophical equipment that I can lay no claim to. (One wonders in what state the matter of them, in the original discussions and lectures, must have left literary students, many of whom would never even have heard of, say, the term "nominalism" before being, no doubt, introduced to it by Dr. Richards.) But even readers without technical qualifications will more than suspect that the ambition is extravagantly disproportionate to the justifying argument: it is one thing to observe that "to inquire about words is to inquire about everything" and that "knowledge in all its varieties—scientific, moral, religious—has come to seem a vast mythology with its sub-orders divided according to their different pragmatic sanctions" (p. 227), and much more another thing than Dr. Richards seems to recognize to give such observations the rigour and precision of development and statement that are necessary if any problem is to be left where it wasn't before. If one gets the impression that Dr. Richards, in these brief chapters, is offering to settle all problems—at any rate, to show us the way to settle them—one is left also with the impression of having been reminded of a number of commonplace philosophic considerations from which strict thinking might start.

Certainly the pretensions are inordinate, and it needs no philosopher (or psychologist or semasiologist) to detect unacceptable compressions and ellipses in key places—failure to make, or to make clearly and hold to, essential distinctions (a debility sorting oddly with the show of analytic rigour, and, it seems, escaping the author's notice by reason of this semasiological zeal itself). For instance, we are given four Natures, IV being the scientist's, and we are told (p. 161):

> Nature, then, even in Senses III and IV, even when all the reflections from our perceiving activity that can be eliminated have been eliminated, remains radically a production of our perceptions.

On p. 170 we read:

> We live, to-day, half in and half out of two projected Natures. One is a Nature in Sense III, confused, through lack of reflection, with the unprojected ingressive Nature of Sense I. The other is a Nature in Sense II—shot through and through with our feelings and thus a mythology for them. These two Natures are at war. The enormous development in our conception of Nature in Senses III and IV, by seeming to threaten the sanctions of these projected feelings, is making them sickly, exaggerated and hysterical.

"Nature" and "conception (or view) of Nature," Dr. Richards thus reminds us, are interchangeable; where he says "Nature," we may, if we like, as here—"The two conceptions or views of Nature are at war"—expand it into the longer expression.

Then we remind ourselves that we have just read, on the preceding page (169), that "the perceptions sought by the man of science" result in a Nature over which our power of control is increasing with embarrassing leaps and bounds. And through this Nature (the world of natural science) it will soon be *possible* for us to remove most of the physical ills that oppress humanity.

Is it over a conception (or view) of Nature that our power is increasing so embarrassingly? Surely it is by means of, with the aid of, our conception that our power is increasing? If so, over what? Over, Dr. Richards answers (I suppose), Nature in Sense I—"The influences, of whatever kind, to which the mind is subject from whatever is without and independent of itself" (p. 157), a Nature that is "outside our knowledge," but "in response to" which we "take," "through the perceptive and imaginative activities of the mind," certain "images," "figments," "things," "existences," or "realities" "to be the world we live in" (p. 157). And by the time we come to the passage about "control" we have been thoroughly warned against naïve assumptions:

> But *figment* and *real* and *substantial* are themselves words with no meaning that is not derived from our experience. To say of anything that it is a figment seems to presuppose things more real than itself; but there is nothing within our knowledge more real than these images. [p. 165]

Here, clearly, we are in regions where only the technically qualified should venture comment, and I refrain without difficulty from suggesting the points in Dr. Richards's epistemology at which such a critic would press his questions and his analysis. I return to the laxity of expression I seem to myself to have detected in that passage about our embarrassing power to control (not itself a figment, I assume): a mere minor laxity of expression? I do not think so. If in itself minor, then it is (to adopt a phrase of Dr. Richards's) "a model for enormous evils." It is in any case a laxity without which the subtlety of the following, a subtlety that belongs to the essential purpose of Dr. Richards's book, would have been impossible:

> But dissent is not merely probable but certain if this account is applied to all myths or—to put it the other way—if *all* views of Nature are taken to be projections of the mind, and the religions as well as sciences are included among myths. [p. 177]

This is indeed disarming, the religious reader must feel—very different from the crude attitude of *Science and Poetry* (in reviewing which Mr. Douglas Garman,* not criticizing from a religious

---

* See *Towards Standards of Criticism*, p. 170.

point of view, rudely spoke of the author's "lick-spittle attitude" to science); if dissent is probable, the dissenter has the emollient assurance that at any rate science and religion are placed on a level and treated with equal respect. The equality, of course, is in courtesy merely. Science is a "special kind of myth"—"Other myths do not derive from knowledge in the sense in which science is knowledge" (p. 174)—and the "fundamentally important difference between the myths of natural science and the myths of poetry is the unrestricted claim upon our overt action of the former (getting out of the way of motor-cars, for example)" (p. 178) is so fundamentally important that, as we see, all other kinds of myth, contrasted with science, fall together under "poetry."

I write, not as an indignant religionist who has seen through Dr. Richards's blarney, but as a person of literary interests who is nevertheless concerned for rigorous thinking. I have my eye on that term "myth," which is so generously inclusive, and which does so much of Dr. Richards's work for him. Science and "poetry" are two fundamentally different kinds of things; science and "poetry" are the same kind of thing (for some purposes)—anyway, they are both myths, or mythologies. Obviously, the possibilities here of confusion and unconscious sleight are considerable if (as Dr. Richards, for his own purposes, does) one insists on using "myth" as a key-term. Naturally, keeping a sharp watch upon the purpose (Tone and Intention, as one registers them locally, are not such as to reassure the suspicious), one looks to the argument for a vigilance and a scrupulousness corresponding to the dangers and temptations. One decidedly does not find what one has a right to expect: it is, indeed, difficult not to conclude, unkindly, that one advantage of a training in the Multiple Definition technique is a certain freedom from inhibition in "getting it both ways."

In any case, the conviction remains that the problems Dr. Richards offers to deal with lie among the distinctions and differences covered by that embracing concept "myth" (and its associates), and that he shows nothing approaching an adequate concern for those distinctions and differences. The one difference that is firmly grasped has, as he proffers it, the effect of making science the one kind of myth to be taken seriously ("one gets out of the way of motor-cars"). This may seem unfair, and I am sure that Dr. Richards will think so, for, as we shall see, he takes an unusually exalted view of poetry. But "poetry"—here is another of his embracing terms: it is his lack of interest in the differences he covers with it that produces the effect just noted. I cannot believe that, if you were taking adequate account of the other things besides what I should call "poetry" that Dr. Richards includes under that head, you could be content to leave them there with as little attention to the differences as Dr. Richards shows (any more than I can believe that, if you take no more account of the differences, you are, whatever your theories, really a friend to poetry).

Such attention as he does pay to the differences seems merely to emphasize his lack of interest. For instance, on pp. 174-5 we read:

> For the claim to be knowledge, in this sense, is simply the claim to unrestricted, unconditional control over Action. . . . We step out of the way of the oncoming motor-bus. But our response to any myth is restricted and conditional. What has gone into it determines what we may properly and wisely take from it. "We receive but what we give." If we try to take more from the myth than has gone into it we violate the order of our lives.

If we recognize no more in the way of difficulty here than Dr. Richards shows any sign of recognizing, then "order" (I will risk saying, without indicating where in "the paradigm of the fluctuations of the word *word*" (p. 103) this use comes) remains, it seems to me, a mere word. Just what has gone into the various necessary myths, how it went, how it determines what we may "properly and rightly" take, and how we may keep sufficiently supplied with "myths" into which the appropriate something has somehow "gone" —these are obviously the important problems, and Dr. Richards hardly gives a sign of having noticed them (I will risk, again, adding that he seems to me curiously prone to an uncritical satisfaction with words). He does indeed, extending—in spite of the lapse by which, in the passage just quoted, science, or the motor-bus, becomes contradistinguished from myth—the term "Action" to the non-scientific "mythologies," recognize in a general way that there are various modes of "Accordant Action" (Belief): "It includes intellectual assent, feeling, submission in desire, attitude and will—all modes of response to the myth from mere contemplation to overt behaviour" (p. 173). But here, in what it includes, and remains including—"intellectual assent, feeling, submission in desire, attitude and will"—are the problems: problems to which successions of distinguished spirits have devoted themselves and concerning which there are important traditions ("wisdom," as Dr. Richards uses it, seems to me another mere word).

When he says (p. 176), "I have been taking the largest and the smallest myths together," one can only exclaim: "You have indeed!" He continues, a sentence or two further on, characteristically: "Probably the application of my remarks to the larger myths will have most occupied the reader. But an account of the origin and function of myths is more conveniently tested on lesser examples." "Conveniently" certainly seems the right word here. But the instances of "testing" that he adduces—his dealing (to be referred to later) with Landor and the *Immortality Ode*—make the coolness (for I don't know how else to describe it) of the procedure something for gaping admiration. And actually, whatever might be established or not about the "larger myths" by analysing bits of poems, nowhere in his book, it must be said, does Dr. Richards seriously attempt even such analysis.

To say this, of course, is, by the terms of his own challenge, to dismiss the pretension of the book. But even if, groping one's way through the largenesses of the philosophic argument, one had slipped by the small testings and failed to keep the challenge in mind, and, in philosophic modesty, had concluded that there was a swarm of doubts of which Dr. Richards ought to have the benefit, one would, even in one's worst state of dazed fatigue, have been quite sure by the last chapter that something had gone badly wrong—sure, because of where Dr. Richards exhibits himself as left by the argument:

> To put the burden of constituting order for our minds on the poet may seem unfair. It is not the philosopher, however, or the moralist who puts it on him, but birth. [p. 227]

The intended force of this claim for "the poet," so stated apart from the context, would be uncertain, and, indeed, remains so; but that we are to take the claim at the extreme of romantic inflation the context leaves us no room for doubt. Dr. Richards had asserted, basing himself mainly on a suggested comparison between Defoe's description of Crusoe's seashore and Mr. Joyce's of Stephen Dedalus's, that there has been a "dissolution of consciousness" such that "the whole machinery through which self-examination with a view to increased order could be conducted by Defoe has lapsed" (pp. 222-3). It is, as a rule, impossible to pin Dr. Richards down locally to any precise meaning; here, for instance, "machinery" appears to be grammatically in apposition with "the nomenclature of the faculties, of the virtues and the vices, of the passions, of the moods . . ." and while, on the one hand, "nomenclature" when used by Dr.

Richards is a term to watch very warily, "increased order," on the other hand, is moderate in suggestion. But a reading of the sequence of pages makes it plain that we are to take "dissolution" as meaning (for some purposes, at any rate) the effective disappearance of the very principles of order—of the main lines of organization once represented by the old nomenclature and the current "vocabulary"—and the absence of anything in the nature of appropriate "mythology." "Without his mythologies man is only a cruel animal without a soul" (p. 171); and it is in any case plain that birth will have to have bestowed on the poet something very considerable indeed beside a burden.

> The dissolution of consciousness exhibited in such prose [as that of *Jacob's Room* or *Ulysses*—odd collocation] . . . forces the task of reconstituting a less relaxed, a less adventitious order for the mind upon contemporary poetry. [p. 235]

I still don't understand just how prose is related to poetry in this argument, and the expectation entertained of "the poet" seems to me preposterously extravagant, but it is nevertheless pleasant to be able to agree that contemporary poetry is, or ought to be, important. Further agreement would seem to follow: agreement, let us say, in the aims represented by *Scrutiny*. It follows, for instance, that it is important to get poetry read—to work towards providing for it, what does not exist at present, an informed, intelligent, and influential public. And having made this very obvious point, we find ourselves contemplating the problems presented by the state of current criticism—we find ourselves committed to desiderating (shall we say?) and supporting, when they appear, some serious critical journals; we find ourselves, moreover, committed to hoping (at any rate) that something may come of a determined, concerted, and sustained effort in the educational field. And if we take these commitments seriously we shall before long find ourselves contemplating economic and political problems. In any case we shall not be light-hearted.

And here, in this last sentence, I have come to a reason for not being confident that any such measure of agreement as should, I have suggested, follow a common recognition of the importance of poetry does really exist between Dr. Richards and myself. He is decidedly light-hearted. He writes, for instance, on p. 229:

> Eras that produced no poetry that is remembered have been as disordered as ours. There are better reasons, in the work of modern

poets, to hope that a creative movement is beginning and that poetry, freed from a mistaken conception of its limitation and read more discerningly than heretofore, will remake our minds and with them our world.

Clearly there would be no point in asking for—what would nevertheless be very interesting—a little specificity here; there may be three times as many modern poets, and poets three times as promising, as any I know of, but that would not make Dr. Richards's optimism regarding their influence critically respectable. In fact, poetry in general for Dr. Richards—and for him it is always in general—is, it becomes impossible in these places to doubt, a myth that has very little to do with any particular actualities of poetry, or with the actualities of the world in which poets have to produce their work. It is a large private myth into which, seeing what he gets from it, one concludes a great deal must have gone: with the aid of it he evades the motor-buses and other difficulties and dangers in his theoretical path, slipping into the empyrean by something very like the Indian rope-trick.

His view of poetry is unrealistic to a degree almost incredible. Having, for instance, laid the burden upon "the poet," he says (p. 227):

> There is a figure of speech here, of course, for the burden is not on individual poets, but on the poetic function. With Homer, Dante and Shakespeare in mind, however, the importance of the single poet is not to be under-estimated.

Dr. Richards would seem to favour an idealist-individualism that amounts to a naïve Marxism inverted. In any case, to suggest that we may reasonably look for anything approaching a modern Homer, Dante, or Shakespeare is to endorse the crudest romantic notion of inspired genius: does Dr. Richards know nothing about the general cultural conditions represented by the achievements of those poets (if we are to call Homer *a* poet in the same sense as Dante or Shakespeare)—conditions, in each case, essential to the achievement, and beyond the capacity of the greatest individual genius to provide? If the nature and significance of such conditions had been present to him he could hardly have been so light-hearted about the "dissolution of consciousness" that he envisages—he could hardly, even if there had been a wide public for poetry in our time and no Book Societies, Hollywoods, and Northcliffes, have talked of the necessary new myths as something that a few individual poets, or a Poetic Renaissance, could improvise. It is, as a matter of fact, the very

absence of such conditions in our time that he is asking the poet—
or the poetic function—to remedy.

These problems raised by the mention of Homer, Dante, and
Shakespeare get no hint of recognition. Instead we find (p. 229):

> Such an estimate of the power of poetry may seem extravagant; but
> it was Milton's no less than Shelley's, Blake's or Wordsworth's. It
> has been the opinion of many with whom we need not be ashamed to
> agree . . . [Quotation from Ben Jonson follows.]

We haven't yet decided whether this is a careless insult to our intelligence, or merely an incredibly innocent peroration, when we discover that it is modesty. These exalted and reverberant generalities, it turns out, express merely a certain embarrassment at the approach of the real claim—at the shift from oblique statement to the direct. The real claim is not for the poet, but for the semasiologist:

> With Coleridge we step across the threshold of a general theoretical
> study of language capable of opening to us new powers over our minds
> comparable to those which systematic critical inquiries are giving us
> over our environment. The step across was of the same type as that
> which took Galileo into the modern world. It required the shift from
> a preoccupation with that What and Why to the How of language.
> [p. 232]

The step, it appears, has already been taken; something has been established in this book:

> And it has this consequence, that critics in the future must have a
> theoretical equipment of a kind which has not been felt to be necessary in the past. So physicists may sigh for the days in which less mathematics was required by them. But the critical equipment will not be
> *primarily* philosophical. It will be rather a command of the methods
> of general linguistic analysis. As the theory of Poetry develops, what
> is needed will be disengaged from philosophy, much as the methodology of physics has been disengaged [p. 233]

Dr. Richards's book, we are to understand, has both demonstrated the possibility and nature of the new science and provided a start towards the necessary "mathematics."

What is there in the book to justify these pretensions? Bluntly, nothing. There are recurrent hints at the revolutionary new technique and its epoch-making potentialities, but, for demonstration, not even a beginning in the serious critical analysis of poetry.

The most determined show of demonstrating the technique and inaugurating the science is Chapter IV, "Imagination and Fancy," in which Dr. Richards tries to turn Coleridge's distinction into a precise (or, to be fair, useful) laboratory instrument. Taking Coleridge's own example from *Venus and Adonis,* he notices that in the Fancy passage—

> *Full gently now she takes him by the hand,*
> *A lily prison'd in a gaol of snow,* etc.

—there is no "relevant interaction, no inter-inanimation," between the "units of meaning." Shakespeare, he says justly, is not attempting to realize in words the contact of hands, either as felt by the actors or seen by us. "He is making pleasing collocations that are *almost* wholly unconnected with what he is writing about." The commentary continues, characteristically:

> Why he is doing this (and what it is) are large questions. The answer would be partly historical . . . It would be partly psychological . . .

But why not, one asks, make the obvious and essential point that Shakespeare with his "lily," "snow," "ivory," and "alabaster" is being conventional—conventional in a mode readily illustrated from any anthology of Elizabethan verse (or from the *Oxford Book*)?

Those "large questions" are merely a nuisance: they distract Dr. Richards from noticing that the decorative-conventional element, pervasive in the poem, conditions such passages as that which he takes, in isolation, as imaginative. At any rate, if he notices, he says nothing about it, but gives a very misleading account of:

> *Look! how a bright star shooteth from the sky*
> *So glides he in the night from Venus' eye.*

He does not point out how, when we come to these lines in their place in the poem, "realization" is limited and conditioned, the situation "distanced," so that we suffer no such profound imaginative stir as his analysis suggests (p. 83).

He will no doubt reply that he is deliberately restricting his commentary, for the moment, to the enforcement of a given point. To this one has to rejoin that he nowhere in the book goes any further or deeper, or suggests the limitations and dangers of this superficial inspection of odds and ends, or incites to the discipline required for the serious analysis of poetry. He encourages instead the wholly misdirected kind of ingenuity represented by the footnote on p. 80. The triviality of the demonstration—and, I repeat, we get nothing more serious—offers an odd contrast with the portentous prelude, "The Coalescence of Subject and Object," which we are invited to wrestle with as essential to the understanding of

Fancy and Imagination (the book in general is characterized by such a contrast—the contrast, sometimes amusing, between the difficulty of the philosophic argument and the critical greenness presumed in the reader).

This triviality is inherent in the ambition of the undertaking. The explanation lies in the following sentence (p. 84):

> This, then, is an *observable* difference from which we set out, though it is unhappily not true that all can observe it equally or equally clearly.

That *"observable"* explains why, after the setting out, there is no advance. Why is it italicized? Clearly, in order to suggest—the claim is implicit—that here we have the beginnings of a laboratory technique. This is the point as which, in unavoidable nakedness, the nature of the process of "reinterpreting" Coleridge in Benthamite terms (or of uniting the realms of Coleridge and Bentham [see p. 18]) lies exposed, clear for a moment of metaphysics and semasiology. What do we propose to bring for treatment into the laboratory? Poetry, or bits of poetry. But the data can be possessed only by a delicate inner discipline, and in such possession as is incompatible with producing them in any laboratory, or in any way that the analogy of "laboratory" does not completely misreprsent. Dr. Richards himself (who does not use the word "laboratory," but merely italicizes "observable") has said as much again and again, sometimes in quite admirable formulations; for example (*Practical Criticism*, p. 291):

> It might be said, indeed, with some justice, that the value of poetry lies in the difficult exercise in sincerity it can impose upon its readers even more than upon the poet.

But the new science has somehow to be got started. So we find Dr. Richards trying to explain how "something rather like a refreshed atomism—a counting of relations—appears again as we develop and apply Coleridge's doctrine" (p. 70). This counting must not be crudely confused with valuation—the valuation that involves exercises in sincerity and so confronts laboratory technique with extremely delicate problems. These problems may be postponed and dealt with later. Coleridge, of course, used the terms Imagination and Fancy as implying different values. "The conception [Imagination] was devised as a means of describing the wider and deeper powers of some poetry" (p. 96). Nevertheless, we can, if we wish

> make the terms purely descriptive. We shall then have instances of imagination which are valuable and instances which are not, and we must then go on to contrive a further theory, a theory of values which will explain (so far as we are able to do so at present) these differences of value. [This is the procedure I attempted to follow in *Principles of Literary Criticism.*] [p. 96]

There is, perhaps, something admirable in the candour of that square-bracketed parenthesis: Dr. Richards will hardly contend at this date that the theory of values expounded in *Principles of Literary Criticism* is of any use for any respectable purpose whatever, or that it does anything but discredit the ambition to make criticism a science. In any case, the confusion obscuring the scientific project remains, and it is not lessened by Dr. Richards's appearing to put the case against himself in the latter part of the chapter (pp. 97-9). (He has an odd way of suggesting that by being on both sides at once—or by slipping unobtrusively from one to the other—one reconciles them.)

Coleridge's critical doctrine, of course, cannot be "developed and applied" into a science; to attempt such development and application is to abandon him for (shall we say?) Bentham. Dr. Richards, in his account of the bent of interest and the training that produced the doctrine, curiously slights one important head. Metaphysics and psychology get full insistence:

> It is to be expected then that what he found to say after his inquiries will not be understood by those without a similar training. This is true of all special studies. Psychology, however, is peculiar in that those who are not students in it feel ready so often to correct those who are. [p. 37]

Against this it seems to me important to set—we have Coleridge's own words *—another aspect of his training:

> O! when I think of the inexhaustible mine of virgin treasure in our Shakespeare, that I have been almost daily reading him since I was ten years old—that the thirty intervening years have been unintermittingly and not fruitlessly employed in the study of the Greek, Latin, English, Italian, Spanish and German belle-lettrists . . .

With these intense literary interests and this training, Coleridge (he was indeed a "subtle-souled psychologist") was equipped to think rigorously about poetry and to understand the nature and condition of the process of analysing it. Even if the theoretical knowledge "available" in his time had equalled the modern psy-

---
* *Coleridge's Shakespearean Criticism,* Raysor, Vol. I, p. 220.

chologist's, he could hardly have asked (at any rate, with Dr. Richards's intention): "Do we yet know enough about what we are doing when we try to analyse a passage of poetry to settle its merits or demerits *by argument?*" (p. 127). I say "with Dr. Richards's intention" because the question is not unambiguous. But (though—or is it "though"?—Dr. Richards says that, with our present knowledge, "the answer must be a firm 'No' ") the dealings with the *Immortality Ode* that follow compel us to interpret "settle by argument" in the way the pervasive laboratory pretension suggests.

Dr. Richards undertakes to dispose of Coleridge's strictures on the "Mighty Prophet! Seer blest!" passage. Some of the replies admit of very damaging rejoinders, but few readers interested in poetry will bother to argue with Dr. Richards: it is so plain that the piece of arguing he offers (though—see p. 176—it is a large proportion of the illustrative practice on which he bases his science) neither illustrates, nor furthers, the analysis of poetry. It will perhaps be enough (space being limited) to quote his conclusion:

> My comments on Coleridge's misunderstandings do not aver that the Ode is a piece of scientific psychology. Nor would I say that—apart from some twenty lines, five or six of which are "truths that wake, to perish never"—it is at Wordsworth's highest level. But its weakest lines deserve respect as the frame of what they support. [p. 137]

No critic who had gone through the Ode in (to use Dr. Richards's own admirable phrase) "experimental submission" could have committed himself to this summing-up or have supposed that the argument leading to it was doing anything but distract from the relevant analysis. (Of course, an account of the Ode is assumed here that I am, naturally, ready to supply.)

Coleridge's interest in developing his theories was a kind that did not tempt him to forget the nature of "experimental submission" (without which, whatever it is that is analysed, it is not poetry). And the central passage on the Imagination, we do well to remind ourselves, begins with the sentence about the poet's bringing "the whole soul of man into activity, with the subordination of its faculties to each other according to their relative worth and dignity." It is one thing for Coleridge to point, by means of examples, to the kind of way in which Imagination manifests itself locally. It is very much another thing to suppose that one is developing his theory into precision when, by much argument about isolated odds and ends of verse, one arrives at this (p. 91):

> But Imagination, as I have described it, can be shown in trivial examples. And Fancy can be shown in important matters. . . . In Imagination, as I have taken it, the joint effect (worthless or not) . . .

Coleridge's theory can be developed only in an arduous and scrupulous exploration of the organic complexities of poetry by a developing analysis—by an analysis going deeper and deeper and taking wider and wider relations into account; that is, becoming less and less distinguishable as laboratory technique. Dr. Richards's procedure, heading away from the concrete, leaves him (it is an ironical fate for one who warns us so much against this sort of thing) the happy servant of a set of abstract terms. It is comment enough on the new science that it should enable him, in the effort to explain how "the sense of musical delight," which is a "gift of the imagination," can be given by *The Faerie Queene*, which is "chiefly a work of Fancy," to discover in that poem

> an architectural, which is here an imaginative unity. And it may be this other unity which produces "the sense of musical delight." It is thus that Spencer "has an imaginative fancy." [p. 120]

The ingenious undergraduate will certainly find that the new apparatus has its uses.

It is plain that when Dr. Richards remarks (p. 137) that "persons with literary interests to-day frequently suffer from lack of exercise in careful and sometimes arduous thinking," he lays himself open to the retort that, if one is going to think with effect about literature, there must be no lack of intensity in one's literary interests. They must be intense enough to ensure disinterestedness. It is here that Dr. Richards, in certain very obvious ways, fails. That his literary interests derive from an interest in theory rather than his theory from his literary interests has never been a secret. The fact is apparent (Dr. Richards insists upon one's coming out with this delicate kind of judgement) in his prose. Mr. Eliot made a radical criticism when he corrected that "'enormity" in the Ritual for Sincerity. The insensitiveness is pervasive. (Even in descending to slang one should respect the peculiar force of the given expression, and I take the occasion here to protest against the jocular reference to Coleridge as the "Highgate spell-binder" [p. 22]: "spell-binding" surely implies a combination of contempt for one's audience with desire to impress it, and Coleridge, I imagine, was at no period guilty of that sort of thing.)

But the disability that beyond any question matters is that

apparent both in the infrequency, in Dr. Richards's theorizing, of any approach to the concrete and in the quality of such approach as he ventures on. *Practical Criticism,* for instance, is valuable in spite of the title's being a misnomer; and the theoretical considerations—the hints thrown out, the questions asked—would have been more valuable if they had derived from a more adequate interest in particulars. That book, too, offers depressing instances of the relation between insufficiency of interest and lack of disinterestedness, the most remarkable of them being Dr. Richards's "case" about the Longfellow poem. No one concerned merely to see what was there in front of him could have found that poem "extremely urbane" and "rather witty" (references to "Dryden, Pope and Cowper"); or have supposed that the case made out, with "suppleness (not subtlety)," was even faintly plausible.

The offence (there are others of the kind in *Practical Criticism*) is a very serious one in a champion of the serious study of poetry. It is shocking to find Dr. Richards, in the present book, impenitent about another offence of the same kind. He refers back to his "Fifteen Lines of Landor" as a serious experiment. But I have not been able to discover that he has replied anywhere to the letter from Mr. Bonamy Dobrée printed in *The Criterion* for October, 1933. Mr. Dobrée there points out that "Dr. Richards deliberately made a puzzle for his students by omitting to inform them what Landor was talking about" (the information being necessary because of the wresting of the passage from its context). "It is one thing," comments Mr. Dobrée, "to conduct scientific experiments on the reactions of people to certain collections of words, another to discover, by a little calm thought, what a poet was talking about." Mr. Dobrée, moreover, in his closing sentence, puts his finger on the irrelevant "idea," the imported interest, that led Dr. Richards to set his students at exercises so much the reverse of conducive, in nature and spirit, to the sensitive reading of poetry.

The last chapter of the present book is called "The Bridle of Pegasus" and it is especially full of irresponsible generalities, bright ideas, and uncritical tips. Who, for instance, are these '"newfanglers" who are unable to construe the "meaning structures" of "Shelley, Keats or Wordsworth" (and what have the "meaning structures" of these three poets in common?)? Is it, again, a critical, or scientific, proceeding to base any conclusion about the development of consciousness on a comparison between Daniel Defoe and James Joyce? Ought Dr. Richards to throw out such large generalizations about the history of reading capacity so lightly, and so lightly to "decline the invidious task of demonstration"? Is it helpful to point out that the "agèd eagle" passage in *Ash Wednesday* is "dramatic," without noting too that it falls (its significance being that it does so) within a poem an essential characteristic of which is to be much less "dramatic" than most of Mr. Eliot's work? Has Dr. Richards not read the *Mad Prince's Song* since he wrote *Science and Poetry* that he should still think that poem (in which Mr. de la Mare makes a characteristic use of Ophelia) a "quintessence" of *Hamlet*? Does he still (see the foot-note on p. 207) think that Mr. Yeats in *The Wind Among the Reeds* was writing "an unusually simple and direct kind of love poetry" (*Science and Poetry*, p. 73)?

But I must leave the rest of my notes unused. It is depressing to realize, in any case, that this commentary has been so completely adverse. But Dr. Richards does seem to me to be heading completely away from any useful path—and to be heading others: his past work has won him prestige enough to make this explicitness unavoidable. It is a great pity, when one thinks of what, had he limited himself by any given discipline, he might have accomplished. As it is, one can only turn against him the terms of his own challenge:

> But the study of poetry, for those born in this age, is more arduous than we suppose. It is therefore rare. Many other things pass by its name and are encouraged to its detriment. [p. 230]

(1935)

Virginia Woolf

(1) MRS. WOOLF AND LIFE

The Years, by Virginia Woolf

Reviewed by W. H. Mellers

Mrs. Woolf, we all know, is a Poet in Prose; or rather she has—perhaps one should say had—a range of sensuous impressions which would have stood a great poet in good stead. But sensuous impressions, though they are immensely important and perhaps the only means whereby a poet can make his apprehensions and his attitudes concrete and comprehensible, are not an end in themselves; if they were, most normally sensitive children would be great poets. Of course, Mrs. Woolf is an "intelligent woman," but, as a reviewer in *The Calendar* pointed out * on the publication of *Mrs. Dalloway,* her intellectual capacity is oddly disproportionate to, and immature compared with, her sensitiveness, and, if she ventures outside the narrow range imposed on her by her sensuousness, she becomes a child. Since the range of experience implied in sensuous apprehension purely and simply is, indeed, necessarily so limited, it is perhaps significant that the only occasion when she has been able to use her impressions, in their various subtle interrelations, to form an organization, a whole, has been when she was concerned, to some extent at least, with personal reminiscence; and it is probable, moreover, that what she did in *To the Lighthouse* could only be done once.

In this book, anyway, Mrs. Woolf used her impressions triumphantly as imaginative concepts, and she perfected an original technique to express the order which she apprehended within these impressions. As she is a sensuous artist, and what the senses perceive is transitory and mutable, she saw them as dominated by Time; and she found a central symbol for her theme so just and integral that it is not as over-simple as it may superficially appear to say that what differentiates *To the Lighthouse* from Mrs. Woolf's other books is precisely that in this work alone *something really happens*—the trip to the Lighthouse. And here, because she has kept within her limi-

---

* See *Towards Standards of Criticism,* p. 48 ff.

tations, her conception of human relationships and of moral values is delicate and sure. (Mrs. Ramsay has positive life, is something compelling and potent.) But how limited this conception nevertheless is is suggested by the somewhat suspicious easiness of the middle section (Time Passes). Even in this book, where her poetry is so consummately incarnated, her attitude is ultimately that of the "sensitive" young girl who, growing old in years, looks back and remembers.

When she had written *To the Lighthouse* there were three courses open to Mrs. Woolf. Either she could enlarge her scope, do something fresh; or she could stop writing altogether; or she could cheat by way of technique. She chose the last of these alternatives. In *The Waves* there is a fatal falsification between what her impressions actually are and what they are supposed to signify—they are pinned to her prose like so many dead butterflies. Mrs. Woolf goes through the appropriate gestures (doors open, doors shut), uses the appropriate formulae (the rose blossoms, the petal falls), but the champing beast on the shore confessed itself a mechanical toy, and the artificially artful parallel with the waves hardly pretends to be anything more than a parallel. The artfulness of the method makes the immediacy and hence the quality of the impressions themselves deteriorate. The rhythm loses the subtle flexibility of the earlier books, falling at times to the bathos of the magazine-story ("But if one day you do not come after breakfast, if one day I see you in some looking-glass perhaps looking after another, if the telephone buzzes and buzzes in your empty room, I shall then after unspeakable anguish, I shall then—for there is no end to the folly of the human heart—seek another, find another, you. Meanwhile, let us abolish the ticking of time's clock with one blow. Come closer."); while many of the "poetical" images betray only too patently their genesis. ("A crack of light knelt on the wall.") A rudimentary analysis of any characteristic passage suffices to prove, indeed, that, shorn of the "original" technique, what Mrs. Woolf has to say about the relationship between her characters, about the business of living, is both commonplace and sentimental.

The hero-worship of Percival (a "great master of the art of living") is perhaps a minor point, though symptomatic; but the radical weakness and falsity of the book is revealed in the central position occupied by Bernard, the maker of phrases. "Now you tug at my skirts, looking back, making phrases . . . I shall be a clinger to the outsides of words all my life. . . . There is some flaw in me, some fatal hesitancy, which if I pass it over, turns to foam and falsity." There could be no more accurate description of what Mrs. Woolf is doing in *The Waves;* essentially her attitude is that of the undergraduette—or Bloomsbury-poet. "There are stories, but what are stories? What is the thing that lies behind the semblance of the thing?" Our lives are shrouded in obscurity, and knowing nothing we turn on our wistfullest smiles and tread our way to the grave. It is difficult to see how an honest reader can discover any more "profundity" in *The Waves* than this; and if there *is* any form in these multiple incoherencies the trick lies in Bernard's "I retrieve them from formlessness with words." It is only a trick, and a pretty threadbare one at that. We must note, too, the complete disappearance of the irony that gave such subtlety of poise to *To the Lighthouse;* though Mrs. Woolf is "critical," there is no evidence that she hasn't, with Bernard, a sympathy which amounts to an implicit self-identification.

Whatever lingering doubts we may have entertained about the validity of *The Waves* are resolved with dismal finality when we consider Mrs. Woolf's new novel, *The Years,* in which, without the superficial screen of Experimental Technique, she reveals the same sentimentalities and ineptitudes. Presumably the explicit theme is one which had been implicit in the earlier books, the inevitable theme of the sensuous impressionist, "the passage of time and its tragedy." Only, as Mrs. Woolf presents it, it isn't tragic, but merely fatuous. It is impossible to find tragedy in the aging of persons who are non-existent, and, far from having the rounded vitality of Mrs. Ramsay, the characters in this novel have not even the factitious existence of the collections of phrases that make up the *personae* of *The Waves*. These people are phantoms; they grow old, but they cannot change because they have never been alive; in so far as they exist at all it is as a bundle of memories. The book is a document of purposelessness. Either life is supremely meaningless, or, as the years go by, there is perhaps a pattern (what has been will be), yet there is no point in the pattern. The discovery of it entails, indeed, a degree of falsification. The repetitions, the cooing doves and the bonfire smoke, are sly and artful, the jig-saw of the *littérteur*. "Does everything then come over again a little differently? She thought. If so, there a pattern, a theme, recurring, like music . . . ? But who makes it? Who thinks it? Her mind slipped. She could not finish her thought." The atmosphere of uncertainty, of ambiguity, is, of course, traded upon. Conversations are misunderstood, thought is incommunicable. "Who's right? Who's wrong? . . . We cannot make laws and religions that fit because we do not know ourselves. . . . If we do not know ourselves how can we know other people?" And consequent upon this purposelessness is a sense of oppressive frustration. People are always having "the truth" on the tip of the tongue, but are unable (and it is God alone that knows why) to utter it. The "climax"—pathetic paradox—comes when Nicholas, attempting to make the speech that would at last reveal the secret of their lives, is prevented. "It was to have been a miracle. A masterpiece! But how can one speak when one is always interrupted . . . I was going to drink to the human race. . . . He brought his glass down with a thump on the table. It broke."

The long final section on the Present Day is, indeed, easily the best part of the book, and here the ambiguity and purposelessness, the frustration, becomes less artful and, paradoxical as it may seem, more sharply focussed, with a quality of passive desolation which is comparable with the neurasthenic weariness and fatigue of Kurt Weill's queerly documentary ballet, *The Seven Deadly Sins,* though it entirely lacks the negative intensity of Weill's music.

> Rest, rest, let me rest. How to deaden, how to cease to feel; that was the cry of the women bearing children; to rest, to cease to be . . . not to live; not to feel; to make money, always money, and in the end, when I'm old and worn like a horse, no, it's a cow. . . .

The extraordinarily inert, incantory rhythm of the prose, and the remotely reminiscent nature of the images—as though the scene were viewed not immediately but in retrospect, distantly as through a mirror or through the glass of an aquarium—produces an effect oddly similar to the grey, drab exhaustion, the unreal nightmarish atmosphere of Weill's music, but it is, of course, superficially more "refined" more precious.

To speak of Mrs. Woolf's refinement reminds us of her celebrated femininity, which quality seems to go hand in hand with the curiously tepid Bloomsbury prose into which she has always, in unguarded moments, been inclined to trickle. Here, anyway, it only enforces the feeling of weakness and sterility, and one can but reflect dismally on the inanity of a world in which the only positives seem to be "silence and solitude." These incoherently reminiscent mumblings seem purposely to ignore the human will and all it entails; and although we have no right to blame an artist for not doing what he didn't intend to do, the complete omission, in a work which embraces the passage of time during the last fifty years, of (for instance) physical desire may strike us at least as odd. Of course it is obvious enough that Mrs. Woolf's social world is a minute one. The phrase "feminine intuition," used in connexion with Mrs. Woolf, inevitably invites comparison with Jane Austen, and if the latter has social decorum, Mrs. Woolf can only be said to have social decorousness. But, even at her best, for all her air of abysmal profundity, is Mrs. Woolf's spiritual world either quite as far-reaching as it seems? Some of us may perhaps think that, as a novelist, Mrs. Woolf is too concerned about Life to be concerned, as was Miss Austen, very adequately about living. And if it be objected that Mrs. Woolf is not using the novel *qua* novel but for a poetical end, we return to the point from which we started; and conclude that she is, in the long run, only a very minor sort of poet.

(1937)

(II) CATERPILLARS OF THE COMMONWEALTH UNITE!

Three Guineas, by Virginia Woolf

Reviewed by Q. D. Leavis

This book is not really reviewable in these pages because Mrs. Woolf implies throughout that it is a conversation between her and her friends, addressed as she constantly says to "women of our class," though bits of it are directly and indirectly aimed at those women's menfolk. What "our class" is turns out to be the people whose fathers function at Westminster, who "spend vast sums annually upon party funds; upon sport; upon grouse moors . . . lavish[es] money upon clubs—Brook's, White's, the Travellers', the Reform, to mention the most prominent." Mrs. Woolf would apparently be surprised to hear that there is no member of that class on the contributing list of this review. On the other hand, readers of this review will be surprised to hear that Mrs. Woolf thinks this class— the relatively very few wealthy propertied people in our country—is to be identified with "the educated class" and contains at this date the average educated man and the average student of the women's colleges of the older universities. This is the first of many staggering intimations for the reader that Mrs. Woolf is not living in the contemporary world: almost the first thing we notice is that the author of *Three Guineas* is quite insulated by class. What respectable ideas inform this book belong to the ethos of John Stuart Mill. What experience there is of domineering and hostile man (for that purports to justify the undertaking) is second-hand and comes from hearsay.*

It is no use attempting to discuss the book for what it claims to be, which is a sort of chatty restatement of the rights and wrongs of women of Mrs. Woolf's class, with occasional reflections, where convenient, on the wrongs of other kinds of Englishwomen. Mrs. Woolf, by her own account, has personally received considerably more in the way of economic ease than she is humanly entitled to and, as this book reveals, has enjoyed the equally relaxing ease of an uncritical (not to say flattering) social circle: she cannot be supposed to have suffered any worse injury from mankind than a rare unfavourable review. Writing this book was evidently a form of self-indulgence—altruism exhibits a different tone, it is not bad-tempered, peevishly sarcastic, and incoherent as this book is throughout. As a reviewer I must say it impresses me as unpleasant self-indulgence, and as a member of a class of educated women Mrs. Woolf has apparently never heard of I feel entitled to add it is also highly undesirable. The reviewers have indeed all blessed the book, but any man who objected would lay himself open to the obvious charges of (a) being no gentleman and (b) expressing a resentment easily explicable in psychological terms, while any woman who refused to vote solid would of course be a traitress to the cause. Nevertheless, I venture to voice what I know to be the opinion of many educated women, that Mrs. Woolf's latest effort is a let-down for our sex. *A Room of One's Own* was annoying enough, causing outpourings of disgust in the very quarters in which Mrs. Woolf, one gathered, expected to earn gratitude; but this book is not merely silly and ill-informed, though it is that too; it contains some dangerous assumptions, some preposterous claims, and some nasty attitudes.

The method is a deliberate avoidance of any argument—its unity is emotional. She tries in fact to make a weapon of feminine inconsequence, and I felt sympathetic with another reader of *Three*

---

*Often unreliable. Mrs. Woolf instances as one burning injustice: "Not a single educated man's daughter is thought capable of teaching the literature of her own language at either university." There are at present six women regularly on the lecture-list for the English Tripos and I believe at no time in the last ten years has there been less than four—a generous representation for two colleges. Again: "The great majority of your sex [Englishmen] are to-day in favour of war."

Guineas, of course of the wrong sex, who remarked to me that Mrs. Woolf's mental processes reminded him of Mrs. Nickleby's. The result affects me like Nazi dialect without Nazi convictions. Take pages 39 to 40. They run like this (I preserve Mrs. Woolf's wording where possible): men dress up in their professional capacities as warriors, lawyers, courtiers, dons; they forbid us women to wear such uniform, but don't let them suppose that they are anything but a ridiculous spectacle to us; preserving archaic costume for public ritual in the universities emphasizes the superiority of educated men over other people; this arouses competition and jealousy, emotions making for war; women therefore can help to prevent war by refusing to wear academic dress (though they have at present a legitimate grievance in not being allowed to wear it at Cambridge) or to accept public honours; and by openly despising the men who do. I cannot understand all this as anything but phrases which have no meaningful connexion with each other, but it is a fair specimen of the rhetoric in which the "argument" of *Three Guineas* is conducted. This passage, moreover, is illustrated with photographs, but as they are evidently selected with malice and as the thought perforce leaps to mind how a corresponding selection, probably as stupid-looking or ridiculous, could be compiled of eminent women's faces and persons in gala dress, the method defeats itself. As does another artifice. This is to write as though the defects of human nature existed only in the male branch (if deliberate, it's bad tactics because it outrages common sense, and if unconscious, as there seems reason to suppose, it discounts the whole undertaking). For example, Mrs. Woolf gives much space to the Victorian father who almost without exception, she thinks, kept his daughters in intellectual and economic subservience. I do not myself believe that the bourgeois fathers at any period were worse than the mothers, or that both varieties of parent are not at all times equally inclined to proprietary behaviour wherever unchecked by self-knowledge, whatever the state of the law and public opinion. Mrs. Woolf writes as though the Victorian fathers whom she adduces as jealous of their daughters' marrying or achieving economic independence were not to be paralleled in many ages, including our own, by the common case of mothers who try to run their sons' lives (D. H. Lawrence's mother is a well-known type), and it is even arguable that the moral and emotional pressure exerted by mothers upon their children, particularly sons, is worse than the economic dependence of daughters and wives.

In fact, the release of sex hostility that this kind of writing represents is self-indulgent because it provides Mrs. Woolf with a self-righteous glow at the cost of furnishing an easy target for unsympathetic males, and at the still greater cost of embarrassing those women who are aware that the only chance of their getting accepted as intellectual equals by intelligent men (and so ultimately by the men who run the institutions and professions) is by living down their sex's reputation for having in general minds as ill-regulated as Mrs. Woolf's is here seen to be. It is a reputation that will die the harder for *Three Guineas*.

For just think of the proposals made here for improving the position of educated women. There is her proposal for reforming the evils of the professions by women refusing to acquiesce in them. Instances given are: refuse to approve of academic dress and decorations because these somehow cause wars; accept university lectureships in literature and then refuse to lecture because all such lectures and all teaching of literature (except by creative writers to those itching to become such themselves) is "vain and vicious"; refuse to pander to "adultery of the brain" by writing for journals or publishers (alternative source of income for professional women writers not inheriting five hundred a year and rooms of their own not indicated). Then there is the plan for abolishing the man-made university with its examinations, degrees, and distinctions based on native ability, and substituting the ideal college as conceived by and for women. At a time when all responsible educationists are expressing radical dissatisfaction both with the existing college system and with the accepted idea of university education this attracts our attention as a hopeful sign. But as a nice practical start Mrs. Woolf won't hear of university students being prepared in any way to earn a living, even by studying specialties. She thinks that adults from eighteen to twenty-one can justify their existence as burdens on the state by studying what she calls the art of living. Most people might feel that the art of living is best acquired incidentally to some discipline, either that given by brute circumstances when one is forced to stand on one's own feet (ideal: Robinson Crusoe) or that acquired in the pursuit of specialist studies—and many educationists now think it would be an improvement to combine the two. Without some such discipline the art of living becomes a pitiful affair. Mrs. Woolf's conception of it turns out to be the variety implied in the prospectus of an Arts Theatre I once received, which announced something like this, that it would be a place where people who appreciated the arts of dress, epicurism, and conversation would be able, in appropriate surroundings, to feed a corresponding taste for the art of drama. It seems to me the art of living as conceived by a social parasite. Mrs. Woolf wants studies in her college to be pursued by "the clever and the stupid" side by side, without any troublesome distinctions or standards to spoil things. But if an institution for the higher education of adults is to defend human values, as Mrs. Woolf in theory at any rate desiderates, it can only do so by jealously maintaining the highest possible standards where the arts are concerned and conducting the most rigorous scrutiny of intellectual processes generally. Hence its very first duty would be to inculcate the critical attitude and its second to develop in its students the ability to discriminate, judge, and reject, along with the practice of responsible thinking and conduct. Mrs. Woolf, however, feels even more strongly than about the wrongs of women of her class the wrongs of writers like Sir Edmund Gosse and Tennyson (specified along with Keats as objecting to criticism—a few instances of better-known objectors to criticism, such as Miss Edith Sitwell and Marie Corelli, would have made the point clearer), and her most cherished project of all is to uproot criticism, root and branch, in the Nazi manner. With access to some practical control Mrs. Woolf would evidently develop into a high-powered persecutor; this throws a pretty light on her conception of truth, freedom, and intellectual liberty, which she calls upon educated women to maintain. She wants to penalize specialists in the interests of amateurs, and so her university, in spite of a promise that learning should be studied there for its own sake, could only be a breeding-ground for boudoir scholarship (a term I once heard applied to the learning of one of Mrs. Woolf's group) and belletrism. I cannot believe that anyone else would think this an improvement on the existing kind of university study, or that such a higher '"education" would be more successful than the present kind in discouraging meanness of spirit, hostility to freedom of thought, and hatred of disinterestedness. Mrs. Woolf's is no doubt a feminine conception of congenial study, as opposed to the existing masculine one of disciplined studies towards an end, but is it the kind of education women have struggled for admission to in the past? *Three Guineas* draws freely on the impressive biographies of the leaders of female emancipation, but from the quotations she gives I conclude the desires of these women were the same as mine and those of most men on entering college, the desire to continue a general education by disciplined specialist studies under the best available instructors (who, shameful admission, still happen to be men in most fields) and as far as possible in the company of those students able to set the highest standards and work with the greatest degree of maturity (who also happen to be men, which explains why sensible women would never dream of imitating Mrs. Woolf's feminist heroics). The least damning thing you might say about Mrs. Woolf's proposals is that they are irresponsible.

Out of these babblings the noble and dignified utterances of Josephine Butler, the vigorous good sense with which Sophia Jex-Blake pursued her reasonable demands, the humility of Anne Clough, appeal to Heaven against the context in which they find themselves. I think such women would rather not have had the claims of their sex advocated by Mrs. Woolf's methods. I myself stipulate that any piece of female writing advocating equality of opportunity for the sexes should prove its author to have a highly developed character and a respectable intellect, to be free from mere sex-hostility, to have an at least masculine sense of responsibility and that capacity for self-criticism which impresses us as a mark of the best kind of masculine mind, and over and above that to come from a woman capable of justifying her existence in any walk of life. There really are quite a number of women like that about. I would rather the men who need converting from gross prejudice against women's abilities read not *Three Guineas* but, among other recent women's books, *Highland Homespun* (Margaret M. Leight), *Can I Help You, Madam?* (Ethyle Campbell), *I'm Not Complaining* (Ruth Adams), *Sex and Temperament in Savage Society* (Margaret Mead)—books which in varied ways exhibit women capable of doing a job (farming, business, education, social sciences) which demands sterling qualities of mind and character. These books are impressive documentation of women's right to share interests and occupations that have sometimes been considered suitable only for men.

But I have passed over Mrs. Woolf's plan for the complete emancipation of women of her class from the prison-house she considers every part of the home other than the drawing-room to be. To judge from *Three Guineas* Mrs. Woolf wants the women of her class to have the privileges of womanhood without the duties and responsibilties traditionally assumed by them, and to have the advantages of man's education without being subsequently obliged, as nearly all men are, to justify it. Thus she urges the re-endowment of the almost extinct class of "idle, charming, cultivated women" whose function would be to provide those dinner-tables and drawing-rooms where the art of living, as previously defined, is to be practised, and she is indignant that the early students of Girton and Newnham had to make their own beds and suffer plain living—though some responsible educationists now advocate university reform in the direction of obliging even men to conduct their education in the more realistic surroundings provided by the absence of servants.

On the other hand, "Daughters of educated men have always done their thinking from hand to mouth. . . . They have thought while they stirred the pot, while they rocked the cradle. It was thus that they won us the right," etc. I agree with someone who complained that to judge from the acquaintance with the realities of life displayed in this book there is no reason to suppose Mrs. Woolf would know which end of the cradle to stir. Mrs. Woolf, in fact, can hardly claim that she has thus helped to win us the right, etc. I myself, however, have generally had to produce contributions for this review with one hand while actually stirring the pot, or something of that kind, with the other, and if I have not done my thinking while rocking the cradle it was only because the daughters even of uneducated men ceased to rock infants at least two generations ago. Well, I feel bound to disagree with Mrs. Woolf's assumption that running a household and family unaided necessarily hinders or weakens thinking. One's own kitchen and nursery, and not the drawing-room and dinner-table where tired professional men relax among the ladies (thus Mrs. Woolf), is the realm where living takes place, and I see no profit in letting our servants live for us. The activities Mrs. Woolf wishes to free educated women from as wasteful not only provide a valuable discipline; they serve as a sieve for determining which values are important and genuine and which are conventional and contemptible. It is this order of experience that often makes the conversation of an uncultivated, charmless woman who has merely worked hard and reared a family interesting and stimulating, while its absence renders a hypertrophied conversation piece like *Three Guineas* tiresome and worthless. Mrs. Woolf's plan for a new society intrigues me, nevertheless. We have to have one kind of educated women, the idle, charming, cultivated women, who are to be subsidized as hostesses for the art of social intercourse (it is presumably to spare the sensibilities of these exquisite creatures that criticism of literature is to be prohibited—perhaps because they tend to dabble in letters themselves). Then we are to have a sterner kind of educated woman, the professional woman, for whose benefit the men's colleges are to be thrown open and all the available scholarship money divided equally between the sexes—the women who are to be just like men only more high-minded. Both these kinds are the five-hundred-a-year-by-the-right-of-birth-as-daughters-of-the-ruling-classes women. Then there are to be the base-born women who come in on the edge of the picture as drudges, to relieve both the other kinds of women of their natural duties (I mean, of course, nursing and rearing their own infants) as well as the routine of home-making. To impress hired labour for such work is enlightened ("'remember we are in the twentieth century now," writes Mrs. Woolf, and quotes a feminist writer to the effect that a mother is only incapacitated from pursuing her profession for two months per child), but Mrs. Woolf's ancestors, who thought it advisable to send their daughters about London accompanied by a personal maid, are the objects of much laboured irony (see p. 294). Then there are the unfortunate men who are to marry these daughters of educated men. If their wives choose to have babies—for women are to avert war by refusing to bear children, but apparently not indefinitely—they must from the start share the work of tending their offspring. A thorough-going revolution in their wage-earning pursuits, and so a regular social reorganization, unenvisaged by Mrs. Woolf, must take place to allow this. I like to think of the professional man hurrying home at four-hour intervals to spend upwards of half an hour giving the baby its bottle (for breast-feeding will only be able to survive among the uneducated)—among other duties; and presently he will have little time to give to his profession if he has any unenlightened doubts about trusting the growing mentality and sensibilities of his child to hirelings. But perhaps Mrs. Woolf does not mean to be taken as seriously as this. Or perhaps she is advocating the Soviet system of handing the child over to the state to rear at the earliest possible age. If so, she should say as much and clear up her projects; they are at present all too nebulous.

I should like to end by making one part of them a little less so. It will be necessary to draw upon the disagreeable facts of experience instead of confining ourselves with Mrs. Woolf to assertions and wishful prophecy; but to import even a little reality into such a discussion should be a service. The position then with regard to further female emancipation seems to be that the onus is on women to prove that they are going to be able to justify it, and that it will not vitally dislocate (what it has already seriously disturbed—and no responsible person can regard that without uneasiness) the framework of our culture. It is no use starting all over again with the theory with which the Victorian emancipators began; we have to look at the results of fifty years of experience and consider facts which worry thoughtful women. One is that it is the exceptional and not the average woman student who is the intellectual equal of the average serious undergraduate in the same subject. "Every year I have from one to two dozen men reading my subject [one of the humanities, taken by a comparable number of each sex, in which women generally get better preparation at school than men] with whom I can discuss it as equals. I have learned from long experience that among the women students there will be only one such in three years, if that." Observations of this kind from perfectly open-minded witnesses are not unusual, and substantiate the regular complaint of outstanding women students that there is a dearth of congenial intellectual company to be found in college— whereas the men can always find such company. Either, that is, the women's colleges do not cream the country as the men's do, or else there is precious little intellectual cream available for them to skim off. In relation to this, we may examine Mrs. Woolf's implication that women are victimized because they are restricted to about ten per cent of the students at both Oxford and Cambridge. It is an open secret that even at present the entrance lists can hardly be filled without lowering the standard of admission undesirably—this may well be because it is harder for intelligent girls at the lower end of the economic scale to get to college than for their brothers, but Mrs. Woolf is assured that none of these if up to honours standard is ever prevented from entering Oxford or Cambridge because the quota is filled. Again, Mrs. Woolf thinks it monstrous that the men's scholarship list at Cambridge is more than six times the length of the women's, but the general informed opinion seems to be that to throw all scholarships open to both sexes would mean that women would probably get fewer scholarships than at present, and rarely any in some subjects (scholarships being awarded on evidence of promise as well as of acquirements). To say that this is because women have not had the educational advantages of men, that is, of being taught by men at school, only puts the difficulty further back. The obvious course is to advocate co-education at an earlier stage than college, as a preliminary to women's storming the older universities. Mrs. Woolf's guns should have been trained not on the protectionists of the men's colleges, but on the women of her own class who don't give their daughters the chance to start fair with their brothers, but send them to conventual establishments where they never come up against masculine standards. Mrs. Woolf should logically be campaigning for two things—co-education from the primary to the boarding schools, and a change in the social structure which will allow the daughters of *any* men to enter upon the highest course of studies they are fitted for. As for the daughters of Mrs. Woolf's class, evidence suggests that they value the opportunities offered by the universities less than in the early days when these had to be struggled for. "I am in the minority of those who go there to work, and they think it funny," the daughter of an educated man, in her first year at one of the Oxford colleges, remarked to me recently. Perhaps related to this is the complaint often heard from intelligent Oxford undergraduates that the women students there make themselves a nuisance. It suggests another reason for deploring the tone of *Three Guineas*. One hears there is still plenty of sex-hostility about in the common-rooms and combination-rooms; but Mrs. Woolf only cites the indefensible manifestations of such an attitude, but women cannot afford to give such prejudice any grounding.

If from evidence of what limited progress we have made in equalizing the sexes we wish to move to a more profitable attack on theory than *Three Guineas* makes, there is *Sex and Temperament in Savage Society*. Miss Mead's investigation of different kinds of societies, where (*a*) the women are "masculine" in temperament and activities and the men "feminine," (*b*) both sexes are "masculine," (*c*) both are "feminine," provides real evidence (assuming the other anthropolgists have checked the sources) that many qualities and habits of feeling which we think sex-linked are the arbitrary results of social forms. If a competent social psychologist were to apply the findings of this book to the problems connected with emancipating women within our culture we might get somewhere at last. Certainly there is no longer any use in this field of speculation for the non-specialist like Mrs. Woolf.

(1938)

APPENDICES

APPENDIX A

Leavis and *The Calendar*

The relevance of The Calendar of Modern Letters *was suggested in the Introduction. F. R. Leavis published excerpts from it under the title* Towards Standards of Criticism. *Here is his Introduction, entitled "The Standards of Criticism":*

The Calendar of Modern Letters was founded in 1925, and died two a half years later, having been first a monthly and then a quarterly. How good it was while it lasted the following selection of criticism from its pages will show—evidence the more impressive when it is remembered that they had already yielded, among other things,* a volume of critical essays (*Scrutinies I*, edited by Edgell Rickword). *The Calendar* commanded the services of half a dozen really distinguished critics, each one better than any that finds frequent employment in existing periodicals, and was able to count on good work from a number of others. It was lively as well as intelligent. And yet it couldn't live. No one will suggest (it would, at any rate, be a misleading way of putting it) that it was killed by competition, or that the band of critics who served it disappeared from current criticism because, the function being over-provided-for, their talents were superfluous. They dispersed and did in effect disappear; and admiration for their work and concern to get it recognized and, if possible, bring them back into criticism would have been incentive enough to this selection, even if such admiration and concern had not necessarily involved a preoccupation with the general significance of their enterprise and fate, with the general plight that the history of *The Calendar* illustrates.

The force of the illustration depends, of course, upon the intrinsic value of the work represented. This value, it may be well to repeat, is such that, for the most part, no further significance was necessary

---

* E.g., *A Pamphlet against Anthologies*, by Laura Riding and Robert Graves, which appeared in its first form in *The Calendar; Anonymity*, by E. M. Forster; and some of the contents of *Transition* by Edwin Muir.

to justify the reprinting. Indeed, it had better be confessed at once (certain of the critics represented will probably not like the idea) that the undertaking was not altogether free from a pedagogic incentive: the bound volumes of *The Calendar* have been serving a certain educational purpose incomparably well, and further sets are unobtainable. Good criticism and intelligent discussion of literature are not common; *The Calendar* abounds with them in great variety—so far, in fact, as to be unique; and an introduction to it might make all the difference between a creditable "Arts" course product and the development of a mature intelligence. It will be gathered, then, that the intrinsic value is very high.

But, at the moment, it is the general significance that takes the stress—the decay in a modern civilized community of the function so admirably served by *The Calendar*. For if *The Calendar* could not find enough support, what hope (in default of generous patrons) can there be for any serious critical journal? And, as a matter of fact, in ways that everyone can instance—degeneration and decease —the signs have become decidly worse since the last issue of *The Calendar*: there is no need to particularize.

But perhaps "function," three sentences above, takes too much for granted; inquiry may start by considering how its own function appeared to *The Calendar*. The preliminary statement is cautious, but with a caution that derives, not from vagueness, timidity, or lack of conviction, but from a subtle appreciation of the problem in view:

> A preconceived idea is, as the artist knows, a tyrant dangerous to the proper organization of the impulse, definable in no other terms than those of the finished work which compels him to his strange exertion. The same reticence is necessary even in the humble creation of a Review, in which activity, since it is to some extent an aesthetic one, there is virtue not in intentions but in achievement only. We lay down no programme as to *The Calendar*'s performance nor prophecy as to its character, since these things cannot interest our readers till they have a tangible existence, and then we shall be ready to join our own criticism with theirs. A conviction of the value of spontaneous growth (or of growth which looks spontaneous to the watching mind), and of unpoliced expression, is as near as we can come to any public challenge or editorial doctrine.

Nevertheless, something more had to be there from the outset, since, as *The Calendar* says later in reviewing *The New Criterion*, "not even the bulkiest review can be boundlessly eclectic, and as soon as the element of choice is introduced the question of a principle or a programme becomes paramount"; and about its own "principle" *The Calendar* is, at the outset, explicit:

> In reviewing we shall base our statements on the standards of criticism, since it is only then that one can speak plainly without offence, or give praise with meaning.

These "standards of criticism" are assumed; nothing more is said about them. Nothing more needed to be said; for if we can appreciate—which is not necessarily to agree with—the reviewing in *The Calendar,* we know what they are, and if we cannot, then no amount of explaining or arguing will make much difference. (What is said of the reviewing bears, of course, on the choice of creative work.)

But the assumption of "standards of criticism" qualifies the previous account, briefly suggested, of the modern disintegration: "Today there is only the race, the biological-economic environment, and the individual." Where the recognition of standards of criticism can be counted on, then there is more than the individual; there is also some remnant of tradition, the common mind, the something more-than-individual that *The Calendar* refers to in its "Valediction":

> The value of a review must be judged by its attitude to the living literature of the time (which includes such works of the past as can be absorbed by the contemporary sensibility). . . .

Where there is a "living literature of the time" there is also a "contemporary sensibility," and it is always the business of criticism (whatever it may appear to be doing immediately) to define—that is, help to form—and organize this, and to make conscious the "standards" implicit in it. (This "contemporary," of course, as the passage just quoted indicates, includes the past, or as much of it as there is any access to.)

When disintegration, social and cultural, has set in, the business of criticism becomes very difficult of performance. In what senses there has been disintegration, and with what embarrassing consequences for the critic, the following extract from a review of Mrs. Woolf's *The Common Reader* suggests:

> The Victorians . . . took advantage of the lull before the storm and produced the last examples of the literature which retains its expressive value along the whole range of group-sensibilities. Since then, the reading-public has split. We have the small body of educated sharp-witted readers from whom a small spark of intelligence sometimes flickers, but being passionate, if at all, only about values and

not experience, ultimately uncreative; and themselves so frequently practitioners as to be unsatisfactory even as audience. Beyond lies the vast reading-public which is led by the nose by the high-class literary-journalist-poet type and its tail tweaked by the paragraphist with pretensions not rising above personal gossip.

Disintegration, it is plain, involves more than "splitting," and where it has gone so far that the "contemporary sensibility" depends on a negligible few—negligible, that is, in influence on the contemporary world—then the assertion of "standards," now indeed a matter of assertion, becomes "dogmatism": intellectuals, by way of discrediting a study of cultural decline, will remark that in it "'there are assumed certain standards of taste, which if properly understood and applied by a sensitive person, make it possible to estimate the value of any piece of literary work, and to *place* it in relation to any other literary work whatever." What such characteristic phrasing makes one hopeless of getting properly understood is the nature of "standards," the "standards" invoked in literary criticism—how, if they are not certified weights and measures lying ready to be picked up and applied from the outside, it should not then necessarily follow that they must be merely "immobilized personal preferences." *

Explanation is impotent where the "contemporary sensibility," the traditional "mind," with its memory (living—really living, and so changing—always in the present or not at all) and its sense of relative value, is not there to appeal to: discussion of values in the abstract, engaging nowhere, remains a barren academic exercise. When the "contemporary sensibility" is active, then the general doubt, of the form exemplified above, does not arise to be dealt with. Nor does the abstract possibility of estimating the value of any piece of literary work, and "placing" it in "relation to any other literary work whatever," propose itself for consideration or need to be considered. There may be a good deal of room for difference about particular valuations, but there is enough common understanding of what value is to make differences discussible, and enough agreement to make the question whether there has been a cultural decline in the past two centuries, say, a real and urgent one, and to make the effort towards standards fruitful in further and more conscious agreement.

In the conditions of disintegration contemplated above, the function (the corresponding importance of which was at the same time implicitly brought out) of defining and organizing the contem-

---

* ". . . *des préférences personnelles immobilisées.*"—Jules Lemaître.

porary sensibility must be at best extremely arduous. "The reader we have in mind, the ideal reader," though (*The Calendar* adds) he may not be "one with whom we share any particular set of admirations and beliefs," is the Common Reader, representing the "standards of criticism"; but a Common Reader who has to be created rather than addressed, though *The Calendar* puts the undertaking modestly:

> . . . the readers of a paper have their share in the formation of its individuality, though it may be designed in the first place with some imagined kind of reader in the foreground. As this hypothesis is corrected by the reality, the balance of sympathies and antipathies is adjusted into an unpredictable harmony.

At any rate, enough of the literary tradition survives to make the crystallization of a Common Reader a reasonable calculation.

The fact that the other traditional continuities have, as the introductory statement of *The Calendar* points out, so completely disintegrated, makes the literary tradition correspondingly more important, since the continuity of consciousness, the conservation of the collective experience, is the more dependent on it: if the literary tradition is allowed to lapse, the gap is complete. But what gives the literary tradition its unique importance also makes it desperately precarious. Can it last, we ask, in isolation, unsupported by extra-literary sanctions, and not merely in isolation, but in a hostile environment?

The question was, in a sense, raised in the brush that *The Calendar* had with *The Criterion*. For the "intellectualist reaction" and the "neo-classicism" animadverted upon represent a preoccupation with the pre-conditions of literature, with extra-literary traditions and sanctions. This is not the place to discuss the profitableness of the preoccupation in that particular instance, or the justice or otherwise of *The Calendar*'s animadversions. But it is the place, and fair, to remark the superior liveliness of *The Calendar* and its great critical superiority: there would at any rate seem to be little profit in a concern for tradition and for sanctions that is not associated with the "standards of criticism." Literary criticism provides the test for life and concreteness; where it degenerates, the instruments of thought degenerate too, and thinking, released from the testing and energizing contact with the full living consciousness, is debilitated, and betrayed to the academic, the abstract, and the verbal. It is of little use to discuss values if the sense for value in the concrete—the experience and perception of value—is absent.

> One can have little respect for the periodical which flaunts a pretension to philosophic righteousness and yet makes as many blunders with regard to the actual works of poetry or literature before it as the most unenlightened of its Georgian predecessors.

It is the praise of *The Calendar* that it had a right, in pronouncing its valediction, to say this.

At any rate, the sententious consolation may perhaps be permitted that there are worse things than death; for *The Calendar* it was that died. But it is a poor consolation if it leaves us to conclude that no intelligent review can support itself in the present age. The conclusion cannot be easily evaded; it is what the history of *The Calendar* seems to prove, and the subsequent history of critical journalism to corroborate. Anyway, it is certain, not merely that no good critic can now hope to make anything like a living by the exercise of his talents, but that he will be lucky if he is allowed to employ them, in public, at all. The situation is in that respect, as everyone qualified to report will agree, very much worse than it was before the episode of *The Calendar*.

And yet the Editors, in their "Valediction Forbidding Mourning," a finely poised piece of work, admirable in tone and phrasing, do not suggest hopelessness:

> We have decided to scuttle the ship, rather than have the leaks periodically stopped by a generous patron, because the present literary situation requires to be met by a different organization, which we are not now in a position to form. Could such an organization be formed, we should find means to bring it into play.

It would be interesting to know what kind of organization they have in mind. Beyond insisting that the standards of literary criticism—"the freedom to exercise an independent judgement on contemporary work"—must not be compromised, they give no hint.

Their insistence shows, at least, that they have not surrendered to the Marxist conclusion—or (it becomes convenient to change the tense) had not in 1927. Some readers, perhaps, have been waiting for the force of that conclusion to be recognized here. Tacit recognition might appear to have been conceded already in the picture of disintegration drawn above. When things have, by avowal, gone so far, does not worry about a moribund literary tradition condemn itself as patently futile? Can the intelligent and courageous justify to themselves any but a concern, a direct concern, with fundamentals, with the task of social regeneration—social regeneration, which means, in the first place, revolution, economic and political? The case looks strong. And it is unlikely that anyone who has been interested enough to read the present disquisition as far as this does not hold economic and political action to be urgent. But some may feel that "fundamentals," above, covers a dangerous simplification.

There can be no pretence of dealing fairly with the Marxist position here. A different position must merely be asserted—that of those who think that the inevitability (and desirability) of drastic social changes makes an active concern for cultural continuity the more essential, and that the conditions of clear thinking, and of wisdom with regard to human values and ends, do not need the less attention because we are, inevitably, to suffer more confusion and disorientation.

Nevertheless, the episode of *The Calendar* has a certain finality. There would be no point in repeating the experiment. It will be a radically "different organization" that offers any hope. A review, to have any chance of surviving, must enlist a far more active support than can be won for any merely literary review, however lively and intelligent. No one doubts (is it safe to say?) that there are in the English-speaking world some thousands of potential readers of such a review as *The Calendar*: that is implied in the possibility of referring to the "contemporary sensibility." But if, amid the distractions of the modern scene, they are to be marshalled in sufficient numbers, it must be by finding some way of enlisting a very active conviction that the "contemporary sensibility" matters very much to the contemporary world: the function and the conviction cannot now be taken for granted as they might in other days.

Indeed, one cannot think of success merely in terms of a review. "Organization" would involve a "movement" of some kind, a more general reaction, provoked by the extremity of the plight; for one must count on such a reaction as natural, and be ready to exploit it, if one finds hope worth entertaining and the cause important.

This attempt to enlarge on *The Calendar*'s hint of "a different organization" hardly gets closer to particularity: its negative effect, emphasizing the desperateness of the case, will for most readers be the predominant. This is inevitable, for, as *The Calendar,* in its "Valediction," says: "such a combination as we envisage is dependent on the happy meeting of many contingencies." It must be a matter of quickness to take advantage of opportunities, and if one sees them, the only effective account of them will be the actual enterprise.

This much more may be ventured by way of suggesting possibilities—a kind of earnest of seriousness, a hostage; for, in face of the situation recognized above, only the kind of seriousness that drives directly at practice, and invites that test, has the right to persist in hope: if a campaign for standards in literary criticism, together with the relevant attention to contemporary civilization in general, could be effectively associated with a movement in the educational field—it is perhaps best to leave it at the aposiopesis, though this will not be found, by many, exhilarating, for "academic" and "scholastic" are discouraging words. Yet if corporate spirit (this is not to entertain illusions about the average quality of the profession in any branch—"average" says little) can be anywhere effectively mobilized for disinterested ends it is in education. A fantastic hope?—"such a combination . . . is dependent on the happy meeting of many contingencies."

It is now time to turn to the contents of the present volume. These are all critical. It must be said in passing that in the creative work it published *The Calendar* maintained the "standards of criticism" as seriously as in its essays and reviews, although, inevitably, the level of actual, achieved, intrinsic quality is not so consistent. It printed, among others of distinction, D. H. Lawrence (it printed some of his best criticism, too) and T. F. Powys. The generosity with which it supported contemporary literature would count for much in the "leaks" that led to the "scuttling" of the ship. But the review that cannot attempt a similar generosity is gravely limiting its function.

The main difficulty, other than economic, is to be sufficently encouraging to experimental and young work without any serious damage to standards. Of reviewing, too, the editors say, in their introductory statement: "It is difficult to keep those standards in a little space and still to be just to contemporary work which is perhaps immature." In the ways in which it tackled this difficulty *The Calendar* can fairly be held up as a model for a critical journal. The illustrations in this selection are of critical method—procedure in actual reviewing. There is no need to specify examples of the analysis that is more interesting than the book reviewed: of the pretentious book disposed of with judicial quietness as a typecase; of the serious, but unachieved, intention that is, as undiscouragingly as possible, "placed" and made the opportunity for generalizations. The variety of procedure, of profitable critical practice, illustrated is not even suggested in these remarks; but, in any case, it hardly needs insisting on.

The point is that all this is possible where there are real critics and an intelligent conception of criticism. Where there is a grasp of principle, on the one hand, and an intelligent interest in the contemporary situation, on the other, some sense of its outlines, structure, and points of tension, then the ordinary year's publishing offers enough opportunities for profitable criticism to keep a serious review going. But to ask for these qualifications is to ask a great deal. For instance, where is a critic to find help with "principles" in criticizing fiction, the head under which the bulk of the output demanding attention will come? With little more than a few hints from Henry James—from the prefaces and *Notes on Novelists*—he will have to do everything for himself.

Or, rather, would, if there were not *The Calendar* to hand. For *The Calendar* contains—this selection from it contains—as good an introduction to the criticism of the novel as one can reasonably ask for, as much help as a potentional critic needs. Not only is its critical practice good; it offers an examination and statement of principle that should have become a *locus classicus*. If anyone is still wondering why it is that Mr. Percy Lubbock's *Craft of Fiction,* for all its scholarly nicety, seems to make no difference, let him read "A Note on Fiction," by C. H. Rickword.* The answer is given at the outset, in the axiom from which the "Note" starts: "the problem of language, the use of the medium in all its aspects, is the basic problem of any work of literature." All preoccupation with "form," "structure," "method," "technique," that is not controlled by this axiom must be more or less barren.

A novel, like a poem, is made of words; there is nothing else one can point to. We talk of a novelist as "creating characters," but the process of "creation" is one of putting words together. We discuss the quality of his "vision," but the only critical judgements we can attach directly to observable parts of his work concern particular arrangements of words—the quality of the response they evoke. Criticism, that is, must be in the first place (and never cease being) a matter of sensibility, of responding sensitively and with precise discrimination to the words on the page. But it must, of course, go on to deal with the larger effects, with the organization of the total response to the book. The "total response," what is it? We speak of "form":

---

* Reprinted in *Forms of Modern Fiction* ed. O'Connor (1948).

. . . the form of a novel only exists as a balance of response on the part of the reader. Hence schematic plot is a construction of the reader's that corresponds to an aspect of that response and stands in merely diagrammatic relation to the source. Only as precipitate from the memory are plot or character tangible; yet only in solution have either any emotive valency. The composition of this fluid is a technical matter. The technique of the novel is just as symphonic as the technique of the drama and as dependent, up to a point, on the dynamic devices of articulation and control of narrative tempo. But, though dependent, it is dependent as legs are on muscles, for the *how* but not the *why* of movement; and, interesting as functional technique may be to the mechanical minded and to workers in the same medium on the look-out for tips, the organic is the province of criticism.

Here we have, in more explicit form, the comment on such studies as *The Craft of Fiction*. Few reviewers will be grateful for it; it hardly makes the business of criticism any easier. And the remark that " 'Character' is merely the term by which the reader alludes to the pseudo-objective image he composes of his responses to the author's verbal arrangements" will not deter the ordinary critic or conversationalist from wondering why it is that D. H. Lawrence, though not interested in character, appears to matter, or from assuming that to note the "unreality" of T. F. Powys's characters is to make an adverse criticism on *Mr. Weston's Good Wine*.

But for those who are concerned to develop for themselves a critical technique for the novel there is more here than a warning against the usual divagations and irrelevances. The positive approach is suggested, and its general nature made unmistakably plain. No one can be fitted with critical sensibility, but, having that, one can be helped to apply it. The problem is to go beyond the words on the page without losing touch with them; to develop a technique for keeping the sensibility always in control in one's inevitable dealings with abstractions and "precipitates from the memory." When the problem is so envisaged, it becomes plain that one can no more be given a detailed technique than one can be given a sensibility. Such help as C. H. Rickword offers must remain, in the nature of the case, fairly general. But that is not to go back on the judgement that he offers a great deal—as much, essentially, as can be taken. The generality of the following, for instance, will be rich in particular profit for those capable of taking anything. He is considering Professor Gaselee's pronouncement that, "Brought up on good novels, we are bored with their rude predecessors of antiquity," since, in these last, "Of psychology there is barely a trace ... any attempt indeed at character-drawing is faint and rough."

> If we offered him Homer, even Homer in an English prose translation, we should hear, instead of these wails of hunger, the happy noises of prolonged mastication. Now, it cannot be contended that the addition of a little psychology and character-drawing to a chain of events makes all the difference between aesthetic starvation and satisfaction, but some quality inherent in those events. And it is this quality that is common to all great works of literature, in no matter what genre. It is a unity among the events, a progressive rhythm that includes and reconciles each separate rhythm. As manifested in the novel, it resolves, when analysed, chiefly into character and plot in a secondary, schematic sense—qualities that are purely fictitious.

This bringing together of fiction and poetry is the more richly suggestive because of the further assimilation it instigates. The differences between a lyric, a Shakespeare play, and a novel, for some purposes essential, are in no danger of being forgotten; what needs insisting on is the community. And this for the sake not merely of critical principle, but of immediate profit in critical technique (principle that does not bear on technique is of little interest).

"Rhythm," as the term is used in the passage just quoted, and as explicated by Dr. I. A. Richards in *The Principles of Literary Criticism,* is comparatively easy to understand and to illustrate in a lyric. *Macbeth* is extremely more complex, yet the same approach and essentially the same method apply; the development is continuous, as suggested in the elaborate account of "rhythm" (*The Principles of Literary Criticism,* p. 137):

> Grammatical regularities, the necessity for completing the thought, the reader's state of conjecture as to what is being said, his apprehension in dramatic literature of the action, of the intention, situation, state of mind generally, of the speaker, all these and many other things intervene. . . . This texture of expectations, satisfactions, disappointments, surprisals, which the *sequence of syllables* brings about, is rhythm.

One may feel that "rhythm" in this development becomes a very elusive concept, but the formulation is full of sound suggestion for approach and critical method, and has the virtue of constantly referring one back to "the sequence of syllables" (italicized above for the present purpose)—to the words on the page. It suggests what the critical analysis of a Shakespeare play would be. If one adds that it suggests, what would be the critical analysis of a novel, no one will now suppose that novel and play are thus assimilated because they both contain characters.

It is in the opposite direction that the argument points, and the room it has taken will have been justified if this proposition is now seen to have some force: that if one is not intelligent about poetry one is unlikely to be intelligent about fiction, and the connoisseur of fiction who disclaims an interest in poetry is probably not interested in literature. And the proposition holds as essentially of novels where the staple medium appears to be much like that of the essayist or the historian as of those which C. H. Rickword, anticipating a recent observation of Mr. T. S. Eliot, has in mind here: "the main thing to be noted about the new 'subjective' novelists is their increasing tendency to rely for their effects not on set pieces of character-drawing, but directly on the poetic properties of words."

To the reader who complains that he has still been brought no nearer to a working technique of criticism it must be repeated that nothing more can be done for him—unless, perhaps, by the example of good practice. Of this last there is abundance in *The Calendar*. Monthly reviewing, of course, gives little opportunities for elaborate exhibitions of critical method, and the ordinary year's publishing little occasion. But, working within the inevitable limitations, *The Calendar*'s critics performed their function exemplarily.

"A Note on Fiction," then, together with the varied reviews assembled with it in a section of the present book, constitutes an incomparable aid to the intelligent criticism of novels. This section alone would make the book important.

If the section relating to poetry has not the same kind of importance, that is not because it is less remarkable, interesting, and intelligent, but because the need here is less acute: criticism of poetry is rather less desperately backward than that of fiction. Nevertheless, to do justice to the achievement of *The Calendar,* one should remind oneself of a few comparative dates. *The Calendar* was, for instance, in time to review *The Principles of Literary Criticism.* By the time the *Poems* of Mr. Eliot appeared for review, it had, in reviews and essays, laid down the grounds of criticism upon which Mr. Eliot was to be duly appraised, so that the recognition of his significance came as a matter of course. This is easily said and may not sound impressive. But let the reader compare *The Calendar*'s criticism of poetry with that of any other critical journal over those three years, and *The Calendar* will be found to stand alone. It *assumed* that re-education which was necessary before the contemporary re-orientation of English poetry could be recognized and appreciated. But where at that time, apart from Mr. Eliot's essays, were the incitements and aids to such a re-education to be found?

The Calendar provided these, for its "assuming" was a very active matter. Thus we find Mr. Edgell Rickword noting, in 1925, in a discussion of "The Use of the Negative Emotions":

> The modern poet is to his audience an author, not a man. It is interested in his more generalized emotions, not in his relations with the life and people round him. Yet to himself the poet should be in the first place a man, not an author. He should not be conscious of the distinction between the sensations he gets from his immediate contact with things and the sensations he uses as the material of his art. At present he is inhibited from using a set of emotions (those we call negative emotions) because of a prejudice against them. . . .

At about the same date, Mr. Douglas Garman, glancing over contemporary criticism, is forced to conclude:

> The inference, that poetry is looked upon as being unconnected with a radically intelligent activity, is only too well supported by the facts. . . .

In the two essays from which these quotations come the reorientation of the last decade is defined, and the critical basis established for appreciating Mr. Eliot, Mr. Pound, and their successors.

From this brief account it must be plain that the intrinsic quality of the section "Poetry" is high. It contains some admirable treatment of general questions, some very fine examples of "practical criticism," and a number of patterns for reviewers—illustrations, among other things, of the critical profit that intrinsically uninteresting work can be made to yield (see *e.g.*, the notices of Mr. Noyes and Mr. Binyon).

Some indication has now been given of the arrangement adopted in this book. After "Fiction" and "Poetry" comes the classification, "General Criticism." Under this head are included, with some unavoidable arbitrariness, items of various kinds, dealing with the theory and method of criticism and with general questions—essays, articles, and reviews of critical works.

The last head, "Miscellaneous," needs no comment.

It may be well, before ending, to anticipate some criticism. The characteristic fault of *The Calendar*'s critical writing may be described as corrugation—excessive difficulty. In determining, with severe effort, what the author meant, one may find, rather too often, clearer ways of saying it. But explanations enough of the fault suggest themselves at once: to have to start so much from the beginning and do everything for oneself does not conduce to smoothness of exposition. And that the difficulty is worth wrestling with is usually obvious at once.

Again, some readers may object to the tone of certain reviews, as being unnecessarily inurbane and unkind. All that need be said here is that not everything chosen was chosen for its judicial poise, and that a critical organ that cannot on occasion take the kind of liberty represented is in danger of something worse than inurbanity and injustice. And what one of the editors writes, discussing the "Audience," would cover far more than all that might be found to need excusing in *The Calendar*:

> There is no longer a body of opinion so solid as that represented by *The Quarterly, The Edinburgh* and *Blackwood's*. The fact that they pronounced a vigorous aesthetic creed, and were, therefore, of the greatest benefit to a lively interest in poetry, is forgotten, because they were sometimes ungentlemanly, and their place has been taken, but not filled, by the torrential journalistic criticism which is poured out daily, weekly, and monthly, and is so enlightened and refined that the fulfillment of its obvious function is overlooked in its efforts to be open-minded and polite. There has never been such a rubbishy flow of poetry as that which is vomited by contemporary publishers, yet the reading public has never expressed its opinion through such mealy-mouthed critics. Smut alone has moved their costive sensibilities to a definite opinion, and then their violence was only equalled by their obtuseness. For the most part their opinions are diluted with the oils of snobbism or social decorum.

It has, then, been answered—the inevitable question: why reprint the reviewing of an obscure periodical that died half a dozen years ago? If the answer is not found convincing the fault is with the answerer, for the case intrinsically is as strong as one could ask for. But the following pages, if read, will answer for themselves.

(1933)

APPENDIX B

The Contents of *Scrutiny*, Volumes I to XV, (1932-1948)

The present anthology can hardly suggest the full range of *Scrutiny*, 1932-1948. Nor is *Scrutiny* the kind of magazine that is shown off to best advantage by excerpts. It is distinguished, rather, for the standards it has consistently maintained through thousands of pages. The casual reader may therefore be interested in glancing over the following table of contents. The more zealous reader will not be so easily satisfied. The table, I hope, will send him to the files of *Scrutiny* itself, even if this means, as it probably will, a visit to a university library. *Scrutiny* has not up to now been indexed—even annually. Consequently, those of us who wanted to know if *Scrutiny* contained an article on such and such had to search through the whole file. This appendix should save future investigators a little trouble. It is not, of course, an index, nor, even as a table of contents, is it in all ways complete. (A few books, for instance, which were rather noticed than reviewed have been omitted from the list of titles.) But perhaps it is better than nothing.

Volume I (1932-1933)

No. 1

A Manifesto, by The Editors
A Note on Nostalgia, by D. W . Harding
"The Literary Mind," by F. R. Leavis
Notes on the Style of Mrs. Woolf, by M. C. Bradbrook
On a Grave of the Drowned, a poem, by Ronald Bottrall
The Political Background, by G. Lowes Dickinson
The Development of the Public School, by Martin Crusoe
Release, a Poem, by C. H. Peacock
The Art-Form of Democracy, by William Hunter

BOOKS REVIEWED *

——— *What Would Be the Character of a New War? (H. L. Elvin)*
Angell, Norman: *The Unseen Assassins (H. L. Elvin)*

----
* Reviewers' names in parentheses.

Chase, Stuart: *The Nemesis of American Business (Q. D. Leavis)*
The Tragedy of Waste (Q. D. Leavis)
Men and Machines (Q. D. Leavis)
Mexico (Q. D. Leavis)
Culpin, Millais, and Smith, May: *The Nervous Temperament (D. W. Harding)*
Flexner, Abraham: *Universities: American, English and German (Willard Thorp)*
Fox, Charles: *The Mind and its Body (D. W. Harding)*
Fuller, Major-General J. F. C.: *The Dragon's Teeth (H. L. Elvin)*
Huxley, Aldous: *Brave New World (Joseph Needham)*
Leavis, F. R.: *New Bearings in English Poetry (D. W. Harding)*
Murchison, Carl, ed.: *Psychologies of 1930 (D. W. Harding)*
Read, Herbert, and Dobrée, Bonamy, ed.: *The London Book of English Prose (L. C. Knights)*
Tennant, F. R.: *Philosophy of the Sciences (J. L. Russell)*
Wells, H. G.: *The Work, Wealth and Happiness of Mankind (F. R. Leavis)*
Wingfield-Stratford, Esmé: *They that Take the Sword (H. L. Elvin)*

No. 2

"Enlightened" Education, by Alan Keith-Lucas
The Chinese Renaissance, by I. A. Richards
The New Bentham, by Michael Oakeshott
What's Wrong with Criticism?, by F. R. Leavis
Eagles and Trumpets for the Middle Classes, by H. L. Elvin
Excursion, a Poem, by C. H. Peacock

BOOKS REVIEWED

Allen, Frederick Lewis: *Only Yesterday (Donald Culver)*
Auden, W. H.: *The Orators: An English Study (Douglas Garman)*
Bradby, C. F.: *About English Poetry (Denys Thompson)*
Chesterton, G. K.: *Chaucer (H. M. R. Murray)*
Coleridge, Samuel Taylor: *Unpublished Letters of,* ed. Griggs *(Edmund Blunden)*
Dos Passos, John: *Manhattan Transfer (F. R. Leavis)*
The Forty-Second Parallel (F. R. Leavis)
Nineteen-Ninteen (F. R. Leavis)
Dreiser, Theodore: *Tragic America (Donald Culver)*
Faulkner, William: *Sartoris (Willard Thorp)*
Fowler, J. H.: *The Art of Teaching English (Denys Thompson)*

APPENDICES

Kimmins, C. W., and Rennie, Belle: *The Triumph of the Dalton Plan (W. H. Auden)*
Lyon, P. H. B.: *The Discovery of Poetry (Denys Thompson)*
Maclean, Catherine Macdonald: *Dorothy Wordsworth: The Early Years (Edmund Blunden)*
Marcy, W. Nichols: *Reminiscences of a Public Schoolboy (W. H. Auden)*
Percy, Lord Eustace, ed.: *The Year Book of Education (W. H. Auden)*
Richards, I. A.: *Mencius on the Mind (D. W. Harding)*
Ridley, M. R.: *Poetry and the Ordinary Reader (Denys Thompson)*
Shillan, David: *Exercises in Criticism (Denys Thompson)*
Smith, Elsie: *An Estimate of William Wordsworth, by his Contemporaries, 1793-1822 (Edmund Blunden)*
Strong, L. A. G.: *Common Sense About Poetry (Denys Thompson)*
Westermarck, Edward: *Ethical Relativity (James Smith)*
Wilson, Edmund: *Devil Take the Hindmost (Donald Culver)*
Wilson, J. Dover: *The Essential Shakespeare (Douglas Garman)*

No. 3

Editorial Note
Under Which King, Bezonian? (Editorial), by F. R. Leavis
Festivals of Fire, Section I, by Ronald Bottrall
Surréalisme, by Henri Fluchère
Two Poems, by Selden Rodman
Marvell's "Garden," by William Empson
Advertising God, by Denys Thompson
Will Training Colleges Bear Scrutiny?, by L. C. Knights
From "Coolstone Park," a Novel, by C. H. Peacock

BOOKS REVIEWED

Barbusse, Henri: *Zola (Q. D. Leavis)*
Blake, William: *Visions of the Daughters of Albion (F. R. Leavis)*
Burns, C. Delisle: *Leisure in the Modern World (F. R. Leavis)*
Butler, A. S. G.: *The Substance of Architecture (Donald Culver)*
Church, Richard: *News from the Mountain (Gilbert Armitage)*
Crowther, J. G.: *Industry and Education in Soviet Russia (Montagu Slater)*
Filene, Edward A.: *Successful Living in This Machine Age (F. R. Leavis)*
Haldane, J. B. S.: *The Causes of Evolution (S. A. Asdell)*

Lawrence, D. H.: *The Letters of*, ed. Huxley *(F. R. Leavis)*
Lewis, Wyndham: *The Doom of Youth (Douglas Garman)*
　　　　　　　　Filibusters in Barbary (Douglas Garman)
　　　　　　　　The Enemy of the Stars (Douglas Garman)
　　　　　　　　Snooty Baronet (Douglas Garman)
Meiklejohn, Alexander: *The Experimental College (F. R. Leavis)*
Piaget, J.: *The Moral Judgement of the Child (D. W. Harding)*
Pope, Arthur: *An Introduction to the Language of Painting and Drawing (Donald Culver)*
Shaw, Bernard: *Music in London 1890-94 (Bruce Pattison)*
Trotsky, Leon: *The History of the Russian Revolution*, Vol. I *(W. A. Edwards)*
Van Doren, Mark: *The Poetry of John Dryden (Sherard Vines)*
Warner, Sylvia Townsend: *The Salutation (Q. D. Leavis)*
Wölfflin, Heinrich: *Principles of Art History (Donald Culver)*
Woolf, Virginia: *The Common Reader: Second Series (Denys Thompson)*

No. 4

Appeal to Readers
Restatements for Critics (Editorial), by F. R. Leavis
Culture and Leisure, by A. L. Morton
Evaluations (I): I. A. Richards, by D. W. Harding
History and the Marxian Method, by H. Butterfield
Notes on Comedy, by L. C. Knights
English Work in the Public School, by Martin Crusoe
Wordsworth and Professor Babbitt, by Roy Morrell

BOOKS REVIEWED

Angell, Norman: *The Press and the Organization of Society (Geoffrey Grigson)*
Bentham, Jeremy: *Theory of Fictions*, ed. Ogden *(I. A. Richards)*
Churchill, the Rt. Hon. Winston S.: *Thoughts and Adventures (W. H. Auden)*
Eliot, T. S.: *Selected Essays (Edgell Rickword)*
Goodman, Richard, ed.: *Oxford Poetry 1932 (Gilbert Armitage)*
Hunter, William: *Scrutiny of Cinema (J. Isaacs)*
Knight, G. Wilson: *The Shakespearean Tempest (M. C. Bradbrook)*
Porteus, Hugh Gordon: *Wyndham Lewis, a Discursive Exposition (T. R. Barnes)*
Potocki, Count of Montalk: *Snobbery with Violence (Gilbert Armitage)*

Read, Herbert: *Form in Modern Poetry (James Smith)*
Squire, J. C.: *A Face in Candlelight (Geoffrey Grigson)*
Squire, J. C., ed.: *Younger Poets of To-Day (Geoffrey Grigson)*

Vol. II (1933-1934)

No. 1

A Cure for Amnesia, by Denys Thompson
Revaluations (I): John Webster, by W. A. Edwards
Festivals of Fire, Section II, by Ronald Bottrall
Evaluations (II): Croce, by James Smith
English Tradition and Idiom, by Adrian Bell
The French Novel of To-Day, by Henri Fluchère
"Hero and Leander," by M. C. Bradbrook

BOOKS REVIEWED

——— *Essays in Order,* No. 1 to No. 8 *(L. C. Knights)*
——— *New Verse,* Nos. 1 and 2 *(F. R. Leavis)*
Aldington, Richard: *The Eaten Heart (F. R. Leavis)*
Barton, J. E.: *Purpose and Admiration (Donald Culver)*
Campbell, Roy: *Flowering Reeds* (F. R. Leavis)
Chambers, Sir Edmund, ed.: *The Oxford Book of Sixteenth Century Verse (W. A. Edwards)*
Chestov, Leo: *In Job's Balances (Michael Oakeshott)*
Crosby, Harry: *Transit of Venus (F. R. Leavis)*
               Torchbearer (F. R. Leavis)
               Chariot of the Sun (F. R. Leavis)
               Sleeping Together (F .R. Leavis)
Dudley, Dorothy: *Dreiser and the Land of the Free (F. R. Leavis)*
Dunbar, William: *The Poems of,* ed. Mackenzie *(John Speirs)*
Elton, Oliver: *The English Muse (Douglas Garman)*
Faulkner, William: *Light in August (F. R. Leavis)*
Fausset, Hugh I'Anson: *The Lost Leader, a Study of Wordsworth (T. R. Barnes)*
Fry, Roger: *Characteristics of French Art (Donald Culver)*
Kaines-Smith, S. C.: *Art and Commonsense (Donald Culver)*
Lewis, C. Day: *The Magnetic Mountain (F. R. Leavis)*
Monroe, Harriet, ed.: *Poetry, a Magazine of Verse (F. R. Leavis)*
Pink, Alderton: *A Realist Looks at Democracy (Denys Thompson)*
               If the Blind Lead (Denys Thompson)
Reavey, George: *Faust's Metamorphoses (F. R. Leavis)*

Roberts, Michael, ed.: *New Signatures (F. R. Leavis)*
New Country (F. R. Leavis)
Spender, Stephen: *Poems (F. R. Leavis)*
Wilenski, R. H.: *The Meaning of Modern Sculpture (Donald Culver)*
Yeats, W. B.: *Words for Music Perhaps: and other Poems (M. C. Bradbrook)*

No. 2

XXX Cantos of Ezra Pound, by Ronald Bottrall
Milton's Verse, by F. R. Leavis
Scrutiny of Examinations, by L. C. Knights
To Maecenas, a Poem, by C. H. Peacock
Will Economics Follow the Robbins Road?, by Donald K. Kitchin
Mr. Kitchin on the Insignificance of Economics, by Harold E. Batson.

BOOKS REVIEWED

―――― *transition 22* etc., *(F. R. Leavis)*
Arnheim, Rudolf: *Film (William Hunter)*
Beckett, Samuel, and others: *Our Exagmination* etc. *(F. R. Leavis)*
Céline, L. F.: *Voyage au Bout de la Nuit (Douglas Garman)*
Dewey, John, and others: *The Educational Frontier (L. C. Knights)*
Edwards, W. A.: *Plagiarism: An Essay on Good and Bad Borrowing (John Speirs)*
Evans, B. Ifor: *English Poetry in the Later Nineteenth Century (Gorley Putt)*
Hausleiter, L.: *The Machine Unchained* (Denys Thompson)
Hecker, Julius F.: *Moscow Dialogues (Montagu Slater)*
Housman, A. E.: *The Name and Nature of Poetry (Gorley Putt)*
Jolas, Eugene: *The Language of Night (F. R. Leavis)*
Joyce, James: *Anna Livia Plurabelle (F. R. Leavis)*
Haveth Childers Everywhere (F. R. Leavis)
Two Tales of Shem and Shaun (F. R. Leavis)
Kellett, E. E.: *Literary Quotation and Allusion (John Speirs)*
Knight, G. Wilson: *The Christian Renaissance (F. R. Leavis)*
MacLeish, Archibald: *Conquistador* (F. R. Leavis)
Sitwell, Sacheverell: *Canons of Giant Art: Twenty Torsos in Heroic Landscapes (Frank Chapman)*
Ward, Harry F.: *In Place of Profit (Montagu Slater)*
Wolfe, Humbert: *Romantic and Unromantic Poetry (Gorley Putt)*

Wood, H. G.: *The Truth and Error of Communism (Montagu Slater)*

No. 3

On Metaphysical Poetry, by James Smith
French Literary Periodicals, by Henri Fluchère
Prospectus for a Weekly, by Denys Thompson
The Criticism of William Empson, by M. C. Bradbrook
The Significance of Economics Thus Conceived, by D. K. Kitchin
Foot-note to the Above, by H. Batson
Sonnet by Gongora and Translation, by E. M. Wilson
Revaluations (II): The Poetry of Pope, by F. R. Leavis

BOOKS REVIEWED

―― *Recent Social Trends in the United States (D. W. Harding)*
Bolitho, Hector: *Alfred Mond: First Lord Melchett (W. H. Auden)*
Eddington, Sir Arthur: *The Expanding Universe (C. A. Meredith)*
Eliot, T. S.: *The Use of Poetry and the Use of Criticism (D. W. Harding)*
Henryson, Robert: *The Poems and Fables of,* ed. Wood *(John Speirs)*
Isaacs, S. S.: *Social Development in Young Children (D. W. Harding)*
Jeans, Sir James: *The New Background of Science (C. A. Meredith)*
Leavis, F. R., ed.: *Towards Standards of Criticism (I. M. Parsons)*
Pound, Ezra, ed.: *Active Anthology (F. R. Leavis)*
Robertson, H. M.: *Aspects of the Rise of Economic Individualism (L. C. Knights)*
Stonier, G. W.: *Gog-Magog (Hugh Gordon Porteus)*
Strachey, Lytton: *Characters and Commentaries (T. R. Barnes)*
Sullivan, J. W. N.: *The Limitations of Science (C. A. Meredith)*
Taba, Hilda: *The Dynamics of Education (Raymond O'Malley)*
Woolf, Leonard, ed.: *The Intelligent Man's Way to Prevent War (H. L. Elvin)*
Yeats, W. B.: *The Winding Stair and Other Poems (F. R. Leavis)*

No. 4

Editorial
Revaluations (III): Burns, by John Speirs
The Scientific Best Seller, by J. L. Russell
The Irony of Swift, by F. R. Leavis

What Shall We Teach? by Denys Thompson
Fleet Street and Pierian Roses, by Q. D. Leavis

BOOKS REVIEWED

——— *Music and the Community* [Cambridgeshire Report] *(Bruce Pattison)*
Bulley, Margaret: *Art and Counterfeit (J. M. and D. W. Harding)*
Charques, R. D.: *Contemporary Literature and Social Revolution (Frank Chapman)*
Churchill, Charles: *Poems of,* ed. Lavev *(H. J. Edwards)*
Goldenweiser, Alexander: *History, Psychology, and Culture (D. W. Harding)*
Hennell, T.: *Change in the Farm (Adrian Bell)*
Madelin, Louis: *Le Consulat et l'Empire (H. Butterfield)*
Murry, J. Middleton: *William Blake (T. R. Barnes)*
Powell, Lord Baden: *Lessons from the Varsity of Life (W. H. Auden)*
Read, Herbert: *Art Now (J. M. and D. W. Harding)*
Roberts, Michael, ed.: *Elizabethan Prose (L. C. Knights)*
Sparrow, John: *Sense and Poetry (Hugh Gordon Porteus)*
Wilenski, R. H.: *The Modern Movement in Art (J. M. and D. W. Harding)*

Vol. III (1934-1935)

No. 1

Evaluations (III): Alfred North Whitehead, by James Smith
Revaluations (IV): Hardy the Novelist, by Frank Chapman
Amateurism and Professionalism in Economics, by H. E. Batson
The Work of L. H. Myers, by D. W. Harding
The Return of Odysseus, a Poem, by Richard Eberhart

BOOKS REVIEWED

Auden, W. H.: *Poems (F. R. Leavis)*
    The Dance of Death (F. R. Leavis)
Barker, George: *Thirty Preliminary Poems (Hugh Gordon Portens)*
    Alanna Autumnal (Hugh Gordon Porteus)
Biaggini, E. G.: *English in Australia (W. A. Edwards)*
Birch, Lionel: *The Waggoner on the Footplate (H. E. Batson)*
Bottrall, Ronald: *Festivals of Fire (F. R. Leavis)*
    The Loosening and Other Poems (F. R. Leavis)
Brooks, Collin: *The Economics of Human Happiness (H. E. Batson)*

Cole, G. D. H.: *The Intelligent Man's Review of Europe To-Day*
  [with Margaret Cole] *(H. E. Batson)*
    *The Intelligent Man's Guide through World
  Chaos (H. E. Batson)*
Cole, G. D., ed.: *What Everybody Wants to Know about Money
  (H. E. Batson)*
Mavrogordato, John: *Elegies and Songs (F. R. Leavis)*
Monro, Alida, ed.: *Recent Poetry 1923-1933 (F. R. Leavis)*
Muir, Edwin: *Variations on a Theme (F. R. Leavis)*
Palmer, Herbert: *Summit and Chasm (F. R. Leavis)*
Peers, R., ed.: *Adult Education in Practice (W. A. Edwards)*
Pekin, L. B.: *Progressive Schools, Their Principles and Practice
  (Eric Capon)*
Pudney, John: *Spring Encounter (F. R. Leavis)*
Read, Herbert: *The End of a War (F. R. Leavis)*
Sassoon, Siegfried: *The Road to Ruin (F. R. Leavis)*
Stoll, Elmer Edgar: *Art and Artifice in Shakespeare (L. C. Knights)*
Swingler, Randall: *Difficult Morning (F. R. Leavis)*
Thompson, Denys: *Reading and Discrimination (W. A. Edwards)*
Tillyard, E. M. W.: *Poetry Direct and Oblique (D. W. Harding)*
Turner, W. J.: *Jack and Jill (F. R. Leavis)*

No. 2

Oxford Letter, by H. A. Mason
Why Universities? by F. R. Leavis
Revaluations (V): Shakespeare's Sonnets, by L. C. Knights
History in the Classroom, by W. E. Brown
Advertising and Economic Waste, by C. H. P. Gifford

BOOKS REVIEWED

———*Modern Schools Handbook (Denys Thompson)*
——— *The Old School (Denys Thompson)*
Boughton, Rutland: *The Reality of Music (Bruce Pattison)*
Céline: *Journey to the End of the Night,* tr. Marks *(William
  Hunter)*
Curry, W. B.: *The School (Denys Thompson)*
Eliot, T. S.: *The Rock (D. W. Harding)*
    After Strange Gods (F. R. Leavis)
Hartley, Dorothy: *Here's England (Adrian Bell)*
Hecker, Julius F.: *Russian Sociology (H. W. Durant)*
Joad, C. E. M., ed.: *Manifesto (F. R. Leavis)*

Lambert, Constant: *Music Ho! (Bruce Pattison)*
Pound, Ezra: *A B C of Reading (H. A. Mason)*
Pundit, Ephraim, ed.: *Superman (H. A. Mason)*
Reavey, George, and Slonin, Marc, ed.: *Soviet Literature. An Anthology (D. S. Mirsky)*

No. 3

Culture and Early Environment, by Raymond O'Malley
Revaluations (VI): Wordsworth, by F. R. Leavis
The Novels of Jean Giono, by Henri Fluchère
The Religion of Progress, by J. L. Russell
Correspondence: from "Ephraim Pundit," John Sparrow, George Reavey, and Ronald Bottrall

BOOKS REVIEWED

Barker, Granville H., and Harrison, G. B., ed.: *A Companion to Shakespeare Studies (L. C. Knights)*
Dobrée, Bonamy: *Modern Prose Style (Frank Chapman)*
Dos Passos, John: *In All Countries (Frank Chapman)*
Eliot, T. S.: *Elizabethan Essays (L. C. Knights)*
Fitzgerald, F. Scott: *Tender Is the Night (D. W. Harding)*
Forster, E. M.: *Goldsworthy Lowes Dickinson (W. H. Auden)*
Henn, T. R.: *Longinus and English Criticism (James Smith)*
Heppenstall, Rayner: *John Middleton Murry (D. W. Harding)*
Lewis, C. Day: *A Hope for Poetry (H. A. Mason)*
McDougall, W.: *Religion and the Sciences of Life (C. E. Lucas)*
Murry, J. Middleton: *Aspects of Literature (D. W. Harding)*
Willey, Basil: *The Seventeenth Century Background (H. J. C. Grierson)*

No. 4

Proletarian Literature, by William Empson
Revaluations (VII): George Chapman (I) by James Smith
Unpublished Poems, by Isaac Rosenberg
Aspects of the Poetry of Isaac Rosenberg, by D. W. Harding
Musical History, by Bruce Pattison

BOOKS REVIEWED

Aiken, Conrad: *Landscape West of Eden (H. A. Mason)*
Bell, Adrian: *The Balcony (Sylvia Legge)*
Cantwell, Robert: *The Land of Plenty (Frank Chapman)*
Cecil, Lord David: *Early Victorian Novelists (Frank Chapman)*

Charles, Enid: *The Twilight of Parenthood (C. E. Lucas)*
Engle, Paul: *American Song (H. A. Mason)*
Gibbs, Evelyn: *The Teaching of Art in Schools (J. M. Harding)*
Ginsberg, Morris: *Sociology (H. W. Durant)*
Gould, Gerald, Lehmann, John, Roberts, D. K., ed.: *The Year's Poetry (H. A. Mason)*
Graves, Robert: *Claudius the God (D. W. Harding)*
Griffith, Lt. Wyn: *Branwen (H. A. Mason)*
Haskell, Arnold L.: *Balletomania (Erik Mesterton)*
Kendon, Frank: *Tristram (H. A. Mason)*
La Valette, John de, ed.: *The Conquest of Ugliness (J. M. Harding)*
Mangan, Sherry: *No Apology for Poetrie (H. A. Mason)*
Pound, Ezra: *Homage to Sextus Propertius (John Speirs)*
Pudney, John: *Open the Sky (H. A. Mason)*
Read, Herbert: *Art and Industry (J. M. Harding)*
Richards, I. A.: *Coleridge on Imagination (F. R. Leavis)*
Spender, Stephen: *Poems (H. A. Mason)*
      Vienna (H. A. Mason)
Taggard, Genevieve, and Fitts, Dudley, ed.: *Ten Introductions (H. A. Mason)*
Thomas, Dylan: *18 Poems (H. A. Mason)*
Tomlinson, R. R.: *Picture Making by Children (J. M. Harding)*
Wilenski, R. H.: *The Study of Art (J. M. Harding)*

Vol. IV (1935-1936)

No. 1

Preamble to a Great Adventure, a Poem, by Ronald Bottrall
Propaganda and Rationalization in War, by D. W. Harding
Approach to Ariosto, by J. H. Whitfield
A Hundred Years of the Higher Journalism, by Denys Thompson
The Scottish Ballads, by John Speirs
Revaluations (VII): George Chapman (II), by James Smith
Correspondence: from J. B. S. Haldane, J. L. Russell, W. Empson, and P. Mansell Jones

BOOKS REVIEWED

Anand, Mulk Raj: *Untouchable (Boman Mehta)*
Bateson, F. W.: *English Poetry and the English Language (F. R. Leavis)*
Boyle, Kay: *My Next Bride (H. A. Mason)*

Bradbrook, M. C.: *Themes and Conventions of Elizabethan Tragedy* (L. C. Knights)
Caldwell, Erskine: *American Earth* (H. A. Mason)
Clare, John: *The Poems of*, ed. Tibble *(John Speirs)*
Faulkner, William: *Pylon* (H. A. Mason)
Kingsmill, Hugh: *The Sentimental Journey (Frank Chapman)*
Lagerkvist, Pär: *The Eternal Smile,* tr. Harding and Mesterton (J. M. Parsons)
Moore, Marianne: *Selected Poems* (F. R. Leavis)
Murry, John Middleton: *Between Two Worlds* (D. W. Harding)
Myers, L. H.: *The Root and the Flower* (D. W. Harding)
Powys, T. F.: *Captain Patch* (H. A. Mason)
Saroyan, William: *The Daring Young Man on the Flying Trapeze* (H. A. Mason)
Smith, E. Sherwood: *The Faith of a Schoolmaster* (Raymond O'Malley)

No. 2

Lady Novelists and the Lower Orders, by Q. D. Leavis
"Intelligent Ideals of Urban Life," by Uno Åhrén
Tradition and Ben Jonson, by L. C. Knights
Revaluations (VIII): Shelley, by F. R. Leavis
Correspondence

BOOKS REVIEWED

Aldington, Richard: *Life Quest (John Speirs)*
Auden, W. H., and Isherwood, Christopher: *The Dog Beneath the Skin; or, Where Is Francis?* (T. R. Barnes)
Barker, George: *Poems (John Speirs)*
Benedict, Ruth: *Patterns of Culture* (D. W. Harding)
Brierley, W.: *Means Test Man* (W. H. Auden)
Crowther, J. G.: *British Scientists of the Nineteenth Century* (C. E. Lucas)
Eliot, T. S.: *Murder in the Cathedral* (T. R. Barnes)
Gurrey, P.: *The Appreciation of Poetry* (Frank Chapman)
Henderson, Philip: *Literature and a Changing Civilization* (L. C. Knights)
Hilton, Jack: *Caliban Shrieks* (W. H. Auden)
Holt, William: *I Was a Prisoner* (W. H. Auden)
Hopkins, Gerard Manley: *The Letters of*, ed. Abbott *(F. R. Leavis)*
Johnson, Alan Campbell, ed.: *Growing Opinions* (W. H. Auden)
Lewis, C. Day: *A Time to Dance (John Speirs)*

Maugham, W. Somerset: *Don Fernando (E. M. Wilson)*
Pound, Ezra: *A Draft of Cantos XXXI-XLI (John Speirs)*
Potter, Stephen: *Coleridge and S. T. C. (R. G. Cox)*
Read, Herbert: *Poems 1914-1934 (John Speirs)*
Spender, Stephen: *The Destructive Element (H. A. Mason)*

No. 3

English Poetry in the Seventeenth Century, by F. R. Leavis
The Maddermarket Theatre, by T. R. Barnes
Thomas Hobbes, by Michael Oakeshott
The Critical Writings of George Santayana, by Q. D. Leavis

BOOKS REVIEWED

Aiken, Conrad: *King Coffin (Q. D. Leavis)*
Auden, W. H., and Garrett, John: *The Poet's Tongue (Denys Thompson)*
Barker, George: *Janus (Frank Chapman)*
Doughty, Charles M.: *Selected Passages from "The Dawn in Britain,"* ed. Fairley *(F. R. Leavis)*
Empson, William: *Poems (H. A. Mason)*
Garnett, David: *Beany-Eye (Q. D. Leavis)*
Graham, Angus, ed: *The Golden Grindstone (Unsigned)*
Gropius, Walter: *The New Architecture and the Bauhaus,* tr. Shand *(Herbert Read)*
Macdiarmid, Hugh: *Second Hymn to Lenin and Other Poems (F. R. Leavis)*
Macneice, Louis: *Poems (Frank Chapman)*
Matthiessen, F. O.: *The Achievement of T. S. Eliot (H. A. Mason)*
Millin, Sarah Gertrude: *The South Africans (Unsigned)*
Orage, A. R.: *Selected Essays and Critical Writings of,* ed. Read and Saurat *(F. R. Leavis)*
Richardson, Dorothy: *Clear Horizon (Q. D. Leavis)*
Santayana, George: *The Last Puritan: a Memoir in the Form of a Novel (Q. D. Leavis)*
Spurgeon, Caroline F. E.: *Shakespeare's Imagery and What it Tells Us (R. G. Cox)*
Treener, Anne: *Charles M. Doughty: a Study of his Prose and Verse (F. R. Leavis)*
Tretiakov, S.: *Chinese Testament (Unsigned)*
Waln, Nora: *The House of Exile (Unsigned)*
Ward, Richard Heron: *The Powys Brothers (F. R. Leavis)*

No. 4

Scrutiny of Modern Greats, by E. W. F. Tomlin
English for the School Certificate: a Note, by Frank Chapman
Tragic Philosophy, by G. Santayana
Revaluations (IX): Keats, by F. R. Leavis
Post Obitum: Diaghileff, Pavlova, by Vladimir Kameneff
The Tendencies of Bergsonism, by H. B. Parkes

BOOKS REVIEWED

Bews, J. W.: *Human Ecology (C. E. Lucas)*
Burney, Charles: *A General History of Music*, ed. Mercer *(Bruce Pattison)*
Cummings, A. J.: *The Press (Denys Thompson)*
Davis, H. L.: *Honey in the Horn (Q. D. Leavis)*
Empson, William: *Some Versions of Pastoral (H. A. Mason)*
Fanfani, Anintore: *Catholicism, Protestantism and Capitalism (L. C. Knights)*
Gascoyne, David: *A Short Survey of Surrealism (Geoffrey Walton)*
Grigson, Geoffrey, ed.: *The Arts To-day (Geoffrey Walton)*
Kameneff, V.: *Russian Ballet Through Russian Eyes (D. W. Harding and E. M.)*
Prokosch, Frederic: *The Asiatics (E. S. Huelin)*
Riding, Laura, ed.: *Epilogue: a Critical Summary*, Vol. I *(Geoffrey Walton)*
Stokes, Adrian: *Russian Ballets (D. W. Harding and E. M.)*
Stovin, Harold: *Totem: The Exploitation of Youth (Frank Chapman)*
Woodworth, Mary Katharine: *The Literary Career of Sir Samuel Egerton Brydges (R. G. Cox)*
Young, Stark: *So Red the Rose (Q. D. Leavis)*

Volume V (1936-1937)

No. 1

The Robber Barons, by Denys Thompson
English Poetry in the Eighteenth Century, by F. R. Leavis
Psychology and Criticism, by Richard March
Psychology and Criticism: a Comment, by D. W. Harding
Shakespeare and Profit Inflation, by L. C. Knights
A Note on Hopkins and Duns Scotus, by W. H. Gardner

BOOKS REVIEWED

———— *British Armaments and World Peace (Denys Thompson)*
———— *The Press Campaign for Rearmament (Denys Thompson)*
———— *The Roots of War (Denys Thompson)*
———— *Verbatim Summary of the Evidence presented by the Union of Democratic control before the Royal Commission on the Private Manufacture of and Trading in Arms (Denys Thompson)*
Brown, Alec: *The Fate of the Middle Classes (E. W. F. Tomlin)*
Bonington, R. and B.: *The Citizen Faces War (Denys Thompson)*
Eliot, T. S.: *Essays Ancient and Modern (F. R. Leavis)*
Forster, E. M.: *Abinger Harvest (Q. D. Leavis)*
Hamilton, Mary Agnes: *Newnham (Sylvia Legge)*
Huxley, Aldous: *What Are You Going to Do About It? (Denys Thompson)*
Meldrum, Roy: *An English Technique (T. R. Barnes)*
Murry, John Middleton: *Shakespeare (R. G. Cox)*
Myers, L. H.: *Strange Glory (Geoffrey Walton)*
Parsons, I. M., ed.: *The Progress of Poetry (F. R. Leavis)*
Read, Herbert: *In Defence of Shelley and Other Essays (H. A. Mason)*
Roberts, Michael, ed.: *The Faber Book of Modern Verse (F. R. Leavis)*
Singh, Iqbal: *When One Is in It (Som Nath Chib)*
Spender, Stephen: *The Burning Cactus (E. S. Huelin)*
Verschoyle, Derek, ed.: *The English Novelists (Q. D. Leavis)*

No. 2

Oxford Letter, by E. W. F. Tomlin
Jules Laforgue, by G. M. Turnell
Tight-ropes to Parnassus: a Note on Contemporary Music, by W. H. Mellers
"Antony and Cleopatra" and "All for Love": A Critical Exercise, by F. R. Leavis

BOOKS REVIEWED

———— *The New Survey of London Life and Labour*, Vol. IX, *Life and Leisure (D. W. Harding)*
Ayer, A. J.: *Language, Truth and Logic (E. W. F. Tomlin)*
Bell, Adrian, ed.: *The Open Air, an Anthology of English Country Life (Frank Chapman)*

Blake, Howard: *Prolegomena to Any Future Poetry (Geoffrey Walton)*
Deutsch, Babette: *This Modern Poetry (R. G. Cox)*
Eliot, T. S.: *Collected Poems 1909-1935 (D. W. Harding)*
Hofmannsthal, Hugo von: *Andreas or The United (Q. D. Leavis)*
Huxley, Aldous: *Eyeless in Gaza (Q. D. Leavis)*
Lagerkvist, Pär: *Guest of Reality,* tr. Mestertou and Harding *(Norman Shrapnel)*
Lehmann, Rosamond: *The Weather in the Streets (Q. D. Leavis)*
Leigh, Margaret Mary: *Highland Homespun (Adrian Bell)*
Long, Haniel: *Pittsburgh Memoranda (Geoffrey Walton)*
MacLeish, Archibald: *Panic (Geoffrey Walton)*
Muir, Edwin: *Scottish Journey (John Speirs)*
Neil, A. S.: *Is Scotland Educated? (John Speirs)*
Power, William: *Literature and Oatmeal (John Speirs)*
Prokosch, Frederic: *The Assassins (Geoffrey Walton)*
Simpson, J. H.: *Sane Schooling (R. O'Malley and D. Thompson)*
Thomson, G. M.: *Scotland: That Distressed Area (John Speirs)*

No. 3

French Intellectuals and the Political Crisis, by Henri Fluchère
The Swallow's Egg: Notes on Contemporary Art, by Richard March
Yeats, Synge, Ibsen and Strindberg, by T. R. Barnes
Bernard Van Dieren: Musical Intelligence and "The New Language," by W. H. Mellers
Revaluations (X): "Piers Plowman," by D. A. Traversi
Correspondence

BOOKS REVIEWED

Adams, Henry: *Mont-Saint-Michel and Chartres (Donald Culver)*
Auden, W. H.: *Look, Stranger (F. R. Leavis)*
Auden, W. H., and Isherwood, Christopher: *The Ascent of F. 6 (F. R. Leavis)*
Cole, G. D. H.: *What Marx Really Meant (E. W. F. Tomlin)*
Dos Passos, John: *The Big Money (Q. D. Leavis)*
Eberhart, Richard: *Reading the Spirit (F. R. Leavis)*
Graves, Robert: *Antigua, Penny, Puce (Q. D. Leavis)*
Hecker, Julius: *The Communist Answer to the World's Needs (E. W. F. Tomlin)*
Hook, Sidney: *From Hegel to Marx (E. W. F. Tomlin)*
Irwin, Will: *Propaganda and the News (Denys Thompson)*

Knight, G. Wilson: *The Principles of Shakespearean Production
(T. R. Barnes)*
Lehmann, John, ed.: *New Writing,* Nos. 1 and 2 *(H. A. Mason)*
McDougall, William: *Psycho-analysis and Social Psychology (D. W.
Harding)*
Mehring, Franz: *Karl Marx (E. W. F. Tomlin)*
Murry, J. Middleton, and others: *Marxism (E. W. F. Tomlin)*
Scholes, Percy A.: *Music: The Child and the Masterpiece (Bruce
Pattison)*
Smith, Logan Pearsall: *Reperusals and Re-collections (R. G. Cox)*
Warner, Sylvia Townsend: *Summer Will Show (Q. D. Leavis)*
Yeats, W. B.: *Dramatis Personae (H. A. Mason)*

No. 4

"*The Winter's Tale,*" by F. C. Tinkler
Christopher Dawson, by H. B. Parkes
Literary Criticism and Philosophy, by René Wellek
Delius and Peter Warlock, by W. H. Mellers
Henry James, by F. R. Leavis

BOOKS REVIEWED

Aeschylus: *The Agamemnon of,* tr. Macneice *(H. A. Mason)*
Bell, Adrian: *By-road (Frank Chapman)*
Chib, Som Nath: *Language, Universities and Nationalism in India
(A. A. Hamid)*
Duhamel, Georges: *Salavin (Q. D. Leavis)*
Farrell, James: *Studs Lonigan (Q. D. Leavis)*
Frost, Robert: *Selected Poems (Geoffrey Walton)*
Henderson, Philip: *The Novel To-day (Q. D. Leavis)*
Hopkins, Gerard Manley: *The Notebook and Papers of,* ed. Howes
(R. G. Cox)
Huxley, Aldous: *The Olive Tree (Denys Thompson)*
Mallarmé, *Some Poems of,* tr. Fry *(Martin Turnell)*
Potter, Stephen: *The Muse in Chains (L. C. Knight)*
Wilson, Edmund: *Travels in Two Democracies (H. A. Mason)*
Yeats, W. B., ed.: *The Oxford Book of Modern Verse, 1892-1935
(H. A. Mason)*

Vol. VI (1937-1938)

No. 1

The Great Reviews, by R. G. Cox
Othello and the Mangold-Wurzels: Literacy in the U.S.S.R., by A. Stawar
The Religious Problems in Hopkins, by W. H. Gardner
"Coriolanus," by D. A. Traversi
Literacy Criticism and Philosophy: a Reply, by F. R. Leavis

BOOKS REVIEWED

——— Contemporary Poetry and Prose, Nos. 6-8 (H. A. Mason)
——— Scottish Poetry from Barbour to James VI (John Speirs)
Barker, George: Calamiterror (H. A. Mason)
Brooks, Van Wyck: The Flowering of New England (Donald Culver)
Dyment, Clifford: Straight or Curly? (H. A. Mason)
Gittings, Robert: The Story of Psyche (H. A. Mason)
Heppenstall, Rayner: Sebastian (H. A. Mason)
Knights, L. C.: Drama and Society in the Age of Jonson (L. G. Salinger)
Roberts, D. Kilham, and Lehmann, John, ed.: The Year's Poetry, 1936 (H. A. Mason)
Sherif, Muzafer: The Psychology of Social Norms (D. W. Harding)
Thibaudet, Albert: Histoire de la Littérature Française de 1789 à nos Jours (J. Mansell Jones)
Westrup, J. A.: Purcell (Bruce Pattison)
Woolf, Virginia: The Years (W. H. Mellers)

No. 2

Restoration Comedy: the Reality and the Myth, by L. C. Knights
The Cultural Background of Intelligence Testing, by D. W. Harding
The Great Reviews (II), by R. G. Cox
Abraham Cowley and the Decline of Metaphysical Poetry, by Geoffrey Walton
Correspondence: Literary Criticism and Philosophy, by René Wellek
Christopher Dawson and "Arena," by H. B. Parkes

BOOKS REVIEWED

———, Teaching Poetry (D. Thompson and R. O'Malley)
Bulley, Margaret H.: Art and Understanding (Richard March)

APPENDICES

James, D. G.: *Scepticism and Poetry (F. R. Leavis)*
Lewis, C. Day; ed.: *The Mind in Chains (F. R. Leavis)*
London, Kurt: *The Seven Soviet Arts (Geoffrey Walton)*
Macneice, Louis: *Out of the Picture (H. L. Bradbrook)*
Madge, Charles: *The Disappearing Castle (H. L. Bradbrook)*
Madge, Charles, and Harrison, Tom: *Mass-Observation (D. W. Harding)*
Orr, Sir John Boyd, and others: *What Science Stands For (C. E. Lucas)*
Pound, Ezra: *The Fifth Decad of the Cantos (H. L. Bradbrook)*
Pring, Beryl: *Education, Capitalist and Socialist (F. R. Leavis)*
Richards, I. A.: *The Philosophy of Rhetoric (F. R. Leavis)*
Roberts, Michael: *The Modern Mind (Michael Oakeshott)*
Rosenberg, Isaac: *The Complete Works of,* ed. Harding and Bottomley *(F. R. Leavis)*
Street, A. G.: *Farming England (Adrian Bell)*
Warner, Rex: *Poems (H. L. Bradbrook)*

No. 3

Education by Book Club?, by H. A. Mason
The Role of the Onlooker, by D. W. Harding
Diabolic Intellect and the Noble Hero: a Note on "Othello," by F. R. Leavis
Jean Wiener and Music for Entertainment, by W. H. Mellers
Revengers Against Time, by Ronald Bottrall

BOOKS REVIEWED

Curry, Walter Clyde: *Shakespeare's Philosophical Patterns (R. G. Cox)*
Gide, André: *Retour de l'U.R.S.S. (H. A. Mason)*
    Retouches à mon Retour de l'U.R.S.S. (H. A. Mason)
Jennings, Humphrey, and others, ed: *May the Twelfth (D. W. Harding)*
Lawrence, D. H.: *Phoenix (F. R. Leavis)*
Lynd, Robert S., and Lynd, Helen Merrell: *Middletown in Transition (D. W. Harding)*
MacLeish, Archibald: *The Fall of the City (T. R. Barnes)*
Muir, Edwin: *Journeys and Places (W. H. Mellers)*
Pevsner, Nikolaus: *Industrial Art in England (J. M. Harding)*
Rose, Walter: *The Carpenter's Shop (F. C. Tinkler)*

Sayers, Dorothy: *Gaudy Night (Q. D. Leavis)*
      Busman's Honeymoon (Q. D. Leavis)
Shaw, Bernard: *London Music in 1888-89 as heard by Corno di Bassetto (W. H. Mellers)*
Sloan, Pat: *Soviet Democracy (H. A. Mason)*
Ta-Kao, Ch'u, tr.: *Chinese Lyrics (W. H. Mellers)*
Tate, Allen: *Selected Poems (W. H. Mellers)*
Wright, Louis B.: *Middle-Class Culture in Elizabethan England (L. C. Knights)*
Young, G. M.: *Daylight and Champaign (Geoffrey Walton)*

No. 4

The Modern Universities, by L. C. Knights
A Letter from Ireland, by Grattan Freyer
The Composer and Civilization: Notes on the Later Work of Gabriel Fauré, by W. H. Mellers
"The Revenger's Tragedy" and the Morality Tradition, by L. G. Salingar
Correspondence, from Boris Ford

BOOKS REVIEWED

Caudwell, Christopher: *Illusion and Reality (H. A. Mason)*
Clarke, G. N.: *Science and Social Welfare in the Age of Newton (C. E. Lucas)*
Giraudoux, Jean: *Racine*, tr. Jones *(Martin Turnell)*
Jefferies, Richard: *Jefferies' England, Nature Essays*, ed. Looker *(Q. D. Leavis)*
    Selections of his Work, ed. Williamson *(Q. D. Leavis)*
    Hodge and his Master, ed. Williamson *(Q. D. Leavis)*
Jones, P. Mansell: *French Introspectives (Martin Turnell)*
Lindsay, Jack: *John Bunyan: Maker of Myths (F. R. Leavis)*
Roberts, Denys Kilham, and Grigson, Geoffrey, ed.: *The Year's Poetry, 1937 (Frank Chapman)*
Stebbing, L. Susan: *Philosophy and the Physicists (E. W. F. Tomlin)*
Tillotson, Geoffrey: *On the Poetry of Pope (Geoffrey Walton)*
Tillyard, E. M. W.: *Shakespeare's Last Plays (D. A. Traversi)*
Tindall, William York: *John Bunyan: Mechanick Preacher (F. R. Leavis)*

Vol. VII (1938-1939)

No. 1

The Modern Universities: a Postscript, by L. C. Knights
"Cymbeline," by F. C. Tinkler
The Apotheosis of Post-Impressionism, by Richard March
Wordsworth: a Preliminary Survey, by James Smith
William Dunbar, by John Speirs
Correspondence: Exact Thought and Inexact Language

BOOKS REVIEWED

——— Seventeenth Century Studies Presented to Sir Herbert Grierson (L. C. Knights)
Adam, Ruth: *I'm Not Complaining* (Q. D. Leavis)
Auden, W. H., and MacNeice, Louis: *Letters from Iceland* (Geoffrey Walton)
Brod, Max: *Franz Kafka. Eine Biographie* (R. Wellek)
Burstall, Sara A.: *Frances Mary Buss: an Educational Pioneer* (Sylvia Legge)
De la Mare, Walter: *Memory, and Other Poems* (Geoffrey Walton)
Elliot, J. H.: *Berlioz* (W. H. Mellers)
Gissing, George: *Stories and Sketches* (Q. D. Leavis)
Grierson, Sir Herbert: *Milton and Wordsworth* (F. R. Leavis)
Kohn-Bramstedt, Ernst: *Aristocracy and the Middle-Classes in Germany* (R. Wellek)
Macneice, Louis: *I Crossed the Minch* (Geoffrey Walton)
    The Earth Compels (Geoffrey Walton)
Peacock, C. H.: *Poems* (Geoffrey Walton)
Prokosch, Frederic: *The Carnival* (Geoffrey Walton)
Tillyard, E. M. W.: *The Miltonic Setting* (F. R. Leavis)
Turner, W. J.: *Mozart* (W. H. Mellers)
Upward, Edward: *Journey to the Border* (R. G. Cox)
Warner, Rex: *The Wild Goose Chase* (R. G. Cox)

No. 2

The Philosophy of Marxism, by H. B. Parkes
Baudelaire, by James Smith
The Composer and Civilization (II): Albert Roussel and La Musique Française, by W. H. Mellers
E. M. Forster, by F. R. Leavis

BOOKS REVIEWED

Callan, Norman: *Poetry in Practice (Frank Chapman)*
Hopkins, Gerard Manley: *Further Letters of*, ed. Abbott *(R. G. Cox)*
Mason, Eudo C.: *Rilke's Apotheosis (Richard March)*
Muir, Kenneth, ed.: *English Poetry: a Students' Anthology (Frank Chapman)*
Rilke, Rainer Maria: *Later Poems*, tr. Leishman *(Richard March)*
Roberts, Michael: *T. E. Hulme (H. A. Mason)*
Roll, Erich: *A History of Economic Thought (P. Harris)*
Rose, William, and Houston, G. Craig, ed.: *Rainer Maria Rilke (Richard March)*
Spender, Stephen: *Trial of a Judge (H. A. Mason)*
Starkie, Enid: *Arthur Rimbaud (Martin Turnell)*
    Rimbaud in Abyssinia (Martin Turnell)
Woolf, Virginia: *Three Guineas (Q. D. Leavis)*

No. 3

"*The New Republic*" *and the Ideal Weekly*, by H. A. Mason
Henry James' Heiress: The Importance of Edith Wharton, by Q. D. Leavis
"*The Great and Good Corneille*," by Martin Turnell
"*Troilus and Cressida*," by D. A. Traversi
Revaluations (XI): Arnold as Critic, by F. R. Leavis

BOOKS REVIEWED

—— *Report on the British Press (H. A. Mason)*
Auden, W. H., and Isherwood, Christopher: *On the Frontier (T. R. Barnes)*
Chase, Stuart: *The Tyranny of Words (James Smith)*
Duhamel, Georges: *Défense des Lettres (H. A. Mason)*
    In Defense of Letters, tr. Bozman *(H. A. Mason)*
Kafka, Franz: *America (R. O. C. Winkler)*
Mead, Margaret: *Sex and Temperament in Three Primitive Societies (F. C. Tinkler)*
Palmer, Mary, ed.: *Writing and Action (Frank Chapman)*
Read, Herbert: *Poetry and Anarchism (D. W. Harding)*

No. 4

The American Cultural Scene: (I) Political Thought, by H. B. Parkes
"Wuthering Heights," by Boris Ford
Music in the Melting Pot: Charles Ives and the Music of the Americas, by W. H. Mellers
Leslie Stephen: Cambridge Critic, by Q. D. Leavis
Giovanni Papini and Italian Literature, by D. A. Traversi
Correspondence: The "PEP" Report on the Press

BOOKS REVIEWED

Adam, Ruth: *There Needs No Ghost (Q. D. Leavis)*
Biaggini, E. G.: *Education and Society (Frank Chapman)*
Blom, Eric: *Beethoven's Piano Sonatas Discussed (W. H. Mellers)*
Crane, Hart: *The Collected Poems of (F. R. Leavis)*
Douglas, George: *The House with the Green Shutters (John Speirs)*
Gray, Cecil: *The Forty-eight Preludes and Fugues of J. S. Bach (W. H. Mellers)*
Hackett, C. A.: *Le Lyrisme de Rimbaud (Martin Turnell)*
Kellett, E. E.: *Aspects of History (H. B. Parkes)*
Lane, Margaret: *Edgar Wallace (Q. D. Leavis)*
Macmurray, John: *The Clue to History (D. W. Harding)*
Macneice, Louis: *Modern Poetry (Geoffrey Walton)*
Peacock, Reginald: *Hoelderlin (H. L. Bradbrook)*
Roberts, D. Kilham, and Grigson, Geoffrey, ed.: *The Year's Poetry, 1938 (Geoffrey Walton)*
Stone, Irving: *Sailor on Horseback: the Biography of Jack London (Q. D. Leavis)*
Thomas, Edward: *The Childhood of: a Fragment of Autobiography (F. R. Leavis)*
Thomas, Helen: *As It Was . . . World Without End (F. R. Leavis)*
Traversi, D. A.: *Approach to Shakespeare (R. G. Cox)*
Wais, Kurt: *Mallarmé (James Smith)*
Williams, C. H.: *The Modern Historian (H. B. Parkes)*

Vol. VIII (1939-1940)

No. 1

The American Cultural Scene: (II) Criticism, by H. B. Parkes
The Ideas of Machiavelli, by Grattan Freyer
Classics and Education: a Note, by H. A. Mason

Marlowe's "Dr. Faustus," by James Smith
Edmund Rubbra and Symphonic Form, by W. H. Mellers

BOOKS REVIEWED

Bernal, J. D.: *The Social Function of Science (C. A. Lucas)*
Bronokski, J.: *The Poet's Defense (R. O. C. Winkler)*
Connolly, Cyril: *Enemies of Promise (Q. D. Leavis)*
Eliot, T. S.: *The Family Reunion (Martin Turnell)*
Ewart, Gavin: *Poems and Songs (W. H. Mellers)*
Lewis, C. S.: *Rehabilitations and Other Essays (L. C. Knights)*
Macneice, Louis: *Modern Poetry (Q. D. Leavis)*
  Autumnal Journey (W. H. Mellers)
Marsh, Sir Edward: *A Number of People (Q. D. Leavis)*
Moholy-Nagy, L.: *The New Vision (Storm Jameson)*
Prince, F. T.: *Poems (W. H. Mellers)*
Richards, I. A.: *Interpretation in Teaching (H. A. Mason)*
Smith, Logan Pearsall: *Unforgotten Years (Q. D. Leavis)*
Spender, Stephen: *The Still Centre (W. H. Mellers)*
Trilling, Lionel: *Matthew Arnold (F. R. Leavis)*

No. 2

The Claims of Politics: Richard Church, Geoffrey Davies, Christopher Dawson, George Every, S. S. M., Michael Oakeshott, Olaf Stapledon, L. Susan Stebbing, R. H. Tawney
Literary Criticism in France (I), by Martin Turnell
Harmony and Composition, by Edmund Rubbra
A Classical Education and Eighteenth-Century Poetry, by A. R. Humphreys

BOOKS REVIEWED

Bottrall, Ronald: *The Turning Path (R. O. C. Winkler)*
Henderson, Philip: *The Poet and Society (Marius Bewley)*
Knight, G. Wilson: *The Burning Oracle (R. O. C. Winkler)*
Lewis, Wyndham: *Wyndham Lewis the Artist (Richard March)*
Muir, Edwin: *The Present Age from 1914 (F. R. Leavis)*
Pope, Alexander: *The Twickenham Edition of the Poems of,* Vol. IV: *Imitations of Horace,* ed. Butt *(F. R. Leavis)*
Roberts, R. Ellis: *Portrait of Stella Benson (W. H. Mellers)*
Root, Robert Kilburn: *The Poetical Career of Alexander Pope (F. R. Leavis)*
Watson, Francis: *Art Lies Bleeding (Richard March)*

No. 3

The Spens Report: a Symposium-Review
The American Cultural Scene: (III) Education, by H. B. Parkes
The Tragedy of Blood, by James Smith
Literary Criticism in France (II), by Martin Turnell
Escapism in Literature, by Olaf Stapledon

BOOKS REVIEWED

Collingwood, R. G.: *An Autobiography (J. C. Maxwell)*
Eliot, T. S.: *The Idea of a Christian Society (D. W. Harding)*
Fry, Roger: *Last Lectures (Geoffrey Walton)*
Hemingway, Ernest: *The Fifth Column (W. H. Mellers)*
Maulnier, Thierry: *Introduction à la Poésie Française (Martin Turnell)*
Myers, Rollo H.: *Music in the Modern World (W. H. Mellers)*

No. 4

Regulated Hatred: an Aspect of the Work of Jane Austen, by D. W. Harding
"Athalie" and the Dictators, by Martin Turnell
Searchlight on Tin-Pan Alley, by W. H. Mellers
Revaluations (XII): The Poetry of Coleridge, by Marius Bewley
Correspondence: James Smith, D. W. Harding, Professor Parrott

BOOKS REVIEWED

Evans, B. Ifor: *Tradition and Romanticism (R. G. Cox)*
Hogben, Lancelot: *Dangerous Thoughts (J. C. Maxwell)*
Hutchinson, C. G., and Chapman, F., ed.: *Village Life and Labour (T. R. Barnes)*
King, Alec, and Ketley, Martin: *The Control of Language (T. R. Barnes)*
Thompson, Denys: *Between the Lines, or How to Read a Newspaper (Frank Chapman)*
Willey, Basil: *The Eighteenth Century Background (J. C. Maxwell)*
Yeats, W. B.: *Last Poems and Plays (F. R. Leavis)*

Vol. IX (1940-1941)

No. 1

The American Cultural Scene: (IV) The Novel, by H. B. Parkes
"As You Like It," by James Smith

Tradition and Innovation To-day, by Olaf Stapledon
Music and the Dramatic, By W. H. Mellers
Revaluations (XIII): Coleridge in Criticism, by F. R. Leavis

BOOKS REVIEWED

—— *Folios of New Writing,* Spring 1940 *(R. G. Cox)*
Archer, W. G.: *The Blue Grove: the Poetry of the Uraons (D. W. Harding)*
Jenkinson, A. J.: *What Do Boys and Girls Read? (T. R. Barnes)*
Kitto, H. D. F.: *Greek Tragedy (J. C. Maxwell)*
Rees, Garnet: *Rémy de Gourmont—Essai de Biographie Intellectuelle (G. D. Klingopulos)*
Spender, Stephen: *The Backward Son (W. H. Mellers)*
Thomas, Dylan: *Portrait of the Artist as a Young Dog (W. H. Mellers)*

No. 2

Education and the University (I): Sketch for an English School, by F. R. Leavis
Rubbra's No. 3, by W. H. Mellers
The Significance of Manzoni's "Promessi Sposi," by D. A. Traversi
Prince Hamlet, by L. C. Knights

BOOKS REVIEWED

Auden, W. H.: *Another Time (F. R. Leavis)*
Butterfield, H.: *The Statecraft of Machiavelli (D. A. Traversi)*
Darnton, Christian: *You and Music (W. H. Mellers)*
Dent, E. J.: *Opera (W. H. Mellers)*
Hill, Christopher, ed.: *The English Revolution, 1640 (L. C. Knights)*
MacColl, D. S.: *What Is Art? (Geoffrey Walton)*
Muir, Edwin: *The Story and the Fable (Q. D. Leavis)*
Myers, L. H.: *The Pool of Vishnu (D. W. Harding)*
Orwell, George: *Inside the Whale (Q. D. Leavis)*
Plekhanov, G. V.: *The Role of the Individual in History (L. C. Knights)*
Richards, J. M.: *Modern Architecture (Geoffrey Walton)*
Speirs, John: *The Scots Literary Tradition (J. C. Maxwell)*
Wilenski, R. H.: *Modern French Painters (Geoffrey Walton)*
Yeats, W. B.: *Letters on Poetry (W. H. Mellers)*

No. 3

The Custom of War, and the Notion of Peace, by D. W. Harding
Crime and Punishment in Ben Jonson, by D. J. Enright
Postscript on Verlaine, by Martin Turnell
Education and the University (II): Criticism and Comment, by F. R. Leavis
"Greats," by J. C. Maxwell

BOOKS REVIEWED

——— *Folios of New Writing, Autumn 1940* (R. G. Cox)
——— *Poets of To-morrow: Cambridge Poetry 1940* (W. H. Mellers)
Bartlett, F. C.: *Political Propaganda* (D. W. Harding)
Bradbrook, M. C., and Thomas, M. G. Lloyd: *Andrew Marvell* (L. C. Knights)
Eberhart, Richard: *Song and Idea* (W. H. Mellers)
Eliot, T. S.: *East Coker* (W. H. Mellers)
Empson, William: *The Gathering Storm* (W. H. Mellers)
Parkes, Henry Bamford: *Marxism: a Post-mortem* (Christopher Hill)

No. 4

Education and the University (III): Literary Studies, by F. R. Leavis
The Politeness of Racine, by R. C. Knight
The Theme of "The Ancient Mariner," by D. W. Harding
Mahler as Key-Figure, by W. H. Mellers
"Henry the Fifth," by D. A. Traversi

BOOKS REVIEWED

——— *Science in War* (Penguin Special) (C. E. Lucas)
Ayer, A. J.: *The Foundation of Empirical Knowledge* (R. O. C. Winkler)
Carse, Adam: *The Orchestra in the XVIIIth Century* (Eric Blom)
Hassall, Christopher: *S.O.S. Ludlow* (T. R. Barnes)
Leon, Derrick: *Introduction to Proust* (Martin Turnell)
Lewis, Cecil Day: *Selected Poems* (T. R. Barnes)
                    Poems in Wartime (T. R. Barnes)
Macneice, Louis: *The Poetry of W. B. Yeats* (W. H. Mellers)
Plomer, William: *Selected Poems* (T. R. Barnes)
Prokosch, Frederic: *Death at Sea* (T. R. Barnes)
Shewring, Walter: *Topics: Ten Essays* (J. C. Maxwell)

Vol. X (1941-1942)

No. 1

Correspondence (re-Marxism), by H. B. Parkes
Towards a Musical Academy, by W. H. Mellers
Revaluations (XIV): Joseph Conrad (I), by F. R. Leavis
Nietzsche, by H. B. Parkes
A Critical Theory of Jane Austen's Writings (I), by Q. D. Leavis

BOOKS REVIEWED

Crowther, J. G.: *The Social Relations of Science (C. E. Lucas)*
Hemingway, Ernest: *For Whom the Bell Tolls (W. H. Mellers)*
Macneice, Louis: *Plant and Phantom (R. G. Lienhardt)*

No. 2

Conservatism and Tradition: Post Obitum—
       Donald Francis Tovey
       Hamilton Harty
       Frank Bridge
                      by W. H. Mellers
A Critical Theory of Jane Austen's Writings (II): (i) *"Lady Susan" into "Mansfield Park,"* by Q. D. Leavis
The Development of Modern Italian Poetry (I), by D. A. Traversi
Revaluations (XIV): Joseph Conrad (concluded), by F. R. Leavis

BOOKS REVIEWED

——— *Folios of New Writing*, Spring 1941 *(R. G. Cox)*
Auden, W. H.: *New Year Letter (R. O. C. Winkler)*
Eliot, T. S.: *Points of View*, ed. Hayward *(R. O. C. Winkler)*
Newton, Eric: *European Painting and Sculpture (Stephen Reiss)*
Sampson, George: *The Concise Cambridge History of English Literature (Boris Ford)*
Stebbing, L. Susan: *Ideals and Illusions (J. C. Maxwell)*

No. 3

"First Broadcast Performance," by W. H. Mellers
The Ambiguity of "Measure for Measure," by L. C. Knights
The Greatness of "Measure for Measure," by F. R. Leavis
A Note on Literature and the Irish Tradition, by D. J. Enright
The Significance of the "Princesse de Clèves," by Martin Turnell

A Critical Theory of Jane Austen's Writings (II): (ii) "Lady Susan" into "Mansfield Park" (Concluded), by Q. D. Leavis

BOOKS REVIEWED

Butler, E. M.: *Rainer Maria Rilke (D. J. Enright)*
House, Humphry: *The Dickens World (R. C. Churchill)*
Knight, G. Wilson: *The Starlit Dome (T. R. Barnes)*
Lynd, R. S.: *Knowledge for What? (C. E. Lucas)*
Rowse, A. L.: *Tudor Cornwall (Vera Mellers)*
Waddington, C. H.: *The Scientific Attitude (C. E. Lucas)*
Woolf, Virginia: *Between the Acts (F. R. Leavis)*

No. 4

After Ten Years: Editorial
The Significance of "Cymbeline," by A. A. Stephenson, S. J.
The Criticism of Shakespeare's Late Plays: a Caveat, by F. R. Leavis
Language and Function in American Music, by W. H. Mellers
Dickens, Drama and Tradition, by R. C. Churchill

BOOKS REVIEWED

—— *Poets of To-morrow;* 3rd Selection *(R. G. Lienhardt)*
Collingwood, R. G.: *The Three Laws of Politics (J. C. Maxwell)*
Lennard, Reginald: *Democracy: The Threatened Foundations (J. C. Maxwell)*
Nichols, Ross: *Prose Chants and Poems (R. G. Lienhardt)*
Ridler, Anne, ed.: *A Little Book of Modern Verse (R. G. Lienhardt)*
Roberts, Michael: *The Recovery of the West (R. O. C. Winkler)*
Shchedrin: *Fables,* tr. Volkhovsky *(D. J. Enright)*
Spender, Stephen: *Life and the Poet (L. C. Knights)*.
Thomson, David: *The Democratic Ideal in France and England (J. C. Maxwell)*
Tillotson, Geoffrey: *Essays in Criticism and Research (R. G. Cox)*
Tinker, C. B., and Lowry, H. F.: *The Poetry of Matthew Arnold (R. G. Cox)*

Vol. XI (1942-1943)

No. 1

Towards a Conception of Musical Tradition (I): Melody and Texture, Mediaeval and Modern, by W. H. Mellers
Farewell and Welcome: a Sequence of Poems, by Ronald Bottrall
A Case for Kipling? by Boris Ford

Demigods and Pickpockets: the Augustan Myth in Swift and Rousseau, by J. C. Maxwell
"Measure for Measure," by D. A. Traversi

BOOKS REVIEWED

Eliot, T. S.: *The Dry Salvages (F. R. Leavis)*
Johnson, Samuel: *The Poems of,* ed. Smith and McAdam *(F. R. Leavis)*
Spender, Stephen: *Ruins and Visions (D. J. Enright)*
Treece, Henry: *Invitation and Warning (D. J. Enright)*
Wilson, Edmund: *The Wound and the Bow (F. R. Leavis)*

No. 2

Evidence Evalued, by Ronald Bottrall
Chaucer (I): "Troilus and Criseyde," by John Speirs
A Letter on the Music Criticism of W. H. Mellers, by Boris Ford and Stephen Reiss
A Reply, by W. H. Mellers
Benjamin Constant and "Adolphe," by Martin Turnell

BOOKS REVIEWED

Dampier, Sir William: *A History of Science and Its Relations with Philosophy and Religion (R. O. C. Winkler)*
Elwin, Malcolm: *Savage Landor (F. R. Leavis)*
Hölderlin, Friedrich: *Gedichte,* ed. Closs *(D. J. Enright)*
Lewis, C. S.: *A Preface to Paradise Lost (L. C. Knights)*

No. 3

Education and the University: Considerations at a Critical Time, by F. R. Leavis
New English and American Music, by W. H. Mellers
Cormac's Ruined House: A Survey of the Modern Irish Novel, by D. J. Enright
Chaucer (II): The Canterbury Tales (I), by John Speirs

BOOKS REVIEWED

——— *The Southern Review: Thomas Hardy Centennial Issue,* Summer 1940 *(Q. D. Leavis)*
Blunden, Edmund: *Thomas Hardy (Q. D. Leavis)*
Cecil, Lord David: *Hardy the Novelist (Q. D. Leavis)*

Dent, H. C.: *A New Order in English Education (L. C. Knights)*
Eliot, T. S.: *Little Gidding (D. W. Harding)*
Löwe, Adolf: *The Universities in Transformation (L. C. Knights)*
Menon, V. K. Narayana: *The Development of William Butler Yeats (R. G. Lienhardt)*
Millaud, Pierre: *France (Geoffrey Walton)*
Pick, John: *Gerard Manley Hopkins, Priest and Poet (R. G. Lienhardt)*
Scarfe, Francis: *Auden and After (F. R. Leavis)*

No. 4

"Le Misanthrope" (I), by Martin Turnell
Objections to a Review of "Little Gidding," by R. N. Higinbotham
Reflections on the Above, by F. R. Leavis
Bacon and the Seventeenth-Century Dissociation of Sensibility, by L. C. Knights

BOOKS REVIEWED

—— *Rebuilding Britain, for the R.I.B.A. (Geoffrey Walton)*
Bowra, C. M.: *The Heritage of Symbolism (Martin Turnell)*
Jeans, Sir James: *Physics and Philosophy (R. O. C. Winkler)*
Mann, Thomas: *Stories of Three Decades (D. J. Enright)*
Mumford, Lewis: *The Culture of Cities (Geoffrey Walton)*
Pevsner, Nikolaus: *An Outline of European Architecture (Geoffrey Walton)*
Quiggin, A. H.: *Haddon the Head Hunter (Q. D. Leavis)*

Vol. XII (1943-1944)

No. 1

Literature and Society, by F. R. Leavis
"The Discipline of Letters": A Sociological Note, by Q. D. Leavis
"Le Misanthrope" (II), by Martin Turnell
Chaucer (III): The Canterbury Tales (II), by John Speirs

BOOKS REVIEWED

MacDiarmid, Hugh: *Lucky Poet (John Durkan)*
Pope, Alexander: *The Poems of*, Vol. V: *The Dunciad*, ed. Sutherland *(F. R. Leavis)*
Storrs, Sir Ronald: *Orientations (Q. D. Leavis)*
Tallents, Sir Stephen: *Man and Boy (Q. D. Leavis)*

Thompson, Denys: *Voice of Civilisation: An Enquiry into Advertising (R. C. Churchill)*
Truscot, Bruce: *Redbrick University (L. C. Knights)*

No. 2

Evaluations (IV): Gerard Manley Hopkins, by F. R. Leavis
Rilke and Hoelderlin in Translation, by D. J. Enright
A Critical Theory of Jane Austen's Writings (III): The Letters, by Q. D. Leavis
Towards a Conception of Musical Tradition (II): Voice and Dance in the XVI and XVII Centuries, by W. H. Mellers

BOOKS REVIEWED

Battiscombe, Georgina: *Charlotte Yonge (Q. D. Leavis)*
Bethell, S. L.: *The Literary Outlook (Q. D. Leavis)*
Every, Bro. George, S.S.M.: *Christian Discrimination (Q. D. Leavis)*
Gascoyne, David: *Poems, 1937-1942 (R. G. Lienhardt)*
Nicholson, Norman; ed.: *An Anthology of Religious Verse (R. G. Lienhardt)*
Nicholson, Norman: *Man and Literature (Q. D. Leavis)*
Read, Herbert: *Education Through Art (Geoffrey Walton)*
Ridler, Anne: *The Nine Bright Shiners (R. G. Lienhardt)*
Spencer, Theodore: *Shakespeare and the Nature of Man (L. C. Knights)*

No. 3

Stefan George and the New Empire, by D. J. Enright
George Herbert, by L. C. Knights
Johnson as Critic, by F. R. Leavis
Towards a Conception of Musical Tradition (II): Voice and Dance in the XVI and XVII Centuries (II), by W. H. Mellers

BOOKS REVIEWED

Bebbington, W. G., ed.: *Introducing Modern Poetry (Frank Chapman)*
Bethell, S. L.: *Shakespeare and the Popular Dramatic Tradition (A. I. Doyle)*
Brereton, J. L.: *The Case for Examinations (Denys Thompson)*
Hayek, F. A.: *The Road to Serfdom (J. C. Maxwell)*
Savage, D. S.: *The Personal Principle (R. G. Lienhardt)*

No. 4

Moral Bewilderment, by Morris Ginsberg
Tragedy and the "Medium": a Note on Mr. Santayana's "Tragic Philosophy," by F. R. Leavis
Two Generations of English Music, by W. H. Mellers
"Phèdre," by Martin Turnell
J. B. Leishman and the Art of Translation, by D. J. Enright

BOOKS REVIEWED

——— *Poetry: London,* Vol. 2, No. 9 *(Geoffrey Walton)*
——— *Poetry: Scotland,* I *(Geoffrey Walton)*
Fuller, Roy: *The Middle of a War (Geoffrey Walton)*
  A Lost Season (Geoffrey Walton)
Gardner, W. H.: *Gerard Manley Hopkins, 1844-1889 (R. G. Lienhardt)*
Gascoyne, David: *Poems, 1937-1942 (Geoffrey Walton)*
Gee, Kenneth: *Thirty-two Poems (Geoffrey Walton)*
Grierson, Herbert J. C., and Smith, J. C.: *A Critical History of English Poetry (F. R. Leavis)*
Jennett, Sean: *Always Adam (Geoffrey Walton)*
Keyes, Sidney: *The Cruel Solstice (Geoffrey Walton)*
Shapiro, Karl J.: *Person, Place and Thing (Geoffrey Walton)*
Strassburg, Gottfried von: *Tristan und Isolt: a Poem,* by, ed. Closs *(D. J. Enright)*
Tiller, Terence: *The Inward Animal (Geoffrey Walton)*
Trilling, Lionel: *E. M. Forster (F. R. Leavis)*
Yates, Peter: *The Motionless Dancer (Geoffrey Walton)*

Vol. XIII (1944-1946)
No. 1

The Interpretation of History, by A. J. Woolford
Goethe's "Faust" and the Written Word: (I) *The First Part,* by D. J. Enright
On the Social Background of Metaphysical Poetry, by L. C. Knights
"Thought" and Emotional Quality: Notes in the Analysis of Poetry, by F. R. Leavis

BOOKS REVIEWED

Newsom, John: *Willingly to School (Denys Thompson)*
Schücking, Levin: *The Sociology of Literary Taste (F. R. Leavis)*
Trevelyan, G. M.: *English Social History (F. R. Leavis)*

No. 2

Existentialism and Literature: a Letter from Switzerland, by H. A. Mason
The Controlling Hand: Jane Austen and "Pride and Prejudice," by Reuben A. Brower
Correspondence: Rilke, George, and "Reintegration," by W. Schenk and D. J. Enright
Imagery and Movement: Notes in the Analysis of Poetry, by F. R. Leavis

BOOKS REVIEWED

—— *New Lyrical Ballads: Ballad Book I (A. I. Doyle)*
—— *Personal Landscape: an Anthology of Exile (A. I. Doyle)*
Auden, W. H.: *For the Time Being (R. G. Lienhardt)*
Bottrall, Ronald: *Farewell and Welcome (A. I. Doyle)*
Cobbett, William: *The Opinions of,* ed. Cole, G. D. H. and Margaret *(L. C. Knights)*
Corby, Herbert: *Hampdens Going Over (A. I. Doyle)*
Keyes, Sidney: *Collected Poems of (A. I. Doyle)*
Lipson, E.: *A Planned Economy or Free Enterprise (A. J. Woolford)*
Nicholson, Norman: *Five Rivers (A. I. Doyle)*
Potts, Paul: *Instead of a Sonnet, Ballad Book 2 (A. I. Doyle)*
Read, Herbert: *A World Within a War (A. I. Doyle)*

No. 3

The Dark Ages: Culture and the Oratorio, by W. H. Mellers
Revaluations (XV): George Eliot (I), by F. R. Leavis
Goethe's "Faust" and the Written Word: (II) A Chapter of Accidents, by D. J. Enright
Flaubert (I), by Martin Turnell

BOOKS REVIEWED

Connolly, Cyril: *The Condemned Playground (R. G. Lienhardt)*
Davies, H.: *The Boys' Grammar School (Denys Thompson)*
Grundy, G. B.: *Fifty-Five Years at Oxford (H. A. Mason)*
Palinurus: *The Unquiet Grave (R. G. Lienhardt)*
Stahl, E. L.: *Hoelderlin's Symbolism (D. J. Enright)*

No. 4

"Much Ado About Nothing," by James Smith
Revaluations (XV): George Eliot (II), by F. R. Leavis

Flaubert (Concluded), by Martin Turnell
Goethe's "Faust" and the Written Word: (III) The Second Part, by D. J. Enright

BOOKS REVIEWED

Aragon, Louis: *Les Yeux d'Elsa (A. I. Doyle)*
        Servitude et Grandeurs des Français (A. I. Doyle)
Koestler, Arthur: *The Yogi and the Commissar (H. A. Mason)*
Orwell, George: *Critical Essays (T. R. Barnes)*
Parker, A. A.: *The Allegorical Drama of Calderón (James Smith)*
Roy, Claude: *Aragon (A. I. Doyle)*

Vol. XIV (1946-1947)

No. 1

Les Chemins de la Liberté, by H. A. Mason
Revaluations (XV): George Eliot (III), by F. R. Leavis
Goethe's "Faust" and the Written Word: (III) The Second Part (Concluded), by D. J. Enright

BOOKS REVIEWED

Grigson, Geoffrey, ed.: *The Mint: a Miscellany (R. G. Cox)*
Lewis, C. S.: *The Great Divorce (E. K. T. Dock)*
Malinowski, Bronislaw: *The Dynamics of Culture Change*, ed. Kaberry *(R. G. Lienhardt)*
Preston, Raymond: *"Four Quartets" Rehearsed (H. A. Mason)*
Rowse, A. L.: *The Spirit of English History (A. J. Woolford)*
Thomas, Dylan: *Deaths and Entrances (Wolf Mankowitz)*
Truscott, Bruce: *First Year at the University (H. A. Mason)*

No. 2

M. Camus and the Tragic Hero, by H. A. Mason
The Rhythmical Intention in Wyatt's Poetry, by D. W. Harding
George Eliot (IV): "Daniel Deronda" and "The Portrait of a Lady," by F. R. Leavis

BOOKS REVIEWED

Apollinaire, Guillaume: *Choix de Poésies*, ed. Bowra *(C. D. Klingopulos)*
Koestler, Arthur: *Thieves in the Night (Q. D. Leavis)*
Miller, Henry: *The Cosmological Eye (R. G. Lienhardt)*
Peacock, Ronald: *The Poet in the Theatre (R. G. Cox)*

Reed, Henry: *A Map of Verona* (G. D. Klingopulos)
Rouveyre, André: *Apollinaire* (G. D. Klingopulos)
Sackville-West, V.: *The Garden* (G. D. Klingopulos)
Warner, Rex: *The Cult of Power* (H. A. Mason)

No. 3

André Malraux and His Critics, by H. A. Mason
The Cultural Implications of Planning and Popularization, by G. H. Bantock
The Novel as Dramatic Poem (I): "Hard Times," by F. R. Leavis
Professor Chadwick and English Studies, by A Pupil
Correspondence

BOOKS REVIEWED

Bottrall, Ronald: *Selected Poems* (H. A. Mason)
Bradbrook, M. C.: *Ibsen the Norwegian, a Revaluation* (R. G. Cox)
Downs, Brian W.: *Ibsen, the Intellectual Background* (R. G. Cox)
James, Henry: *Fourteen Stories* by, ed. Garnett (Q. D. Leavis)
Matthiessen, F. O.: *Henry James: the Major Phase* (F. R. Leavis)
Meyer, Ernest: *English Chamber Music* (W. H. Mellers)

No. 4

The Two Henry Jameses, by Quentin Anderson
Professor Chadwick and English Studies: Comments by J. C. Maxwell and Redbrick
The Critical Review of To-day: Prolegomena to a Historical Inquiry, by R. G. Cox
The Novel as Dramatic Poem (II): "Wuthering Heights," by G. D. Klingopulos
Music Chronicle, by W. H. Mellers
Correspondence from R. Bottrall

BOOKS REVIEWED

Camus, Albert: *La Peste* (H. A. Mason)
Elwin, Verrier: *Folk Songs of Chhattisgarh* (D. W. Harding)
James, Henry: *Roderick Hudson* (F. R. Leavis)
Knight, G. Wilson: *The Crown of Life: Essays in Interpretation of Shakespeare's Final Plays* (R. G. Cox)
Lewis, C. Day: *The Poetic Image* (R. G. Cox)
Saurat, Denis: *Modern French Literature, 1870-1940* (C. A. Hackett)

Vol. XV (1947-1948)

No. 1

Henry Sidgwick's Cambridge, by Q. D. Leavis
Henry James, His Symbolism and His Critics, by Quentin Anderson
Contemporary French Criticism, by Henri Peyre and H. A. Mason
"Henry IV—Part I," by D. A. Traversi
Marivaux, by Martin Turnell
Correspondence from T. S. Eliot

BOOKS REVIEWED

Closs, A.: *Die freien Rhythmen in der deutschen Lyrik* (D. J. Enright)
Dupee, F. W., ed.: *The Question of Henry James* (Q. D. Leavis)
Jenkins, Elizabeth: *Young Enthusiasts* (Raymond O'Malley)
Rajan, B., ed.: *T. S. Eliot: a Study of His Writing by Several Hands* (F. R. Leavis)

No. 2

Some Cultural Implications of Freedom in Education, by G. H. Bantock
Henry James and the Function of Criticism, by F. R. Leavis
Reflections on Clarendon's History of the Rebellion, by L. C. Knights
"Henry IV, Part II," by D. A. Traversi
Music Chronicle, by W. H. Mellers
Correspondence re Mr. Bottrall and Mr. Eliot, and "Henry IV—Part I"

BOOKS REVIEWED

Auden, W. H.: *The Age of Anxiety* (H. A. Mason)
Biaggim, E. G.: *Progressive Exercises in Reading* (T. A. Birrell)
"Critique": *The First Two Years* (H. A. Mason)
Empson, William: *Seven Types of Ambiguity* (R. G. Cox)
Grigson, Geoffrey: *The Harp of Aeolus* (Geoffrey Walton)

No. 3

Freedom in Education: Thoughts Provoked by Mr. Bantock, by Boris Ford
Goethe's 'Roman Elegies', by D. J. Enright
Mencken and the American Language, by Marius Bewley
"Timon of Athens," by J. C. Maxwell
The Novel as Dramatic Poem (III): "The Europeans," by F. R. Leavis
Correspondence—Ronald Bottrall
A Note on Intellectual Life in the U.S.A., by H. A. Mason

BOOKS REVIEWED

Bethell, S. L.: *Essays on Literary Criticism and the English Tradition (R. G. Cox)*
Ginsberg, M.: *Reason and Unreason in Society (G. H. Bantock)*
James, Henry: *The Portrait of a Lady (F. R. Leavis)*
Tillyard, E. M. W.: *Five Poems (R. G. Cox)*

No. 4

The Case of Stefan George, by D. J. Enright
Notes From America (II): Kenneth Burke as Literary Critic, by Marius Bewley
Intellectual Life in the U.S.A.: Comment and Reply, by Seymour Betsky
Authority and Method in Education: Some Reflections on Mr. Ford's Rejoinder, by G. H. Bantock
The Progress of Poesy, by F. R. Leavis

BOOKS REVIEWED

Farmer, H. G.: *A History of Music in Scotland (W. H. Mellers)*
Morgenthau, Hans J.: *Scientific Man Versus Power Politics (G. H. Bantock)*
Pattison, Bruce: *Music and Poetry of the English Renaissance (W. H. Mellers)*
Stravinsky, Igor: *The Poetics of Music (W. H. Mellers)*
Toynbee, Arnold: *A Study of History (R. G. Lienhardt)*
Young, Douglas: *A Braird o Thristles (J. H. Speirs)*

Vol. XVI (1949)

No. 1

Measure For Measure: or Anglo-American Exchanges, by H. A. Mason
The Colloquial Mode of Byron, by Marius Bewley
The Moral Basis of Political Conflicts, by Morris Ginsberg
Correspondence from Boris Ford
The Case of John Webster, by Ian Jack
Culture and Dr. Joad, by R. C. Churchill
A Note on Contemporary "Philosophical" Literary Criticism in France, by H. A. Mason

BOOKS REVIEWED

Eliot, T. S.: *Notes Toward a Definition of Culture* (G. H. Bantock)
Heilman, Robert B.: *This Great Stage* (R. G. Cox)
Prior, Moody E.: *The Language of Tragedy* (R. G. Cox)
Sackton, Alexander H.: *Rhetoric as Dramatic Language in Ben Jonson* (R. G. Cox)
Talon, Henri A.: *John Bunyan, l'homme et l'oeuvre* (Maurice Hussey)

No. 2

Arthur Koestler, by G. D. Klingopulos
The "Cortegiano" and the Civilization of the Renaissance, by Wilhelm Schenk
Mill, Beatrice Webb and the "English School," by F. R. Leavis
"The Tempest," by Derek Traversi

BOOKS REVIEWED

Danby, John F.: *Shakespeare's Doctrine of Nature* (L. C. Knights)
Greig, James A.: *Francis Jeffrey of the Edinburgh Review* (R. G. Cox)
Lovejoy, Arthur O.: *The Great Chain of being Essays in the History of Ideas* (Marius Bewley)
Webb, Beatrice: *Our Partnership* (F. R. Leavis)

No. 3

James's Debt to Hawthorne (I): "The Blithedale Romance" and "The Bostonians," by Marius Bewley
The Shakespearean Dialectic: An Aspect of "Antony and Cleopatra," by John F. Danby
Required Literature Courses as a Contribution to Culture, by Margaret Diggle
"The Family Reunion," by John Peter
In Memoriam: W. Schenk, 1918–1949
Correspondence, F. R. Browning, Donald A. Davie, Marius Bewley

BOOKS REVIEWED

Gramont, E. de: *Marcel Proust* (Martin Turnell)
James, Eric: *An Essay on the Content of Education* (G. H. Bantock)
Keynes, John Maynard: *Two Memoirs* (F. R. Leavis)
March, Harold: *The Two Worlds of Marcel Proust* (Martin Turnell)
Mouton, Jean: *Le Style de Marcel Proust* (Martin Turnell)
Treece, Henry: *Dylan Thomas* (R. G. Cox)
Turnell, Martin: *The Classical Moment* (Alan M. Boase)
Wellek, René, and Warren, Austin: *The Theory of Literature* (Seymour Betsky)

No. 4

"Sir Gawain and the Green Knight," by John Speirs
James's Debt to Hawthorne (II): "The Marble Faun" and "The Wings of the Dove," by Marius Bewley
On the Tragedy of Antony and Cleopatra, by L. C. Knights
Correspondence: G. Wilson Knight and John F. Danby
L. H. Myers and the Critical Function: Rebuke and Reply
Poetry Prizes for the Festival of Britain

BOOKS REVIEWED

Every, George: *Poetry and Personal Responsibility* (F. R. Leavis)
Gathorne-Hardy, Robert: *Recollections of Logan Persall Smith* (H. A. Mason)
Nicoll, Allardyce, ed.: *Shakespeare Survey 2* (R. G. Cox)

Vol. XVII (1950-1951)

No. 1

Mr. Eliot and Social Biology, by L. A. Cormican
James's Debt to Hawthorne (III): The American Problem, by Marius Bewley
"The Windhover," by F. N. Lees
The Novel as Dramatic Poem (IV): "St. Mawr," by F. R. Leavis
Correspondence: Leon Edel and Marius Bewley

BOOKS REVIEWED

Bottrall, Ronald: *Palisades of Fear (Peter Lienhardt)*
Bullett, Gerald, ed.: *Silver Poets of the 16th Century (H. A. Mason)*
Eliot, T. S.: *The Cocktail Party (John Peter)*
Evans, Joan: *English Art, 1307–1461 (Peter Ferriday)*
Muir, Kenneth, ed.: *Collected Poems of Sir Thomas Wyatt (H. A. Mason)*
Parkes, Henry Bamford: *The American People (Marius Bewley)*
Tillyard, E. M. W.: *The Poetry of Sir Thomas Wyatt (H. A. Mason)*

No. 2

Appearance and Reality in Henry James by Marius Bewley
James's "What Maisie Knew": A Disagreement, by F. R. Leavis
Correspondence re "Sir Gawain and the Green Knight"
John Marston's Plays, by John Peter
The "Doctor Faustus" of Thomas Mann, by D. J. Enright

BOOKS REVIEWED

Bateson, F. W.: *English Poetry: a Critical Introduction (R. G. Cox)*
Clark, Kenneth: *Landscape into Art (Geoffrey Walton)*
Gombrich, E. H.: *The Story of Art (Geoffrey Walton)*
Pons, Emile: *Sire Gauvain et le Chevalier Vert (John Speirs)*
Rossiter, A. P.: *English Drama from Early Times (Derek Traversi)*
Stokes, Adrian: *Art and Science (Geoffrey Walton)*
Tillyard, E. M. W.: *Shakespeare's Problem Plays (Derek Traversi)*

No. 4

Medieval Idiom in Shakespeare (I): Shakespeare and the Liturgy, by L. A. Cormican
The Novel as Dramatic Poem (V): "Women in Love" (I) by F. R. Leavis
"Wynnere and Wastoure" and "The Parlement of the Three Ages" by John Spiers
Correspondence: "Sir Gawain and the Green Knight" Again by Q. D. Leavis
Maisie, Miles and Flora, the Jamesian Innocents: A Rejoinder by Marius Bewley
Symposium on Mr. Eliot's "Notes" (III) by D. F. Pocock

BOOKS REVIEWED

Berenson, Bernard: *Aesthetics and History* (Geoffrey Walton)
Mahood, M. M.: *Poetry and Humanism* (Geoffrey Walton)
Newton, Eric: *The Meaning of Beauty* (Geoffrey Walton)
Scott, J. W. Robertson: *The Story of the Pall Mall Gazette* (R. G. Cox)

No. 4

Roger North and Political Morality in the Later Stuart Period by T. A. Birrell
Medieval Idiom in Shakespeare (II): Shakespeare and the Medieval Ethic, by L. A. Cormican
The Novel as Dramatic Poem (V): "Women in Love" (II), by F. R. Leavis
Aspects of Modern American Poetry, by Marius Bewley

BOOKS REVIEWED

Craig, Hardin: *The Enchanted Glass* (L. A. Cormican)
Mead, Margaret: *Male and Female* (D. F. Pocock)

Vol. XVIII (1951-1952)

No. 1

Victorian Criticism of Poetry: The Minority Tradition by R. G. Cox
The Novel as Dramatic Poem (VI): "Women in Love" (III) by F. R. Leavis
Matthew Arnold, H.M.I., by G. H. Bantock

BOOKS REVIEWED

Aldington, Richard: *Portrait of a Genius, But . . . (F. R. Leavis)*
Fry, Christopher: *Venus Observed, The Lady's Not For Burning, A Sleep of Prisoners (Marius Bewley)*
Harrod, R. F.: *The Life of John Maynard Keynes (F. R. Leavis)*
Paige, D. D., ed.: *The Letters of Ezra Pound (F. R. Leavis)*
Russell, Peter, ed.: *Ezra Pound: A Collection of Essays (F. R. Leavis)*
Spender, Stephen: *World Within World (F. R. Leavis)*
Tiverton, Fr. William: *D. H. Lawrence and Human Existence (F. R. Leavis)*
Trilling, Lionel: *The Liberal Imagination (Norman Podhoretz)*

No. 2

The Mystery Cycle (I): Some Towneley Cycle Plays by John Speirs
"Reason" and the Restoration Ethos by Harold Wendell Smith
Correspondence: Lawrence and Eliot: Robert D. Wagner and F. R. Leavis
"Troilus and Cressida" Again by L. C. Knights

BOOKS REVIEWED

Auden, W. H.: *The Enchafèd Flood (R. G. Cox)*
Hoggart, Richard: *Auden: an Introductory Note (R. G. Cox)*
Kane, George: *Middle English Literature (John Speirs)*

No. 3

Scott Fitzgerald by D. W. Harding
"The Dissociation of Sensibility" by Harold Wendell Smith
Correspondence: Marjorie Cox, V. de S. Pinto, John Gillard Watson, John Speirs
The Novel as Dramatic Poem (VII): "The Rainbow" (I) by F. R. Leavis
Poetic Satire and Satire in Verse by D. J. Enright
Mr. Pryce-Jones, The British Council and British Culture by F. R. Leavis

BOOKS REVIEWED

Clemen, W. H.: *The Development of Shakespeare's Imagery* (R. G. Cox)
Leishman, J. B.: *The Monarch of Wit* (R. Mayhead)
Harrison, G. B.: *Shakespeare's Tragedies* (R. Mayhead)
Waldock, A. J. A.: *Sophocles the Dramatist* (R. Mayhead)
Wilson, Edmund: *Classics and Commercials* (John Farrelly)

No. 4

The Mystery Cycle (II): Some Townley Plays (concluded) by John Speirs
Scott Fitzgerald: Another View by John Farrelly
The Novel as Dramatic Poem (VII): "The Rainbow" (II) by F. R. Leavis
Nature, Correctness, and Decorum by Harold Wendell Smith

BOOKS REVIEWED

Auden, W. H.: *Nones* (R. Mayhead)
Bradbrook, M. C.: *Shakespeare and Elizabethan Poetry* (L. A. Cormican)

Vol. XIX (1952-1953)

No. 1

Reflections on the Milton Controversy, by John Peter
The Novel as Dramatic Poem (VII): "The Rainbow" (concluded), by F. R. Leavis
Graham Greene: a Comment, by F. N. Lees
"King Lear" (I), by D. A. Traversi

BOOKS REVIEWED

Aldridge, John W., ed.: *Critiques and Essays on Modern Fiction* (R. Mayhead)
Brooks, Cleanth: *Modern Poetry and the Tradition* (R. Mayhead)
Brower, Reuben Arthur: *The Fields of Light* (R. Mayhead)
Chase, Richard: *Emily Dickinson* (John Farrelly)
Evans-Pritchard, E. E.: *Social Anthropology* (D. F. Pocock)
Hall, James, and Steinmann, Martin, eds.: *The Permanence of Yeats* (R. Mayhead)

Radcliffe-Browne, A. R.: *Structure and Function in Primitive Society (D. F. Pocock)*
Sutherland, Donald: *Gertrude Stein (R. Mayhead)*

No. 2

The New Scholarship? by R. G. Cox
Reality and Sincerity: Notes in the Analysis of Poetry by F. R. Leavis
Revaluations (XVI): James Fenimore Cooper by Marius Bewley
"King Lear" (II) by D. A. Traversi

BOOKS REVIEWED

Boase, Alan M., ed.: *The Poetry of France (Henri Fluchère)*
Chiari, Joseph: *Contemporary French Poetry (Henri Fluchère)*
Danby, John F.: *Poets on Fortune's Hill (J. C. F. Littlewood)*
Hackett, C. A., ed.: *Anthology of Modern French Poetry (Henri Fluchère)*
Thomas, Dylan: *Collected Poems, 1934-1952 (Robin Mayhead)*

No. 3

The Responsible Critic: or The Function of Criticism at Any Time by F. R. Leavis
Cowley, Marvell and the Second Temple by Harold Wendell Smith
"King Lear" (II) (concluded) by D. A. Traversi

BOOKS REVIEWED

British Journal of Educational Studies, Vol. I, No. 1 (G. H. Bantock)
Closs, A.: *Die neuere deutsche Lyrik (D. J. Enright)*
Heerikhuizen, F. W. van: *Rainer Maria Rilke (D. J. Enright)*
Holthusen, H. E.: *Rainer Maria Rilke (D. J. Enright)*
MacDonald, Violet M., tr.: *Letters to Merline, 1919-1922 (D. J. Enright)*
Mitchell, Donald, and Keller, Hans, eds.: *Benjamin Britten (Robin Mayhead)*
Prawer, S. S.: *German Lyric Poetry (D. J. Enright)*
Rilke, R. M.: *From the Remains of Count C. W. (D. J. Enright)*

No. 4

Valedictory
Crashaw and "The Weeper" by John Peter
"The Captain's Doll" by F. R. Leavis
"Much Ado About Nothing" by T. W. Craik
Correspondence: "The Responsible Critic," from F. W. Bateson
Reply by F. R. Leavis
Letters from Geoffrey Walton

BOOKS REVIEWED

Fluchère, Henri: *Shakespeare (R. G. Cox)*
Jones, David: *The Anathemata (J. C. F. Littlewood)*
Knight, G. Wilson: *The Shakespearean Tempest (R. G. Cox)*

(The editorial note on page 407, written in 1948, has become partially out of date by 1964. There now does exist a complete index of *Scrutiny*, and this for the complete file of the magazine, Volume I to XIX, the Index itself, with other additional matter, constituting Volume XX. Larger libraries now have a complete set of *Scrutiny* as reprinted in twenty volumes by the Cambridge University Press. But since not many readers of the present book will have quick access to the complete set, I have thought it a sound idea to reprint the table of contents, and bring it down to Volume XIX. There is this point too: If someone wishes to see at a glance what *Scrutiny* printed and in what order, he can do so by leafing through this table of contents; the full Index would not help him.

—E. B.)

Date Due

PENSACOLA JUNIOR COLLEGE LIBRARY
PN501 .S35
Scrutiny.
The importance of scrutin   000
                                210101

3 5101 00053953 1